RACIAL CONFLICT
TENSION AND CHANGE
IN AMERICAN SOCIETY

GARY T. MARX
Harvard University

LITTLE, BROWN AND COMPANY
Boston

ACKNOWLEDGEMENTS

I am grateful to Al Schneider and John Akula for their assistance, as well as to numerous students in classes which, beginning as race relations courses, ended as racial conflict courses. From them I have learned much about the mixture of realistic and nonrealistic elements in conflict situations and the difficulty of reconciling an appreciation of the dimensions and functions of conflict in the abstract with its presence in interpersonal situations.

Library of Congress
Catalog Card No. 76-153184

SECOND PRINTING

Published simultaneously in Canada
by **Little, Brown and Company** (Canada) **Limited**

Printed in the United States of America

CONTENTS

720688

V. CONSEQUENCES OF CONFLICT   441

INTRODUCTION

"Freedom Is a Constant Struggle"—Masthead of Sun Flower County, Mississippi Freedom Newspaper

ALTHOUGH greatly overstated, Disraeli's reported comment that "all is race, there is no other truth" would seem to be even more appropriate in twentieth-century America than in nineteenth-century England. Almost wherever one looks race impinges itself upon the American conscience. The articles collected here reflect perhaps the most dramatic aspect of race relations: conflict. I have chosen to focus on this theme not because conflict is the all, or necessarily the most, important aspect of intergroup relations, but because it is highly significant, rather neglected, and offers a vehicle for considering a number of important areas including social change, inequality, and ideology.

The field of race relations is blessed, or cursed, with an abundance of textbook readers. For the most part they cast a wide net. In the pursuit of variety, and no doubt course adoptions, they usually consider the most diverse materials on a wide array of racial, ethnic, and religious groups. Or in a more recent trend, they focus only on blacks in an effort to capture the black experience. A student may learn a considerable amount from texts which (with sections that are usually tenuously linked) draw on various disciplines to deal with the most varied questions posed by race relations or which are unified by a discussion of only blacks, rather than of both blacks and whites and the interaction between them. Yet the student is not left with a basic framework for analyzing the social world or with a set of integrated questions; nor is he or she left with much of a feeling for the continuity of social structure and process.

The aim of this book is rather more delimited and focused. As the title suggests, it is concerned with racial conflict and social change as they involve both blacks and whites. Widespread racial change and an increase in domestic conflict are among the most salient features of contemporary American life. Though the exact links between conflict and change are not always clear and may vary considerably depending on the context and the level of analysis involved, a crucial factor has been the challenge from organized protest groups, often using nonconventional tactics.

What is *racial conflict*? Put most simply, it is conflict between groups that consider each other racially distinct. The boundaries of the group in question and one's sense of identity with it are determined by racial criteria, as popularly defined.[1]

This of course begs the question of what conflict is. For our purposes *conflict* can be broadly defined as a self-conscious group struggle for resources perceived as scarce and/or values that are taken to be incompatible. A distinction is sometimes made in the literature between "competition" and "conflict." "Competition" is seen to involve struggle over values or scarce resources in a framework of established rules, which limit what opponents can do to each other, with the main objective being the scarcity or desired values, whereas "conflict" is seen to be less bound in by rules and to involve efforts to neutralize, injure, or eliminate one's rivals.[2]

For certain purposes such a conceptual distinction is important. Struggles where the aim is only pursuit of a scarce resource are likely to be very different than those that also involve efforts to directly injure or destroy the opponent. It is important to determine how these relate and when one gives way to the other. However, a definition which stresses efforts to destroy one's opponents would exclude much of the racial struggle of the last twenty years from the category of conflict, at least as it has been carried on by blacks.[3] Although this struggle has often been pursued through noninstitutional means, it has not been primarily directed at destroying whites or white society. Rather, it has been directed toward inclusion and a greater share of wealth and power. Both "competition" and "conflict" are processes of opposition: an important aspect of racial change is the fact of struggle, challenge, and opposition. It is this broad phenomena that for convenience we shall refer to as *conflict*. In so doing we lose something in the way of precision but gain considerably in the way of scope. The pursuit of scarce resources and incompatible values which occurs beyond the framework of established rules can be seen as noninstitutionalized conflict. This may be

---

[1] It is important to stress the social and cultural character of groups defined along racial lines. In American society race is more a social than a biological category. Anyone with any visible African ancestry is classified as Negro. In Brazil it is almost the opposite. Any European ancestry tends to exclude one from being classified as Negro. A large portion of American "Negroes" have just as much European ancestry as they do African and many "whites," particularly in the South have an appreciable degree of African ancestry. Even the term "race" is scientifically problematic. There is little agreement among physical anthropologists about just what race is, what gene pools should define it, or even how many races there are. For a useful discussion summarizing much of the relevant literature, see G. Simpson and M. Yinger, *Racial and Cultural Minorities* (New York: Harper & Row, 1965), chap. 2. Yet such scientific issues aside, if people impute meaning to racial categories, even though their definition is culturally relative, varying from one society to the next, the social analyst must deal with social definitions.

[2] For some conceptual discussions of conflict, see A. Schneider and G. Marx "Violent Intergroup Conflict in American Society," in *American Social Problems,* (ed.) J. Douglas, (New York: Random House, forthcoming); C. Fink, "Some Conceptual Difficulties in the Theory of Social Conflict," *Journal of Conflict Reso-*

lution 12, no. 4; M. Deutsch, "Conflicts Productive and Destructive," *Journal of Social Issues* 15, no. 1: A. Rapoport, *Fights, Games, and Debates* (Ann Arbor, Mich.: Univ. of Michigan Press, 1960); L. Coser, *The Functions of Social Conflict* (New York: Free Press, 1954); R. Mack and R. Snyder, "The Analysis of Social Conflict—Toward an Overview and Synthesis," *Journal of Conflict Resolution* (June 1957); T. Schelling, *The Strategy of Conflict* (Cambridge: Harvard University Press, 1960); R. Dahrendorf, *Class and Class Conflict in Industrial Society* (Palo Alto: Stanford University Press, 1959).

[3] However, such a definition is rather well-suited to the actions of some southern whites in their defense of the status quo. In the 1970's it is increasingly coming to fit the activities of some black protest groups as well.

violent or nonviolent and may or may not involve efforts to injure and destroy the opponent (beyond whatever losses he may suffer if his opponent gains his goals).[4]

The readings in this book deal primarily with groups organized, at least partly, for the pursuit of ends which are incompatible. Prejudice, discrimination, racial etiquette, and inequality are of interest primarily as they become defined as issues around which group struggle takes place, though a very important question is: Under what conditions does the struggle for equal opportunity, dignity, and redistribution of power and income occur, as against strains being ignored, unrecognized, or resulting in displaced hostility toward oneself, other members of one's group, or giving rise to an individualistic and idiosyncratic resistance?

In contemporary American society when we think of racial conflict, we tend to think of challenge to the color line from a subordinate black, Puerto Rican, or Mexican group and reaction on the part of the dominant white group. However, another important type of racial conflict, particularly historically, has been that initiated by whites in establishing the color line and in using prejudice as a tool to further their own ends. Still another common type of racially or ethnically linked conflict in American society has been between more or less equally subordinate minority groups as they struggle in direct competition for the meager resources available to them, in a milieu where they have learned the racism of the larger culture and may displace aggression onto each other. A particularly

interesting and neglected type of conflict has been that within minority groups. Material is presented on each of these conflicts, though because of its direct relevance and current research interests, most attention is given to efforts that challenge the color line. Many of the issues, concepts, and theories apply equally well to other forms of racial conflict.

Struggle over scarce resources and discrepant values may take many forms. A large proportion of social struggle in America is highly regularized, fairly tightly bound in by rules, occurs within a framework of traditional legal standards, and is seen as legitimate by most members of society.

One of the clearest examples of such institutionalized means of struggle is electoral politics. Labor/management disputes resolved through collective bargaining are another. A third area where groups may pursue incompatible claims is the legal system. Still other means are through lobbying, letter writing, or peaceful petitioning. Such conflict is sometimes referred to as "working within the system."

Yet there are other forms of conflict that at least initially may be considered illegal, which can involve threats, coercion, force, and disruption. A relatively powerless and impoverished minority group may find that the negative power to disrupt is the strongest resource it has.

For a group with heightened aspirations and intense grievances, operating within the traditional framework may be seen as slow, cumbersome, and ineffectual. When traditional means are ineffective and serve only to perpetuate the status quo, strong pressure may exist for conflict to be carried out outside of normal channels. Playing by the rules of the game (which may mean other people's rules) sometimes means that one can't play the game.

---

[4] The presence of conflict bounded by rules, and whether or not one is out to hurt his opponent are logically somewhat independent, although empirically the presence of rules, for functional reasons of self-interest, usually tends to limit at least to some degree what groups do to each other.

This reader gives particular attention to some of the less institutionalized kinds of conflict: demonstrations, sit-ins, boycotts, confrontations, and civil disorders. It is important to realize that such tactics may occur simultaneously with efforts carried on within customary channels. Indeed over time a given tactic such as a labor union strike or sit-in may move from being defined as illegal to legal. The ends sought by a conflict group may be seen as illegitimate, as well as the means it uses.

Two kinds of articles are presented here: general theoretical material on conflict and focused, detailed material on actual conflict situations. Beyond gathering together in an orderly way some of the more readable and important materials on conflict and race, this approach permits an assessment of the extent to which the theories can help us gain a deeper understanding of specific case studies and it adds some substance to otherwise rather abstract analytic theories.

The need for a reader such as this became apparent to me as a confused graduate student, preparing for examinations and being pulled back and forth, between abstract, nonsubstantive, general considerations of conflict and concrete, largely atheoretical descriptions of real situations of racial conflict. It was originally hoped to show how a general theory of social conflict could unify and shed light on a particular case of racial conflict. As my reading broadened, my ambitiousness narrowed when it became clear that we are far from a theory of social conflict, if by theory one means a tightly related set of testable propositions of sufficient generality. What we have instead are a number of useful concepts, the specification of some important analytic issues and questions, some middle-range theories, some empirical generalizations, and a view of society which stresses the scarcity of desired resources, competing values and belief systems, the imperfect integration of social structure and culture, and the imperfect nature of socialization, all of which give rise to a conflict potential.

This reader is organized around a number of questions that can be asked about any type of social conflict, as well as some questions that are unique to race conflict and American society: Why do societies have a potential for conflict? What are the main institutional areas within which conflict occurs? What are some of the main types of racial conflict? What affects the form conflict takes? What kinds of social situations make it likely that organized conflict will appear? How is racial conflict distributed in time and place, and what are some of its main correlates and antecedents? What is the role of ideas in mobilizing people to action and in justifying their behavior? What are the implications of different strategies? What kinds of individuals are likely to become active in social conflict situations, and what are some of the things that happen to them in the process? What affects the course of a given conflict? What terminates a given conflict? What are the consequences of conflict for the individual and for society? When do the actions of organized protest groups bring about change? Repression? Both or neither? Just how important is conflict to change?

One of the luxuries of an academic tradition that, in some ways for the better and in others for the worse, seems to be dying out in American social science, is the posing of questions and the raising of issues for their own sake. To begin to understand a field one must know what the questions are. This volume hardly does justice to the questions posed above, though some areas, such as the documentation of inequality in various institutional spheres, are handled far better than others. However, the body of literature included here, it is hoped, contains among the best answers we have that are readily accessible to students.

In general, I started with a set of questions; let this inform the articles to be included, rather than letting the materials suggest the questions.

In putting together such a volume out of existing materials rather than commissioning new materials, one runs into problems of completeness and quality. Important gaps exist and some areas are not treated in sufficient depth. Yet perhaps this very fact can inspire needed studies.

The book is divided into five parts, which roughly correspond to the questions posed above. These parts are organized around various analytic areas and relate logically to each other. They tend to parallel the actual form of a given instance of racial conflict. Thus we move from documenting the potential for realistic conflict to a consideration of what situations are conducive to the appearance of overt conflict, to the role of ideas in mobilizing people, to the actual occurrence of the conflict, and, finally, to the consequences of conflict.

Part I, "General Theoretical Perspectives on Conflict," includes abstract discussions of conflict in society. It offers a view of society as having builtin scarcities and contradictions. Conflict over these scarcities and value differences is seen as a fundamental social process. The essence of race conflict lies here. This level of analysis can be separated from personality factors such as hostility or prejudice. Some types of conflict are specified and the functions of conflict are explored.

The next part, "Social Structure and Racial Conflict," is a less abstract consideration of how social organization affects racial conflict. It is divided into two sections. Section A deals with scarce resources and institutionalized inequality. It considers some of the various things that conflict revolves around, such as political power, money, status, cultural definitions, etc. It does this by studies documenting the poverty and powerlessness of blacks relative to whites. These factors form the basis for realistic conflict. Whether, in fact, conflict occurs depends upon the type of community involved and how people come to define their situation.

Conflict is not all of one kind, nor do all racially stratified societies have an equal likelihood of conflict. Certain social situations are much more conducive to the occurrence of overt conflict than others are. Section B of this part considers antecedents and correlates of conflict. Some of these are at the community level, such as how pluralistic the society is. Others look to the historical nature of the initial contact between racial groups; still others center on the economic and political context, or consider the importance of demographic changes and other disruptions as they bear on the likelihood of racial conflict.

Given a potential for conflict, and historical conditions and a community structure conducive to its emergence, consideration is next given in Part III, "Ideology and Strategy," to the role ideas play in preparing people for action and in indicating what lines of behavior are appropriate and why.[5] In this part rather than presenting articles analyzing the role of ideology, the participants

---

[5] This is not necessarily to imply that objective strains and deprivation always give rise to ideologies of change. It is almost axiomatic among social scientists to note that what counts is not so much objective conditions but how people define them. However, there is no doubt often a reciprocal relationship between ideology and social structure.

speak for themselves. Included are statements by black and white nationalists, moderates and liberals, ranging from the Black Panthers to Martin Luther King and Senator Bilbo of Mississippi to President Johnson. Several articles analyzing strategy are also included.

Given scarce resources, a conducive milieu, and ideas which justify and even demand conflict, Part IV, "The Dynamics of Conflict," considers actual conflict situations. It is divided into parts: social processes and case studies.

The racial conflicts we are concerned with have a dynamic quality to them, though for some purposes they can be analyzed statically. In the social process section, articles are presented which attempt to catch the expressive, emergent quality of such conflict. A disagreement over a minor issue with little emotional involvement on the part of those concerned broadens to include the very basis of the group's consensus and participants come to hate each other. A confrontation that initially involves only a few demonstrators expands to include an entire community, as a result of indiscriminate police action. A group that was previously seen in a favorable or neutral light gradually becomes negatively defined. Although at a very concrete level every instance of conflict is different, the articles in this section attempt to capture certain ideal-typical patterns of development.

The introduction to the case study section raises a large number of questions and offers propositions relevant to understanding the emergence, form, course, and consequences of conflict. These help structure our observations of conflict situations and offer a framework for analysis. Up to this point the student has been exposed to many general ideas about conflict. He or she is now presented with descriptions and

analysis of actual race conflict situations. For example, one case is a disagreement on a university campus, another a controversy over schools; still another deals with the emergence of a community police patrol, another with conflict over passage of antidiscrimination legislation, and another with a rent strike. Hopefully it will be possible for the student to apply some of the perspectives, concepts, and hypotheses presented in this part, and earlier throughout the book, to the case studies, as well as to the conflicts (of a racial nature or otherwise) likely to be found on the campus or the larger community.

The most effective learning is surely that which a person does for him- or herself. By being offered broad concepts, general theoretical perspectives, and various propositions, on the one hand, and substantive accounts, on the other, the student is hopefully challenged to bring the two together and come to appreciate the interplay of theory and fact.[6] Perhaps he or she will also gain some of the joy of discovery, not to mention the increase in knowledge, which can come from being able to suddenly order seemingly unrelated social phenomena, or to see what at first seemed to be an idiosyncratic pattern of development as common to a certain type of conflict, or to be able to make reasoned predictions about a future course of events.

Part V, "Consequences of Conflict," poses a number of questions about conflict and change and considers the implications of racial conflict for society and the individual.

This organization deals with many of the basic aspects of racial conflict and seems to flow fairly naturally out

[6] For a useful discussion of the interdependence of theory and empirical research, see R. Merton, *Social Theory and Social Structure* (New York: Free Press, 1957), chaps. 2, 3.

of the real world.[7] It permits us to look at American racial conflict at a very specific microscopic level and yet offers a minimal organizational framework for a few of the many separate studies on various aspects of racial conflict and the civil rights movement and counter movement.

The criteria for including articles was no doubt far less rational than one might hope, yet other factors being equal, articles have been included that (1) seemed useful in trying to cope with one or more of the questions raised above and which could be generalized to other types of conflict; (2) were clearly written and not so technical or esoteric as to overwhelm the average undergraduate, nor so superficial as to insult him or her; and (3) were current and had not been reprinted elsewhere.

This is not intended to be a reader about blacks any more than it is a reader about whites; rather, it considers a phenomenon intricately involving both groups. There is a tendency in some popular discussion and research to assume that because in certain ways the situation of blacks in unique, it is in all ways unique. This sometimes leads to too narrow a focus only on specific black materials rather than an equivalent concern with more general phenomena, concepts, and perspectives applicable to a much wider array of groups. The same might be said of a focus only on American, rather than worldwide, racial conflict.[8]

In viewing only the specific we are in danger of losing sight of the possible existence of a broader underlying structure and the universality of much of human experience. The serious sins of omission and distortion of the past should not now lead to a similar imbalance, though here the need for political and psychological change may clash with the needs of social science. Hopefully, the student will take from these readings some sense of the essential elements of social conflict, whether it be conflict between whites and blacks, conflict within the black or white group, between blacks and Puerto Ricans, or conflict involving different social classes and religious groups.

For most purposes racial conflict can be usefully conceived of as simply one aspect of the broader phenomena of social conflict. What is most important for sociological understanding is conflict, not race, though racial struggles, where the essential humanity of the opposition can be denied, seem to involve a more violent and macabre potential than strictly political or economic struggles. Racial struggles also seem to have a greater sexual component.

It is true also that in recent decades racial and ethnic conflicts have greatly increased in frequency, partly replacing the religious conflict of earlier years. The conflicts of Hindus and Moslems in India, Malays and Chinese in Singapore, French and British in Quebec, Catholic and Protestants in Northern Ireland, Israelis and Arabs in the Middle East, Ibos and Hausas in Nigeria, and any of dozens of other situations, clearly indicate that the United States is not

---

[7] Though it is not argued that analytic elements such as resource scarcity, a conducive social milieu and ideology necessarily causally affect each other in the order they are presented here, they are interdependent and jointly affect the nature of the conflict. Conflict, once it emerges, can, of course, also have an affect on the way an ideology develops or a social milieu changes.

[8] For some books offering a comparative international perspective, see M. Tumin, *Comparative Perspectives on Race Relations* (Boston: Little Brown, 1969); R. A. Schermerhorn, *Comparative Ethnic Relations* (New York: Random House, 1970); T. Shibutani and K. Kwan, *Ethnic Stratification, a Comparative Approach* (New York: Macmillan, 1965); R. Segal, *The Race War* (New York: Viking Press, 1967).

alone in having problems of intergroup relations. With the decline of colonialism and the rise of nationalism, ethnic and racial problems have joined class and generational problems as a major source of world conflict within, as well as between, countries. Ethnic tensions are probably more in evidence today than at any other time in human history. Such conflicts are certainly deserving of attention, but not primarily because of the presence of unique conflict elements.

PART ONE
GENERAL THEORETICAL PERSPECTIVES ON CONFLICT

TAKING a broad historical and anthropological perspective, Charles Wagley and Marvin Harris argue that minority groups, as we understand them, are a relatively new phenomenon in human history. Their emergence is seen to be dependent on the formation of the nation-state five thousand years ago. This in turn depended on the development of an agricultural surplus and the emergence of cities. The development of the state meant a form of social organization by which culturally and physically different groups sharing a given geographical area could be bound into the same social and administrative unit.

The expansion of Europe beginning in the sixteenth century was an event having profound significance for world ethnic relations. Since then more than seventy million people have left Europe, carrying their culture, technology, diseases, and domination to diverse parts of the world. The origin of a particular minority is often related to migration and the expansion of national states.

Lewis Coser offers a broad overview of social conflict. He notes that conflict has creative as well as destructive components. Conflict is viewed as a basic part of social organization. The intensity of conflict, its means—violent or nonviolent—and its consequences are seen to depend on the kind of social structure in which it appears. Here we must consider factors such as whether conflict occurs in a tightly or loosely integrated setting, whether dissent is encouraged, whether the ideology of conflict involves supra-individual ends, and whether the conflict occurs within a broad framework of consensus or is over this very consensus.

Ralf Dahrendorf contrasts two images of society—one focuses on integration and the other on coercion. One stresses the importance of shared values and social stability, whereas the other stresses the importance of force and the ubiquity of change and conflict. An understanding of society requires attention to the interaction of stability and change, integration and conflict, and consensus and coercion. However, to explain the formation of conflict groups,

Dahrendorf stresses the coercion perspective. He then goes on to consider one important element of social organization which creates a potential for conflict groups: authority relations. The fact that authority and power are not equally distributed serves as a basis around which conflict may take place. Although Dahrendorf explicitly restricts himself to class conflict, much of his discussion has a broader relevance.

Jessie Bernard contrasts some psychological and sociological approaches to conflict. She argues that an objective conflict of group interests underlies much intergroup discord. The clear grounds for such realistic conflict are presented in Part IIA. To understand social conflict it is necessary to look beyond individual subjective feelings of hostility, stereotypes, prejudice, misunderstandings, and lack of knowledge about an outgroup, to the kinds of relations that exist between groups. It is here that Bernard locates the source of group conflict.

Looking at objective group relations of domination and subordination leads to consideration of what groups profit from the status quo and the link between this and ideologies of prejudice. To clearly make her point, Bernard is somewhat polemical. As later articles indicate, misperception, ignorance, stereotypes, and personality needs may have an important bearing on conflict. Rhetoric may greatly overstate the extent of actual incompatibility between two groups. Yet, Bernard calls attention to an important area for analysis.

The large number of variables that figure in any given instance of conflict and a degree of independence between them mean that most researchers work on only one level of analysis. For many purposes this is sufficient. For example, we can ask about the historical origins of a stereotype without trying to determine what kinds of people currently hold the stereotype, or we can look at the personality characteristics of activists without necessarily considering the consequences of different conflict strategies. But ultimately the larger the number of factors that are considered and related to each other, the greater will be our understanding.

The final article by Earl Raab and Seymour Martin Lipset does not discuss conflict directly; rather it offers a useful discussion of prejudice in attitudes and behavior and summarizes much empirical research. In considering concepts that are crucial to an understanding of racial cooperation and antagonism, they stress the importance of the social situation in producing discriminatory behavior, as against the role played by attitudes within the person. Their development of the concept of the "prejudiced society," which shows how thoroughly ingrained and mutually supportive customary patterns of prejudice often are, leads nicely into the articles in Part II, which documents many of the basic sources of racial struggle.

1
The Development of the Nation-State and the Formation of Minorities*

C. WAGLEY and H. HARRIS

With the knowledge provided by archaeology, ethnography, and written history, it is clear that human societies have progressively expanded in size, in complexity, and in territorial scope as man has extended and perfected his technological control over his environ-

*[C. Wagley and H. Harris, "The Development of the Nation-State and the Formation of Minorities," in *Minorities in the New World* (New York: Columbia Univ. Press, 1958), pp. 240–243. By permission of Columbia University Press]

ment. For nearly fifty thousand years our species lived in small wandering bands limited in size by their precarious methods of subsistence. During all this time (and much more, if one considers human species other than Homo sapiens) the necessity of hunting for food with inefficient weapons, or of gathering it with ineffective instruments, kept the population sparse. It was not until about ten thousand years ago that man first became a food producer—an agriculturist and a breeder of animals. This "food-producing revolution," to use V. Gordon Childe's term, occurred independently at least once in the old world and at least once in the New World. From the earliest centers, a knowledge of food-producing techniques spread rapidly over most of the globe until a large proportion of all human societies lived by food production, yet in isolated areas and in more inhospitable environments man continued to live by hunting and gathering. With a secure food supply furnished from his gardens and from his domestic animals, there was for the first time a sedentary life in villages. But these village societies were in one important sense as "primitive" as the remaining nomadic hunting and gathering societies. "Throughout both Paleolithic and Neolithic times each little group was largely self-contained and self-supporting, as the surviving primitive societies, whether hunters or growers of vegetable and animal food, are largely self-contained and self-supporting.[1] During all of this time there were no minority groups.

About five thousand years ago a second great "revolution" gave birth to mankind's first cities, to great public

works—such as irrigation systems and land reclamation projects—writing, standards of weights and measures, the beginnings of science, foreign trade, and to specialized labor of all descriptions. This "urban revolution" seems to have first occurred in the Middle East, and at a later date to have spread elsewhere in the Old World. Again the "urban revolution" took place independently in the New World, where such peoples as the Aztec of Mexico, the Maya of Yucatan, and the Inca of highland South America developed their own indigenous civilizations. For the present purposes, the most important feature of this second great change in human history is that it was associated with the growth of a new form of social organization, namely, what we today call the state. In broadest perspective, it was the formation of state societies which made the existence of minority groups possible. Primitive societies are stateless societies. Although a primitive tribe may have considerable formal political organization, such as tribal councils or a chieftain vested with relatively strong authority, social order is achieved by stressing the obligations and rights due to kinsmen by descent or by marriage. It is therefore characteristic that the various systems of classifying kin among primitive peoples have a greater extension than those used by so-called civilized peoples. In primitive societies an individual often has hundreds of "relatives," including individuals only distantly or even fictitiously related (i.e., all my fellow clan members may be my "brothers"). An individual's world in primitive societies is thus populated largely by "relatives," all of whom speak the same language, practice the same customs, and belong to the same physical stock. In the small band and villages typical of the primitive world, the use of ridicule, noncooperation, and os-

[1] R. Redfield, *The Primitive World and Its Transformation,* New York: Cornell Univ. Press, 1953, p. 7. In the Old World the hunting and gathering period and the early foodproducing period are known respectively as the Paleolithic and the Neolithic periods.

tracism, reinforced by common bonds of culture, is usually sufficient to insure conformity to the "unwritten law." Coercion, external compulsion, and legal procedure, although not entirely absent, are seldom necessary to maintain internal order (Linton, p. 109). Primitive tribes usually have a definite idea of their own territory, and they resist invasion and trespass with force; but the emphasis of their social organization is on "our people," no matter where they live, and not upon the territorial unit. Primitive social organization thus contains no provisions for incorporating into a single social unit groups of individuals who are not related by descent or by marriage, who follow different customs, who stress distinctive values, and who, in sum, are an alien people.

Only with the development of the state did human societies become equipped with a form of social organization which could bind masses of culturally and physically heterogeneous "strangers" into a single social entity. Whereas primitive peoples derive their cohesion largely from a common culture and from kinship and other kinds of personal ties, state societies are held together largely by the existence of a central political authority which claims a monopoly of coercive power over all persons within a given territory. Theoretically, with a sufficiently strong development of the apparatus of government, a state society can extend law and order over limitless subgroups of strangers who neither speak the same language, worship the same gods, nor strive for the same values.

Yet the growth of the state form of organization did not entirely replace the principles by which unity is achieved among primitive peoples. On the contrary, if a thoroughgoing replacement had indeed taken place, minorities, as we know them today, would not exist. In reality, many of the subgroups have

continued to regard themselves as distinctive units within the total society, not because they inhabit the same territory and are subject to the same apparatus of government, but because they share cultural traits different from others and reckon themselves, in a sense, as kinsmen by descent. Moreover, certain of these subgroups, especially the more numerous and more powerful ones, have tended to act as if the population of their state society was like the population of a primitive tribe; have tended to act as if the state society to which they belong ideally ought to consist of their own physical and cultural type; and as if the state were merely the territorial expression of their own people or "nation." Thus, from the persistence of primitive principles of social organization there emerges that strange contradiction of terms known as the "national state." It is the prevalence of this contradiction which guarantees the proliferation of minority situations throughout the modern world.

Of course, there is no absolute reason why a state society cannot also be a nation in the above sense. But the contradiction involved is an historical rather than a logical one. Neither history nor ethnography can provide more than a mere handful of examples of state societies which have consisted solely of racially and culturally homogeneous elements. It need scarcely be said that throughout recorded history the territorial limits of states have been in ceaseless flux, thereby insuring the heterogeneity of their populations. Boundary changes resulting from wars, revolutions, confederations, and conferences have occurred with such frequency as to leave no time for the growth of homogeneous national states. Moreover, the same technological revolution which broke the insularity of the primitive bands and villages and led to the rise of state societies brought with it ever-increasing opportunities for large-scale population shifts. Certainly there is no society in the world today where state and nation may be said to coincide, except as a convenient fiction for novelists and politicians.

And yet, especially during the last few centuries, many conscious and unconscious efforts have been made to achieve the ideal of a national state. In the process, the cultural traditions, the language, and physical type of one of the groups of a state society are proposed as the national language, the national culture, and the national physical type. Usually this dominant or "national" way of life is that of the numerical majority, and the strangers—the minority members—form smaller cultural or racial enclaves. But sometimes a handful of people have, through their superior economic, political, or military power, been able to impose their cultural and physical "ideal" of nationhood on the rest of the society. . . .

While the ancient world had known empires of great extent—such as the Roman, Chinese, Mongol, and Inca— with the growth of the postfeudal European states, empires of unprecedented proportions came to be formed. By the sixteenth century, the revolutionary development of gunpowder weapons, maneuverable sailing vessels, and navigational devices gave to the European states a marked technological superiority over most of the world's societies. With this new equipment the European states were able to overcome hitherto undreamed-of distances for the purposes of state expansion. Within a few hundred years, Africa, North and South America, India, southeast Asia, parts of China, central and northeastern Asia, Indonesia, Melanesia, Polynesia, and Australia were to become, with varying degrees of permanency, subject to European governments. Colonists were sent into many of these areas to establish permanent settlements and to rule over the indigenous populations. But with the waxing and waning of imperial fortunes and with the growth of movements for independence, the political control of these areas shifted from one state society to another, sometimes with bewildering frequency. Thus, in addition to minorities consisting of conquered indigenous peoples, such as the Indians of Mexico and Brazil, the expansion of European states also created a somewhat smaller number of minorities consisting of European colonists or their descendants whose governments lost dominion over the areas they had formerly controlled. The French in Canada are such a minority. . . .

Although slavery is an ancient institution, found even among primitive peoples, the colossal scale on which the New World colonists and their descendants employed slave labor was quite unique. After the Europeans had decimated or driven out the scanty aboriginal populations who inhabited the southern portions of the English colonies, the Antilles, and the coast of Brazil, they found themselves in possession of great tracts of fertile virgin lands. These areas could be made to grow valuable commodities for which the European climate was unsuited; all that was needed was labor to clear the forests and do the work in the fields. Unable to call upon a dense aboriginal population, as the Spanish were able to do, the lowland planters sought to meet their labor requirements by using the population of another continent. They set up trading stations along the African coast and bartered rum, cloth, and other articles of European and American manufacture for human beings. Encouraged by the avarice of the European traders, the Africans raided deep into the continent for men, women, and children who because they belonged to stranger tribes could be delivered to the traders without qualms.

There thus grew up one of the greatest forced transfers of people known in human history. How many people were killed in the African raids by which slaves were captured and how many more died while being transported across the sea under unspeakable conditions will probably never be known with any accuracy.

Among the several forms of migration responsible for the origin of many New World minorities, slavery involved the greatest amount of compulsion and brutality. But there are many other migrant groups in the New World who were to a certain extent "forced" into their trip across the sea. These migrations were prompted by a complex variety of motives; some resulted from various shades and degrees of compulsion other than the extreme represented by the slave trade. Some groups, like the Irish, migrated to escape the threat of imminent death by starvation; others, like the Huguenots and the Quakers, were forced to leave because of religious persecution. Still others, like many of the Germans, hoped for relief from political persecution. Many of the immigrants chose to become indentured laborers in the New World rather than inmates of debtors' prisons in their homelands; untold thousands were recruited by the agents of shipping companies under false pretenses; thousands of others came to avoid serving in European armies. As the economy of the United States and other New World areas shifted toward industrialism, a vast new market for wage laborers grew up, thereby providing an outlet for impoverished, landless, excess populations all over the world. Upon arrival in their new homes, the migrants assumed a variety of statuses fully as diverse as the motives which had prompted their voyages across the sea. Some, as indentured laborers and miserably paid factory workers, lived and worked under conditions not too far removed from the hardships and indignities of slavery. Others found freedom and security, as homesteaders, skilled craftsmen, and merchants. It was Europe, torn by wars, her soils depleted, and with masses of unemployed or marginal workers crowding her cities, which made the greatest contribution to the labor-hungry countries across the sea. Indeed, all of these motives, movements, and results add up to what Robert Park has called the "European diaspora," unquestionably the greatest migratory movement the world has ever seen. . . .

Certain generalizations have already emerged from our analysis of minority groups. First, the appearance of minority groups in the long history of human society is fairly recent and seems to date from the emergence of the state as a form of sociopolitical organization some five thousand years ago. Second, the origin of specific minority groups is always associated closely with the formation and expansion of state organizations or with migration from one state to another. As Louis Wirth once succintly wrote: "The genesis of minorities must therefore be sought in the fact that territory, political authority, people, and culture only rarely coincide[2]". . . .

2
Some Sociological Aspects of Conflict*
LEWIS COSER

Social conflict may be defined as a struggle over values or claims to status,

*["Some Sociological Aspects of Conflict" by L. Coser, Reprinted with permission of the publisher from *International Encyclopedia of the Social Sciences,* David L. Sills, Editor. Volume 3, pages 232–236, Copyright © 1968 by Crowell Collier and Macmillan, Inc.]

[2] Louis Wirth, "The Problem of Minority Groups," in Ralph Linton, ed., *The Science of Man in the World Crisis,* New York: Columbia Univ. Press, 1945, p. 365.

power, and scarce resources, in which the aims of the conflicting parties are not only to gain the desired values but also to neutralize, injure, or eliminate their rivals. Such conflicts may take place between individuals, between collectivities, or between individuals and collectivities. Intergroup as well as intragroup conflicts are perennial features of social life.

Conflict is an important element of social interaction. Far from being always a "negative" factor that "tears apart," social conflict may contribute in many ways to the maintenance of groups and collectivities as well as to the cementing of interpersonal relations.

Nineteenth-century sociology paid much attention to social conflict. In all social thought derived from Hegel, particularly in Marxian thought, conflict is the key explanatory variable. The same is the case with social thinkers directly or indirectly inspired by social Darwinism, such as Herbert Spencer, Gustav Ratzenhofer, Ludwig Gumplowicz, and William Graham Sumner. The struggle for power and influence is one of the themes of Pareto's theories, as well as those of Mosca, Michels, and Sorel. Similarly, in the classical tradition in German sociology, from Tönnies to Simmel and Weber, conflict was considered a major social phenomenon. Weber, for example, insisted that "conflict cannot be excluded from social life. . . . 'Peace' is nothing more than a change in the form of the conflict or in the antagonists or in the objects of the conflict, or finally in the chances of selection" ([1904–1917] 1949, pp. 26–27). Simmel, to whom we owe a classical analysis of various forms of conflict, insisted that "conflict is a form of sociation" and that "a certain amount of discord, inner divergence, and outer controversy, is organically tied up with the very elements that ultimately hold the group together" ([1908] 1955, pp. 17–18).

Similarly, the fathers of American sociology saw in conflict an inherent and ineradicable component of social structures. Most of them agreed with Robert Park that "only where there is conflict is behavior conscious and self-conscious; only here are the conditions for rational conduct" (1924, p. 578).

In a more recent period, the functions of conflict and the study of conflict phenomena were neglected by American sociologists. If conflict was discussed at all, attention was paid mainly to its dissociative aspects. The stress on the need for common values and harmony led a number of social theorists, from Lloyd Warner to Talcott Parsons, to consider conflict a kind of sickness of the body social. Within the last decade, however, a number of theorists opposing the prevailing harmony model have endeavored, partly under the influence of Marx and Simmel, to develop a conflict model of society. The works of Jessie Bernard (1957), Lewis Coser (1956), Ralf Dahrendorf (1957), and Max Gluckman (1956) illustrate this approach.

THE OBJECTIVE BASES OF CONFLICT

The objective bases of social conflict must be sharply separated from subjective elements. Failure to do so results in excessively psychologistic explanations, which cannot do justice to the structure of conflict or to the situations that give rise to it. Such objective bases for contentions vary widely. Conflicts may break out over the distribution of a great variety of scarce values and goods, such as income, status, power, dominion over territory, or ecological position. Such occasions for conflict behavior need to be analyzed separately from dispositions and attitudes such as hostility, aggressiveness, *ressentiment,* hatred, and the like. In certain types of conflicts, such as modern management–labor conflicts, the antagonists may harbor only a minimum of hostile emotions toward each other. Conflicts and hostile sentiments, although often associated, are, in fact, different phenomena.

The distinction between realistic and nonrealistic conflict has proved valuable in analysis. Realistic conflict arises when men clash in the pursuit of claims and the expectation of gain. It is viewed by the participants as a means toward the achievement of specific goals, a means that might be abandoned if other means appear to be more effective. On the other hand, nonrealistic conflict, arising from aggressive impulses that seek expression no matter what the object, allows no functional alternative of means, since it is not aimed at the attainment of a concrete result but at the expression of aggressive impulses. Scapegoating provides an example; the object of attack is secondary to the dispositional need for attack. Thus, in nonrealistic conflict there are functional alternatives for the target, in contrast to realistic conflict in which there are functional alternatives to the means used. In concrete empirical cases, it is likely, of course, that mixtures between the pure types of realistic and nonrealistic conflict will be found to be present.

Hostile attitudes do not necessarily result in conflict; nor need we expect that objective discrepancies in power, status, income, and the like will necessarily lead to the outbreak of conflict, although they can be conceived as potential sources of conflict. Here, as elsewhere, the way men define a situation, rather than the objective features of the situation, must be the focus of analysis. Potential claimants for greater income, status, deference, or power may be deterred from conflict because of fear of consequences or because they consider existing discrepancies in the distribution of valued objects to be legitimate.

THE STRUCTURAL IMPACT OF CONFLICT

The impact of conflict on social structures varies according to the type of such structures. In loosely structured groups and in open, pluralistic societies, conflict that aims at a resolution of tension between antagonists is likely to have stabilizing functions. If the direct expression of rival claims is permitted, such conflicts may serve to eliminate the causes for dissociation and to reestablish unity. In such flexible structures, multiple affiliations of individuals make them participate in a variety of group conflicts so that those who are antagonists in one conflict are allies in another. Thus, multiple conflicts, although varying in intensity, are likely to crisscross one another and thereby prevent cleavages along one axis. The pluralism of associations in such types of societies leads to a plurality of fronts of conflict, and the intensity of any one of these conflicts is likely to be relatively low. Segmental participation in a multiplicity of conflicts constitutes a balancing mechanism within the structure. In this way, conflicts may be said to sew pluralistic society together.

In rigid social structures and in closed groups, on the other hand, the impact of conflict is likely to be quite different. The closer the group, the more intense are conflicts likely to be, that is, the more highly involved the parties. Such groups tend to inhibit the open acting out of hostility since they fear its disruptive effect. Closed groups tend to absorb the total personality of their members; they are jealous of members' affiliation with other groups and desire to monopolize their loyalty. The resultant deep involvement of the members and the intimate association among them is likely to lead to a great deal of hostility and ambivalence, a hostility, however, to which the group denies legitimate outlets. Hence, if conflicts break out in groups that have tried to prevent them, they are likely to be peculiarly intense. This is so because, first, the personality absorption in such groups tends to favor the mobilization of all psychic energies in the conduct of the struggle, and, second, because these conflicts now are not likely to remain limited to the issues at hand but to revive all those grievances that were denied expression previously. All the previously latent causes for conflict are now superimposed upon one another.

A similar situation prevails in large social structures that are organized in unitary and rigid patterns. Here also, conflict, if it occurs at all, is likely to be intense. The lack of multiplicity of crisscrossing associations and multiple allegiances between members is likely to have as a consequence the superimposition of the various latent sources of conflicts. In such structure, a basic division of society into two large hostile classes or groups (the situation envisaged by Marx) becomes a strong probability.

While closeness of association and structural rigidity tend to lead to high intensity of conflict, they do not necessarily lead to a high degree of violence of conflict. Violence, as distinct from intensity, refers to the choice of means for carrying out the conflict rather than to the degree of involvement of the participants. Intensity and violence may vary independently of each other. The more integrated into the society or group are the parties to the conflict, the less likely will the conflict between them be violent. The greater the degree of integration, the higher the likelihood that the conflicting parties will choose weapons that will not permanently menace their common bonds. Violent class struggles or class wars are likely to give way to less militant means, such as institutionalized strikes or regularized contests, in those societies that permit the integration of lower classes or ethnic and other minorities into the social order.

IDEOLOGY AND CONFLICT

Conflicts are likely to be more intense, and more violent as well, to the degree that the contenders are collectivity-oriented rather than self-oriented and hence consider that their struggle is waged for the sake of superindividual ends. Ideological struggles that transcend the merely individual ones allow the participants a "good conscience" in the choice of their means of struggle. Hence, individuals who see themselves acting as representatives of a cause, fighting not for self but only for the ideals of a collectivity they represent, tend to be more radical and merciless than those who fight for personal advantage. The ideological end may justify the means in the eyes of the participants and lead them to consider justifiable, in public ideological contention, means that they might reject in private conflict.

This order of phenomena highlights the importance of intellectuals, that is, the makers and shapers of ideologies in society. Intellectuals who transform conflicts of interests into conflicts of ideas help provide public justification of conflicts and hence to make them more intense. Conflicts may involve the pursuit of personal interests by private individuals or they may arise from the pursuit of the interests of various types of collectivities. Intellectuals, when they function as "ideologists," tend to strip such conflicts of their merely personal or merely interested aspects and to transform them into struggles over eternal truths. They thereby deepen and intensify them. Yet, lest the social role of intellectuals be overrated, it needs to be stressed that they can effectively function as "ideological agents" only in structures that favor the growth of ideologies. In pluralistic societies, crisscrossed by manifold conflicts upon a variety of axes, the role of ideologists is likely to be much less pronounced and their influence considerably reduced; they are likely to assume more important roles in those structures in which the superimposition of conflicts upon one axis favors the emergence of unified ideological fronts.

When manifold conflicts are superimposed upon each other, many and variegated interests can be fused by the adherence to a common ideology.

CONFLICT, CONSENSUS, AND SOCIAL CHANGE

The distinction between conflicts that exceed the limits imposed by societal consensus and those taking place within the basic consensus has informed political thought ever since Aristotle. Conflicts that do not attack the basic consensus and are in effect waged upon the very ground of consensus are likely to lead to adjustments between the various parties and hence to contribute to a closer integration of the society. In contrast, conflicts that attack basic assumptions of collective existence dissociate and split the society into warring camps.

Loosely structured groups and open pluralistic societies, by allowing conflicts to be fought out among a variety of contenders and on a variety of fronts, institute safeguards against types of conflict that might endanger basic consensus. They minimize the danger of divergences touching upon central consensual values. However, in rigid groups or societies the chances are high that if conflict occurs despite the effort to repress it, it will reach down to the basic layers of consensus. For example, if major strata of a society's population are permanently excluded from participation in the society's benefits, they will tend to reject the very assumptions upon which the society is built, and if the systems of legitimation no longer fully operate, they will attempt to attack the social order through revolutionary violence. On the other hand, where no stratum of the population considers itself totally excluded from society's benefits, although all may still engage in multifarious struggles to increase their respective shares of income, wealth, power, or prestige, conflicts will tend to be waged within the limits of a consensus.

Each society contains some elements of strain and potential conflict. Analysis of social change needs to focus attention on these elements, since they provide the dynamics of change. Elements that evade and resist the patterned structure of norms and the habitual balance of power and interests may be considered harbingers of the emergence of new and alternate patterns emerging from an existing structure. Conflict prevents the ossification of social systems by exerting pressures for innovation and creativity; it prevents habitual accommodations from freezing into rigid molds and hence progressively impoverishing the ability to react creatively to novel circumstances. The clash of values and interests, the tension between what is and what some groups or individuals feel ought to be, the conflict between vested interest groups and new strata demanding their share of wealth, power, and status are all productive of social vitality.

Social change can be analyzed only in relation to specified structures. This is why it is necessary to distinguish between changes that take place *within* particular structures and changes that lead to the decay of old structures and the emergence of new ones. We may talk of a change *of* a social system as distinct from changes *within* a social system when all major structural relations, basic institutions, and prevailing value systems have been drastically altered. This theoretical distinction needs to be made, even though it is recognized that the concrete changes *of* a system may be the consequence of previous changes *within* the system.

Whether conflicts within a society will lead to adjustments between existing institutions or to systemic changes of the institutions depends on the degree of flexibility of the social structure. Flexible systems allow progressive rearrangements in their structures in tune with the outcome of various types of group conflict within them. Rigid societies, refusing to make such adjustments and allowing the accumulation of unresolved latent conflicts, are likely to maximize the chances of violent outbreaks attacking the consensual structure and leading to changes *of* social systems.

INGROUP AND OUTGROUP

Sumner's dictum that the distinction between the ingroup (ourselves) and the outgroup (everybody else) is established in, and through, conflict has found general acceptance. One of the prime mechanisms for the strengthening of group bonds and for the emergence of new groups has always been the creation or strengthening among group members of a sense of common values, interests, and purposes, all leading to a mobilization of the group's energies against outsiders. The distinction between "us" and "them," perhaps the most fundamental social distinction, is es-

tablished and periodically reaffirmed in social conflict between insiders and outsiders, between friends and enemies. In homogeneous societies, in which individuals participate in only small numbers of social circles, this distinction is likely to be so encompassing that it allows only minimal relations between the members of all but a few social circles. However, in heterogeneous societies, that is, in societies in which individuals are likely to participate in a great number of social circles in which there will be high degrees of overlapping memberships in a variety of associations and groupings, this sense of exclusiveness will be successfully minimized. In such societies, with their varieties of functionally specific and nongeneralized conflict, men who will be friends in one relationship might well be enemies in another; conflicts with some lead to new alliances with others. If everyone is somebody's ally in some respects and his opponent in many others, such conflicts will draw all into a multifarious and varied group life in which the very crisscrossing of allegiances among men segmentally involved on a variety of fronts prevents exclusiveness and withdrawal.

Peace and feuding, conflict and order, are correlative. Both the cementing and the breaking of the cake of custom constitute part of the dialectic of social life. One is hence ill-advised to distinguish sharply a sociology of order from a sociology of conflict, or a harmony model of society from a conflict model. Such attempts can only result in artificial distinctions. The analysis of social conflicts brings to awareness aspects of social reality that may be obscured if analytical attention focuses too exclusively on phenomena of social order; but an exclusive attention to conflict phenomena may obscure the central importance of social order and needs to be corrected by a correlative concern with the ordered aspects of social life. We deal here not with distinct realities but only with differing aspects of the same reality, so that exclusive emphasis on one or the other is likely to lead the analyst astray. Perhaps we need return now to Charles Horton Cooley's statement: "The more one thinks of it the more he will see that conflict and cooperation are not separable things, but phases of one process which always involves something of both" (1918, p. 39).

REFERENCES

BERNARD, JESSIE, 1957, "The Sociological Study of Conflict." Pages 33–117 in International Sociological Association, *The Nature of Conflict: Studies on the Sociological Aspects of International Tensions.* UNESCO, Tensions and Technology Series. Paris: UNESCO. Contains a comprehensive bibliography.

BOULDING, KENNETH E., 1962, *Conflict and Defense: A General Theory.* A publication of the Center for Research in Conflict Resolution at the University of Michigan. New York: Harper.

COOLEY, CHARLES H., 1918, *Social Process.* New York: Scribner.

COSER, LEWIS A., 1956, *The Functions of Social Conflict.* Glencoe, Ill.: Free Press.

DAHRENDORF, RALF, (1957) 1959, *Class and Class Conflict in Industrial Society.* Rev. & enl. ed. Stanford (Calif.) Univ. Press. First published in German as *Soziale Klassen und Klassen-Konflikt in der industriellen Gesellschaft.*

DAHRENDORF, RALF, 1962, *Gesellschaft und Freiheit: Zur soziologischen Analyse der Gegenwart.* Munich: Piper. This work incorporates a series of papers previously published in English.

GLUCKMAN, MAX, 1956, *Custom and Conflict in Africa.* Oxford: Blackwell; Glencoe, Ill.: Free Press.

MACK, RAYMOND W., and SNYDER, RICHARD S., 1957, "The Analysis of Social Conflict: Toward an Overview and Synthesis." *Journal of Conflict Resolution* 1:212–248.

PARK, ROBERT E., and BURGESS, ERNEST, 1924, *Introduction to the Science of Society.* Univ. of Chicago Press

SIMMEL, GEORG, (1908) 1955, *Conflict: The Web of Group Affiliations.* Glencoe, Ill.: Free Press. These essays originally appeared as "Der Streit" and "Die Kreuzung sozialer Kreise" in Georg Simmel's *Soziologie,* published by Duncker and Humblot, Berlin.

WEBER, MAX, (1904–1917) 1949, *Max Weber on the Methodology of the Social Sciences.* Translated and edited by Edward A. Shils and H. A. Finch. Glencoe, Ill.: Free Press.

3
*Integration and Values Versus Coercion and Interests: The Two Faces of Society**
RALF DAHRENDORF

Throughout the history of Western political thought, two views of society have stood in conflict. Both these views are intended to explain what has been, and will probably continue to be, the most puzzling problem of social philosophy: how is it that human societies cohere? There is one large and distinguished school of thought according to which social order results from a general agreement of values, a *consensus omnium* or *volonté générale* which outweighs all possible or actual differences of opinion and interest. There is another equally distinguished school of thought which holds that coherence and order in society are founded on force and

*[Reprinted from *Class and Class Conflict in Industrial Society* by Ralf Dahrendorf with the permission of the publishers, Stanford University Press and Routledge and Kegan Paul, Ltd. © 1959 by the Board of Trustees of the Leland Stanford University.]

constraint, on the domination of some and the subjection of others. To be sure, these views are not at all points mutually exclusive. The Utopian (as we shall call those who insist on coherence by consensus) does not deny the existence of differences of interest; nor does the Rationalist (who believes in coherence by constraint and domination) ignore such agreements of value as are required for the very establishment of force. But Utopian and Rationalist alike advance claims of primacy for their respective standpoints. For the Utopian, differences of interest are subordinated to agreements of value, and for the Rationalist these agreements are but a thin, and as such ineffective, coating of the primary reality of differences that have to be precariously reconciled by constraint. Both Utopians and Rationalists have shown much ingenuity and imagination in arguing for their respective points of view. This has not, however, led them more closely together. There is a genuine conflict of approach between Aristotle and Plato, Hobbes and Rousseau, Kant and Hegel, and this conflict has grown in intensity as the history of thought has advanced. Unless one believes that all philosophical disputes are spurious and ultimately irrelevant, the long history of the particular dispute about the problem of social order has exposed—if not solved —what appear to be fundamental alternatives of knowledge, moral decision, and political orientation. . . .

Insofar as historical societies are concerned, Karl Marx subscribed to an image of society of the rational variety. He assumed the ubiquity of change and conflict as well as domination and subjection, and I suggest that this view seems particularly appropriate for the analysis of problems of conflict. In any case, it seems more appropriate than the utopian view implicit in the works of Drucker and Mayo, according to which happy cooperation is the normal state

of social life. Marx, or Drucker and Mayo, may not be especially convincing representatives of these views,[1] but the distinction with which we are concerned here is, in any case, not tied to their names. Generally speaking, it seems to me that two (meta-) theories can and must be distinguished in contemporary sociology. One of these, the *integration theory of society,* conceives of social structure in terms of a functionally integrated system held in equilibrium by certain patterned and recurrent processes. The other one, the *coercion theory of society,* views social structure as a form of organization held together by force and constraint and reaching continuously beyond itself in the sense of producing within itself the forces that maintain it in an unending process of change. Like their philosophical counterparts, these theories are mutually exclusive. But—if I may be permitted a paradoxical formulation that will be explained presently—in sociology (as opposed to philosophy) a decision which accepts one of these theories and rejects the other is neither necessary nor desirable. There are sociological problems for the explanation of which the integration theory of society provides adequate assumptions; there are other problems which can be explained only in terms of the coercion theory of society; there are, finally, problems for which both theories appear adequate. For sociological analysis, society is Janus-headed, and its two faces are equivalent aspects of the same reality. . . .

For purposes of exposition it seems useful to reduce each of the two faces of society to a small number of basic tenets, even if this involves some degree of oversimplification as well as overstatement. The integration theory of society, as displayed by the work of Parsons and other structural-functionalists, is founded on a number of assumptions of the following type:

1 Every society is a relatively persistent, stable structure of elements.

2 Every society is a well-integrated structure of elements.

3 Every element in a society has a function, i.e., renders a contribution to its maintenance as a system.

4 Every functioning social structure is based on a consensus of values among its members.

In varying forms, these elements of (1) stability, (2) integration, (3) functional coordination, and (4) consensus recur in all structural-functional approaches to the study of social structure. They are, to be sure, usually accompanied by protestations to the effect that stability, integration, functional coordination, and consensus are only "relatively" generalized. Moreover, these assumptions are not metaphysical propositions about the essence of society; they are merely assumptions for purposes of scientific analysis. As such, however, they constitute a coherent view of the social process[1] which enables us to comprehend many problems of social reality.

However, it is abundantly clear that the integration approach to social analysis does not enable us to comprehend all problems of social reality. Let us look at two undeniably sociological problems of the contemporary world which demand explanation. (1) In recent years, an increasing number of industrial and commercial enterprises have introduced the position of personnel manager to cope with matters of hiring and firing, advice to employees,

etc. Why? And: what are the consequences of the introduction of this new position? (2) On the 17th of June, 1953, the building workers of East Berlin put down their tools and went on a strike that soon led to a generalized revolt against the communist regime of East Germany. Why? And: what are the consequences of this uprising? From the point of view of the integration model of society, the first of these problems is susceptible of a satisfactory solution. A special position to cope with personnel questions is functionally required by large enterprises in an age of rationalization and "social ethic"; the introduction of this position adapts the enterprise to the values of the surrounding society; its consequence is therefore of an integrative and stabilizing nature. But what about the second problem? Evidently, the uprising of the 17th of June is neither due to, nor productive of, integration in East German society. It documents and produces not stability, but instability. It contributes to the disruption, not the maintenance, of the existing system. It testifies to dissensus rather than consensus. The integration model tells us little more than that there are certain "strains" in the "system." In fact, in order to cope with problems of this kind we have to replace the integration theory of society by a different and, in many ways, contradictory model.

What I have called the coercion theory of society can also be reduced to a small number of basic tenets, although here again these assumptions oversimplify and overstate the case:

1 Every society is at every point subject to processes of change; social change is ubiquitous.

2 Every society displays at every point dissensus and conflict; social conflict is ubiquitous.

3 Every element in a society renders a contribution to its disintegration and change.

4 Every society is based on the coercion of some of its members by others.

[1] It is important to emphasize that "stability" as a tenet of the integration theory of society does not mean that societies are "static." It means, rather, that such processes as do occur (and the structural-functional approach is essentially concerned with processes) serve to maintain the patterns of the system as a whole. Whatever criticism I have of this approach, I do not want to be misunderstood as attributing to it a "static bias" (which has often been held against this approach without full consideration of its merits).

If we return to the problem of the German workers' strike, it will become clear that this latter model enables us to deal rather more satisfactorily with its causes and consequences. The revolt of the building workers and their fellows in other industries can be explained in terms of coercion.[2] The revolting groups are engaged in a conflict which "functions" as an agent of change by disintegration. A ubiquitous phenomenon is expressed, in this case, in an exceptionally intense and violent way, and further explanation will have to account for this violence on the basis of the acceptance of conflict and change as universal features of social life. I need hardly add that, like the integration model, the coercion theory of society constitutes but a set of assumptions for purposes of scientific analysis and implies no claim for philosophical validity —although, like its counterpart, this model also provides a coherent image of social organization.

Now, I would claim that, in a sociological context, neither of these models can be conceived as exclusively valid or applicable. They constitute complementary, rather than alternative, aspects of the structure of total societies as well as of every element of this structure. We have to choose between them only for the explanation of specific problems; but in the conceptual arsenal of sociological analysis they exist side by side. Whatever criticism one may have of the advocates of one or the other of these models can therefore be directed only against claims for the exclusive validity of either.[3] Strictly speaking, both models are "valid" or, rather, useful and necessary for sociological analysis. We cannot conceive of society unless we realize the dialectics of stability and change, integration and conflict, function and motive force, consensus and coercion. . . .

While logically feasible,[4] the solution of the dilemma of political thought which we have offered here for the more restricted field of sociological analysis nevertheless raises a number of serious problems. It is evidently virtually impossible to think of society in terms of either model without positing its opposite number at the same time. There can be no conflict, unless this conflict occurs within a context of meaning, i.e., some kind of coherent "system." No conflict is conceivable between French housewives and Chilean chess players, because these groups are not united by, or perhaps "integrated into," a common frame of reference. Analogously, the notion of integration makes little sense unless it presupposes the existence of different elements that are integrated. Even Rousseau derived his *volonté générale* from a modified *bellum omnium contra omnes*. Using one or the other model is therefore a matter of emphasis rather than of fundamental difference; and there are . . . many points at which a theory of group conflict has to have recourse to the integration theory of social structure.

Inevitably, the question will be raised, also, whether a unified theory of

---

[2] For purposes of clarity, I have deliberately chosen an example from a totalitarian state. But coercion is meant here in a very general sense, and the coercion model is applicable to all societies, independent of their specific political structure.

[3] This, it seems to me, is the only—if fundamental —legitimate criticism that can be raised against Parsons' work on this general level. In *The So-*

cial System, Parsons repeatedly advances, for the integration theory of society, a claim that it is the nucleus of "the general" sociological theory—a claim which I regard as utterly unjustified.

[4] As is demonstrated most clearly by the fact that a similar situation can be encountered in physics with respect to the theory of light. Here, too, there are two seemingly incompatible theories which nevertheless exist side by side, and each of which has its proper realm of empirical phenomena: the wave theory and the quantum theory of light.

society that includes the tenets of both the integration and the coercion models of society is not at least conceivable —for as to its desirability there can be little doubt. Is there, or can there be, a general point of view that synthesizes the unsolved dialectics of integration and coercion? So far as I can see, there is no such general model; as to its possibility, I have to reserve judgment. It seems at least conceivable that unification of theory is not feasible at a point which has puzzled thinkers ever since the beginning of Western philosophy.

For the explanation of the formation of conflict groups out of conditions of social structure, we shall employ a model that emphasizes the ugly face of society. . . . I shall try to show how, on the assumption of the coercive nature of social structure, relations of authority become productive of clashes of role interest which under certain conditions lead to the formation of organized antagonistic groups within limited social organizations as well as within total societies. . . .

AUTHORITY RELATIONS

From the point of view of the integration theory of social structure, units of social analysis ("social systems") are essentially voluntary associations of people who share certain values and set up institutions in order to ensure the smooth functioning of cooperation. From the point of view of coercion theory, however, the units of social analysis present an altogether different picture. Here, it is not voluntary cooperation or general consensus but enforced constraint that makes social organizations cohere. In institutional terms, this means that in every social organization some positions are entrusted with a right to exercise control over other positions in order to ensure effective coercion; it means, in other words, that there is a differential dis-

tribution of power and authority. One of the central theses of this study consists in the assumption that this differential distribution of authority invariably becomes the determining factor of systematic social conflicts of a type that is germane to class conflicts in the traditional (Marxian) sense of this term. The structural origin of such group conflicts must be sought in the arrangement of social roles endowed with expectations of domination or subjection. Wherever there are such roles, group conflicts of the type in question are to be expected. Differentiation of groups engaged in such conflicts follows the lines of differentiation of roles that are relevant from the point of view of the exercise of authority. Identification of variously equipped authority roles is the first task of conflict analysis;[5] conceptually and empirically all further steps of analysis follow from the investigation of distributions of power and authority. . . .

In the present study we are concerned exclusively with relations of authority, for these alone are part of social structure and therefore permit the systematic derivation of group conflicts from the organization of total societies and associations within them. The significance of such group conflicts rests with the fact that they are not the product of structurally fortuitous relations of power but come forth wherever authority is exercised—and that means in all societies under all historical conditions. (1) Authority relations are always relations of super- and subordination. (2) Where there are authority relations, the superordinate element is socially expected to control, by orders

---

[5] To facilitate communication, I shall employ in this study a number of abbreviations. These must not however be misunderstood. Thus, "conflict analysis" in this context stands for "analysis of group conflicts of the class type, class being understood in the traditional sense." At no point do I want to imply a claim for a generalized theory of social conflict.

and commands, warnings and prohibitions, the behavior of the subordinate element. (3) Such expectations attach to relatively permanent social positions rather than to the character of individuals; they are in this sense legitimate. (4) By virtue of this fact, they always involve specification of the persons subject to control and of the spheres within which control is permissible.[6] Authority, as distinct from power, is never a relation of generalized control over others. (5) Authority being a legitimate relation, noncompliance with authoritative commands can be sanctioned; it is indeed one of the functions of the legal system (and of course of quasi-legal customs and norms) to support the effective exercise of legitimate authority. . . .

I have assumed in the preceding remarks that authority is a characteristic of social organizations as general as society itself. Despite the assertion of Renner—and other modern sociologists—that in some contemporary societies the exercise of authority has been eliminated and replaced by the more anonymous "rule of the law" or other nonauthoritative relations, I should indeed maintain that authority is a universal element of social structure. It is in this sense more general than, for example, property, or even status. . . . Generally speaking, however, the universality of authority relations would seem evident as soon as we describe these relations in a "passive" rather than in an "active" sense.

[6] This element of the definition of authority is crucial. It implies that the manager who tries to control people outside his firm, or the private lives of people inside his firm, trespasses the borderline between authority and power. Although he has authority over people in his firm, his control assumes the form of power as soon as it goes beyond the specified persons and spheres of legitimate control. This type of trespassing is of course frequent in every authority relation; and an empirical phenomenon well worth investigating is to what extent the fusion of authority and power tends to intensify group conflicts.

Authority relations exist wherever there are people whose actions are subject to legitimate and sanctioned prescriptions that originate outside them but within social structure. This formulation, by leaving open who exercises what kind of authority, leaves little doubt as to the omnipresence of some kind of authority somehow exercised. For it is evident that there are many forms and types of authority in historical societies. There are differences of a considerable order of magnitude between the relations of the citizen of classical Athens and his slaves, the feudal landlord and his villeins and serfs, the nineteenth-century capitalist and his worker, the secretary of a totalitarian state party and its members, the appointed manager of a modern enterprise and its employees, or the elected prime minister of a democratic country and the electorate. No attempt will be made in this study to develop a typology of authority. But it is assumed throughout that the existence of domination and subjection is a common feature of all possible types of authority and, indeed, of all possible types of association and organization. . . .

4
The Conceptualization of Intergroup Relations with Special Reference to Conflict*
JESSIE BERNARD

INTRODUCTION: THE SEVERAL TYPES OR LEVELS OF INTERGROUP CONCEPTUALIZATION

. . .The psychological approach is characterized by an emphasis on subjective factors, for the psychologist, because of the nature of his science,

*[Reprinted from *Social Forces*, 1951, pp. 243–251 by permission of the publisher, University of North Carolina Press.]

sees primarily what goes on in the human mind. The psychological *Tendez* is of necessity, therefore, in the direction of an "it's all in the mind" orientation. Thus in conceptualizing intergroup relations the tendency is to minimize objective conditions and to concentrate on such phenomena as stereotypes, prejudice, hostility, aggression, threat orientation, and to lay great emphasis on the allegedly nonrational nature of these subjective phenomena.

At the present time, therefore, the conceptualization of intergroup relations may be thought of in terms of a continuum so far as emphasis on subjective factors is concerned. At one extreme we have the ecologist's theoretical system with its concepts of symbiosis, commensalism, predation, parisitism, etc., in which there is little if any room for recognition of subjective factors, or, indeed, of individuals at all. Next comes the economist's system, which in its analyses of the division of labor, especially in the international market, verges closely on the ecological point of view, but makes room for some emphasis on subjective factors in its considerations of value. (The Marxist conceptualization of intergroup relations, of course, makes room for a good deal of subjective emphasis.) Next on the continuum would probably come the political scientist's system which, with its emphases on nations and nationalism, has a large component of subjective material. Then comes the sociologist's formulations which place considerable stress on objective relations, but also deal with subjective factors in his emphases on cultural factors. Finally we have the psychologist's conceptual system which is wholly in terms of subjective elements.

. . .Sociological research in intergroup relations has lagged behind psychological research. In the field of conflict, for example, we know more about the personality mechanisms underlying hostility, prejudice, aggression, and group stereotypes than we do about the techniques for determining whether or not a conflict exists and of measuring the extent of incompatibility of group goals, if it does.

The psychological or subjective approach has a great deal of value, and nothing said here is intended to disparage it in any sense. It does, however, raise a number of theoretical questions. Are intergroup relations to be conceived as existing independently of, or at least separately from, the inner reactions or the interpersonal relations of members, as the social sciences have tended to conceptualize them; or are they to be conceived subjectively, either as the sum-total of individual interpersonal relations among members of the groups, or as the subjective reactions of the members of the groups, as the psychologists tend to conceive them? Can one always tell what the intergroup relations are from a scrutiny, however careful, of interpersonal relations? Does the fact that Group A has no prejudice, hostility, or wrong stereotypes of Group B mean in fact that there is no conflict between them?

The present article, written by a sociologist with, presumably, a sociological bias, will deal primarily with the contrast between the sociological and the psychological conceptualizations of conflict in intergroup relations, omitting reference to the ecological, economic, and political.

SOCIOLOGICAL AND PSYCHOLOGICAL CONCEPTUALIZATIONS CONFLICT

Sociologically speaking, conflict exists between groups when there is a fundamental incompatibility in their values, goals, interests, etc., so that if one group gets what it wants, the other group cannot get what it wants.[1] Conflict so conceived can exist independently of the subjective reactions of members of the groups. The members of the groups in conflict may and, indeed, often do need and bear affection toward one another, as in the case of the conflict between the sexes or age groups. Nor is hostility a necessary concomitant of conflict, viewed sociologically. Conflict in this sociological sense should be distinguished from misunderstanding; in a misunderstanding, groups may feel that a conflict exists when in fact none does. Nor should conflict be confused with aggression. Aggression may occur where there is no conflict; and conflict may occur without aggression. It is not, in fact, always possible to determine whether a conflict actually exists, that is, whether the goals, values, interests, etc., of two groups are actually incompatible.

In contrast to this concept is that of the psychologist according to which conflict appears to exist in the minds of group members. There is, for example, much written on "threat orientation" but little on actual threat. In a recent text in social psychology, the author is at great pains to emphasize that groups may conceive of one another as threats,[2] but he lays little stress on the fact that maybe this threat-consciousness is well based in fact. Sociologically speaking, one group may actually constitute a threat to another and the threat-consciousness of the threatened group is not nonrational but well-founded in fact, as we shall indicate below.

INTERGROUP RELATIONS CONCEIVED AS THE SUM-TOTAL OF INTERPERSONAL RELATIONS AMONG GROUP MEMBERS

One way to conceptualize intergroup relations psychologically is to view them as the sum-total of interpersonal relations among members of the groups. Although this point of view is not usually precisely formulated, it often lies back of practical programs for improving intergroup relations. The assumption is made that improving interpersonal relations will ipso facto improve the relationship between the groups. It is basic to the principle that "getting people together," or "getting people to work on a common project" will improve intergroup relations. . . .

In brief, a thousand friendships between members of two groups—German and American scientists, for example, or a thousand love affairs between soldiers and forbidden enemy women —will not add up to friendly group relations. Nor conversely, will a thousand quarrels between American tourists and French taxidrivers add up to Franco–American conflict.

For the laws which govern interpersonal relations are not necessarily the same as those which regulate intergroup relations.[3] We recognize this fact in intersexual relations. Men and women have found themselves attracted to one another in spite of the widest and deepest group barriers. Negro and white, Mongolian and Caucasian, Oriental and Occidental, Jew and gentile, Greek and barbarian, conqueror and vanquished have leaped group barriers from time immemorial. Even among men, personal attractions have often subverted intergroup patterns. In static trench warfare, as in World War I, fraternization between

[1] Jessie Bernard, *American Community Behavior* (New York: Dryden, 1949), Chaps. 3 and 6 and Part III.
[2] Theodore Newcomb, *Social Psychology* (New York: Dryden, 1950).
[3] This fact is elaborated in Jessie Bernard, *op. cit.,* pp. 116–117, 358–359.

enemies can be a constant danger to intergroup hostility. It is reported that in both world wars American soldiers often found their enemies, the Germans, personally more congenial than their allies, the French. We are told that even in Nazi Germany many high officials had their "pet" Jews of whom they were fond and whom they wished to protect.

Nothing here said should be interpreted as opposing any effort to bring the members of conflicting groups into warm, friendly relations. The argument is, simply, that such relations will not necessarily bring about equally friendly group relations. This interpersonal approach might be labeled the "cosmetic" approach; it glosses over the surface but does not always come to grips with the fundamental bases for group conflict.

INTERGROUP RELATIONS CONCEIVED AS SUBJECTIVE REACTIONS OF GROUP MEMBERS

More often explicitly stated is the psychological conceptualization of group relations in terms of the subjective reactions of group members. The tendency of psychologists to conceptualize group conflict in terms of stereotypes, prejudice, hostilities, and aggressions is illustrated in a number of recent works. Otto Klineberg, in his outstanding and valuable memorandum on *Tensions Affecting International Understanding,*[4] deals with such topics as personality in relation to nationality, national stereotypes, attitudes and their modification, and influences making

[4]Otto Klineberg, *Tensions Affecting International Understanding,* Social Science Research Council Bulletin 62, 1950. It should be pointed out that although Klineberg is a psychologist and therefore oriented toward the subjective emphasis in intergroup relations he is critically aware of the inadequacy of the psychological viewpoint taken alone.

for aggression. He recognizes the existence of demographic and technological factors in intergroup relations but —justifiably—begs to be excused from discussing them, as outside the competence of a psychologist. Newcomb, who as professor of both psychology and sociology, could be expected to represent a sociological orientation (and does, more than most psychologists), in a chapter in his recent text on group conflict discusses prejudices, hostilities, stereotypes, barriers to communication (especially segregation), lynching, and the reduction of hostility (by reducing personal susceptibility to threat orientation, reducing barriers to communication, changing norms through joint participation). These two important works illustrate a conceptualization of intergroup conflict held by many psychologists.

The question may perhaps legitimately be raised as to whether such a frame of reference even deals with intergroup relations at all. It certainly deals with human beings and tells us a good deal about them. Does it, however, tell us anything about group relations?

An important embodiment of the psychological conceptualization of intergroup relations is the basic psychological premise on which the UNESCO constitution rests, namely that "wars begin in the minds of men."[5] This type of statement has a specious kind of authenticity about it which sounds well until one tries to interpret it. It is either a truism, meaning that war is a kind of human behavior, which is conceived and executed through the human mind. Or else it is, unless considerably modified and qualified, something of a fallacy. For what, exactly, does it mean? No one save perhaps orthodox Freudian psychoanalysts would argue today that war is the result

[5] Quoted by Klineberg, *op. cit.,* p. 4.

of an instinct (of pugnacity or aggression, or what-have-you) that periodically requires mass expression. Modern warfare is a highly complex technological enterprise for which nothing in man's instinctive equipment prepares him. Indeed, modern warfare is so contrary to our instincts that a considerable amount of training, indoctrination, and outside motivation is necessary to convert men into fighters. Modern psychologists do not, therefore, invoke instincts (excepting again the psychoanalysts who posit a death instinct) to explain wars. But they have created a number of concepts to substitute for the concept of instinct. They are, as we have seen, such concepts as stereotypes, prejudice, hostility, aggression and threat orientation.

Stereotypes

The current doctrine with respect to stereotypes tends to challenge the older "kernel of truth" theory and to emphasize the wholly nonrational element in them. It is argued, although not demonstrated, that stereotypes among nations are more important than the facts about the nations themselves. "More important than the truth about America is what Europe thinks about America—if we view the matter from the standpoint of relationships; for Europe will be more influenced by its own picture of America than by America itself."[6] Klineberg agrees with Den Hollander that stereotypes become "a psychological reality of tremendous importance, which operates in both directions in determining group relations and group behavior."[7]

In support of the argument that stereotypes are independent of actual experience, psychologists offer data to show that whether one has had little or much contact with minority groups, one tends to hold similar stereotypes. The person who has had no contact with Negroes reacts much like one who has had a great deal. How then could his picture of Negroes be based on fact?[8] It is, obviously, true that the origin of stereotypes within the individual does not require first-hand experience with the stereotyped group. But vicarious experience can be, and in fact is, just as effective. Teachers and propagandists depend on it as a matter of course. . . . Most people must of necessity acquire their stereotypes of other peoples of the world through this kind of vicarious rather than through direct contacts. But this tells us little about the accuracy of the stereotype itself; it may be favorable or unfavorable, accurate or innaccurate whether it is acquired directly or vicariously. But none of this informs us about the origin or the validity of the stereotypes as collective representations in the first place. We can explain why John Smith, who has had little contact with Negroes, has a stereotype of the Negro as superstitious and lazy, or of the Arapesh as cherishing and gentle. But this explanation does not account for the origin of the stereotype in John Smith's world. Are stereotypes wholly arbitrary? If so, can we invent arbitrary stereotypes about any group and make them stick? Why are certain adjectives chosen as part of the stereotypes of particular groups? If there is little in the "kernel of truth" theory, it should be possible to create any kind of stereotype about any people. . . .

Whether or not stereotypes do or do not have a "kernel of truth" as their base, no evidence has been presented to show that they cause or prevent intergroup conflict. The stereotypes of

[6] W. A. Visser't Hooft, quoted by Otto Klineberg, *ibid.*, p. 123.
[7] *Ibid.*
[8] Newcomb, *op. cit.*, p. 582.

German children with respect to America resemble those of French children more than they do those of British children; all are fairly friendly and favorable.[9] Yet twice in this century Germany and the United States have fought wars. Most Americans hold unfavorable stereotypes about, let us say, the Turks. These stereotypes are not likely to lead us to war with the Turks; nor do they even imply the existence of conflict.

Hostile stereotypes are more likely to be the result of conflict than its cause. When a conflict exists, each side attempts to create hostile stereotypes of the enemy in order to whip up fighting drive. It is, in fact, one of the functions of propagandists to create such stereotypes—of the ruthless Hun, of the aggressive communist, of the sneaking Jap, etc. Stereotypes, in brief, may be used as weapons in intergroup conflict; they have not been shown to be causes of such conflict.

Prejudice

Prejudice is undoubtedly an important sociological as well as psychological fact. Yet its relationship to intergroup conflict is no more clear and unequivocal than that of the stereotype. As in the case of the stereotype, prejudice appears to be one of the results rather than a cause of intergroup conflict. Can we, for example, say that the slave trader was prejudiced against the Africans he captured and sold? There certainly was a conflict here; was it a consequence of prejudice? Was prejudice responsible for the conflict between the American Indian and the white colonist? Or was it a consequence? Thousands if not millions of Americans during the thirties were, if anything, prejudiced in favor of the Russians. Many found it difficult to accept the

[9] Unpublished study by Marie Jahoda, cited by Klineberg, *op. cit.*, pp. 108–110.

existence of conflict between the Soviet Union and the United States in the post-war forties; some do not still. There has been little if any prejudice against the Germans in this country. Nevertheless conflict has existed.

In brief, the existence of a causal relationship between prejudice and group conflict objectively considered has yet to be demonstrated. In order to prove such a relationship we would have to show that prejudice existed between the parties of all intergroup conflict and that no such prejudice existed where no conflict existed. Prejudice, like the hostile stereotype, is a weapon in intergroup conflict; it is used in conflict; it does not cause conflict. Until a causal relationship can be established between prejudice and intergroup conflict, the conceptualization of intergroup conflict in terms of prejudice has limited significance.

Hostility

Conflict objectively considered can exist between groups without hatred or hostility on the part of the members. Conversely, hostility can exist without conflict. Hostility, like adverse stereotypes and prejudice, results from, rather than causes, conflict. . . .

Threat orientation

The subjective or psychological concept which seems to have the most direct bearing on intergroup conflict is that dealing with the consciousness of threat on the part of group members. The chief limitation to this concept lies in the fact that the psychologist as psychologist can tell us only what the members of a group conceive as threats; he cannot tell us whether or not an actual threat exists. . . .

Prejudice may result from the objective conflict of group interests. There is a good, that is, rational basis for "prejudice" if such "prejudice" will preserve one's privileges or help one fight for privileges. Such "prejudices" may not be gentlemanly or Christian or "American" in the ideal sense, but they are certainly not nonrational in a threat situation. They represent an empirically reasonable technique in conflict. Carey McWilliams has called anti-Semitism "a mask for privilege." Perhaps all kinds of discriminatory prejudices have something of this character. A threat to privilege may produce them.

It is the sociologist who should be able to tell us something of the "real" or "objective" relations between groups, regardless of how they may appear subjectively within the minds of the members; he should be able to tell us whether or not a threat exists. To be sure, no group is likely to think of itself as a threat to any other group; on the contrary, members of one group are likely to conceive of other groups as threats to themselves. The sociologist should, however, be able to tell whether the threat actually exists and in which direction. The psychologist, training his microscope on the subjective reactions of his subjects, is not in a position to tell us about the outside world, however much he may know of threat orientation. Was the white man a threat to the American Indian? Was the American Indian a threat to the white man? The psychologist cannot answer such questions because his theoretical conceptualization of intergroup relations makes no room for such problems. He can tell us what the white man felt and thought about the Indian, but not whether or not an objective conflict existed. . . .

The concept of threat-orientation comes nearer than the others so far discussed to the heart of intergroup conflict; it is the logical subjective counterpart to objective conflict, for in true conflict one group actually is a threat to the other. The difficulty is, however, that threat-orientation may exist independent of an objectively based conflict of interest. . . .

VALUES AS CLEWS TO INTERGROUP CONFLICT

The above discussion does not imply that subjective factors in intergroup relations are to be discounted. There is a sense in which it may be said that wars and other conflicts begin in the minds of men. Men have certain hierarchies of values in their minds. War is, for most people, low on their list. But there are, again for most people, certain things that are worse than war. . . . Few people actually want war. But there are other things they want even less. Historically the cultures and peoples that have been willing to pay any price at all to avoid war have probably been destroyed as separate cultures and peoples by other groups that were not willing to pay the price of culture self-destruction in order to maintain peace. It is in the values in men's minds, not in their stereotypes, prejudices, hostilities, and aggressions, that one must, perhaps, look for the subjective "causes" of conflict. When these values are incompatible, so that one set can survive only at the expense of the other, we have intergroup conflict, no matter how the individual members may feel toward one another personally. . . .

5
The Prejudiced Society*
EARL RAAB
and SEYMOUR MARTIN LIPSET

The problem of prejudice, as it presents itself to society, consists of overt acts which deny equal status or opportunity

*[From American Race Relations Today by Earl Raab. Copyright © 1962 by Earl Raab. Reprinted by permission of Doubleday and Company, Inc.]

to people because of their racial, religious, or ethnic identity. However, "prejudice" is often used in a specialized sense to describe an individual's state of mind or attitude. There has long been a popular tendency to reify "prejudiced attitude"; to conceive of it as a little mental package tucked away in a corner of the brain, waiting for the proper stimulus to bring it to life. According to this view, if a person has "a prejudiced attitude" against Filipinos, then when a Filipino brushes up against him, or enters the same room he's in, or applies to him for a job, or tries to move next door, this attitude would be triggered and the "prejudiced person" would act accordingly.

The evidence clearly indicates, however, that prejudiced attitudes are very far from being neat little mental packages; and that, at the very least, they do not predetermine prejudiced behavior.

Gordon Allport has partly defined an attitude as a "mental and neural state of readiness."[1] The meaningful reference here is to the fact that an attitude is a "mental and neural" state and not just to the fact that it is a state of readiness. A mechanical jack-in-the-box, crouched on its springs, might be said to have an attitude of readiness. Its attitude is such that it will jump up when the cover is removed. But a human attitude describes an internal state that has an independent existence, apart from any resultant behavior. If a child were simulating a jack-in-the-box in a school play, his attitude towards jumping out of the box in which he was crouched might consist of a combination of elements, e.g.: he may be displeased about the physical prospect of jumping out; on the other hand, he may have a strong fear of the derision

he will face if he fails to jump. Both of these elements comprise his "attitude about jumping" at a given point. The attitude exists as a real fact even if the show is cancelled and he never does have the opportunity of jumping or not jumping.

Hostility and stereotype

It is common to think of the prejudiced attitude as consisting of both hostility and an overgeneralization or stereotype. It is even common to think of the hostility as flowing from the stereotype. But, in fact, it is possible for an individual to have the stereotype without the hostility, or the hostility without the stereotype. It is possible to cloak two groups with the same stereotype, and have different feelings about them. Saenger and Flowerman questioned some· 450 college students as to their feeling of dislike for a number of human groups. They also asked these students to indicate the characteristics which they believed marked these groups. Presumably their likes or dislikes would be based on the kinds of characteristics which they attributed to these groups. This was not the case. Students who expressed a dislike for Jews ascribed to them characteristics which they also ascribed to other groups for whom they did *not* express a dislike. For example, 31 percent of the students complained that the Jews were mercenary; but 24 percent of them complained that Americans were mercenary, and 38 percent that businessmen were mercenary. However, Jews were more often disliked for this quality than were Americans or businessmen.

In a study made by B. M. Kramer, he marked off five "distance zones" from an area in which Negroes were moving and interviewed white residents in each of the zones. Zone 1 was the closest to this area of expanding Negro movement. Zone 5 was the most

[1] Gorden Allport, "Attitudes," in *A Handbook of Social Psychology,* edited by C. Murcheson (Worcester: Clark University Press, 1935), p. 798.

remote, three miles away. There was a general desire among white residents in all five zones to exclude Negroes from their neighborhoods. Kramer checked the stereotypes held by these white residents about Negroes, e.g., that Negroes were personally unclean or diseased. In zone 1, where the white residents had the closest contact with the Negroes, only 5 percent offered such stereotypes as reasons for exclusion; as against 25 percent of the residents in zone 5. However, the intensity of hostility in zone 1 was higher than in zone 5; in zone 1, 64 percent of the residents made spontaneous expressions of hostility, as against only 4 percent in zone 5. Whatever else may have been involved in the situation, it was clear that hostility and stereotype were not tied to each other.

A negative stereotype may exist without hostility; hostility without a negative stereotype; a combination of both cognitive and emotional elements may exist with varying degrees of intensity and with varying targets. A prejudiced attitude is indeed not a homogeneous mental package. Prejudiced attitude 1 is different from prejudiced attitude 2, and there is almost an endless variety of possibilities.

Frame of reference — the situational factor

Not only do prejudiced attitudes differ widely from one individual to another, but they tend to differ from one situation to another for any given individual. For an attitude is not a thing, it is a process; it is an interaction. It is an interaction involving not only the person and the object, but all other factors that are present in any situation. A crude illustration: In his own hometown, Jones may have the deepest contempt for Smith, who lives up the block. He considers Smith a rough character with bad manners and worse taste,

socially unacceptable and intellectually barren. Jones has a *feeling* of distaste when he thinks of Smith, and avoids him conscientiously. It happens that Jones, alone on an unguided world tour, has a transportation breakdown in a primitive village in a backward country. The villagers are unfriendly, unlettered, and unsanitary. Into this unhappy and improbable scene, after a couple of days, rides Smith. Jones may well greet him with a joyful embrace, rather than with distaste. His image of Smith as a boor may be replaced by the image of a man who at least has the good sense to speak English and to wash his hands before eating. Whether or not this feeling and image will carry over in any way when the two men return to their home town is another matter — but the fact remains that a different external situation has evoked a different attitude.

Sherif and Cantril have called this situational factor "frame of reference." They write:

The term "frame of reference" is simply used to denote the functionally related factors (present and past) which operate at the moment to determine the particular properties of a psychological phenomenon (such as perception, judgment, affectivity).

In psychological literature, the critical importance of the situational factor is supported by experiments on many levels. Wever and Zener had subjects judge the weight of a series of objects as "light" or "heavy." When the series of objects was changed from a light series to a heavy series, the same object that was formerly judged heavy was now perceived as light. McGarvey had her subjects rate the "social prestige" of various occupations and found that the desirability of any given occupation was dependent on the kind of occupational series with which it appeared.

Many research roads lead to the

understanding that prejudiced attitudes can be highly situational in character. One evening at a summer camp, thirty young men were tested as to their attitudes towards Japanese–Americans. Following this, they were scheduled to attend a show at a local theatre. Instead, their show-going was cancelled, and they were forced to accomplish a series of complicated tasks. The same night, following the tasks, their attitudes towards Japanese–Americans were retested, and were found to be less favorable than they had been earlier in the evening. Nothing had changed in the interim with respect to the young men vis-a-vis Japanese–Americans, but some other factors in the situation had changed.

Deitrich Reitzes examined a situation, in which a group of white people had favorable attitudes towards Negroes at work and in shopping centers, but had unfavorable attitudes towards them living in their residential neighborhood. He traced these inconsistencies to different attitudinal "fields"; that is, each of these situations had different external forces operating to form the interaction of attitude. The unions to which the white people belonged were actively committed to intergroup equality at work. The Chamber of Commerce and business groups in the area involved were actively seeking Negro trade. The neighborhood civic club, however, was actively exclusionist. There were different "collective interests" involved in the different situations. In short, an individual does not typically have "an attitude" towards Negroes; he has many different attitudes depending on the circumstances.

There are a number of different ways in which this "situational" character of prejudice may be described:

A general attitude, about Negroes, for example, does not predetermine specific attitudes about Negroes. In other words, if a person has a general stereotype of Negroes, and a general hostility towards Negroes, this does not automatically mean that he will have an unfavorable attitude towards working in the same factory with Negroes.

One specific attitude towards Negroes, e.g., working with them, may have a quite different texture from another specific attitude, e.g., living next to them.

The same person may have one attitude about working next to Negroes in one situation, and a different attitude about working next to them in another situation.

In sum, a prejudiced attitude may shift from one moment and situation to another.

Disparity between the attitude and the act

The situational nature of prejudice is evident, too, in the mass of evidence concerning the disparity between *expressed* attitudes and behavior.

A Chinese couple traveled twice across the United States, and up and down the Pacific Coast. During the course of this trip, they asked for service in hundreds of hotels, auto camps, tourist homes, and restaurants. They were refused accommodations in only one sleeping place, and in none of the eating places. Six months after their trip, R. T. LaPiere sent a mail questionnaire to each of these places asking if Chinese could be accommodated. Over 90 percent of the forty-seven sleeping places and of the 81 eating places that replied said that Chinese would *not* be accommodated.

In a Northeastern suburban community, three young women, two white and one Negro, entered eleven restaurants. They encountered no problems, and received nothing less than exemplary service. Two weeks later a letter was sent to the same restaurants asking for reservations for a similar group. There was no answer to the letters, and great resistance to the follow-up phone calls.

Saenger and Gilbert studied customer reactions to the employment of Negro sales personnel in New York City department stores. One group they interrogated had been observed as customers in stores where there were both Negro and white clerks. Twenty percent of those who had bought from Negro clerks said they would disapprove of the policy of employing Negro clerks in the department stores; 21 percent of those who had bought from white clerks expressed the same attitude. In other words, prejudice towards Negro clerks did not cause customers to avoid them in the stores. Over 40 percent of those who said they would not buy in a store with Negro clerks had actually been observed not only in such a store but at a counter where there was a Negro clerk. One-third of those who said they would never buy from a Negro clerk had been observed buying from a Negro clerk less than an hour before they were interviewed.

The behavior—not the attitude

It is true, of course, that the *expression* of an attitude may be different from, or at least only a surface part of, an attitude. A person who is asked whether he would have any objection to rooming with someone of another racial extraction may honestly say, and honestly believe, that he is free of such prejudiced attitudes. But he may find, to his own shock, that when it comes down to it, he does have internal resistance to such a relationship; or indeed, without realizing it himself, he may find reasons and devices for avoiding such a relationship. Likewise, he may say that he *does* have objections, and when it comes down to it, he may not have these objections, or may not find them operative. His initial response may depend

on the circumstances: who asks him and where. His ultimate reaction may also depend on the circumstances. This disparity between attitude as expressed and as it ultimately affects behavior merely reemphasizes the *situational* character of the whole complex of prejudice. And it is the act of prejudice, not the attitude itself, which is the social problem of prejudice as earlier defined.

Andrew Kapos surveyed the attitudes of thirty segregated white gentile fraternities at the University of Michigan in 1953. He found a more intensive feeling of general prejudice against Jews than against Negroes. But he also found more willingness to admit Jews than Negroes to the fraternities, possibly because of the group standards which the fraternity members felt existed in the world around them. The attitudes of almost a thousand Texas manufacturers towards Negroes were tested; and the results were compared with the actual hiring practices of these manufacturers. It was found that the general attitude of a man towards Negroes had little to do with whether or not he employed them. An employer's willingness to hire Negroes was not significantly related to the degree of general hostility he felt or expressed towards Negroes.

In Panama there are places where one side of a street falls in the American Canal Zone, and the other side of the same street falls in Panamanian territory. Biesanz and Smith found that Panamanian Negroes tend to conform to discriminatory practices when they go to the Zone side of the street; while white Americans tend to adjust to nondiscriminatory practices when they go to the Panamanian side.

Whether in the fraternities of Ann Arbor, the factories of Texas, or the streets of Panama, it is not the prejudiced attitude which is itself important to the social problem of prejudice. It is the act of excluding Negroes from the fraternities and from the factories that makes prejudice a problem for society. The attitudes are important to that problem only insofar as they *cause* these acts. It is clear, however, that a prejudiced attitude is not a kind of pushbutton, nor a constant psychic bundle; it is, more accurately, an interaction in any given situation. It is clear that general attitudes of prejudice do not necessarily predetermine prejudiced behavior; it is clear that a specific attitude at one moment does not predetermine the act that will eventuate at another moment. What, then, *is* the relationship between attitudes and behavior?

LEARNING PREJUDICE

Prejudiced behavior typically shapes and alters prejudiced attitudes. The learning of prejudice is affected primarily by the kinds of social situations in which people live.

The fact that attitudes do not necessarily predetermine behavior, does not mean that attitudes and behavior do not typically accompany each other. The human being is not a mechanical jack-in-the-box. We do normally have feelings and conceptions that accompany our behavior. But our feelings and conceptions—our attitudes—do not necessarily *precede* our behavior. The attitude of the boy who is going to jump out of the box in the school play may be altered by the very fact that he is going to jump out of the box; just as his attitude immediately after his act may be shaped by the bare fact that he did jump out.

In brief, behavior typically shapes and alters attitudes. Cantril examined attitude polls on the subject of "lend-lease" assistance to the Allies before the United States was involved in World

War II. He found that immediately after Congress actually passed lend-lease legislation, attitudes toward such legislation became more favorable by about 10 percent. The point, according to Cantril, is that public opinion tends to follow accomplished fact.

Stouffer and his associates asked white soldiers: How would you like it if your division had companies which included both Negro and white platoons? Seven percent of those who already were in a company with Negro platoons replied that they disliked the situation; 20 percent of those questioned who were in the same regiment but not in the same company as Negro platoons replied that they would dislike it; 24 percent of those who were in the same division but not the same regiment as Negro platoons replied that they would dislike it; 62 percent of those questioned who were not even in the same division as Negro platoons replied that they would dislike it. The further they were from the accomplished fact, the more they disliked it.

Deutsch and Collins surveyed attitudes of white residents in four different public housing projects in New York. In two, Negro and white families were assigned indiscriminately to the same apartment buildings. In the other two, Negroes were assigned to different buildings within the same project.

In all cases, the assignments were made under an automatic procedure that did not take into account the preference of those assigned. Asked if they would dislike living in the same buildings with Negroes, about three-quarters of the white respondents in the segregated projects said they would, as against only about one-quarter of those already living in the fully integrated units. About 50 percent of those in the integrated projects said they desired to be friendly with their Negro neighbors, as against only about 10 percent in the segregated projects. General attitudes towards Negroes seemed to be affected as well: about 75 percent of those in the integrated units said they respected Negroes in general, as against well below 50 percent of those in the segregated projects.

Attitudes after the fact

Many research studies show that specific attitudes change after the fact, e.g.: attitudes towards living in the same neighborhood, serving in the same Army company. These studies are evidence that specific attitudes do shape themselves to specific behavior. However these studies do *not* indicate that a shift in one specific attitude towards a minority group will necessarily affect other specific attitudes towards the same group; or that a shift in a specific attitude will always affect the expression of a general attitude as it apparently did in the Deutsch and Collins study.

Harding and Hogrefe studied the attitudes of white employees towards Negro coworkers in department stores. The white employees were divided into three groups according to the nature and extent of their contact with Negroes. Group I included those who had worked in departments where there had been at least one Negro whose job was on an equal or superior plane. Group II included those who had worked in departments where Negroes had been of lower working status than themselves. Those in group III had never worked in a department with Negroes.

They were all asked: "How would you feel about taking a new job in which there were both Negroes and white people doing the same kind of work as you?" Seventy-three percent of group I, 61 percent of group II, and 48 percent of group III said they would be favorable. But there was no significant difference between the three groups when they were asked, for example, whether they would want to sit next to Negroes on the bus or train. The experience of working with Negroes apparently only produced a more favorable attitude towards Negroes in that specific "fellow-employee" frame of reference.

A further clue may be found in the study of Daniel Wilner and his associates of attitudes of white residents in public housing projects. This three-year study compared two kinds of white tenants: those who lived close to Negroes and those who lived at a relative distance. In neither case was the distance a matter of choice for the white residents who had been assigned to their quarters in these public projects. As in the Deutsch–Collins study, it was discovered that attitudes changed favorably as the distance to the Negroes decreased. Not only was there a significant difference in the specific attitude (i.e., living near Negroes), but again an apparent shift in general attitudes. In one project, for example, where Negroes and whites lived in the same buildings, 53 percent of the respondents said that they generally liked and respected Negroes; in another project where the buildings were all-white and all-Negro, only 36 percent of the respondents said that they generally liked and respected Negroes.

However, the Wilner study went further. Among one group of women who lived close to Negroes, 32 percent who had no personal contact with their Negro neighbors beyond casual greetings had a high degree of general esteem for Negroes; 45 percent who, in addition, had extended street conversation with their Negro neighbors had a high degree of general esteem for Negroes; and 74 percent who had neighborly associations with Negroes, i.e., behaved like neighbors, had a high degree of esteem generally for Negroes.

Proximity was not a matter of choice

but of automatic assignment. The greater the proximity, the more likely was there to be neighbor-like activity. A point made by the Wilner study is that the shift in general attitudes came not so much from mere contact or proximity, but from a changed pattern of behavior. The white residents who *acted* like neighbors came most often to *feel* like neighbors on many levels.

I. N. Brophy found a very marked reduction in general anti-Negro prejudice among white merchant seamen who, without the benefit of choice, had worked with Negro sailors. Thirty-three percent of those who had never shipped with Negroes were rated as unprejudiced; 46 percent of those who had shipped with Negroes once; 62 percent who had shipped with Negroes twice; and 82 percent of those who had shipped with Negroes five or more times were rated as unprejudiced. This was in sharp contrast to the Harding and Hogrefe study of the limited shifts in general attitudes for whites who had worked with Negroes in department stores. But these seamen not only worked together very closely, but also lived together twenty-four hours a day. And neighborly relationships are, of course, more general and encompassing than working relationships.

Behavior shapes attitude

In other words, evidence indicates that specific attitudes shape themselves to behavior. People who actually work with Negroes, especially as equals, develop attitudes favorable towards working with Negroes. People who actually are neighbors of Negroes develop attitudes favorable toward being neighbors of Negroes. Evidence also indicates that general attitudes shape themselves to behavior only if that behavior is itself general in nature. People who behave towards Negroes as full equals on every level tend to develop attitudes toward them as full equals on every level.

Thus, the mass of modern evidence runs counter to the "attitudes-first" fallacy, which holds that prejudice is a lurking state of mind that spills over into overt behavior. It might be more accurate to say that the prejudiced state of mind if typically a function of behavior; except for the danger that *this* formula might be oversimplified into a kind of reverse fallacy. Actually, there emerges an understanding that the key to prejudice must be found *outside* the realm of attitude-behavior relationships. The evidence has demonstrated how both attitudes and behavior are affected by the social frame of reference in which they occur.

In an integrated housing situation, attitudes and behavior are different than in a segregated housing situation. In an integrated army situation, attitudes and behavior are different than in a segregated army situation. In a shopping center situation attitudes and behavior towards Negroes are different than in a neighborhood situation. On one side of a Panamanian street, a white man's behavior towards Negroes may be different than on the other side of the street. It is this *situational* factor which is central to both attitude and behavior; which can stand outside any behavior-attitude spiral and avoid the fruitless question: "Which comes first?"

The effect of the situational factor on the social problem of prejudice can be found in the dramatic story of post-war integration in the armed forces. A military installation comprises a kind of community in itself, with its own community practices and patterns. Soldiers, sailors, marines, and airmen for the most part live as well as work within the military setting. Traditionally, the armed forces community had followed the racial patterns of the nation's lowest common denominator: the deep South. The assumption was made that only in this way could the armed forces accommodate the young men from the South as well as from other parts of the country who entered the services with deep-set attitudes of prejudice. Segregation was the rule on almost every level. Most military leaders expected it to stay that way indefinitely. In 1948, however, an edict was handed down by administrative order from President Truman's office: the armed forces were to be thoroughly and effectively integrated.

In its own inimitable way, the armed forces implemented this edict by a series of direct military orders. Today, there is effective integration throughout all the branches of service. In 1953, in an extensive survey of the effects of the desegregation edict five years after it was issued, Lee Nichols was able to report that Negroes and whites, from all parts of the country were not just training and fighting together, but were also eating at the same tables, sleeping in the same quarters, drinking beer together, going to church and the movies together.

Beyond the call of duty

A typical illustration of the process has been provided by Brigadier General Frank McConnell who had been assigned, shortly after the integration edict, to command a major training base in South Carolina. Customarily, as the recruits poured in, the Negroes were separated from the whites and established in separate organizations. General McConnell issued an order that the next fifty-five draftees who arrived would comprise a platoon, regardless of their color, and that this procedure would be followed with all subsequent arrivals. The order was issued verbally and "that," he said "was the end of segregation in Fort Jackson." There were no interracial incidents then or thereafter.

"I would see recruits, Negro and white, walking down the street, all buddying together," said the general. "The attitude of the southern soldiers was that this was the army way; they accepted it the same way they accepted getting booted out of bed at 5:30 in the morning."

This was the army way This was the new social situation, the new set of practices which surrounded the white soldier who had been accustomed to quite another way of life. His new community accepted it, he accepted it. There were no incidents of any consequence. Scattered grumbling that was heard when the policy was announced, but before it was implemented, disappeared when integration actually took place. Apprehension had been unwarranted. A congressional committee reported that "the almost total absence of opposition that had been anticipated in the enlisted men is a contributing factor in the success of this policy. The men were more ready for equality of treatment than the officer corps had realized." Commanders reported that interracial incidents had *lessened* under the policy of integration, as a result of the lessening of tensions.

The servicemen did not necessarily retain these specific attitudes or behavior patterns when they returned to their hometowns: the situational factors had shifted back again. In many cases, their *general* attitudes may have altered somewhat, at least temporarily, because of their total-living experiences in integration; and the aspiration levels of the Negro servicemen may also have been raised as a result. But they settled back without difficulty in the segregated patterns of their home communities. More definitively, the practices of the armed forces had a direct impact on certain practices in the nonmilitary community. Negro and white soldiers sat side by side on a city bus in Columbia, South Carolina, where such mingling was actually prohibited by law. Restaurants near military posts decided to admit Negroes along with white soldiers, partly because white and Negro soldiers began to accompany each other in town. In Amarillo, Texas, the USO club was opened to Negro airmen for the first time. Amarillo University began to admit Negroes to its extension classes. George L. P. Weaver, formerly of the CIO, told Lee Nichols that the elimination of segregation in the armed forces opened new job opportunities for Negroes with government contractors; indeed in the integrated military, Negro servicemen were often able to learn vocational skills which they otherwise could have had no opportunity to learn.

At the very least, within the relatively uncomplicated society bounded by the armed forces, the *social problem* of prejudice had been virtually eliminated by the outlawing of prejudiced practices. Equality of opportunity is in effect. The aspirations of the nonwhites within the military setting are being met. Interracial "incidents" and tensions have been reduced. This is not really being enforced at bayonet point, but has come to be accepted by servicemen. In terms of attitudes, they have, by and large, responded "beyond the call of duty," in their fraternization with fellow servicemen of another race. Not only has behavior changed, which is the crux of the social problem, but behavior has patently shaped attitudes.

The situation or the personality

Perhaps then the most effective and workable approach to understanding the phenomenon of prejudice is through an investigation of the kinds of *social situations* which give rise to and sustain prejudiced behavior and attitudes. This is a sharply different approach from that which would investigate what kinds of *people* are prone to prejudice.

This is not to underestimate the special validity of an approach to prejudice from the vantage point of personality and personality differences. There are good reasons for making such a psychological approach. Prejudice serves an emotional function for many people. It helps them to shift blame from themselves to others, to rationalize their aggressions, or otherwise provides an outlet for their special emotional needs. Some people with special emotional needs have a special susceptibility to prejudice. In attempting to understand or remedy the particular virulence or persistence of a given individual's prejudice, it is often necessary to understand his psychological history.

One white factory worker got along very well with his coworker who happened to be Negro. They were friendly, ate their lunches together, worked together harmoniously. Suddenly the white worker began to have severe marital troubles and seemed headed towards a divorce. He began to make slurring references to the Negro's race and they finally had to be separated. Another man, bitter because he was making no progress in his business firm, blamed the "Jews" in top management and became vocally anti-Semitic, although it turned out that there weren't any Jews in the management of the firm. One study of veterans found that those who were generally frustrated and felt that they had been subject to "bad breaks" in the service were more often prejudiced than those who felt they had experienced "good breaks" in the service. There is evidence that many of those who stigmatize the Negro as hypersexual are indeed guilt-ridden by their own sexuality, and are attempting to rid themselves of that guilt by projecting it onto the Negro.

The body of psychological knowledge which throws light on these reactions is extremely helpful in explaining individual differences and in helping to treat individual problems. Since certain emotional needs are universal, in one degree or another, this knowledge even helps to explain the special "attractiveness" that prejudice seems to have for human beings in general.

But it does not explain the specific *social problem* of prejudice with which our society is currently burdened. Presumably the factory worker who was having trouble with his wife would have found *some* scapegoat, even if there were no Negro available. It might have been the thinnest man in the factory, or the fattest, or the one with red hair, or perhaps just the one with whom he was most incompatible. The need to blame other people instead of oneself, irrelevantly to work out on other people one's guilt or aggressiveness or fear, is an unhealthy condition in itself. It is a problem in mental health. Those who have this problem are undoubtedly more susceptible to prejudice and to other social aberrations than those who do not have such a problem. But this condition itself does not create the specific social evils attending prejudice as described earlier. It is only when these problems are displaced on groups and help establish a deep-going pattern of denying equal opportunity to specific groups that the social problem of prejudice emerges. In short, the factory worker's psychological reaction does not create the social problem of prejudice, it merely operates within the social framework of a pattern of prejudice which already exists.

Furthermore, the psychological approach, as valuable as it is, does not explain the preponderance of people who engage in prejudiced behavior, but do *not* have special emotional problems. It does not explain the widespread pattern of prejudice. It does not explain why prejudice is more intense in one place and time than in another.

The lessons of social situations

These aspects of the social problem of prejudice are explainable only in terms of our *learning* prejudice much as we learn our other basic patterns of social behavior. But people do not typically learn their social values and social behavior in the same way that they learn the arithmetic table. It is not a matter of formal training or mere intellectual acceptance. A child may "learn" the social precept that it is wrong to steal, but may steal nonetheless. He has effectively learned the social value of honesty only to the extent that he has "internalized" that value; i.e., to the extent that this social value has become a natural and unthinking part of his behavior. It is not that he weighs consequences, but that it would "go against his grain" to steal.

This is not the kind of learning which basically is effected in the classroom, or even at the mother's knee. It is shaped fundamentally not by lecture or exhortation, but, in a kind of "creeping socialization," by the kinds of social situations in which people live, and, especially, in which they grow up.

It then becomes necessary to define more precisely the nature of "social situation" as it applies to prejudice and to discover the kinds of social situations which give rise to and sustain prejudice.

THE PREJUDICED COMMUNITY

The pattern of community practices is the fountainhead of prejudice: of prejudiced behavior and of prejudiced attitudes.

The growing child learns his social behavior primarily by following the modes and models of behavior around him. Indeed, he has little choice. He learns how to behave towards people of other racial and religious groups by seeing how other people behave, and by automatically participating in the behavior patterns which already exist.

Consider the extreme but not atypical case of a community where the Negro population has been traditionally subordinate on every level. The Negro with whom the young child comes into contact is a domestic in his home; or an elevator operator or janitor or a worker in some other menial capacity. The Negroes he knows are not as well-educated as the white people he knows, nor as well-dressed, nor as well-housed. The white people in his community do not socialize with Negroes, nor share the same public accommodations with them. No Negroes sit down at the same dinner table with him or with the people he knows; Negroes are not customers in the restaurants or hotels to which he is taken. Negroes are addressed by their first name, but always address the white people as "Mr." or "Mrs." They do not go to the same school as white children. They sit in separate sections of the bus. They use different rest rooms in the bus stations. If there is a tight fit on the sidewalk, it is the Negro pedestrian who gives way.

These are the social situations, i.e., the overt sets of relationships with which the child is surrounded. He does not have to be *told* that Negroes are "inferior," or what his relationships to them are supposed to be. These are apparent. Even more important, he is part of the white community and necessarily he *behaves* within the framework of these existing relationships. It is not just that his parents use a different restroom than do the Negroes. *He* uses a different restroom than the Negroes. *He* sits in the white section of the bus. *He* behaves towards them as social inferiors, and naturally comes to accept them as social inferiors. It isn't necessary to inculcate in him explicit attitudes about the social inferiority of Negroes. More likely, it is necessary for him to develop attitudes that do not conflict with his behavior.

Negroes conform to the prevailing patterns in such a community not only because they must, but also in part because they have accepted the values of the dominant community, and for the same reasons. They have been part of the same behavior patterns.

This process takes place at an early age. In one nursery school study, when preschool Negro children were given a white and Negro doll to play with, they almost uniformly preferred the white doll.

Schools for prejudice

There is a tendency to believe that these kinds of prejudicial behavior patterns are to be found preponderantly in the deep South. It is often startling to those in the northern and western parts of the country to find, by the most casual self-survey, the extent to which their own communities are "schools for prejudice" by dint of similar ongoing situations.

In the North and West, Negroes and whites typically live in different neighborhoods. That these Negro neighborhoods are usually inferior to the white is a fact readily apparent to the young observer. The proportion of substandard housing occupied by Negroes in 1952, according to United States Census standards, was six times as great as that occupied by whites. This was a uniform condition around the country. Nor is residential separatism restricted to the racial level. The Anti-Defamation League found, in a 1959 survey, that housing segregation on a religious basis was becoming more prevalent than was thought to be the case. For example, it found that a number of residential communities in the Chicago area were almost completely closed to Jews, and others had "large areas where Jews are barred."

Negroes typically work in lower-status jobs in communities throughout the nation. An index of this comparative status is the fact that the average earnings of the Negro worker is little more than half that of the white worker. This is partly the result of the history of educational and economic disadvantage which is the heritage of the Negro. But it is to a large extent the result of current prejudice. Where surveys have been made of job orders by employers in the North and West, in communities as widely separated as Los Angeles and Chicago, it has been found that at least 75 percent of the job orders for white collar workers specify "white only." At least 25 percent of these job orders specify "Christian only." (In 1959, the state of California took steps to remedy this situation with the passage of a Fair Employment Practices Act.)

It has been estimated that about one-quarter of the Negro school children *outside* the South go to schools that are in fact substantially all-Negro, and about half go to school where there is only token mixing. This is largely a result of segregated housing patterns.

John P. Dean supervised a study of 248 cities, ranging in population from 10,000 to 500,000 to determine the extent to which American Jews were thoroughly integrated. Three tests were used: admission to Junior League; admission to country clubs and city clubs; admission to exclusive residential areas. In one-third of the cities, Jews are denied admission to all three. In only twenty out of the 248 cities are some Jews accepted in all three, and these twenty are smaller cities. In more than half of the fifty largest cities in the study, Jews are denied admission to all three categories; and in only one are they admitted to all three.

These behavior patterns are not only the substance of prejudice as a social problem; they are also the breeding conditions of prejudice. In a very real sense, prejudiced behavior reproduces itself; carries within it its own seeds of continuity. In the same sense, prejudice is a dramatic example of the "self-fulfilling prophecy." The prejudiced image of a Negro as a constitutionally menial worker is sustained by the prejudiced behavior which in fact freezes him as a menial worker.

The projection of prejudice

The learning of prejudice is a natural result of actual participation in patterns of prejudiced behavior; or of first-hand observation of the patterns of prejudiced behavior in the community; but it may also result from *vicarious* participation, or *second-hand* observation of the patterns of prejudiced behavior. A society provides many "cues" for social behavior, e.g.: "white" and "colored" signs above public drinking fountains; or classified ads in the newspapers which read "gentile only"; or house-for-sale signs which read "white only" or "restricted."

In these several ways, then, it is on the level of actual behavior situations that the normal reproduction of prejudice is effected. It is within the framework of these behavior situations that individual differences, except perhaps the most pathological, operate. It is on the base of these behavior situations that the behavior-attitude spiral of prejudice builds. Attitudes and explicit ideologies are most firmly constructed on the foundation of these existing social situations.

Indeed, the attitudes which must develop to accompany human behavior are *implied* in this behavior and it is in this way that such attitudes are primarily learned rather than by direct instruction. By the time a child is told for the first time that "Negroes are inferior," he is already convinced of it. On the other hand, by the time he is told for the first time that "Negroes are *not* inferior" it is already often too late. He will resist the idea. Or, if he is finally intellectually convinced of the fact that Negroes are not inferior, he may evade the consequences. He may find some other reason for behaving towards the Negroes *as though* they were inferior. It is axiomatic in all learning situations that rhetorical exhortations have little chance of success when they are in battle against actual behavior patterns. For example, a child will not tend to be honest because his father tells him to be, if the same father is constantly engaged in dishonest practices himself.

Studies of the development of prejudice in children show that young children who have not yet been involved in prejudiced behavior patterns may pick up prejudiced talk, but this doesn't affect their unprejudiced behavior. Later, after having become involved in prejudiced behavior patterns, they may pick up democratic language in the schools or elsewhere, but this doesn't affect their prejudiced behavior. By the age of fifteen, Gordon Allport points out, "considerable skill is shown in imitating the adult pattern."[2]

They are now able to rationalize their prejudiced behavior whenever necessary and resort to the prejudiced ideologies which do not precede but follow prejudiced behavior patterns.

In brief, the pattern of *community practices* serves as the primary source of prejudice in behavior and attitude. This does not mean that we are merely back on the causative merry-go-round, where behavior chases attitude and attitude chases behavior in a dismally unending circle. "Community practices" connotes more than just the sum total

of individual behavior at any given time. It means customary collective behavior. It means collective habits which tend to perpetuate themselves with their own momentum, such as the collective habit of smoking tobacco or drinking coffee.

Similarly, prejudiced community practices typically reproduce themselves by force of *custom*. All other things being equal, these practices are passed automatically from one generation to the next. John Dollard, after studying traditional patterns of prejudice in a southern town, wrote:

The master defense against accurate social perception . . . is always . . . the tremendous conviction of rightness about any behavior form which exists. What is done is de facto right and is justified by the consideration that it has not been invented by current culture bearers but comes to them through sacred tradition.

The persistence of prejudice

The sheer power of custom recreates prejudiced community practices—which in turn, typically, breeds individual practices of prejudice, and, then, individual attitudes of prejudice. As a matter of fact, it is possible for prejudiced custom to persist without building up *any* corresponding attitudes.

For example, it has become commonplace for investigators of prejudiced employment practices to find the following kind of situation:

A personnel officer in a large firm tells a Jewish applicant, in effect, that he is sorry but the firm does not hire Jews as salesmen. A complaint is brought to the head of the firm, who expresses genuine astonishment. "What difference does it make?" he asks. "A good salesman is a good salesman." A visit is then made to the personnel officer who himself expresses genuine astonishment. No Jews had ever been

---

[2] Gordon W. Allport, *The Nature of Prejudice* (Cambridge: Addison-Wesley, 1954), p. 310.

hired by that firm, and he had just assumed that it was policy.

The department stores of a city with a fairly large Negro population had never hired a Negro clerk. As the store owners were approached on this situation, one by one, they indicated that they really had no objection to employing Negroes, and really hadn't given the matter much thought. It just "hasn't been done." One department store departed from the custom and hired Negro clerks; the others followed cheerfully and without incident.

These customary community practices, with or without corresponding attitudes, are the "frame of reference," the *situational* key to the prevention of and altering of the widespread phenomenon of prejudiced behavior and prejudiced attitudes. This pattern of community practices is the basic remedial target, rather than emotional maladjustment, or any given set of prejudiced attitudes. When this pattern of community practice changes—whether by law, direct action, or otherwise; whether willingly or reluctantly—the prevailing pattern of community attitudes will be likely to change accordingly. Laws prohibiting the sale of liquor in the United States have dramatically failed to change attitudes about liquor; but these laws have failed to change community practices in the first place. There is impressive indication, however, that in the area of social relationships, and specifically in the area of intergroup relationships, community practices *can* be changed prior to corresponding attitudinal changes, and will then serve to effect such attitudinal changes.

PART TWO
SOCIAL STRUCTURE AND RACIAL CONFLICT

SECTION A

SCARCE RESOURCES AND INSTITUTIONALIZED INEQUALITY: THE BASIS FOR REALISTIC CONFLICT

THE articles in this section are concerned with some of the basic scarcities, practices, and differing values and beliefs which can generate conflict.

In the last part it was argued that certain of society's resources are inherently scarce. Here this concept is documented for particular kinds of resources and institutional areas by contrasting whites with blacks.

Laymen as well as supposed specialists often err in their view of racial conflict. For the concerned laymen race tension may be seen to stem from ignorance, a lack of communication, moral sickness and ill will, or psychological aberrations of activists, rather than being seen as a "natural" consequence of a social stratification system.

On the other hand, some presumably hard-headed, "realistic" sociologists often err in the other direction.[1] They may deny the presence of irrational hostility, ignorance, misperception, and nonrealistic conflict, choosing instead to see all intergroup tension as irreconcilable and stemming from a fundamental group struggle after inherently scarce and indivisible resources that can only end in bloodshed. They may ignore or deny the possibility of cooperation across racial lines in addition to denying that race is only one component of humanity's complex identity which includes factors such as sex, age, class, and region as well as institutional and ideological components.

Be that as it may, this part, and indeed the entire book, emphasizes the rational aspects of the conflict process, though it is not limited to this.

That blacks and other poor groups are challenging the society suggests that they want something they don't have. That this challenge meets with resistance suggests that some groups and individuals gain from the racial status quo. The question of who gains in what ways from the American pattern of race relations has been too little studied by American social scientists (as has the question of what it costs).

The articles in this part deal with white advantage and black disadvantage. These advantages, by and large, are not random or idiosyncratic, rather they are "institutionalized" and a part of the normal way of doing society's business.

Although in particular detail the range of things over which social groups can be in conflict is enormous, at a more abstract level much conflict can be seen to stem around inequality and disagreement over the distribution of three scarce social resources noted by Max Weber: class, status, and power.[2] Inequality with respect to these factors is found in all industrial societies. However, the degree of inequality and the extent to which it is related to ascribed characteristics such as race or sex vary appreciably. Stripped to its skeletal form, much of American racial conflict lies in the struggle for these resources.

[1] In a sense this represents an advance over the 1950's when the view many sociologists held of conflict more closely approximated that of the laymen sketched above.

[2] M. Weber, *Essays in Sociology,* trans. H. H. Gerth and C. Wright Mills (New York: Oxford Univ. Press, 1946).

How are power and authority distributed? Who is dominant, and who is subordinate? What spheres of activity are influenced? Who will lead? If there is an election, how are candidates chosen? Who can vote? How are electoral boundaries drawn? Who will be appointed to positions of political power? Which groups and interests have the most behind the scenes influence on decision making? What means are used to control subordinates?

Similar questions can be asked about almost any voluntary or involuntary organization such as: schools, welfare and police departments, churches, factories, labor unions, private clubs, charities, etc. Who has the power? Who has authority to make and enforce the rules? Which groups benefit or are hurt the most by this?

With respect to questions of social class and economics: How is material property distributed? Who owns what? What are an individual's chances in the marketplace? How do the actions of the government affect the above? What kinds of people will fill what jobs? Who will be promoted? How much or how little will they be paid? What criteria are used to determine membership in labor unions? Will pay for the same job vary depending on ascribed characteristics? What are the constraints and limitations placed on the behavior of merchants and employers or customers and employees?

As the earlier article by Dahrendorf implied, authority is not something restricted to elections and government. In this sense many of the above economic issues are subordinate to questions of power and authority.[3] To ask about hiring practices and salaries in

a southern textile mill or membership criteria in a northern craft union is, in an important sense, to deal with questions of power and authority. It is in this sense that Dahrendorf argued that much conflict at bottom revolves around issues of authority. However, this is less direct and pronounced in the case of disagreement over status issues.

Here we ask: What attributes of individuals and groups are highly valued in the society? How do various life conditions affect the honor an individual receives? How are various class, national, religious, ethnic and racial groups, and life styles ranked in terms of their desirability? Who gives deference to whom? What special privileges are associated with a high status ranking, or degradations with a lowly one, and what are the symbolic and ritualized practices which go along with these? How are status, prestige, and honor distributed in the society?

Social status and the evaluations placed on one's major group affiliations are of course partly determined by the distribution of income and power. Yet, at least in the short run, status has a meaning independent of these.

Status involves an important and often neglected component of American racial struggle. The issue often goes far beyond squalor to questions of sovereignty and dignity. This helps explain how sometimes issues which may seem trivial from the perspective of the dominant group come to be of great importance to the minority group member. Struggle and assertion, as ceremonial and even ritualized acts which communicate a symbolic meaning regarding a group's conception of itself, may be as important as actually gaining one's concrete ends. Compromise often seems more difficult in issues where fundamental questions of honor are involved. Moral legiti-

---

[3] At a more abstract level even differences of belief and value conflicts may be seen as a struggle over the scarce resources of power, in such cases, the power to enforce one's definition of the world on others.

mations may play a greater role, giving such struggles a more bitter and perhaps irrational character than those involving economic issues.[4]

Concretely demanding status and dignity and a reversal of traditional societal evaluations that may be related to its history and firmly embedded in a group's culture and psyche is rather more difficult than gaining the right to vote or an end to discrimination by a particular employer, which can be effected by agreements and laws. Yet the struggle for status may be seen in an attack on particular incidents of a racially demeaning character and in the attack on traditional racial insults or etiquette such as: enforced segregation, calling blacks "boy" or "girl" or always by their first names, spelling "Negro" with a small "N," the use of racial epithets, and the kind of deference expected of blacks by southern etiquette. These are at issue precisely because they symbolically reaffirm the relative status positions of whites and blacks. When such practices are challenged, they make manifest the underlying status structure.

In the American racial context when differences in life styles, cultural standards, and valued symbols are not allowed expression they offer a potential for conflict. Unlike the struggle for scarce resources such as status or money, where as one group gains, another must lose, demands for pluralism, tolerance of social variation, and the end to demeaning restrictions on cultural expression do not so clearly mean losses for whites.

Protest over such issues may more often meet with success because the cost to whites in any direct sense is relatively slight and they may be consistent with American values of indi-

[4] For example, see J. Gusfield, *Symbolic Crusade* (Urbana: Univ. of Illinois Press, 1963).

vidualism and liberty. Among examples of such conflict are recent black protests over the refusal of various employers, schools, and the armed services to permit the wearing of Afro hair styles or clothes, the playing of soul music, and the serving of soul food; the refusal to make Malcolm X's birthday a school holiday; the lily-white nature of Miss America beauty contests; and interpretations of American and world history offered in schools.

Another important source of conflict stems from the advocacy of incompatible beliefs and values rather than direct disagreement about how power, money, and status will be distributed, though these of course may underlie or be affected by such conflicts. This has been an important source of conflict throughout world history. Holy wars are a good example.

Though some of the conflicts that the Muslims and Black Panthers have been involved in are an exception, in recent decades most American racial conflict, at least in the North, has not been highly ideological and has stemmed more from the struggle over scarce resources and the demands to change certain social practices. Still it should be noted that this may give rise to competing belief systems such as those that stress that positions in schools, welfare and police departments should be filled by those representatives of the community they serve, rather than filled on the basis of presumed (and sometimes questioned) abstract criteria of merit, theoretically regardless of race, though actually such universalistic standards often serve to effectively rule out blacks, given a cumulative heritage of disadvantage. The failure to meaningfully change distribution patterns of income and power seems to be leading to an increase in conflict related to incompatible beliefs, as an ever larger number of determined blacks come to question the legitimacy of the system itself and to deny that it is in any way binding on them. Examples are the refusal to be drafted or salute the flag and urban guerrilla activities. This has major implications for conflict resolution. A dispute over hiring can be negotiated, but what is there to negotiate over, short of the overthrow of the system, when the legitimacy of the very social order itself is denied? Here the ends sought shift from reforming and modifying existing institutions to a revolutionary effort to create wholly new institutions.

The articles in this section include discussions of schools, welfare, housing, unions, merchants, political representation, income and occupation, and police practices. They use statistical data, institutional analysis, and journalistic descriptions in considering the entire nation, various regions and cities, and particular incidents. But the essential point in all of them is documenting and/or describing institutionalized inequality and practices that are capable of generating challenge and conflict from blacks.

Robert Blauner offers a conceptual framework for approaching black inequality and subordination. His emphasis on colonialism as a process permits him to note many parallels between the situation of American blacks and colonial people's in Africa and Asia.

Inequality and problems in the area of education, welfare, and housing are considered by the excerpt from the report of the Kerner commission.

Harold M. Baron, by a careful analysis of the number of blacks holding high offices in government and industry in Chicago, reveals the extent of black powerlessness.

Herbert Hill considers the racial

practices of some businesses and organized labor, and documents appreciable economic inequality and discrimination against blacks.

David Caplovitz's empirical study reveals some of the many ways in which unscrupulous merchants may take advantage of the low income consumer.

Art Goldberg and Gene Marine in "The Killing of George Baskett and the Acquittal of Officer O'Brien" describe an encounter between a white policeman and a black citizen.

Rather than focusing directly on black disprivilege, the article by Norval Glenn considers some of the gains that whites receive from black subordination, particularly in the South.

Although many of the facts documented here may not be surprising to the politically concerned college student, it is well to keep in mind that most white Americans seem unaware of them. For example, the July 1968 Gallup poll found only 1 percent of whites believing that blacks are treated "badly," while 75 percent felt "Negroes are treated the same as whites."

Some of the ways in which the nature of the issue affects the conflict are considered in the introduction to Part IV, Section B, yet several important points can be noted here. One of the things that makes racial conflict so prevalent and so difficult to resolve relative to union conflicts, or conflicts over floridation, is the coalescence of such a large number of grievances around skin color. Of course, skin color is often incidental, but because of its presence and visibility things easily come to be defined as racial issues, even though to the outside observer they may sometimes seem to be class, rural-urban, or generational issues. The large number of issues involved and the presence of a large number of varied conflict groups may make bargaining and negotiation and eventual resolution more difficult.

6
Internal Colonialism and Ghetto Revolt*
ROBERT BLAUNER

It is becoming almost fashionable to analyze American racial conflict today in terms of the colonial analogy. I shall argue in this paper that the utility of this perspective depends upon a distinction between colonization as a process and colonialism as a social, economic, and political system. It is the experience of colonization that Afro-Americans share with many of the nonwhite people of the world. But this subjugation has taken place in a societal context that differs in important respects from the situation of "classical colonialism." . . . [S]ome major developments in black protest— the urban riots, cultural nationalism, and the movement for ghetto control— [can be seen] as collective responses to colonized status. Viewing our domestic situation as a special form of

*[Reprinted from *Social Problems*, vol. 16, no. 4, Spring 1969, pp. 393–408 by permission of the Society for the Study of Social Problems. This is a revised version of a paper delivered at the University of California Centennial Program, "Studies in Violence," Los Angeles, June 1, 1968. For criticisms and ideas that have improved an earlier draft, I am indebted to Robert Wood, Lincoln Bergman, and Gary Marx. As a good colonialist I have probably restated (read: stolen) more ideas from the writings of Kenneth Clark, Stokely Carmichael, Frantz Fanon, and especially such contributors to the Black Panther Party (Oakland) newspaper as Huey Newton, Bobby Seale, Eldridge Cleaver, and Kathleen Cleaver than I have appropriately credited or generated myself. In self-defense I should state that I began working somewhat independently on a colonial analysis of American race relations in the fall of 1965.]

colonization outside a context of a colonial system will help explain some of the dilemmas and ambiguities within these movements.

The present crisis in American life has brought about changes in social perspectives and the questioning of long accepted frameworks. Intellectuals and social scientists have been forced by the pressure of events to look at old definitions of the character of our society, the role of racism, and the workings of basic institutions. The depth and volatility of contemporary racial conflict challenge sociologists in particular to question the adequacy of theoretical models by which we have explained American race relations in the past.

For a long time the distinctiveness of the Negro situation among the ethnic minorities was placed in terms of color, and the systematic discrimination that follows from our deepseated racial prejudices. This was sometimes called the caste theory, and while provocative, it missed essential and dynamic features of American race relations. In the past ten years there has been a tendency to view Afro-Americans as another ethnic group not basically different in experience from previous ethnics and whose "immigration" condition in the North would in time follow their upward course. The inadequacy of this model is now clear—even the Kerner report devotes a chapter to criticizing this analogy. A more recent (though hardly new) approach views the essence of racial subordination in economic class terms: black people as an underclass are to a degree specially exploited and to a degree economically dispensable in an automating society. Important as are economic factors, the power of race and racism in America cannot be sufficiently explained through class analysis. Into this theory vacuum steps the model of internal colonialism. Problematic and imprecise as it is, it gives hope of becoming a framework that can integrate the insights of caste and racism, ethnicity, culture, and economic exploitation into an overall conceptual scheme. At the same time, the danger of the colonial model is the imposition of an artificial analogy which might keep us from facing up to the fact (to quote Harold Cruse, 1968) that "the American black and white social phenomenon is a uniquely new world thing (p. 214)."

During the late 1950's, identification with African nations and other colonial or formerly colonized peoples grew in importance among black militants.[1] As a result the United States was increasingly seen as a colonial power and the concept of domestic colonialism was introduced into the political analysis and rhetoric of militant nationalists. During the same period black social theorists began developing this frame of reference for explaining American realities. As early as 1962, Cruse characterized race relations in this country as "domestic colonialism."[2] Three years later in *Dark Ghetto,* Kenneth Clark (1965) demonstrated how the political, economic, and social structure of Harlem was essentially that of a colony. Finally in 1967, a full-blown elaboration of "internal colonialism" provided the theoretical framework for Carmichael and Hamilton's widely read *Black Power* (1967). The following year the colonial analogy gained currency and new "respectability" when Senator McCarthy habit-

[1] Nationalism, including an orientation toward Africa, is no new development. It has been a constant tendency within Afro–American politics. See Cruse (1968a, especially Chaps. 5–7).

[2] This was six years before the publication of *The Crisis of the Negro Intellectual* (1968b), which brought Cruse into prominence. Thus the 1962 article was not widely read until its reprinting in Cruse (1968a).

ually referred to black Americans as a colonized people during his campaign. While the rhetoric of internal colonialism was catching on, other social scientists began to raise questions about its appropriateness as a scheme of analysis.

The colonial analysis has been rejected as obscurantist and misleading by scholars who point to the significant differences in history and social-political conditions between our domestic patterns and what took place in Africa and India. Colonialism traditionally refers to the establishment of domination over a geographically external political unit, most often inhabited by people of a different race and culture, where this domination is political and economic, and the colony exists subordinated to, and dependent upon, the mother country. Typically the colonizers exploit the land, the raw materials, the labor, and other resources of the colonized nation; in addition a formal recognition is given to the difference in power, autonomy, and political status, and various agencies are set up to maintain this subordination. Seemingly the analogy must be stretched beyond usefulness if the American version is to be forced into this model. For here we are talking about group relations within a society; the mother country-colony separation in geography is absent. Though whites certainly colonized the territory of the original Americans, internal colonization of Afro–Americans did not involve the settlement of whites in any land that was unequivocally black. And unlike the colonial situation, there has been no formal recognition of differing power since slavery was abolished outside the South. Classic colonialism involved the control and exploitation of the majority of a nation by a minority of outsiders. Whereas in America the people who are oppressed were themselves originally outsiders and are a numerical minority.

This conventional critique of "internal colonialism" is useful in pointing to the differences between our domestic patterns and the overseas situation. But in its bold attack it tends to lose sight of common experiences that have been historically shared by the most subjugated racial minorities in America and nonwhite peoples in some other parts of the world. For understanding the most dramatic recent developments on the race scene, this common core element—which I shall call colonization—may be more important than the undeniable divergences between the two contexts.

The common features ultimately relate to the fact that the classical colonialism of the imperialist era and American racism developed out of the same historical situation and reflected a common world economic and power stratification. The slave trade for the most part preceded the imperialist partition and economic exploitation of Africa, and in fact may have been a necessary prerequisite for colonial conquest—since it helped deplete and pacify Africa, undermining the resistance to direct occupation. Slavery contributed one of the basic raw materials for the textile industry which provided much of the capital for the West's industrial development and need for economic expansionism. The essential condition for both American slavery and European colonialism was the power domination and the technological superiority of the Western world in its relation to peoples of non-Western and nonwhite origins. This objective supremacy in technology and military power buttressed the West's sense of cultural superiority, laying the basis for racist ideologies that were elaborated to justify control and exploitation of nonwhite people. Thus because

classical colonialism and America's internal version developed out of a similar balance of technological, cultural, and power relations, a common *process* of social oppression characterized the racial patterns in the two contexts—despite the variation in political and social structure.

There appear to be four basic components of the colonization complex. The first refers to how the racial group enters into the dominant society (whether colonial power or not). Colonization begins with a forced, involuntary entry. Second, there is an impact on the culture and social organization of the colonized people which is more than just a result of such "natural" processes as contact and acculturation. The colonizing power carries out a policy which constrains, transforms, or destroys indigenous values, orientations, and ways of life. Third, colonization involves a relationship by which members of the colonized group tend to be administered by representatives of the dominant power. There is an experience of being managed and manipulated by outsiders in terms of ethnic status.

A final fundament of colonization is racism. Racism is a principle of social domination by which a group seen as inferior or different in terms of alleged biological characteristics is exploited, controlled, and oppressed socially and psychically by a superordinate group. Except for the marginal case of Japanese imperialism, the major examples of colonialism have involved the subjugation of nonwhite Asian, African, and Latin American peoples by white European powers. Thus racism has generally accompanied colonialism. Race prejudice can exist without colonization—the experience of Asian-American minorities is a case in point—but racism as a system of domination is part of the complex of colonization.

The concept of colonization stresses

the enormous fatefulness of the historical factor, namely the manner in which a minority group becomes a part of the dominant society.[3] The crucial difference between the colonized Americans and the ethnic immigrant minorities is that the latter have always been able to operate fairly competitively within that relatively open section of the social and economic order because these groups came voluntarily in search of a better life, because their movements in society were not administratively controlled, and because they transformed their culture at their own pace—giving up ethnic values and institutions when it was seen as a desirable exchange for improvements in social position.

In present-day America, a major device of black colonization is the powerless ghetto. As Kenneth Clark (1964) describes the situation:

Ghettos are the consequence of the imposition of external power and the institutionalization of powerlessness. In this respect, they are in fact social, political, educational, and above all—economic colonies. Those confined within the ghetto walls are subject peoples. They are victims of the greed, cruelty, insensitivity, guilt, and fear of their masters. . . . (pp. 10–11)

The community can best be described in terms of the analogy of a powerless colony. Its political leadership is divided, and all but one or two of its political leaders are shortsighted and dependent upon the larger political power structure. Its social agencies are financially precarious and dependent upon sources of support outside the community. Its churches are isolated or dependent. Its economy is dominated by small businesses which are largely

owned by absentee owners, and its tenements and other real property are also owned by absentee landlords.

Under a system of centralization, Harlem's schools are controlled by forces outside of the community. Programs and policies are supervised and determined by individuals who do not live in the community. . . . (pp. 79–80)

Of course many ethnic groups in America have lived in ghettos. What make the black ghettos an expression of colonized status are three special features. First, the ethnic ghettos arose more from voluntary choice, both in the sense of the choice to immigrate to America and the decision to live among one's fellow ethnics. Second, the immigrant ghettos tended to be a one and two generation phenomenon; they were actually waystations in the process of acculturation and assimilation. When they continue to persist as in the case of San Francisco's Chinatown, it is because they are big business for the ethnics themselves and there is a new stream of immigrants. The black ghetto on the other hand has been a more permanent phenomenon, although some individuals do escape it. But most relevant is the third point, European ethnic groups like the Poles, Italians, and Jews generally only experienced a brief period, often less than a generation, during which their residential buildings, commercial stores, and other enterprises were owned by outsiders. The Chinese and Japanese faced handicaps of color prejudice that were almost as strong as the blacks faced, but very soon gained control of their internal communities, because their traditional ethnic culture and social organization had not been destroyed by slavery and internal colonization. But Afro–Americans are distinct in the extent to which their segregated communities have remained

---

[3] As Eldridge Cleaver (1968a) reminds us, "Black people are a stolen people held in a colonial status on stolen land, and any analysis which does not acknowledge the colonial status of black people cannot hope to deal with the real problem" (p. 51).

controlled economically, politically, and administratively from the outside. One indicator of this difference is the estimate that the "income of Chinese–Americans from Chinese-owned businesses is in proportion to their numbers forty-five times as great as the income of Negroes from Negro-owned businesses" (Glazer & Moynihan, 1963, p. 37). But what is true of business is also true for the other social institutions that operate within the ghetto. The educators, policemen, social workers, politicians, and others who administer the affairs of ghetto residents are typically whites who live outside the black community. Thus the ghetto plays a strategic role as the focus for the administration by outsiders which is also essential to the structure of overseas colonialism.

The colonial status of the Negro community goes beyond the issue of ownership and decision making within black neighborhoods. The Afro–American population in most cities has very little influence on the power structure and institutions of the larger metropolis, despite the fact that in numerical terms, Blacks tend to be the most sizable of the various interest groups. A recent analysis of policy making in Chicago (Baron, 1968) estimates that "Negroes really hold less than 1 percent of the effective power in the Chicago metropolitan area. [Negroes are 20 percent of Cook County's population.] Realistically the power structure of Chicago is hardly less white than that of Mississippi."

Colonization outside of a traditional colonial structure has its own special conditions. The group culture and social structure of the colonized in America is less developed; it is also less autonomous. In addition, the colonized are a numerical minority, and furthermore they are ghettoized more totally and are more dispersed than

people under classic colonialism. Though these realities affect the magnitude and direction of response, it is my basic thesis that the most important expressions of protest in the black community during the recent years reflect the colonized status of Afro–America. Riots, programs of separation, politics of community control, the black revolutionary movements, and cultural nationalism each represent a different strategy of attack on domestic colonialism in America. Let us now examine some of these movements.

RIOT OR REVOLT?

The so-called riots are being increasingly recognized as a preliminary if primitive form of mass rebellion against a colonial status. There is still a tendency to absorb their meaning within the conventional scope of assimilation-integration politics: some commentators stress the material motives involved in looting as a sign that the rioters want to join America's middle class affluence just like everyone else. That motives are mixed and often unconscious, that black people want good furniture and television sets like whites is beside the point. The guiding impulse in most major outbreaks has not been integration with American society, but an attempt to stake out a sphere of control by moving against that society and destroying the symbols of its oppression.

In my critique of the McCone Report (Blauner, 1966) I observed that the rioters were asserting a claim to territoriality, an unorganized and rather inchoate attempt to gain control over their community or "turf." In succeeding disorders also the thrust of the action has been the attempt to clear out an alien presence, white men and officials, rather than a drive to kill whites as in a conventional race riot. The main attacks have been directed at the property of white business men and at the police who operate in the black community "like an army of occupation" protecting the interests of outside exploiters and maintaining the domination over the ghetto by the central metropolitan power structure. . . .

One of the most significant consequences of the process of colonization is a weakening of the colonized's individual and collective will to resist his oppression. It has been easier to contain and control black ghettos because communal bonds and group solidarity have been weakened through divisions among leadership, failures of organization, and a general disspiritment that accompanies social oppression. The riots are a signal that the will to resist has broken the mold of accommodation. In some cities as in Watts they also represented nascent movements toward community identity. In several riot-torn ghettos the outbursts have stimulated new organizations and movements. If it is true that the riot phenomenon of 1964–68 has passed its peak, its historical import may be more for the "internal" organizing momentum generated than for any profound "external" response of the larger society facing up to underlying causes. . . . Despite the differences in objective conditions, the violence of the 1960's seems to serve the same psychic function, assertions of dignity and manhood for young blacks in urban ghettos, as it did for the colonized of North Africa described by Fanon (1963) and Memmi (1967).

CULTURAL NATIONALISM

Cultural conflict is generic to the colonial relation because colonization involves the domination of Western technological values over the more communal cultures of non-Western peoples. Colonialism played havoc with the national integrity of the peoples it brought under its sway. Of course, all traditional cultures are threatened by industrialism, the city, and modernization in communication, transportation, health, and education. What is special are the political and administrative decisions of colonizers in managing and controlling colonized peoples. . . .

The most total destruction of culture in the colonization process took place not in traditional colonialism but in America. As Frazier stressed, the integral cultures of the diverse African peoples who furnished the slave trade were destroyed because slaves from different tribes, kingdoms, and linguistic groups were purposely separated to maximize domination and control. Thus language, religion, and national loyalties were lost in North America much more completely than in the Caribbean and Brazil where slavery developed somewhat differently. Thus on this key point America's internal colonization has been more total and extreme than situations of classic colonialism. For the British in India and the European powers in Africa were not able—as outnumbered minorities—to destroy the national and tribal cultures of the colonized. Recall that American slavery lasted two hundred and fifty years and its racist aftermath another one hundred. Colonial dependency in the case of British Kenya and French Algeria lasted only seventy-seven and one hundred and twenty-five years respectively. In the wake of this more drastic uprooting and destruction of culture and social organization, much more powerful agencies of social, political, and psychological domination developed in the American case.

The colonizers use their culture to socialize the colonized elites (intellectuals, politicians, and middle class) into an identification with the colonial system. Because Western culture has the prestige, the power, and the key to open the limited opportunity that a minority of the colonized may achieve, the first reaction seems to be an acceptance of the dominant values. Call it brainwashing as the Black Muslims put it; call it identifying with the aggressor if you prefer Freudian terminology; call it a natural response to the hope and belief that integration and democratization can really take place if you favor a more commonsense explanation, this initial acceptance in time crumbles on the realities of racism and colonialism. The colonized, seeing that his success within colonialism is at the expense of his group and his own inner identity, moves radically toward a rejection of the Western culture and develops a nationalist outlook that celebrates his people and their traditions. As Memmi (1967) describes it:

Assimilation being abandoned, the colonized's liberation must be carried out through a recovery of self and of autonomous dignity. Attempts at imitating the colonizer required self-denial; the colonizer's rejection is the indispensable prelude to self-discovery. That accusing and annihilating image must be shaken off: oppression must be attacked boldly since it is impossible to go around it. After having been rejected for so long by the colonizer the day has come when it is the colonized who must refuse the colonizer. . . .(p. 128)

Cultural revitalization movements play a key role in anticolonial movements. They follow an inner necessity and logic of their own that comes from the consequences of colonialism on groups and personal identities; they are also essential to provide the soli-darity which the political or military phase of the anticolonial revolution requires. In the United States an Afro-American culture has been developing since slavery out of the ingredients of African worldviews, the experience of bondage, southern values and customs, migration and the northern lower class ghettos, and most importantly, the political history of the black population in its struggle against racism.[4] That Afro-Americans are moving toward cultural nationalism in a period when ethnic loyalties tend to be weak (and perhaps on the decline) in this country is another confirmation of the unique colonized position of the black group. (A similar nationalism seems to be growing among American Indians and Mexican-Americans.)

THE MOVEMENT FOR GHETTO CONTROL

The call for black power unites a number of varied movements and tendencies.[5] Though no clear-cut program has yet emerged, the most important emphasis seems to be the movement for control of the ghetto. Black leaders and organizations are increasingly

[4] In another essay, I argue against the standard sociological position that denies the existence of an ethnic Afro-American culture and I expand on the above themes. The concept of "Soul" is astonishingly parallel in content to the mystique of "Negritude" in Africa; the Pan-African culture movement has its parallel in the burgeoning black culture mood in Afro-American communities. See Rose (1969).

[5] Scholars and social commentators, black and white alike, disagree in interpreting the contemporary black power movement. The issues concern whether this is a new development in black protest or an old tendency revised; whether the movement is radical, revolutionary, reformist, or conservative; and whether this orientation is unique to Afro-Americans or essentially a black parallel to other ethnic group strategies for collective mobility. For an interesting discussion of black power as a modernized version of Booker T. Washington's separatism and economism, see Harold Cruse (1968a, pp. 193–258).

concerned with owning and controlling those institutions that exist within or impinge upon their community. The colonial model provides a key to the understanding of this movement, and indeed ghetto control advocates have increasingly invoked the language of colonialism in pressing for local home rule. The framework of anticolonialism explains why the struggle for poor people's or community control of poverty programs has been more central in many cities than the content of these programs and why it has been crucial to exclude whites from leadership positions in black organizations.

The key institutions that anticolonialists want to take over or control are business, social services, schools, and the police. Though many spokesmen have advocated the exclusion of white landlords and small businessmen from the ghetto, this program has evidently not struck fire with the black population and little concrete movement toward economic expropriation has yet developed. Welfare recipients have organized in many cities to protect their rights and gain a greater voice in the decisions that affect them, but whole communities have not yet been able to mount direct action against welfare colonialism. Thus schools and the police seem now to be the burning issues of ghetto control politics. . . .

There is a growing recognition that the police are the most crucial institution maintaining the colonized status of black Americans. And of all establishment institutions, police departments probably include the highest proportion of individual racists. This is no accident since central to the workings of racism (an essential component of colonization) are attacks on the humanity and dignity of the subject group. Through their normal routines the police constrict Afro–Americans

to black neighborhoods by harassing and questioning them when found outside the ghetto; they break up groups of youth congregating on corners or in cars without any provocation; and they continue to use offensive and racist language no matter how many intergroup understanding seminars have been built into the police academy. They also shoot to kill ghetto residents for alleged crimes such as car thefts and running from police officers.[6]

Police are key agents in the power equation as well as the drama of dehumanization. In the final analysis they do the dirty work for the larger system by restricting the striking back of black rebels to skirmishes inside the ghetto, thus deflecting energies and attacks from the communities and institutions of the larger power structure. . . .

Of all the programs of decolonization, police autonomy will be most resisted. It gets to the heart of how the state functions to control and contain the black community through delegating the legitimate use of violence to police authority.

The various "black power" programs that are aimed at gaining control of individual ghettos—buying up property and businesses, running the schools through community boards, taking

---

[6] A recent survey of police finds "that in the predominantly Negro areas of several large cities, many of the police perceive the residents as basically hostile, especially the youth and adolescents. A lack of public support—from citizens, from courts, and from laws—is the policeman's major complaint. But some of the public criticism can be traced to the activities in which he engages day by day, and perhaps to the tone in which he enforces the 'law' in the Negro neighborhoods. Most frequently he is 'called upon' to intervene in domestic quarrels and break up loitering groups. He stops and frisks two or three times as many people as are carrying dangerous weapons or are actual criminals, and almost half of these don't wish to cooperate with the policeman's efforts." Peter Rossi et al. (1968, p. 114).

over antipoverty programs and other social agencies, diminishing the arbitrary power of the police—can serve to revitalize the institutions of the ghetto and build up an economic, professional, and political power base. These programs seem limited; we do not know at present if they are enough in themselves to end colonized status.[7] But they are certainly a necessary first step.

THE ROLE OF WHITES

What makes the Kerner report a less-than-radical document is its superficial treatment of racism and its reluctance to confront the colonized relationship between black people and the larger society. The report emphasizes the attitudes and feelings that make up white racism, rather than the system of privilege and control which is the heart of the matter.[8] With all its discussion of the ghetto and its problems, it never faces the question of the stake that white Americans have in racism and ghettoization.

This is not a simple question, but this paper should not end with the impression that police are the major villains.[9] All white Americans gain some privileges and advantage from the colonization of black communities. The majority of whites also lose something from this oppression and division in society. Serious research should be directed to the ways in which white individuals and institutions are tied into the ghetto. In closing let me suggest some possible parameters.

[7] Eldridge Cleaver (1968b) has called this first stage of the anticolonial movement *community* liberation in contrast to a more long-range goal of *national* liberation.

[8] For a discussion of this failure to deal with racism, see Marx (1968).

[9] Such a statement is easier to assert than to document but I am attempting the latter in a forthcoming book tentatively titled *White Racism, Black Culture,* to be published by Little Brown, 1970.

1 It is my guess that only a small minority of whites make a direct economic profit from ghetto colonization. This is hopeful in that the ouster of white businessmen may become politically feasible. Much more significant, however, are the private and corporate interests in the land and residential property of the black community; their holdings and influence on urban decision making must be exposed and combated.

2 A much larger minority have occupational and professional interests in the present arrangements. The Kerner commission reports that 1.3 million non-white men would have to be upgraded occupationally in order to make the black job distribution roughly similar to the white. They advocate this without mentioning that 1.3 million specially privileged white workers would lose in the bargain (National Advisory Commission on Civil Disorders, 1968). In addition there are those professionals who carry out what Lee Rainwater (1967) has called the "dirty work" of administering the lives of the ghetto poor: the social workers, the school teachers, the urban development people, and of course the police. The social problems of the black community will ultimately be solved only by people and organizations from that community; thus the emphasis within these professions must shift toward training such a cadre of minority personnel. Social scientists who teach and study problems of race and poverty likewise have an obligation to replace themselves by bringing into the graduate schools and college faculties men of color who will become the future experts in these areas. For cultural and intellectual imperialism is as real as welfare colonialism, though it is currently screened behind such unassailable shibboleths as universalism and the objectivity of scientific inquiry.

3 Without downgrading the vested interests of profit and profession, the real nitty-gritty elements of the white stake are political power and bureaucratic security. Whereas few whites have much understanding of the realities of race relations and ghetto life, I think most give tacit or at least subconscious support for the containment and control of the black population. Whereas most whites have extremely distorted images of black power, many—if not most—would still be frightened by actual black political power. Racial groups and identities are real in American life; white Americans sense they are on top, and they fear possible reprisals or disruptions were power to be more equalized. There seems to be a paranoid fear in the white psyche of black dominance; the belief that black autonomy would mean

unbridled license is so ingrained that such reasonable outcomes as black political majorities and independent black police forces will be bitterly resisted.

On this level the major mass bulwark of colonization is the administrative need for bureaucratic security so that the middle classes can go about their life and business in peace and quiet. The black militant movement is a threat to the orderly procedures by which bureaucracies and suburbs manage their existence, and I think today there are more people who feel a stake in conventional procedures than there are those who gain directly from racism. For in their fight for institutional control, the colonized will not play by the white rules of the game. These administrative rules have kept them down and out of the system; therefore they have no necessary intention of running institutions in the image of the white middle class.

The liberal, humanist value that violence is the worst sin cannot be defended today if one is committed squarely against racism and for self-determination. For some violence is almost inevitable in the decolonization process; unfortunately racism in America has been so effective that the greatest power Afro–Americans (and perhaps also Mexican–Americans) wield today is the power to disrupt. If we are going to swing with these revolutionary times and at least respond positively to the anticolonial movement, we will have to learn to live with conflict, confrontation, constant change, and what may be real or apparent chaos and disorder.

A positive response from the white majority needs to be in two major directions at the same time. First, community liberation movements should be supported in every way by pulling out white instruments of direct control and exploitation and substituting technical assistance to the community

when this is asked for. But it is not enough to relate affirmatively to the nationalist movement for ghetto control without at the same time radically opening doors for full participation in the institutions of the mainstream. Otherwise the liberal and radical position is little different than the traditional segregationist. Freedom in the special conditions of American colonization means that the colonized must have the choice between participation in the larger society and in their own independent structures.

REFERENCES

BARON, H. M., "Black Powerlessness in Chicago," *Trans-Action,* 1968, 61, 27–33.

BLAUNER, R., "Whitewash over Watts: The Failure of the McCone Report," *Trans-Action* 1966, 3, 3–9, 54.

CARMICHAEL, S., and HAMILTON, C., *Black Power,* New York: Random House, 1967.

CLARK, K. B., *Youth in the Ghetto,* New York: Haryou Associates, 1964.

———, *Dark Ghetto,* New York: Harper and Row, 1965.

CLEAVER, E., "The Land Question," *Ramparts,* 1968(a), 6, 51.

———, "Community Imperialism," *The Black Panther,* May 18, 1968(b).

CRUSE, H., *Rebellion or Revolution,* New York: Morrow, 1968 (a)

———, *The Crisis of the Negro Intellectual,* New York: Morrow, 1968(b).

FANON, F., *Wretched of the Earth,* New York: Grove, 1963.

GLAZER, N., and MOYNIHAN, D., *Beyond the Melting Pot,* Cambridge, Mass: M.I.T. Press, 1963.

MARX, G. T., "Two Cheers for the Riot Commission Report," in J. Szwed (ed.), *Black Americans: A Second Look,* New York: Basic Books, 1970.

MEMMI, A., *The Colonizer and the Colonized,* Boston: Beacon Press, 1967.

RAINWATER, L., "The Revolt of the Dirtyworkers," *Trans-Action,* 1967, 5 (1).

ROSE, P., (ed.), *Americans from Africa,* New York: Atherton, 1969.

ROSSI, P., et al., "Between Black and White—the Faces of American Institutions and the Ghetto," in *Supplemental Studies for the National Advisory Commission on Civil Disorders,* July 1968.

7
*Inequality in Education,
Welfare, and Housing**
KERNER COMMISSION

A. EDUCATION

Education in a democratic society must equip the children of the nation to realize their potential and to participate fully in American life. For the community at large, the schools have discharged this responsibility well. But for many minorities, and particularly for the children of the racial ghetto, the schools have failed to provide the educational experience which could help overcome the effects of discrimination and deprivation.

This failure is one of the persistent sources of grievance and resentment within the Negro community. The hostility of Negro parents and students toward the school system is generating increasing conflict and causing disruption within many city school districts. . . .

The bleak record of public education for ghetto children is growing worse. In the critical skills—verbal and reading ability—Negro students fall further behind whites with each year of school completed. For example, in the metropolitan Northeast Negro students on the average begin the first grade with somewhat lower scores on standard achievement tests than white, are about 1.6 grades behind by the sixth grade, and have fallen 3.3 grades behind white students by the twelfth grade.[1] The failure of the public schools to equip these students with basic ver-

bal skills is reflected in their performance on the Selective Service Mental Test. During the period June 1964– December 1965, 67 percent of Negro candidates failed the examination. The failure rate for whites was 19 percent.

The result is that many more Negro than white students drop out of school. In the metropolitan North and West, Negro students are more than three times as likely as white students to drop out of school by age 16–17.[2] As reflected by the high unemployment rate for graduates of ghetto schools and the even higher proportion of employed workers who are in low-skilled, low-paid jobs, many of those who do graduate are not equipped to enter the normal job market, and have great difficulty securing employment.[3]

Several factors have converged to produce this critical situation.

Segregation

The vast majority of innercity schools are rigidly segregated. In seventy-five major central cities surveyed by the United States Commission on Civil Rights in its study, "Racial Isolation in the Public Schools," 75 percent of all Negro students in elementary grades attended schools with enrollments that were 90 percent or more Negro. Almost 90 percent of all Negro students attended schools which had a majority of Negro students. In the same cities, 83 percent of all white students in those grades attended schools with 90 to 100 percent white enrollments.

Racial isolation in the urban public schools is the result principally of resi-

---

*[*Kerner Commission* (New York: Bantam Books, 1968).]

[1] "Equality of Educational Opportunity," U.S. Department of HEW, Office of Education (1966), p. 20. This report, generally referred to as the "Coleman report," was prepared pursuant to Section 402 of the Civil Rights Act of 1964.

[2] The actual nonenrollment rate for Negro students in these areas is 20 percent, as opposed to 6 percent for white students. Coleman report, p. 31.

[3] Employment figures reflect discriminatory practices as well. The contribution of inadequate education to unemployment, while not quantified, is clearly substantial.

dential segregation and widespread employment of the "neighborhood school" policy, which transfers segregation from housing to education. The effect of these conditions is magnified by the fact that a much greater proportion of white than Negro students attend private schools. Studies indicate that in America's twenty largest cities approximately four out of ten white students are enrolled in nonpublic schools, as compared with only one out of ten Negro pupils. The differential appears to be increasing.[4]

Segregation in urban schools is growing. In a sample of fifteen large northern cities, the Civil Rights Commission found that the degree of segregation rose sharply from 1950 to 1965. As Negro enrollments in these fifteen cities grew, 97 percent of the increase was absorbed by schools already over 50 percent Negro and 84 percent by schools more than 90 percent Negro.[5] By 1975, it is estimated that if current policies and trends persist, 80 percent of all Negro pupils in the twenty largest cities, comprising nearly one-half of the nation's Negro population, will be attending 90 to 100 percent Negro schools. . . .[6]

Teachers

The schools attended by disadvantaged Negro children commonly are staffed by teachers with less experience and lower qualifications than those attended by middle class whites.[7] For example, a 1963 study ranking Chicago's public high schools by the socioeconomic status of surrounding neighborhoods found that in the ten lowest-ranking schools only 63.2 percent of all teachers were fully certified and the median level of teaching experience was 3.9 years. In three of these schools, the median level was one year. Four of these lowest ranking schools were 100 percent Negro in enrollment and three were over 90 percent Negro. By contrast eight of the ten highest ranking schools had nearly total white enrollments, and the other two were more than 75 percent white. In these schools, 90.3 percent of the teachers were fully certified and the median level of teaching experience was 12.3 years.

Testifying before the commission, Dr. Paul Daniel Dodson, director of the New York University Center for Human Relations and Community Services, stated that:

Innercity schools have not been able to hold teaching staff. Between 1952 and 1962 almost half the licensed teachers of New York City left the system. Almost two out of every five of the 50,000 teaching personnel of New York City do not hold regular permanent licenses for the assignments they have.

In another school system in one of the large cities, it was reported of one innercity school that of eighty-four staff members, forty-one were temporary teachers, twenty-five were probationaries, and eighteen

[4] "Big City School Desegregation: Trends and Methods," Dentler and Elsbery, National Conference on Equal Educational Opportunity, November, 1967, p. 3.

[5] While the proportion of Negroes attending all-Negro schools in southern and border states has declined in the fourteen years since the Supreme Court's school desegregation decision, the number of Negro students attending schools with all or nearly all-Negro enrollments has risen. "Racial Isolation in the Public Schools," p. 10.

[6] "Big City School Desegregation: Trends and Methods," op. cit.

[7] The Civil Rights Commission's survey found no major national differences in the educational attainment (years completed) of teachers in majority-Negro or majority-white schools. However, many large cities did not take part in the basic studies which supplied the data for this conclusion. It is precisely in these cities that teachers of disadvantaged Negro students tend to be the least experienced. Moreover, the commission did conclude that Negro students, more often than whites, had teachers with nonacademic college majors and lower verbal achievement levels.

[were] tenure teachers. However, only one of the tenure teachers was licensed in academic subjects.

United States Commissioner of Education, Harold Howe, testified that many teachers are unprepared for teaching in schools serving disadvantaged children, "have what is a traumatic experience there and don't last." Moreover, the more experienced teachers normally select the more attractive schools in white neighborhoods, thereby relegating the least experienced teachers to the disadvantaged schools. This process reinforces the view of ghetto schools as inferior.

As a result, teachers assigned to these schools often begin with negative attitudes toward the students, and their ability and willingness to learn. These attitudes are aggravated by serious discipline problems, by the high crime rates in areas surrounding the schools, and by the greater difficulties of teaching students from disadvantaged backgrounds. These conditions are reflected in the Coleman report's finding that a higher proportion of teachers in schools serving disadvantaged areas are dissatisfied with their present assignments and with their students than are their counterparts in other schools.[8]

Studies have shown that the attitudes of teachers toward their students have very powerful impacts upon educational attainment. The more teachers expect from their students—however disadvantaged those students may be—the better the students perform. Conversely, negative teacher attitudes act as self-fulfilling prophecies: the teachers expect little from their students; the students fulfill the expectation. As Dr. Kenneth Clark observed, "Children who are treated as if they

are uneducable invariably become uneducable."[9]

In disadvantaged areas, the neighborhood school concept tends to concentrate a relatively high proportion of emotionally disturbed and other problem children in the schools. Disadvantaged neighborhoods have the greatest need for health personnel, supplementary instructors, and counsellors to assist with family problems, provide extra instruction to lagging students, and deal with the many serious mental and physical health deficiencies that occur so often in poverty areas.

These conditions which make effective teaching vastly more difficult, reinforce negative teacher attitudes. A 1963 survey of Chicago public schools showed that the condition creating the highest amount of dissatisfaction among teachers was lack of adequate provision for the treatment of maladjusted, retarded, and disturbed pupils. About 79 percent of elementary school teachers and 67 percent of high school teachers named this item as a key factor. The need for professional support for teachers in dealing with these extraordinary problems is seldom, if ever, met.

Although special schools or classes are available for emotionally disturbed and mentally handicapped children, many pupils requiring such help remain in regular classes because of negligence, red tape, or unavailability of clinical staff. An example is provided by a National Education Association Study of Detroit:[10]

Before a disturbed child can receive psychological assistance, he must receive diag-

---

[8] Coleman report, p. 12.

[9] "Dark Ghetto," Dr. Kenneth Clark (1965), p. 128.

[10] "Detroit, Michigan: A Study of Barriers to Equal Educational Opportunity in a Large City," National Commission on Professional Rights and Responsibilities of the National Education Association of the United States, March, 1967, p. 66.

nostic testing. But before this happens, the teacher must fill in a form . . . to be submitted . . . to a central office committee. . . . If the committee decides that psychological testing is in order, the teacher must fill out a second form . . . to be submitted to the psychological clinic. The child may then be placed on the waiting list for psychological testing. The waiting period may last for several weeks, several months, or several years. And while he waits, he "sits in" the regular classroom. . . . Since visiting teachers are scarce and special classes insufficient in number, the child who has been tested is usually returned to the regular classroom to serve more time as a "sit-in."

Teaching in disadvantaged areas is made more difficult by the high rate of student turnover. In New York City during 1963–1964, seven of ten students in the average, segregated Negro–Puerto Rican elementary school either entered or left during the year.[11] Similar conditions are common to other inner-city schools. Continuity of education becomes exceedingly difficult—the more so because many of the students entering ghetto schools during the school year come from rural southern schools and are thus behind even the minimum levels of achievement attained by their fellow northern-born students.

Enrollments

In virtually every large American city, the innercity schools attended by Negroes are the most overcrowded. We have cited the vast population exchange —relatively affluent whites leaving the city to be replaced by Negroes— which has taken place over the last decade. The impact on public education facilities has been severe. . . .

Negroes now comprise a majority or near majority of public school students in seven of the ten largest American cities, as well as in many other cities. . . .

Because this rapid expansion of Negro population has been concentrated in segregated neighborhoods, ghetto schools have experienced acute overcrowding. Shortages of textbooks and supplies have developed. Double shifts are common; hallways and other nonclassroom space have been adapted for class instruction; and mobile classroom units are used. Even programs for massive construction of new schools in Negro neighborhoods cannot always keep up with increased overcrowding.

From 1951 to 1963, the Chicago Board of Education built 266 new schools or additions, mainly in all-Negro areas. Yet a special committee studying the schools in 1964 reported that 40 percent of the Negro elementary schools had more than thirty-five students per available classroom, as compared to 12 percent of the primarily white elementary schools. Of the eight Negro high schools, five had enrollments over 50 percent above designed capacity. Four of the ten integrated high schools, but only four of the twenty-six predominantly white high schools, were similarly overcrowded. Comparable conditions prevail in many other large cities.

The Civil Rights Commission found that two-thirds of the predominantly Negro elementary schools in Atlanta were overcrowded. This compared with 47 percent of the white schools. In 1965, all Atlanta Negro high schools were operating beyond their designed capacity; only one of three all-white high schools, and six of eight predominantly white schools were similarly overcrowded.[12]

Washington D.C. elementary schools

---

[11] The comparable rate in the white schools was four out of ten.

[12] Atlanta report for Civil Rights Commission, pp. 32–34.

with 85–100 percent Negro enrollments operated at a median of 115 percent of capacity. The one predominantly white high school operated at 92.3 percent, an integrated high school at 101.1 percent, and the remaining schools—all predominantly Negro—at 108.4 percent to 127.1 percent of capacity.

Overcrowded and inadequately supplied schools have severe effects upon the quality of education, the most important of which is that teachers are forced to concentrate on maintaining classroom discipline, and thus have little time and energy to perform their primary function—educating the students.

Facilities and curricula

Innercity schools are not only overcrowded, they also tend to be the oldest and most poorly equipped.

In Detroit, thirty of the school buildings still in use in these areas were dedicated during the administration of President Grant.[13] In Cincinnati, although from 1950 to 1965 Negro student population expanded at a faster pace than white, most additional school capacity planned and constructed was in predominantly white areas. According to a Civil Rights Commission report on Cincinnati, the added Negro pupil population was housed, for the most part, in the same central-city schools vacated by the whites.[14]

With respect to equipment, the Coleman report states that "Negro pupils have fewer of some of the facilities that seem most related to achievement. They have less access to physics, chemistry, and language laboratories; there are fewer books per pupil in their

libraries; their textbooks are less often in sufficient supply."[15]

The quality of education offered by ghetto schools is diminished further by use of curricula and materials poorly adapted to the life-experiences of their students. Designed to serve a middle class culture, much educational material appears irrelevant to the youth of the racial and economic ghetto. Until recently, few texts featured any Negro personalities. Few books used or courses offered reflected the harsh realities of life in the ghetto, or the contribution of Negroes to the country's culture and history. This failure to include materials relevant to their own environment has made students skeptical about the utility of what they are being taught. Reduced motivation to learn results.

Funds

Despite the overwhelming need, our society spends less money educating ghetto children than children of suburban families. Comparing the per capita education costs for ghetto schools with suburban, one educator, in testimony before this commission, said:

If the most educated parents with the highest motivated children find in their wisdom that it costs $1,500 per child per year to educate their children in the suburbs, isn't it logical that it would cost an equal amount to educate the less well motivated, low income family child in the inner city? Such cost would just about double the budget of the average innercity school system.[16]

Twenty-five school boards in communities surrounding Detroit spent up to $500 more per pupil per year to educate their children than the city.

---

[13] Testimony of Norman Drachler, Superintendent of Schools, Detroit.
[14] Cincinnati report for the Civil Rights Commission, pp. 21–25.

[15] Coleman report, pp. 9–12.
[16] Testimony of Dr. Dodson.

Merely to bring the teacher/pupil ratio in Detroit in line with the state average would require an additional 16,650 teachers at an annual cost of approximately $13 million.[17]

There is evidence that the disparity in educational expenditures for suburban and innercity schools has developed in parallel with population shifts. In a study of twelve metropolitan areas, the Civil Rights Commission found that, in 1950, ten of the twelve central cities spent more per pupil than the surrounding suburbs; by 1964, in seven of the twelve the average suburb spent more per pupil than the central city in seven.[18]

This reversal reflects the declining or stagnant city tax base, and increasing competition from nonschool needs (police, welfare, fire) for a share of the municipal tax dollar. The suburbs, where nonschool needs are less demanding, allocate almost twice the proportion of their total budgets to education as the cities.[19]

State contributions to city school systems have not had consistent equalizing effects. The Civil Rights Commission found that although state aid to city schools has increased at a rate proportionately greater than for suburban schools, states continue to contribute more per pupil to suburban schools in seven of the twelve metropolitan areas studies. Table 1 illustrates the findings.

Community-School relations

Teachers of the poor rarely live in the community where they work and sometimes have little sympathy for the life styles of their students. Moreover, the growth and complexity of the administration of large urban school systems has compromised the accountability of the local schools, to the communities which they serve, and reduced the ability of parents to influence decisions affecting the education of their children. Ghetto schools often appear to be unresponsive to the community, communication has broken down, and parents are distrustful of officials responsible for formulating educational policy.

The consequences for the education of students attending these schools are serious. Parental hostility to the schools is reflected in the attitudes of their children. Since the needs and concerns of the ghetto community are rarely reflected in educational policy formulated on a citywide basis, the schools are often seen by ghetto youth as being irrelevant. . . .

The absence of effective community-school relations has deprived the public education system of the communication required to overcome this divergence of goals. In the schools,

TABLE 1 Revenues per Pupil from State Sources

Place	Amount per Pupil 1950	Amount per Pupil 1964	Percent Increase 1950–1964
Baltimore City	$ 71	$171	140.8
Suburbs	90	199	121.1
Birmingham City	90	201	123.3
Suburbs	54	150	177.7
Boston City	19	52	173.7
Suburbs	30	75	150.0
Buffalo City	135	284	110.4
Suburbs	165	270	63.6
Chattanooga City	62	136	119.4
Suburbs	141	152	7.8
Chicago City	42	154	266.6
Suburbs	32	110	243.8
Cincinnati City	51	91	78.4
Suburbs	78	91	16.7
Cleveland City	50	88	76.0
Suburbs	39	88	125.6
Detroit City	135	189	40.0
Suburbs	149	240	61.1
New Orleans City	152	239	57.2
Suburbs	117	259	121.4
St. Louis City	70	131	87.1
Suburbs	61	143	134.4
San Francisco City	122	163	33.6
Suburbs	160	261	63.1

Source: "United States Commission on Civil Rights, Racial Isolation in the Public Schools."

---

[17] Testimony of Norman Drachler, Superintendent of Schools, Detroit.
[18] "Racial Isolation in the Public Schools," p. 27.
[19] "Racial Isolation in the Public Schools," p. 26.

as in the larger society, the isolation of ghetto residents from the policy-making institutions of local government is adding to the polarization of the community and depriving the system of its self-rectifying potential. . . .

B. THE WELFARE SYSTEM

The commission believes that our present system of public assistance contributes materially to the tensions and social disorganization that have led to civil disorders. The failures of the system alienate the taxpayers who support it, the social workers who administer it, and the poor who depend on it. As Mitchell Ginsberg, head of New York City's Welfare Department, stated before the commission, "The welfare system is designed to save money instead of people and tragically ends up doing neither."

The system is deficient in two critical ways:

First, it excludes large numbers of persons who are in great need, and who, if provided a decent level of support, might be able to become more productive and self-sufficient.

Second, for those who are included, it provides assistance well below the minimum necessary for a decent level of existence, and imposes restictions that encourage continued dependency on welfare and undermine self-respect.

In short, while the system is indispensable because for millions—mostly children—it supports basic needs, drastic reforms are required if it is to help people free themselves from poverty. . . .

States and local governments contribute an average of about 45 percent of the cost of supporting the AFDC program, with each state setting the level of grants for its own residents. Monthly payments vary widely from state to state. They range from $9.30 per AFDC recipient monthly in Mississippi to a high of $62.55 in New York. In fiscal year 1967, the total annual cost of the AFDC program, including federal, state, and local contributions, was approximately $2.0 billion, providing an average of about $36 monthly for each recipient.

This sum is well below the poverty subsistence level under any standard. The National Advisory Council on Public Welfare has commented:

The national average provides little more than half the amounts admittedly required by a family for subsistence; in some low income states, it is less than a quarter of that amount. The low public assistance payments contribute to the perpetuation of poverty and deprivation that extend into future generations.

Over the last six years, despite the longest sustained period of economic progress in the history of this country, the AFDC caseload has risen each year while the unemployment rate has fallen. . . . Yet, it has been estimated in 1965, nationwide, over 50 percent of persons eligible to receive assistance under welfare programs were not enrolled.

In addition to the AFDC program, almost all states have a program of general assistance to provide minimum payments based largely or entirely on need. During calendar year 1966, the states spent $336 million on general assistance. No federal funds have ever been available for this program. In fact, no federal funds have ever been available for men or women, however needy, who are neither aged, severely handicapped nor the parents of minor children.

The dimension of the "pool" of poor but unassisted individuals and families—either ineligible under present programs or eligible but unenrolled—is indicated by the fact that in 1966 there were 21.7 million nonaged persons in the United States with incomes below the "poverty level" as defined by the Social Security Administration. Only a third of these received assistance from major public welfare programs:

[T]he bulk of the nonaged poor live in families where there is a breadwinner who works either every day or who had worked a part of the year, so that the picture that people have of who the poor are is quite a different thing from an analysis of the poverty population. And what we have done in effect is carve out, because of our categorical approach to public assistance, a certain group of people within that overall poverty population to give help to.

Seventy percent of the nonaged poor families were headed by men, and 50 percent of these held full-time jobs and 86 percent of them worked at least part of the year, so that the typical poor family is much like the typical American family, except they don't make enough money. And they have been historically excluded from the AFDC program. [20]

The gaps in coverage and low levels of payments are the source of much of the long-term dissatisfaction with the system. The day-to-day administration of the system creates even sharper bitterness and dissatisfaction, because it serves to remind recipients that they are considered untrustworthy, ungrateful, promiscuous, and lazy. Among the most tension-producing statutory requirements, administrative practices, and regulations are the following:

First, in most states benefits are available only when a parent is absent from the home. Thus, in these states an unemployed father whose family needs public assistance in order to

[20] Testimony before the commission of Lisle C. Carter, Jr., Assistant Secretary for Individual and Family Services, Department of Health, Education and Welfare.

survive, must either abandon his family or see them go hungry. This so-called man-in-the-house rule was intended to prevent payments to children who have an alternative potential source of support. In fact, the rule seems to have fostered the breakup of homes and perpetuated reliance on welfare. The irritation caused by the rule is aggravated in some states by regular searches of recipients' homes to ferret out violations.

Second, until recently *all* amounts earned by adult welfare recipients on outside jobs, except for small allowances for expenses, were deducted directly from the welfare payments they would otherwise have received. This practice, required by federal law, appears to have taken away from many recipients the incentive to seek part- or full-time employment. The 1967 amendments to the welfare laws permit retention of the first $30 earned by a recipient each month and one-third of all earnings above that amount. This is a start in the right direction but does not go nearly far enough. New York City has, for example, begun experimenting with a promising program that allows welfare mothers to keep the first $85 of earnings each month and a percentage of amounts above that.

Third, in most states, there is a residency requirement, generally averaging around a year, before a person is eligible to receive welfare. These state regulations were enacted to discourage persons from moving from one state to another to take advantage of higher welfare payments. In fact, they appear to have had little, if any, impact on migration and have frequently served to prevent those in greatest need— desperately poor families arriving in a strange city—from receiving the boost that might give them a fresh start.

Fourth, though large amounts are

being spent on social service programs for families, children, and young people, few of these programs have been effective. In the view of the Advisory Council on Public Welfare, the inadequacies in social services

are themselves a major source of such social evils as crime and juvenile delinquency, mental illness, illegitimacy, multigenerational dependency, slum environments, and the widely deplored climate of unrest, alienation, and discouragement among many groups in the population.

A final source of tension is the brittle relationship that exists between many welfare workers and the poor. The cumulative abrasive effects of the low levels of assistance, the complicated eligibility requirements, the continuing efforts required by regulations to verify eligibility—often by means that constitute flagrant invasions of privacy— have often brought about an adversary relationship between the case worker and the recipient family. This is intensified by the fact that the investigative requirements not only force continuing confrontations but, in those states where the same worker performs both investigative and service functions, leave the worker little time to provide service.

As was stated by Lisle Carter, Assistant Secretary of Health, Education and Welfare, in testimony before the commission:

[W]e think [it] is extremely important that welfare recipients begin to feel that the welfare worker is on their side instead of on the side of the agency. There have been statements made that the welfare workers are among the most hated persons in the ghetto, and one of the studies shows that the recipients tend to feel that what the workers says is something that cannot be challenged. Nowhere do you get the feeling that . . . the worker is there to really go

to bat for recipients in dealing with the other pressures that they face in the community. . . .

An altered and expanded welfare system by extending support to more of those in need, by raising levels of assistance on a uniform national basis, and by eliminating demeaning restrictions could begin to recapture the rich human resources that are being wasted by poverty. . . .

C. HOUSING

The passage of the National Housing Act in 1934 signaled a new federal commitment to provide housing for the nation's citizens. Fifteen years later Congress made the commitment explicit in the Housing Act of 1949, establishing as a national goal, the realization of "a decent home and suitable environment for every American family."

Today, after more than three decades of fragmented and grossly underfunded federal housing programs, decent housing remains a chronic problem for the disadvantaged urban household. Fifty-six percent of the country's nonwhite families live in central cities today, and of these, nearly two-thirds live in neighborhoods marked by substandard[21] housing and general urban blight. For these citizens, condemned by segregation and poverty to live in the decaying slums of our central cities, the goal of a decent home and suitable environment is as far distant as ever.

During the decade of the 1950's, when vast numbers of Negroes were migrating to the cities, only four million of the 16.8 million new housing units constructed throughout the nation

---

[21] The Department of Housing and Urban Development classifies substandard housing as that housing reported by the United States Census Bureau as (1) sound but lacking full plumbing, (2) deteriorating and lacking full plumbing, or (3) dilapidated.

were built in the central cities. These additions were counterbalanced by the loss of 1.5 million central-city units through demolition and other means. The result was that the number of non-whites living in substandard housing increased from 1.4 to 1.8 million, even though the number of substandard units declined.

Statistics available for the period since 1960 indicate that the trend is continuing. There has been virtually no decline in the number of occupied dilapidated units in metropolitan areas, and surveys in New York City and Watts actually show an increase in the number of such units. These statistics have led the Department of Housing and Urban Development to conclude that while the trend in the country as a whole is toward less substandard housing, "There are individual neighborhoods and areas within many cities where the housing situation continues to deteriorate. . . . "[22]

Substandard, old, and overcrowded structures

Nationwide, 25 percent of all nonwhites living in central cities occupied sub-

[22] U.S. Senate, *Hearings before the Subcommittee on Executive Reorganization of the Committee on Government Operations,* 89th Congress, 2nd Session, August 16, 1966, p. 142.

standard units in 1960 compared to 8 percent of all whites. Preliminary Census Bureau data indicate that by 1966, the figures had dropped to 16 and 5 percent respectively. However, if "deteriorating" units and units with serious housing code violations are added, the percentage of nonwhites living in inadequate housing in 1966 becomes much greater. . . .

The commission carried out special analyses of 1960 housing conditions in three cities, concentrating on all Census Tracts with 1960 median incomes of under $3,000 for both families and individuals. It also analyzed housing conditions in Watts. The results showed that the vast majority of people living in the poorest areas of these cities were Negroes and that a high proportion lived in inadequate housing:

Negroes, on the average, also occupy much older housing than whites. In each of ten metropolitan areas analyzed by the commission, substantially higher percentages of nonwhites than whites occupied units built prior to 1939.

Finally, Negro housing units are far more likely to be overcrowded than those occupied by whites. In United States metropolitan areas in 1960, 25 percent of all nonwhite units

TABLE 2

Item	Detroit	Washington, D.C.	Memphis	Watts Area of Los Angeles
Total population of study area	162,375	97,084	150,827	49,074
Percentage of study area nonwhite	67.5%	74.5%	74.0%	87.3%
Percentage of housing units in study area:				
— Substandard by HUD definition	32.7%	23.9%	35.0%	10.5%
— Delapidated, deteriorating, or sound but lacking full plumbing	53.1%	37.3%	46.5%	29.1%

Source: United States Department of Commerce, Bureau of the Census.

were overcrowded by the standard measure (that is, they contained 1.01 or more persons per room). Only 8 percent of all white occupied units were in this category. Moreover, 11 percent of all nonwhite occupied units were seriously overcrowded (1.51 or more persons per room), compared with 2 percent for white occupied units.

Higher rents for poorer housing

Negroes in large cities are often forced to pay the same rents as whites and receive less for their money, or pay higher rents for the same accommodations.

The first type of discriminatory effect—paying the same amount but receiving less—is illustrated by data from the 1960 census for Chicago and Detroit.

In certain Chicago census tracts both whites and nonwhites paid median rents of $88, and the proportions paying various specific rents below that median were almost identical. But the units rented by nonwhites were typically:

Smaller (the median number of rooms was 3.35 for nonwhites versus 3.95 for whites).
In worse condition (30.7 percent of all nonwhite units were deteriorated or dilapidated units versus 11.6 percent for whites).
Occupied by more people (the median household size was 3.53 for nonwhites versus 2.88 for whites).
More likely to be overcrowded (27.4 percent of nonwhite units had 1.01 or more persons per room versus 7.9 percent for whites).

In Detroit, whites paid a median rental of $77 as compared to $76 among nonwhites. Yet 27.0 percent of nonwhite units were deteriorating or dilapidated, as compared to only 10.3 percent of all white units.

The second type of discriminatory effect—paying more for similar housing—is illustrated by data from a study of housing conditions in disadvan-taged neighborhoods in Newark, New Jersey. In four areas of that city, nonwhites with housing essentially similar to that of whites paid rents that were from 8.1 percent to 16.8 percent higher. Though the typically larger size of nonwhite households, with consequent harder wear and tear, may partially justify the difference in rental, the study found that nonwhites were paying a definite "color tax" of apparently well over 10 percent on housing. This condition prevails in most racial ghettos.

The combination of high rents and low incomes forces many Negroes to pay an excessively high proportion of their income for housing. This is shown dramatically by the following chart, showing the percentage of renter households paying over 35 percent of their incomes for rent in ten metropolitan areas:

TABLE 3   Percentages of White and Non-white Occupied Units with Households Paying 35 Percent or More of Their Income for Rent in Selected Metropolitan Areas

Metropolitan Area	White Occupied Units	Nonwhite Occupied Units
Cleveland	8.6	33.8
Dallas	19.2	33.8
Detroit	21.2	40.5
Kansas City	20.2	40.0
Los Angeles–Long Beach	23.4	28.4
New Orleans	16.6	30.5
Philadelphia	19.3	32.1
St. Louis	18.5	36.7
San Francisco–Oakland	21.2	25.1
Washington, D.C.	18.5	28.3

Source: United States Department of Commerce, Bureau of the Census.

The high proportion of income that must go for rent leaves less money in such households for other expenses. Undoubtedly, this hardship is a major reason many Negro households regard housing as one of their worst problems.

Discrimination in housing code enforcement

Thousands of landlords in disadvantaged neighborhoods openly violate building codes with impunity, thereby providing a constant demonstration of flagrant discrimination by legal authorities. A high proportion of residential and other structures contain numerous violations of building and housing codes. Refusal ro remedy these violations is a criminal offense, one which can have grievous effects upon the victims—the tenants living in these structures. Yet in most cities, few building code violations in these areas are ever corrected, even when tenants complain directly to municipal building departments.

There are economic reasons why these codes are not rigorously enforced. Bringing many old structures up to code standards and maintaining them at that level often would require owners to raise rents far above the ability of local residents to pay. In New York City, rigorous code enforcement has already caused owners to board up and abandon over 2,500 buildings rather than incur the expense of repairing them. Nevertheless, open violation of codes is a constant source of distress to low income tenants and creates serious hazards to health and safety in disadvantaged neighborhoods. . . .

Poverty and housing deterioration

The reasons many Negroes live in decaying slums are not difficult to discover. First and foremost is poverty. Most ghetto residents cannot pay the rent necessary to support decent housing. This prevents private builders from constructing new units in the ghettos or from rehabilitating old ones, for either action involves an investment that would require substantially higher rents than most ghetto dwellers can pay. It also deters landlords from maintaining units that are presently structurally sound. Maintenance requires additional investment, and at the minimal rents that innercity Negroes can pay, landlords have little incentive to provide it.

The implications of widespread poor maintenance are serious. Most of the gains in Negro housing have occurred through the turnover which occurs as part of the "filtering down" process—as the white middle class moves out, the units it leaves are occupied by Negroes. Many of these units are very old. Without proper maintenance, they soon become dilapidated, so that the improvement in housing resulting from the filtering-down process is only temporary. The 1965 New York City survey points up the danger. During the period that the number of substandard units was decreasing, the number of deteriorating units increased by 95,000.

Discrimination

The second major factor condemning vast numbers of Negroes to urban slums is racial discrimination in the housing market. Discrimination prevents access to many nonslum areas, particularly the suburbs, and has a detrimental effect on ghetto housing itself. By restricting the area open to a growing population, housing discrimination makes it profitable for landlords to break up ghetto apartments for denser occupancy, hastening housing deterioration. By creating a "back pressure" in the racial ghettos, discrimination keeps prices and rents of older, more deteriorated housing in the ghetto higher than they would be in a truly free and open market.

Existing programs

To date, federal building programs have been able to do comparatively little to provide housing for the disadvantaged. In the thirty-one-year history of subsidized federal housing, only about 800,000 units have been constructed, with recent production averaging about 50,000 units a year. By comparison, over a period only three years longer, FHA insurance guarantees have made possible the construction of over ten million middle- and upper-income units.

Federal programs also have done little to prevent the growth of racially segregated suburbs around our cities. Until 1949, FHA official policy was to refuse to insure any unsegregated housing. It was not until the issuance of Executive Order 11063 in 1962 that the agency required nondiscrimination pledges from loan applicants.

8
Black Powerlessness
in Chicago*

HAROLD M. BARON with HARRIET
STULMAN, RICHARD ROTHSTEIN,
and RENNARD DAVIS

Until recently, the three principal targets of the civil rights movement in the North were discrimination and inferior conditions in (1) housing for Negroes, (2) jobs for Negroes, and (3) the education of Negroes. But after failing to bring about major changes, many Negroes realized that one reason the status quo in housing, jobs, and education continues is that the black community lacks control over decision making. Negroes remain second-class

*[Reprinted with permission from *Trans-action*, November 1968. Copyright © November, 1968 by Trans-action, Inc., New Brunswick, New Jersey.]

citizens partly because of the discrimination of individual whites, but mainly because of the way whites control the major institutions of our society. And therefore the fourth major goal of Negro organizations and the civil rights movement has become the acquisition of power.

It was because of this concern with power for black people that more than two years ago, the Chicago Urban League—a social welfare organization dedicated to changing institutions so as to achieve full racial equality—started to study the decision-making apparatus in Cook County, Ill., and particularly how it affects or ignores Negro citizens. (Cook County takes in the city of Chicago, and two-thirds of the population of surrounding suburban ring included in the Chicago Standard Metropolitan Statistical area.) Among the questions we posed were:

What is the extent of Negro exclusion from policy-making positions in Chicago?

Where Negroes are in policy-making positions, what types of positions are these, and where are Negroes in greatest number and authority?

Do Negroes in policy-making positions represent the interests of the Negro community? and

How might an increase in the percentage of Negro policymakers affect socioeconomic conditions for Negroes in general?

What we found was that in 1965 some 20 percent of the people in Chicago were Negro. Yet the representation of Negroes in policy-making positions was minimal. Of the top 10,997 policy-making positions in the major Cook County institutions included in our study, Negroes occupied only 285—or 2.6 percent.

In government, out of a total of 1,088 policy-making positions Negroes held just 58. This 5 percent is about one-fourth of the percentage of Negroes in the total county population. Of the 364, elective posts in the survey, however, Negroes occupied twenty-nine, or 8 percent, indicating that the franchise has helped give Negroes representation. Yet Negroes had the most positions, percentagewise, on appointed supervisory boards, such as the Board of Education and the Chicago Housing Authority. There they occupied ten of the seventy-seven policy-making positions, or about 13 percent.

Negroes were better represented on appointed supervisory boards and in elected (nonjudicial) offices that they were in local administrative positions, or in important federal jobs based in Chicago. Thus, Negroes held 12 percent of the nonjudicial elected posts in Chicago's government, but only a little over 1 percent of the appointive policy-making positions in the city administration. The same anomaly appears at the federal level. There is one Negro out of the thirteen United States Congressmen from Cook County (8 percent), but Negroes held only one out of thirty-one presidential appointments (3 percent), and eight of the 368 top federal civil service posts (2 percent).

Nonetheless, Negroes have—proportionately—2½ times as many important posts in the public sector as they have in the private sector. Negroes are virtually barred from policy-making positions in the large organizations that dominate the private institutions in the Chicago area. Out of a total of 9,909 positions, Negroes fill a mere 227. This 2 percent representation is only the one-tenth of the proportionate Negro population.

The whitest form of policy making in Chicago is in the control of economic enterprises. Out of 6,838 positions identified in business corporations,

Negroes held only forty-two (six-tenths of 1 percent). Thirty-five of these were in insurance, where Negroes occupy 6 percent of the 533 posts. But all thirty-five were in two all-Negro insurance firms. The other seven positions were in four smaller banks. In banks in general, Negroes, occupied three-tenths of 1 percent of the policy posts. There were no Negro policymakers at all in manufacturing, communications, transportation, utilities, and trade corporations.

Out of the 372 companies we studied, the Negro-owned insurance companies were the only ones dominated by blacks. And if we had used the same stringent criteria for banks and insurance companies that we used for nonfinancial institutions, there would have been no black policymakers in the business sector at all.

Now, amazingly enough, Chicago has proportionately more Negro-controlled businesses, larger than neighborhood operations, than any other major city in the North. Therefore, similar surveys in other northern metropolitan areas would turn up an even smaller percentage of Negro policymakers in the business world.

The legal profession, represented by corporate law firms, had no Negroes at high policy levels. We are convinced that the same situation would be found in other professions, such as advertising and engineering.

The very prestigious universities—the University of Chicago, Northwestern University, Loyola University, DePaul University, Roosevelt University, the Illinois Institute of Technology, and the University of Illinois (the only public university of the seven) —had a negligible 1 percent Negro representation. Most of these universities had few Negro students, faculty members, or administrators. Five of the seven had no Negro policymakers.

The University of Illinois had one. Roosevelt University, the sole institution that had a number of Negroes at the top, was the newest and the one with the least public support. When this university was founded, its leaders had made a forthright stand on racial questions and a firm commitment to liberal principles.

We included these major universities in our survey because other institutions—public and private—have been placing increasingly greater value on them. Every year hundreds of millions of dollars in endowment and operating funds are given to the Chicago-area schools. After all, their research activities, and their training of skilled personnel, are considered a key to the region's economic growth. One indication of the tremendous influence these universities have is that they have determined the nature of urban renewal more than any other institutional group in Chicago (aside from the city government). Without a doubt, the universities have real—not nominal—power that only five out of 380 policy-making positions in these universities are held by Negroes.

The exclusion of Negroes from the private sector carries over to its voluntary organizations: Negroes are found in only 1 percent of the posts there. It is in the voluntary associations that it is easiest to make symbolic concessions to the black community by giving token representation, yet even here Negroes were underrepresented—which highlights the fundamental norms of the entire sector.

The sectors and individual groups in the Chicago area with the highest Negro representation were those visory boards, labor unions, and religious and welfare organizations. These four groups accounted for 216 of the posts held by Negroes, or 75 percent, al-though these four groups have only 19 percent of all the policy-making positions we studied. Labor unions had a larger percentage—13 percent—than any other institution in the private sector. In welfare and religious organizations, whose constituents were often largely Negro, Negroes occupied 8 percent of the positions, the same percentage of the elected public offices they held.

Now, either the black constituency elected the Negroes directly (in the case of elective offices and trade unions); or the Negroes were appointed to posts in an operation whose clients were largely Negro (principal of a Negro school, for example); or Negroes were given token representation on bodies that had a broad public purpose (like religious organizations).

By "token representation," we mean—following James Q. Wilson—that "he is a man chosen because a Negro is 'needed' in order to legitimate (but not direct) whatever decisions are made by the agency."

Of the three ways a black constituency had of getting itself represented, the most important was the first. The statistics clearly show the importance of the Negro vote. The elected political offices and the elected trade union offices account for only 11 percent of all the policy-making positions in Cook County. Yet almost half of all the Negro policymakers were found in these two areas—137 out of 285.

Nonetheless, even in the major areas where Negro representation was the greatest—labor unions, elective offices, supervisory boards, and religious and welfare organizations—many institutions still excluded Negroes from positions of authority.

There are, of course, few Negroes in the building trade unions, most of which bar Negroes from membership. Only two out of the twelve building trade union organizations we studied had even one Negro in a decisive slot. These two Negroes made up a mere 1½ percent of the policy-making positions in the building trade unions.

The greatest degree of black representation was found in the former CIO industrial unions. Only one-fourth of these units in the survey totally excluded Negroes from leadership. In almost half, the percentage of Negro policymakers was over 15 percent— which is above token levels.

The former AFL unions (not including those in the building trades) had a higher rate of exclusion than those of the CIO. Two-fifths of these AFL unions had no Negroes at all in policy-making posts. But one-third of this group had leaderships that were 15 percent or more Negro. And the only two black-controlled locals large enough to be included in this study were in AFL unions.

In elective offices, the Negro vote certainly does give Negroes some representation—though far below their proportionate number. In public administration, however, where advancement to policy-making offices comes through appointment and influence, Negroes are all but excluded from decisive posts, at both the federal and local levels. Although a very high percentage of all Negro professionals are in public service, they do not reach the top.

The only major governmental operation that had a goodly number of Negroes at the upper level of the bureaucratic hierarchy was the public school system. Nine percent of the top positions were occupied by Negroes. This unique situation is the result of some fairly recent appointments, made as concessions after an intense civil rights campaign directed at the Chicago Board of Education. In this instance, one can consider these civil rights ac-

tions as a proxy for Negro votes. Still, this high-level representation in the Chicago school hierarchy did not seem to reflect any uniform policy of including Negroes in management. At the level of principalship that was not included as a policy-making position in this study, only 3 percent of the positions were occupied by blacks.

The voluntary welfare and religious associations that were sufficiently important to be included in the study usually had at least a few Negro policymakers. Only two out of fourteen bodies had no Negroes in policy positions, while four organizations had token representation — below 5 percent. None had a Negro majority in the key posts. Only the Chicago Urban League (with 43 percent) had Negroes in more than 15 percent of its policy slots. If individual religious denominations had been among the organizations counted in the survey, there would have been some black-dominated groups. As it was, Negro representation in the United Protestant Federation, which was included, came largely from the traditionally Negro denominations. It is of interest to note that, in recent years, Protestant groups have provided some of the few instances in which Negroes have been elected to important offices by a constituency that was overwhelmingly white.

Not only were Negroes grossly underrepresented in Chicago's policy-making posts, but even where represented they had less power than white policymakers.

As we have seen, Negroes were virtually excluded from policy making in the single most powerful institutional sector—the business world. In all sectors they were generally placed in positions in which the authority was delegated from a higher administrator or divided among a board. Rarely were Negroes in positions of ultimate authority, either as chief executive or as top board officer.

When Negroes ran for a board or for a judicial office on a slate, their number had been limited by the political parties apportioning out the nominations. The percentage of Negroes on such boards or (especially) in judicial offices tended to run lower than the number of Negroes in legislative posts, for which Negroes run individually.

It is also true that no Negro has ever been elected to one of the key citywide or countywide executive positions, such as mayor, city clerk, or president of the Cook County Board. These are the positions with the greatest power and patronage.

In welfare agencies, where Negroes have token representation, they are virtually excluded from the key posts of executive director. Only five of the 135 directors of medium and large welfare agencies were Negro.

Now, it was in the trade union sector that the highest percentage of Negroes had policy posts—13 percent. We asked several experts on the Chicago trade union movement to list the number of Negroes among the one hundred most powerful trade unionists in the area. Among the one hundred people they named, the number of Negroes ranged from two to five.

This did not surprise us, for it was compatible with our general knowledge of the number of Negroes with truly powerful posts in other sectors.

The exclusion of Negroes from important posts in Chicago is not limited to legitimate spheres of activity. Thirty years ago, gambling was one of the few areas in which Negroes held tangible power in Chicago. Today, Negroes have lost even this.

Although the syndicate, with its billion-dollar-a-year Chicago operation was not included in our formal survey,

it is worthwhile noting the Chicago Crime Commission's data on this powerful, influential organization. There were no Negroes among the top thirteen leaders in the syndicate; and while five Negroes were on the Crime Commission's 1967 list of 216 major and minor syndicate members, only one is reputed to have even minor authority. As *The Wall Street Journal* has noted, in the rackets as in legitimate business, Negroes are effectively barred from the executive suite.

A RULE OF THUMB ON NEGRO POWER

All in all, then, we would suggest the following rule of thumb: *The actual power vested in Negro policymakers is about one-third as great as the percentage of the posts they hold.*

Thus when Negroes elected other Negroes to office, these officers tended to represent small constituencies. For example, the greatest number of Negroes in legislative posts came from relatively small districts that happen to have black majorities. Indeed, according to Cook County tradition, Negroes simply do not hold legislative posts in city, state, or federal government *unless* they represent a district that is mostly black. No district with Negroes in the minority had a Negro representative, even when Negroes constituted the single largest ethnic group. And some districts with a Negro majority had a *white* representative.

Then too, the smaller the district, the more likely it would be homogeneous, and the greater the chances of its having a black majority that could return a Negro to office. In the Chicago area, consequently, Negroes were best represented on the city council, which is based on fifty relatively small wards, each representing about 70,000 people;

Negroes were represented most poorly in the United States House of Representatives, for which there are only nine rather large districts in Chicago, each representing almost 500,000 people.

Most of the government policymaking posts that Negroes had been appointed to were in operations that had a large Negro clientele, if not a majority—as in the case of the Chicago public schools, or in operations that had largely Negro personnel, as in the case of the post office. On the appointed supervisory boards, in fact, those with as many as two Negro members were the Chicago Board of Education and the Board of Health, both of which serve very large numbers of Negroes.

This limiting of Negro policymakers to Negro constituencies was quite as evident in the private sector. Three of the four banks with Negroes in policymaking posts were in Negro neighborhoods; and two were the smallest of the 102 banks we studied, and the other two were not much larger. The two insurance firms had mainly Negro clients, and were among the smallest of the thirty studied. In the voluntary organizations, the more they served Negroes, the higher the percentage of Negroes on their boards (although representation was by no means proportionate). Thus, the five Negro executive directors of welfare organizations we studied headed all-Negro constituencies: Three directed moderate-sized neighborhood settlements in the ghetto; one directed a virtually all-Negro hospital; and one directed an interracial agency that has traditionally had a Negro executive.

Still another way of limiting the power of Negro policymakers, we discovered, was by "processing" them. Public and private institutions, as indicated, tend to have a token representation of Negroes. And many Negroes in these positions have totally identified with the traditional values and goals of the institution, regardless of what they mean to the mass of Negroes. Some of these Negro policymakers, because of their small numbers and lack of an independent source of power, are neutralized. Others, if they are firm in representing the needs and outlook of the black community, are isolated. The two Negro members of the Chicago Board of Education represented these extremes. Mrs. Wendell Green, a longtime board member and the elderly widow of a former judge, had been the most diehard supporter of Benjamin Willis, the former schools superintendent, through all of his fights against the civil rights movement. The other Negro—Warren Bacon, a business executive—sympathized with the campaign against inferior, segregated housing and, as a result, has been largely isolated on the board. He was rarely consulted on critical questions. His vote was usually cast with a small minority, and sometimes alone.

The fact is that the norms and traditions of *any* organization or enterprise limit the amount of power held by black policymakers. It is no longer bold to assert that the major institutions and organizations of our society have an operational bias that is racist, even though their *official* policies may be the opposite. The Negro policymaker in one of these institutions (or in a small black-controlled organization dependent upon these institutions, such as the head of a trade union local) has a certain degree of conflict. If he goes along with the institution, from which he gains power and prestige, he ends up by implementing operations that restrict his minority group. Edward Banfield and James Q. Wilson have neatly pinpointed this dilemma in the political sphere:

Not only are few Negroes elected to office, but those who are elected generally find it necessary to be politicians first and Negroes second. If they are to stay in office, they must soft-pedal the racial issues that are of the most concern to Negroes as Negroes.

This pattern is seen in the failure of William Dawson, Cook County's one Negro Congressman, to obtain many presidential appointments or top federal civil service posts for Negroes. Theoretically he is in a more strategic position to influence government operations than any other Chicago-based Congressman, since he has twenty-three years' seniority and holds the important chairmanship of the Government Operations Committee. Yet in 1965 Negroes held only 2 percent of the top federal jobs in Chicago.

Any examination of the real power of Negroes in Chicago requires an examination of the strongest single organization in the Negro community—the Democratic Party. Wilson's study, *Negro Politics,* points out that the strength and cohesiveness of the Negro Democratic organization is largely dependent upon the strength of the total Cook County Democratic organization. The Negro organization is a "submachine" within the larger machine that dominates the city. The Negro submachine, however, has basically settled for lesser patronage positions and political favors, rather than using its considerable strength to try to make or change policy. Therefore, this Negro organization avoids the controversial questions and seeks to avoid differences with the central organization on such vital issues as urban renewal and the schools.

In short, then, not only are Negroes underrepresented in the major policy-making positions in Cook County, but even where represented their actual power is restricted, or their representatives fail to work for the long-term interests of their constituency. It is therefore safe to estimate that Negroes really hold less than 1 percent of the effective power in the Chicago metropolitan area. Realistically, the power structure of Chicago is hardly less white than that of Mississippi.

From these figures it is clear that, at this time, Negroes in the Chicago area lack the power to make the changes in the areas of housing, jobs, and education. The basic subjugation of the black community, however, would not end if there were simply more Negroes in policy-making posts. We have seen the prevalence of tokenism, of whites choosing Negro leaders who are conservative, of their boxing in Negro leaders who are proved to be liberal, of their giving these leaders less actual power than they give themselves.

Our analysis suggests that the best way to increase both the number *and* the power of Negro policymakers is through unifying the black constituency. Access to policy-making positions could come through both the development of large, black-controlled organizations, and through getting Negroes into white-dominated organizations. If the constituency lacks its own clear set of goals and policies, however, things will surely remain the same. For success depends not just upon the formal unity, but upon the nature of the goals set by the black community. In this situation, the overcoming of black powerlessness seems to require the development of a self-conscious community that has the means to determine its own interests, and the cohesiveness to command the loyalty of its representatives. We can safely predict that more and more Negroes will be moved into policy-making positions. The fundamental conflict, therefore, will take place between their cooptation into the established institutions and their accountability to a black constituency.

9
Racial Inequality in Employment: The Patterns of Discrimination*
HERBERT HILL

Optimistic assumptions regarding the Negro's progress in American society must be reexamined in the light of the Negro's current economic plight. The great mass of Negroes, especially in the urban centers, are locked in a permanent condition of poverty. This includes the long-term unemployed as well as the working poor, who know only a marginal economic existence and who increasingly are forced into the ranks of the unemployed.

THE UNEMPLOYMENT CRISIS

The Negro community throughout the United States is today experiencing a crisis of unemployment. Negroes now constitute a very large part of the hard-core, permanently unemployed group in American society. In northern industrial centers one out of every three Negro workers was unemployed for varying lengths of time between 1958 and 1963, and a very high proportion exhausted all of their unemployment compensation benefits. More than 50 percent of all the unskilled Negro workers in the country have been unemployed for substantial periods since 1958. Furthermore, it is evident that the unskilled Negro worker, forty-five years of age and over, who has lost his job, will never again work at productive gainful employment.

Of great significance is the fact that, since 1951, the differential in the average income of Negro and white workers has been increasing. By December of 1951, the Negro median wage was approaching 57 percent of the white workers' average income. Since that time, however, the gap between the income of white and Negro workers has been growing steadily greater. In Michigan, for example, the ratio of average Negro income to white income dropped from 87 percent in 1949 to 76 percent in 1958, and has continuously deteriorated since that time.[1]

During the period of 1960–1961 in Chicago, Negroes, who constitute 20 percent of the total labor force, were 43 percent of Chicago's unemployed. This does not include the significant number of Negroes who, in Chicago, as elsewhere, have dropped out of the labor force and, therefore, are no longer counted among the unemployed.

During 1960–1961, white males in Chicago between the ages of 25 and 44 had an unemployment rate of only 2.2 percent—minimal unemployment; however, in the Negro ghetto in Chicago, and in other urban industrial centers, unemployment has become a way of life. In thirty-one all-Negro census tracts, the unemployment rate was over 15 percent, while only three white census tracts have a ratio that high. Labor force projections indicate that there will be 450,000 more workers in Chicago's metropolitan area in 1970 than there were in 1960. More than one-third of these will be Negro. Yet the trend of employment potentiality indicates that only 150,000 new positions will be created by 1970. The future holds only the prospect of increasing long-term unemployment for the Negro wage earner.[2]

As a result of automation and other technological changes in the economy, unskilled and semiskilled job occupations are disappearing at the rate of 35,000 a week, or nearly two million

*[Reprinted with permission from *The Annals of the American Academy of Political and Social Science*, vol. 357, January 1965, pp. 31–47. (There has been some progress in hiring and the opening of labor unions to blacks since this article was written, but in broad outline the patterns remain very similar.)]

a year. It is in these job classifications that there has been a disproportionate displacement of Negro workers.

The economic well-being of the entire Negro community is directly and adversely affected by the generations of enforced overconcentration of Negro wage earners in the unskilled and menial job classifications in the industrial economy. A continuation of this pattern will cause even greater crises in the years to come unless fundamental and rapid changes take place in the occupational characteristics and mobility of Negro labor in the United States. In March of 1964, the United States Department of Labor announced that Negroes constitute 20.6 percent of the nation's unemployed, although Negroes comprise only 10 percent of the population. To quote *The New York Times,* "Unemployment of these proportions, were it general, would be a national catastrophe. . . ."

THE NEGRO IN THE SOUTH

There can be no doubt that in the southern states there exists a rigid and systematic pattern of employment discrimination based on race. Industrial management and organized labor, as well as state agencies and the federal government, are responsible for the continued existence of the pattern of racial job discrimination. An immense industrial development has been taking place in the southeastern states since the end of World War II, but a most disturbing aspect of the rapid growth of manufacturing facilities in the South has been the serious inability of the Negro worker to register significant employment gains in the new southern industrial economy.

Investigations indicate that in the textile industry, still the basic manufacturing industry of the South, Negroes are in a most marginal position. According to state government figures, the number of textile workers employed in South Carolina was 48,000 in 1918 and 122,000 in 1960, while the percentage of Negroes in the textile labor force fell from 9 percent to 4.7 percent over this period. On July 6, 1961, the National Association for the Advancement of Colored People filed an extensive series of complaints against major textile manufacturing companies with the President's Committee on Equal Employment Opportunity. Three years later there is little change in the racial occupational pattern in the southern textile industry. Negroes remain concentrated in menial and unskilled classifications and comprise about 2 percent of the work force. . . .

In heavy industry, the gains of Negro labor throughout the southern states are most limited. Negro employment is negligible in such major industrial operations as the General Motors plants in Atlanta and Doraville, Georgia, and the Ford Motor Company plants in Atlanta, Memphis, Norfolk, and Dallas. The employment study made by the United States Commission on Civil Rights confirms our opinion that very little progress has been made by the southern Negro in heavy industry. The commission's findings are summarized in part in its published report as follows:

This commission's investigations in three cities — Atlanta, Baltimore, and Detroit — and a commission hearing in Detroit revealed that in most industries studied, patterns of Negro employment by federal contractors conformed to local industrial employment patterns. In Atlanta, the two automobile assembly plants contacted employed no Negroes in assembly operations. Except for one driver of an inside power truck, all Negro employees observed were in janitorial work — sweeping, mopping, carrying away trash. Lack of qualified applicants cannot account for the absence of Negroes from automotive assembly jobs in Atlanta. Wage rates are relatively high for the locality and the jobs are in great demand. The work is at most semiskilled and educational requirements are extremely low.[3]

A major problem for Negro workers in southern industry is the operation of separate racial seniority lines in collective bargaining agreements entered into by management and labor unions. Investigations of the status of Negro workers in pulp and papermaking operations, in chemical and oil refining, in steel and tobacco manufacturing, as well as in other important sectors of the southern industrial economy, clearly indicate that Negroes are usually hired exclusively in classifications designated as "common laborer" or "yard labor" or "nonoperating department" or "maintenance department." These are the euphemisms for the segregated all-Negro labor departments established by the separate racial promotional lines in many labor-management contracts throughout southern industry. As a result of these discriminatory provisions, white persons are initially hired into production or skilled craft occupations which are completely closed to Negro workers. The Negro worker who is hired as a laborer in the "maintenance department" or "yard labor department" is denied seniority and promotional rights into desirable production classifications and is also denied admission into apprentice and other training programs. In these situations Negro seniority rights are operative only within certain all-Negro departments, and Negro workers therefore have an extremely limited job mobility. Thus Donald Dewey, of Columbia University, reports that most southerners believe that their economy is divided into "white" and "Negro" jobs.[4] The North Carolina Advisory Com-

mittee to the United States Commission on Civil Rights reports that "North Carolina in common with states of its region, has traditions which more or less automatically assign Negroes to menial or unskilled positions."[5]

The pulp and papermaking industry is one of the fastest growing manufacturing industries in the South. Company management and the trade unions which have jurisdiction in this important southern industry are responsible for a rigid pattern of discriminatory practices including separate racial promotional lines in union contracts which limit Negro workers to menial, unskilled job classifications at low pay and which violate their basic seniority rights. The two dominant unions in this industry are the United Papermakers' and Paperworkers' Union and the International Brotherhood of Pulp, Sulphite, and Paper Mill Workers' Union, both affiliated with the AFL-CIO. In virtually every paper mill in the South where they hold collective bargaining agreements, these two unions operate segregated locals and include discriminatory provisions in their union contracts. A compelling example of the operation of segregated locals with separate racial seniority lines is to be found at the large manufacturing plant of the Union Bag-Camp Paper Corporation in Savannah, where thousands of persons are employed. This plant has the largest single industrial payroll in Savannah.

The tobacco industry is important in the southern industrial economy, and here, too, we find a pattern of separate racial seniority lines in virtually all collective bargaining agreements between the major tobacco manufacturing companies and the Tobacco Workers International Union, AFL-CIO. In one of the largest manufacturing plants, that of the Liggett & Myers Tobacco Company in Durham,

North Carolina, colored workers are employed in unskilled and janitorial jobs with limited seniority rights operative only in all-Negro designated classifications. Investigations made by the NAACP indicate that in this tobacco manufacturing plant, as in so many others, Negroes are initially hired only as sweepers, janitors, and toilet attendants and are promoted exclusively within the limited "Negro" seniority line of progression.

Negro railway workers throughout the South are the victims of a traditional policy of job discrimination as a result of collusion between railway management and railroad labor unions. In St. Petersburg, the Atlantic Coast Line Railroad, and, in Memphis, the St. Louis–San Francisco Railroad Company, for example, have entered into agreements with the Brotherhood of Railroad Trainmen to deny qualified Negro railway workers opportunities for promotion and advancement. These are typical of similar practices elsewhere.

The Brotherhood of Railroad Trainmen, an AFL-CIO affiliate, removed the "Caucasian Only" clause from its constitution in 1959. However, this was apparently for public relations purposes only, as the union continues in most cities to exclude qualified Negro railroad employees. Frequently, in collusion with management, Negro brakemen are classified as "porters" and then refused membership in the union under the pretext of their being outside its jurisdiction. This, however, does not prevent the Trainmen's Union from negotiating wages and other conditions of employment for these so-called porters who have no representation in the collective bargaining unit.

STATE EMPLOYMENT SERVICES

Another extremely serious problem confronting Negro workers is the dis-criminatory practices of state employment services whose operation, in southern states, is characterized by a pattern of racial segregation and discrimination. These states include Alabama, Florida, Georgia, Louisiana, Mississippi, North Carolina, South Carolina, and, partially, Virginia and Tennessee. Job orders are racially designated, and job referrals are made on the basis of race. Major industrial corporations operating with federal government contracts cannot possibly be in compliance with the president's Executive Order banning employment discrimination where such contractors in the South are using the facilities of the state employment services. The United States government is completely responsible for providing the operating costs of all state employment services. Federal funds are disbursed by the Department of Labor, which administers the Federal-State Employment Services program. It obviously makes no sense for the administration to issue executive orders banning employment discrimination by government contractors while agencies of the federal government subsidize such discriminatory practices. The NAACP has repeatedly called upon the United States Department of Labor to take decisive action to eliminate the pattern of discrimination and segregation in the operation of state employment services.

FEDERAL SUPPORT OF DISCRIMINATION

Even in the North, the operation of the state employment services represents a serious problem to Negro workers. The state employment services receive funds and awards from the federal government based to a very large degree on the number of gross placements made during the year. This inevitably places operating personnel in the position of responding to arbitrary and discriminatory job requirements in referring workers for jobs and in selecting them for admission into training facilities. A further problem is the usual tacit assumption by local employment service personnel that there are "white" jobs and "colored" jobs. This is a result of the prevailing hiring pattern in many localities and the reluctance of state employment services to innovate changes in the established racial patterns.

Because the colored worker is extremely vulnerable to long-term unemployment as a result of the combined factors of racial discrimination and technological change, Negro workers more than any other group in the work force qualify for training under the Federal Manpower Development and Training Act. However, investigations made by the NAACP clearly indicate that Negroes, with some few exceptions, are being limited to programs that simply perpetuate the traditional concentration of Negroes in menial and unskilled jobs. Thus, in Portland, Oregon, there was an all-Negro training program for hotel waiters, and in Pensacola, Florida, there were all-Negro programs for chambermaids and waitresses. In Birmingham, Alabama, there are all-white training programs in electronics and arc welding, but Negroes are limited to training as laundry-machine operators and shirt-pressers. In Beaufort, South Carolina, there is a training program for Negro waiters, while in Greenville, South Carolina, there is an all-white program for general machine and tool machine workers. *The Courier-Journal,* Louisville, Kentucky, December 11, 1962, in a news report headlined "200 Retrainees Can't Get Jobs" states: "One course was held for Negro clerk-stenographers but it developed that employers in that area wanted only white clerical help."

On May 3, 1963, Clarence Mitchell, director of the NAACP Washington Bureau, in a strongly worded letter to Representative Carl D. Perkins, chairman of the General Subcommittee on Education of the House Committee on Education and Labor, protested against the racial practices of Manpower Development and Training Act (MDTA) programs. The association requested the correction of policies which force Negroes to be shunted into training programs for "chambermaids, shirt pressers, service station attendants, waiters and waitresses." Although expressing support for the MDTA general program, the NAACP statement condemned practices "which foster racial segregation and also continue to promote the antiquated idea that the kitchen is the only place for colored wage earners."

In addition to the pattern of racial segregation in the training programs conducted under the Manpower Development and Training Act in Alabama, Georgia, Mississippi, South Carolina, and other southern states, reports from northern communities indicate that because of the statutory requirement that there shall be "reasonable expectation of employment" as a basis for entry into training programs, unemployed low-skilled Negro workers are very frequently screened out of admission into desirable programs for skilled craft training. The consequences of the Manpower Development and Training Act for Negroes have been no training or segregated training or training for the lowest and least desirable job classifications. A continuation of this pattern will simply extend and deepen the job gap between white and Negro workers.

The Department of Health, Education, and Welfare each year distributes $55 million of federal funds for education under the Smith-Hughes Act; a very large part of this is given to vocational training programs in which Negroes are totally excluded or limited to unequal segregated facilities. Vocational and trade schools in the southern states receive a substantial part of these federal funds, but in most southern urban areas where there has been a tremendous growth of manufacturing operations, we find that the limited programs offered in Negro vocational schools are obsolete in terms of modern industrial technology. Thus, while white students in vocational schools are preparing for advanced technology in electronics and for the automotive and aerospace industries, Negroes are limited to "home economics" and other traditional service occupations, and here also the federal government has a direct responsibility for helping to perpetuate the pattern that makes the Negro worker an unskilled worker and most vulnerable to large-scale permanent unemployment.

APPRENTICESHIP AND VOCATIONAL TRAINING

. . . A major factor contributing to the irrational, wasteful, and socially harmful operation of the nation's apprenticeship and vocational training programs is the color discrimination and racial exclusion which characterize training programs in major sectors of the economy in the North as well as the South. Discrimination in job-training programs is also greatly responsible for the very high rate of Negro unemployment.

For many occupations the only way a worker can be recognized as qualified for employment is to successfully complete apprenticeship training programs. This is true for the printing trades, among machinists and metal workers, in the various crafts in the building and construction trades industry, and many others.

Studies, such as that made by the New York State Commission Against Discrimination,[6] as well as by the National Association for the Advancement of Colored People, clearly indicate that no significant advances have been made by Negroes in those craft union apprenticeship training programs which have historically excluded nonwhites. An examination of the available data makes it evident that less than 1 percent of the apprentices in the building and construction industry throughout the United States are Negro. In the ten-year period, 1950–1960, in the State of New York, the increase of Negro participation in building trades apprenticeship programs rose from 1.5 to 2 percent.

Open access to plumbing and pipe-fitting apprenticeship controlled by the Plumbers Union is a very rare experience for young Negroes in the North as well as the South. Similarly, Negro youths are excluded from apprenticeship programs controlled by the Sheet Metal Workers Union, the International Brotherhood of Electrical Workers, the Lathers and Plasterers Union, the Boilermakers, the Structural Iron Workers Union, and from other important craft unions operating in the construction industry.

Almost equally exclusive are the printing trades unions. In a survey made by the National Association for the Advancement of Colored People of the seven major New York City newspapers in 1962, we find that, with the exclusion of building services and maintenance personnel, less than 1 percent of those employed on the major New York newspapers are Negro.

In many training programs the role of the labor union is decisive because the trade union usually determines who is admitted into the training program and, therefore, who is admitted into the union membership.

Labor unions also exercise control over apprenticeship programs through hiring hall procedures in de facto closed shop situations. In these circumstances, craft unions have the power either to promote or to prevent the admission of individuals or of an entire class of persons. By means of a variety of formal and informal controls, craft unions are frequently the decisive factor in the recruitment process in many apprenticeship programs and often directly prevent Negro youth from becoming skilled craft workers via the established route of apprenticeship.

On the level of the small shop and local union, the tradition of racial discrimination has now become deeply institutionalized. A form of caste psychology impels many workers to regard their own positions as "white man's jobs, " to which no Negro should aspire. These workers, and often their union leaders, regard jobs in their industries as a kind of private privilege, to be accorded and denied by them as they see fit. Often Negroes are not alone in being barred from such unions which have much of the character of the medieval guild, but Negroes as a group suffer the most from these practices. On the local level, the tradition which sustains discrimination is to be found among skilled workers in heavy industry as well as in the craft occupations, and in the North almost as commonly as in the South.

The Bureau of Apprenticeship and Training of the United States Department of Labor, in giving certification to an apprenticeship program, provides the legal basis for public subsidies to apprenticeship programs. The federal government, through grants-in-aid from the United States Office of Education of the Department of Health, Education, and Welfare, provides funds which subsidize apprenticeship training programs in many states. The federal government, therefore, is directly subsidizing discrimination in the skilled trades whenever a trade union or employer excludes Negroes and members of other minority groups from admission into a registered apprenticeship training program.

THE RACIAL PRACTICES OF ORGANIZED LABOR

The Report on Employment[7] of the United States Commission on Civil Rights indicated the significant extent of discrimination within organized labor, and stated that the "efforts of the AFL-CIO have proved to be largely ineffective" in curbing discrimination and that the impact of union discrimination, especially in skilled craft occupations, was a basic factor in contributing to the concentration of Negroes in menial, unskilled jobs in industry, their virtual exclusion from construction and machinist crafts, and accounted for the extreme vulnerability of Negro labor to long-term unemployment both of a cyclical and structural nature. The report urged passage of federal legislation for prohibiting discrimination by unions and stressed the inability of the AFL-CIO to take action on its own initiative against the broad pattern of union racist practices.

The course of events in the past decade, and especially since the merger of the AFL with the CIO in 1955, clearly indicates that the social consciousness of the industrial unions with their sensitivity to the problems of the Negro wage earner has now all but totally vanished. Instead, trade unions are responding like other conservative institutions in American society to the intensified demands of the Negro for full equality. A significant indication of this conservatism was the refusal of the AFL-CIO Executive Council to support the August 28, 1963, March on Washington, the greatest Negro demonstration in the nation's history. . . .[8]

Currently, the Negro worker is confronted not with a trade union movement that is a force for social change, but, on the contrary, with a national labor organization that has become a very conservative and highly bureaucratized institution, defending the status quo which is now directly attacked by the Negro in virtually every area of American life.

Many trade unions lag behind the progress made by other institutions in the community. In East St. Louis, Illinois, and Tulsa, Oklahoma, for example, Negro children attend integrated schools during the day, but their parents attend segregated union meetings at night, if they are admitted into labor unions at all. Recently A. Philip Randolph, president of the Brotherhood of Sleeping Car Porters, called "for a crusade to desegregate the Southern AFL-CIO State Conventions and City Central bodies" and stated that "this is a problem probably not less significant or difficult than the desegregation of public schools in the South."

There is a deep distrust among many Negro wage earners and others within the Negro community toward trade unions. It is a distrust well-founded in experience. For today, as in the past, there is a profound disparity between the public image presented by the national AFL-CIO and the day-to-day realities as experienced by many Negro workers. This is true in the North as well as the South. There are few exceptions, especially in the mass production industries where, historically, there has been a large concentration of Negro workers and in some unions such as the United Automobile Workers (UAW), the United Packinghouse Workers (UPW), and the National Maritime Union (NMU) where there is an ideological sensitivity to the "Negro question."

But for the Negro in major areas of the economy, in the building and construction trades, in the railroad industry, among the Seafarers and the Boilermakers and the oil and chemical workers and machinists, in pulp, tobacco, and paper manufacturing, in metal working, in the printing trades, and in many other industries highly unionized for a long period of time, trade union practices are characterized by a broad pattern of discrimination and segregation.

AFL-CIO affiliated unions engage in four basic categories of discriminatory racial practices. They are: exclusion of Negroes from membership, segregated locals, separate seniority lines in collective bargaining agreements, and refusal to admit qualified Negroes into apprenticeship training programs controlled by unions.

The Brotherhood of Railway and Steamship Clerks which operates many segregated local lodges in northern as well as southern cities is among the important international unions responsible for a broad pattern of segregation.

The United Brotherhood of Carpenters and Joiners, for over a half-century, has been among the most important of all the building trades unions, and, with very few exceptions, organizes Negroes and whites into separate locals insofar as it permits Negroes to join the union at all. In the South there seems to be no exception to this rule, and it is most often followed in northern cities as well. In Memphis and Chicago, for example, Negro carpenters in segregated local unions found that members of the white locals refused to work on the same job with them.

The white locals are in control of the union hiring hall, and, because of frequent arrangements with municipal and county political machines, all hiring for major public as well as private construction projects is done through the "lily-white" union hiring hall. Quite frequently Negroes are excluded altogether from work in white neighborhoods. This means that Negro carpenters are restricted to marginal maintenance and repair work within the Negro community and that they seldom are permitted to work on the larger construction projects. The same practices are true for other building trades unions in many cities throughout the country. . . .

It is the economic structure of the building industry which concentrates in the local unions the power to decide who obtains employment and who gets admitted to the craft. The men who are engaged in construction work are recruited from labor pools controlled exclusively by the various unions in the craft jurisdictions of building trades. The union is the sole employment agency, and the men who appear on the jobs are those whom the union has referred to the job site. Contractors are thus completely dependent upon local unions for their labor supply. This factor further increases the power of local craft unions to control the employment process. . . .

Rather than admit Negro members, the unions frequently encourage the use of out-of-town labor. Based upon direct interviews, Shaughnessy found that commuters travel as much as 120 miles per day from Connecticut and elsewhere to find steady employment in New York, when the available local union membership supply is exhausted. But local sources of skilled Negro manpower are deliberately ignored. During the spring and summer of 1963, there were approximately 1,200 plumbers with "travelling cards" from other cities working in New York City. . . .

Out-of-town construction workers commute over a hundred miles daily to jobs in New York City, while local Negroes and Puerto Ricans are denied employment and entry to union-controlled jobs and apprenticeship programs. . . .

As long as union membership remains a condition of employment in many trades and crafts and Negroes are barred from union membership solely because of their color, then trade union discrimination is the decisive factor in determining whether Negro workers in a given industry shall have an opportunity to earn a living for themselves and their families. This is especially true in the printing trades, the construction industry, and other occupations where labor unions exercise a high degree of control over access to employment.

. . . With one or two exceptions, state and municipal fair employment practices commissions are drastically limited in their effectiveness by inadequate funds and inadequate staff. Most of these agencies are simply complaint-taking bureaus that often take years to resolve an individual complaint received from an aggrieved citizen. We know that, in practice, only a very small fraction of all individuals who are the victims of employment discrimination because of race or religion ever file complaints with state or municipal commissions; therefore, because of the complexities in eliminating discriminatory employment practices, the fundamental approach must be towards the initiation of affirmative action based upon the overall pattern of employment discrimination. In addition, one must note the unfortunate inability of state and municipal fair employment practices commissions to eliminate discriminatory racial practices in many important areas of the active job market. . . .

Discriminatory racial practices by trade unions are not simply isolated or occasional expressions of local bias against colored workers, but rather, as the record indicates, a continuation of the institutionalized pattern of anti-Negro employment practices that is traditional in important sectors of the American economy.

The pattern of union responsibility for job discrimination against Negroes is not limited to any one area of the country or to some few industries or union jurisdictions, but involves many labor organizations in a wide variety of occupations in manufacturing and construction on the railroads and in the maritime trades. An example of this is the Seafarers International Union (SIU) which operates union-controlled hiring halls on Great Lakes ports such as Duluth, Chicago, Detroit, Buffalo, and Cleveland. As a systematic practice this union will dispatch Negro workers for menial jobs only as "mess boys" and cooks in the galley departments of ships operating under SIU collective bargaining agreements. Over the years Negro members of the Seafarers International Union have repeatedly protested this practice, but to no avail, as the union continues discriminatory job assignments in its hiring halls. . . .

The Negro is now making the same demands upon organized labor that are being made upon all other institutions in American society, and it is certain that the attacks upon racism within trade unions will proceed with the same intensity as against other organizations that impose restrictions based on race and color. . . .

Year after year, thousands of nonwhite students graduate from vocational high schools in the major urban centers of the nation, but after satisfactorily completing their courses of study in a variety of craft skills, young Negro workers ready to enter the labor market are denied employment opportunities in the printing industry, among machinists, or in building and construction trades and are forced to take low-paying menial or unskilled jobs if they are to work at all. Many of them are forced completely to abandon hope for work in the craft for which they were trained. Is it any wonder that there are many school dropouts each year among Negro youth in vocational training schools, who soon enough learn the realities of the racial practices of craft unions in New York City, Chicago, Philadelphia, and elsewhere and express their feeling of futility by leaving school at an early age?

Negroes may be winning the broad legal and social struggles for equality in the United States, but they are losing the battle for equal employment opportunity and economic justice. At the present time, the historic civil rights gains won by Negroes in the past twenty years are in danger of being destroyed by the growing crisis of unemployment and underemployment that directly affects the well-being of the entire Negro community and leads to acute social dislocation and despair.

The emergence of a large "underclass" of the Negro unemployed, the growth of a permanent black lumpenproletariat, might very well alter the character of the Negro civil rights movement—a movement that in the past has operated in the classic tradition of protest and reform—and thus lead to developments that have the gravest implication for the whole of American society.

FOOTNOTES

[1] HERMAN P. MILLER, *Rich Man, Poor Man* (New York: Thomas Y. Crowell, 1964), p. 88.

[2] HAROLD BARON, "Negro Unemployment—A Case Study," *New University Thought*, Vol. 3 No. 2 (September–October 1963), p. 43.

[3] U.S. COMMISSION ON CIVIL RIGHTS, *Employment, 1961*, Report No. 3, pp. 65–66.

[4] DONALD DEWEY, "Negro Employment in Southern Industry," *Journal of Political Economy*, LX (August 1952), pp. 279–293.

[5] *Equal Protection of the Laws in North Carolina: Report of the North Carolina Advisory Committee to the United States Committee on Civil Rights,* 1962, Washington, D.C., p. 87.

[6] NEW YORK STATE COMMISSION AGAINST DISCRIMINATION, *Apprentices, Skilled Craftsmen and the Negro: An Analysis* (New York, 1960); Herbert Hill, *The Negro Wage-Earner and Apprenticeship Training Programs* (New York: National Association for the Advancement of Colored People, 1960).

[7] UNITED STATES COMMISSION ON CIVIL RIGHTS, *Report on Employment,* Washington, D.C., 1961.

[8] For a discussion of trade union racial practices see Herbert Hill, "Labor Unions and the Negro," *Commentary* (December 1959), pp. 479–488; "Racism within Organized Labor," *The Journal of Negro Education, 1961,* No. 2, pp. 109–118; and "Has Organized Labor Failed the Negro Worker?" *The Negro Digest* (May 1962), pp. 41–49.

10
*Exploitation of the Low Income Consumer**
DAVID CAPLOVITZ

The numerous accounts of exploitation fall under several general headings.[1] Some reveal the high-pressure sales techniques to which these families are subjected. Others relate to the misrepresentation of the price of goods. And still others refer to the substitution of inferior goods for those ordered. Included here are accounts of the sale of reconditioned goods as new.

The repetitiveness of the incidents is quite striking. Some families were victimized by unethical television repairmen, a few by the same company. Another group were victims of the

pots-and-pans salesmen; encyclopedia salesmen show up in several of the accounts, as do the peddlers selling sink attachments.

As we shall see, the incidents touch upon a number of themes. These include the role of the mass media in setting off the chain of events with alluring ads; the anonymity of many of the credit transactions to the point where the consumer is not sure who the merchant is; the bewilderment of the consumer in the face of powerful forces brought into play by the merchant; and the hopelessness, frustration, and resignation of many in the face of exploitation.

BAIT ADVERTISING AND THE SWITCH SALE

A sizable number of the families had been victimized by "bait" advertising. Responding to advertisements for sewing machines, phonographs, washing machines, and other items offered at unusually low prices, they succumbed to the salemen's "switch-sale" technique by buying a much more expensive model.

The technique is illustrated by the story of a 26-year-old Negro housewife:

I saw a TV ad for a $29 sewing machine, *so I wrote to the company and they sent down a salesman who demonstrated it for me. It shook the whole house, but I wanted to buy it anyway. But he kept saying it would disturb all the neighbors by being so noisy, and* went out to the hall and brought in another model costing $185. . . .

I actually had to pay $220. He promised if I paid within a certain amount of time I would get $35 back. But since my husband was out of work, we couldn't pay within the time period, *so I didn't get the refund.* . . . I was taken in by the high-pressure sales talk.

* [From David Caplovitz, *The Poor Pay More,* Copyright © 1967 by The Free Press, A Division of the Macmillan Company.]

[1] It should be kept in mind that the difficulties to be described were experienced by less than half of the families we interviewed. Moreover, we have deliberately selected the more detailed and complicated incidents for illustrative purposes.

A middle-aged Puerto Rican husband was victimized by a variant of this racket. Instead of responding to an ad, he received a call from a salesman saying that his wife had won a sewing machine:

He brought the machine to the house. It was worth $25, and we ended up buying another one for $186. A friend of mine bought a similar machine, maybe better than mine, for $90. They tricked me into buying the machine for $186 on credit.

In these cases, the reactions are much the same, the feeling of being tricked by a high-pressure salesman. In each instance, a purchase was made at a price higher than the anticipated one.

The "switch sale" is by no means limited to sewing machines. A 28-year-old Negro housewife told the following story about a phonograph sale:

I saw an advertisement in the paper for a $49 Hi-Fi set. *The ad said: "Phone for free demonstration," so I did. The salesman came a few days later, bringing a set that was different from the one I saw advertised. I told him it wasn't the set I saw in the paper, but he said it was, so we hassled for a while. He kept high-pressuring me, saying he had one in the car he knew I would like. So finally, I told him to bring it up. He did, and played it for me.*

I asked him to leave it so my husband could hear it, but he said "no." Then I asked him to come back later when my husband would be home and he said "no" again. Well I decided to gamble and signed the papers. [*Later they mailed a coupon book. The set came to $175.*]

He asked me for a down-payment, so I gave him my old radio and got $10 off. And right after that, my husband came in. He didn't want the set, but the salesman told him we couldn't return it. *Later my husband examined the set. The salesman had said it contained four woofers and two*

tweeters, but my husband found out they didn't exist. We called the store, but they said we couldn't change it, so we had to pay the full amount.

Once the set stopped working. We phoned the store and got free repairs. But the second time the set broke down, we called the store and were told that the company no longer dealt in Hi-Fi sets, only in sewing machines.

One law of the commercial jungle facing the low income consumer is vividly dramatized in this irreversibility of the credit transaction. Tacit in all dealings with ethical merchants is the right to exchange merchandise if the customer is not satisfied. Not so in the low income market. Once the signature is obtained on the contract, the sale is consummated. It should be noted that the husband returned in time to register his displeasure to the salesman. But the concept of the satisfied customer is foreign to such hit-and-run transactions. Even when the couple discovered that the phonograph did not measure up to the salesman's claims, they were still unable to exchange it. As we shall see, this is not an isolated occurrence. Other families also discovered that the principle of exchange does not apply to them. The runaround this couple received when seeking service is also fairly typical. The explanation given seems quite thin, and yet it was apparently enough to free the store from the complaining customer. The incident also illustrates the way "easy credit" breaks through traditional constraints upon consumption. However reluctant at first, this housewife was still able to indulge her impulse to buy without consulting her husband.

Bait advertising was reported by a 37-year-old Negro mother living on welfare. She had seen a newspaper ad, placed by a 125th Street furniture store, announcing the reupholstering of couches with good material for $49.95:

I phoned them and they sent out a salesman. I told him I saw the ad and wanted my couch covered for $49.95. I asked him to show me the material. He pulled out some patterns and looked at them and said, "These aren't so hot. I really want to give customers something they'll be satisfied with." Then he flipped to the higher-priced patterns — but I didn't know they were higher-priced then. I picked out a pattern and asked him how much. He told me $149. But I only had $49 in cash and wanted to pay only in cash, so I told him that this was too high. He praised the material so much, talking about its quality and durability, that I finally told him that if I could get an account I'd take it. He gave me a contract. I just took a quick look and signed it. They sent for the couch and returned it two weeks later. The work on the seams of the pillows was awful. . . . Six months later, the wire in the spring popped out the side and the other side had a pointed end on it.

By now the elements of the process are familiar: the "bait ad," the high-pressure salesman, the purchase of a much more expensive item, and, as often happens, dissatisfaction with the merchandise. Of particular interest in this case is the fact that the woman had every intention of paying cash when she responded to the ad but was converted into a credit buyer inspite of her intent. . . .

The idea of the unusual bargain takes other forms besides bait advertising. Sometimes the consumer is "hooked" by the promise of free merchandise. . . .

One variant of the "something for nothing" appeal is based on the principle of the "pyramid club." Consumers are promised a refund if they help the salesman find a certain number of customers. One instance, reported by an 18-year-old Negro housewife, involved

the added inducement of an outright monetary gift:

My mother sent the vacuum cleaner salesman here. He said that he would give me $5 just to talk to me. Then he said that if I got him nine more sales I could have the vacuum cleaner free. I wasn't able to find any customers and I can't work the vacuum cleaner with all its attachments. I don't want it and I've stopped making the payments on it.

Here we see an example of the great disparity between the more traditional logic of these consumers and the law of installment buying. Whether or not the consumer wants the merchandise has no bearing on the merchant's right to payment once the contract is signed. . . .

MISREPRESENTATION OF PRICES

The preceding incidents illustrate various schemes through which low income families are pressured into buying. Other incidents exhibit another fairly common form of duplicity: the misrepresentation of price, particularly in credit transactions. Although the merchant is required by law in New York State to enter both the cash price and the finance charges on the installment contract, some circumvent this law either by not explaining the terms of the contract or by not sending the customer his copy of the contract until sometime after the sale is consummated. In several instances we found that the consumer did not learn the full cost of his merchandise until he received the payment coupons sometime after the sale. This practice is illustrated by the following typical episodes:

[41-year-old Puerto Rican Husband, welfare family] I was cheated on a TV set I bought. At first the price was supposed to be $220. After I signed the contract I found

out that it was really $300. But then it was too late.

[*34-year-old Puerto Rican housewife*] *I was told by the salesman that the credit price for the Hi-Fi set was $299.* When I got the payment book, I found out that I had to pay them $347.

[*28-year-old Negro housewife*] *I heard an ad on the radio about a special bargain on washing machines for only $100. After I ordered it and had it installed, I got a bill for $200. I said I wouldn't pay it and they took it away.* I paid a $50 down payment, and they never gave it back to me. I'm just glad I did not have to pay the balance.

In the last case, we see that the misleading price appeared in an ad. The consumer made the purchase over the telephone, and therefore the true cost was not revealed until after the installation. It should also be noted that the misleading advertisement led to the loss of a $50 down payment. The vulnerable position of many low income consumers is suggested by this woman's feeling of relief that she did not lose even more money.

The manner in which salesmen lie to families about the cost of goods is revealed by another incident involving a door-to-door salesman selling washing machines:

[*Husband and wife, aged 33 and 27, Puerto Rican*] *A salesman came to the door about three months ago and showed us a pamphlet with pictures of washing machines. He said it would be simple to buy it on credit. We met him at the furniture company,* where he showed us the machine and said it would not cost more than $290. So we signed the papers and didn't have to pay any cash. *When the machine was installed it didn't work.*

We called the store three times and were promised a mechanic, but he never came. And we got a credit-payment book in the mail for $462.66, *saying we were supposed to pay $18 a month.* [They also received a

sales slip, and on this bill there is a typed statement to the effect that a down payment of $29.30 was made by Mr. R. Both Mr. and Mrs. R. deny any cash payments.] *A month later we got a statement saying that payments were overdue and we would have to pay 93¢ more. We don't want this machine and they're going to sue us.*

In this incident the true price was almost 60 percent more than the one quoted by the salesman. Perhaps the mysterious down payment credited to this family was made by the peddler-intermediary in order to reassure the merchant.

A number of families told us that peddlers frequently misrepresented the price of their merchandise, quoting lower prices initially and then demanding higher ones on later visits. Typical of these accounts is the story of a 36-year-old Puerto Rican mother on welfare:

In March 1960, a peddler knocked at my door and insisted so much that I said I'd take a lamp for $29. *I gave him a $3 deposit. When he came back with the account book the next week,* the price had gone up to $42. *I said I wouldn't pay it.* So he took away the lamp, but he never gave me back the $3.

Again we see the loss of a down payment as the outcome of this practice. . . .

SUBSTITUTION OF GOODS

Not only are prices misrepresented in the low income market, but so is quality. Some families were sold reconditioned merchandise that had been represented as new, and others received merchandise inferior to that ordered.

The sale of used merchandise as new is of course illegal. Yet, some merchants hinted that their competitors engaged in this practice. The following reports indicate that this does indeed happen. A 36-year-old Puerto Rican mother on welfare gave this account:

I bought a TV set from a First Avenue store. It was a used set which was sold as new. *After seven days it broke down. The store took it back and returned it in two weeks. It broke down again and they took it for thirty days. They brought it back and it broke down one week later. They took it away again and I* asked for a refund because there was a guarantee of ninety days which had not run out. But they wouldn't give me back my $100 or bring me another TV. *I went to the store several times but with no results.*

A basic inequality in the merchant consumer relationship is pointed up by this incident. When the low income consumer fails to live up to his obligations of payment, the merchant is able to utilize the law to protect his rights. When the merchant fails to respect a guarantee, however, the consumer is more likely to lose his initial investment than to obtain justice. In part, this is due to his ignorance of the laws which protect him and the agencies which can help him. But this inequality also partly stems from the merchant's superior resources. He can turn the job of collecting over to lawyers, collection agencies, and the courts. The consumer, on the other hand, must invest his own time in at least initiating legal action, time which, as we have seen, he cannot easily take from his job.

In another incident the sale of a used TV set as new was confirmed by a repairman. A 39-year-old Puerto Rican mother living on welfare had this experience:

I got a new TV set and some beds for $452.67. The TV alone was $280. It broke down after two years, and I paid $30 for

repairs. The TV repairman said that the set was a reconditioned one in a new cabinet.

The substitution of merchandise is illustrated by an incident told by a 26-year-old Negro husband:

We've spent more money repairing the TV than it cost. The store sent a different one than we asked for and it didn't look new. *We complained to the store and they offered a trade for $25 on another one.*

Another example of delivering the "wrong" item was provided by a 53-year-old white mother. In this case only a part of the equipment was delivered.

A peddler high-pressured my daughter into ordering a Hi-Fi from the catalogue he had. He then delivered a pickup instead of a phonograph. He kept insisting that my daughter had marked a pickup, and he wouldn't exchange it. [She has already paid $167 which is twice the current market price for this item.]

THE ANONYMITY OF CREDIT TRANSACTIONS

Several families responded to the question about cheating by describing pots-and-pans salesmen, who sold them poor quality merchandise at exorbitant prices. The details of these stories are similar. The salesman shows up either with the goods or with a catalogue. He stresses the unusually low payments, gets the housewife to sign a contract, extracts a small down payment, and then disappears. Sometime later the family receives a payment book from a finance company and frequently learns only then that the set of pots and pans will cost as much as $60. What is striking about these accounts is the anonymity of the transaction. Several interviewees reported that they tried unsuccessfully to find out the name of the store from which they had bought the merchandise. The high pressure techniques of these salesmen as well as the theme of anonymity are illustrated in this report by a 30-year-old Puerto Rican husband:

This happened about four or five days after we moved in. My wife was home and a man knocked at the door. He was selling pots and he pressured my wife to look at them. He said that they would cost only $5 a month and that he would leave her a piggy bank so she could save for other things. Then he told her to "sign here," and when all the payments were made she'd get a present. He then asked her if he could just leave the pots for a second while he went downstairs. But since she was signed up he never came back. We got a coupon book and mailed $5 each month to a bank in New Jersey. . . .I don't know the name of the store but I guess it's somewhere in Fenway, New Jersey. I have no records of it.

[*Another young Puerto Rican husband gave a similar account:*] *A salesman came around selling aluminum pots and pans. They're not worth a damn. I gave him a dollar down and then the bank sent me a book and I had to send in payments.* Some bank in New Jersey. I tried to find out the store's name, but I couldn't. *The set cost $60—$5 a month for twelve months.*

These incidents illustrate the various ways in which merchants take advantage of low income consumers. They show the high pressure tactics, the substitution of goods, the exorbitant prices, and the shoddy merchandise that are commonplace in the low income market. . . .

11
The Killing of George Baskett and the Acquittal of Officer O'Brien*
ART GOLDBERG and
GENE MARINE

The scene: *San Francisco. Its climate is moderate; tempers do not flare; passions are not abraded by the heat. It is renowned for an easy-going, live-and-let-live attitude. It prides itself on its cultural diversity.*

Michael O'Brien was returning with some friends from a Sunday outing at Lake Berryessa. The double date had not gone well: O'Brien had been drinking and was in an unpleasant mood. At one point, he made his date get out of the car with him and told her to "be a little more affectionate" or walk home. She calmed him down a little, though, and they got back into the car.

On the way across the San Francisco-Oakland Bay Bridge, he suddenly brandished a .38 revolver. After a minute he put the gun away, and a few minutes later they were at Brush Place.

You'd have to be a pretty determined San Franciscan to know where Brush Place is. About two and a half blocks from the ugly new Hall of Justice, there's a little dead-end alley off Folsom Street called Hallam Street. Off that alley there's an even smaller alley, also a

*[Reprinted by permission of the Editors from *Ramparts*, Vol. 8, no. 1, July 1969, pp. 10–16, 18. Copyright Ramparts Magazine, Inc. 1969. This article reports an instance of a policeman killing a black and being acquitted by a white jury. The authors of the article clearly have strong feelings about the case. As the article indicates Officer O'Brien and those whose testimony supported him saw events very differently and do not share the same feelings. Were they to have written this article it would no doubt be rather different. Yet even if the events reported here were entirely fictitious, the article is important because it describes a type of situation which sometimes does occur and, however infrequently, occurs disproportionately to minorities and the poor.]

dead end. That's Brush Place. O'Brien kept his boat in one of the garages in Brush Place that are rented out for that purpose.

Carl Hawkins, a mild-mannered black streetcar motorman, seems to have scraped O'Brien's boat trailer with his car. Hawkins immediately stopped and got out.

This is how all the witnesses who were not police described what happened next:

One thing quickly led to another. O'Brien yelled at Hawkins, "If you scrape my car, I'll shoot you!" People in the neighborhood, many of them black, came out or looked out their windows to see what was happening. Suddenly O'Brien pulled out his .38 and shouted, "Get your heads back in, niggers, or I'll kill all of you. I'll blow your heads off." Hawkins' wife went inside to phone the police; Mike's companion, Willis Garriott, went out toward Folsom Street on the same errand.

As Garriott returned with Special Patrol Officer Raymond Adkins (a private policeman, but one with a uniform and a gun), there was the sound of a shot and confusion in the street; O'Brien had three black men at gunpoint, their hands against the wall at the end of the alley. O'Brien was getting nastier by the minute; according to witnesses, he said, "I want to kill a nigger—I want to kill a nigger so goddamned bad I can taste it!"

A black truck driver and neighbor of Hawkins, George Baskett—five inches shorter than O'Brien and 75 pounds lighter—picked up a slat out of a chair back, a thin piece of wood about 23 inches long and about an inch and a half wide, and tried to knock the gun away from O'Brien. Garriott and the special cop had their guns out by now and watched as O'Brien growled, "Drop the stick, drop it, goddammit."

He counted in a rapid cadence, "One ... two ... three. ..." There was a sharp crack. The bullet ripped through Baskett's chest, severing a major artery. As Baskett lay moaning and dying in the street, O'Brien approached him. "Shut up, dammit," he growled, "shut up." He kicked at Baskett's side, turning his victim over on his back. Baskett's pregnant wife ran out toward her husband. "Get out of here, you black bitch," O'Brien shouted, forcing her down the street. Then he looked up at the black faces peering down from the windows above him. "Get your heads back in niggers," he shouted, "before I blow them off." Within minutes, Baskett, twenty-eight years old and the father of five children, was dead. Michael O'Brien had killed his nigger.

The police came, including San Francisco's head-cracking Tactical Squad. They immediately began questioning "suspects." They arrested Mr. and Mrs. Carl Hawkins, Mrs. Hawkins' son Richard Dickerson, and Otis Baskett, on charges of conspiracy, assault to commit murder, and assault with a deadly weapon. Then they helped the dazed O'Brien out of the alley and away from the angry crowd.

O'Brien of course was white. And although he had never said so to anybody in Brush Place, that night or at any other time, Michael O'Brien was a cop. "If he had only identified himself as a policeman," recalled the soft-spoken Carl Hawkins, a man of fifty, "this whole business would never have happened." And then—not apparently conscious himself of the ironic significance with which his words illuminated the growing chasm between law and people in the country as a whole—"People around here have a lot of respect for a police officer."

Within four hours of the shooting of George Baskett in Brush Place, the official police investigation of the incident had been conducted and concluded. The two officers who submitted the report admitted in court that it had been rewritten three times on the orders of their superior, Lieutenant Daniel Mahoney, who had specifically ordered them not to mention any witnesses other than the policemen present. The report concluded that the killing of Baskett was "justifiable homicide." It was only *after* reaching this conclusion that the police questioned the arrested blacks, who for three hours had been kept handcuffed in the paddy wagon outside the Hall of Justice. Early Monday morning, Chief Thomas Cahill told reporters that the whole affair was a "sad situation," but "a man has a right to defend himself." He termed the shooting "accidental" and informed them that his own private investigation was closed.

But it was soon clear that sweeping the "accident" under the rug was not going to be quite so easy. Word had spread fast, and an aroused black community was soon denouncing Cahill's expeditious review of the case as a police department "whitewash." On top of this came some exceptional newspaper reporting by two local journalists, Birney Jarvis and Charles Raudebaugh. The police story stank. They knew it and they said so—on the front pages of *The San Francisco Chronicle*.

By October 1, Cahill was forced to announce a reopening of the investigation. On October 9, Michael O'Brien was arrested and formally charged with murder.

In these times of popular backlash against "coddling" of accused criminals, it is instructive to note what kind of support is available to a rank-and-file policeman with no "connections" who has killed a black citizen. First, of course, there are his comrades-in-arms, who came through with two

crucial commodities: money and testimony.

The accused O'Brien had other help. He did not, for instance, have to resort to the public defender or to penny ante private counsel. The earliest moves in his case were handled by prominent San Francisco attorney Edward Dullea. Dullea's brother is president of the prestigious Catholic University of San Francisco, whose law school has given the city a large proportion of its judges (including Judge Karesh, who ended up trying the case). The father of the Dullea brothers was a former San Francisco chief of police.

But Dullea was soon replaced on the case by his even more prominent partner—through whom still other lines of influential support became available to the humble cop—the fire-eating, legendary trial lawyer, Jake Ehrlich.

THE LEGEND OF SAM BENEDICT

Jake Ehrlich is the "best criminal lawyer" in San Francisco. That doesn't mean that he is the best criminal lawyer in San Francisco; it means that that's his local title, though it rests mostly on past laurels—he doesn't have to work much any more. His reputation rests on the fact that while he has occasionally compromised on conviction for manslaughter, he has never had a client convicted of murder—and he's handled over fifty murder cases. . . .

Ehrlich is also, now and for some time past, the attorney for the Police Officers' Association—a voluntary organization which when you become a cop, you join if you're white and stay away from if you aren't.

One of the things that Ehrlich has going for him is that any jury that could conceivably be put together in San Francisco is going to be in awe just because it's the nearly legendary Jake Ehrlich before the bench. He's not only

Sam Benedict; he's Perry Mason, Judd, and the Defender, all at once.

Another thing about Jake is that he will use whatever will win; if racism will win, he'll use that. And so he did. He played it like a fiddle.

Although almost everyone had assumed that murder is unbailable in California, a municipal judge released O'Brien after he was booked. Black leaders were furious, and the noise was so loud for a day or so that a second municipal judge overruled his colleague and ordered O'Brien back to jail.

Then Ehrlich moved in, going up to Superior Court where he obtained a ruling granting $25,000 bail. "This man is not going to run," the judge explained.

Half the bail came from a bail bondsman. The other half was put up by [financier] Louis Lurie. "If this is a murder case," Ehrlich's friend told a reporter, "I'm the Pope of Rome."

He's not; and Michael O'Brien never was, and never will be, tried for the murder of George Baskett.

The grand jury members, as always, were prosperous middle-class, predominantly white, and predominantly male. They meet in closed session and the district attorney tells them pretty much what he wants them to know.

After hearing witnesses, the grand jury deliberated for 15 minutes and indicted Michael O'Brien—not for murder, but for manslaughter.

The foreman said that, in the light of the testimony, there wasn't that much difference between murder and manslaughter in this case. (Huey Newton, who was ultimately convicted of manslaughter, was indicted for first degree murder by the Alameda County grand jury across the bay, without benefit of eyewitness testimony or a murder weapon.)

The city's black leaders hit the roof. A blistering statement was issued charging that law enforcement agencies had "connived and conspired to thwart justice."

Jake Ehrlich, on the other hand, had the grace to concede that manslaughter is a better rap than murder, though he still insisted it was justifiable homicide. "But this is one of those political footballs," he went on. "Everyone wants to be heard, and all they're doing is creating class feelings."

O'Brien's bail was reduced to $3,125.

THE JUDGE

Superior Court Judge Joseph Karesh grew up in South Carolina, but that does not make him a bigot. In fact, he is proud of the fact that his father, a rabbi, taught Hebrew to the local black ministers. Like Jake Ehrlich and Mayor Joseph Alioto, Karesh is a liberal. When a probation officer was fired for having a beard, Karesh ordered him rehired with back pay. He ruled that the city could have topless joints and ordered the police to allow performances of Michael McClure's play, "The Beard."

He has, however, a couple of minor hangups. He doesn't like student dissidents, he loves cops, and he appears to have a somewhat racist way of not being a bigot.

One local attorney recalls, "In many previous dealings I had with Karesh, he seemed to have a very strong block against perceiving that any policeman could be guilty of any misconduct. One sure way to arouse his anger would be to suggest that the police were guilty of any impropriety. It would sort of destroy his world if he thought O'Brien really called those people 'niggers' or shot to kill."

And a local reporter notes that ". . . in his chambers he'd cut up prosecution witnesses, and talk about how the blacks are getting away with everything, how juries are afraid to convict them, how they are arrested one day and walk away free the next day."

THE BLACK-WHITE ENTANGLEMENT

On January 13, 1969, in the Superior Court of California, Joseph Karesh presiding, Michael O'Brien went on trial for manslaughter in the death of George Baskett.

Two days later George Baskett's sixth child was born.

It took only one day to choose a jury. Ehrlich used two peremptory challenges: one eliminated airlines' supervisor George A. Buckner, Jr., the only black called. No "Personal reflection," said Ehrlich.

Similarly, *any* lawyer can insure an all-white jury by use of his allotment of peremptory challenges, which the judge cannot review.

Ehrlich made it quite clear, when questioning jurors, what the trial was going to be about. A key issue, he said, would be "this black-white entanglement." Judge Karesh found nothing to criticize in that formulation.

Attention on the second day focused on Elizabeth Hawkins, a tall, striking woman who said flatly that she had watched Michael O'Brien deliberately murder George Baskett. The next day, Ehrlich moved in, contempt dripping from his tiny frame. He accused Mrs. Hawkins of having lied outright on three occasions.

But she refused to be Ehrlich's pigeon. After she insisted again that she had seen O'Brien kick the dying Baskett:

Ehrlich: "What kind of shoes did O'Brien have on?"

Mrs. Hawkins: "Sneakers, I think."

Ehrlich: "Then he couldn't have hurt Baskett much if he kicked him, could he?"

Mrs. Hawkins: "I have no idea—I have never been shot and then kicked."

Carl Hawkins followed his wife to the stand and corroborated her story, with additional details. During the early part of the incident, he said, his stepson, Richard Dickerson, had arrived and asked a neighbor, Mrs. Anne Thomas, what was going on.

"Your father's having trouble with the white man," she replied.

That, she testified, angered O'Brien further. "Shut up, you goddamn nigger bitch!" he yelled.

Mrs. Thomas promptly yelled back, "Ask God why he made me a nigger bitch and made you a honky."

Baskett had picked up a stick and tried to use it to knock the pistol from O'Brien's hand, but O'Brien ordered him to drop it and began to count.

"O'Brien," Hawkins testified, "extended his arm, braced his right arm with his left hand to steady the pistol, and fired one shot. I saw the flash of the gun."

Otis Baskett, the dead man's brother, appeared and told the same story.

Ehrlich tore into him, shouting that he was a "professional liar." Assistant District Attorney Walter Giubbini, who prosecuted the case, called the use of the phrase "disgusting." Karesh, however, let Ehrlich rant.

But the next witness—Special Officer Adkins—had seen none of this at all. What *he* had seen was a silent confrontation, no words at all, in which Baskett was beating O'Brien on the head. "O'Brien stumbled backwards, kind of shaking his head. Mr. Baskett was preparing to strike him again when the gun discharged." Later he said that O'Brien was "tensing up, trying to regain his balance," but that he was off balance and "back-pedaling," leaning backward with his gun "straight out in his hand," when it went off.

On redirect examination Adkins admitted to consulting with Ehrlich about a week after the shooting. The police department had been "harassing" him to talk to the district attorney, he explained. Ehrlich interrupted to say that he had advised Adkins only to tell the truth.

Dickerson's turn came next, and his story varied from that of the other black witnesses only in the quotation from O'Brien, which he remembered as, "Drop it—drop it, goddamn it, nigger, I'll kill you." Then the count.

The score, by witnesses, was: four who matched each other almost exactly, one who differed. Up to this point memory divided along racial lines.

THE TRAITOR TO HIS RACE

David Anderson, the eighteen-year-old son of an elementary school principal, testified that he was listening to a rock record "when I heard shots and a big commotion." He went up on his roof, which commanded an excellent view of Brush Place, to see what was going on, and he told the court what he saw.

David Anderson is not only white, he's "clean": his father's professional job is in San Leandro, just south of Oakland across the bay, and the family lives in the pristine suburb of Castro Valley. Anderson had taken his apartment while going to college.

From the roof, he said, he saw three black men spread-eagled against the wall and a white man with a gun; he identified the white man as O'Brien. Then, Anderson went on, a fourth black picked up a stick and swung it, hitting O'Brien either in the left side or on the left elbow. As Baskett backed away, crouching, O'Brien deliberately shot him.

Shortly thereafter, he went on, O'Brien held his gun on one of the men leaning against the wall, and deliberately kicked him in the seat of the pants. "Just give me an excuse—just give me a reason and I'll shoot you!" O'Brien was

quoted as shouting. Then O'Brien moved back and yelled at the people looking out of the apartments to get their heads back in.

Ehrlich was faced with a calm and believable young witness, and one who was white—apparently beyond the reach of simple racism. But he knew his judge, and he knew his jurors. The key lay in Anderson's attendance at San Francisco State College, and the possibility of making the young man appear a traitor to his race.

Ehrlich immediately asked whether Anderson was participating in the strike there; Anderson answered that he was. There followed a barrage of questions about Black Panthers, hair, SDS, prejudice, and a number of other subjects, none of which were particularly relevant, though they seemed to fascinate the judge, and Giubbini gave up trying to stem the flow.

What Anderson actually said was fairly mild. He is not a member of Students for a Democratic Society, though he is in sympathy with some of its aims (which no one asked about). He thinks students and teachers have a right to strike. He hopes the strike will help to end institutional racism.

But this alone doesn't convey the effect. Ehrlich met Giubbini's objection to the whole line of questioning by saying that he was trying to prove bias, because "these people who are part of SDS think every white policeman is a pig." He asked Anderson: "If there is any feeling between white man and black man, you are standing against the white man?"

Ehrlich kept Anderson on the stand for two more days, hammering at left-wing associations that weren't there and ideas that Anderson refused to agree with. He demanded that Anderson show his draft card and pretended surprise when Anderson produced one.

Having raised the specter of SDS, the bombastic attorney made another try, this time with the Black Panthers. He asked whether Anderson knew Richard E. Brown, a Panther who had given a lower apartment in the same building as his address when arrested five times between March and November 1968. Anderson said he didn't know Brown, but that he had moved into the building in September and that no blacks lived there.

Finally, Ehrlich said that he "had been informed" that a police report, dated the night after the shooting, involved Anderson's apartment, and that the report said a black youth was living with Anderson and his white roommate, David Dixon, and that the apartment was decorated with "Free Huey," "Black Revolution," and Che Guevara posters. Anderson merely noted that his apartment is decorated with travel posters, not revolutionary posters, and that he and Dixon have no other roommate.

By a strange coincidence, the Tactical Squad was called out in the area of Rodgers Street "to protect fire engines against possible sniper fire" on the night following the Brush Place shooting. And a couple of the boys just happened to bust into the front of, and out the back of, 35 Rodgers Street, where that stupid white punk lived who had backed up the black people's story about what happened the night before.

When they busted in, one Tac Squad member testified, he saw somebody else going out the back; he trained his pistol on the man and told him to stop—then discovered that it was Richard Brown, who cried out, "We live here, we live here."

The cops were there, of course, without a warrant, without any cause to break into the apartment, and without permission. They didn't even call out that they were police.

John Coate is white, but he has long hair and is obviously another traitor to his race. Coate, it seems, was visiting David Anderson on the night of September 30, when the Tac Squad came, and he said there was no black man there and no revolutionary posters on the walls. Ehrlich decided Coate was biased against the police, too, and started on the same bit with questions about State; Coate replied that he believes in nonviolence and is opposed to both police and student violence on the campus. Anderson, he said, is "a rather conscientious person who cares about the world in which he lives."

And the jury apparently just plain didn't hear Anderson's father, the school principal, because he was there that night too, and while he left before the cops came, he left Coate and Anderson and Dixon alone. He also described the posters on the wall. He could describe them, he said, because he had provided them—they were travel posters.

At one point during the testimony, Ehrlich found reason to thunder an accusation which, in its wording, effectively let the jury know which side Anderson was supposed to be on. "This is a white and black fight," Ehrlich shouted. "This man Anderson is an unmitigated liar. Any man who would sit there and lie a man's life away is not entitled to a fair trial—he should be taken out and shot."

For this bit of legal theory from the city's foremost criminal attorney, the judge had not a word of rebuke.

But that wasn't Ehrlich's most extravagant shot for the day. He made his position, his tactics, and his opinion of the judge all very clear just a short time later, when a Tac Squad officer said that he believed Richard Brown was in the courtroom.

Ehrlich strode to the railing separating the spectators from the front of the court, leaned over, and bellowed, "What's your name? Stand up, *boy!*"

There were some audible gasps in the courtroom, but Ehrlich ignored them. The black youth, after a brief but obvious struggle for control, said quietly, "My name is not 'boy.' My name is Richard Brown."

Ehrlich walked back to the counsel table, threw himself into the chair, and said, "Why don't you lock him up?" That's a little obscure, but that's what he said.

Judge Karesh leaned solicitously forward and said, "I'm sure you didn't mean to offend anybody, Mr. Ehrlich."

Jake took the cue and leaped up again. Facing the jury, he thundered, "Some black people seem to think it disgraceful to be called 'boy.' My grandfather and father called me that. What's wrong with it? I don't understand this childish, infantile feeling. I have defended these people many times without fee. I have no hatred for these people, no feeling for them at all. But I won't take any backtalk out of them, either!"

Karesh finally decided that maybe it was time for the jury to leave. When they were gone, he repeated to Ehrlich, "I did not mean to imply earlier that you meant any offense to anyone."

O'BRIEN'S TESTIMONY

Michael O'Brien told his own story earnestly and well. He'd had a few nips of the Red Mountain burgundy, it was true, but he wasn't drunk at all. He would never do a thing like threatening a girl with a long walk home—he was only a little put out because she had turned moody and was spoiling his "fun day."

When Baskett attacked him with a stick, he said, he tried to shoot him "between the knee and the thigh, but the gun clicked and didn't go off," so he thought it was empty.

"Here's this man with a club," O'Brien explained. "He made a real lunge at me. I backed away but he caught me across the right side of the head. I fell backward and hit the ground. As I'm falling backward the gun discharged."

The stick, he said, looked bigger in the alley.

And, when they told him in the police station that Baskett was dead, he said, "I couldn't talk any more. I was crying."

He also said that his "Gas Huey" tie clip (which he wore in the Hunter's Point ghetto during Huey Newton's trial) was only a gag. It didn't have anything to do with gassing Huey.

O'Brien was convincing, and the jury probably didn't pay all that much attention to the one serious use of physical evidence by Giubbini, who asked O'Brien to demonstrate what had happened.

When he demonstrated, his gun arm—inevitably—moved upward. Giubbini quietly pointed out that (1) the bullet that killed Baskett traveled *downward,* and (2) there were no powder burns on Baskett's clothes, as there would have had to have been according to O'Brien's reenaction. (A .38 police revolver will spray powder into clothing three feet away. It's hard to hit a guy over the head with a 23-inch stick from more than three feet away.)

Giubbini got in a description of another episode in O'Brien's life—when on a drinking spree at a Broadway topless joint called Pierre's, he took off after a topless waitress and chased her into her dressing room, waving his .38 all the way. O'Brien tried to say that it was a water pistol, then backtracked when Giubbini seemed to know what he was talking about. But after hearing it all, Karesh decided it was irrelevant and ruled the whole thing inadmissible.

The rest of the witnesses all supported the prosecution in one way or another, and several demonstrated that there was a conscious attempt to alter evidence in O'Brien's favor. But by then the jury had the message: black people lie; white people tell the truth, unless they're traitors to their race and belong to SDS and fraternize with Black Panthers, in which case they lie about that too.

Finally, nobody listened when Giubbini—who had started out in mild-mannered enough fashion, but who got increasingly incensed as he watched the Ehrlich-Karesh racism tandem—blasted the police department for the errors and omissions in its reports and investigations, and said that the original report (written without any black witnesses having been questioned) showed "some effort to . . . reflect what the lieutenant thought it should reflect, not what the facts were. . . . We're talking," he told the jury, "about credibility in this case. We have to keep our eyes open."

But he was the only one talking about credibility. The others were talking about niggers.

HYENAS

Jake Ehrlich spent six days on his summation. Not preparing it—*giving* it. It was the longest defense summation in the history of San Francisco criminal law. It was also the most vicious, bigoted, nauseating, low, and piggish performance any local courtroom has ever seen. Contrary to press suggestions, it was not racist, it was nothing that subtle. It is a disgrace to the Bar that the Bar Association did not meet the next day with censure and possible disbarment in mind; it is a disgrace to the bench that Joseph Karesh was not hounded out of his robes—and out of town as well—for letting it happen. Any Mississippi backwoods judge in the past ten years would have told an attorney making the same speech to tone it down.

Ehrlich started things off by referring to Brush Place as "a hellhole, with 200 hyenas in there."

He slashed at Alioto for "ordering" the trial because the mayor is "looking for the minority vote."

Banging on a lectern with the stick used by Baskett, he shouted, "Mike didn't do what I would have done. I would have shot him then and there. But he backed away, remembering his policeman's training."

Mrs. Hawkins, he shouted, "should be in jail for perjury. The blood of Baskett is on her hands. I don't know how she can sleep at night."

He repeatedly returned to racism, and told the jury that the residents of Brush Place had manufactured "a false facade of lies, chicanery, and trickery," and that Giubbini had "patched up all these stories to make them fit one mold." The "litany of lies" was to be expected, however: "You must realize we're dealing here with people of little or no moral honesty or integrity."

Carl Hawkins, in Ehrlich's peroration, became "Mr. Holier than Thou," "Old Mr. Prayer Meeting," and, most often, "The Deacon," after Ehrlich said that Hawkins reminded him of "the old prayer meetings down home." Hawkins "manufactured" the story of O'Brien kicking Baskett, Ehrlich said, and was in any case "a sanctimonious little liar."

In the middle of the attack on Hawkins, Ehrlich suddenly said, "I'd better stick to the record; otherwise, I'll be accused . . . of being a racist or something."

"These people," Ehrlich told the jury, apparently relishing the hated phrase, "would have killed . . . O'Brien, and they would have killed you, too, if you'd been there. They have absolutely no respect for an oath, the truth or for common decency. They would just as soon sacrifice you as they did this boy here."

Otis Baskett, whom Ehrlich accused of "bobbing, weaving, and double-talking," became "that big phony." And what David Anderson became was something else again.

"This boy is a member of SDS and hates police as sure as I'm standing here. He hates them and would shoot them if he had a chance. . . . [He] is a vicious young punk who wants to destroy our government . . . our homes, our children, 200 years of American democracy, and the flag and all that it stands for."

But it wasn't America that Ehrlich wanted the jury to see Anderson as betraying; that was incidental.

"I can realize our black brethren sticking together," the tiny lawyer intoned. "They do things I don't approve of, but I can understand. What I can't understand is Anderson coming apparently from a good home and selling his soul to prove his hatred for a policeman, what he calls a pig." (Anderson testified that he never uses the term "pig.")

Ehrlich called one or another witness "liar," "punk," "knucklehead," "little fool," "perjurer," "killer." He charged that Giubbini had deliberately implied that all nineteen policemen who testified were liars and had "manufactured evidence," and he added, "This breaks my heart when I see it."

Finally, he wound up with an almost tearful plea for poor, victimized Mike O'Brien, begging, "Don't sacrifice this boy on the altar of chicanery to get a few lousy, dirty votes. If you don't find O'Brien not guilty, there is only one answer—the Golden Gate Bridge." He didn't say for whom.

Unaccountably, Ehrlich and Giub-

bini seem to have made an agreement in advance not to interrupt each other's closing statements—and Giubbini is a gentleman, though it must have taken considerable effort.

For Judge Karesh, there is not even that excuse. He sought to interrupt Ehrlich only when Ehrlich launched into a tirade against the *Chronicle,* and then only on the grounds that the jury had been instructed to avoid or ignore all mention of communications media during the trial!

One lawyer who was there put his opinion graphically: "Any judge with any balls would have cut Ehrlich off right away. A member of the Bar is not allowed to make racist remarks." A reporter who was at many of the trial sessions said that Karesh's role in the entire trial was vital: "The judge practically turned into a defense attorney" (the same reporter also called Ehrlich "a racist of the Bilbo type" and said that "at times, the word 'nigger' slipped out of his mouth accidentally").

The jury reported itself deadlocked, ten to two (for acquittal, it turned out), but the judge sent them back. The jury asked for instructions as to whether they should give weight to O'Brien's police training—whether, in effect, they should expect more restraint from him than from an ordinary twenty-seven-year-old kid with a gun and a jug of Red Mountain. The judge refused to give such an instruction (Giubbini wanted it, Ehrlich didn't); shortly thereafter the jury acquitted Michael O'Brien.

AFTERMATH

Michael O'Brien was freed on March 20. On March 30, Patrolman Gerald Roberts, with his gun drawn, chased Alvert Joe Linthcome into a record shop, erroneously suspecting him of stealing a car. Linthcome's younger sister, who was standing outside the store, screamed at Roberts, "Don't shoot him, please, don't shoot him."

Linthcome, black, nineteen, and unarmed, turned around and put his elbows on the counter behind him. Roberts stepped into the doorway and killed him. The police, and ultimately the coroner, said it was justifiable homicide. Patrolman Roberts said, "I thought he had a gun."

John L. Brennan, attorney for the Linthcome family, has been denied permission to see the police report on the case. Elmo E. Ferrari, president of the civilian police commission, told him: "I'm sure Chief Cahill will give you all the documents he thinks you should have. . . . We'll leave this in the chief's good hands."

The polarization deepens at all levels. The mayor courts the backlash by spewing hysteria about the Black Panthers: he informs a Presbyterian group that the Panthers' ten-point program calls for "robbing and raping." The police raid the Panther office in force, on the pretext of a sound permit violation, sparking a near riot in the angry neighborhood that is quelled, according to reporters, only by the Panthers themselves. The mayor is not impressed: "The young men who did react so quickly and so well were probably mistaken for Panthers."

A group called Officers for Justice is formed representing nearly all of the city's 78 black policemen—the highest ranking blacks are two sergeants, the total police force is 1,800—as an alternative to the white Police Officers Association. The new group cheers Reverend Cecil Williams when he calls the POA "the most racist organization we have in San Francisco." The businessmen's Downtown Association on the other hand cosponsors with the POA a testimonial dinner for O'Brien's attorney, Jake Ehrlich.

One black policeman, Robert Jeffrey, on the force for more than four years, resigned four days after George Baskett was killed, saying, ". . . I can no longer be the recipient of this hatred and outright prejudice. . . . I can no longer go forth into the community and tell the people of the ghetto areas that everything is all right if we just wait a little longer."

A few years ago in the South, blacks, refusing any longer to wait and trust in the white man's justice to protect them, armed and organized themselves into the Deacons for Defense. Northern liberals, convinced that no other channel of justice existed for the black man in the South, reluctantly accepted this. Now they must face the fact that if the liberal cities of the North are going to practice Mississippi justice, a similar response from northern blacks may have to be accepted as well.

12
White Gain from
Negro Subordination*
NORVAL GLENN

A question of considerable theoretical and practical importance is the extent of any occupational and economic benefits that whites in the United States derive from the subordination of Negroes. Certainly the initial subordination, through slavery, was for economic gain, and almost as certainly economic considerations were among the primary motives for continued Negro subordination after emancipation. Many students of contemporary American race relations believe that economic functions

*[Reprinted from Social Problems, Vol. 14, no. 2, Fall 1966, pp. 159–178 by permission of the Society for the Study of Social Problems. A grant from the University of Texas Research Institute financed the research reported here. The author is indebted to S. Dale McLemore for a critical reading of the manuscript.]

of discrimination to a large extent account for its perpetuation. Others, however, believe that noneconomic motives now largely determine white policy and action toward Negroes. Two sociologists recently claimed that the economic need for the Negro is virtually gone, that if he disappeared tomorrow, he would hardly be missed.[1]

Inspite of the importance and controversy attached to the question, it has been subjected to little empirical investigation,[2] probably because of the difficulty in ascertaining that whites would be more prosperous and have more favorable occupations if Negroes

were not present and subordinated. Published data on the subject do not allow conclusions of maximum certainty. In general, they support the view that whites derive appreciable occupational and economic benefits from the low status of Negroes, but since the data are for 1950 and earlier, one cannot be confident that recent changes in the economy and in the demand for different kinds of labor have not ended any previous white benefits.

The present study, though not definitive, is designed to supply more recent and more nearly conclusive data. Based on 1960 census data, it is similar to a study the author did with 1950 data,[3] but the analysis is modified and extended.

THE PROBLEM AND METHODS

Negro subordination, as the term is used here, refers to the disparity between Negroes and whites in such stratification variables as power, income, and occupations, and therefore it is not synonymous with discrimination. Subordination of Negroes results from both present discrimination and the remaining effects of past discrimination, including the poorer average qualifications of Negro workers. The most extreme subordination would exist if all Negroes were below all whites with respect to the stratification variable being considered, and there would be no subordination if Negro and white status were equal. Overlaping of the Negro and white distributions constitutes intermediate subordination; the greater the overlap, the smaller the subordination. The question of whether or not whites benefit from Negro subordination is, then, a question of whether or not white status is absolutely higher than it would be if Negroes were

[1] Sidney M. Willhelm and Edwin H. Powell, "Who Needs the Negro?" *Trans*-Action, 1 (September-October, 1964), pp. 3–6.

[2] To the author's knowledge, the only recent studies designed specifically to investigate this question are reported in Norval D. Glenn, "Occupational Benefits to Whites from the Subordination of Negroes," *American Sociological Review*, 28 (June, 1963), pp. 443–448; and Phillips Cutright, "Negro Subordination and White Gains" *American Sociological Review*, 30 (February, 1965), pp. 110–112. See also Norval D. Glenn, "Reply to Cutright on Negro Subordination," *American Sociological Review*, 30 (June, 1965), p. 416. The classic statement of the alleged white economic gain from Negro subordination is in John Dollard, *Class and Caste in a Southern Town*, New Haven: Yale University Press, 1937, chap. 6. However, Dollard's conclusions are impressionistic and are based primarily on observations in one small southern community. Several authors give data that relate to but do not systematically test the hypothesis of white benefits. For instance, Myrdal noted in the early 1940's that the occupational status of southern whites was somewhat higher, in certain respects, than that of northern whites, and he attributed the difference to the whites' near monopoly on higher jobs in the South (Gunnar Myrdal, *An American Dilemma*, New York: Harper and Row, 1944, p. 297). However, this white gain noted by Myrdal plays no important role in his theory of discrimination and prejudice. Blalock reports that in 1950 certain aspects of white status were higher in those southern counties with higher concentrations of Negroes, but he does not conclude that the higher white status resulted from the subordination of the numerous Negroes. See Hubert M. Blalock, Jr., "Per Cent Non-White and Discrimination in the South," *American Sociological Review*, 22 (December, 1957), p. 681.

[3] Glenn, "Occupational Benefits," *op. cit.*

not below whites. If the answer is yes, then rational considerations of self-interest could lie behind white resistance to Negro advancement.

The manner in which whites are assumed to benefit from Negro subordination is simple; the concentration of Negroes near the bottom of the occupational and economic hierarchies allegedly keeps whites up. For instance, to the extent that Negroes do low-paying and unpleasant work, whites are assumed able to escape such work. Discrimination and relatively low qualifications handicap Negroes in the competition for high-paying jobs, thus supposedly making it easier for whites to rise into and keep these jobs. In addition, it is believed that the concentration of Negroes in unskilled and semiskilled work increases the supply of labor at those levels and thus decreases labor costs—a possible detriment to unskilled and semiskilled white workers but a benefit to white employers.

It is not inevitable or obvious that any of these gains acrue to whites. For instance, the concentration of Negroes in low level jobs could simply increase the proportion of such jobs and/or increase unemployment instead of helping whites to rise and stay up in the job hierarchy. An abundance of unskilled Negro labor might retard mechanization and prevent the most efficient utilization of labor rather than appreciably reducing the costs of employers. Even if sizable occupational gains do acrue to whites, these gains could be offset by detrimental economic consequences of Negro subordination. Inefficient use of Negro talent undoubtedly reduces the productivity of the economy perhaps by several billions of dollars annually.[4]

This waste of productive potential primarily hurts Negroes but it also hurts whites to some extent. For instance, Negro poverty hurts white-owned businesses that offer goods and services to the Negro market, and the direct and indirect consequences of the Negro disadvantage cost white taxpayers an incalculable amount in welfare, relief, and law enforcement expenses. Although discrimination and the effects of past discrimination give whites a larger proportion of the total wealth, they do not necessarily increase the absolute size of the white share.[5]

Determining the exact extent of beneficial and detrimental consequences to whites from Negro subordination seems impossible. The detrimental effects are particularly hard to measure. It would be very difficult if not impossible to arrive at even a defensible rough estimate of the extent to which Negro subordination lowers total productivity, increases the tax burden, increases unemployment, and affects the occupational structure. About the best that one can hope to do is estimate the extent and nature of benefits and detriments to particular segments of the white population. Such estimates can have considerable theoretical and practical utility even if one cannot estimate with comparable accuracy the balance of gains and losses to the total white population. For example, the knowledge that whites in certain parts of the country benefit in some ways from Negro subordination can help explain prejudice, discrimination, and interracial conflict, irrespective of what the overall consequences of the Negro disadvantage may be.

Probably the most fruitful approach

---

[4] George Eaton Simpson and J. Milton Yinger, *Racial and Cultural Minorities: An Analysis of Prejudice and Discrimination,* New York: Harper and Row, 1965, p. 137.

[5] See Simpson and Yinger, *op. cit.,* pp. 187–190, and Norval D. Glenn, "The Role of White Resistance and Facilitations in the Negro Struggle for Equality," *Phylon,* 26 (Summer, 1965), pp. 110–111.

to discovering the partial consequences of Negro subordination is ecological analysis. Most of any white benefits and some of the detriments that result from low Negro status are not evenly distributed geographically but are primarily on localities in which Negroes are a large percentage of the population. For instance, the white workers who are likely to benefit from the competitive handicap of Negroes are those who actually are, or who in the absence of discrimination would be, competing against Negroes. Competition for jobs is not strictly local, of course, but for many kinds of jobs it is largely so, and therefore any positive effects of the Negro handicap would be primarily upon whites who live near large Negro populations. Consequently, if whites do gain appreciably in occupational and income status from Negro subordination, one would expect, in the absence of offsetting influences, a positive ecological association of the percentage of the population that is Negro and measures of white status. If there were no other plausible explanations, such an association would suggest that Negro subordination benefits at least some of the whites in the localities with the larger percentages of Negroes.

In order to study possible white gains from Negro subordination the relationship between percentage of an area that is nonwhite and various measures of white status are examined.

The localities used for this study are the 179 urbanized areas designated in the 1960 census reports for which separate data for whites and nonwhites are reported. Limiting the study to urbanized areas very roughly controls those influences upon white status that vary by community size, and separate analyses by region are performed to control those influences that vary by region. Several additional control variables, including the percentage of

the labor force in manufacturing industries (an index of industrialization), were at first used, but none of these controls appreciably altered the relationship between percentage nonwhite and white status.

The measures of white status used here are a summary index of occupational status of employed males (abbreviation IOS),[6] percentage of employed males in nonmanual and skilled occupations, percentage of families with annual income of $10,000 or more, percentage of families with income below $3,000, and percentage of the male civilian labor force unemployed.

---

[6] The IOS is computed by assigning a value to each of the census "occupational groups," assigning to each worker the value of his occupational group, and taking the average of the individual values of all workers in an urbanized area or a category of urbanized areas. The values for the occupational groups are arrived at by the following formula:

IOS for an occupational group =

$$(a/A + b/B) \times 100 = (a/A + b/B) \times 50$$

When

$a =$ median earnings of experienced male civilian workers in the occupational group in 1959

$A =$ median earnings of all experienced male civilian workers in 1959

$b =$ median years of school completed by experienced male civilian workers in the occupational group as of 1960

$B =$ median years of school completed by all experienced male civilian workers as of 1960

The value is above one hundred if both the earnings and education of the workers in the occupational group were above the medians for all workers, and the value is below one hundred if both earnings and education were below parity. The values for the occupational groups are as follows: professional, technical, and kindred workers (146); farmers and farm managers (63); managers, officials, and kindred workers (108); sales workers (111); craftsmen, foremen, and kindred workers (104); operatives and kindred workers (88); service workers, including private household (77); farm laborers and foremen (43); laborers, except farm and mine (70). A similar but more refined measure is Duncan's Socioeconomic Index for the occupational groups, but the IOS has the advantage of being based on 1960 rather than 1950 census data. Both the SEI and IOS were used for parts of this study with virtually the same results.

The following hypotheses are offered:

1 The higher the percentage of the population that is nonwhite, the higher will be the overall measure of white occupational status.

2 The higher the percentage of the population that is nonwhite, the higher will be the percentage of white males in nonmanual and skilled occupations.

3 The higher the percentage of the population that is nonwhite, the higher will be the percentage of white families with an annual income of $10,000 or more.

4 The higher the percentage of the population that is nonwhite, the lower will be the percentage of white families with annual incomes of below $3,000.

5 The higher the percentage of the population that is nonwhite, the lower will be the percentage of the white male civilian labor force that is unemployed.

FINDINGS

In Tables 1 and 2 the relationships are all in the predicted direction. The larger the percentage of nonwhite, the higher various measures of white status are, whether considered in terms of percentages or correlations. Does this then offer strong proof of greater white gains the more blacks there are in an area? Not necessarily. It is possible that measures of status for blacks also increase as the proportion of blacks in an area increases. That is the higher total status (of blacks as well as whites) in areas with a larger percentage of blacks may account for the above findings. However, in most instances this does not seem to be the case as can be seen by looking at the figures for all races.[7]

Even if the proportion of black and measures of white status vary together, without measures of black status varying in a similar fashion, this does not necessarily mean that the former causes the latter. Perhaps they are both caused by some third factor and are not directly related to each other. A higher rate of economic growth could be such a factor. The greatest opportunities for whites to advance occupationally and economically and to avoid unemployment are almost certainly in the urbanized areas with the most rapidly expanding economies, and these same localities may be most likely to attract large numbers of Negro migrants. The large influx of Negroes, in turn, might reduce the status measures for the total populations of these urbanized areas below the measures for less rapidly developing localities.

This alternate explanation cannot be ruled out for the North and West. Rate of population growth is a fairly good index of rate of economic expansion, and the average population increase from 1950 to 1960 was 28.2 percent in the urbanized areas with less than 10 percent of nonwhites and 31.7 percent in those with larger proportions of nonwhites. Furthermore, earnings within broad occupational classes averaged higher in the urbanized areas with the larger Negro population concentrations. This suggests that certain influences for prosperity were greater in these communities and that in the absence of the larger numbers of Negroes some of the measures of total status might have been higher.[8] Some of the whites in the urbanized areas

---

[7] Exceptions are the lower unemployment percentage and larger percentage of families with incomes of over $10,000. Among whites in the border urbanized areas and the higher score on the index of status and larger percentage of families with incomes of over $10,000 in the North and West, which may be largely explained by more favorable conditions for people of all races in these urban areas with large nonwhite populations.

[8] The urbanized areas with the larger proportions of nonwhites had larger populations on the average (2,104,560 compared with an average of 305,375 in the other northern and western urbanized areas), and population size is positively associated with occupational and economic status. See Leo Schnore, "Some Correlates of Urban Size: A Replication," *American Journal of Sociology,* 69 (September, 1963), pp. 185–193.

TABLE 1   Various Measures of Status and Percentage Nonwhite

	Whites Percentage Nonwhite				All Races Percentage Nonwhite			
	0–9.9	10–19.9	20–29.9	30 and up	0–9.9	10–19.9	20–29.9	30 and up
Percentage in nonmanual and skilled occupations, 1960	66.0	68.3	74.1	75.6	64.6	64.2	63.0	60.8
IOS	106.1	107.2	109.5	110.3	105.5	105.4	104.8	103.5
Percentage of the civilian male labor force unemployed, in urbanized areas, 1960	4.7	4.0	3.7	3.6	5	4.7	4.4	5.2
Percentage of families in urbanized areas with income less than $3,000, 1959	12.8	11.2	13.8	14.0	13.7	13.7	20.6	26.1
Percentage of families in urbanized areas with income more than $10,000, 1959	18.7	22.9	18.2	17.3	17.5	20.9	15.0	12.6

TABLE 2 Product Moment Coefficients of Correlation between Percentage Nonwhite and Status Variables

Dependent Variable	North and West		Border		South	
	Whites	All Races	Whites	All Races	Whites	All Races
Index of occupational status	+.14	+.10	+.65	+.36	+.33	−.23
Percentage of male civilian labor force unemployed	−.19	+.02	−.45	−.30	−.42	−.10
Percentage of families with income below $3,000	−.22	+.01	−.56	−.10	−.55	+.44
Percentage of families with income of $10,000 and up	+.34	+.22	+.62	+.54	+.27	−.06
Number of employed private household servants (all races) per 1,000 families		+.25		+.27		+.72

in the North and West with the larger numbers of Negroes may benefit from Negro subordination, but the data of this study do not in themselves prove any benefits.

The South is a different story. The more favorable white status in the urbanized areas with 25 percent or more of nonwhites cannot be explained by recent, more rapid economic growth in those localities. On the average their populations increased 36.9 percent from 1950 to 1960, compared with an average growth of 65.1 percent in the other southern urbanized areas. Nor is there any other apparent reason why the southern whites in the localities with the larger percentages of nonwhites should have had greater opportunities for advancement in recent years. In 1960 these urbanized areas were very similar to others in the South in average population size, percentage of workers in manufacturing, and earnings within broad occupational classes.[9] The percentage of nonwhites in the southern urbanized areas apparently depends more upon the historical Negro density in their hinterlands than upon economic factors that have made them relatively attractive or unattractive to Negro migrants. The fact that whites in the southern urbanized areas with large Negro populations have unusually favorable occupational status and employment rates and higher incomes than other southern whites is very likely the consequence of the presence and subordination of the Negroes.

What is the extent and probable nature of white occupational gains in the southern urbanized areas? The concept of "white bonus jobs" intro-

[9] The average population size of urbanized areas with 25 percent or more of nonwhites was 240,498 and other southern urbanized areas averaged 231,347. Average percentage of workers in manufacturing industries was 21.3 and 23.1 respectively in the two classes of urbanized areas.

duced by Cutright is useful here.[10] White bonus jobs are high level jobs available to whites because Negroes are present and subordinated. In other words, they are jobs filled by whites that would be filled by Negroes if the Negroes were not subordinated and that would not exist if the Negroes were not present. In this study, the number and nature of these jobs in the eight southern urbanized areas with 35 percent or more nonwhites are estimated by guessing what the total male occupational distribution would be if Negroes were not present or subordinated. This is done by matching these urbanized areas with eight nonsouthern urbanized areas that had the same proportions of their employed labor forces in manufacturing industries but had no more than 5 percent of nonwhites. Since degree of industrialization is a major determinant of occupational structure, it is assumed that the occupational structure in the southern communities would resemble that in the matched nonsouthern communities if the former had few or no Negroes. The estimated proportion of whites in bonus jobs in the southern urbanized areas is calculated by subtracting the proportion of workers in each class of high level occupations in the estimated total distribution from the proportion in that occupational class in the real white distribution (Table 3).

The greatest apparent numbers of white bonus jobs were as managers, officials, and proprietors, and as sales workers—precisely the occupations in which Negro representation is smallest and in which the greatest numbers of white bonus jobs would be expected.[11]

There also were apparently a sizable number of bonus jobs as craftsmen and foremen and a smaller number as clerical workers—a pattern again congruent with Negro representation in these occupations. An estimated 10 percent of the employed white males in the eight urbanized areas were in bonus jobs, but this apparent gain was partially offset by a smaller-than-normal proportion of whites in professional and technical work. On the other hand, probably many more than 10 percent of the whites in these urbanized areas benefited from the unusually high white occupational distribution. If the whites in the bonus jobs had not been in them, it is unlikely that they would have been at the very lowest levels, where there was the greatest deficit in white jobs. Rather, they would have been at only slightly lower levels, where they would have displaced other whites to slightly lower levels, and so on. Therefore, whites in almost all occupations except the very lowest ones and the professions may have benefited from Negro subordination. Whatever white gains there were may have accrued in some small measure to a majority of the whites in these communities.

CONCLUSIONS AND IMPLICATIONS

The evidence is convincing though not conclusive that many whites in southern urbanized areas benefit occupationally and economically from the presence and subordination of a large disadvantaged Negro population. The primary beneficiaries apparently are middle class southern housewives and white workers in proprietary, managerial, sales, and upper level manual occupations. A majority of these beneficiaries apparently have intermediate rather than high incomes. A good many whites may escape poverty, but few seem to receive very high income as the

---

[10] Cutright, *op. cit.*

[11] For data on Negro representation in the occupational groups in 1960, see Leonard Broom and Norval D. Glenn, *Transformation of the Negro American,* New York: Harper and Row, 1965, p. 110.

TABLE 3 Estimated White Bonus Jobs in Eight Southern Urbanized Areas with 35 Percent or More of Nonwhites, 1960[a]

Occupational Group	Percentage Distribution of All Employed Males in Eight Northern and Western Urbanized Areas	Percentage Distribution of Employed White Males in Eight Southern Urbanized Areas	Difference	Estimated Percentage of White Males in Bonus Jobs in Southern Urbanized Areas	Estimated Number of White Males in Bonus Jobs in Southern Urbanized Areas
Professional, technical, and kindred workers	14.2	12.3	−1.9	—	—
Farmers and farm managers	0.3	0.2	−0.1	—	—
Managers, officials, and proprietors, except farm	13.4	18.0	+4.6	25.6	12,189
Clerical and kindred workers	9.5	9.8	+0.3	3.1	803
Sales workers	9.6	12.6	+3.0	23.8	7,919
Craftsmen, foremen, and kindred workers	21.0	23.1	+2.1	9.1	5,570
Operatives and kindred workers	18.1	17.0	−1.1	—	—
Private household workers	0.1	0.03	−0.1	—	—
Service workers, except private household	6.9	4.0	−2.9	—	—
Farm laborers and foremen	0.4	0.1	−0.3	—	—
Laborers, except farm and mine	6.5	2.8	−3.7	—	—
Total	100.0	100.0		10.0	26,481

[a] Each southern urbanized area is matched with a northern or western urbanized area with the same percentage of its workers (within one percentage point) employed in manufacturing but with less than 5 percent of its population nonwhite. The southern urbanized areas are Albany, Georgia: Birmingham, Alabama; Durham, North Carolina; Jackson, Mississippi; Macon. Georgia; Memphis, Tennessee; Monroe, Louisiana; and Savannah, Georgia. The northern and western urbanized areas are Albany-Schenectady-Troy, New York; Denver, Colorado; Minneapolis-St. Paul, Minnesota; Portland, Oregon-Washington; Reading, Pennsylvania: Salt Lake City, Utah; Sioux City, Iowa-Nebraska-South Dakota; and Spokane, Washington.

The northern and western urbanized areas were larger on the average (515,215) than the southern ones (215,113). Since occupational status is generally somewhat more favorable in larger communities (Schnore, *op. cit.*), any bias introduced by the larger northern and western urbanized areas is toward underestimating the white bonus jobs.

result of the presence and subordination of numerous Negroes.

This study reveals little evidence for the alleged economic dysfunctions of Negro subordination to low level whites. In 1959 earnings within low level occupations were somewhat lower in the urbanized areas with the greater proportions of nonwhites than in other southern urbanized areas, but this difference probably reflects lower earnings of nonwhites rather than of whites. Therefore, the findings of this study do not support the Marxist view that discrimination against Negroes benefits the "capitalist class" but hurts white workers.

The data of this study by themselves are not an adequate basis for conclusions concerning the balance of beneficial and detrimental economic influences of Negro subordination upon the total white population. The detriments may well outweigh the benefits, but the benefits suggested by the data are important nevertheless. However great the detrimental effects may be, they are probably rather widely distributed and may be incurred in some small measure by almost all whites. Taxpayers throughout the country help pay the costs of Negro poverty, and almost everyone is indirectly affected by the relatively low level of Negro buying power. The detrimental effects may be so diffuse and widely distributed that few people are aware of them or are greatly concerned if they are aware of them. Therefore, the detrimental consequences of Negro subordination probably have little effect upon the attitudes and actions of most whites toward Negroes. Any beneficial consequences, by contrast, seem to be concentrated upon relatively few whites, and these whites are more likely to be aware of the effects of Negro subordination. Even those whites who are unaware of the benefits they receive may act in accordance

with their self-interest, since they may adhere to a racial ideology shaped by the interests of earlier generations of whites. If the traditional southern racial ideology continues to be congruent with white economic interests, as the data presented here suggest, the interests will tend to reinforce and perpetuate it, even if many whites who gain from Negro subordination fail to perceive their gain.[12]

It is unlikely that any present white gains from Negro subordination will soon disappear.[13] In time, much lower level work now performed by Negroes will be done by machines, and Negroes will not be so needed to relieve whites of menial tasks. However, there will always be a job hierarchy; intermediate level jobs of today will become low level jobs of tomorrow, and so long as most Negroes are employed and subordinated, they will probably continue to reduce the proportion of white workers at the lowest levels. Since the nonwhite employment rate in the summer of 1965 was virtually the same as it was fifteen years earlier, the unemployment of a majority of Negroes does not seem imminent.[14] And at re-

---

[12] For fuller discussion of the ways in which the interests of whites may affect their action toward Negroes, see Glenn, "The Role of White Resistance," *op. cit.*

[13] The white gain apparently declined little from 1950 to 1960. In his study with 1950 data, the author found that the percentage of employed white nonagricultural males in nonmanual and skilled work was 61.2 in standard metropolitan areas with less than 3 percent Negroes and that it was 73.8 in SMA's with 25 percent or more Negroes—a spread of 12.6 percentage points. The present study reveals that 64.8 percent of the employed white males in urbanized areas with less than 3 percent nonwhites were in nonmanual and skilled occupations, compared with 76.3 percent in urbanized areas with 25 percent or more nonwhites—a spread of 11.5 percentage points.

[14] Nonwhite unemployment was near 8 percent at both dates, but it was somewhat higher (near 10 percent) during much of the early 1960's. Eventually, automation may rapidly increase nonwhite unemployment, as Willhelm and Powell predict, *op. cit.*

cent rates of closure of the Negro-white occupational and income gaps, Negro subordination will remain considerable for many decades.[15]

Therefore, it seems that Negro-white antagonism in the United States is and will long remain partly a matter of realistic conflict. Negroes cannot advance without the loss of traditional white benefits, and it is unlikely that most of the whites who benefit from the inferior status of Negroes will willingly allow Negro advancement.[16] This is not to say that race prejudice and social discrimination against Negroes are strictly or even largely an expression of economic rationality. However, white economic interests and whites' perceptions of these interests very likely play a major role in prompting white resistance to the so-called Negro revolt.

[15] See Leonard Broom and Norval D. Glenn, "When Will America's Negroes Catch Up?" *New Society,* March 25, 1965, pp. 6–7.

[16] However, as the author has pointed out elsewhere, white resistance to Negro advancement is almost certainly reduced in periods of rapid economic growth and rapid upward shifts in the occupational structure, when Negroes can advance without whites incurring any absolute losses in income or occupational status. Even at such times, closing the Negro-white gap entails loss of a white competitive advantage, but whites who nevertheless are moving up are likely to be less aware of and less concerned about this loss. See Norval D. Glenn, "Changes in the American Occupational Structure and Occupational Gains of Negroes," *Social Forces,* 61 (December, 1962), pp. 188–195 and "Some Changes in the Relative Status of American Nonwhites, 1940 to 1960," *Phylon,* 24 (Summer, 1963), pp. 109–122.

SECTION B

ANTECEDENTS AND CORRELATES OF RACIAL CONFLICT

THE articles in the preceding section have documented some factors which create a potential for conflict. Whether or not it occurs depends on the social setting and how people come to define their situation. A degree of institutionalized inequality is a constant feature of most societies; yet the mere fact of inequality, or differences in belief systems, does not in itself result in the appearance of organized conflict groups.

The articles in this section consider some conditions that increase the likelihood of conflict and some factors that affect the form it takes. Unlike the general theoretical articles in Part I, this material deals explicitly with racial conflict, though in several cases (such as Breed's discussion of the effect of pluralism on conflict) propositions are offered which presumably would also hold for nonracial conflict as well. It is important in thinking about a phenomenon such as racial conflict to look for more general propositions and patterns which apply to international, class, generational, or interpersonal conflict as well.

Considering all the diverse forms of racial and ethnic conflict, there have been relatively few comparable efforts to measure how its different forms are interrelated and distributed in terms of time, place, institution, and the nature of participants. We don't even have very good measures for getting at the degree of racial conflict in a given area. In the United States most attention has been given to the distribution of slave revolts, lynchings, sitins, demonstrations, riots, the attitudes of black and white population, and elections or court cases where race is

a salient issue. Attention could also be given to the degree of competition for jobs and housing and interracial fights, assaults, and crime. One measurement problem is the diverse number of phenomena that can be considered instances of racial conflict and the fact that inequality as such is not equivalent to conflict. Another is the variability with respect to factors such as intensity and duration that may exist even among substantively similiar conflict phenomena.

If we had an adequate mapping of how different kinds of conflict were distributed, we could more easily make inferences about what comes before it and what goes along with it, and in this way begin to deal with the conditions which are necessary and sufficient for the occurrence of various kinds of racial conflict.

The logic of inquiry followed by many of the articles in this section is to start with some basic pattern of variation and seek to explain it: for example, the greater questioning of segregation in the North than in the South, the greater questioning of segregation today than in other time periods, differences in racial conflict patterns in industrial and nonindustrial societies, or the difference in protest orientation between religious and nonreligious blacks.

Warren Breed's article is a good example of the sociological level of analysis. It does not deal directly with the individual, with historical development, or with cultural traditions. Rather, it considers an aspect of group structure: the degree of pluralism.

The South, having fewer organizations and fewer individuals and interests represented in the political process, is seen as less pluralistic than the North. This affects the likelihood of conflict occurring. In the South, most of the groups and institutions that do exist are organized around the value of white supremacy. A single party system, the relative absence of labor unions, and a white population, overwhelmingly Anglo-Saxon and Protestant, lead to greater control by a traditional elite and make it much more difficult for issues of a controversial nature to enter the public arena than is the case in the North with its more diverse groups. In such a closed and monolithic system, successful change, particularly in the beginning, is partly dependent on forces outside the system, such as actions of the federal government, nonindigenous activists, and national businesses or churches.

Stanley Lieberson, rather than looking at the nature of current group structure, focuses on the form of the initial historical contact between the dominant and minority group. He shows how this factor may greatly condition the subsequent patterns of race relations and conflict. He identifies two basic patterns of contact: those where a native population is made subordinate by a migrant group, as in black-white relations in South Africa, and those where a migrant population is made subordinate in the country to which it moves, as in the case of blacks or Japanese in the United States. The former is more likely to see acrimonious conflict of a nationalist variety, whereas in the latter situation emphasis is more likely to be put on inclusion and assimilation.

Pierre Van Den Berghe argues that, regardless of the always unique factors in a given ethnic contact situation, attention to very broad political and economic factors can tell us a considerable amount about the nature of intergroup relations. Considering such

factors, he identifies two types of racial systems: paternalistic and competitive. These correspond broadly to the distinction between rural-nonindustrial and urban-industrial societies. Racial patterns in these two systems are contrasted in terms of a number of variables such as etiquette, forms of aggression, segregation, and stereotypes. Competitive systems, such as our own society, are marked by much greater overt racial conflict and antagonism than are paternalistic systems such as nineteenth-century colonial regimes.

Tamotsu Shibutani and Kian M. Kwan ask: What are some of the conditions under which an already established color line breaks down? What leads an ethnic group to actively challenge institutionalized inequality? Using a wide range of historical and comparative material, they note the importance of technological innovations, demographic shifts, wars, conquest, and the diffusion of new ideas which upset customary adjustments and lead to a questioning of the status quo.

The changes that Shibutani and Kwan look at often lead a minority to actively question its subordinate position. Their challenge then leads to response from the dominant group. Conflict is a reciprocal process where contending groups interact with each other and respond to the actual and expected moves of their opponents. Much recent American research has gone into minority group protest and violence. Yet of equal or greater historical significance has been the conflict and violence initiated by those with power against minority racial, ethnic, and religious groups. Sometimes this is in establishing the color line, sometimes when minority groups rise to question it, but very often it is as a scapegoating device which may force mass indignation away from its basic source and/or aid in the exploitation of the minority. The article by George Simpson and Milton Yinger focuses on the latter type of dominant group initiated conflict. They note that ideas of prejudice and attacks on minority groups are often a tool in the struggle for scarce resources. Racial oppression is more likely when it is economically profitable for the dominant group. Attacks on minorities and scapegoating are also seen to be more likely during periods of economic depression and general social upheaval when anxiety and frustration may be more pronounced.

The article by James A. Geschwender looks at a particular question at one point in time. What accounts for the emergence of the contemporary civil rights movement? Five hypotheses are presented and then considered in light of data contrasting the economic condition of whites and blacks. These hypotheses deal with objective "structural" conditions that involve the position of whites and blacks in relation to each other. The easy assumption that the greater the inequality, the greater the overt conflict does not seem to hold. Changes in objective conditions are seen to cause feelings of relative deprivation on the part of blacks, which in turn increases the likelihood of challenges to the status quo.

Here we see assumptions being made about the connection between objective social conditions, such as the relative position of groups to each other or over time, and the perceptions and attitudes of particular individuals. Although the relationship is by no means one to one, particular social conditions are likely to give rise to certain individual attitudes.

This brings us to another level at which the correlates of conflict involvement may be considered: that of the individual and his or her feelings and perception. Here one studies the demographic, social, and psychological characteristics of particular people. In the article on religion and protest I ask how the social institution of religion affects individual black protest attitudes and note that it generally has an inhibiting effect. Further analysis of this data elsewhere reveals that a protest orientation is more likely among those who are better-educated, more-involved in voluntary organizations, and who have a positive self-image, high morale, and a sophisticated world view.[1]

However, the mere holding of ideas or an ideology that calls forth conflict action is not sufficient. For such attitudes to lead to activism an individual must first be "available" and in a position to undertake the often considerable hardships and risks involved. This partly explains the greater involvement of the young, those with few, if any, familial responsibilities, and those not in occupations that would subject them to sanctioning for their involvement.

Furthermore, individuals who hold attitudes that are conducive to conflict action and are "available" for action are more likely to actually become involved when they are in communities with certain characteristics. In the South, for example, during the beginning phases of the civil rights movement, other factors being equal, black protest was more likely in relatively urbanized communities, those with a higher socioeconomic level, those where organizations such as the NAACP were viable before the beginning of the current struggle and where a Negro college was located, and those where blacks were a relatively smaller percentage of the population. These factors, in turn, no doubt act back on the nature of the attitudes an individual holds.

[1] G. Marx, *Protest and Prejudice* (New York: Harper & Row, Torchbook edition, 1969).

13
A Societal Theory of Race and Ethnic Relations*
STANLEY LIEBERSON

"In the relations of races there is a cycle of events which tends everywhere to repeat itself."[1] Park's assertion served as a prologue to the now classical cycle of competition, conflict, accommodation, and assimilation. A number of other attempts have been made to formulate phases or stages ensuing from the initial contacts between racial and ethnic groups.[2] However, the sharp contrasts between relatively harmonious race relations in Brazil and Hawaii and the current racial turmoil in South Africa and Indonesia serve to illustrate the difficulty in stating—to say nothing of interpreting—an inevitable "natural history" of race and ethnic relations.

Many earlier race and ethnic cycles were, in fact, narrowly confined to a rather specific set of groups or contact situations. Bogardus, for example, explicitly limited his synthesis to Mexican and Oriental immigrant groups on the

west coast of the United States and suggested that this is but one of many different cycles of relations between immigrants and native Americans.[3] Similarly, the Australian anthropologist Price developed three phases that appear to account for the relationships between white English-speaking migrants and the aborigines of Australia, Maoris in New Zealand, and Indians of the United States and Canada.[4]

This paper seeks to present a rudimentary theory of the development of race and ethnic relations that systematically accounts for differences between societies in such divergent consequences of contact as racial nationalism and warfare, assimilation and fusion, and extinction. It postulates that the critical problem on a societal level in racial or ethnic contact is initially each population's maintenance and development of a social order compatible with its ways of life prior to contact. The crux of any cycle must, therefore, deal with political, social, and economic institutions. The emphasis given in earlier cycles to one group's dominance of another in these areas is therefore hardly surprising.[5]

Although we accept this institutional approach, the thesis presented here is that knowledge of the nature of one group's domination over another in the political, social, and economic spheres is a necessary but insufficient prerequisite for predicting or interpreting the final and intermediate stages of racial and ethnic contact. Rather, institutional factors are considered in terms of a distinction between two major types of contact situations: contacts involving subordination of an indigenous population by a migrant group, for example, Negro-white relations in South Africa;

*[Reprinted by permission of the author from the *American Sociological Review*, Vol. 26, no. 6, December 1961, pp. 902–910.]

[1] Robert E. Park, *Race and Culture*, Glencoe, Ill.: The Free Press, 1950, p. 150.

[2] For example, Emory S. Bogardus, "A Race-Relations Cycle," *American Journal of Sociology*, 35 (January, 1930), pp. 612–617; W. O. Brown, "Culture Contact and Race Conflict" in E. B. Reuter, ed., *Race and Culture Contacts*, New York: McGraw-Hill, 1934, pp. 34–47; E. Franklin Frazier, *Race and Culture Contacts in the Modern World*, New York: Alfred A Knopf, 1957, pp. 32ff.; Clarence E. Glick, "Social Roles and Types in Race Relations" in Andrew W. Lind, ed., *Race Relations in World Perspective*, Honolulu: Univ. of Hawaii Press, 1955, pp. 243–262; Edward Nelson Palmer, "Culture Contacts and Population Growth" in Joseph J. Spengler and Otis Dudley Duncan, ed., *Population Theory and Policy*, Glencoe, Ill.: The Free Press, 1956, pp. 410–415; A. Grenfell Price, *White Settlers and Native Peoples*, Melbourne: Georgian House, 1950. For summaries of several of these cycles, see Brewton Berry, *Race and Ethnic Relations*, Boston: Houghton Mifflin, 1958, chap. 6.

[3] Bogardus, *op. cit.*, p. 612.

[4] Price, *op. cit.*

[5] Intraurban stages of contact are not considered here.

and contacts involving subordination of a migrant population by an indigenous racial or ethnic group, for example, Japanese migrants to the United States.

After considering the societal issues inherent in racial and ethnic contact, the distinction developed between migrant and indigenous superordination will be utilized in examining each of the following dimensions of race relations: political and economic control, multiple ethnic contacts, conflict and assimilation. The terms "race" and "ethnic" are used interchangeably.

DIFFERENCES INHERENT IN CONTACT

Most situations of ethnic contact involve at least one indigenous group and at least one group migrating to the area. The only exception at the initial point in contact would be the settlement of an uninhabited area by two or more groups. By "indigenous" is meant not necessarily the aborigines, but rather a population sufficiently established in an area so as to possess the institutions and demographic capacity for maintaining some minimal form of social order through generations. Thus a given spatial area may have different indigenous groups through time. For example, the indigenous population of Australia is presently largely white and primarily of British origin, although the Tasmanoids and Australoids were once in possession of the area.[6] A similar racial shift may be observed in the populations indigenous to the United States.

Restricting discussion to the simplest of contact situations, i.e., involving one migrant and one established population, we can generally observe sharp differences in their social organization at the time of contact. The indigenous population has an established and presumably stable organization prior to the

arrival of migrants, i.e., government, economic activities adapted to the environment and the existing techniques of resource utilization, kinship, stratification, and religious systems.[7] On the basis of a long series of migration studies, we may be reasonably certain that the social order of a migrant population's homeland is not wholly transferred to their new settlement.[8] Migrants are required to make at least some institutional adaptations and innovations in view of the presence of an indigenous population, the demographic selectivity of migration, and differences in habitat.

For example, recent postwar migrations from Italy and the Netherlands indicate considerable selectivity in age and sex from the total populations of these countries. Nearly half of 30,000 males leaving the Netherlands in 1955 were between twenty and thirty-nine years of age whereas only one quarter of the male population was of these ages.[9] Similarly, over 40,000 males in this age range accounted for somewhat more than half of Italy's male emigrants in 1951, although they comprise roughly 30 percent of the male population of Italy.[10] In both countries, male emigrants exceed females in absolute numbers as well as in comparison with the sex ratios of their nation. That these cases are far from extreme can be illustrated with Oriental migration data. In 1920, for example, there were 38,000 foreign-born Chinese adult males in the United States, but only 2,000 females of the same group.[11]

[6] Price, op. cit., chaps. 6 and 7.

[7] Glick, op. cit., p. 244.
[8] See, for example, Brinley Thomas, "International Migration" in Philip M. Hauser and Otis Dudley Duncan, eds., The Study of Population, Chicago: University of Chicago Press, 1959, pp. 523–526.
[9] United Nations, Demographic Yearbook, 1957, pp. 147, 645.
[10] United Nations, Demographic Yearbook, 1954, pp. 131, 669.
[11] R. D. McKenzie, Oriental Exclusion, Chicago: University of Chicago Press, 1928, p. 83.

In addition to these demographic shifts, the new physical and biological conditions of existence require the revision and creation of social institutions if the social order known in the old country is to be approximated and if the migrants are to survive. The migration of eastern and southern European peasants around the turn of the century to urban industrial centers of the United States provides a well-documented case of radical changes in occupational pursuits as well as the creation of a number of institutions in response to the new conditions of urban life, e.g., mutual aid societies, national churches, and financial institutions.

In short, when two populations begin to occupy the same habitat but do not share a single order, each group endeavors to maintain the political and economic conditions that are at least compatible with the institutions existing before contact. These conditions for the maintenances of institutions can not only differ for the two groups in contact, but are often conflicting. European contacts with the American Indian, for example, led to the decimation of the latter's sources of sustenance and disrupted religious and tribal forms of organization. With respect to a population's efforts to maintain its social institutions, we may therefore assume that the presence of another ethnic group is an important part of the environment. Further, if groups in contact differ in their capacity to impose changes on the other group, then we may expect to find one group "superordinate" and the other population "subordinate" in maintaining or developing a suitable environment.

It is here that efforts at a single cycle of race and ethnic relations must fail. For it is necessary to introduce a distinction in the nature or form of subordination before attempting to predict whether conflict or relatively harmonious assimilation will develop. As we shall shortly show, the race relations cycle in areas where the migrant group is superordinate and indigenous group subordinate differs sharply from the stage in societies composed of a superordinate indigenous group and subordinate migrants.[12]

POLITICAL AND ECONOMIC CONTROL

Emphasis is placed herein on economic and political dominance since it is assumed that control of these institutions will be instrumental in establishing a suitable milieu for at least the population's own social institutions, e.g., educational, religious, and kinship, as well as control of such major cultural artifacts as language.

Migrant superordination

When the population migrating to a new contact situation is superior in technology (particularly weapons) and more tightly organized than the indigenous group, the necessary conditions for maintaining the migrants' political and economic institutions are usually imposed on the indigenous population. Warfare, under such circumstances, often occurs early in the contacts between the two groups as the migrants begin to interfere with the natives' established order. There is frequently conflict even if the initial contact was friendly. Price, for example, has observed the following consequences of white invasion and subordination of the indigenous populations of Australia, Canada, New Zealand, and the United States:

During an opening period of pioneer invasion on moving frontiers the whites decimated the natives with their diseases; occupied their lands by seizure or by pseudo-purchase, slaughtered those who resisted;

[12] See, for example, Reuter's distinction between two types of direct contact in E. B. Reuter, ed., *op. cit.*, pp. 4–7.

intensified tribal warfare by supplying white weapons; ridiculed and disrupted native religions, society, and culture, and generally reduced the unhappy peoples to a state of despondency under which they neither desired to live, nor to have children to undergo similar conditions.[13]

The numerical decline of indigenous populations after their initial subordination to a migrant group, whether caused by warfare, introduction of venereal and other diseases, or disruption of sustenance activities, has been documented for a number of contact situations in addition to those discussed by Price.[14]

In addition to bringing about these demographic and economic upheavals, the superordinate migrants frequently create political entities that are not at all coterminous with the boundaries existing during the indigenous populations' supremacy prior to contact. For example, the British and Boers in southern Africa carved out political states that included areas previously under the control of separate and often warring groups.[15] Indeed, European alliances with feuding tribes were often used as a fulcrum for the territorial expansion of whites into southern Africa.[16] The bifurcation of tribes into two nations and the migrations of groups across newly created national boundaries are both consequences of the somewhat arbitrary nature of the political entities created in regions of migrant superordination.[17] This incorporation of diverse indigenous populations into a single territorial unit under the dominance of a migrant group has consider-

able importance for later developments in this type of racial and ethnic contact.

Indigenous superordination

When a population migrates to a subordinate position considerably less conflict occurs in the early stages. The movements of many European and Oriental populations to political, economic, and social subordination in the United States were not converted into warfare, nationalism, or long-term conflict. Clearly, the occasional labor and racial strife marking the history of immigration of the United States is not on the same level as the efforts to expel or revolutionize the social order. American Negroes, one of the most persistently subordinated migrant groups in the country, never responded in significant numbers to the encouragement of migration to Liberia. The single important large-scale nationalistic effort, Marcus Garvey's Universal Negro Improvement Association, never actually led to mass emigration of Negroes.[18] By contrast, the indigenous American Indians fought long and hard to preserve control over their habitat.

In interpreting differences in the effects of migrant and indigenous subordination, the migrants must be considered in the context of the options available to the group. Irish migrants to the United States in the 1840's, for example, although clearly subordinate to native whites of other origins, fared better economically than if they had remained in their mother country.[19] Further, the option of returning to the homeland often exists for populations migrating to subordinate situations.

[13] Price, *op. cit.,* p. 1.

[14] Stephen Roberts, *Population Problems of the Pacific,* London: George Routledge & Sons, 1927.

[15] John A. Barnes, "Race Relations in the Development of Southern Africa" in Lind, ed., *op. cit.*

[16] *Ibid.*

[17] Witness the current controversies between tribes in the newly created Congo Republic. Also, for a list of tribes living on both sides of the border of the Republic of Sudan, see Karol

Józef Krótki, "Demographic Survey of Sudan" in *The Population of Sudan,* report on the sixth annual conference, Khartoum: Philosophical Society of Sudan, 1958, p. 35.

[18] John Hope Franklin, *From Slavery to Freedom,* 2d ed., New York: Alfred Knopf, 1956, pp. 234–238, 481–483.

[19] Oscar Handlin, *Boston's Immigrants,* rev. ed., Cambridge, Mass.: The Belknap Press of Harvard University Press, 1959, chap. 2.

Jerome reports that net migration to the United States between the midyears of 1907 and 1923 equaled roughly 65 per cent of gross immigration.[20] This indicates that immigrant dissatisfaction with subordination or other conditions of contact can often be resolved by withdrawal from the area. Recently subordinated indigenous groups, by contrast, are perhaps less apt to leave their habitat so readily.

Finally, when contacts between racial and ethnic groups are under the control of the indigenous population, threats of demographic and institutional imbalance are reduced since the superordinate populations can limit the numbers and groups entering. For example, when Oriental migration to the United States threatened whites, sharp cuts were executed in the quotas.[21] Similar events may be noted with respect to the decline of immigration from the so-called new sources of eastern and southern Europe. Whether a group exercises its control over immigration far before it is actually under threat is, of course, not germane to the point that immigrant restriction provides a mechanism whereby potential conflict is prevented.

In summary, groups differ in the conditions necessary for maintaining their respective social orders. In areas where the migrant group is dominant, frequently the indigenous population suffers sharp numerical declines and their economic and political institutions are seriously undermined. Conflict often accompanies the establishment of migrant superordination. Subordinate indigenous populations generally have no alternative location and do not control the numbers of new ethnic popula-

tions admitted into their area. By contrast, when the indigenous population dominates the political and economic conditions, the migrant group is introduced into the economy of the indigenous population. Although subordinate in their new habitat, the migrants may fare better than if they remained in their homeland. Hence their subordination occurs without great conflict. In addition, the migrants usually have the option of returning to their homeland and the indigenous population controls the number of new immigrants in the area.

MULTIPLE ETHNIC CONTACTS

Although the introduction of a third major ethnic or racial group frequently occurs in both types of societies distinguished here, there are significant differences between conditions in habitats under indigenous domination and areas where a migrant population is superordinate. Chinese and Indian migrants, for example, were often welcomed by whites in areas where large indigenous populations were suppressed, but these migrants were restricted in the white mother country. Consideration of the causes and consequences of multiethnic contacts is therefore made in terms of the two types of racial and ethnic contact.

Migrant superordination

In societies where the migrant population is superordinate, it is often necessary to introduce new immigrant groups to fill the niches created in the revised economy of the area. The subordinate indigenous population frequently fails, at first, to participate in the new economic and political order introduced by migrants. For example, because of the numerical decline of Fijians after contact with whites and their unsatisfactory work habits, approximately 60,000

---

[20] Harry Jerome, *Migration and Business Cycles,* New York: National Bureau of Economic Research, 1926, pp. 43–44.

[21] See George Eaton Simpson and J. Milton Yinger, *Racial and Cultural Minorities,* rev. ed., New York: Harper & Brothers, 1958, pp. 126–132.

persons migrated from India to the sugar plantations of Fiji under the indenture system between 1879 and 1916.[22] For similar reasons, as well as the demise of slavery, large numbers of Indians were also introduced to such areas of indigenous subordination as Mauritius, British Guiana, Trinidad, and Natal.[23] The descendants of these migrants comprise the largest single ethnic group in several of these areas.

McKenzie, after observing the negligible participation of the subordinated indigenous populations of Alaska, Hawaii, and Malaya in contrast to the large numbers of Chinese, Indian, and other Oriental immigrants, offers the following interpretation:

The indigenous peoples of many of the frontier zones of modern industrialism are surrounded by their own web of culture and their own economic structure. Consequently they are slow to take part in the new economy especially as unskilled laborers. It is the individual who is widely removed from his native habitat that is most adaptable to the conditions imposed by capitalism in frontier regions. Imported labor cannot so easily escape to its home village when conditions are distasteful as can the local population.[24]

Similarly, the Indians of the United States played a minor role in the new economic activities introduced by white settlers and, further, were not used successfully as slaves.[25] Frazier reports that Negro slaves were utilized in the West Indies and Brazil after unsuccessful efforts to enslave the indigenous

Indian populations.[26] Large numbers of Asiatic Indians were brought to South Africa as indentured laborers to work in the railways, mines, and plantations introduced by whites.[27]

This migration of workers into areas where the indigenous population was either unable or insufficient to work in the newly created economic activities was also marked by a considerable flow back to the home country. For example, nearly 3.5 million Indians left the Madras Presidency for overseas between 1903 and 1912, but close to 3 million returned during this same period.[28] However, as we observed earlier, large numbers remained overseas and formed major ethnic populations in a number of countries. Current difficulties of the ten million Chinese in Southeast Asia are in large part due to their settlement in societies where the indigenous populations were subordinate.

Indigenous superordination

We have observed that in situations of indigenous superordination the call for new immigrants from other ethnic and racial populations is limited in a manner that prevents the indigenous group's loss of political and economic control. Under such conditions, no single different ethnic or racial population is sufficiently large in number of strength to challenge the supremacy of the indigenous population.

After whites attained dominance in Hawaii, that land provided a classic case of the substitution of one ethnic group after another during a period when large numbers of immigrants were needed for the newly created and expanding plantation economy. According to Lind, the shifts from Chinese to

[22] K. L. Gillion, "The Sources of Indian Emigration to Fiji," *Population Studies,* 10 (November, 1956), p. 139; I. M. Cumpston, "A Survey of Indian Immigration to British Tropical Colonies to 1910," *ibid.,* pp. 158–159.

[23] Cumpston, *op. cit.,* pp. 158–165.

[24] R. D. McKenzie, "Cultural and Racial Differences as Bases of Human Symbiosis" in Kimball Young, ed., *Social Attitudes,* New York: Henry Holt, 1931, p. 157.

[25] Franklin, *op. cit.,* p. 47.

[26] Frazier, *op. cit.,* pp. 107–108.

[27] Leo Kuper, Hilstan Watts, and Ronald Davies, *Durban: A Study in Racial Ecology,* London: Jonathan Cape, 1958, p. 25.

[28] Gillion, *op. cit.,* p. 149.

Japanese and Portuguese immigrants and the later shifts to Puerto Rican, Korean, Spanish, Russian, and Philippine sources for the plantation laborers were due to conscious efforts to prevent any single group from obtaining too much power.[29] Similarly, the exclusion of Chinese from the United States mainland stimulated the migration of the Japanese and, in turn, the later exclusion of Japanese led to increased migration from Mexico.[30]

In brief, groups migrating to situations of multiple ethnic contact are thus subordinate in both types of contact situations. However, in societies where whites are superordinate but do not settle as an indigenous population, other racial and ethnic groups are admitted in large numbers and largely in accordance with economic needs of the revised economy of the habitat. By contrast, when a dominant migrant group later becomes indigenous, in the sense that the area becomes one of permanent settlement through generations for the group, migrant populations from new racial and ethnic stocks are restricted in number and source.

CONFLICT AND ASSIMILATION

From a comparison of the surge of racial nationalism and open warfare in parts of Africa and Asia or the retreat of superordinate migrants from the former Dutch East Indies and French Indochina, on the one hand, with the fusion of populations in many nations of western Europe or the "cultural pluralism" of the United States and Switzerland, on the other, one must conclude that neither conflict nor assimilation is an inevitable outcome of racial and ethnic contact. Our distinction, how-

ever, between two classes of race and ethnic relations is directly relevant to consideration of which of these alternatives different populations in contact will take. In societies where the indigenous population at the initial contact is subordinate, warfare and nationalism often—although not always—develop later in the cycle of relations. By contrast, relations between migrants and indigenous populations that are subordinate and superordinate, respectively, are generally without long-term conflict.

Migrant superordination

Through time, the subordinated indigenous population begins to participate in the economy introduced by the migrant group and, frequently, a concomitant disruption of previous forms of social and economic organization takes place. This, in turn, has significant implications for the development of both nationalism and a greater sense of racial unity. In many African states, where Negroes were subdivided into ethnic groups prior to contact with whites, the racial unity of the African was created by the occupation of their habitat by white invaders.[31] The categorical subordination of Africans by whites as well as the dissolution and decay of previous tribal and ethnic forms of organization are responsible for the creation of racial consciousness among the indigenous populations.[32] As the indigenous group becomes increasingly incorporated within the larger system, both the saliency of their subordinate position and its significance increase.

---

[29] Andrew W. Lind, *An Island Community*, Chicago: University of Chicago Press, 1938, pp. 218–229.

[30] McKenzie, *Oriental Exclusion, op. cit.*, p. 181.

[31] For a discussion of territorial and tribal movements, see James S. Coleman, "Current Political Movements in Africa," *The Annals of the American Academy of Political and Social Science*, 298 (March, 1955), pp. 95–108.

[32] For a broader discussion of emergent nationalism, see Thomas Hodgkin, *Nationalism in Colonial Africa*, New York: New York University Press, 1957; Everett C. Hughes, "New Peoples" in Lind, ed., *op. cit.*, pp. 95–115.

No alternative exists for the bulk of the native population other than the destruction or revision of the institutions of political, economic, and social subordination.

Further, it appears that considerable conflict occurs in those areas where the migrants are not simply superordinate, but where they themselves have also become, in a sense, indigenous by maintaining an established population through generations. In Table 1, for example, one can observe how sharply the white populations of Algeria and the Union of South Africa differ from those in nine other African countries with respect to the percent born in the country of settlement. Thus, two among the eleven African countries for which such data were available[33] are outstanding with respect to both racial turmoil and the high proportion of whites born in the country. To be sure,

TABLE 1   Nativity of the White Populations of Selected African Countries, Circa 1950

Country	Percent of Whites Born in Country
Algeria	79.8
Basutoland	37.4
Bechuanaland	39.5
Morocco[a]	37.1[b]
Northern Rhodesia	17.7
Southern Rhodesia	31.5
South West Africa[c]	45.1
Swaziland	41.2
Tanganyika	47.6
Uganda	43.8
Union of South Africa	89.7

[a] Former French zone.

[b] Persons born in former Spanish zone or in Tangier are included as native.

[c] Excluding Walvis Bay.

Source: United Nations, *Demographic Yearbook,* 1956, Table 5.

Note: Other nonindigenous groups included when necessary breakdown by race is not given.

[33] United Nations, *Demographic Yearbook, 1956,* Table 5.

other factors operate to influence the nature of racial and ethnic relations. However, these data strongly support our suggestions with respect to the significance of differences between indigenous and migrant forms of contact. Thus where the migrant population becomes established in the new area, it is all the more difficult for the indigenous subordinate group to change the social order.

Additionally, where the formerly subordinate indigenous population has become dominant through the expulsion of the superordinate group, the situation faced by nationalities introduced to the area under earlier conditions of migrant superordination changes radically. For example, as we noted earlier, Chinese were welcomed in many parts of Southeast Asia where the newly subordinated indigenous populations were unable or unwilling to fill the economic niches created by the white invaders. However after whites were expelled and the indigenous populations obtained political mastery, the gates to further Chinese immigration were fairly well closed and there has been increasing interference with the Chinese already present. In Indonesia, where Chinese immigration had been encouraged under Dutch domain, the newly created indigenous government allows only token immigration and has formulated a series of laws and measures designed to interfere with and reduce Chinese commercial activities.[34] Thompson and Adloff observe that

Since the war, the Chinese have been subjected to increasingly restrictive measures throughout Southeast Asia, but the severity and effectiveness of these has varied with the degree to which the native nationalists are in control of their countries and feel

[34] B. H. M. Vlekke, *Indonesia in 1956,* The Hague: Netherlands Institute of International Affairs, 1957, p. 88.

their national existence threatened by the Chinese.[35]

Indigenous superordination

By contrast, difficulties between subordinate migrants and an already dominant indigenous population occur within the context of a consensual form of government, economy, and social institutions. However confused and uncertain may be the concept of assimilation and its application in operational terms,[36] it is important to note that assimilation is essentially a very different phenomenon in the two types of societies distinguished here.

Where populations migrate to situations of subordination, the issue has generally been with respect to the migrants' capacity and willingness to become an integral part of the on-going social order. For example, this has largely been the case in the United States where the issue of "new" versus "old" immigrant groups hinged on the alleged inferiorities of the former.[37] The occasional flurries of violence under this form of contact have been generally initiated by the dominant indigenous group and with respect to such threats against the social order as the cheap labor competition of Orientals on the west coast,[38] the nativist fears of Irish Catholic political domination of Boston in the nineteenth century,[39] or the desecration of sacred

principles by Mexican "zoot-suiters" in Los Angeles.[40]

The conditions faced by subordinate migrants in Australia and Canada after the creation of indigenous white societies in these areas are similar to that of the United States; that is, limited and sporadic conflict, and great emphasis on the assimilation of migrants. Striking and significant contrasts to the general pattern of subordinate immigrant assimilation in those societies, however, are provided by the differences between the assimilation of Italian and German immigrants in Australia as well as the position of French Canadians in eastern Canada.

French Canadians have maintained their language and other major cultural and social attributes whereas nineteenth- and twentieth-century immigrants are in process of merging into the predominantly English-speaking Canadian society. Although broader problems of territorial segregation are involved,[41] the critical difference between French Canadians and later groups is that the former had an established society in the new habitat prior to the British conquest of Canada and were thus largely able to maintain their social and cultural unity without significant additional migration from France.[42]

Similarly, in finding twentieth-century Italian immigrants in Australia more prone to cultural assimilation than

[35] Virginia Thompson and Richard Adloff, *Minority Problems in Southeast Asia,* Stanford, California: Stanford University Press, 1955, p. 3.

[36] See, for example, International Union for the Scientific Study of Population, "Cultural Assimilation of Immigrants," *Population Studies,* supplement, March, 1950.

[37] Oscar Handlin, *Race and Nationality in American Life,* Garden City, New York: Doubleday Anchor Books, 1957, chap. 5.

[38] Simpson and Yinger, *op. cit.*

[39] Oscar Handlin, *Boston's Immigrants, op. cit.,* chap. 7.

[40] Ralph Turner and Samuel J. Surace, "Zoot-Suiters and Mexicans: Symbols in Crowd Behavior," *American Journal of Sociology,* 62 (July, 1956), pp. 14–20.

[41] It is, however, suggestive to consider whether the isolated settlement of an area by a racial, religious, or ethnic group would be permitted in other than frontier conditions. Consider, for example, the difficulties faced by Mormons until they reached Utah.

[42] See Everett C. Hughes, *French Canada in Transition,* Chicago: University of Chicago Press, 1943.

were German migrants to that nation in the 1800's, Borrie emphasized the fact that Italian migration occurred after Australia had become an independent nation-state. By contrast, Germans settled in what was a pioneer colony without an established general social order and institutions. Thus, for example, Italian children were required to attend Australian schools and learn English, whereas the German immigrants were forced to establish their own educational program.[43]

Thus the consequences of racial and ethnic contact may also be examined in terms of the two types of superordinate-subordinate contact situations considered. For the most part, subordinate migrants appear to be more rapidly assimilated than are subordinate indigenous populations. Further, the subordinate migrant group is generally under greater pressure to assimilate, at least in the gross sense of "assimilation" such as language, than are subordinate indigenous populations. In addition, warfare or racial nationalism—when it does occur—tends to be in societies where the indigenous population is subordinate. If the indigenous movement succeeds, the economic and political position of racial and ethnic populations introduced to the area under migrant dominance may become tenuous.

A FINAL NOTE

It is suggested that interest be revived in the conditions accounting for societal variations in the process of relations between racial and ethnic groups. A societal theory of race relations, based on the migrant-indigenous and superordinate-subordinate distinctions de-

veloped above, has been found to offer an orderly interpretation of differences in the nature of race and ethnic relations in the contact situations considered. Since, however, systematic empirical investigation provides a far more rigorous test of the theory's merits and limitations, comparative cross-societal studies are needed.

14
Paternalistic versus Competitive Race Relations*
P. VAN DEN BERGHE

A TYPOLOGY OF RACE RELATIONS

Many scholars, such as Wirth, Cox, Simpson and Yinger, Wagley, Lieberson, and Merton and Frazier, have presented typologies of race relations, but their schemes have been of restricted use. These typologies have generally failed to relate race relations to the total society; some have been based on a single criterion such as aspirations of the subordinated group, policies of the dominant group, the indigenous or immigrant status of the dominant group, or the basis of group definition. Others have been constructed around the interrelation of two dichotomous variables, using the device of the two-by-two table. Others have been little more than ad hoc lists of situations without clarifying the variables along which the distinctions were made.

In an attempt to transcend the limitations of these approaches, I tried, by the Weberian ideal-type method, to arrive at a classification meeting the following criteria:

[43] W. D. Borrie assisted by D. R. G. Packer, *Italians and Germans in Australia,* Melbourne: F. W. Cheshire, 1954, *passim.*

*[Reprinted from *Race and Racism,* pp. 24–34 by permission of the publisher, John Wiley and Sons, Inc.]

1 Comparative applicability, at least to the multiracial societies created by the expansion of Europe since the fifteenth century which together account for most of the world's racially stratified societies.

2 Historical usability in analyzing the evolution of race relations within a given society.

3 Specification of the dimensions or variables along which the typology is constructed.

4 Integration of the specific syndrome of race relations with the rest of the social structure.

Students of comparative race relations cannot but note basic similarities in social structure which transcend cultural differences. Thus, as rightly noted by Tannenbaum, the racial attitudes of the Spanish and Portuguese and the legal and religious status of slaves in Latin America were quite different from those in the English Colonies.[1] Overriding these differences were close similarities in structure between the slave plantations of northeastern Brazil and the antebellum southern United States. (Gilberto Freyre, in comparing these two slave regimes, used the phrase "latifundiary monoculture" to describe them.[2] Indeed, race relations in eighteenth-century Brazil resemble those in the antebellum southern United States more closely than the antebellum situation resembles contemporary United States race relations.

If two societies with widely different cultural traditions can more or less independently develop similar racial situations and institutions, if, conversely, the history of a given country can be marked by profound changes and discontinuities, and, furthermore, if abrupt qualitative changes in race relations can be shown to coincide with structural changes in the society at large, it is reasonable to accept that basic as-

[1] Frank Tannenbaum, *Slave and Citizen,* New York, Knopf, 1947.
[2] Gilberto Freyre, *The Master and the Slave,* New York, Knopf, 1946.

pects of the social structure exert a considerable degree of determinism on the prevailing type of race relations. Such is the fundamental argument underlying the typology of race relations which I shall present shortly.

By stressing similarities between several societies of the same type, I do not reject, of course, the notion that important differences also exist between them, for indeed differences always exist between any two societies which have developed independently of one another. In other terms, *the factors or variables that we shall examine do not account for all of the variance in race relations.* My argument is simply that cultural idiosyncracies specific to a given place and time, far from preventing cross cultural uniformities and making generalizations impossible, leave a large residual of similarities unaccounted for except in terms of the broad economic and political infrastructure.

On the basis of this general formulation, I suggest that it is useful to analyze race relations in terms of two ideal types, which, for lack of better words, I have called "paternalistic" and "competitive."

1 Race relations in a *paternalistic* system follow the master-servant model. The dominant group, often a small minority of less than 10 percent of the total population, rationalizes its rule in an ideology of benevolent despotism and regards members of the subordinate group as childish, immature, irresponsible, exuberant, improvident, fun-loving, good humored, and happy-go-lucky; in short, as inferior but lovable as long as they stay in "their place." In the subordinate group there is generally an ostensible accommodation to inferior status and sometimes even an internalization of inferiority feelings expressed through self-deprecation.

Roles and statuses are sharply defined along racial lines, with a rigidly ascriptive division of labor and a great asymmetry and complementarity in social relationships. Social distance between racial castes is maximized and symbolized by an elaborate and punctilious etiquette involving nonreciprocal terms of address, sumptuary regulations, and repeated manifestations of subservience and dominance. This great degree of social distance allows close symbiosis and even intimacy, without any threat to status inequalities. Consequently, physical segregation is not prominently used as a mechanism of social control and may, in fact, be totally absent between masters and servants living together in a state of "distant intimacy." Miscegenation in the form of institutionalized concubinage between women of the subordinate group and men of the dominant group is not only frequent but accepted by the ruling group as another of its legitimate prerogatives and forms of exploitation. The offspring of such unions is either assimilated to the subordinate group (often with a somewhat privileged status within it) or it develops into a distinct intermediate group. Racial prejudice on the part of the ruling group is, of course, present but seems to be related more directly to economic and social position than to any deep underlying psychodynamics. This prejudice often takes the form of "pseudotolerance" as exemplified by professions of love for the subordinate group as long as inequality is unchallenged. Genteel benevolence and noblesse oblige rather than virulent hatred characterize the paternalistic brand of bigotry. Open, collective aggression in a paternalistic system originates almost invariably from the subordinate group in the form of slave rebellions, and revivalistic, messianistic, or nationalistic movements.

A paternalistic type of race relations is characteristic of fairly complex but preindustrial societies, in which agriculture and handicraft production constitute the bases of the economy. Large-scale production of a cash-crop on slave plantations is a common and perhaps the "purest" case of paternalistic relations as shown by the pre-abolition regimes in northeastern Brazil, the Western Cape Province of South Africa, the West Indies, and the southern United States. Colonial regimes using various forms of forced labor, the *encomienda* system in Spanish Americ.., and other types of land-based serfdom or indenture also exhibit many of the characteristics of paternalism.

Such societies are rigidly stratified into racial castes which are separated by a wide gulf in status, occupation, education, health standards, income, life style, and sometimes also in cultural tradition. The class distinctions that may exist within castes are less important than the caste barrier, which is horizontal in the sense that there is no overlap in class status between castes. The color line allows no mobility except within castes, and even emancipation in slavery systems often does not appreciably improve the freedman's status. Race is, with age and sex, the major criterion for the division of labor: manual work, whether in agriculture, domestic service, or handicraft, is the sole occupation open to members of the subordinate group or groups, and conversely supervisory, managerial, governmental, and professional functions are monopolized by the dominant caste. An elaborate ideology of racism and caste superiority buttresses such regimes, which, in relatively stable agrarian societies, can show great resilience and longevity. Conflict is, of course, present as in all social systems, but paternalistic regimes are based at least partly on the acquiescence of the subordinate group. Close face-to-face ties between masters and servants reinforce the status quo and supplement the use of coercion. Government in this type of social system tends to be vested in a feudal, land-owning aristocracy which often also owns, or at least closely controls, the labor force. Colonial or white settler bureaucracies are another type of paternalistic government. Paternalistic regimes are thus extreme examples of tyranny over, and exploitation of, the many by the few. The relative stability of these regimes is partly a product of coercion but, at least as importantly, of close, intimate, albeit highly unequal symbiosis. The very asymmetry and complementarity of economic ties between racial castes makes for a tightly integrated pattern of economic interdependence. In addition, miscegenation and other forms of unequal but intimate social relations create powerful affective (although often ambivalent) bonds across caste lines.

2 The *competitive* type of race relations represents the polar opposite of the paternalistic type. It is characteristic of industrialized and urbanized societies with a complex division of labor and a manufacturing basis of production. The dominant group is frequently a majority or a large minority (more than 20 or 25 percent). There is still a color bar, and racial membership remains ascribed, but *class* differences become more salient relative to caste; that is, there is a greater range of class status within castes, whereas the gap in education, income, occupation, and living style between castes tends to narrow. Typically, there is even an overlap in class status between castes, so that the caste line is best described as oblique rather than horizontal. Racial membership still plays a role in the division of labor, but achieved criteria of selection take precedence over strictly ascriptive ones. In a complex industrial economy that requires high skill levels the labor force has to be relatively free and mobile, and race is no longer workable as the paramount criterion for job selection; at least a heavy price in productivity has to be paid if racial ascription of occupations is to be retained. The political system often takes the form of a *"Herrenvolk* democracy," that is, a parliamentary regime in which the exercise of power and suffrage is restricted, de facto, and often de jure, to the dominant group.

In such a dynamic industrial society, with its great geographical mobility and its stress on impersonal market mechanisms and universalistic and achieved criteria of occupational selection, race relations are quite different from what they are under agrarian conditions. The master-servant model with its elaborate caste etiquette and

TABLE 1   A Schematic Outline of the Paternalistic and the Competitive Types of Race Relations

| | A. *"Independent" Variables*[a] | |
	Paternalistic	Competitive
1. Economy	Nonmanufacturing, agricultural, pastoral, handicraft; mercantile capitalism; plantation economy	Typically manufacturing, but not necessarily so; large-scale industrial capitalism
2. Division of labor	Simple ("primitive") or intermediate (as in preindustrial large-scale societies). Division of labor along racial lines. Wide income gap between racial groups	Complex (manufacturing) according to "rational" universalistic criteria; narrow gap in wages; no longer strictly racial

	Paternalistic	Competitive
3. Mobility	Little mobility either vertical or horizontal (slaves, servants, or serfs "attached" in space)	Much mobility both vertical and horizontal (required by industrial economy)
4. Social stratification	Caste system with horizontal color bar; aristocracy versus servile caste with wide gap in living standards (as indexed by income, education, death and birth rates); homogeneous upper caste	Caste system but with tendency for color bar to "tilt" to vertical position; complex stratification into classes within castes; narrower gaps between castes and greater range within castes
5. Numerical ratio	Dominant group a small minority	Dominant group a majority
6. Value conflict	Integrated value system; no ideological conflict	Conflict at least in Western "Christian," "democratic," "liberal" type of society

B. "Dependent" Variables[a]

	Paternalistic	Competitive
1. Race relations	Accommodation; everyone in "his place" and "knows it"; paternalism; benevolent despotism	Antagonism; suspicion, hatred; competitiveness (real or imaginary)
2. Roles and statuses	Sharply defined roles and statuses based on ascription, particularism, diffuseness, collectivity orientation, affectivity; unequal status unthreatened	Ill-defined and based on achievement, universalism, specificity, self-orientation, affective neutrality; unequal status threatened
3. Etiquette	Elaborate and definite	Simple and indefinite
4. Forms of aggression	Generally from lower caste: slave rebellions; nationalistic, revivalistic, or messianistic movements; not directly racial	Both from upper and lower caste; more frequent and directly racial: riots, lynchings, pogroms; passive resistance, sabotage, organized mass protests
5. Miscegenation	Condoned and frequent between upper caste males and lower caste females; institutionalized concubinage	Severely condemned and infrequent
6. Segregation	Little of it; status gap allows close but unequal contact	Much of it; narrowing of status gap makes for increase of spacial gap
7. Psychological syndrome	Internalized subservient status; no personality "need" for prejudice; no "high F"; "pseudotolerance"	"Need" for prejudice; "high F"; linked with sexuality, sadism, frustration; scapegoating
8. Stereotypes of lower caste	Childish, immature, exuberant, uninhibited, lazy, impulsive, fun-loving, good-humored; inferior but lovable	Aggressive, uppity, insolent, oversexed, dirty; inferior, despicable, and dangerous
9. Intensity of prejudice	Fairly constant	Variable and sensitive to provocative situations

C. "Social Control" Variables

	Paternalistic	Competitive
1. Form of government	Aristocratic, oligarchic, autocratic, either centralized or "feudal"; colonial	Restricted or pseudodemocratic
2. Legal system	Lower caste has definite legal status; law on side of racial status quo	Lower caste has no definite legal status, resort to extralegal sanctions (e.g., lynchings)

[a] By "independent" variables I mean here those basic structural factors that determine to a large extent the prevailing type of race relations in a given society. By "dependent" variables, I mean more specifically aspects or components of the racial situation.

its mechanisms of subservience and social distance breaks down to be replaced by acute competition between the subordinate caste and the working class within the dominant group. To the extent that social distance diminishes, physical segregation is introduced as a second line of defense for the preservation of the dominant group's position. The amount of contact between castes declines as the society becomes increasingly compartmentalized into racially homogeneous ghettos with their nearly self-sufficient institutional structure. Miscegenation decreases in frequency and becomes more clandestine and stigmatized in both dominant and subordinate groups.

Given the more advanced state of industrialization characteristic of competitive societies, the division of labor makes for more "organic solidarity" and greater complementarity of roles than in a paternalistic system. However, role complementarity and asymmetry cut across racial cleavages in competitive societies. The racial cleavages no longer follow lines of economic interdependence but rather express themselves through spacial segregation at the ecological level and duplication of analogous institutions (e.g., in parallel church organizations and school systems) at the level of social structure. In other words, in a competitive system racial cleavages make for *segmentation without differentiation* and, in so doing, conflict with economic imperatives in a way that is not true of paternalistic systems in which caste lines combine the features of segmentation *and* differentiation. The growth of interdependence on lines other than racial ones and the structural and ecological fragmentation of competitive societies then pull in opposite directions and constitute one of the major sources of strain and disequilibrium in such systems.

The dominant group's image of the lower caste changes from one of backward but ingratiating grownup children to one of aggressive, insolent, "uppity," clannish, dishonest, underhanded competitors for scarce resources and challengers of the status quo. Virulent hatred replaces condescending benevolence and the psychopathology of bigotry finds a social outlet in scapegoating. Political consciousness develops in the oppressed group or groups; conflict is endemic and frequently erupts in both dominant and subordinate groups in the form of lynching, pogroms, race riots, and terrorism as well as in disciplined mass movements of political opposition ranging from ordinary demonstrations to passive resistance. Situations exhibiting the characteristics of competitive race relations include modern United States, Britain, and South Africa, Eastern European anti-Semitism, and anti-Chinese or anti-Indian prejudice in such countries as Kenya, British Guiana, Malaya, and Indonesia.

It should be apparent that the typology of race relations just outlined closely parallels the well-known distinction in social science between *Gemeinschaft* and *Gesellschaft.* The scheme just outlined represents little more than an application and elaboration of this useful dichotomy to the field of race relations. The main variables that make up the social, economic, and political structure of a society are not only complexly interrelated but they determine to a considerable extent the type of race relations prevailing in that society at a given period in time. The formulation I have just sketched does meet the four conditions mentioned earlier: it specifies the factors that differentiate the two types; it relates the syndrome of race relations to the rest of the social structure; and it can be used both synchronically to compare societies and diachronically to study the evolution of a given society through time.

Thus, using the scheme, slave societies can be compared with one another and important similarities can become evident. Alternatively, by examining, say, the United States before and after the Civil War, we can relate changes in patterns of race relations meaningfully to more fundamental transformations in the economic, social, and political structure. . . . Naturally, given empirical cases seldom exhibit all the characteristics of an ideal type, which must be regarded as an analytical tool rather than as a shorthand description of a given situation. At best, one finds only approximations, and given instances typically show varying mixtures of the characteristics of both ideal types. For example, in the process of a society's evolution from a paternalistic to a competitive situation a number of "survivals" of the paternalistic type can linger on for long periods, even though the society as a whole clearly moves toward a closer approximation to competitive conditions; or, as in South Africa, governmental policies may endeavor to reestablish a paternalistic utopia in an acutely competitive situation. . . .

15
Changes in Life Conditions Conducive to Interracial Conflict*

TAMOTSU SHIBUTANI
and KIAN M. KWAN

Much of the current interest in "race relations" arises from concern over tension and conflict. The extended

* [From Shibutani and Kwan, *Ethnic Stratification.* Copyright © 1965 by The Macmillan Company.]

periods during which people of different ethnic categories live together in peace and mutual respect tend to be overlooked, and discussions of the subject frequently bring to mind organizations such as the Ku Klux Klan, the Mau Mau, the Nazi Storm Troopers, and the Sinn Fein. Because of their spectacular character, bombings, assassinations, riots, guerrilla warfare, lynchings, and pogroms attract a disproportionate share of attention, and even historians tend to focus upon these outbreaks of violence, which are episodic and ephemeral and constitute but a small part of what happens in the contact of peoples. . . .

Insofar as conflict is a joint transaction, the course of events can be understood only as a succession of reciprocating adjustments that the combatants make to one another. What each side does is a response to the actual or anticipated moves of its opponents; thus, the course of events is built up in social interaction.

The more spectacular clashes between ethnic groups generally occur in periods of transition, when the degree of institutionalization of stratified systems is low. Disorders of all kinds arise in situations characterized by uncertainty, either before a color line has been established or when it is breaking down. Ironically, where the color line is well-established, tension is usually at a minimum. To be sure, the calm of a stable society is occasionally disturbed by a mutiny led by a resourceful rebel who becomes a thorn in the side of the authorities. But such incidents are rare and seldom a serious threat to the ascendancy of the dominant group. In stable societies minority peoples are either reasonably satisfied with their lot or do not dare challenge the existing order. What, then, are the conditions under which an already established color line breaks down? . . .

THE WEAKENING
OF STRATIFIED SYSTEMS

Since conflicts are not likely to occur unless members of minority groups challenge the prerogatives of their rulers, we may begin our study by examining the conditions under which minority groups become dissatisfied with their lot. The social institutions of any community represent collective adjustments to life conditions. If these circumstances change, some of the accepted procedures become inadequate, and new and better-suited arrangements eventually develop. This suggests that the various forms of opposition between ethnic groups constitute a phase in a larger process through which social structures are transformed.

Among the most important changes in life conditions are technological innovations. A social system is geared to a given material environment, and the introduction of new techniques generally disrupts the old patterns. The new ways often create new tastes, and they force changes in social relationships so that they can be utilized more effectively.[1] Sometimes a new elite group is formed, while those who had previously enjoyed high standing suddenly find themselves obsolete. For example, the invention of an automatic cotton picker has diminished the demand for cheap farm labor in the South, and it has driven many marginal farmers into bankruptcy. Both Negro and white people have been leaving the South in large numbers, and the pattern of ethnic stratification throughout the United States is being altered. Transformations may occur with the sudden loss of people with specialized skills, as in the departure of the Moors from Spain.

There can be little question that the widespread adoption of automation will also lead to changes in the structure of our society. As the demand for highly skilled specialists increases and the need for unskilled labor decreases, many social dislocations can be anticipated.

When there are drastic changes in the prevailing mode of production, new interests develop that clash with customary procedures. Marked changes follow the introduction into a community of mass production—with its specialization of tasks, separation of ownership from management, and huge impersonal labor force. In the South, for example, absentee employers were not concerned with the pedigree of their workers; there was no opposition to hiring Negroes, especially if they were willing to work for somewhat lower wages.[2] Wherever there is a shortage of labor, employers tend to encourage a spirit of tolerance and good will so that they can recruit the necessary manpower from alien sources. The voluntary segregation of minority groups also collapses from economic necessity. When the Molokans lived in agricultural settlements in Russia, they were largely self-sufficient. When they settled in Los Angeles, however, they could not possibly produce everything that they needed, and they were forced to seek employment outside their colony.[3] Gypsies were traditionally coppersmiths, musicians, bear tamers, peddlers, horse dealers, and fortune tellers; and there is little demand for their specialties in industrial societies. In the United States their campsites have

---

[1] Cf. William F. Ogburn, *Social Change,* New York: Viking Press, 1937.

[2] A. Davis and B. Gardner, *Deep South,* Chicago: Univ. of Chicago Press, 1941, p. 478. Cf. Rudolf Heberle, "Social Consequences of the Industrialization of Southern Cities," *Social Forces,* XXVII (1948), 29–37.

[3] P. Young, *The Pilgrims of Russian Town,* Chicago: Univ. of Chicago Press, 1932, pp. 122–123.

virtually disappeared. Many have gone to cities, where they now express an interest in vocational training, permanent housing, and an education for their children. Perhaps one reason for the recent granting of independence to their colonial subjects by so many European powers is that the practical advantages of colonialism have been declining. As the natives insist upon higher wages and better economic opportunities, they no longer serve as a source of cheap labor. Furthermore, the growing unrest among subject peoples makes the cost of maintaining order too great.[4]

One of the consequences of such changes in the economic system is that people in minority groups may acquire new competitive advantages. The industrialization of Europe, for example, gave many of the Christians and Jews living in the millets of the Middle East advantages over their Moslem neighbors. Because of their aptitude for European languages and ways of thought, governments and commercial organizations drew a disproportionately large number of their minor employees from these minority groups, thus helping to create a bourgeoisie.[5] When members of minority groups acquire skills that make them an integral part of the labor force, they become indispensable to their employers. Those in the dominant group whose livelihood depends upon the cooperation of these people are among the first to make concessions. The practice of hiring Negroes in the urban North, for example, was not altered by the subsequent influx of large numbers of white people from the South. Negro workers had already proved their worth, and employers were

not willing to risk alienating them just to accommodate newcomers of uncertain value. In many cases the southerners found themselves treated contemptuously as "hillbillies"; most of them had to accept the prevailing conditions of work or do without jobs.[6] Higher wages and better jobs mean not only a better standard of living but greater purchasing power. Although some scholars question whether the economic position of Negroes has actually improved relative to other Americans, the purchasing power of Negroes is now so great that few entrepreneurs can afford to antagonize them.[7] Furthermore, better economic circumstances also give minority groups organized bargaining power. During World War II, when imports to Nigeria fell, Nigerians were forced to produce many of their own goods. War production not only increased the productive capacity of the area but stimulated the growth of labor unions from twelve with 4,337 members in 1940 to 177 unions with 165,130 members in 1955.[8]

The repudiation of customary practices while pursuing economic interests is relatively easy in a capitalistic society, where a high value is placed upon profit and upon private property. It is further facilitated by the impersonal character of money, for as the popular saying goes, "One man's money is as good as another's." Many merchants are not particular with whom they trade, and where there is respect for the operation

[4] R. Kennedy, "Colonial Crisis and the Future," in R. Linton (ed.) *Science of Man in the World Crisis,* New York: Columbia Univ. Press, 1945, p. 345.

[5] A. Hourani, *Minorities in the Arab World,* London: Oxford Univ. Press, 1947, pp. 25–26.

[6] Lewis M. Killian, "The Effects of Southern White Workers on Race Relations in Northern Plants," *American Sociological Review,* XVII (1952), 327–31.

[7] E. Franklin Frazier, "The Negro in the United States," in Lind, *Race Relations in World Perspective,* Honolulu: Univ. of Hawaii Press, 1955, pp. 348–351. Cf. Gary S. Becker, *The Economics of Discrimination,* Chicago: University of Chicago Press, 1957.

[8] J. Coleman, *Nigeria Background to Nationalism,* Berkeley: Univ. of Calif. Press, 1958.

of a free market, others are reluctant to interfere. Should people in minority groups produce goods more cheaply or be willing to sell their labor for a lower price, there are bound to be business-men who will find them attractive. In addition, economic gains of minority groups are protected by reluctance to interfere with property rights, one of the cornerstones of a laissez-faire economy. Even under the "black codes" of the Reconstruction period, for example, when Negroes were stripped of most of their rights, their right to own property was not taken away.[9] One of the major barriers faced by proponents of *apartheid* in South Africa is that the program conflicts with economic interests. If the proposed separation of ethnic groups is actually carried out, many industries would not be able to operate. Thus far, this phase of the program has not been implemented.[10]

Another type of change in life conditions is the transformation of demographic structure. A social system is geared to a particular demographic balance. The educational institutions of a community depend upon a particular age distribution, just as prostitution is more likely to be profitable where the sex ratio favors males. The preservation of a rigid color line also depends upon retaining roughly the same proportion of people in each category; any change in relative numbers may disrupt the old patterns. The demographic structure of a community may be upset by migration. People in a minority group may leave, or a large number of one ethnic minority may enter. For example, only half of the 6 million people in Malaya in 1960 were Malay; about 37 percent

were Chinese and 11 percent were Indian or Pakistani. The Chinese were so numerous and their economic power so great that their political demands could not be ignored. The demographic structure of a community may also be altered by differential rates of growth. We live in the kind of society we do partly because the American pioneers who pushed westward enjoyed a much higher reproduction rate than the Indians. The demographic structure may also be altered by a changing sex ratio. When the sex ratio is balanced on both sides of the color line, segregation is easier to maintain. Should the sex ratio in one ethnic group become unbalanced, however, there is likely to be pressure for permitting intermarriage.

Of particular importance in inter-ethnic contacts is an increase in the density of population. The growth of cities alters many customary practices; cities have tended to be melting pots, and industrial cities in particular have been graveyards for traditions. Senti-mental ties to one's own group are often weakened, and new patterns of conduct are attempted. The Molokans found it extremely difficult to maintain their isolation in Los Angeles. Their adversary was protean, informal, in-sidious, and therefore difficult to han-dle. There were no direct attacks upon them by Americans. But the desire to distinguish themselves as a select group diminished among the younger people, and the comforts of the new way of life to which they were exposed became more appealing.[11] Nigerian cities were aggregations of tribal units, and tribal homogeneity was to a large extent pre-served in the heart of each of the quar-ters. But in the peripheral sectors there was a weakening of ancestral ties; new tastes were created, new values adopt-ed, and new patterns emulated. In these

[9] Allison Davis, "Caste, Economy, and Violence," *American Journal of Sociology,* LI (1945), 13–14.
[10] Leo Kuper, "The Control of Social Change: A South African Experiment," *Social Forces,* XXXIII (1954), 26–28.

[11] P. Young, *op. cit.,* p. 158.

areas people felt insecure and frustrated, and it was here that nationalist activities centered.[12] Even in the well-established caste system of India the exigencies of city life have forced many Hindus to alter their notions of ritual purity. In restaurants one had to eat food prepared by people of other castes, generally without even knowing who they were, and in hotels one had to eat in the company of whoever happened to be present.[13]

Drastic changes in systems of ethnic stratification sometimes follow a major catastrophe. Disasters that affect the entire community—such as floods, epidemics, famine, or invasion by a common foe—strike everyone in the same manner and require cooperation for survival. In periods of grave crisis customary barriers are usually relaxed somewhat in the face of more pressing considerations. The exigencies of life force men to respect one another for their intrinsic qualities rather than for the conventional status symbols they bear.

The relative position of various ethnic groups may also be altered by war and conquest. This has been a frequent occurrence in Europe and in the Middle East, where national boundaries have changed back and forth. The annexation of Bosnia and Herzogovina by Austria–Hungary in the early twentieth century stimulated the development of Slav nationalism. The earlier loss of German-speaking Silesia to Prussia and the strengthening of the Slavic peoples by the acquisition of Polish and Ruthenian areas also changed the relative numerical strength of the various ethnic groups in the empire.[14]

When Timbuctoo was conquered by the French soon after the turn of the century, the guild system of hereditary crafts broke down, for the new rulers forbade the use of force to keep former slaves out of the occupations they desired. Furthermore, the Arma were no longer able to pillage the wealthy Gabibi, who in turn found it unnecessary to plunder their subordinates to recoup their losses. Since armed robbery was prohibited, the upper classes in the various ethnic groups had to learn to live by commerce.[15] During the Japanese occupation of Southeast Asia in World War II the European colonists were placed at the bottom of the social scale. Although the Japanese were disliked, the puppet regimes they sponsored helped develop native leadership and stimulated nationalistic sentiment.[16]

Perhaps the most important change in life conditions is the transformation of values. When new ideas are introduced, especially those that challenge values previously taken for granted, an ethnic group is on its way to developing new cultural attributes. The doctrine of "white supremacy," which many subjects in European colonies had accepted, was first challenged by the success of the Japanese in the Russo-Japanese War. The defeat of the Russians in 1905 was the first concrete proof that white men were not invincible. The numerous dislocations of World War II resulted in additional doubts. Throughout Southeast Asia achievements of the Japanese in employing the industrial inventions and military methods of the white man gave the idea of the inferiority of colored

[12] Coleman, Nigeria, op. cit., pp. 72–79.
[13] G. Ghurye, Caste and Class in India, Bombay: Popular Book Depot, 1950, pp. 186–187.
[14] Robert A. Kann, The Habsburg Empire, New York: Frederick A. Praeger, 1957, p. 31.

[15] H. Miner, The Primitive City of Timbuctoo, Princeton: Princeton Univ. Press, 1953, pp. 55–57, 181, 252–253.
[16] W. Wertheim, Indonesian Society in Transition, The Hague: W. Van Houeve, 1956, pp. 152–166.

people a stunning blow.[17] In New Guinea the presence of Negro troops in the U.S. Army was convincing proof to the natives that colored people, if given an opportunity, could attain the same level of accomplishment as white people.[18] In Nigeria, which was a station for troops and supplies going to the battlefields of North Africa, failure of a large number of European troops unconnected with colonial governments to observe customary aloofness provided opportunities to learn that the white man had all the vices of the colored.[19]

Despite the efforts of rulers to insulate their subjects from outside influence, knowledge of conditions in the rest of the world often reaches minority peoples. Travellers bring word of life in other lands. Those who had once regarded their conditions as inevitable learn that there are people much like themselves who enjoy a very different way of life. When members of minority groups learn of democratic ideals, they become critical and restive. During the nineteenth century the ideas of the Enlightenment could not be kept out of Latin America. The people rejected the doctrine of the divine right of kings, and independence came to the entire area within fifty years of the French Revolution.[20] The ideological conflict in World War II focused attention upon such basic issues as political liberty, economic opportunity, intellectual freedom, and social justice. The publication of the Atlantic Charter and the subsequent discussion of the third clause, ". . . the right of all peoples to choose the form of government under which they will live. . . ," aroused nationalistic aspirations throughout the colonial world. The pursuit of a virulent racist policy by the Nazis made such views even more important. Allied propaganda urging freedom and equality for all played an important part in sowing discontent among subjugated peoples, and in areas dominated by the Axis powers many of the natives joined resistance movements and fought courageously. The British Labor Party pledged itself to an anticolonial policy, and public opinion in the ruling nations also underwent transformation. The entire institution of colonialism was weakened, and Prime Minister Churchill's postwar declaration that he would not preside over the liquidation of the British Empire was interpreted as a betrayal of a promise. When some colonial powers attempted to reestablish their hold after the war, they discovered that their presence was no longer welcomed. Once the ideals of freedom and equality had been released, they could not be conveniently recalled.[21]

In industrial societies the most important channel of upward social mobility is education. In Africa, the Europeans taught that education was an indispensable prerequisite to economic progress and political privilege, and the Africans accepted this belief. The educational gains of minority groups usually result in the transformation of perspectives. The people not only learn new skills but new ideas as well. Merely learning to read opens new vistas, and educated Africans have played an im-

[17] R. Emerson et al., Government and Nationalism in Southeast Asia, New York Institute of Pacific Relations, 1942, p. 16; N. Chaudhuri, Autobiography of an Unknown Indian, New York: MacMillan, 1951, pp. 104–105; and Kennedy, op. cit., p. 312.

[18] H. Hogbin, Transformation Scene: The Changing Culture of a New Guinea, London: Routledge and Kegan Paul, 1951, p. 288.

[19] Coleman, Nigeria, op. cit., pp. 25–54.

[20] G. Blanksten, "Politics of Latin America" in G. Almond and J. S. Coleman (eds.), Politics of Developing Areas, Princeton: Princeton

Univ. Press, 1960, p. 490; C. Harring, The Spanish Empire in America, New York, Oxford Univ. Press, 1947.

[21] Cf. Coleman, Nigeria, op. cit., pp. 79–80, 231–49; and Kennedy, op. cit., pp. 338–40, 345–46.

portant part in transmitting new ideas of freedom to their illiterate fellows. News of the achievements of American Negroes provided inspiration throughout Africa. In India, the educated Hindu learned that European history was a struggle for freedom, and the revolutionary leaders of Europe became the heroes of Indian intellectuals. Missionary education gave an increasing number of Africans powerful weapons for the Christian ideals of equality and brotherhood challenge the ethical basis of colonial rule.[22] Thus, education not only raises the competitive advantages of minority peoples but also gives them access to ideas that challenge the existing order. The schools now being established throughout the world through foreign aid funds and by UNESCO will not only help people to raise their standard of living but will undoubtedly alter their thinking about social status.

As ethnic minorities acquire new cultural characteristics, they are better able to compete for jobs and for space. Through their new competitive advantages they acquire more political power. Systems of ethnic stratification begin to break down when minority peoples develop new self-conceptions and refuse to accept subordinate roles. As they become more aware of their worth in comparison to members of the dominant group, what they had once accepted as natural becomes unbearable. What had once appeared to be special privileges for superior persons is redefined as the rights of all human beings. . . .

Once something has occurred to disturb the existing social order, there is a period of transition before a new social system is established. This period varies considerably in length, but it is almost always marked by misunder-

standing and tension. Social structure rests upon consensus; concerted action is possible because men share common understandings. Social change of any kind involves a change of perspectives, and this is not likely to occur simultaneously for everyone in a community. A transitional period is one in which consensus has broken down. It is a period of uncertainty, for people are not quite sure of what to expect of one another. Frequently there is external conformity to outdated norms. Status symbols of the old order may still be honored ostensibly, even when they are no longer accepted. Some members of the dominant group realize that their claims to superiority are unjustified, and people in minorities may feign subservience to avoid possible trouble. There may be a flat contradiction between overt behavior and inner dispositions. As long as each person believes that the others still support the old order, external compliance with traditional patterns continues. What makes the reestablishment of consensus so difficult is that many refuse to reveal their inner feelings. Thus, human beings often support one another for some time on views that only a few of them actually hold. Under these circumstances the resentment of those in minority groups becomes intensified.

The transformation of the color line does not result in the abolition of inequality. In most cases one system of social stratification is replaced by another, and distinctions are made on some basis. A system of ethnic stratification may become transformed into a class system. This is frequently the case in a capitalistic economy. As members of a subordinate group in increasing numbers acquire the culture of the dominant group, ethnic identity becomes secondary, and people begin to identify on the basis of occupation and

[22] Cf. Coleman, *Nigeria, op. cit.*, p. 101; Franck, *op. cit.*, pp. 116–37; and Leakey, *op cit.*, p. 71.

income level. In some cases, ethnic groups change their relative ranks, while the system itself remains the same. This is what has happened in the United States. A century ago the Irish were at the bottom of the social scale, doing the least desired jobs and being despised for it. Then, as they improved their lot, they were replaced by a succession of new immigrants. The system itself has not changed fundamentally, but the strata have been occupied by different ethnic groups. Thus, when a system of ethnic stratification breaks down, it is not likely to be replaced by an unstratified society. . . .

16
Prejudice As a Weapon in the Struggle for Power, Income, and Prestige*
GEORGE EATON SIMPSON
and L. MILTON SINGER

Several factors in American history encouraged the use and elaboration of race prejudice. As the colonists became numerous and began to press deeper into the Indians' lands, sharp conflicts inevitably arose. Few of the settlers seriously considered that the Indians might have some rights to the land. It was easier to develop a picture of the lying, thieving, murdering savage, pagan in religion, racially stupid except for a kind of animal cunning. Such a person has no rights; the only good Indian is a dead Indian. This picture was frequently not held by the trappers and traders who moved individually among the Indians. They gained by friendly contact and therefore tended to judge the Indian differently. But the prejudice of the farmer-settler prevailed. There

*[From pp. 87–93 in *Racial and Cultural Minorities: An Analysis of Prejudice and Discrimination*, Third Edition, by George Eaton Simpson and J. Milton Yinger. Copyright © 1958, 1965 by George Eaton Simpson and Y. Milton Yinger. Copyright, 1953 by Harper and Row, Publishers, Inc. Reprinted by permission of the publishers.]

were qualifications and exceptions and ambivalent feelings of course. These were never strong enough, however, to prevent the continuing seizure of Indian lands with a minimum of compensation, the decimation of the Indian population to scarcely more than one-third its original size, and the development of a rationalizing prejudice that moved with the white man across the continent. In recent decades categorical race prejudice against the Indian has sharply declined—and so has the economic function which that prejudice formerly served.

The development and entrenchment of prejudice against the Negro are also made more meaningful by an examination of the economic situation in which it throve. The situation before the American Revolution had potentialities for several different attitudes, and economic factors were important in helping to select the one that finally became dominant. Many of the Negroes who came to America first were indentured servants, not slaves; there were also white indentured servants. From this situation it was possible that both Negro and white bondsmen would move toward freedom as the settlements became more stable, or that both would sink into a permanent status of inferiority (whether of slavery or some other legal form), or that one group would break out of servitude while the other was kept in. Before the revolution the first possibility seemed most likely; in the seventeenth century a Virginia court had upheld the right of one Negro to claim the perpetual service of another Negro—showing that no categorical race line had yet been drawn. With the failure of tobacco, rice, and indigo to support the plantation economy, the settlers became lukewarm toward slavery.

In Granville County, North Carolina, a full-blooded Negro, John Chavis, educated at Princeton, conducted a private school for white children, and was a licentiate under the local Presbytery, preaching to white congregations in the state. One of the pupils became governor of North Carolina, another was the state's Whig senator. Two were sons of the chief justice of North Carolina. He was not stopped until the Denmark Vesey uprising in South Carolina (the first state to show promise of economic prosperity through the cotton industry) threatened the whole structure of slavery.[1]

Myrdal states that in the first two decades of the nineteenth century the abolitionist movement was as strong in the South as in the North, if not stronger.[2]

Despite these signs of contradictory tendencies in the South, the legal and institutional structure of slavery had developed, since the late seventeenth century, into a system of great clarity and consistency focused primarily on one goal: the maximization of profit. No matter how harsh or beneficient might be the personal relationship of master to slave, in the last analysis the slave was property, without personal rights, without family rights, without religious rights.

If the legal clarity of an unmitigated slave system in the United States was not fully matched by practice in the seventeenth and eighteenth centuries, in the first half of the nineteenth century almost all the ambiguities were eliminated. Economic forces were of great importance in this development. The invention of the cotton gin and other mechanical devices for the processing of cotton cloth began to make cotton agriculture profitable. In 1793, 500,000 pounds of cotton were exported

to Europe. The cotton gin was patented in 1794, and the next year six million pounds were exported. By a decade later, 1805, the amount had grown to forty million pounds.[3] The price of cotton rose, the value of slaves doubled, and land values increased sharply; "and with every increase in value the difficulty of breaking the status of Negro slavery increased."[4] The belief in slavery, which had been on the decline for a century or more, began to revive in the South. After 1803 an extensive literature to justify slavery appeared. It attempted to show that slavery was contrary neither to nature nor to religion, and that since the Negro was inferior and subhuman, it was even harmonious with democracy. Occasionally a writer would recognize the economic foundation of these beliefs. In *Sociology for the South,* 1854, George Fitzhugh wrote, "Our southern patriots at the time of the Revolution, finding Negroes expensive and useless, became *warm antislavery* men. We, their wiser sons, having learned to make cotton and sugar, find slavery very useful and profitable, and think it is a most excellent institution. We of the South advocate slavery, no doubt, from just as selfish motives as induce the Yankees and English to deprecate it."[5] But Fitzhugh hastened to add, "We have, however, almost all human and divine authority on our side of the argument. The Bible nowhere condemns, and throughout recognizes slavery."[6]

IMMIGRATION INTO THE UNITED STATES

That racial distinctions by themselves are unimportant in explaining prejudice

---

[1] Charles S. Johnson, "Race Relations and Social Change," in E. T. Thompson (ed.), *Race Relations and the Race Problem,* Duke, 1939, pp. 275 ff.

[2] Gunnar Myrdal, *An American Dilemma,* Harper & Row, 1944, p. 86.

[3] W. D. Weatherford and Charles S. Johnson, *Race Relations,* Heath, 1934, p. 136.

[4] Johnson, *op. cit.,* p. 282.

[5] Quoted by Myrdal, *op. cit.,* p. 1188.

[6] *Ibid.*

in group conflict is shown in a study of the changing attitude toward immigrants in the United States. Since many of the same arguments and beliefs are involved in the treatment of white and of colored immigrants, one must conclude that something other than "race difference" lies behind the situation. This conclusion is also supported by the fact that an immigrant group that is accepted and even welcomed in one circumstance, despite a racial difference, may be condemned and attacked in another situation "because" of its race. It is obviously impossible to explain the changing amount of prejudice by the racial constant.

The belief is rather widespread that there was no "immigrant problem," no prejudice against the newcomers to America, until the late nineteenth century. A careful study of our early history will show this to be false. It is easy today to assume that the early immigrants were readily accepted because of their passion for liberty, their thrift, their industry. Their contemporaries, however, were as likely to complain of the immigrants' foreign ways, criminality, and filth. The agitation of the Know-Nothing Order was directed against the Irish and Germans. The supposed contrast between the "new" immigration (from south and east Europe) and the "old" immigration (from north Europe) that was drawn so sharply by many writers in the early twentieth century is interestingly paralleled by a writer comparing the "new" and the "old" of 1835: "Then our accessions of immigration were real accessions of strength from the ranks of the learned and the good, from the enlightened mechanic and artisan and intelligent husbandman. Now, immigration is the accession of weakness, from the ignorant and vicious, or the priest ridden slaves of Ireland and Germany, or the outcast tenants of the poorhouses and prisons of

Europe."[7] Compare that with the writers of 1910–1920 who were exalting the quality of the early immigrants in order to condemn the newcomers. Lothrop Stoddard writes:

> ... The white race divides into three main subspecies—the Nordics, the Alpines, and the Mediterraneans. All three are good stocks, ranking in genetic worth well above the various colored races. However, there seems to be no question that the Nordic is far and away the most valuable type. . . . Our country, originally settled almost exclusively by Nordics, was toward the close of the nineteenth century invaded by hordes of immigrant Alpines and Mediterraneans, not to mention Asiatic elements like Levantines and Jews. As a result, the Nordic native American has been crowded out with amazing rapidity by the swarming, prolific aliens. . . .[8]

It is easy to see from such statements that things are not as good as they used to be—and perhaps they never were.[9]

Racial differences or supposed differences, national, religious, cultural differences, or simply a general "inferiority" are the reasons ordinarily given to explain opposition to immigrants. Do these "explanations" hide,

[7] Quoted by Isaac A. Hourwich, *Immigration and Labor,* Putnam, 1912. For other valuable historical studies of immigration, see Oscar Handlin, *The Uprooted,* Little, Brown, 1951; and Maldwyn Jones, *American Immigration,* Univ. of Chicago Press, 1960. Technical treatment of immigrant statistics and absorption can be found in E. P. Hutchinson, *Immigrants and Their Children, 1850–1950,* Wiley, 1956; and E. P. Hutchinson, "Notes on Immigration Statistics of the United States," *Journal of The American Statistical Association,* December 1958, no. 284, pp. 963–1025.

[8] Lothrop Stoddard, *The Rising Tide of Color Against White World-Supremacy,* Scribner, 1920, pp. 162–165.

[9] For an interesting discussion of the "old" and "new" immigration into Australia see Stanley Lieberson, "The Old-New Distinction and Immigrants in Australia," *ASR,* August 1963, pp. 550–565. For the most part, Lieberson found that rates of adaptation and assimilation in Australia were similar for South and North Europeans.

perhaps even from the person who uses them, economic and political conflicts which are the more basic causes of the attitude? . . .

The evidence seems to indicate clearly a tradition of opposition to immigrants, who are accepted targets for aggression partly because of economic and political conflicts. There seems to be a direct correlation between the peaks of "nativist" activity and the valleys of economic depression. The Native American party of the 1830's, the Know-Nothing Order of the 1850's, the American Protective Association in the last two decades of the nineteenth century, and the scores of anti-alien, one-hundred-per-cent-American groups in the 1930's—these all show the tendency to try to bolster a shaky economic situation by prejudice against recent immigrant groups.[10] This correlation between prejudice and economic insecurity is low because many other variables influence the strength of prejudice, and they may operate strongly in different circumstances from those that encourage the use of prejudice as an economic weapon. Anti-Semitic activities may increase in the United States because of political factors in Germany which have reverberations here. Such activities may have no direct relation to economic stresses in the United States except as those stresses create a favorable setting for the borrowing of the German pattern. It should also be noted that economic forces may encourage prejudice in "good times" (and among the economically powerful), hope of gain rather than fear of loss being the underlying motive. In a multiple-factor situation, such as prejudice, it is important not to assume that because the course of events does not follow the pattern indicated by one factor (economic crisis, for example) the factor in question isn't operative. Its influence may simply be canceled out by other factors which obscure its effects. . . .

RESTRICTIVE LEGISLATION

The most convincing evidence that anti-immigrant prejudice reflects economic forces in part is the story of federal legislation that gradually controlled and restricted immigration after 1882. Many people supported this legislation who had no economic interest—probably, in fact, in opposition to their long-run economic interest. But some of the strongest proponents of restriction were groups who could see some immediate economic advantage in weakening or getting rid of immigrant competitors. The arguments used were partly racial or biological—continued immigration means "blood pollution" or "mongrelization"; they were partly religious and cultural—"our capacity to maintain our cherished institutions stands diluted by a stream of alien blood." But the economic factor was occasionally stated in undisguised fashion. "The Chinaman is here because his presence pays, and he will remain and continue to increase so long as there is money in him. When the time comes that he is no longer profitable *that* generation will take care of him and will send him back."[11]

Vigorous exclusionist sentiments developed first on the west coast, where a visible racial minority with a unifying cultural tradition came into economic competition with some of the "native" whites, who in exploiting the resources of a new era were accustomed to a conflict pattern and a vigilante tradition. When unskilled workers were needed to build railroads and to begin the develop-

[10] See Donald Young, *Research Memorandum on Minority Groups in the Depression,* SSRC, 1937.

[11] Quoted from the Sacramento *Record Union,* Jan. 10, 1879, by Oliver C. Cox, *Caste, Class and Race,* Doubleday, 1948, p. 413.

ment of the resources of the West, many Chinese were imported and welcomed. Agitation against the Chinese began, perhaps, in the 1860's. During this decade the Central Pacific Railroad was completed, so that competition for jobs among the unskilled was intensified. The gold boom began to fade and unemployment to rise. Serious economic crises in the 1870's, accompanied by extensive migration of unemployed persons from the East, brought sharper and sharper demands from the white workers that the continuing Chinese immigration be stopped. In 1876 both major parties in California had anti-Chinese planks in their platforms, and a statewide vote in 1879 was overwhelmingly for exclusion.[12]

The changing economic situation was accompanied by a shifting stereotype of the Chinese. From worthy, industrious, sober, law-abiding citizens they rather suddenly developed into unassimilable, deceitful, servile people smuggling opium. "There were no new personal experiences to account for the contrast. There was no increase in native aggressiveness on the part of the white group. There was no heightening of an instinctive consciousness of kind. There was, however, a change in the economic conditions in California which made it to the advantage of the whites to eliminate the Chinese as a factor in competition, and the attitude toward them was an effect of this situation."[13]

In 1882 Congress passed a law that suspended all immigration of Chinese labor for ten years. The legislation was renewed from time to time and in 1904 the time limit was removed. . . .

The exclusion of Japanese immigrants followed much the same pattern.

At first they were welcomed; but by 1900 there were demands that the Japanese be excluded, and these grew more and more insistent. On March 1, 1905, the California legislature, by a vote of 28-0 and 70-0 in the two houses, passed a resolution urging Congress to exclude Japanese from the country.[14] In 1906 the San Francisco school board passed a resolution that barred Japanese children from white schools. This was repealed, under pressure from the federal government, but continued agitation finally led to the "gentlemen's agreement" of 1907 in which the Japanese government agreed to issue no more passports to skilled or unskilled workers, except those who had previously resided in the United States or their wives or their children under 21 years of age. The immigration of women to become the wives of Japanese already in the United States was permitted until 1920, when Japan agreed to refuse emigration to the "picture brides." The act of 1924 stopped all immigration from Japan.

Anti-Japanese activity had not stopped with the virtual cutting off of immigration by the gentlemen's agreement. Newspaper headlines and editorials, nativist organizations such as the Native Sons of the Golden West, mob action, political oratory, and legal enactments all continued to show the extent of the prejudice, particularly in California. Gradually the federal government became involved after having tried for several decades to restrain California's anti-Japanese expressions because of the difficulties they created in international diplomacy. By the Immigration Act of 1924, and by the resettlement policy of 1942, the federal government expressed agreement with the racial sentiments involved.

---

[12] See B. Schreike, *Alien Americans,* Viking, 1936, pp. 3–22.

[13] Otto Klineberg, *Social Psychology,* Holt, Rinehart and Winston, 1940, pp. 385–386.

[14] Carey McWilliams, *Prejudice—Japanese–Americans: Symbol of Racial Intolerance,* Little, Brown, 1944, p. 19.

It is our concern to ask at this point: Who profited, or thought they profited, from such moves? Perhaps the most tangible and continuous gains accrued to men running for office or in office, who, by striking out at the Japanese, could create in-group feeling, could sponsor a cause, could exploit the tensions of the average voter, and could avoid reference to any of the critical issues which might have two opposing sides that were difficult to occupy simultaneously. Many California politicians since 1900 have made use of prejudice against the Japanese to win an election. If the existing fund of prejudice was not enough to make the tactic effective, their supporting newspapers could manufacture enough to help. Before World War II there was a strong correlation between the waves of anti-Japanese agitation and election years. Since the Japanese group was small and politically and economically weak, candidates could attack it almost without fear of reprisals; it was as politically safe to be against the Japanese as to be against sin. Even Woodrow Wilson, speaking in California during the presidential election of 1912, declared: "The whole question is one of assimilation of diverse races. We cannot make a homogeneous population of a people who do not blend with the Caucasian race." McWilliams reports that the Democratic party distributed over 100,000 copies of this relatively innocuous statement around the state.

There were doubtless economic as well as political motives involved in the anti-Japanese activities on the west coast after 1900. At various times trade unions and small landowners took part in these agitations, but organized opposition stemmed most directly from the owners of the huge estates which characterize parts of California. These men certainly did not fear the competition of the few Japanese farmers with their relatively small holdings. What they did fear was the opposition of the small white landowners who found it difficult to compete with the estates, the struggles for improvement of their own very badly paid field hands, the traditions in favor of family-sized farms and homesteads, and federal legislation that prevented them from monopolizing the water supplied through governmentally sponsored irrigation projects. If they could divert attention from their own control of the land by attacking the Japanese farmer as the cause of everybody's difficulties, they might funnel off some of the hostility to which they were vulnerable and get political support for laws favorable to them.

17
Group Structure and Resistance to Desegregation in the Deep South*
WARREN BREED

Existing approaches to the southern race problem tend to be either reductionist or unsystematic, in that they fail to include elements basic to sociological analysis—patterns of social structure and social process. This paper will discuss the Deep South as a region, with specific focus on its organization and its social processes, and will contrast the South with the North along these dimensions. The past four decades have seen only scattered discussion of this kind.[1] In addition, the emphasis

*[Reprinted from *Social Problems*, vol. 10, no. 1, Summer 1962, pp. 84–94 by permission of the Society for the Study of Social Problems. The author is indebted to Robert E. Barnes for a critical reading of the manuscript.]
[1] See, e.g., Augustus W. Hayes, *Rural Community Organization* (Chicago: University of Chicago Press, 1921), p. 52; Wayland J. Hayes, "The Southern Crisis and Social Control," *Social Forces,* 15 (October, 1936), p. 29; Frank D. Alexander, "Constructive Measures for Southern Rural Communities," *Social Forces,* 24

will shift the question from the "causation" of prejudice to current resistance to desegregation, or the *persistence* of a social problem, and will suggest that the variables of group structure and political process are crucial to the problem. While considerable school desegregation occurred in the fall of 1961, it will be argued that structural forces of resistance remain to constitute still-considerable barriers to further attempts to changing racial patterns.

Of the existing approaches, the psychological study of southern attitudes is most frequently used, and it is clear that most southerners favor segregation. One of the best-known approaches, the "authoritarian personality" argument,[2] has failed to be borne out when applied to the South;[3] more relevant is the "vicious circle" hypothesis.[4] A focus on the distribution of attitudes and their developmental dynamics is relevant, but more knowledge is needed about how these are expressed, or not expressed, at the community level; attitudes can be a symptom, as well as a causal agent, of social structure.

Many sociologists[5] have made this point, holding that institutional structure as well as behavior is relevant to the racial situation. Another way of stating it is to say the focus will be on the sociology of knowledge, rather than the psychology of prejudice. Likewise, demographic, caste-and-class, and various politico-historical accounts have failed to consider the patterns of social structure and social process which are the focus of this paper. We take these studies as a point of departure into an investigation of the social structure and political behavior of the Deep South (defined broadly as the former plantation areas running from South Carolina to Louisiana). Theoretical guidelines are furnished by two theories, which will now be reviewed briefly.

GROUP STRUCTURE AND POLITICAL PROCESS

A pluralistic society is one in which numerous groups have public access to one another and to government, so that a relatively large proportion of individuals are involved in public discussion. These groups form only with the development of society beyond the folk stage, and become crucial in complex, interdependent modern societies, operating to mediate changes in the relationships between groups and strata.[6] As such they function as a key element in the political system. Korn-

(December, 1945), pp. 182–183; Rudolf Heberle, "A Sociological Interpretation of Social Change in the South," *Social Forces,* 25 (October, 1946), p. 14; Herman H. Long, "Race Prejudice and Social Change," *American Journal of Sociology,* 57 (July, 1951), pp. 18–19; the selections by Harold F. Kaufman, Floyd Hunter, Henry A. Bullock and H. C. Nixon in Rupert B. Vance and Nicholas J. Demerath, *The Urban South* (Chapel Hill: Univ. of North Carolina Press, 1954); and Roland J. Pellegrin and Charles H. Coates, "Absentee-Owned Corporations and Community Power Structure," *American Journal of Sociology,* 61 (March, 1956), p. 414. For a comprehensive view see Gunnar Myrdal, Richard Sterner, and Arnold Rose, *An American Dilemma* (New York: Harper, 1944), pp. 44–49.

[2] T. W. Adorno *et al., The Authoritarian Personality* (New York: Harper, 1950).

[3] E. T. Prothro, "Ethnocentrism and Anti-Negro Attitudes in the Deep South," *Journal of Abnormal and Social Psychology,* 47 (1952), 105–108.

[4] Myrdal, *op. cit.,* chap. 3.

[5] R. K. Merton, "Discrimination and the American Creed," in R. M. MacIver, *Discrimination and National Welfare* (New York: Harper, 1949); Joseph D. Lohman and Dietrich R. Reitzes, "Note on Race Relations in Mass Society," *American Journal of Sociology,* 58 (November, 1952), pp. 240–246; Reitzes, "Institutional Structure and Race Relations," *Phylon,* 20 (Spring, 1959), pp. 48–66.

[6] R. M. MacIver, *The Web of Government* (New York: Macmillan, 1947), chaps. 2 and 3; David B. Truman, *The Governmental Process* (New York: Knopf, 1959).

hauser[7] has contrasted pluralistic society with three other types of political forms—the folk, the mass, and the totalitarian. He characterizes pluralistic society as having the most freedom, because of the presence of intermediate associations which provide access to government for all segments of society and prevent the elite from manipulating the population.

A companion frame of reference, that of process of public opinion formation, provides a dynamic mechanism for the theory of pluralist society. In focusing on process rather than other aspects of public opinion, we follow the distinction drawn by MacIver,[8] who specified three parts of "the public opinion system": ground of consensus, structure of communication, and opinion alignment. The first includes values and other cultural elements, and the third embraces the end product of the process, as seen in the results of opinion polls. The second element is under consideration here. It revolves around communication of all sorts, whether in the mass media or in the deliberations and exchanges in and between groups, formal and informal. This group-communication aspect is basic to many works dealing with the formation of public opinion.[9] Simultaneously, these groups are the intermediate associations central to the

theory of pluralist society, mechanisms through which the clash of interests brings various segments of society into the political forum and produces pressures for change.

THE NONPLURALISM OF THE DEEP SOUTH

The central contention of this paper is that the Deep South is the least pluralistic of the regions and harbors less "public opinion process" in the sense of controversial public discussion, and that these characteristics inhibit change toward desegregation. This general thesis will be analyzed in terms of five more specific propositions dealing with pluralistic structure and participation:

1 There are fewer organizations—of all kinds except those related to churches—in South than North, and these have lower membership than elsewhere.

2 Of the kinds of groups which stimulate political controversy in the North, at least four are either nonexistent or weaker in the Deep South.

3 When northern and southern communities are compared with respect to political behavior, more pluralism and wider participation are found in the northern city.

4 All the Deep South institutions—familial, political, economic, and religious—are organized around the values of white supremacy, making segregation itself a structural principle of the region.

5 Those few organizations which do oppose segregation express themselves but rarely and cautiously on the race issue, and are continually subject to reprisals and threats which in turn maintain the pressure for continued caution.

The data which follow constitute the body of the paper. The evidence has been taken from a variety of sources, mostly studies conducted with other purposes in mind, and also from the observation of the writer. Documentation of the first proposal—a very broad one—is perhaps the least satisfactory, but no evidence has been found which

[7] William Kornhauser, *The Politics of Mass Society* (Glencoe: The Free Press, 1959).

[8] R. M. MacIver, *Academic Freedom in the United States* (New York: Columbia University Press, 1954).

[9] Carroll D. Clark, "The Concept of the Public," *Southwestern Social Science Quarterly,* 13 (March, 1933), pp. 311, 320; Nelson M. Foote and Clyde W. Hart, "Public Opinion and Collective Behavior," in Muzafer Sherif and M. O. Wilson (eds.), *Group Relations at the Crossroads* (New York: Harper, 1953); Herbert Bluner, "Collective Behavior," in A. M. Lee (ed.), *New Outline of the Principles of Sociology* (New York: Barnes and Noble, 1946), pp. 189–196; W. Phillips Davison, "The Public Opinion Process," *Public Opinion Quarterly,* 22 (Summer, 1958), pp. 91–102.

contravenes the trend. Taken together, the five propositions present a pattern that suggests a general, although tentative, support of the hypothesis.

Proposition 1 : There is less organizational activity in the Deep South

The South rated lowest among the four regions on most of the organizational indices used in the Bureau of Agricultural Economics studies of 140 villages a generation ago.[10] This was true for number of organizations, average organizations per village, and average membership in organizations of various types. Only in attendance did southern groups perform on a par with the other regions. In the category "social organizations per 1,000 community population" southern villages ranked far below the other regions. As shown in Table 1, where the shopping center was less than twenty-five miles away and over 25,000 population, southern villages had 1.8 social organizations per 1,000 population, as against 7.7 for the country as a whole.

Although the gap was smaller than this in the remaining subcategories, the difference was always substantial and in the same direction. In a more

recent study, Payne[11] found higher religious membership in two southern rural areas than in comparative northern sections, but again, lower membership in agricultural extensions and Grange programs, the difference being considerable. It would appear that a smaller proportion of the Deep South population participates in the "intermediate associations" typical of pluralist society.

Proposition 2: Four types of groups crucial to controversial political activity are absent or weak in the Deep South

On the American political scene there are several types of organizations which contribute to much of the controversy, in the form of demands and campaigns to secure these demands. Among these groups are the two major political parties, industrial groups (management and labor), religious groups, ethnic groups, farm groups and veterans', women's, professional and many other types of groups representing and cutting across the various interests of the society. When the Deep South is analyzed, however, the picture changes enormously: opposition groups of the first four types listed above are either absent or relatively weak, and all others

[10] Edmund deS. Brunner and Irving Lorge, *Rural Trends in Depression Years* (New York: Columbia Univ. Press, 1937), chap. 10; and Edmund deS. Brunner and J. H. Kolb, *Rural Social Trends* (New York: McGraw-Hill, 1933).

[11] Raymond Payne, "Some Comparisons of Participation in Rural Mississippi, Kentucky, Ohio, Illinois and New York," *Rural Sociology,* 18 (June, 1953), pp. 171-172.

TABLE 1   Social Organizations per 1,000 Community Population by Size of Shopping Center and Distance from That Center and by Region—140 Villages

	Under 25 miles	25–50 Miles	50 Miles and More
		Under 10,000 population	
All regions	6.0	7.5	4.1
South	2.5	4.0	1.3
		10,000 to 25,000 population	
All regions	4.7	5.7	4.6
South	2.7	3.0	3.2
		25,000 and over	
All regions	7.7	5.9	6.1
South	1.8	1.6	2.3

Source: Edmund deS. Brunner and J. H. Kolb, *Rural Social Trends* (New York: McGraw-Hill, 1933), p. 372. The data were gathered in 1930. Three other regions were included in the table: Middle Atlantic, Middle West, and Far West.

are perhaps weaker as well. This absence of "countervailing" groups prevents all effective challenges to the system.

Political The Republican party is weak or totally absent in the "Solid South." While Republicans have won numerous votes in recent Presidential elections, they receive few—averaging perhaps from 5 to 20 percent—of the votes when they run for governor or United States Senator.[12]

Several political patterns can be discerned in the Deep South, but V. O. Key and others have found a strong tendency to domination by big farmers and city financial and industrial leaders. Historically, while cleavages and dissent were countenanced prior to about 1830,[13] and expressed again around the turn of the century by the Populists, later generations have seen less structured clamor from opposition groups. Historians relate this to several factors: the potentially threatening presence of the Negro, the war and reconstruction, the one-party system, the successful repulsion of labor organizers, and poverty and rural folk patterns. There is some agreement among historians that an understanding was reached between the ruling Bourbons and the Populists around the turn of the century when the Populists showed they could arouse the southern working classes; in effect, all factions agreed not to woo the Negro vote. White supremacy continued to hold ultimate priority, so that class issues were muted.[14] (The appeal to the lower classes by Huey Long in Louisiana was an exception to the general pattern.) "Within this framework of a limited suffrage," according to Key, "at times state-wide campaigns are but personal rivalries uncomplicated by substantial social and economic issues."[15] It was in this connection that Key came closest to the argument being presented in this paper: "The factional system simply provides no institutionalized mechanism for the expression of lower-bracket viewpoints."[16] Key did not go on to develop this theme. A related observation was made by Floyd Hunter:[17] "Power groups in Old State . . . must depend upon speed in spotting and isolating dissident elements in the body politic." As will be suggested below, the chances for the continuing public operation of an organizational vehicle which challenged this power were exceedingly slim; legitimation of the system was strong at all points.

Labor Union strength is least evident in the South among the regions. Repeated drives to "organize Dixie" have stalled. This resistance has a historical base; Cash[18] has described at length how labor organizers for decades were routed with violence and the charge of communism. The large supply of cheap labor and the absence of other sympathetic class-oriented organizations are factors in this weakness. For the category "percent of nonagricultural employment organized," the five Deep South states rank well below the national average:

Alabama: 25 percent
Georgia: 15 percent
Louisiana: 20 percent
Mississippi: 15 percent

[12] Richard M. Scammon (ed.), *America Votes 3* (Pittsburgh: Univ. of Pittsburgh Press, 1959).

[13] Clement Eaton, *Freedom of Thought in the Old South* (Durham: Duke Univ. Press, 1940).

[14] C. Vann Woodward, *Origins of the New South* (Baton Rouge: Louisiana State Univ. Press, 1951); Francis B. Simkins, *A History of the South* (New York: Knopf, 1959).

[15] V. O. Key, *Southern Politics* (New York: Knopf, 1949), p. 308

[16] *Ibid.*, p. 309.

[17] Floyd Hunter, *Community Power Structure* (Chapel Hill: University of North Carolina Press, 1953), p. 160.

[18] W. J. Cash, *The Mind of the South* (New York: Knopf, 1941), pp. 351–368.

South Carolina: 9 percent
United States: 33 percent[19]

The general situation of labor in the Deep South is reflected in the fact that southern groups seeking industry have advertised the docility of their unorganized labor, in the fact that these states have been among the slowest to pass laws for workmen's compensation, child labor, and female labor, and have been lax in administering such laws as were put on the books.[20] Finally, southern unions are probably less militant than those in the North.

Ethnic groups Demographic data reveal a striking degree of homogeneity among whites of the region. With the exception of the big cities and parts of the Gulf Coast, most counties in the Deep South show proportions of Anglo-Saxon heritage well over 90 percent. Among the regions the area contains by far the smallest proportions of foreign-born, mixed parentage, and eastern and southern European stock.[21] Hence there is simply no militant "hyphenated" pressure-group organization, nor the potentiality for one.

Religious groups Stemming in large part from the Anglo-Saxon homogeneity of the region, there is also less potential for sociopolitical dissent from the religious sector. Most of the churches are Protestant; the sometimes energetic civic activity arising from Catholic, Jewish, and Greek Orthodox churches in other American cities is precluded. Where Protestant churches themselves differ from the more educated, higher class urban denomina-

tions, they take on another characteristic which removes them from political activity: a focus upon the salvation of the individual person rather than on any kind of "social gospel."

Other types of groups Voluminous data establish the relative weakness of Republican, labor, ethnic, and church groups in the Deep South. It is possible, moreover, that the pattern goes deeper, but clear evidence on the relative impotence of other kinds of groups is lacking. Women's groups in the South have made no record comparable to that forged by comparable groups in New England. Feminism became a powerful force in nineteenth-century New England, mobilizing three movements which led to constitutional amendments: abolition of slavery, women's suffrage, and prohibition. Scattered southern women's groups have conducted successful campaigns as with antilynching, but more typically they deal with "culture," gardening, and the past. Another type of group—farm organizations—were found by Payne to be larger and more numerous in North than South, and in the four pairs of cities (cited below) they show more influence in the North. Still another type of group, the Boy Scouts, a youth-civic organization, keeps membership records in its various branches state by state; for 1959, per capita scout membership (including adults) was 42 percent higher in the rest of the country than in the five Deep South states. Finally, a nationwide study of group participation showed that persons widely found in the South—rural, less educated, Democrats—are the least likely to belong to formal organizations.[22] On the other hand, such prom-

---

[19] Alexander Heard, *The Costs of Democracy* (Chapel Hill: University of North Carolina Press, 1960), p. 174.

[20] Charles W. Pipkin, "Social Legislation," in W. T. Couch (ed.), *Culture in the South* (Chapel Hill: University of North Carolina Press, 1934).

[21] E. P. Hutchinson, *Immigrants and Their Children* (New York: Wiley, 1956, chap. 3).

[22] Julian L. Woodward and Elmo Roper, "Political Activity of American Citizens," *American Political Science Review*, 44 (December, 1950), pp. 872–885.

inent groups as the United Daughters of the Confederacy, with chapters in many Deep South communities, were formed to reinforce the traditional system.

Proposition 3: Less political behavior is found when comparing pairs of northern and southern communities

Using published studies, it is possible to perform a secondary analysis of four pairs of communities, a northern and a southern city in each pair, studying the dynamics of political participation in each pair. Size is roughly even within pairs, except for the fourth pair. The smallest are Springdale and Cottonville: going up in size are Jonesville and Old Town: Yankee City and Talladega; and the two largest, Steelport and Regional City.[23] The communities were visted at different times, and no claim to representativeness of the regions can be made, but these were the only four available studies of Deep South communities.

All eight communities are run in oligarchic fashion, northern as well as southern. All contain churches, civic clubs, fraternal groups, and other associations. In each pair, however, more pluralism, dissent, and a consequent wider distribution of access are present

in the northern city. The nearest exception is found in the smallest northern town, Springdale, where the Democrats are weak and most people are antiunion. Yet union men live there, the Democrats win some elections, and the Poles, Finns, and Norwegians of the North are either unknown or minimally present in the native-born Protestant South.

The greatest contrast, perhaps, obtains between the two largest cities, Steelport and Regional City. Although Steelport is much the smaller, its burgeoning democratization stands in striking contrast to the well-known domination by business elites in Regional City. Labor in Steelport "took off" in 1937 with the CIO and shortly gained considerable power. The Democratic party concurrently was able to challenge the traditional Republican hegemony, bringing further access to the city's majority of Catholic and Greek Orthodox European groups. In Regional City, on the other hand, only two of the top forty leaders are unionists. Within the two main factions of the Democratic party, ranks are closed in the face of a threat from challengers who would open public discussion of basic issues, as shown in the case of the denial of the ballot to the Progressive party in 1948.[24]

A fifth Deep South locality, "Plantation County,"[25] could be added to the above set of comparisons were it not so small (three hundred families) that the ethnographer chose to study the entire county. The paternalistic pattern with the planter as overlord, although preserving a *noblesse oblige* spirit toward Negroes in the face of the newcomer merchants, falls within the pat-

---

[23] The studies are, respectively, Arthur J. Vidieh and Joseph Bensman, *Small Town in Mass Society* (Garden City: Doubleday, 1960); Hortense Powdermaker, *After Freedom* (New York: Viking, 1939); W. L. Warner, *Democracy in Jonesville* (New York: Harper, 1949); Allison Davis, Burleigh B. Gardner, and Mary R. Gardner, *Deep South* (Chicago: Univ. of Chicago Press, 1941); W. L. Warner and Paul S. Lunt, *The Social Life of a Modern Community* (New Haven: Yale Univ. Press, 1941); Solon T. Kimball and Marion Pearsall, *The Talladega Story* (University, Alabama: The Univ. of Alabama Press, 1954); James B. McKee, "The Power to Decide," in Meyer Weinberg and Oscar E. Shabat, *Society and Man* (Englewood Cliffs: Prentice-Hall, 1956), pp. 528–538; Floyd Hunter, *Community Power Structure* (Chapel Hill: Univ. of North Carolina Press, 1953).

[24] Hunter, *op. cit.,* p. 160.

[25] Morton Rubin, *Plantation County* (Chapel Hill: Univ. of North Carolina Press, 1951). This study is significant for its sensitivity to social change.

tern sketched for the other four Deep South communities. No opposition groups are present; the new merchants maintain not only the white domination, but cooperate with the older planters on crucial policies. Because the plantation is the hub of its own community, little is said about associations, except that the "more important associations . . . have to do with securing white supremacy and the general status of the groups already in power."[26] Also, "the whites control politics above all."[27] Aside from the planter-merchant rift, almost the only case of "public opinion" in the county apparently was kept virtually private, i.e., out of official, public notice, such as courts and press. Two white boys beat up a Negro; the sheriff held the boys overnight and released them, and no trial took place. "The white community continued to discuss the incident for several months,"[28] but apparently at the interpersonal, gossip level, permitting the institutional structure once again to escape official public examination.

Proposition 4: Southern institutions are built around the structural principle of segregation

Human groups operate, not in a vacuum, but within a cultural system which structures behavior through norms and roles. In the culture of the Deep South, segregation is a vital part of each of the main institutions. The family socializes the young into the system, and is the haven of "racial purity"; the obligations of kinship and the idealization of women both are often noted as greater in the South than elsewhere. Religion offers the less-educated minister a biblical justification for segregation and the hierarchical order in general; southern churches stress old testament revivalism

and personal salvation more than the social gospel, and almost all churches are segregated in membership. Economic life in all forms but retailing operates with a color differential, and job discrimination is a mechanism for continuing the pattern. Politics are played around the Negro issue, and through political control the system perpetuates itself; chauvinism against "meddling by outsiders" characterize the region, as does a low respect for law and a high frequency of violence. The principle of segregation pervades the region in all areas: the mass media, like education, are less prominent in southern life,[29] and offer little challenge to the system; the memory of the Civil War is kept alive in speeches and in Confederate caps and flags, and the band playing Dixie marching past the Civil War statue in the town square. It is this institutionalization of segregation as an organizing principle of southern life, plus the lack of opposition groups to challenge the tradition, and not merely the internalization of prejudices, that is required to understand the persistence of individual attitudes of prejudice in millions of persons.

Proposition 5: Existing organizations in the Deep South rarely express their opposition to segregation and are strongly sanctioned when they do

It was into the institutional setting sketched above that the Supreme Court decision of 1954 was issued. The reaction could have been predictable from a knowledge of the nonpluralism of the region. Without opposition forces to develop a public opinion situation, groups such as the White Citizens' Councils organized to mobilize the region and express protest and reaffirmation of the traditional way of life.

[26] *Ibid.*, p. 182.
[27] *Ibid.*, p. 99.
[28] *Ibid.*, p. 102.

[29] Harry E. Moore, "Mass Communication in the South," *Social Forces,* 29 (March 1951), pp. 365–376.

They quickly gained a "monopoly of propaganda"—virtually unobtainable in other regions with more pluralistic organization—and were able to use the classic propaganda strategy of appealing to values already held by the audience—those of segregation and sectional virtue and autonomy. Reinforcement through primary group channels followed, and the region remained solidary.

With segregation groups dominating the scene, white opposition groups—the few that existed—made sporadic attempts to challenge the system. Statewide affiliates of the Southern Regional Council and similar local groups found few white recruits and were stigmatized and harassed. Such groups were typically led by clergymen, social workers, and professors, many from the North. The attempt to attract power personnel failed. In New Orleans professionals tried for two years to mobilize business leaders, without success. Much of the work remained underground, but once in the open, sanctions from the majority were quickly forthcoming. Letters to the editor called forth a counterbarrage. Members who spoke at meetings, testified at hearings, or gave their names as group officers were subjected to night telephone calls, taxis sent to their homes, and threats against life, children, and property.[30] Even within the groups, as Foreman[31] has pointed out, a splintering arose over questions of timing, scope, and tactics, and these impasses often led to preoccupation with administrative details and little community

action. Few, if any, dissenting roles, in other words, promised rewards.

THE PATTERN OF CHANGE

One finds very little exception to this pattern. No Deep South community has voluntarily desegregated its schools. Cities that did so shortly after the 1954 decision were in border areas with existing groups ready to work for compliance. In Nashville, for example, Anna Holden reported at least 17 organizations which publicly worked for desegregation, including the American Association of University Women, B'nai B'rith, Fellowship of Southern Churchmen, League of Women Voters, Middle Tennessee Mental Health Association, Nashville Association of Churches, National Association of Social Workers, Council of Colored Parent-Teacher Associations, Council of Parent-Teacher Associations, CIO Council, AFL Trades and Labor Council, Nashville Ministerial Association, National Council of Jewish Women, Tennessee State Nurses Association, United Church Women, and the Young Women's Christian Association.[32] Similar organizational opposition to resistance developed in Washington, D. C., Louisville, Baltimore, St. Louis, and Kansas City.

In cities farther to the South, much less group activity is discovered. In Little Rock the organized antisegregation forces during the crisis period were confined to the clergy in higher-class churches and the Arkansas Council on Human Relations. In Virginia, "the Committee for Public Schools stepped in to fill a void left by the initial failure of other groups. . . ."[33] Three inte-

---

[30] In such a situation the phenomenon of "pluralistic ignorance" tends to suggest to people that "everybody else" still holds the traditional attitudes. Warren Breed and Thomas Ktsanes, "Puralistic Ignorance in the Process of Opinion Formation," *Public Opinion Quarterly,* 25 (Fall, 1961), pp. 382–392.

[31] Paul B. Foreman, "Local Interracial Groups in the Deep South," and "A Script for the Washington Panel" (dittoed), 1957.

[32] Anna Holden, "A First Step Toward School Integration," pamphlet published by the Congress of Racial Equality, June, 1958, pp. 11–12.

[33] William M. Lightsey, "Organization to Save Public Schools," pamphlet published by the Virginia Committee for Public Schools, n.d., p. 1.

grationist organizations formed in New Orleans after 1954, but all met with reprisals and were inactive by 1960.[34] In each case, the development of a moderate organizational structure waited until the issuance of final court orders and the threat—or in the case of Little Rock and Norfolk, the reality— of closed public schools.

Social change, in fact, has come only under certain conditions, and two of these are forces from outside the system. One is the federal government and its court orders and in the extreme case (Little Rock) the use of troops. The other is the previously docile Negro community and its court suits, boycotts, sit-ins, and Freedom Rides, all reflecting a new organizational form and a new ideology of equality. Precisely because they were in many ways outside the old system, they were more insulated from the sanctions inhibiting challenge from the white liberals.

The third major new condition was the threat of closed schools. These added conditions point to a kind of "natural history" of the Deep South community as it confronts desegregation, and the process can be seen in terms of the theoretical scheme of increasing pluralism and the development of a public opinion situation. Several stages occur roughly in this order: (1) a monopoly of community sentiment in favor of segregation; (2) a federal court suit brought by the Negro community; (3) rallying of heightened resistance efforts; (4) a court order to desegregate; (5) the threat of closed schools; (6) the mushrooming of moderate groups in the white community favoring compliance, law and order, and open schools—and thus a public opinion situation; (7) the crisis with possible violence by segregationists; and (8) the start of gradual desegregation, with continued resistance. The details differ with each city, but the two sets of outside forces and the threat of school closing have always brought opposition groups to the fore and the development of pluralism and the open exchange of opinions. The function of the process is to bring change, toward a more universalistic definition of the situation, while permitting the community to struggle with all available means to maintain tradition.

CONCLUSION

The thesis that the Deep South has a less-pluralistic social structure and less political participation than other regions has been supported by diverse data coming from numerous published studies of the South, and from the observation of the writer. Evidence exists to suggest that the Deep South has fewer organizations and lower membership than elsewhere, and that this is strikingly true with respect to such politically relevant groups as a major opposition political party, labor unions, and ethnic and religious minority groups. Within this structure, it is not surprising that southern communities appear to exhibit less widespread political participation on the part of various segments of the population, but rather to show greater control by a traditional set of elites. These leaders through the years have demonstrated a tendency to keep issues of a potentially controversial sort from entering the public arena, and to run public affairs on a personalistic basis. Thus "public opinion" in the sense of group structure and discussion process is absent in the sense known to other regions. Few channels for feedback are provided in the system, so that the

[34] Warren Breed, "The Process of Moderate Opinion Formation in the New Orleans School Desegregation Crisis of 1960" (dittoed), 1961.

power structure goes unchallenged by what would constitute opposition groups elsewhere. All of this activity takes place within a set of institutions which are themselves built around traditions like segregation and are highly operative whenever social change is threatened; in addition the widespread distribution of segregationist attitudes reinforces institutional practices. Thus the few groups which would express anti-segregation sentiments do so softly and even then are strongly pressured, by various techniques of social control, to refrain from providing legitimation for new ideologies. It remained for the threat of closed public schools, and the continuing pressure of the federal government and Negro groups, which were basically outside the system, for countervailing groups finally to mobilize in several large southern cities.

DISCUSSION

This study has been exploratory in nature, and further work will be required for validation. More intensive study of the size and provenience of politically relevant groups and how they operate to represent or discriminate against various interests is indicated, for the non-South as well as the South. In addition, the region presents a laboratory for the study of problems and processes of public opinion formation through the observation of groups—old or new—and how they adapt to new situations by either maintaining nativist orientations or seeking to shift to new positions and still keep their membership and their legitimacy in the community. The groups can be analyzed along the dimensions of "social movements,"[35] and the sociology

of knowledge. At the level of community, the question might be raised as to the similarity or dissimilarity of the cohesiveness and the viability of communities within different societal arrangements—as between North and South, or between these regions and various societies (feudal, totalitarian, colonial, etc.) in other parts of the world.[36] Such comparative study, treating institutions as well as groups and political participation, is indicated if the theories of institutional structure and change are to be advanced. The focus could shift to changes within the system as a response to external pressures, and material could be organized around "the four functional problems" —with the Deep South being forced to restructure its behavior with respect to goal attainment and adaptation, with consequent problems of pattern-modification and integration.

At the level of personality, as stated earlier, "attitudes" may be symptoms of social situations as well as their cause; the relationship of nonpluralism and "southern personality structure" (sometimes considered to be ingenuous, self-assured, arrogant, etc.) offers a possibility for study.[37] It may be that the kind of social environment which facilitates the operation of the "vicious circle" of continued attitudinal prejudice also fails to provide the individual southerner with any serious controversial opposition through which to achieve the more universalistic attitude structures found more widely in the non-South.

[35] Clarence E. Glick, "Collective Behavior in Race Relations," *American Sociological Review*, 13 (June, 1948), pp. 287-294.

[36] Compare Deep South social structure with those countries described in Lucian W. Pye, "Communication Patterns and the Problems of Representative Government in Non-Western Societies," *Public Opinion Quarterly*, 20 (Spring, 1956), pp. 249-257.

[37] See the discussions of southern personality by two southern observers, Josephine Pinckney and Clarence E. Cason, in Couch, *op. cit.*

18
Social Structure and the Negro Revolt: An Examination of Some Hypotheses*
JAMES A. GESCHWENDER

Five general types of hypotheses which attempt to explain current black protest have appeared in the sociological literature.

The first of these might be called the "vulgar Marxist hypothesis." It could be so named because of the general belief that this is the manner in which Marx believed revolutions originated.[1] This hypothesis may be stated: *As a group experiences a worsening of its conditions of life, it will become increasingly dissatisfied until it eventually rebels.* It is questionable if this is the correct interpretation of Marx's analysis of the cause of the revolutions.[2] Nevertheless, this hypothesis has received support from Sorokin in his analysis of revolution and qualifies as a candidate hypothesis.[3]

The second type of hypothesis might be called the "rising expectations hypothesis." This hypothesis may be stated: *As a group experiences an improvement in its conditions of life it will also experience a rise in its level of desires. The latter will rise more rapidly than the former, leading to dissatisfaction and rebellion.* The classic statement of this hypothesis was presented by L. P. Edwards though others have presented similar formulations.[4]

The third kind of explanation might be called the "sophisticated Marxist hypothesis," after its author, or the "relative deprivation hypothesis," after its nature. This hypothesis may be stated: *As a group experiences an improvement in its conditions of life and simultaneously observes a second group experiencing a more rapid rate of improvement, it will become dissatisfied with its rate of improvement and rebel.* Marx saw the chain of events—including the alienation of labor, the development of class consciousness, and the proletarian revolution—as having its inception with feelings of relative deprivation resulting from a set of changes in objective conditions.[5]

The fourth type of hypothesis might be called the "rise and drop hypothesis." It may be worded: *As a group experiences an improvement in its conditions of life followed by a sharp reversal of this improvement, it will become dissatisfied and rebel.* James C. Davies formulated this hypothesis.[6]

The fifth type of hypothesis might be called the "status inconsistency hypothesis," and may be worded: *A group which possesses a number of status attributes which are differently ranked on the various status heirarchies will be dissatisfied and prone toward rebellion.* This hypothesis is probably best known through Lenski's work in status crystallization but is similar to

---

*[Reprinted from *Social Forces,* vol. 43, no. 2, December 1964, by permission of the University of North Carolina Press.]
[1] Cf. James C. Davies, "Toward a Theory of Revolution," *American Sociological Review,* 27 (February 1962), pp. 5–18, esp. p. 5.
[2] Cf. Reinhard Bendix and Seymour Martin Lipset, "'Karl Marx' Theory of Social Classes," Reinhard Bendix and Seymour Martin Lipset (eds.), *Class, Status and Power* (Glencoe, Illinois: The Free Press, 1953), pp. 32–33.
[3] Pitirim A. Sorokin, *The Sociology of Revolution* (Philadelphia: J. B. Lippincott Co., 1925), p. 367.

[4] Lyford P. Edwards, *The Natural History of Revolution* (Chicago: The Univ. of Chicago Press, 1927). See also the passage quoted from A. de Tocqueville in Davies, *op. cit.,* p. 6; and Crane Brinton, *The Anatomy of Revolution* (New York: W. W. Norton Co., 1938), esp. pp. 74–78 and pp. 44–46.
[5] See citations in Davies, *op. cit.,* p. 5; Bendix and Lipset, *op. cit.,* pp. 32–33.
[6] Davies, *op. cit.,* p. 6.

propositions of Broom, Hughes, and Sorokin.[7]

To evaluate these hypotheses, census data are used to analyze changes in the position of Negroes and whites between 1940 and 1960 with respect to education, occupation, and income. These categories are chosen because they are important determinants of life chances and style.

The nonwhite is improving his educational level relative to previous generations of nonwhites and also is improving his educational level relative to whites. The data are ambiguous as to proportional gains in the upper educational categories.

When considered as a totality, the data on occupational changes indicate that nonwhites are leaving the farms more rapidly than whites; are being occupationally upgraded relative to previous generations of nonwhites; and are experiencing some occupational upgrading relative to whites but possibly not at the highest occupational status levels. Nonwhite income has shown a relatively steady increase in both current and constant dollars from 1939 to 1961. White income has shown a similar increase in both current and constant dollars.

However, the rate of increase for whites has been relatively greater than that for blacks. Up to 1961 nonwhites had raised their standard of living but not as rapidly as whites.

[7] Gerhard Lenski, "Status Crystalization: A Non-Verbal Dimension of Social Status," *American Sociological Review,* 19 (August 1954), p. 412; Leonard Broom, "Social Differentiation and Stratification," Robert K. Merton, Leonard Broom and Leonard S. Cottrell (eds.), *Sociology Today* (New York: Basic Books, Inc. 1959), pp. 429–41; Everett C. Hughes, "Social Change and Status Protest: An Essay on the Marginal Man," *Phylon,* 10 (First Quarter 1949), pp. 58–65; Pitirim A. Sorokin, *Society, Culture and Personality* (New York: Harper & Bros., 1947).

EVALUATION OF HYPOTHESIS

What are the implications of these changes for the above hypotheses?

The "vulgar Marxist hypothesis," which predicted rebellion as a result of a worsening of conditions of life, is clearly inconsistent with these data. The position of the Negro is improving educationally, occupationally, and incomewise.

The "rising expectations hypothesis," which predicted rebellion as a result of improvements in conditions of life, is consistent with the data examined. Negroes have improved their level of education; they have better jobs; and they are earning more money with which they may purchase more things. One might assume a more rapid rise in level of aspirations.

The "sophisticated Marxist hypothesis," which gave a relative deprivation basis for its prediction of rebellion, is also consistent with these data. Negroes have improved their level of education and have done so more rapidly than have whites. But education is not a direct measure of living conditions either socially or economically. It is one source of status and, as such, it carries with it certain satisfactions. Occupation may be viewed as a second source of status. The Negro has improved his occupational level, thus improving his status rewards as well as receiving other rewards in terms of better working conditions. The evidence is not clear as to the relative occupational level, thus improving his status rewards as well as receiving other rewards in terms of better working conditions. The evidence is not clear as to the relative occupational gains or losses experienced by the Negro. He appears to be moving more rapidly than whites into the middle status occupations, but if urban occupations only are considered, he is moving more slowly into the higher status occupations. Whether this situation would produce feelings of relative loss or relative gain is a moot question which could only be settled through further empirical studies.

The area of income most directly affects conditions of life and presents the clearest picture. Negroes are improving their incomes in terms of both current and constant dollars. The gap between white and Negro incomes is also increasing in terms of both current and constant dollars. Thus, Negroes are improving their material conditions of life but are not doing so at the same rate as whites. This is the perfect situation to create feelings of relative deprivation leading to rebellion.

The "rise and drop hypothesis," which predicted rebellion as a result of the reversal of past progress in conditions of life, is not consistent with the data examined. There appears to be a relatively steady improvement in level of education, level of occupation, and income in both current and constant dollars. No reversal may be observed.

The "status inconsistency hypothesis," which predicted rebellion as a result of an increase in the proportion of status inconsistents, is consistent with the data examined. There has been an increase in the proportion of status inconsistents among Negroes. This is true in both a trivial and a significant sense. Current research in status inconsistency emphasizes the dimensions of occupation, income, education, and ethnicity as the crucial ones for American society. Negroes have retained their low ethnic status, but they have improved their position on each of the other status dimensions. Thus, they have increased their status inconsistency in the trivial sense. They have increased the combination of low ethnic status

with higher rankings on other dimensions.

Negroes have also increased their status inconsistency in a more significant sense. These data show that they are not only improving their level of education, but they are doing so at a more rapid rate than whites, while in the area of occupational gains there has not been as significant a gain relative to that of whites.

Even if we ignore their ethnicity, Negroes are becoming increasingly status inconsistent as a result of the fact that they are raising their level of education but are being denied the occupational mobility or income level which would "normally" be associated with such progress.

DISCUSSION

Only two out of the five proposed hypotheses have been rejected. This leaves the task of either choosing among the remaining hypotheses or somehow reconciling them. It is a relatively simple task to reconcile the "sophisticated Marxist hypothesis" with the "status inconsistency hypothesis," as the essence of each is the concept of the relative deprivation. The former is explicitly stated in these terms, while the latter's thesis is implied. It is the association between statuses which generally prevails in a society that determines what is status consistency. Deviations from this prevailing association are what constitute status inconsistency. It is the experiencing of these deviations to one's own detriment which causes the propensity to revolt among status inconsistents.[8]

It is also possible to reconcile the "rising expectations hypothesis" with

[8] Cf., George C. Homans, *Social Behavior: Its Elementary Forms* (New York: Harcourt, Brace & World, 1961), pp. 232–264.

the "status inconsistency hypothesis." Both Edwards and Brinton see blockages of social mobility as an essential basis for the "rising expectations hypothesis."[9] People feel that they have legitimate aspirations which are blocked, thus interfering with the circulation of the elite, and creating a status inconsistent group. This is very similar to the interpretation that Broom gives to the "status inconsistency hypothesis."

It seems that "relative deprivation" is the essence of all three hypotheses that are consistent with the observed data. It is only by observing the process of social mobility in society that one will develop aspirations for such mobility. Observation of the criteria used to select successful aspirants are legitimate. Possession of these characteristics without subsequent mobility creates status inconsistency. Without comparing one's own experiences with those of others in society and subsequently developing feelings of relative deprivation, no rebellion would take place. This should not be misinterpreted as a claim that the psychological state of possessing feelings of relative deprivation will, regardless of objective conditions, produce rebellion. In contrast, the suggestion proposed herein is that certain types of objective conditions will produce feelings of relative deprivation, which will, in turn, produce rebellion.

The Negro in the United States has been exposed to just such a set of objective conditions. He is handicapped by blockages in the circulation of the elite, especially in the area of the professions. He is acquiring the education which is normally the key to occupational mobility and economic gain. He is not experiencing as rapid a rate of occupa-

[9] Brinton, op. cit., pp. 78–79; Edwards, op. cit., p. 30.

tional mobility to which he feels he is entitled. He is not receiving the economic rewards which he feels he has earned. As a result, he is becoming increasingly status inconsistent and he sees himself falling further and further behind the white.

19
Religion: Opiate or Inspiration of Civil Rights Militancy among Negroes?*
GARY T. MARX

Let justice roll down like waters, and righteousness like a mighty stream. [Amos 5:24]

But God . . . is white. And if his love was so great, and if he loved all his children, why were we the blacks, cast down so far? [James Baldwin]

The relationship between religion and political radicalism is a confusing one. On the one hand, established religious institutions have generally had a stake in the status quo and hence have supported conservatism. Furthermore, with the masses having an otherworldly orientation, religious zeal, particularly as expressed in the more fundamentalist branches of Christianity, has been seen as an alternative to the development of political radicalism. On the other hand, as the source of universal humanistic values and the strength that can come from believing one is carrying out God's will in political matters, religion has occasionally played a strong

*[Reprinted from the American Sociological Review, vol. 32, no. 1, 1969, by permission of the American Sociological Association. Revision of paper read at the annual meeting of the American Sociological Association, August 1966. This paper may be identified as publication A-72 of the Survey Research Center, University of California, Berkeley. I am grateful to Gertrude J. Selznick and Stephen Steinberg for their work on the early phase of this project, and to the Anti-Defamation League for support.]

positive role in movements for radical social change.

This dual role of religion is clearly indicated in the case of the American Negro and race protest. Slaves are said to have been first brought to this country on the "good ship Jesus Christ."[1] While there was occasional controversy over the effect that religion had on them it appears that most slaveowners eventually came to view supervised religion as an effective means of social control. Stampp, in commenting on the effect of religion, notes:

. . . through religious instruction the bondsmen learned that slavery had divine sanction, that insolence was as much an offense against God as against the temporal master. They received the Biblical command that servants should obey their masters, and they heard of the punishments awaiting the disobedient slave in the hereafter. They heard, too, that eternal salvation would be their reward for faithful service . . .[2]

In discussing the period after the Civil War, Myrdal states that ". . . under the pressure of political reaction, the Negro church in the South came to have much the same role as it did before the Civil War. Negro frustration was sublimated into emotionalism, and Negro hopes were fixed on the after world."[3] Many other analysts, in considering the consequences of Negro religion from

the end of slavery until the early 1950's reached similar conclusions about the conservatizing effect of religion on race protest.[4]

However, the effect of religion on race protest throughout American history has by no means been exclusively in one direction. While many Negroes were no doubt seriously singing about chariots in the sky, Negro preachers such as Denmark Vesey and Nat Turner and the religiously inspired abolitionists were actively fighting slavery in their own way. All-Negro churches first came into being as protest organizations and later some served as meeting places where protest strategy was planned, or as stations on the underground railroad. The richness of protest symbolism in Negro spirituals and sermons has often been noted. Beyond this symbolic role, as a totally Negro institution, the church brought together in privacy people with a shared problem. It was from the church experience that many leaders were exposed to a broad range of ideas legitimizing protest and obtained the savoir faire, self-confidence, and organizational experience needed to chal-

---

[1] Louis Lomax, *When the Word Is Given,* New York: New American Library, 1964, p. 34. It has often been noted that when the missionaries came to Africa they had the Bible and the people had the land. When the missionaries left, they had the land and the Africans had the Bible.

[2] Kenneth Stampp, *The Peculiar Institution,* New York: Alfred A. Knopf, 1956, p. 158.

[3] Gunnar Myrdal *et al., An American Dilemma,* New York: Harper, 1944, pp. 851–853. About the North he notes that the church remained far more independent "but on the whole even the northern Negro church has remained a conservative institution with its interests directly upon other-worldly matters and has largely ignored the practical problems of the Negro's fate in this world."

[4] For example Dollard reports that "religion can be seen as a mechanism for the social control of Negroes" and that planters have always welcomed the building of a Negro church on the plantation but looked with less favor upon the building of a school. John Dollard, *Caste and Class in a Southern Town,* Garden City: Doubleday Anchor, 1957, p. 248. A few of the many others reaching similar conclusions are, Benjamin E. Mays and J. W. Nicholson, *The Negro's Church,* New York: Institute of Social and Religious Research, 1933; Hortense Powdermaker, *After Freedom,* New York: Viking Press, 1939, p. 285; Charles Johnson, *Growing Up in the Black Belt,* Washington, D.C.: American Council of Education, 1941, pp. 135–136; Horace Drake and St. Clair Cayton, *Black Metropolis,* New York: Harper and Row, 1962, pp. 424–429; George Simpson and Milton Yinger, *Racial and Cultural Minorities,* New York: Harper, rev. ed., 1958, pp. 582–587. In a more general context this social control consequence of religion has of course been noted throughout history from Plato to Montesquieu to Marx to Nietzsche to Freud to contemporary social theorists.

lenge an oppressive system. A recent commentator states that the slave churches were "the nucleus of the Negro protest" and another that "in religion Negro leaders had begun to find sanction and support for their movements of protest more than 150 years ago."[5]

Differing perceptions of the varied consequences religion may have on protest have continued to the present time. While there has been very little in the way of empirical research on the effect of the Negro church on protest,[6] the literature of race relations is rich with impressionistic statements which generally contradict each other about how the church either encourages and is the source of race protest or inhibits and retards its development. For example, two observers note, "as primitive evangelism gave way to a more sophisticated social consciousness, the church became the spearhead of Negro protest in the deep South,"[7] while another indicates "the Negro church is a sleeping giant. In civil rights participation its feet are hardly wet."[8] A civil rights activist, himself a clergyman, states: ". . . the church today is central to the movement . . . if there had been no Negro church, there would have been no civil rights movement today."[9] On the other hand, a sociologist, commenting on the more involved higher status ministers, notes: ". . . middle class Negro clergymen in the cities of the South generally advocated cautious gradualism in race activities until the mid-1950's when there was an upsurge of protest sentiment among urban Negroes . . . but most of them [ministers] did not embrace the more vigorous techniques of protest until other leaders took the initiative and gained widespread support."[10] Another sociologist states, "Whatever their previous conservative stance has been, the churches have now become 'spearheads of reform.'"[11] Still another indicates: ". . . the Negro church is particularly culpable for its general lack of concern for the moral and social problems of the

---

[5] Daniel Thompson, "The Rise of Negro Protest," *Annals of the American Academy of Political and Social Science,* 357 (January, 1965).

[6] The empirical evidence is quite limited. The few studies that have been done have focused on the Negro minister. Thompson notes that in New Orleans Negro ministers constitute the largest segment of the Negro leadership class (a grouping which is not necessarily the same as "protest leaders") but that "The vast majority of ministers are primarily interested in their pastoral role . . . their sermons are essentially biblical, dealing only tangentially with social issues." Daniel Thompson, *The Negro Leadership Class,* Englewood Cliffs, New Jersey: Prentice-Hall, 1963, pp. 34–35. Studies of the Negro ministry in Detroit and Richmond, California, also stress that only a small fraction of Negro clergymen show any active concern with the civil rights struggle. R. L. Johnstone, *Militant and Conservative Community Leadership among Negro Clergymen,* Ph.D. dissertation, University of Michigan, Ann Arbor, 1963, and J. Bloom, *The Negro Church and the Movement for Equality,* M.A. thesis, University of California, Berkeley, Department of Sociology, 1966.

It is worthy of mention that, although the number of cases was small, the Negro ministers in our sample had the lowest percentage militant of any occupational group. With respect to the sons of clergymen, the situation seems somewhat different. While the myth of the preacher's son gone bad is almost a part of American folklore, one would think that a comparable myth might develop within the Negro community—that of the preacher's son gone radical. Malcolm X, James Baldwin, A. Philip Randolph, Martin Luther King, James Farmer, Adam Clayton Powell, Elijah Muhammad, and a number of others had clergymen as fathers. To be taken into consideration is that clergymen make up a relatively larger segment of the Negro middle than of the white middle class.

[7] Jane Record and Wilson Record, "Ideological Forces and the Negro Protest," *Annals, op. cit.,* p. 92.

[8] G. Booker, *Black Man's America,* Englewood Cliffs, N.J.: Prentice-Hall, 1964, p. 111.

[9] Rev. W. T. Walker, as quoted in William Brink and Louis Harris, *The Negro Revolution in America,* New York: Simon and Schuster, 1964, p. 103.

[10] N. Glenn, "Negro Religion in the U.S." in L. Schneider, *Religion, Culture and Society,* New York: John Wiley, 1964.

[11] Joseph Fichter, "American Religion and the Negro," *Daedalus* (Fall, 1965), p. 1087.

community . . . it has been accommodating. Fostering indulgence in religious sentimentality, and riveting the attention of the masses on the bounties of a hereafter, the Negro church remains a refuge, and escape from the cruel realities of the here and now."[12]

Thus one faces opposing views, or at best ambiguity, in contemplating the current effect of religion. The opiating consequences of religion are all too well known as is the fact that the segregated church is durable and offers some advantages to clergy and members that might be denied them in a more integrated society. On the other hand, the prominent role of the Negro church in supplying much of the ideology of the movement, many of its foremost leaders, and an institution around which struggle might be organized—particularly in the South—can hardly be denied. It would appear from the bombings of churches and the writings of Martin Luther King and other religiously inspired activists that for many, religion and protest are closely linked.

Part of this dilemma may lie in the distinction between the church as an institution in its totality and particular individual churches within it, and the further distinctions among different types of individual religious concern. This paper is concerned with the latter subject; it is an inquiry into the relationship between religiosity and response to the civil rights struggle. It

first considers how religious denomination affects militancy, and then how various measures of religiosity, taken separately and together, are related to civil rights concern. The question is then asked of those classified as "very religious" and "quite religious," how an "otherworldly orientation"—as opposed to a "temporal" one—affects militancy.

In a nationwide study of Negroes living in metropolitan areas of the United States, a number of questions were asked about religious behavior and beliefs as well as about the civil rights struggle.[13] Seven of the questions dealing with civil rights protest have been combined into an index of conventional militancy.[14] Built into this index are a number of dimensions of racial protest such as impatience over the speed of integration, opposition to discrimination in public facilities and the sale of property, perception of barriers to Negro advancement, support of civil rights demonstrations, and expressed willingness to take part in a demonstration. Those giving the militant response to five or more of the questions are considered militant, those giving such a response to three

---

[12] E. U. Essien-Udom, *Black Nationalism,* New York: Dell Publishing Co., 1962, p. 358.

Many other examples of contradictory statements could be offered, sometimes even in the same volume. For example, Carleton Lee stresses the importance of religion for protest while Rayford Logan sees the Negro pastor as an instrument of the white power structure (in a book published to commemorate one hundred years of emancipation). Carleton Lee, "Religious Roots of Negro Protest," and Rayford Logan, "Educational Changes Affecting American Negroes," both in Arnold Rose, *Assuring Freedom to the Free,* Detroit: Wayne University Press, 1964.

[13] This survey was carried out in 1964 by the Survey Research Center, University of California, Berkeley. A nonsouthern metropolitan area probability sample was drawn as well as special area samples of Negroes living in New York City, Chicago, Atlanta, and Birmingham. Since the results reported here are essentially the same for each of these areas, they are treated together. More than 90 percent of the interviews were done with Negro interviewers. Additional methodological details may be found in Gary Marx, *Protest and Prejudice: A Study of Belief in the Black Community,* New York: Harper & Row, Torch book edition, 1969.

[14] Attention is directed to conventional militancy rather than to that of the Black Nationalist variety because a very small percentage of the sample offered strong and consistent support for Black Nationalism. As in studying support for the KKK, the Birch Society or the Communist party, a representative sample of normal size is inadequate.

or four of the questions, moderate, and fewer than three, conservative.[15]

DENOMINATION

It has long been known that the more fundamentalist sects such as the Holiness groups and the Jehovah's Witnesses are relatively uninterested in movements for secular political change.[16] Such transvaluational movements, with their otherworldly orientation and their promise that the last shall be first in the great beyond, are said to solace the individual for his lowly status in this world and to divert concern away from efforts at collective social change which might be brought about by man. While only a minority of Negroes actually belong to such groups, the proportion is higher than among whites. Negro literature is rich in descriptions of these churches and their position on race protest.

In Table 1 it can be seen that those belonging to sects are the least likely to be militant; they are followed by those in predominantly Negro denominations. Ironically those individuals in largely white denominations (Episcopalian, Presbyterian, United Church of Christ, and Roman Catholic) are those most likely to be militant, in spite of the perhaps greater civil rights activism of the Negro denominations. This pattern emerged even when social class was held constant.

In their comments members of the less conventional religious groups clearly expressed the classical attitude of their sects toward participation in the politics of the secular world. For example, an Evangelist in the Midwest said, "I don't believe in participating in politics. My church don't vote—they just depends on the plans of God." And an automobile serviceman in Philadelphia stated, "I, as a Jehovah's Witness, cannot express things involving the race issue." A housewife in the Far West ventured, "In my religion we do not approve of anything except living like it says in the Bible; demonstrations mean calling attention to you and it's sinful."

The finding that persons who belong to sects are less likely to be militant than the nonsect members is to be expected; clearly this type of religious involvement seems an alternative for most people to the development of radicalism. But what of the religious style of those in the more conventional churches which may put relatively less stress on the afterlife and encourage various forms of secular participation? Are the more religiously inclined within these groups also less likely to be militant?

---

[15] Each of the items in the index was positively related to every other and the index showed a high degree of internal validity. The index also received external validation from a number of additional questions. For example, the percentage belonging to a civil rights organization went from zero among those lowest in militancy to 38 percent for those who were highest, and the percentage thinking that civil rights demonstrations had helped a great deal increased from 23 percent to 58 percent. Those thinking that the police treated Negroes very well decreased from 35 percent to only 2 percent among those highest in militancy.

[16] Liston Pope, *Millhands and Preachers,* New Haven: Yale University Press, 1942, p. 137. J. Milton Yinger, *Religion, Society, and the Individual,* New York: The Macmillan Company, 1957, pp. 170–173.

TABLE 1   Proportion Militant (%) by Denomination*

Denomination	% Militant
Episcopalian	46 (24)
United Church of Christ	42 (12)
Presbyterian	40 (25)
Catholic	40 (109)
Methodist	34 (142)
Baptist	32 (658)
Sects and Cults	20 (106)

* Twenty-five respondents are not shown in this table because they did not specify a denomination, or belonged to a non-Christian religious group, or other small Christian group.

RELIGIOSITY

The present study measured several dimensions of religious involvement. Those interviewed were asked how important religion was to them, several questions about orthodoxy of belief, and how frequently they attended worship service.[17] Even with the sects excluded, irrespective of the dimension of religiosity considered, the greater the religiosity, the lower the percentage militant. (See Tables 2, 3, and 4.) For example, militancy increases consistently from a low of only 29 percent among those who said religion was "extremely important" to a high of 62 percent for those who indicated that religion was "not at all important" to them. For those very high in orthodoxy (having no doubt about the existence of God or the devil) 27 percent were militant while for those totally rejecting these ideas 54 percent indicated great concern over civil rights. Militancy also varies inversely with frequency of attendance at worship service.[18]

TABLE 2   Militance by Subjective Importance Assigned to Religion*

Importance	% Militant
Extremely important	29 (668)
Somewhat important	39 (195)
Fairly important	48 (96)
Not too important	56 (18)
Not at all important	62 (13)

* Sects are excluded here and in all subsequent tables.

TABLE 3   Militancy by Orthodoxy

Orthodoxy	% Militant
Very high	27 (414)
High	34 (333)
Medium	39 (144)
Low	47 (68)
Very low	54 (35)

TABLE 4   Militancy by Frequency of Attendance at Worship Services

Frequency	% Militant
More than once a week	27 (81)
Once a week	32 (311)
Once a month or more but less than once a week	34 (354)
Less than once a month	38 (240)

Each of these items was strongly related to every other; when taken together they help us to better characterize religiosity. Accordingly they have been combined into an overall measure of religiosity. Those scored as "very religious" in terms of this index attended church at least once a week, felt that religion was extremely important to them, and had no doubts about the existence of God and the devil. For progressively lower values of the index, frequency of church attendance, the importance of religion, and acceptance of the belief items decline consistently until, for those scored

[17] These dimensions and several others are suggested by Charles Y. Glock in "On the Study of Religious Commitment," *Religious Education Research Supplement,* 57 (July-August, 1962), pp. 98–100. For another measure of religious involvement, the number of church organizations belonged to, the same inverse relationship was noted.

[18] There is a popular stereotype that Negroes are a "religious people." Social science research has shown that they are "over-churched" relative to whites, i.e., the ratio of Negro churches to the size of the Negro population is greater than the same ratio for whites. Using data from a nationwide survey of whites, by Gertrude Selznick and Stephen Steinberg, some comparison of the religiosity of Negroes and whites was possible. When these various dimensions of religiosity were examined, with the effect of education and region held constant, Negroes appeared as significantly more religious *only* with respect to the subjective importance assigned to religion. In the North, whites were more likely to attend church at least once a week than were Negroes; while in the South rates of attendance were the same. About the same percentage of both groups had no doubts about the existence of God.

While Negroes were more likely to be sure about the existence of a devil, whites, surprisingly, were more likely to be sure about a life beyond death. Clearly, then, any assertions about the greater religiosity of Negroes relative to whites are unwarranted unless one specifies the dimension of religiosity.

"not at all religious," church is rarely if ever attended, religion is not considered personally important and the belief items are rejected.

Using this measure for nonsect members, civil rights militancy increases from a low of 26 percent for those labeled "very religious" to 30 percent for the "somewhat religious" to 45 percent for those "not very religious" and up to a high of 70 percent for those "not at all religious"[19] (Table 5).

[19] When the sects are included in these tables the results are the same. The sects have been excluded because they offer almost no variation to be analyzed with respect to the independent variable. Since virtually all of the sect members scored as either "very religious" or "somewhat religious," it is hardly possible to measure the effect of their religious involvement on protest attitudes. In addition the import of the relationships shown in these tables is con-

Religiosity and militancy are also related to age, sex, education, religious denomination, and region of the country. The older, the less educated, women, southerners, and those in Negro denominations are more likely to be religious and to have lower percentages scoring as militant. Thus it is possible that the relationship observed is simply a consequence of the fact that both religiosity and militancy are related to some third factor. In Table 6 it can be seen, however, that even when these variables are controlled, the relationship is maintained. That is, even among those in the North, the younger, male,

siderably strengthened when it is demonstrated that religious involvement inhibits militancy even when the most religious and least militant group, the sects, are excluded.

TABLE 5   Militancy by Religiosity

Religiosity	Very Religious	Somewhat Religious	Not Very Religious	Not at All Religious
% Militant	26	30	45	70
N	(230)	(523)	(195)	(36)

TABLE 6   Proportion Militant (%) by Religiosity, for Education, Age, Region, Sex, and Denomination

	Very Religious	Somewhat Religious	Not Very Religious	Not at All Religious
Education				
Grammar school	17 (108)	22 (201)	31 (42)	50 (2)
High school	34 (96)	32 (270)	45 (119)	58 (19)
College	38 (26)	48 (61)	59 (34)	87 (15)
Age				
18–29	33 (30)	37 (126)	44 (62)	62 (13)
30–44	30 (53)	34 (180)	48 (83)	74 (19)
45–59	25 (71)	27 (131)	45 (33)	50 (2)
60+	22 (76)	18 (95)	33 (15)	100 (2)
Region				
Non-South	30 (123)	34 (331)	47 (159)	70 (33)
South	22 (107)	23 (202)	33 (36)	66 (3)
Sex				
Men	28 (83)	33 (220)	44 (123)	72 (29)
Women	26 (147)	28 (313)	46 (72)	57 (7)
Denomination				
Episcopalian, Presbyterian, United Church of Christ	20 (15)	27 (26)	33 (15)	60 (5)
Catholic	13 (15)	39 (56)	36 (25)	77 (13)
Methodist	46 (24)	22 (83)	50 (32)	100 (2)
Baptist	25 (172)	29 (354)	45 (117)	53 (15)

more educated, and those affiliated with predominantly white denominations, the greater the religiosity, the less the militancy.

The incompatibility between piety and protest shown in these data becomes even more evident when considered in light of comments offered by the respondents. Many religious people hold beliefs which clearly inhibit race protest. For a few there was the notion that segregation and a lowly status for Negroes was somehow God's will and not for man to question. Thus a housewife in South Bend, Indiana, in saying that civil rights demonstrations had hurt Negroes, added: "God is the Creator of everything. We don't know why we all dark-skinned. We should try to put forth the effort to do what God wants and not question."[20]

A Negro spiritual contains the lines "I'm gonna wait upon the Lord till my change comes." For our respondents a more frequently stated belief stressed that God as the absolute controller of the universe would bring about change in his own way and at his own time, rather than expressing segregation as God's will. In indicating her unwillingness to take part in a civil rights demonstration, a Detroit housewife said, "I don't go for demonstrations. I believe that God created all men equal and at His appointed time He will give every man his portion, no one can hinder it." And in response to a question about whether or not the government in Washington was pushing integration too slowly, a re-

tired clerk in Atlanta said: "You can't hurry God. He has a certain time for this to take place. I don't know about Washington."

Others who desired integration more strongly and wanted immediate social change felt that (as Bob Dylan sings) God was on their side. Hence man need do nothing to help bring about change. Thus a worker in Cleveland, who was against having more civil rights demonstrations, said: "With God helping to fight our battle, I believe we can do with fewer demonstrations." And in response to a question about whether Negroes should spend more time praying and less time demonstrating, an Atlanta clergyman, who said "more time praying," added "praying is demonstrating."[21]

RELIGION AMONG THE MILITANTS

Although the net effect of religion is clearly to inhibit attitudes of protest it is interesting to consider this relationship in the opposite direction, i.e., observe religiosity among those characterized as militant, moderate, and conservative with respect to the civil rights struggle. As civil rights concern increases, religiosity decreases (Table 7). Militants were twice as likely to be scored "not very religious" or "not at all religious" as were conservatives. This table is also of interest because it shows that, even for the militants, a majority were scored either "very religious" or "somewhat religious." Clear-

---

[20] Albert Cardinal Meyer notes that the Catholic Bishops of the United States said in their statement of 1958: "The heart of the race question is moral and religious." "Interracial Justice and Love," in M. Ahmann, ed., *Race Challenge to Religion,* Chicago: H. Regnery, 1963, p. 126. These data, viewed from the perspective of the activist seeking to motivate Negroes on behalf of the civil rights struggle, suggest that this statement has a meaning which Their Excellencies no doubt did not intend.

[21] A study of ministers in Richmond, California, notes that although almost all questioned were opposed to discrimination, very few had taken concrete action, in part because of their belief that God would take care of them. One minister noted, "I believe that if we all was as pure . . . as we ought to be, there would be no struggle. God will answer my prayer. If we just stay with God and have faith. *When Peter was up, did the people march to free him? No. He prayed, and God did something about it.*" (Bloom, *op. cit.,* italics added.)

TABLE 7   Religiosity by Civil Rights Militancy

	Militants	Moderates	Conservatives
Very religious	18%	24%	28%
Somewhat religious	48	57	55
Not very religious	26	17	16
Not at all religious	8	2	1
Total	100	100	100
N	332	419	242

ly, for many, a religious orientation and a concern with racial protest are not mutually exclusive.

Given the active involvement of some churches, the singing of protest spirituals, and the ideology of the movement as it relates to Christian principles of love, equality, passive suffering,[22] and the appeal to a higher moral law, it would be surprising if there were only a few religious people among the militants.

A relevant question accordingly is: Among the religious, what are the intervening links which determine whether religion is related to an active concern with racial matters or has an opiating effect?[23] From the comments reported above it seemed that, for some, belief in a highly deterministic God inhibited race protest. Unfortunately the study did not measure beliefs about the role of God as against the role of men in the structuring of human affairs. However, a related variable was measured which would seem to have much relevance—the extent to which these religious people were concerned with the here and now as opposed to the afterlife.

The classical indictment of religion

from the Marxist perspective is that by focusing concern on a glorious afterlife the evils of this life are ignored. Of course there are important differences among religious institutions and among individuals with respect to the importance given to otherworldly concerns. Christianity, as with most ideologies, contains within it, if not out-and-out contradictory themes, then certainly themes which are likely to be in tension with one another. In this fact, no doubt, lies part of the explanation of religion's varied consequences for protest. One important strand of Christianity stresses acceptance of one's lot and glorifies the afterlife;[24] another is more concerned with the realization of Judeo–Christian values in the current life. King and his followers clearly represent

[24] The Muslims have also made much of this theme within Christianity, and their militancy is certainly tied to a rejection of otherworldly religiosity. The Bible is referred to as a "poison book" and the leader of the Muslims states, "No one after death has ever gone any place but where they were carried. There is no heaven or hell other than on earth for you and me, and Jesus was no exception. His body is still . . . in Palestine and will remain there." (As quoted in C. Eric Lincoln, *The Black Muslims in America,* Boston: Beacon Press, 1961, p. 123).

However, while they reject the otherworldly theme, they nevertheless rely heavily on a deterministic Allah; according to E. U. Essien-Udom, this fact leads to political inactivity. He notes, "The attainment of black power is relegated to the intervention of "Almighty Allah" sometime in the future. . . . Not unlike other religionists, the Muslims too may wait for all eternity for the coming of the Messiah, the predicted apocalypse in 1970 notwithstanding." E. U. Essien-Udom, *Black Nationalism, op. cit.,* pp. 313–314.

[22] Nonviolent resistance as it relates to Christianity's emphasis on suffering, sacrifice, and privation, is discussed by James W. Vander Zanden. "The Non-Violent Resistance Movement against Segregation." *American Journal of Sociology,* 68 (March, 1963), pp. 544–550.

[23] Of course, a most relevant factor here is the position of the particular church that an individual is involved in. Unfortunately, it was difficult to obtain such information in a nationwide survey.

this latter "social gospel" tradition.[25] Those with the type of temporal concern that King represents would be expected to be higher in militancy. A measure of temporal versus otherworldly concern has been constructed. On the basis of two questions, those interviewed have been classified as having either an otherworldly or a temporal orientation.[26] The evidence is that religiosity and otherworldly concern increase together. For example, almost 100 percent of the "not at all religious" group were considered to have a temporal orientation, but only 42 percent of the "very religious" (Table 8). Those in predominantly white denominations were more likely to have a temporal orientation than those in all-black denominations.

Among the religious groups, if concern with the here and now is a relevant factor in overcoming the opiating effect of religion then it is to be anticipated that those considered to have a tempo-

ral religious orientation would be much higher in militancy than those scored as otherworldly. This is in fact the case. Among the otherworldly religious, only 16 percent were militant; this proportion increases to almost 40 percent among those considered "very religious" and "somewhat religious" who have a temporal religious outlook (Table 9). Thus it would seem that an important factor in determining the effect of religion on protest attitudes is the nature of an individual's religious commitment. It is quite possible, for those with a temporal religious orientation, that—rather than the effect of religion being somehow neutralized (as in the case of militancy among the "not religious" groups)—their religious concern serves to inspire and sustain race protest. This religious inspiration can, of course, be clearly noted among some active civil rights participants.

CONCLUSION

The effect of religiosity on race protest depends on the type of religiosity involved. Past literature is rich in suggestions that the religiosity of the funda-

[25] He states: "Any religion that professes to be concerned with the souls of men and is not concerned with the slums that damn them, the economic conditions that strangle them, and the social conditions that cripple them is a dry-as-dust religion." He further adds, perhaps in a concession, that "such a religion is the kind the Marxists like to see—an opiate of the people." Martin Luther King, *Stride toward Freedom*, New York: Ballantine Books, 1958, pp. 28–29.

John Lewis, a former SNCC leader and once a Baptist Divinity student, is said to have peered through the bars of a southern jail and said, "Think not that I am come to send peace on earth. I came not to send peace, but a sword." (Matthew 10:34.)

[26] The two items used in this index were: "How sure are you that there is a life beyond death?"; and "Negroes should spend more time praying and less time demonstrating." The latter item may seem somewhat circular when observed in relation to civil rights concern. However, this is precisely what militancy is all about. Still it would have been better to measure otherworldly versus temporal concern in a less direct fashion; unfortunately, no other items were available. Because of this the data shown here must be interpreted with caution. However it does seem almost self-evident that civil rights protest which is religiously inspired is related to a temporal religious outlook.

TABLE 8 Proportion (%) with Temporal (as against Otherworldly) Concern, by Religiosity

Religiosity	Percent with Temporal Concern
Very Religious	42 (225)
Somewhat religious	61 (531)
Not very religious	82 (193)
Not at all religious	98 (34)

TABLE 9 Proportion Militant (%) by Religiosity and Temporal or Otherworldly Concern

Concern	Very Religious	Somewhat Religious
Temporal	39 (95)	38 (325)
Otherworldly	15 (130)	17 (206)

mentalist sects is an alternative to the development of political radicalism. This seems true in the case of race protest as well. However, in an overall sense even for those who belong to the more conventional churches, the greater the religious involvement, whether measured in terms of ritual activity, orthodoxy of religious belief, subjective importance of religion, or the three taken together, the lower the degree of militancy.

Among sect members and religious people with an otherworldly orientation, religion and race protest appear to be, if not mutually exclusive, then certainly what one observer has referred to as "mutually corrosive kinds of commitments."[27] Until such time as religion loosens its hold over these people or comes to embody to a greater extent the belief that man as well as God can bring about secular change, and focuses more on the here and now, religious involvement may be seen as an important factor working against the widespread radicalization of the Negro public.

However, it has also been noted that many militant people are nevertheless religious. When a distinction is made among the religious between the "otherworldly" and the "temporal," for many of the latter group, religion seems to facilitate or at least not to inhibit protest. For these people religion and race protest may be mutually supportive.

Thirty years ago Donald Young wrote: "One function which a minority religion may serve is that of reconciliation with inferior status and its discriminatory consequences . . . on the other hand, religious institutions may also develop in such a way as to be an incitement and support of revolt against inferior status."[28] The current civil rights struggle and the data observed here certainly suggest that this is the case. These contradictory consequences of religion are somewhat reconciled when one distinguishes among different segments of the Negro church and types of religious concern among individuals.

[27] Rodney Stark, "Class, Radicalism, and Religious Involvement," *American Sociological Review*, 29 (October, 1964), p. 703.

[28] Donald Young, *American Minority Peoples*, New York: Harper, 1937, p. 204.

These data are also consistent with Merton's statement that it is premature to conclude that "all religion everywhere has only the one consequence of making for mass apathy" and his insistence on recognizing the "multiple consequences" and "net balance of aggregate consequences" of a given institution such as religion. Robert Merton, *Social Theory and Social Structure*, Glencoe: Free Press, 1957, revised edition, p. 44.

PART THREE
IDEOLOGY AND STRATEGY

A STRICT sociological definition of "ideology" would be a relatively authoritative, closed, and explicit belief system which commands obedience from adherents, covers a wide range of situations, and is organized around one or a few preeminent values such as salvation or equality.[1] Among examples of well-developed ideologies are early Christianity and communism. In this part ideology is used in a much more general sense to refer to the body of ideas people bring with them to racial conflict. Unlike other articles in the book which tend to be analytical or descriptive accounts by outside observers, the first eight articles in this section are statements of conflict positions by those actively involved. They vary from black nationalist to white supremacist.

Ideology, by serving as a cognitive map and a source of values and direction, may help people order a confused, frustrated, and crisis-filled world in a fashion meaningful to them. Ideologies tend to simplify and often to distort what may be highly complex, multiply determined social phenomena, though in so doing they may enable a large number of people to account for difficulties they face. The significance of an ideology does not lie in how objectively or fairly it portrays the world. Sometimes it is only through exaggerated claims and grandiose rhetoric that people are moved to action. Ideology may have a strong effect on people's behavior, leading them to actions on behalf of their cause that they would not normally take. This is particularly true to the extent that the ideology comes to have a sacred quality to it. Courage and the motivation to act may be greatly enhanced by the belief that one is unselfishly acting for his or her group on behalf of ultimately right principles. Such justifications also may define the relationship of means and ends for the activist and ease any doubts he or she may have about acting in the name of a broader social group when he or she lacks a formal mandate from that group to act on its behalf.

[1] For a general discussion of ideology, see the articles by E. Shils and H. M. Johnson in the *International Encyclopaedia of Social Science* (New York: Macmillan, 1968), 7: 66–85. See also the classic discussion by Karl Mannheim, *Ideology and Utopia* (New York: Harcourt, 1955); N. Smelser, *Theory of Collective Behavior* (Englewood Cliffs, N.J.: Prentice-Hall, 1965), chap. 5; and the articles by Bendix, Geertz, and Converse in D. Apter, ed., *Ideology and Discontent* (New York: Free Press, 1964).

Domination, inequality, and scarce resources do not necessarily give rise to organized group conflict. India and South Africa, with much stronger caste systems and much greater inequality, have relatively little overt conflict, compared with the United States. This is partly explained by the absence of a belief-legitimating struggle. Most members of the dominant group, and many of the subordinate group, take the latter to be inferior or polluted and thus do not come to actively question their lower status position, though there are also fewer constraints on repression in those countries.

It is only when people come to define their position as unjust and illegitimate that conflict challenging the color line emerges (assuming a conducive social setting). In defining their position in this way they make assumptions about the nature of the social world, what's wrong with it (or threatens it), how it got that way, what it should be like and why, through what means it can and must be changed, and predictions about what the future is likely to hold.

Intellectuals may play an important role here in developing and systematizing a critique of the society and in raising a concrete disagreement or conflict of interest between separate individuals not identifying themselves as part of a larger social category, to the level of perhaps more bitter struggle over broader values and ultimate principles, between more cohesive and self-conscious social groups.

Though even given the presence of an ideology, its importance in motivating, sustaining, and directing conflict actions varies considerably among individuals and situations.[2] And once

conflict has begun, events often are too diverse and fast moving for rigid pre-programmed ideologies. As the conflict evolves, new justifications and interpretations may emerge, as well as the elaboration of old ones.

Most of the statements presented in this section are arguments for particular strategies, or attempts to justify the status quo or to legitimate the need for change, rather than being fully developed ideologies.

Much of the civil rights movement between 1954–1967 consisted of what Shils has called a "program" rather than a fully developed ideology.[3] A program takes seriously certain of the values of the society and seeks their fulfillment within the existing order. It accepts much of the prevailing institutional and value systems, although it strongly rejects one sector. The thrust of the ideas dominant in the civil rights movement at this time was for the full inclusion of blacks and the realization of the American dream. American values of democracy, freedom, equal protection of the laws, and equal opportunity as expressed in the constitution and the Judeo-Christian heritage serve to legitimate and even call forth struggle. In this sense black demands were relatively conservative, seeking not to overthrow, but to share in the American promise.

The relative absence until recently of well-developed ideologies in the context of American racial conflict has permitted flexibility in strategies and tactics and has made possible bargaining and negotiations. Much racial conflict during recent decades has tended to occur within a framework of some consensus (at least at a national level), rather than to be over the very basis of this consensus.

Partly as a result of a more pragmatic ethos, ideology has traditionally played

---

[2] There is often a tendency by the outside observer to impute disinterested ideological motivations to activists whose positions he agrees with and to explain the behavior of those he disagrees with in terms of personal pathology or opportunism, denying them even the dignity of a misguided ideological motivation.

[3] Shils, *op. cit.,* p. 71.

a less important role in American struggles than is the case in Europe. Even for many American activists there tend to exist reformist sentiments involving a gut feeling that something is wrong and that action of some type is required, rather than a clearly articulated, all-encompassing worldview regarding the problem, though this may be changing as the student and black movements, once scornful of traditional rigid ideologies that did not seem to apply to American society, now seek models in the third world.

There are of course numerous dimensions by which ideologies can be classified and many types of ideology, such as revolutionary versus reform, those that stress active involvement versus passive withdrawal, and those that hope to recreate some golden age in the past versus those oriented toward a utopian future. Many of the questions raised elsewhere (Parts IIA and IVA) about the nature of the issue involved in the conflict can also be seen as questions about ideology. Among some additional questions useful to understanding and comparing ideologies involved in conflict situations are the following:

What are the intellectual and historical sources of the ideology?

How is the ideology affected by the social millieu in which it appears?

How has the ideology evolved and what leads to changes in it?

What social conditions are conducive to the emergence of ideologies?

What kinds of legitimations and symbols does it draw upon?

How highly systematized and explicit is it?

How absolutist is it?

How important is the ideology in structuring day-to-day conflict action?

To what degree are its claims subject to objective validation by outside observers?

How are inconsistencies and uncomfortable facts dealt with?

To what degree is the ideology a self-serving device for a manipulative elite, as is often the case with scapegoating?

What assumptions about the relationship between means and ends does it make?

What is the time table for proposed changes?

How important are the actions of adherents seen to be in obtaining the changes desired?

What social and psychological characteristics do people who come to hold the ideology have?

If the ideology contains marked distortions, how is it that some people nevertheless come to accept it?

What role do intellectuals play in defining the issues and developing the belief system?

What role is played by a charismatic leader in spreading the ideology?

THE ARTICLES

Martin Luther King explains his philosophy of nonviolence and argues for its superiority over violent means in bringing about change. Certain features common to many ideological statements may be seen here, such as the religious (as well as pragmatic) justification of both means and ends, the moral obligation to resist tyranny and join the struggle ("to accept passively an unjust system is to cooperate with that system"), the belief that suffering and self-sacrifice will be rewarded by victory ("unearned suffering is redemptive") and that in the future his cause will indeed triumph ("the universe is on the side of justice"). Of particular interest is King's observation that nonviolent resistance may serve to bring about change without the ever-deepening spiral of conflict and hostility (considered later in Part IVA by James Coleman) that is seen to characterize violent struggle.

This excerpt is taken from *Stride toward Freedom* which tells the story of the 1955 Montgomery bus boycott which gave national prominence to, and helped further, the then emerging direct action phase of the civil rights movement. Even though there have been rapid changes on the civil rights front since King wrote these words and his tragic death, his courage, vision, ethical sense, and insights have a timeless quality of heroic proportions. Appearing as a charismatic leader, at a particular time in history when social conditions were conducive, he inspired a national and international revolution on behalf of human rights and helped unite diverse segments of the black movement as well as bridge the gap between an angry black constituency and a moderate white majority, some of whose leaders were willing to listen.[4]

In "What We Want" Stokely Carmichael discusses the concept of black power which as a leader of SNCC he helped develop.[5] He stresses the importance of blacks defining and doing things for themselves and involving people more in the decisions which effect them. Although denying that black power is synonymous with separation, he offers a critique of integration as a solution because it is seen to ignore the problems of poorer blacks and to devalue blackness. Color is a significant factor in American society and cannot be ignored. American ghettos are seen as colonies suffering from the same domination faced by people of color in the third world.

As some of the articles in Part IV will suggest, conflict and disagreement within racial groups may be more pronounced than between them. In "'Black Power' and Coalition Politics" we see evidence of this as Bayard Rustin, coordinator of the 1963 March on Washington and a major civil rights strategist, takes a much more critical perspective to the idea of black power than does Carmichael. He argues that it isolates blacks from potential allies, encourages antiblack forces, focuses attention

away from racial injustice, and is primarily rhetoric without a concrete program for action.

In this book of readings our primary interest is how ideas affect social conflict, yet one can also raise the reverse question of how conflict effects ideas. Here Rustin's observation is instructive: the rise of the black power movement and the stress on the need to build a strong black community emerged partly out of despair over the failure to obtain meaningful integration in the face of great struggle and sacrifice. There are historical parallels here to the inward turn taken by the black movement during the time of Booker T. Washington and Marcus Garvey.

The statement by Huey P. Newton, a leader of the Black Panther Party, locates the source of American racial problems in the structure of the economy and argues that racism cannot be eliminated until capitalism is. Newton argues that the government lacks legitimacy because it fails to meet the people's needs. It therefore must be replaced. Blacks as well as whites are seen to be lacking in freedom. Until freedom is achieved, he predicts that the country will suffer chaos, revolt, and eventually revolution. Panther ideology is constantly evolving; its eclectic nature is a good example of the diverse sources from which an ideology may draw. For example, among others it shows the influence of Malcolm X, Marxism, Maoism, Ho Chi Minh, Che Guevara, and Al Fatah. Many of the ends sought by the Panthers in the ten-point statement included here, such as freedom, justice, peace, full employment, education, decent housing, and an end to police brutality are consistent with at least one interpretation of the American value system (indeed the United States constitution is drawn upon to justify demands). Like most statements of an ideological

[4] For a useful discussion of King's role in the civil rights movement, see: A. Meier, "On the Role of Martin Luther King," *New Politics* (Winter 1965), pp. 52–59.

[5] For example, see S. Carmichael and C. Hamilton, *Black Power and the Politics of Liberation in America* (New York: Random House, 1967).

nature, the concrete form and the mechanisms which will bring them about are not specified.

A classic statement of the virulently racist southern white position may be seen in the speech by Senator Bilbo to the Mississippi legislature. Though delivered in 1944 and dated in parts, it nevertheless illustrates many of the basic arguments for maintaining racial separation. Although in an age when crude racism is on the decline, some of these concepts are often disguised or not openly acknowledged. His remarks were inspired by a pending anti–poll tax bill and new black demands for equal treatment growing out of World War II. His argument for racial separation rests upon scientifically untenable assertions about the purity and superiority of the "blood" of the "white race" (itself a highly heterogeneous group). He wrongly asserts that culture and life styles are determined by race, and thus that segregation is necessary to prevent intermarriage.

Less blatantly racist, although also serving to justify the southern status quo, is the statement by Richard Morphew in the aftermath of the crisis triggered by the enrollment of James Meredith at the University of Mississippi.[6] Unlike Bilbo, he does not seek to justify segregation by referring to an erroneous, even comical (if its consequences were not so tragic), interpretation of world history; nor does he locate the superiority of his group in its reproductive organs. Rather he seeks justifica-

tion in the guarantee to the states of powers not explicitly granted to the United States government by the constitution. The Supreme Court and the preponderant weight of judicial opinion in the last thirty years reject this opinion by arguing that segregation and discrimination clearly fall within the province of the United States government as a result of the thirteenth, fourteenth, and fifteenth amendments to the constitution. It is interesting to observe Morphew seeking legitimation in the same symbols and valued words such as the "constitution," "democratic process," and "freedom" as do civil rights activists.

The very abstractness of the values, a lack of consistency between them (e.g., the value of equality may clash with the value of liberty), and the absence of a firm link between values and the concrete ways they are implemented help account for similiar references to American values. Though the very abstractness and ambiguity of values may be necessary given the variety of specific social situations and may aid in integration among diverse groups, it also ensures that most conflict groups can find some way of legitimating their claims and will have sincere feelings of self-righteousness.

John W. Gardner, former secretary of health, education, and welfare and head of the Urban Coalition, takes a position held by many moderates and liberals. He asks for social reform, yet requests those he sees as rightfully indignant over American problems to always work responsibly and reasonably within the confines of the system that produced and produces these problems and which up to now has been unable to solve them. He is particularly critical of coercive demonstrations. Gardner also argues that solving social problems is a very difficult and gradual process, and he rejects the view that

[6] For a fuller collection of segregationist writings from which these two statements are taken, see I. Newby, ed., *The Development of Segregationist Thought* (Homewood, Ill.: Dorsey Press, 1968). For compilations of black protest thought, see H. Brotz, ed., *Negro Social and Political Thought 1850–1920* (New York: Basic Books, 1966); and F. Broderick and A. Meier, eds., *Negro Protest Thought in the Twentieth Century* (Indianapolis: Bobbs-Merrill, 1965).

people are essentially good but made corrupt by faulty social institutions.

President Johnson's commencement address at Howard University is an example of what could be called the mid-sixties' enlightened-optimistic-establishment position. It implies that with a little effort racial justice will gradually be achieved. It holds a melting pot–assimilationist image of the American ethnic experience and looks forward to the day when the "only difference between whites and Negroes is skin color." President Johnson also sees "the courts, the congress, the president, and most of the people" as allies of racial progress. Public opinion polls and election results tell a rather different story. From a national leader seeking broad consensus, this plea to end racial inequality is designed to appeal to diverse groups. Thus he argues that we must go beyond merely providing equality of opportunity since "freedom is not enough. You do not wipe away the scars of centuries by saying now you're free to go where you want and do as you desire." But at the same time he locates a major cause of racial problems within the black community itself, particularly in what he sees as the breakdown of the black family.[7]

It is well to note that President Johnson did more for civil rights than any president this century. Yet in this speech which stresses the need to end racial injustice and asks Americans to have an "understanding heart," there is remarkably little in the way of concrete policy recommendations, other than mention of the voting rights bill and a call for a conference, though it is rich in vague references (which help perform a consensus and integrative function) to "justice," "freedom," "opportunity," "equality," and "the Great Society."

Many aspects of an ideology are essentially statements of value, asserting that one form of social organization is preferable to another, or predictions about the future, yet other aspects such as explanations for current problems, or assertions about the consequences of various strategies, are more in the realm of fact and hence more subject to objective analysis. The last three articles in this section, rather than being calls to action or discussions of particular viewpoints, seek to analyze strategies for change.

Merton Deutsch asks: "What can a powerless group do to gain its ends?" He specifies tactics likely to elicit cooperation as well as resistance from the dominant group.

James Q. Wilson looks at a similar question in considering strategies of protest available specifically to blacks. He considers how these bear upon the different kinds of demands, issues, and goals likely to be raised by blacks. His argument should be considered in light of the kinds of institutionalized inequality discussed in Part IIA.

James W. Vander Zanden attempts to analyze the degree of success obtained by the method of nonviolent resistance in the South. He suggests that for the southern black, nonviolent resistance helped mediate between the traditional role of accommodation and the hostility felt toward southern racial patterns.

20
Nonviolent Resistance*
MARTIN L. KING

. . . In this period of social change, the Negro must come to see that there is

---

[7] For consideration of some of the implications of this, see C. Rainwater and W. Yancey, *The Moynihan Report and the Politics of Controversy* (Cambridge: M.I.T. Press, 1967).

*[Abridgement of pp. 102–103, 104, 106–107, 211–222, 223–224 in *Stride Toward Freedom*, by Martin Luther King, Jr. Copyright © 1958 by Martin Luther King, Jr. By permission of Harper and Row Publishers, Inc. and Joan Daves. The following passage does not follow the strict chronological order of the original. It has been taken from pp. 172–174, 81–83, and 174–184 as indicated by asterisks in the text.]

much he himself can do about his plight. He may be uneducated or poverty-stricken, but these handicaps must not prevent him from seeing that he has within his being the power to alter his fate. The Negro can take direct action against injustice without waiting for the government to act or a majority to agree with him or a court to rule in his favor.

Oppressed people deal with their oppression in three characteristic ways. One way is acquiescence: the oppressed resign themselves to their doom. They tacitly adjust themselves to oppression, and thereby become conditioned to it. In every movement toward freedom some of the oppressed prefer to remain oppressed. Almost 2,800 years ago Moses set out to lead the children of Israel from the slavery of Egypt to the freedom of the promised land. He soon discovered that slaves do not always welcome their deliverers. They become accustomed to being slaves. They would rather bear those ills they have, as Shakespeare pointed out, than flee to others that they know not of. They prefer the "fleshpots of Egypt" to the ordeals of emancipation.

There is such a thing as the freedom of exhaustion. Some people are so worn down by the yoke of oppression that they give up. A few years ago in the slum areas of Atlanta, a Negro guitarist used to sing almost daily: "Ben down so long that down don't bother me." This is the type of negative freedom and resignation that often engulfs the life of the oppressed.

But this is not the way out. To accept passively an unjust system is to cooperate with that system; thereby the oppressed become as evil as the oppressor. Noncooperation with evil is as much a moral obligation as is cooperation with good. The oppressed must never allow the conscience of the oppressor to slumber. Religion reminds every man that he is his brother's keeper. To accept injustice or segregation pas-sively is to say to the oppressor that his actions are morally right. It is a way of allowing his conscience to fall asleep. At this moment the oppressed fails to be his brother's keeper. So acquiescence—while often the easier way—is not the moral way. It is the way of the coward. The Negro cannot win the respect of his oppressor by acquiescing; he merely increases the oppressor's arrogance and contempt. Acquiescence is interpreted as proof of the Negro's inferiority. The Negro cannot win the respect of the white people of the South or the peoples of the world if he is willing to sell the future of his children for his personal and immediate comfort and safety.

A second way that oppressed people sometimes deal with oppression is to resort to physical violence and corroding hatred. Violence often brings about momentary results. Nations have frequently won their independence in battle. But in spite of temporary victories, violence never brings permanent peace. It solves no social problem; it merely creates new and more complicated ones.

Violence as a way of achieving racial justice is both impractical and immoral. It is impractical because it is a descending spiral ending in destruction for all. The old law of an eye for an eye leaves everybody blind. It is immoral because it seeks to humiliate the opponent rather than win his understanding; it seeks to annihilate rather than to convert. Violence is immoral because it thrives on hatred rather than love. It destroys community and makes brotherhood impossible. It leaves society in monologue rather than dialogue. Violence ends by defeating itself. It creates bitterness in the survivors and brutality in the destroyers. A voice echoes through time saying to every potential Peter, "Put up your sword." History is cluttered with the wreckage of nations that failed to follow this command.

If the American Negro and other

victims of oppression succumb to the temptation of using violence in the struggle for freedom, future generations will be the recipients of a desolate night of bitterness, and our chief legacy to them will be an endless reign of meaningless chaos. Violence is not the way.

The third way open to oppressed people in their quest for freedom is the way of nonviolent resistance. Like the synthesis in Hegelian philosophy, the principle of nonviolent resistance seeks to reconcile the truths of two opposites —acquiescence and violence—while avoiding the extremes and immoralities of both. The nonviolent resister agrees with the person who acquiesces that one should not be physically aggressive toward his opponent; but he balances the equation by agreeing with the person of violence that evil must be resisted. He avoids the nonresistance of the former and the violent resistance of the latter. With nonviolent resistance, no individual or group need submit to any wrong, nor need anyone resort to violence in order to right a wrong.

It seems to me that this is the method that must guide the actions of the Negro in the present crisis in race relations. Through nonviolent resistance the Negro will be able to rise to the noble height of opposing the unjust system while loving the perpetrators of the system. The Negro must work passionately and unrelentingly for full stature as a citizen, but he must not use inferior methods to gain it. He must never come to terms with falsehood, malice, hate, or destruction.

Among the basic aspects of the philosophy of nonviolence are the following:*

First, it must be emphasized that nonviolent resistance is not a method for cowards; it does resist. If one uses

* This material is drawn from pp. 81–83.

this method because he is afraid or merely because he lacks the instruments of violence, he is not truly nonviolent. This is why Gandhi often said that if cowardice is the only alternative to violence, it is better to fight. He made this statement conscious of the fact that there is always another alternative: no individual or group need submit to any wrong, nor need they use violence to right the wrong; there is the way of nonviolent resistance. This is ultimately the way of the strong man. It is not a method of stagnant passivity. The phrase "passive resistance" often gives the false impression that this is a sort of "do-nothing method" in which the resister quietly and passively accepts evil. But nothing is further from the truth. For while the nonviolent resister is passive in the sense that he is not physically aggressive toward his opponent, his mind and emotions are always active, constantly seeking to persuade his opponent that he is wrong. The method is passive physically, but strongly active spiritually. It is not passive nonresistance to evil; it is active nonviolent resistance to evil.

A second basic fact that characterizes nonviolence is that it does not seek to defeat or humiliate the opponent, but to win his friendship and understanding. The nonviolent resister must often express his protest through noncooperation or boycotts, but he realizes that these are not ends themselves; they are merely means to awaken a sense of moral shame in the opponent. The end is redemption and reconciliation. The aftermath of nonviolence is the creation of the beloved community, while the aftermath of violence is tragic bitterness.

A third characteristic of this method is that the attack is directed against forces of evil rather than against persons who happen to be doing the evil.

It is evil that the nonviolent resister seeks to defeat, not the persons victimized by evil. If he is opposing racial injustice, the nonviolent resister has the vision to see that the basic tension is not between races. As I like to say to the people in Montgomery: "The tension in this city is not between white people and Negro people. The tension is, at bottom, between justice and injustice, between the forces of light and the forces of darkness." . . .

A fourth point that characterizes nonviolent resistance is a willingness to accept suffering without retaliation, to accept blows from the opponent without striking back. "Rivers of blood may have to flow before we gain our freedom, but it must be our blood," Gandhi said to his countrymen. The nonviolent resister is willing to accept violence if necessary, but never to inflict it. He does not seek to dodge jail. If going to jail is necessary, he enters it "as a bridegroom enters the bride's chamber."

One may well ask: "What is the nonviolent resister's justification for this ordeal to which he invites men, for this mass political application of the ancient doctrine of turning the other cheek?" The answer is found in the realization that unearned suffering is redemptive. . . .

A fifth point concerning nonviolent resistance is that it avoids not only external physical violence but also internal violence of spirit. The nonviolent resister not only refuses to shoot his opponent but he also refuses to hate him. At the center of nonviolence stands the principle of love. The nonviolent resister would contend that in the struggle for human dignity, the oppressed people of the world must not succumb to the temptation of becoming bitter or indulging in hate campaigns. To retaliate in kind would do nothing but intensify the existence of hate in the universe. Along the way of life, someone must have sense enough and morality enough to cut off the chain of hate. This can only be done by projecting the ethic of love to the center of our lives.

In speaking of love at this point, we are not referring to some sentimental or affectionate emotion. It would be nonsense to urge men to love their oppressors in an affectionate sense. Love in this connection means understanding, redemptive good will. . . .

A sixth basic fact about nonviolent resistance is that it is based on the conviction that the universe is on the side of justice. Consequently, the believer in nonviolence has deep faith in the future. This faith is another reason why the nonviolent resister can accept suffering without retaliation. For he knows that in his struggle for justice he has cosmic companionship. It is true that there are devout believers in nonviolence who find it difficult to believe in a personal God. But even these persons believe in the existence of some creative force that works for universal wholeness. Whether we call it an unconscious process, an impersonal Brahman, or a Personal Being of matchless power and infinite love, there is a creative force in this universe that works to bring the disconnected aspects of reality into a harmonious whole.

Nonviolent resistance makes it possible for the Negro to remain in the South and struggle for his rights.* The Negro's problem will not be solved by running away. He cannot listen to the glib suggestion of those who would urge him to migrate en masse to other sections of the country. By grasping his great opportunity in the South he can make a lasting contribution to the moral strength

* The remaining material is taken from pp. 174–184.

of the nation and set a sublime example of courage for generations yet unborn.

By nonviolent resistance, the Negro can also enlist all men of good will in his struggle for equality. The problem is not a purely racial one, with Negroes set against whites. In the end, it is not a struggle between people at all, but a tension between justice and injustice. Nonviolent resistance is not aimed against oppressors but against oppression. Under its banner consciences, not racial groups, are enlisted.

If the Negro is to achieve the goal of integration, he must organize himself into a militant and nonviolent mass movement. All three elements are indispensable. The movement for equality and justice can only be a success if it has both a mass and militant character; the barriers to be overcome require both. Nonviolence is an imperative in order to bring about ultimate community.

A mass movement of a militant quality that is not at the same time committed to nonviolence tends to generate conflict, which in turn breeds anarchy. The support of the participants and the sympathy of the uncommitted are both inhibited by the threat that bloodshed will engulf the community. This reaction in turn encourages the opposition to threaten and resort to force. When, however, the mass movement repudiates violence while moving resolutely toward its goal, its opponents are revealed as the instigators and practitioners of violence if it occurs. Then public support is magnetically attracted to the advocates of nonviolence, while those who employ violence are literally disarmed by overwhelming sentiment against their stand.

Only through a nonviolent approach can the fears of the white community be mitigated. A guilt-ridden white minority lives in fear that if the Negro should ever attain power, he would act without restraint or pity to revenge the injustices and brutality of the years. It is something like a parent who continually mistreats a son. One day that parent raises his hand to strike the son, only to discover that the son is now as tall as he is. The parent is suddenly afraid—fearful that the son will use his new physical power to repay his parent for all the blows of the past.

The Negro, once a helpless child, has now grown up politically, culturally, and economically. Many white men fear retaliation. The job of the Negro is to show them that they have nothing to fear, that the Negro understands and forgives and is ready to forget the past. He must convince the white man that all he seeks is justice, *for both himself and the white man.* A mass movement exercising nonviolence is an object lesson in power under discipline, a demonstration to the white community that if such a movement attained a degree of strength, it would use its power creatively and not vengefully.

Nonviolence can touch men where the law cannot reach them. When the law regulates behavior it plays an indirect part in molding public sentiment. The enforcement of the law is itself a form of peaceful persuasion. But the law needs help. The courts can order desegregation of the public schools. But what can be done to mitigate the fears, to disperse the hatred, violence, and irrationality gathered around school integration, to take the initiative out of the hands of racial demagogues, to release respect for the law? In the end, for laws to be obeyed, men must believe they are right.

Here nonviolence comes in as the ultimate form of persuasion. It is the method which seeks to implement the just law by appealing to the conscience of the great decent majority who through blindness, fear, pride, or irrationality have allowed their consciences to sleep.

The nonviolent resisters can summarize their message in the following simple terms: We will take direct action against injustice without waiting for other agencies to act. We will not obey unjust laws or submit to unjust practices. We will do this peacefully, openly, cheerfully because our aim is to persuade. We adopt the means of nonviolence because our end is a community at peace with itself. We will try to persuade with our words, but if our words fail, we will try to persuade with our acts. We will always be willing to talk and seek fair compromise, but we are ready to suffer when necessary and even risk our lives to become witnesses to the truth as we see it.

The way of nonviolence means a willingness to suffer and sacrifice. It may mean going to jail. If such is the case the resister must be willing to fill the jail houses of the South. It may even mean physical death. But if physical death is the price that a man must pay to free his children and his white brethren from a permanent death of the spirit, then nothing could be more redemptive.

What is the Negro's best defense against acts of violence inflicted upon him? As Dr. Kenneth Clark has said so eloquently, "His only defense is to meet every act of barbarity, illegality, cruelty, and injustice toward an individual Negro with the fact that one hundred more Negroes will present themselves in his place as potential victims." Every time one Negro school teacher is fired for believing in integration, a thousand others should be ready to take the same stand. If the oppressors bomb the home of one Negro for his protest, they must be made to realize that to press back the rising tide of the Negro's courage they will have to bomb hundreds more, and even then they will fail.

Faced with this dynamic unity, this amazing self-respect, this willingness to suffer, and this refusal to hit back, the oppressor will find, as oppressors have always found, that he is glutted with his own barbarity. Forced to stand before the world and his God splattered with the blood of his brother, he will call an end to his self-defeating massacre.

American Negroes must come to the point where they can say to their white brothers, paraphrasing the words of Gandhi: "We will match your capacity to inflict suffering with our capacity to endure suffering. We will meet your physical force with soul force. We will not hate you, but we cannot in all good conscience obey your unjust laws. Do to us what you will and we will still love you. Bomb our homes and threaten our children; send your hooded perpetrators of violence into our communities and drag us out on some wayside road, beating us and leaving us half dead, and we will still love you. But we will soon wear you down by our capacity to suffer. And in winning our freedom we will so appeal to your heart and conscience that we will win you in the process."

Realism impels me to admit that many Negroes will find it difficult to follow the path of nonviolence. Some will consider it senseless; some will argue that they have neither the strength nor the courage to join in such a mass demonstration of nonviolent action. As E. Franklin Frazier points out in *Black Bourgeoisie,* many Negroes are occupied in a middle class struggle for status and prestige. They are more concerned about "conspicuous consumption" than about the cause of justice, and are probably not prepared for the ordeals and sacrifices involved in nonviolent action. Fortunately, however, the success of this method is not dependent on its unanimous acceptance. A few Negroes in every community, unswervingly committed to the nonviolent way, can persuade hundreds of others at least to use nonviolence as a technique and serve as the moral force to awaken the slumbering national conscience. Thoreau was thinking of such a creative minority when he said: "I know this well, that if one thousand, if one hundred, if ten men whom I could name— if ten honest men only—aye, if one honest man, in the state of Massachusetts, ceasing to hold slaves, were actually to withdraw from the copartnership, and be locked up in the county jail therefore, it would be the abolition of slavery in America. For it matters not how small the beginning may seem to be, what is once well done is done forever."

Mahatma Gandhi never had more than one hundred persons absolutely committed to his philosophy. But with this small group of devoted followers, he galvanized the whole of India, and through a magnificent feat of nonviolence challenged the might of the British Empire and won freedom for his people.

This method of nonviolence will not work miracles overnight. Men are not easily moved from their mental ruts, their prejudiced and irrational feelings. When the underprivileged demand freedom, the privileged first react with bitterness and resistance. Even when the demands are couched in nonviolent terms, the initial response is the same. Nehru once remarked that the British were never so angry as when the Indians resisted them with nonviolence, that he never saw eyes so full of hate as those of the British troops to whom he turned the other cheek when they beat him with lathis. But nonviolent resistance at least changed the minds and hearts of the Indians, however impervious the British may have appeared. "We cast away our fear," says Nehru. And in the end the British not only granted freedom to India but came to have a new respect for the Indians. Today a mutual friendship based on complete equality exists between these two peoples within the commonwealth.

In the South too, the initial white reaction to Negro resistance has been bitter. I do not predict that a similar happy ending will come to Montgomery in a few months, because integration is more complicated than independence. But I know that the Negroes of Montgomery are already walking straighter because of the protest. And I expect that this generation of Negro children throughout the United States will grow up stronger and better because of the courage, the dignity, and the suffering of the nine children of Little Rock, and their counterparts in Nashville, Clinton, and Sturges. And I believe that the white people of this country are being affected too, that beneath the surface this nation's conscience is being stirred.

The nonviolent approach does not immediately change the heart of the oppressor. It first does something to the hearts and souls of those committed to it. It gives them new self-respect; it calls up resources of strength and courage that they did not know they had. Finally it reaches the opponent and so stirs his conscience that reconciliation becomes a reality.

I suggest this approach because I think it is the only way to reestablish the broken community. Court orders and federal enforcement agencies will be of inestimable value in achieving desegregation. But desegregation is only a partial, though necessary, step toward the ultimate goal which we seek to realize. Desegregation will break down the legal barriers, and bring men together physically. But something must happen so to touch the hearts and souls of men that they will come together, not because the law says it, but because it is natural and right. In other words, our ultimate goal is integration which is genuine intergroup and interpersonal living. Only through nonviolence can this goal be attained, for the aftermath of nonviolence is reconciliation and the creation of the beloved community.

It is becoming clear that the Negro is in for a season of suffering. As victories for civil rights mount in the federal courts, angry passions and deep prejudices are further aroused. The mountain of state and local segregation laws still stands. Negro leaders continue to be arrested and harassed under city ordinances, and their homes continue to be bombed. State laws continue to be enacted to circumvent integration. I pray that, recognizing the necessity of suffering, the Negro will make of it a virtue. To suffer in a righteous cause is to grow to our humanity's full stature. If only to save himself from bitterness, the Negro needs the vision to see the ordeals of this generation as the opportunity to transfigure himself and American society. . . .

Nonviolence is a way of humility and self-restraint. We Negroes talk a great deal about our rights, and rightly so. We proudly proclaim that three-fourths of the people of the world are colored. We have the privilege of watching in our generation the great drama of freedom and independence as it unfolds in Asia and Africa. All of these things are in line with the work of providence. We must be sure, however, that we accept them in the right spirit. In an effort to achieve freedom in America, Asia, and Africa we must not try to leap from a position of disadvantage to one of advantage, thus subverting justice. We must seek democracy and not the substitution of one tyranny for another.

Our aim must never be to defeat or humiliate the white man. We must not become victimized with a philosophy of black supremacy. God is not interested merely in the freedom of black men, and brown men, and yellow men; God is interested in the freedom of the whole human race.

The nonviolent approach provides an answer to the long debated question of gradualism *versus* immediacy. On the one hand it prevents one from falling into the sort of patience which is an excuse for do-nothingism and escapism, ending up in standstillism. On the other hand it saves one from the irresponsible words which estrange without reconciling and the hasty judgment which is blind to the necessities of social process. It recognizes the need for moving toward the goal of justice with wise restraint and calm reasonableness. But it also recognizes the immorality of slowing up in the move toward justice and capitulating to the guardians of an unjust status quo. It recognizes that social change cannot come overnight. But it causes one to work as if it were a possibility the next morning.

Through nonviolence we avoid the temptation of taking on the psychology of victors. Thanks largely to the noble and invaluable work of the NAACP, we have won great victories in the federal courts. But we must not be self-satisfied. We must respond to every decision with an understanding of those who have opposed us, and with acceptance of the new adjustments that the court orders pose for them. We must act in such a way that our victories will be triumphs for good will in all men, white and Negro.

Nonviolence is essentially a positive concept. Its corollary must always be growth. On the one hand nonviolence requires noncooperation with evil; on the other hand it requires cooperation with the constructive forces of good.

Without this constructive aspect nonco-operation ends where it begins. There-fore, the Negro must get to work on a program with a broad range of positive goals. . . .

This then must be our present pro-gram: Nonviolent resistance to all forms of racial injustice, including state and local laws and practices, even when this means going to jail; and imagina-tive, bold, constructive action to end the demoralization caused by the legacy of slavery and segregation, inferior schools, slums, and second-class citi-zenship. The nonviolent struggle, if conducted with the dignity and courage already shown by the people of Mont-gomery and the children of Little Rock, will in itself help end the demoraliza-tion; but a new frontal assault on the poverty, disease, and ignorance of a people too long ignored by America's conscience will make victory more certain.

In short, we must work on two fronts. On the one hand, we must continue to resist the system of segregation which is the basic cause of our lagging stan-dards; on the other hand we must work constructively to improve the standards themselves. There must be a rhythmic alternation between attacking the causes and healing the effects.

This is a great hour for the Negro. The challenge is here. To become the instruments of a great idea is a privilege that history gives only occasionally. Arnold Toynbee says in *A Study of History* that it may be the Negro who will give the new spiritual dynamic to Western civilization that it so desper-ately needs to survive. I hope this is possible. The spiritual power that the Negro can radiate to the world comes from love, understanding, good will, and nonviolence. It may even be possi-ble for the Negro, through adherence to nonviolence, so to challenge the nations of the world that they will seriously

seek an alternative to war and destruc-tion. In a day when Sputniks and Ex-plorers dash through outer space and guided ballistic missiles are carving highways of death through the strato-sphere, nobody can win a war. Today the choice is no longer between vio-lence and nonviolence. It is either non-violence or nonexistence. The Negro may be God's appeal to this age—an age drifting rapidly to its doom. The eternal appeal takes the form of a warn-ing: "All who take the sword will perish by the sword."

21
What We Want*
STOKELY CARMICHAEL

One of the tragedies of the struggle against racism is that up to now there has been no national organization which could speak to the growing militancy of young black people in the urban ghetto. There has been only a civil rights movement, whose tone of voice was adapted to an audience of liberal whites. It served as a sort of buffer zone between them and angry young blacks. None of its so-called leaders could go into a rioting community and be listened to. In a sense, I blame our-selves—together with the mass media—for what has happened in Watts, Har-lem, Chicago, Cleveland, Omaha. Each time the people in those cities saw Martin Luther King get slapped, they became angry; when they saw four little black girls bombed to death, they were angrier; and when nothing hap-pened, they were steaming. We had nothing to offer that they could see, except to go out and be beaten again. We helped to build their frustration.

For too many years, black Americans

*[Reprinted with permission from the *New York Review of Books,* September 22, 1966, pp. 5–7. Copyright © 1966 Student Nonviolent Co-ordinating Committee.]

marched and had their heads broken and got shot. They were saying to the country, "Look, you guys are supposed to be nice guys and we are only going to do what we are supposed to do—why do you beat us up, why don't you give us what we ask, why don't you straighten yourselves out?" After years of this, we are at almost the same point—because we demonstrated from a position of weakness. We cannot be expected any longer to march and have our heads broken in order to say to whites: come on, you're nice guys. For you are not nice guys. We have found you out.

An organization which claims to speak for the needs of a community—as does the Student Nonviolent Coordinating Committee—must speak in the tone of that community, not as somebody else's buffer zone. This is the significance of black power as a slogan. For once, black people are going to use the words they want to use—not just the words whites want to hear. And they will do this no matter how often the press tries to stop the use of the slogan by equating it with racism or separatism.

An organization which claims to be working for the needs of a community—as SNCC does—must work to provide that community with a position of strength from which to make its voice heard. This is the significance of black power beyond the slogan.

Black power can be clearly defined for those who do not attach the fears of white America to their questions about it. We should begin with the basic fact that black Americans have two problems: they are poor and they are black. All other problems arise from this two-sided reality: lack of education, the so-called apathy of black men. Any program to end racism must address itself to that double reality.

Almost from its beginning, SNCC sought to address itself to both con-ditions with a program aimed at winning political power for impoverished southern blacks. We had to begin with politics because black Americans are a propertyless people in a country where property is valued above all. We had to work for power, because this country does not function by morality, love, and nonviolence, but by power. Thus we determined to win political power, with the idea of moving on from there into activity that would have economic effects. With power, the masses could *make or participate in making* the decisions which govern their destinies, and thus create basic change in their day-to-day lives.

But if political power seemed to be the key to self-determination, it was also obvious that the key had been thrown down a deep well many years earlier. Disenfranchisement, maintained by racist terror, makes it impossible to talk about organizing for political power in 1960. The right to vote had to be won, and SNCC workers devoted their energies to this from 1961 to 1965. They set up voter registration drives in the Deep South. They created pressure for the vote by holding mock elections in Mississippi in 1963 and by helping to establish the Mississippi Freedom Democratic Party (MFDP) in 1964. That struggle was eased, though not won, with the passage of the 1965 Voting Rights Act. SNCC workers could then address themselves to the question: "Who can we vote for, to have our needs met—how do we make our vote meaningful?"

SNCC had already gone to Atlantic City for recognition of the Mississippi Freedom Democratic Party by the Democratic convention and been rejected; it had gone with the MFDP to Washington for recognition by Congress and been rejected. In Arkansas, SNCC helped thirty Negroes to run for school board elections; all but one were defeated, and there was evidence of fraud and intimidation sufficient to cause their defeat. In Atlanta, Julian Bond ran for the state legislature and was elected—twice—and unseated— twice. In several states, black farmers ran in elections for agricultural committees which make crucial decisions concerning land use, loans, etc. Although they won places on a number of committees, they never gained the majorities needed to control them.

All the efforts were attempts to win black power. Then, in Alabama, the opportunity came to see how blacks could be organized on an independent party basis. An unusual Alabama law provides that any group of citizens can nominate candidates for county office and, if they win 20 percent of the vote, may be recognized as a county political party. The same then applies on a state level. SNCC went to organize in several counties such as Lowndes, where black people—who form 80 percent of the population and have an average annual income of $943—felt they could accomplish nothing within the framework of the Alabama Democratic Party because of its racism and because the qualifying fee for this year's elections was raised from $50 to $500 in order to prevent most Negroes from becoming candidates. On May 3, five new county "freedom organizations" convened and nominated candidates for the offices of sheriff, tax assessor, members of the school boards. These men and women are up for election in November—if they live until then. Their ballot symbol is the black panther: a bold, beautiful animal, representing the strength and dignity of black demands today. A man needs a black panther on his side when he and his family must endure—as hundreds of Alabamians have endured—loss of job, eviction, starvation, and sometimes death, for political activity. He may

also need a gun and SNCC reaffirms the rights of black men everywhere to defend themselves when threatened or attacked. As for initiating the use of violence, we hope that such programs as ours will make that unnecessary; but it is not for us to tell black communities whether they can or cannot use any particular form of action to resolve their problems. Responsibility for the use of violence by black men, whether in self-defence or initiated by them, lies with the white community.

This is the specific historical experience from which SNCC's call for "black power" emerged on the Mississippi march last July. But the concept of black power is not a recent or isolated phenomenon: it has grown out of the ferment of agitation and activity by different people and organizations in many black communities over the years. Our last year of work in Alabama added a new concrete possibility. In Lowndes county, for example, black power will mean that if a Negro is elected sheriff, he can end police brutality. If a black man is elected tax assessor, he can collect and channel funds for the building of better roads and schools serving black people—thus advancing the move from political power into the economic arena. In such areas as Lowndes, where black men have a majority, they will attempt to use it to exercise control. This is what they seek: control. Where Negroes lack a majority, black power means proper representation and sharing of control. It means the creation of power bases from which black people can work to change statewide or nationwide patterns of oppression through pressure from strength—instead of weakness. Politically, black power means what it has always meant to SNCC—the coming-together of black people to elect representatives and *to force those representatives to speak to their needs.* It does not mean merely putting black faces into office. A man or woman who is black and from the slums cannot be automatically expected to speak to the needs of black people. Most of the black politicians we see around the country today are not what SNCC means by black power. The power must be that of a community, and emanate from there.

SNCC today is working in both North and South on programs of voter registration and independent political organizing. In some places, such as Alabama, Los Angeles, New York, Philadelphia, and New Jersey, independent organizing under the black panther symbol is in progress. The creation of a national "black panther party" must come about: it will take time to build, and it is much too early to predict its success. We have no infallible master plan and we make no claim to exclusive knowledge of how to end racism; different groups will work in their own different ways. SNCC cannot spell out the full logistics of self-determination, but it can address itself to the problem by helping black communities define their needs, realize their strength, and go into action along a variety of lines which they must choose for themselves. Without knowing all the answers, it can address itself to the basic problem of poverty, to the fact that in Lowndes County, 86 white families own 90 percent of the land. What are black people in that county going to do for jobs, where are they going to get money? There must be reallocation of land, of money.

Ultimately, the economic foundations of this country must be shaken if black people are to control their lives. The colonies of the United States —and this includes the black ghettos within its borders, North and South— must be liberated. For a century, this nation has been like an octopus of exploitation, its tentacles stretching from Mississippi and Harlem to South America, the Middle East, southern Africa, and Vietnam; the form of exploitation varies from area to area but the essential result has been the same—a powerful few have been maintained and enriched at the expense of the poor and voiceless colored masses. This pattern must be broken. As its grip loosens here and there around the world, the hopes of black Americans become more realistic. For racism to die, a totally different America must be born.

This is what the white society does not wish to face; this is why that society prefers to talk about integration. But integration speaks not at all to the problem of poverty, only to the problem of blackness. Integration today means the man who "makes it," leaving his black brothers behind in the ghetto as fast as his new sports car will take him. It has no relevance to the Harlem wino or to the cotton-picker making three dollars a day. As a lady I know in Alabama once said, "The food that Ralph Bunche eats doesn't fill my stomach."

Integration, moreover, speaks to the problem of blackness in a despicable way. As a goal, it has been based on complete acceptance of the fact that *in order to have* a decent house or education, blacks must move into a white neighborhood or send their children to a white school. This reinforces, among both black and white, the idea that "white" is automatically better and "black" is by definition inferior. This is why integration is a subterfuge for the maintenance of white supremacy. It allows the nation to focus on a handful of southern children who get into white schools, at great price, and to ignore the 94 percent who are left behind in unimproved all-black schools. Such situations will not change until black people have power—to control their own school boards, in this case. Then Negroes become equal in a way that means something, and integration ceases to be a one-way street. Then integration doesn't mean draining skills and energies from the ghetto into white neighborhoods; then it can mean white people moving from Beverly Hills into Watts, white people joining the Lowndes County Freedom Organization. Then integration becomes relevant.

Last April, before the furor over black power, Christopher Jencks wrote in a *New Republic* article on white Mississippi's manipulation of the anti-poverty program:

The war on poverty has been predicated on the notion that there is such a thing as a community *which can be defined geographically and mobilized for a collective effort to help the poor. This theory has no relationship to reality in the Deep South. In every Mississippi county there are* two *communities. Despite all the pious platitudes of the moderates on both sides, these two communities habitually see their interests in terms of conflict rather than cooperation. Only when the Negro community can muster enough political, economic, and professional strength to compete on somewhat equal terms, will Negroes believe in the possibility of true cooperation and whites accept its necessity. En route to integration, the Negro community needs to develop greater independence—a chance to run its own affairs and not cave in whenever "the man" barks. . . . Or so it seems to me, and to most of the knowledgeable people with whom I talked in Mississippi. To OEO, this judgment may sound like black nationalism. . . .*

Mr. Jencks, a white reporter, perceived the reason why America's anti-poverty program has been a sick farce in both North and South. In the South, it is clearly racism which prevents the poor from running their own programs;

in the North, it more often seems to be politicking and bureaucracy. But the results are not so different: in the North, nonwhites make up 42 percent of all families in metropolitan "poverty areas" and only 6 percent of families in areas classified as not poor. SNCC has been working with local residents in Arkansas, Alabama, and Mississippi to achieve control by the poor of the program and its funds; it has also been working with groups in the North, and the struggle is no less difficult. Behind it all is a federal government which cares far more about winning the war on the Vietnamese than the war on poverty; which has put the poverty program in the hands of self-serving politicians and bureaucrats rather than the poor themselves; which is unwilling to curb the misuse of white power but quick to condemn black power.

To most whites, black power seems to mean that the Mau Mau are coming to the suburbs that night. The Mau Mau are coming, and whites must stop them. Articles appear about plots to "get Whitey," creating an atmosphere in which "law and order must be maintained." Once again, responsibility is shifted from the oppressor to the oppressed. Other whites chide, "Don't forget—you're only 10 percent of the population; if you get too smart, we'll wipe you out." If they are liberals, they complain, "what about me?—don't you want my help any more?" These are people supposedly concerned about black Americans, but today they think first of themselves, of their feelings of rejection. Or they admonish, "you can't get anywhere without coalition," when there is in fact no group at present with whom to form a coalition in which blacks will not be absorbed and betrayed. Or they accuse us of "polarizing the races" by our calls for black unity, when the true responsibility for polarization lies with whites who will not accept their responsibility as the majority power for making the democratic process work.

White America will not face the problem of color, the reality of it. The well-intended say: "We're all human, everybody is really decent, we must forget color." But color cannot be "forgotten" until its weight is recognized and dealt with. White America will not acknowledge that the ways in which this country sees itself are contradicted by being black—and always have been. Whereas most of the people who settled this country came here for freedom or for economic opportunity, blacks were brought here to be slaves. When the Lowndes County Freedom Organization chose the black panther as its symbol, it was christened by the press "the Black Panther party"—but the Alabama Democratic party, whose symbol is a rooster, has never been called the White Cock party. No one ever talked about "white power" because power in this country *is* white. All this adds up to more than merely identifying a group phenomenon by some catchy name or adjective. The furor over that black panther reveals the problems that white America has with color and sex; the furor over "black power" reveals how deep racism runs and the great fear which is attached to it.

Whites will not see that I, for example, as a person oppressed because of my blackness, have common cause with other blacks who are oppressed because of blackness. This is not to say that there are no white people who see things as I do, but that it is black people I must speak to first. It must be the oppressed to whom SNCC addresses itself primarily, not to friends from the oppressing group.

From birth, black people are told a set of lies about themselves. We are told that we are lazy—yet I drive through the Delta area of Mississippi and watch black people picking cotton in the hot sun for fourteen hours. We are told, "If you work hard, you'll succeed"—but if that were true, black people would own this country. We are oppressed because we are black—not because we are ignorant, not because we are lazy, not because we're stupid (and got good rhythm), but because we're black.

I remember that when I was a boy, I used to go to see Tarzan movies on Saturday. White Tarzan used to beat up the black natives. I would sit there yelling, "Kill the beasts, kill the savages, kill 'em!" It was as if a Jewish boy watched Nazis taking Jews off to concentration camps and cheered them on. Today, I want the chief to beat hell out of Tarzan and send him back to Europe. But it takes time to become free of the lies and their shaming effect on black minds. It takes time to reject the most important lie: that black people inherently can't do the same things white people can do, unless white people help them.

The need for psychological equality is the reason why SNCC today believes that blacks must organize in the black community. Only black people can convey the revolutionary idea that black people are able to do things themselves. Only they can help create in the community an aroused and continuing black consciousness that will provide the basis for political strength. In the past, white allies have furthered white supremacy without the whites involved realizing it—or wanting, I think. Black people must do things for themselves; they must get poverty money they will control and spend themselves, they must conduct tutorial programs themselves so that black children can identify with black people. This is one reason Africa has such importance: the reality of black men ruling their own natives gives blacks elsewhere a sense of possibility, of power, which they do not now have.

This does not mean we don't welcome help, or friends. But we want the right to decide whether anyone is, in fact, our friend. In the past, black Americans have been almost the only people whom everybody and his momma could jump up and call their friends. We have been tokens, symbols, objects — as I was in high school to many young whites, who liked having "a Negro friend." We want to decide who is our friend, and we will not accept someone who comes to us and says: "If you do X, Y, and Z, then I'll help you." We will not be told whom we should choose as allies. We will not be isolated from any group or nation except by our own choice. We cannot have the oppressors telling the oppressed how to rid themselves of the oppressor.

I have said that most liberal whites react to "black power" with the question, What about me?, rather than saying: Tell me what you want me to do and I'll see if I can do it. There are answers to the right question. One of the most disturbing things about almost all white supporters of the movement has been that they are afraid to go into their own communities — which is where the racism exists — and work to get rid of it. They want to run from Berkeley to tell us what to do in Mississippi; let them look instead at Berkeley. They admonish blacks to be nonviolent; let them preach nonviolence in the white community. They come to teach me Negro history; let them go to the suburbs and open up freedom schools for whites. Let them work to stop America's racist foreign policy; let them press this government to cease supporting the economy of South Africa.

There is a vital job to be done among poor whites. We hope to see, eventually, a coalition between poor blacks and poor whites. That is the only coalition which seems acceptable to us, and we see such a coalition as the major internal instrument of change in American society. SNCC has tried several times to organize poor whites; we are trying again now, with an initial training program in Tennessee. It is purely academic today to talk about bringing poor blacks and whites together, but the job of creating a poor-white power bloc must be attempted. The main responsibility for it falls upon whites. Black and white can work together in the white community where possible; it is not possible, however, to go into a poor southern town and talk about integration. Poor whites everywhere are becoming more hostile — not less — partly because they see the nation's attention focused on black poverty and nobody coming to them. Too many young middle-class Americans, like some sort of Pepsi generation, have wanted to come alive through the black community; they've wanted to be where the action is — and the action has been in the black community.

Black people do not want to "take over" this country. They don't want to "get whitey"; they just want to get him off their backs, as the saying goes. It was for example the exploitation by Jewish landlords and merchants which first created black resentment toward Jews — not Judaism. The white man is irrelevant to blacks, except as an oppressive force. Blacks want to be in his place, yes, but not in order to terrorize and lynch and starve him. They want to be in his place because that is where a decent life can be had.

But our vision is not merely of a society in which all black men have enough to buy the good things of life. When we urge that black money go into black pockets, we mean the communal pocket. We want to see money go back into the community and used to benefit it. We want to see the co-operative concept applied in business and banking. We want to see black ghetto residents demand that an ex-ploiting storekeeper sell them, at min-imal cost, a building or a shop that they will own and improve coopera-tively; they can back their demand with a rent strike, or a boycott, and a com-munity so unified behind them that no one else will move into the building or buy at the store. The society we seek to build among black people, then, is not a capitalist one. It is a so-ciety in which the spirit of community and humanistic love prevail. The word "love" is suspect; black expectations of what it might produce have been betrayed too often. But those were expectations of a response from the white community, which failed us. The love we seek to encourage is within the black community, the only Ameri-can community where men call each other "brother" when they meet. We can build a community of love only where we have the ability and power to do so: among blacks.

As for white America, perhaps it can stop crying out against "black supremacy," "black nationalism," "racism in reverse," and begin facing reality. The reality is that this nation, from top to bottom, is racist; that racism is not primarily a problem of "human relations" but of an exploitation main-tained—either actively or through silence—by the society as a whole. Camus and Sartre have asked, can a man condemn himself? Can whites, particularly liberal whites, condemn themselves? Can they stop blaming us, and blame their own system? Are they capable of the shame which might be-come a revolutionary emotion?

We have found that they usually cannot condemn themselves, and so we have done it. But the rebuilding of this society, if at all possible, is basi-cally the responsibility of whites—not blacks. We won't fight to save the pres-ent society, in Vietnam or anywhere else. We are just going to work, in the way *we* see fit, and on goals *we* define, not for civil rights but for all our human rights.

22
*"Black Power" and Coalition Politics**
BAYARD RUSTIN

There are two Americas—black and white—and nothing has more clearly revealed the divisions between them than the debate currently raging around the slogan of "black power." Despite—or perhaps because of—the fact that this slogan lacks any clear definition, it has succeeded in galvanizing emo-tions on all sides, with many whites seeing it as the expression of a new racism and many Negroes taking it as a warning to white people that Negroes will no longer tolerate brutality and violence. But even within the Negro community itself, black power has touched off a major debate—the most bitter the community has experienced since the days of Booker T. Washington and W. E. B. Du Bois, and one which threatens to ravage the entire civil rights movement. Indeed, a serious split has already developed between advo-cates of black power like Floyd Mc-Kissick of CORE and Stokely Car-michael of SNCC on the one hand, and Dr. Martin Luther King of SCLC, Roy Wilkins of the NAACP, and Whitney Young of the Urban League on the other.

There is no question, then, that great passions are involved in the de-bate over the idea of black power; nor,

*[Reprinted from *Commentary*, by permission. Copyright © 1966 by the American Jewish Committee.]

as we shall see, is there any question that these passions have their roots in the psychological and political frustrations of the Negro community. Nevertheless, I would contend that black power not only lacks any real value for the civil rights movement, but that its propagation is positively harmful. It diverts the movement from a meaningful debate over strategy and tactics, it isolates the Negro community, and it encourages the growth of anti-Negro forces.

In its simplest and most innocent guise, black power merely means the effort to elect Negroes to office in proportion to Negro strength within the population. There is, of course, nothing wrong with such an objective in itself, and nothing inherently radical in the idea of pursuing it. But in Stokely Carmichael's extravagant rhetoric about "taking over" in districts of the South where Negroes are in the majority, it is important to recognize that southern Negroes are only in a position to win a maximum of two congressional seats and control of eighty local counties.* (Carmichael, incidentally, is in the paradoxical position of screaming at liberals—wanting only to "get whitey off my back"—and simultaneously needing their support: after all, he can talk about Negroes taking over Lowndes County only because there is a fairly liberal federal government to protect him should Governor Wallace decide to eliminate this pocket of black power.) Now there might be a certain value in having two Negro congressmen from the South, but obviously they could do nothing by themselves to reconstruct the face of America. Eighty sheriffs, eighty tax assessors, and eighty school board members might ease the tension for a while in their communities, but

they alone could not create jobs and build low cost housing; they alone could not supply quality integrated education.

The relevant question, moreover, is not whether a politician is black or white, but what forces he represents. Manhattan has had a succession of Negro borough presidents, and yet the schools are increasingly segregated. Adam Clayton Powell and William Dawson have both been in Congress for many years; the former is responsible for a rider on school intergration that never gets passed, and the latter is responsible for keeping the Negroes of Chicago tied to a mayor who had to see riots and death before he would put sprinklers on water hydrants in the summer. I am not for one minute arguing that Powell, Dawson, and Mrs. Motley should be impeached. What I am saying is that if a politician is elected because he is black and is deemed to be entitled to a "slice of the pie," he will behave in one way; if he is elected by a constituency pressing for social reform, he will, whether he is white or black, behave in another way.

Southern Negroes, despite exhortations from SNCC to organize themselves into a Black Panther party, are going to stay in the Democratic party—to them it is the party of progress, the New Deal, the New Frontier, and the Great Society—and they are right to stay. For SNCC's Black Panther perspective is simultaneously utopian and reactionary—the former for the by-now obvious reason that one-tenth of the population cannot accomplish much by itself, the latter because such a party would remove Negroes from the main area of political struggle in this country (particularly in the one-party South, where the decisive battles are fought out in Democratic primaries), and would give priority to the issue of race pre-

* See "The Negroes Enter Southern Politics" by Pat Watters, *Dissent,* July-August 1966.

cisely at a time when the fundamental questions facing the Negro and American society alike are economic and social. It is no accident that the two main proponents of "black power," Carmichael and McKissick, should now be cosponsoring a conference with Adam Clayton Powell and Elijah Muhammad, and that the leaders of New York CORE should recently have supported the machine candidate for surrogate—because he was the choice of a Negro boss—rather than the candidate of the reform movement. By contrast, Martin Luther King is working in Chicago with the Industrial Union Department of the AFL-CIO and with religious groups in a coalition which, if successful, will mean the end or at least the weakening of the Daley–Dawson machine.

The winning of the right of Negroes to vote in the South ensures the eventual transformation of the Democratic party, now controlled primarily by northern machine politicians and southern Dixiecrats. The Negro vote will eliminate the Dixiecrats from the party and from Congress, which means that the crucial question facing us today is who will replace them in the South. Unless civil rights leaders (in such towns as Jackson, Mississippi; Birmingham, Alabama; and even to a certain extent Atlanta) can organize grassroots clubs whose members will have a genuine political voice, the Dixiecrats might well be succeeded by black moderates and black southern-style machine politicians, who would do little to push for needed legislation in Congress and little to improve local conditions in the South. While I myself would prefer Negro machines to a situation in which Negroes have no power at all, it seems to me that there is a better alternative today—a liberal-labor-civil rights coalition which would work to make the Democratic party truly responsive to the aspirations of the poor,

and which would develop support for programs (specifically those outlined in A. Philip Randolph's $100 billion Freedom Budget) aimed at the reconstruction of American society in the interests of greater social justice. The advocates of black power have no such programs in mind; what they are in fact arguing for (perhaps unconsciously) is the creation of a *new black establishment.*

Nor, it might be added, are they leading the Negro people along the same road which they imagine immigrant groups traveled so successfully in the past. Proponents of black power —accepting a historical myth perpetrated by moderates—like to say that the Irish and the Jews and the Italians, by sticking together and demanding their share, finally won enough power to overcome their initial disabilities. But the truth is that it was through alliances with other groups (in political machines or as part of the trade union movement) that the Irish and the Jews and the Italians acquired the power to win their rightful place in American society. They did not "pull themselves up by their own bootstraps"—no group in American society has ever done so; and they most certainly did not make isolation their primary tactic.

In some quarters, black power connotes not an effort to increase the number of Negroes in elective office but rather a repudiation of nonviolence in favor of Negro "self-defense." Actually this is a false issue, since no one has ever argued that Negroes should not defend themselves as individuals from attack.* Nonviolence has been advocated as a *tactic* for organized demonstrations in a society where Negroes are

---

* As far back as 1934, A. Philip Randolph, Walter White, then executive secretary of the NAACP, Lester Granger, then executive director of the Urban League, and I joined a committee to try to save the life of Odell Waller. Waller, a sharecropper, had murdered his white boss in self-defense.

a minority and where the majority controls the police. Proponents of nonviolence do not, for example, deny that James Meredith has the right to carry a gun for protection when he visits his mother in Mississippi; what they question is the wisdom of his carrying a gun while participating in a demonstration.

There is, as well, a tactical side to the new emphasis on "self-defense" and the suggestion that nonviolence be abandoned. The reasoning here is that turning the other cheek is not the way to win respect, and that only if the Negro succeeds in frightening the white man will the white man begin taking him seriously. The trouble with this reasoning is that it fails to recognize that fear is more likely to bring hostility to the surface than respect; and far from prodding the "white power structure" into action, the new militant leadership, by raising the slogan of black power and lowering the banner of nonviolence, has obscured the moral issue facing this nation, and permitted the president and vice president to lecture us about "racism in reverse" instead of proposing more meaningful programs for dealing with the problems of unemployment, housing, and education.

Black power is, of course, a somewhat nationalistic slogan and its sudden rise to popularity among Negroes signifies a concomitant rise in nationalist sentiment (Malcolm X's autobiography is quoted nowadays in Grenada, Mississippi, as well as in Harlem). We have seen such nationalistic turns and withdrawals back into the ghetto before, and when we look at the conditions which brought them about, we find that they have much in common with the conditions of Negro life at the present moment: conditions which lead to despair over the goal of integration and to the belief that the ghetto will last forever. . . .

Thus, as in roughly similar circum-

stances in the past—circumstances, I repeat, which in the aggregate foster the belief that the ghetto is destined to last forever—Negroes are once again turning to nationalistic slogans, with black power affording the same emotional release as "Back to Africa" and "Buy Black" did in earlier periods of frustration and hopelessness. This is not only the case with the ordinary Negro in the ghetto; it is also the case with leaders like McKissick and Carmichael, neither of whom began as a nationalist or was at first cynical about the possibilities of integration.* It took countless beatings and twenty-four jailings—that and the absence of strong and continual support from the liberal community—to persuade Carmichael that his earlier faith in coalition politics was mistaken, that nothing was to be gained from working with whites, and that an alliance with the black nationalists was desirable. In the areas of the South where SNCC has been working so nobly, implementation of the Civil Rights Acts of 1964 and 1965 has been slow and ineffective. Negroes in many rural areas cannot walk into the courthouse and register to vote. Despite the voting-rights bill, they must file complaints and the Justice Department must be called to send federal registrars. Nor do children attend integrated schools as a matter of course. There, too, complaints must be filed and the Department of Health, Education and Welfare must be notified. Neither department has been doing an effective job of enforcing the bills. The feeling of isolation increases among SNCC workers as each legislative victory turns out to be only a token victory —significant on the national level, but not affecting the day-to-day lives of Negroes. Carmichael and his colleagues

*On Carmichael's background, see "Two for SNCC" by Robert Penn Warren in the April 1965 *Commentary*—Ed.

are wrong in refusing to support the 1966 bill, but one can understand why they feel as they do.

It is, in short, the growing conviction that the Negroes cannot win—a conviction with much grounding in experience —which accounts for the new popularity of black power. So far as the ghetto Negro is concerned, this conviction expresses itself in hostility first toward the people closest to him who have held out the most promise and failed to deliver (Martin Luther King, Roy Wilkins, etc.), then toward those who have proclaimed themselves his friends (the liberals and the labor movement), and finally toward the only oppressors he can see (the local storekeeper and the policeman on the corner). On the leadership level, the conviction that the Negroes cannot win takes other forms, principally the adoption of what I have called a "no-win" policy. Why bother with programs when their enactment results only in "sham"? Why concern ourselves with the image of the movement when nothing significant has been gained for all the sacrifices made by SNCC and CORE? Why compromise with reluctant white allies when nothing of consequence can be achieved anyway? Why indeed have anything to do with whites at all?

On this last point, it is extremely important for white liberals to understand—as, one gathers from their references to "racism in reverse," the president and the vice president of the United States do not—that there is all the difference in the world between saying, "If you don't want me, I don't want you" (which is what some proponents of black power have in effect been saying) and the statement, "Whatever you do, I don't want you" (which is what racism declares). It is, in other words, both absurd and immoral to equate the despairing response of the victim with the contemptuous assertion of the oppressor. It would, moreover, be tragic if white liberals allowed verbal hostility on the part of Negroes to drive them out of the movement or to curtail their support for civil rights. The issue was injustice before black power became popular, and the issue is still injustice.

In any event, even if black power had not emerged as a slogan, problems would have arisen in the relation between whites and Negroes in the civil rights movement. In the North, it was inevitable that Negroes would eventually wish to run their own movement and would rebel against the presence of whites in positions of leadership as yet another sign of white supremacy. In the South, the well-intentioned white volunteer had the cards stacked against him from the beginning. Not only could he leave the struggle any time he chose to do so, but a higher value was set on his safety by the press and the government—apparent in the differing degrees of excitement generated by the imprisonment or murder of whites and Negroes. The white person's importance to the movement in the South was thus an ironic outgrowth of racism and was therefore bound to create resentment.

But again: however understandable all this may be as a response to objective conditions and to the seeming irrelevance of so many hard-won victories to the day-to-day life of the mass of Negroes, the fact remains that the quasi-nationalist sentiments and "no-win" policy lying behind the slogan of black power do no service to the Negro. Some nationalist emotion is, of course, inevitable, and black power must be seen as part of the psychological rejection of white supremacy, part of the rebellion against the stereotypes which have been ascribed to Negroes for three hundred years. Nevertheless, pride, confidence, and a new identity cannot be won by glorifying blackness or attacking whites; they can only come from meaningful action, from good jobs, and from real victories such as were achieved on the streets of Montgomery, Birmingham, and Selma. When SNCC and CORE went into the South, they awakened the country, but now they emerge isolated and demoralized, shouting a slogan that may afford a momentary satisfaction but that is calculated to destroy them and their movement. Already their frustrated call is being answered with counter-demands for law and order and with opposition to police review boards. Already they have diverted the entire civil rights movement from the hard task of developing strategies to realign the major parties of this country, and embroiled it in a debate that can only lead more and more to politics by frustration.

On the other side, however—the more important side, let it be said—it is the business of those who reject the negative aspects of black power not to preach but to act. Some weeks ago President Johnson, speaking at Fort Campbell, Kentucky, asserted that riots impeded reform, created fear, and antagonized the Negro's traditional friends. Mr. Johnson, according to *The New York Times,* expressed sympathy for the plight of the poor, the jobless, and the ill-housed. The government, he noted, has been working to relieve their circumstances, but "all this takes time."

One cannot argue with the President's position that riots are destructive or that they frighten away allies. Nor can one find fault with his sympathy for the plight of the poor; surely the poor need sympathy. But one can question whether the government has been working seriously enough to eliminate the conditions which lead to frustration politics and riots. The President's very words, "all this takes time," will be understood by the poor for precisely what they are—an excuse instead of a real program, a cover-up for the failure to establish real priorities, and an indication that the administration has no real commitment to create new jobs, better housing, and integrated schools.

For the truth is that it need only take ten years to eliminate poverty—ten years and the $100 billion Freedom Budget recently proposed by A. Philip Randolph. In his introduction to the budget (which was drawn up in consultation with the nation's leading economists), . . . Mr. Randolph points out: "The programs urged in the Freedom Budget attack all of the major causes of poverty—unemployment and underemployment, substandard pay, inadequate social insurance and welfare payments to those who cannot or should not be employed; bad housing; deficiencies in health services, education, and training; and fiscal and monetary policies which tend to redistribute income regressively rather than progressively. The Freedom Budget leaves no room for discrimination in any form because its programs are addressed to all who need more opportunity and improved incomes and living standards, not to just some of them."

The legislative precedent Mr. Randolph has in mind is the 1945 Full Employment Bill. This bill—conceived in its original form by Roosevelt to prevent a postwar depression—would have made it public policy for the government to step in if the private economy could not provide enough employment. As passed finally by Congress in 1946, with many of its teeth removed, the bill had the result of preventing the Negro worker, who had finally reached a pay level about 55 percent that of the white wage, from making any further progress in closing that discriminatory gap; and instead, he was pushed back by the chronically high unemployment rates of the 1950's. Had the original bill been passed, the public sector of our economy would have been able to ensure fair and full employment. Today, with the spiraling thrust of automation, it is even more imperative that we have a legally binding commitment to this goal.

Let me interject a word here to those who say that Negroes are asking for another handout and are refusing to help themselves. From the end of the nineteenth century up to the last generation, the United States absorbed and provided economic opportunity for tens of millions of immigrants. These people were usually uneducated and a good many could not speak English. They had nothing but their hard work to offer and they labored long hours, often in miserable sweatshops and unsafe mines. Yet in a burgeoning economy with a need for unskilled labor, they were able to find jobs, and as industrialization proceeded, they were gradually able to move up the ladder to greater skills. Negroes who have been driven off the farm into a city life for which they are not prepared and who have entered an economy in which there is less and less need for unskilled labor, cannot be compared with these immigrants of old. The tenements which were jammed by newcomers were way-stations of hope; the ghettos of today have become dead-ends of despair. Yet just as the older generation of immigrants—in its most decisive act of self-help—organized the trade union movement and then in alliance with many middle class elements went on to improve its own lot and the condition of American society generally, so the Negro of today is struggling to go beyond the gains of the past and, in alliance with liberals and labor, to guarantee full and fair employment to all Americans.

Mr. Randolph's Freedom Budget not only rests on the Employment Act of 1946, but on a precedent set by Harry Truman when he believed freedom was threatened in Europe. In 1947, the Marshall Plan was put into effect and 3 percent of the gross national product was spent in foreign aid. If we were to allocate a similar proportion of our GNP to destroy the economic and social consequences of racism and poverty at home today, it might mean spending more than $20 billion a year, although I think it quite possible that we can fulfill these goals with a much smaller sum. It would be intolerable, however, if our plan for domestic social reform were less audacious and less far reaching than our international programs of a generation ago.

We must see, therefore, in the current debate over black power, a fantastic challenge to American society to live up to its proclaimed principles in the area of race by transforming itself so that all men may live equally and under justice. We must see to it that in rejecting black power, we do not also reject the principle of Negro equality. Those people who would use the current debate and/or the riots to abandon the civil rights movement leave us no choice but to question their original motivation.

If anything, the next period will be more serious and difficult than the preceding ones. It is much easier to establish the Negro's right to sit at a Woolworth's counter than to fight for an integrated community. It takes very little imagination to understand that the Negro should have the right to vote, but it demands much creativity, patience, and political stamina to plan, develop, and implement programs and priorities. It is one thing to organize sentiment behind laws that do not disturb consensus politics, and quite another to win battles for the redistribution of wealth. Many people who marched in Selma are not prepared to support a bill for a $2.00 minimum wage, to say nothing of supporting a redefinition of work or a guaranteed annual income.

It is here that we who advocate coalitions and integration and who object to the black power concept have a massive job to do. We must see to it that the liberal-labor-civil rights coalition is maintained and, indeed, strengthened so that it can fight effectively for a Freedom Budget. We are responsible for the growth of the black power concept because we have not used our own power to ensure the full implementation of the bills whose passage we were strong enough to win, and we have not mounted the necessary campaign for winning a decent minimum wage and extended benefits. Black power is a slogan directed primarily against liberals by those who once counted liberals among their closest friends. It is up to the liberal movement to prove that coalition and integration are better alternatives.

23
The Black Panther Party*
HUEY P. NEWTON

The Black Panther party is the people's party. We are fundamentally interested in one thing, that is, freeing all people from all forms of slavery in order that every man will be his own master.

At present men are engaged in a struggle for self-determination on both an ethnic and an international level. People everywhere want to eliminate the slavemaster in order to gain sacred freedom. People must be involved in this struggle so as to control the decisions that effect them. A basic tenet of this struggle and its object also is the principle that things we all commonly use and commonly need should be commonly owned. In other words, the people should collectively decide exactly what they need and they should share fully in the wealth they produce. To this end the whole administration of the government should be subject to the dictates of the people, something that doesn't occur in present capitalistic society. If the needs of the people are neither being met by the present form of government administration nor by the present economic philosophy we call capitalism, both should be replaced.

The Black Panther party feels that the present government and its subsidiary institutions are illegitimate because they fail to relate to the people and they fail to meet the needs of the people. Therefore, they have no right to exist. The Black Panther party feels that in the interest of the people's new institutions, both political and economic, should be established, and that the old institutions should disappear.

There are steps that will lead to that society. The Black Panther party recognizes that blacks are in a unique position in America. Because of our heritage, we are the one national minority that has always been deprived of all freedom in determining our destiny. We now demand to be free to structure our own communities so that we can determine the institutions of the community that will perpetuate our culture.

The Black Panther party believes that in order for ethnic minorities to be free, we will have to have administrators who are responsive to the needs and desires of the people. They will be in office solely for the purpose of answering those needs, and the people will be in a position to make the final decision of what will be done.

In a capitalistic society, the capitalist is not interested in a national

*[Huey P. Newton, "The Black Panther Party," *The Black Panther*, August 23, 1969.]

minority because it has no profit value to him. Black people can only begin to experience self-determination when the profit motive behind production disappears. That is why self-determination can only work in a socialistic context. We realize that not only are blacks kept in a slave condition, all persons in this country are essentially in that condition. In order for us to become free, all citizens will have to be free.

There are divisions in the black community that impede the path to self-determination and freedom. One of these divisions is between cultural nationalists and revolutionary nationalists.

The cultural nationalist seeks refuge by retreating to some ancient African behavior and culture, and he refuses to take into consideration those forces that are acting both on his own group and on the world as a whole. The revolutionary nationalist sees that there is no hope for cultural or individual expression, or even hope that his people can exist as a unique entity in a complex whole as long as the bureaucratic capitalist is in control.

The Black Panthers are revolutionary nationalists. We do not believe that it is necessary to go back to the culture of eleventh-century Africa. In reality, we must deal with the dynamic present in order to forge a progressive future. We feel no need to retreat to the past, although we respect our African heritage. The things that are useful in the African heritage we will use to deal with the forces that are working on us today. Those things that are outdated, that are antique, we will look upon with respect, and a fact of our heritage, but not as the basis for a pattern of behavior to follow in the present time.

The revolutionary nationalist respects people, particularly the oppressed people, everywhere and he realizes all men's common struggle for freedom.

And this is what the Black Panther Party is primarily interested in.

There is another division among us, one that the new administration under Richard Nixon is trying to widen. It is a cruel division and a hoax perpetrated on many sincere but misguided black people who still believe they can find their freedom and security in the capitalist system. The talk today is for a type of black capitalism to parallel white capitalism. (Is this a return to separate but equal institutions?) A part of the black bourgeoisie seems to be committed to developing, or attempting to develop, a form of capitalism within the black community, or the black colony as we call it. As far as the masses are concerned it would merely be trading one master for another. A small group of blacks would control our destiny if this development came to pass.

Such a notion is reminiscent of our earlier history when we had black slavemasters. A small percentage of the blacks owned slaves; they were our first black bourgeoisie. What we have today are their spiritual descendants. And just as the earlier black slave holders failed to alleviate the suffering of their slaves, so today the black capitalists (those few in existence) do nothing to alleviate the suffering of their oppressed black brothers.

But in a greater sense, black capitalism is a hoax. Black capitalism is represented as a great step toward black liberation. It isn't. It is a giant stride *away* from liberation. No black capitalist can function unless he plays the white man's game. Worse still, while the black capitalist wants to think he functions on his own terms, he doesn't. He is always subject to the whims of the white capitalist. The rules of black capitalism, and the limits of black capitalism are set by the white power structure.

As a matter of fact, there can be no

real black capitalism because no blacks control the means of production. All blacks can do is have illusions. They can dream of the day when they might share ownership of the means of production. But there is no free enterprise in America. We have monopoly capitalism which is a closed society of white industrialists and their protectors, white politicians in Washington.

While strictly speaking there can be no black capitalism, there is a black bourgeoisie made up primarily of black professionals and small business operators. All, regardless of wealth or accomplishment, are subject to and controlled by the industrialists.

Still, within the black community there is something of a close relationship between all black people, regardless of class or position, because of racism in this country. It would be in the interest of the black bourgeoisie to eliminate racism in order to enhance their prospects, but racism cannot be eliminated until capitalism is eliminated. Historically racism, in the context of developing capitalism, provided the surplus capital that allowed American capitalism to become the monster it is today. Racism is still believed to be a profitable and essential ingredient of capitalism. In our society racism is linked to capitalism. Only by eliminating capitalism and substituting for it socialism will black people, *all* black people, be able to practice self-determination and thus achieve freedom. Freedom means the end of exploitation, something we have suffered from for centuries. And when the Black Panther party calls for freedom, it means freedom *now!*

A capitalistic society can exist only on the basis of a war economy, with its builtin obsolescence and artificially stimulated demands for greater production. The victims of this capitalistic necessity are the black people. Our people are the most drafted and the most killed; it is our contribution toward the preservation of capitalism. In peace we are capitalism's victims, and in war we are its victims. Could anything be more harmful to us as a people and as individuals than to strive for the success of capitalism? What black man wants to die in defense of a system that denies him justice? What black man wants to support an economic system that forces his black brother to go to distant lands to kill and be killed? It is literally a case of black men sending other black men to their deaths so that white men can have bigger profits.

The Panther Community Program is attempting to spur the community into action, creative action, to regain the dignity of the people. We join the struggle of any and all oppressed people all over the world, as well as in this country, regardless of color, who are attempting to gain freedom and dignity. These are the rights of man, and not of any particular group. In some ways the Panthers are like the psychotherapist in that we are trying to make the people well again. The people have been made ill by the forces of oppressive capitalism that have kept them in a position of servitude. The first thing we have to do is make the people aware of these forces that for so long seemed beyond their reach, or control, or understanding. The ruling class has indoctrinated us for so long that we have internalized certain behavior patterns which they want us to have and which we mistakenly think are part of our natural selves. They are not. If we are to be free from economic and social slavery, we must first gain control of our inner selves before we can begin to change the external circumstances of our lives.

The Panther's educational program in the community tries to expose the forces that have shaped our past and our present. On the sociological level we agree with [Karl] Marx that outside forces control man's behavior patterns, and that he will be oppressed until he can control them and can act in his own best interest.

We are not alone in our struggle for freedom. Young whites are beginning to realize more and more each day that they are not free. They have become very angry because the ideas with which they have been indoctrinated have turned out to be lies. They are told that they are free, yet when they try to create and manifest a new form of decision making on the college campuses they are arrested and some are even shot down.

The capitalist ruling class cannot tolerate any challenge from the people. If the people once discover that they are not truly free, they will seek the freedom they lack, thus threatening the existence of the ruling class. In reprisal the ruling class will use any means to put down the people.

Today in some white communities people are suffering from the same repression that we in the black community suffer. The same forces are there—the police, the National Guard, and sometimes even the Regular Army. This will continue to happen time and again in the coming years, thus forming a basis for unity between the peoples of both the black and white communities. Not only are we coming together in unity in this country, we are all part of the international brotherhood of oppressed people.

People all over the world see that their enemy is American imperialism. In Vietnam, one example among many, the people, that is, the National Liberation Front, insist on determining their own destiny. In the pursuit of that goal they will give up their lives rather than forgo the pursuit of freedom that every man deserves. The Panthers stand with the Vietnamese people, and people everywhere, who are attempting to determine their own destinies.

The Panthers are being harassed, persecuted, and killed across the country because we know the truth of our society and we are trying to pass the truth on to the people. Once the people grasp the reality of what we are saying, the ruling class will no longer be able to resist the uprising of the oppressed people. The people of the world are no longer willing to be slaves. The ruling class, of course, is fighting desperately to remain in control.

Until we achieve the freedom we all want, this country will be in a state of chaos. It will suffer revolts and eventually revolution. But the peoples' needs are greater than those of the ruling class. And their will is stronger than that of the ruling class. Man, once awakened to the truth that freedom from oppression and freedom to engage in productive creativity are within his grasp, will never remain content to be a slave.

WHAT WE WANT

1 We want freedom. We want power to determine the destiny of our black community. We believe that black people will not be free until we are able to determine our destiny.

2 We want full employment for our people. We believe that the federal government is responsible and obligated to give every man employment or a guaranteed income. We believe that if the white American businessmen will not give full employment, then the means of production should be taken from the businessmen and placed in the community so that the people of the community can organize and employ all of its people and give a high standard of living.

3 We want an end to the robbery by the *capitalist* of our black community. We believe that this racist government has robbed us and now we are demanding the overdue debt of forty acres and two mules. Forty acres and two mules was promised one hundred years ago as restitution for slave labor and mass murder of black people. We will accept the payment in currency which will be distrib-

uted to our many communities. The Germans are now aiding the Jews in Israel for the genocide of the Jewish people. The Germans murdered six million Jews. The American racist has taken part in the slaughter of over fifty million black people; therefore, we feel that this is a modest demand that we make.

4 We want decent housing, fit for shelter of human beings. We believe that if the white landlords will not give decent housing to our black community, then the housing and the land should be made into cooperatives so that our community, with government aid, can build and make decent housing for its people.

5 We want education for our people that exposes the true nature of this decadent American society. We want education that teaches us our true history and our role in the present-day society. We believe in an educational system that will give to our people a knowledge of self. If a man does not have knowledge of himself and his position in society and the world, then he has little chance to relate to anything else.

6 We want all black men to be exempt from military service. We believe that Black people should not be forced to fight in the military service to defend a racist government that does not protect us. We will not fight and kill other people of color in the world who, like black people, are being victimized by the white racist government of America. We will protect ourselves from the force and violence of the racist police and the racist military, by whatever means necessary.

7 We want an immediate end to *police brutality* and *murder* of black people. We believe we can end police brutality in our black community by organizing black self-defense groups that are dedicated to defending our black community from racist police oppression and brutality. The second amendment to the Constitution of the United States gives a right to bear arms. We therefore believe that all black people should arm themselves for self-defense.

8 We want freedom for all black men held in federal, state, county, and city prisons and jails. We believe that all black people should be released from the many jails and prisons because they have not received a fair and impartial trial.

9 We want all black people when brought to trial to be tried in court by a jury of their peer group or people from their black communities, as defined by the Constitution of the United States. We believe that the courts should follow the United States Constitution so that black people will receive fair trials. The fourteenth amendment of the United States Constitution gives a man a right to be tried by his peer group. A peer is a person from a similar economic, social, religious, geographical, environmental, historical, and racial background. To do this the court will be forced to select a jury from the black community from which the black defendant came. We have been, and are being, tried by all-white juries that have no understanding of the "average reasoning man" of the black community.

10 We want land, bread, housing, education, clothing, justice, and peace. And as our major political objective, a United Nations-supervised plebiscite to be held throughout the black colony in which only black colonial subjects will be allowed to participate, for the purpose of determining the will of black people as to their national destiny.

When, in the course of human events, it becomes necessary for one people to dissolve the political bands which have connected them with another, and to assume, among the powers of the earth, the separate and equal station to which the laws of nature and nature's God entitle them, a decent respect to the opinions of mankind requires that they should declare the causes which impel them to the separation.

We hold these truths to be self-evident, that all men are created equal; that they are endowed by their Creator with certain unalienable rights; that among these are life, liberty, and the pursuit of happiness. That, to secure these rights, governments are instituted among men, deriving their just powers from the consent of the governed; that, whenever any form of government becomes destructive of these ends, it is the right of the people to alter or to abolish it, and to institute a new government, laying its foundation on such principles, and organizing its powers in such form, as to them shall seem most likely to effect their safety and happiness. Prudence, indeed, will dictate that governments long established should not be changed for light and transient causes; and, accordingly, all experience hath shown, that mankind are more disposed to suffer, while evils are sufferable, than to right themselves by abolishing the forms to which they are accustomed. But, when a long train of abuses and usurpations, pursuing invariably the same object, evinces a design to reduce them under absolute despotism, it is their right, it is their duty, to throw off such government, and to provide new guards for their future security.

24
On White Supremacy*
T. BILBO

We in Mississippi are justly proud of the harmonious relations existing here among the races. Our population is almost equally divided and we are glad to have peaceful, law-abiding Negroes within our midst. We ask no Negro to leave our state; at the same time we ask no discontented Negro to remain.

Three-fourths of the nation's 12 million Negroes are living and earning a livelihood in the South. We have an established policy of segregation known and understood by the members of both races. We recognize the right of a Negro to hire Negroes in preference to white people and the white employer has the same right. The right of southern white people to operate political associations and hold their primaries, excluding Negroes, is no more to be questioned than the right of Negroes to form political or social clubs, excluding white people. Certainly Negroes may own and conduct their own restaurants, hotels, and shops exclusively for themselves, just as white people may likewise. The races shall have equal and separate accommodations on buses and trains; and separate public schools shall be maintained. Equal and exact justice shall be accorded both races under the law, but segregation of the races shall be enforced. Honest and intelligent southern white and colored people agree with this policy. In commenting on the recent Detroit race riots, a Negro leader in Arkansas, Rev. Thomas J. Brown, editor of *The Eastern Arkansas World,* made the following statement:

The only way to live peaceably and unmolested in the South, North, East, and West is for every kind to (live to) himself; whether

it be race, clan, or tribe. Henry W. Longfellow wrote, "Birds of a feather flock together. . . ."

The average Negro is proud of his race and its achievement and would not care to undermine its solidarity by amalgamation or intermarriage with other races.

No one needs to be uneasy about the Negro in the South wanting to associate with white folks. He does not even want to live in the same block with them. He does not care to even sit in his front room or eat with him at his table. We don't want to ride with him. We are contented to reside in a Negro section of our towns, go to our own church which is pastored by a black man; send our children to school where they can be under the loving care of Negro teachers. . . .

The Negro race in the South is fortunate to have such a leader as Reverend Brown, and I think he would agree with me that it is difficult, if not impossible, to understand why any group or individual outside the Southland would want to destroy the harmonious race relations which exist here. . . . The three reasons for the destruction of all racial barriers throughout the nation are stated by the *The Militant Church Movement* (of) Louisville, Ky., in the following manner:

The Militant Church Movement affirms:

That color does not affect anything but the outer surface of the skin. . . .

That every act of racial hatred or discrimination is in violation of the will of the founders of this Republic and the principles of Christianity upon which this Nation was built. Thomas Jefferson, who wrote the Declaration of Independence, freed his slaves to prove his sincerity in declaring that all men are born free and equal.

That no church is Christian that is not built on the foundation laid down by its founder, Jesus Christ, namely the fatherhood

*[*Congressional Record,* vol. 90, 78th Congress, March 24–June 12, 1944, Appendix A1795–A1801.]

of God, the brotherhood of man, and the Golden Rule. . . .

Now, I propose to show the falsity of all three of these reasons. First, history and science both defy the statement that "color does not affect anything but the outer surface of the skin." Historical and scientific research has established three propositions beyond all controversy:

First, the white race has founded, developed, and maintained every civilization known to the human race.[1]

Second, the white race, having founded, developed, and maintained a civilization, has never been known, in all history, to lose that civilization as long as the race was kept white.

Third, the white man has never kept unimpaired the civilization he has founded and developed after his bloodstream has been adulterated by the bloodstream of another race, more especially another race so widely diverse in all its inherent qualities as the black race. The superior ability of the white race has been proven craniologically and by six thousand years of planetwide experimentation.

The superior ability of the Caucasian man is evidenced by his endless creation of art, science, law, religion, literature, and every other form of activity known to man down through the ages. Against these achievements, what has the African to offer? What history? What art? What science? What morality? And who will deny the almightiness of heredity? Let the bloodstream be corrupted and nothing can ever restore its purity. If you do not accept this as true, then you brand as false both history and biology. . . .

In the second place, this group has tried to justify full equality of the races in this country in the name of democracy, the name of the founding fathers, and the teaching of Thomas Jefferson. I quote Jefferson's own words:

Nothing is more certainly written in the book of fate, than that these people are to be free; nor is it less certain that the two races, equally free, cannot live in the same government. Nature, habit, opinion have drawn indelible lines of distinction between them.

The founders of this republic never dreamed of it being anything but a white nation. We owe an immeasurable debt to our forefathers who preserved us white through three hundred years of race contact.

The third argument used by the Militant Church group, that of religion, to break down all racial barriers has been frequently used. It was used at one time by the British missionaries in South Africa, and we have before us the practical results of their teachings that all races are of one blood. The mixbreeds of the Cape of Good Hope are evidence of the influence of these ignorant, Negro-loving missionaries who brought disaster along with their teachings. The doctrines of the missionaries were soon changed and they ceased to teach social equality, but who could undo the damage which they had done? The present missionary teaches of the same God and the same Christ and tells the same story of redemption, but one social teaching has been changed. . . .

History clearly shows that the white race is the custodian of the gospel of Jesus Christ and that the white man is entrusted with the spreading of that gospel.

The gospel, of course, is universal; it is missionary in scope; and it is given to all men of all nations. Yet what can be more foreign to the ideals of the Christian religion than amalgamation and miscegenation? Anyone who would,

[1] This of course erroneously credits Caucasians not only for the civilizations of Egypt, the ancient Near East, Greece, and Rome, but also those of India, China, Japan, Mexico (the Aztecs), and Peru (the Incas).

in the name of Christianity, make us a Negroid people betrays his religion and his race.

It should be the desire of both races to maintain racial integrity and have their blood remain pure. If religion teaches the destruction of the races and commits the error of preaching the mixture of all bloods, then what can the missionaries and ministers do to give to the unborn generations the racial heritage which is rightfully theirs? A. H. Shannon, author of *Racial Integrity,* poses this question: "Which is better, a mongrel race, whose origin is sin, and which represents the worst of all races; or a race, whatever its limitations, yet true to its own racial peculiarities and striving to attain, intact, the best and highest of which it is capable? . . ."

Those who would teach us social equality of the races remind us of the fatherhood of God and the brotherhood of man. Why place a fallacious interpretation on these two phrases? If we are to spiritualize "fatherhood of God," then why must we literalize "brotherhood of man"? Both the fatherhood of God and the brotherhood of man are spiritual, and anyone who would interpret the the brotherhood of man in such a manner as to destroy the blood of the white race would destroy the race which has through the centuries proven itself to be the custodian of the gospel of Christ, of his spiritual and ethical teachings. . . .

One of the most pregnant sources of corrupting the minds of our people on the race question is the apostasy of ministers and preachers of practically every denomination expounding the theories of the Christian religion under the favorite texts of brotherhood of mankind, fatherhood of God, and all of one blood. Some of these Negrophilistic preachers with their false interpretations of the real teachings of the Christian religion, pouring out a lot of maudlin sentiment and ecclesiastical rot, tend to make their followers, here in the South and in the North, believe that, under God, the white man is no better than the Negro and that, if you want to go to Heaven, you had better take the sons and daughters of Ethiopia into your fond embraces. . . .

Any preacher or minister who would take advantage of his divine calling to thus destroy the integrity of his race and contaminate and corrupt the blood of his fathers should by his own church be unfrocked and never permitted to smack his traitorous lips on another yellow-legged chicken. . . .

Reduced to its simplest form and laid bare for all the world to judge, we declare that the South is justified in the absolute denial of social equality of the Negroes regardless of what his abilities or accomplishments may be. This the South must do, in behalf of her blood, her essence, and the stock of her Caucasian race.

If we sit with Negroes at our tables, if we entertain them as our social equals, if we discard the color line in all other relations, is it possible to maintain it fixedly in the marriage of the South's Anglo-Saxon sons and daughters? The answer is an emphatic "no. . . ."

Dr. Benjamin Smith, in his book, *The Color Line,* has ably said:

No other conceivable disaster that might befall the South could, for an instant, compare with such miscegenation within her borders. Flood and fire, fever and famine, and the sword even ignorance, indolence, and carpetbaggery she may endure and conquer while her blood remains pure, but once taint the well-spring of her life, and all is lost even honor itself. It is this immediate jewel of her soul that the South watches with such a dragon eye, that she guards with more than vestal vigilance, with a circle of perpetual fire. The blood thereof is the life thereof; he who would de-

file it would stab her in her heart of heart; and she springs to repulse him with the fiercest instinct of self-preservation. It may not be that she is distinctly conscious of her roused antagonism; but the instinct itself is nonetheless just and true and the bulwark of her life.

There are those who would tear away (the) racial pride (of southern whites), knowing full well that it would plunge the Southland into hopeless depths of hybridization. Implant the doctrines of social equality below the Mason-Dixon line, and the result will be a mongrelized Southland. And if the transmitted germ plasma is destroyed, nothing shall ever restore it; neither wealth, nor culture, nor science, nor art, nor morality, nor religion itself.

To southerners this is not a question of individual morality or of self-respect or of individual accomplishments. Every child that is born is born not only of its immediate parents but of all its ancestry. Every child is a child of its race, and heredity plays its part upon it and upon all its descendants. However weak the white man, behind him stands Europe; however strong the black, behind him lies Africa. . . .

We people of the South must draw the color line tighter and tighter, and any white man or woman who dares to cross that color line should be promptly and forever ostracized. No compromise on this great question should be tolerated, no matter who the guilty parties are, whether in the church, in public office, or in the private walks of life. Ostracize them if they cross the color line and treat them as a Negro or as his equal should be treated. . . .

It is imperative that we face squarely and frankly the conditions which confront us. We must not sit idly by, but we must ever be on guard to protect the southern ideals, customs, and traditions that we love and believe in so firmly and completely. There are some issues

that we may differ upon, but on racial integrity, white supremacy, and love of the Southland we will stand together until we pass on to another world.

25
*The Constitution and the Federal Government**
R. MORPHEW

The basic question in the Mississippi crisis was—and remains—this: Whether a contract called the Constitution of the United States means what it says, or whether the power of centralized authority shall be able to overcome this contract at will.

People in Mississippi and California and the other states agree on one point: The laws legally enacted by Congress and the Constitution of the United States should be obeyed. The rub comes when someone acts without legal or constitutional basis, then claims that *his* will must be obeyed instead of the Constitution.

The Constitution of the United States is the contract whereby the sovereign states of our nation—there are now fifty of them—delegate to the federal government certain specific powers, such as those necessary for defense, carrying on foreign affairs, coining money, and so forth. These powers are listed in the Constitution. Then, there follows a specific statement:

The powers not delegated to the United States by the Constitution, nor prohibited by it to the states, are reserved to the states respectively, or to the people.

This is the tenth amendment in the Bill of Rights.

*[R. Morphew, "The Constitution and the Federal Government," in I. A. Newby, ed., *The Development of Segregationist Thought* (Homewood, Ill.: Dorsey Press), pp. 157–163.]

So the issue should really be quite simple. Does the Constitution delegate to the federal government any power to impose its will in regard to educational systems operated by a state? No!

Are states prohibited by the Constitution from running their own schools in their own way? No!

Has Congress passed a law to require any of the things which are being forced at bayonet-point on Mississippi? No!

If those who favor centralized control want to, can they propose a constitutional amendment to make things work their way? Yes!

Have they proposed such an amendment and had it properly ratified? No!

Then shouldn't we be bound by what the Constitution says? Yes!

With these questions clear, then, what is happening? The appointed members of the Supreme Court have determined without law and without authority under the Constitution to impose their will upon the states. They act as legislators in making their own decrees; they act as executives in seeking to carry them out.

In Mississippi, this action ran headon into a determined governor, backed by an unquestioned majority of the people, all of whom believe that the Constitution and the law do not allow what the courts are attempting to force. Since the actions of the courts are without legal authority, the people of Mississippi will not accept them.

Seemingly, then, the situation had reached an impasse. Let us consider for a moment if any action might have been taken to resolve matters while upholding the processes of constitutional government. Can there be a fair solution to this problem, one which reasonable men on both sides could find acceptable?

My answer is an emphatic *yes*— although I hasten to qualify it by saying that I can't realistically expect the advocates of federal force to accept it. They would far rather use centralized power to overcome the Constitution.

But there is an alternative that would wash away all shadow of doubt about illegality and unconstitutionality. There is a way to provide a constitutional answer which persons on both sides could accept in good faith.

Here's how the question could be resolved with justice. At present the Constitution clearly does not provide for the federal government to intervene in educational matters. These affairs are left to the states and to the people. So let's deal with this question by constitutional means!

Let those who uphold the federal position propose an amendment to the Constitution of the United States to allow—without a shadow of a doubt—federal control over education. Such an amendment must win a two-thirds vote in both the House and the Senate then it must be ratified by three-fourths of the states to become a part of the Constitution.

Frankly, I would oppose such an amendment. I do not think it would stand a chance of being adopted. But if it were legally adopted as part of the Constitution, then it would legally become "the law of the land," and would be upheld as such.

However, if such an amendment should fail, then the American people would have spoken, and federal harassment and aggression of the states on matters of education should be dropped forever.

Why hasn't this approach been tried? Simply because some persons in high places are not interested in constitutional government and good will. They are unwilling to take their chances through democratic processes. They prefer to use the centralized force at their command to impose their will, without regard for the Constitution!

And that's exactly what's been done in Mississippi! So many provisions of the Constitution have been violated during the current military occupation of the Oxford, Mississippi area that it would probably be faster to cite the provisions which haven't been shattered. . . .

Less than three weeks ago, the police state came to America! And they didn't even bother to declare martial law!

All this despite the Constitution of the United States—the solemn contract on which our existence as a free people depends.

Article IV, Section 4 of the Constitution says:

The United States shall guarantee to every state in this union a republican form of government, and shall protect each of them against invasion; and on application of the legislature, or of the executive (when the legislature cannot be convened) against domestic violence.

There is no provision whatsoever in the Constitution for sending federal troops into a state, except on application of the legislature, or of the governor if the legislature can't be convened. Now Mississippi's legislature was in session—and it certainly didn't request any troops! Governor Barnett didn't ask for any! So obviously, the sending of federal troops to Mississippi was a plain violation of the Constitution. This is aggression in its simplest form.

The bill of rights has been violated wholesale. Freedom of speech and of assembly were trampled beneath paratroopers' boots on the Ole Miss campus, the first amendment notwithstanding.

The second amendment guarantees that "the right of the people to keep and bear arms shall not be infringed." Yet, everything from BB guns to rocks of throwable size were seized at military roadblocks.

The fourth amendment is supposed to protect us from unreasonable searches and seizures. But the soldiers in Oxford laughed if anyone mentioned a search warrant—or they prodded you with a bayonet, depending on the mood they were in.

The eighth amendment states that excessive bail, excessive fines, and cruel and unusual punishment are prohibited. How can this be squared with the atrocity reports?

Of course, the ninth and tenth amendments, giving certain rights to the states and the people, were again trampled wantonly.

And even the illegally adopted fourteenth amendment, cited by the Warren Court as grounds for outlawing racial segregation, can cut both ways. In all the turmoil over getting James Meredith into Ole Miss what about the rights of the 5,000 legitimate students who were already there in pursuit of an education? This was of no concern to the marshals and troops. Yet, the fourteenth amendment guarantees "equal protection of the laws."

In fact, about the only part of the Constitution still in effect in Mississippi is the sixteenth amendment—the one which permits us to pay the income tax.

Of course, some may say that the situation at Oxford was serious, and that, therefore, the Constitution just couldn't be bothered with. There's no question that the situation was serious —but what made it that way was previous violations of the Constitution.

There's an old saying that one thing leads to another. This has certainly been true in the Mississippi crisis. One violation of the Constitution has led to another, and another, and another . . . until some violations are now being used to justify still more violations.

If you'll stop to think about it, you'll realize that this is the way free governments are destroyed. This is the way constitutional rights and law are cast aside. Some countries in this troubled world could testify that this is the way dictatorship fastens its control upon the people.

That is why it's so important that all of us—we in Mississippi and you in California and others throughout the nation—be ever on the alert, seeing to it that our country's constitutional and legal principles be upheld scrupulously. The real issue is not whether one Negro shall be enrolled in the University of Mississippi. That has been settled. He will remain at Ole Miss only so long as his bodyguards—the troops and marshals—remain. When they leave, Meredith leaves—and he knows it! . . .

But in the Mississippi crisis, if Meredith's enrollment is not the big issue . . . if continued segregation is not the pervading question . . . then what is?

Simply this: the issue is one of dictatorial power versus the constitutional rights of the people. Despite pious protestations to the contrary, the federal action against Mississippi violated the Constitution in a number of ways; therefore, those who dictated it must bear responsibility for the horrible results.

Those who speak of the federal aggression in terms of "law" cannot cite a single section of the Constitution, a single act passed by Congress, or a single treaty that provides them any basis for their emotional, vote-buying, revolutionary position.

The Constitution does not say that a decree by a court—*any* court—is "the law of the land." If it were, Americans would live in a dictatorship, for our federal judiciary is appointed and therefore unresponsive to the people. We would be at the unmerciful mercy of a panel of nine dictators on the Supreme Court who could rule as they willed, and demand federal force to carry out their orders against an enslaved populace.

The Mississippi tragedy has resulted from political, sociological, and demagogic substitution of the decrees of appointed men for law. So when President Kennedy and his partisans speak of upholding "the law," they still find themselves without any law to cite. Thus they expose their hypocrisy and their willingness to take into their own hands powers which are not theirs, all this despite the fact that the president took a solemn oath to "preserve, protect, and defend the Constitution of the United States."

By failing to preserve, protect and defend the Constitution—by substituting dictatorship for it—the president has infringed upon the rights of the states and the people.

For if a mere court decree may upset the Constitution, the law, and previous court rulings on this kind of question which have stood for generations, then what is to prohibit appointed dictators from depriving all Americans of all their freedoms?

If these changes can be wrought contrary to the Constitution and to the law, what is to prevent some appointed court from ruling, for example, that in its "interpretation" of the Constitution, Americans may have free speech—only if the freedom is not extended to criticism of whatever rulers may be in power?

What is to keep appointed judges, if they succeed now, from ruling that freedom of religion may be retained only to the extent of bowing at whatever altar that dictators may designate?

As one portion of freedom goes, so all may go, if we let it!

This issue of federal usurpation is vital to freedom because it is the weapon whereby freedom in America today is most threatened with destruction. No external enemy, communist or any other, so endangers Americans as does unconstitutional government within our nation.

As our enemies rejoice at our misery, let us as Americans seek the course that may yet save our nation.

All of us deplore violence and the situations which create it. But we must do more than that! We must raise a standard of reason and information to enable our people—through the democratic processes—to undo the injustices that have been dictatorially committed, preserving both freedom and the peace.

Let us recognize, as did Jefferson, that "the God who gave us life, gave us liberty at the same time."

Let us strive, as did Jefferson, to "enlighten the people generally, and tyranny and oppressions of body and mind will vanish like evil spirits at the dawn of day."

Finally, let us, along with Jefferson, "swear upon the altar of God eternal hostility against every form of tyranny over the mind of man."

We shall thus realize what the founding fathers must have known. In the clarion words of Patrick Henry, "We are not weak if we make a proper use of those means which the God of Nature has placed in our power. . . . The battle, sir, is not to the strong alone, it is to the vigilant, the active, the brave!"

26
On Protest and Disorder*
JOHN W. GARDNER

Increasingly, here and around the world, the old constraints of tyranny, custom, and stratification that kept a lid on human aspirations have been removed.

When the lid is lifted, what people aspire to—the substantive content of their aspirations—is not unreasonable. They want food, housing, jobs, security, dignity—hardly an irresponsible list. But the time scale on which they want these things poses extraordinary diffi-

*["On Protest and Disorder" was originally given by John Gardner at the Godkin Lectures, Harvard University, 1969, and is incorporated in *Recovery of Confidence* by John W. Gardner. Copyright 1970 by John W. Gardner. Reprinted with the permission of the author and W. W. Norton and Company, Inc.]

culties, given the glacial pace at which human institutions respond to new requirements.

So the stage is set for the most familiar confrontation of modern life—between people who demand change and institutions that resist it. The institutions alter, but never fast enough, and those who seek change are bitterly disappointed.

For this and other reasons, one sees a deepening hostility to institutions—any and all institutions, here and around the world. It is partly understandable in terms of a natural anger over administered frustrations. Men can tolerate extraordinary hardship if they think it inevitable—God's will or Fate or the ancient order of things; but their tempers have a short fuse when hardship results from the decision of another human being, presumably no better than themselves. Yet that is the lot of modern man: it is an administered age.

Related—in what ways we can hardly guess—is a breakdown in authority, in just about every dimension and every way: the authority of parents, religion, custom, social class, the law, and the state.

Without an awareness of these factors—the expectation-despair syndrome, the hostility to institutions, the erosion of authority—one cannot possibly understand the events of the day. The standard phrase concerning social disorders is, "It's only a small group . . .," but that is a misleading assertion. Beyond the fractious few, beyond even the considerable group of sympathizers is the larger number of people who have no fixed views, but are running a chronic low fever of antagonism toward their institutions, toward their fellow man, and toward life in general. They provide the climate in which disorder spreads.

In that climate, unfortunately, our honored tradition of dissent has undergone an unprecedented debasement.

Protest has become a disorderly game for twelve year olds. Reasoned debate has given way to bullhorn obscenities. The loudmouth and the hothead reign unchallenged.

It is hard for the enlightened American to acknowledge that the tradition of dissent may itself be subject to degenerative diseases. He dreads above all to be classed with the know-nothings who would stifle all dissent. But the fact must be faced.

Among the dissenters today we hear a few with a special message. They say, "We don't need reform, we need revolution. The whole system is rotten and should be destroyed."

I have talked long and seriously with people who make that sort of assertion, and have found that most of them don't really mean it. There is an awesome theatricality about today's radicalism, and the apocalyptic assertion is much in vogue. If one patiently questions everyone who makes such assertions, not attacking them but exploring their views, one uncovers a variety of "conventional" radical positions, most of which have been around for a generation or more and have survived peaceably (not necessarily comfortably) within our traditional political structure.

But, of course, some really mean it. At first, one is puzzled by their failure to understand that when a social system is destroyed, the resulting chaos is supremely antagonistic to *any* organized purposes, including the purposes of those who initiated the destruction. The puzzlement clears up when one sees that they have fallen victim to an old and naive doctrine—that man is naturally good, humane, decent, just, and honorable, but that corrupt and wicked institutions have transformed the noble savage into a civilized monster. Destroy the corrupt institutions, they say, and man's native goodness will flower.

There isn't anything in history or anthropology to confirm the thesis but it survives down the generations.

Those who would destroy the system also fail to understand that periods of chaos are followed by periods of iron rule. Those who seek to bring societies down always dream that after the blood bath *they* will be calling the tune; and perhaps that makes the blood bath seem a small price to pay. But after the chaos, no one knows what kind of dictator would emerge. The proposal to destroy the system dissolves under examination.

And yet there is no doubt that today's revolutionary is pursuing that goal with all the energy at his command. And in that pursuit he is wholly cynical in his manipulation of others. The rights of the majority are irrelevant to him; the majority must be manipulated for its own good (as he defines it). He has no interest in rational examination of the issues, indeed will deliberately confuse issues or block communication among groups so as to prevent such examination (for example, by preventing opponents from being heard). He will devise traps to demean those in authority, destroying their dignity where possible. He will exploit the mass media, feeding their hunger for excitement and conflict.

He will plan deliberately provocative confrontations designed to lead authorities to "overreact," knowing that if they do it will bring to his side naive sympathizers who know nothing of the issues but hate to see authorities act repressively. If all people in authority were perfectly wise the tactic would never work. But we shall never have such leaders. If the provocateurs are persistent enough and ingenious enough they can sooner or later trap any official into unwise action.

The fact is that the politics of derision and provocation are not only easy, they yield a kind of twisted pleasure. Sad to say, it's fun to get mad and it's fun to hate. Simple-minded people indulge such emotions without dissembling, and are duly criticized. More guileful people discovered long ago that the big psychic payoff comes in finding a noble cause in which to indulge one's rage and hatred. Then one can draw dividends from both sides of the transaction, satisfying both the new morality and the old Adam. And that is today's fashion. Rage and hate in a good cause! Be vicious for virtue, self-indulgent for higher purposes, dishonest in the service of a higher honesty!

It is easier to understand the existence of a small group of destructive extremists, than to understand why a rather large number of presumably enlightened Americans give them aid and comfort. Generous-minded citizens so fear the censorious role that they fall into a fatuous permissiveness toward destructive behavior. If there is a grain of justification in the behavior, they magnify it to excuse almost any action. They search the status quo for flaws that will make the destructive act seem reasonable. Since there will always be such flaws in an imperfect world, one is left powerless before ruthless opponents. It is hard for the kindly American to recognize that such ruthlessness not only exists in a certain portion of the populace but ripens early. It is hard, too, for him to realize that his very permissiveness may force an escalation of the conflict.

For a long time we have fondly preserved the fiction that the drama of social change is a conflict between dissenters and the top layers of the Establishment. But as the critics fling themselves in kamikazelike assaults on sluggish institutions, they eventually come into headon collision with the people who are most deeply implicated in the sluggishness, namely, the great majority. The stone wall against which many radical reforms shatter is the indifference (or downright hostility) of that majority.

The collision between dissenters and lower middle class opponents is exceedingly dangerous. As long as the dissenters are confronting the top layers of the power structure, they are dealing with people who are reasonably secure, often willing to compromise, able to yield ground without anxiety. But when the dissenters collide with the lower middle class, they confront an insecure opponent, quick to anger and not prepared to yield an inch.

It is at this point that young rebels find great appeal in Herbert Marcuse's ideas. When they think they are attacking the fat cats at the top of the social structure, democratic doctrine seems a serviceable banner to wrap themselves in. But democratic doctrine suddenly becomes a considerable embarrassment when they discover that "the people" they seek to liberate are in fact bitterly opposed to them.

Marcuse deals with that difficulty by saying that democracy and tolerance are themselves barriers to the overthrow of an evil society. He favors a more "directed" society. In doing so, he makes the assumption made by all who fall into authoritarian doctrines—that, in the "directed" society he envisages, people who share his values will be calling the tune. So thought the businessmen who supported Hitler.

The debasement of the critical role makes responsible action for social change increasingly difficult. Those who are engaged in the grueling work of accomplishing institutional change are in desperate need of allies. Responsible social critics can be of enormous help in identifying targets for action, in clarifying and focusing issues, in formulating significant goals and mobilizing support for those goals. That kind of help is not supplied by irresponsible critics.

The responsible critic comes to understand the complex machinery by which change must be accomplished, finds the key points of leverage, identifies feasible alternatives, and measures his work by real results. We have many such critics, and we owe them a great debt.

In contrast, the irresponsible critic never exposes himself to the tough tests of reality. He doesn't limit himself to feasible options. He doesn't subject his view of the world to the cleansing discipline of historical perspective or contemporary relevance. He defines the problem to suit himself. He shrugs off the constraints that limit action in the real world. But the constraints he brushes aside are intrinsic to the problem. Discussions outside that framework are just words.

It's a hard game to lose. If he takes care to stay outside the arena of action and decision, his judgment and integrity will never be tested, never risked, never laid on the line. He can feel a limitless moral superiority to the mere mortals who put their reputation at hazard every day in accountable action. He can spin fantasies of what might be, without the heart-breaking, back-breaking work of building social change into resistant human institutions.

The consequences of such feckless radicalism are predictable. Out of such self-indulgence come few victories. As a result, we are producing a bumper crop of disillusioned and tired exradicals.

It will not be possible to prevent all such disillusionment. Some radicals are so easily disillusioned that one wonders whether the experience feeds some

secret stream of enjoyment. They have perfected the art of being "betrayed" by the world.

The model of the ineffectual radical is the man or woman who spends a few brief years exploding in indignation, posturing, attitudinizing, oversimplifying, shooting at the wrong targets, unwilling to address himself to the exacting business of understanding the machinery of society, unwilling to undergo the arduous training necessary to master the processes he hopes to change.

So those who have mastered the machinery laugh him off. He holds no terror for them. Soon he grows tired and gives up.

The favored instrument of dissent at the moment is the demonstration. And we have to face the fact that the demonstration is a crude, even misleading indicator of the popular will. The coercive demonstration is a threat to the framework of order that makes civil government possible.

Chief among the defects of the demonstration is its enigmatic quality. Whom do the demonstrators represent? How large is their constituency? What kind of mandate do they have from that constituency? What are the merits of their case? If authorities negotiate with them, what is the standing of the agreements reached? If authorities accede to their demands, will that accomplish a net reduction in grievance and injustice within the community? Or will the reduction of this group's grievances leave other groups even more aggrieved and create new injustices as old ones are corrected? Is the protest a true reflection of community sentiment or is it "rigged?" How can you know?

Those are questions that are hard to answer when a crowd of demonstrators appear out of nowhere to disrupt some public function. Precisely because of its enigmatic character, the demonstration lends itself to manipulation by elements within the community who do not in fact have any significant base of community support.

Nevertheless, the demonstration that remains peaceful is a legitimate instrument of social action. Its function is to bring a grievance or an issue to public view.

It is a limited function. The chief means by which citizens make their influence felt must continue to be through the long-tested, well-established procedures of a free society: the ballot, the lawsuit, the strike, the petition, complaints to the press, action through established girevance procedures, and so on.

One hears a special justification in the case of the recent ghetto riots. The riots were necessary, it is argued, to produce fear in the power structure and thereby to get action on the social front. And those who make that argument now insist that the tactic succeeded, and they advocate its continued use.

It is true that the riots provoked fear. But there were a lot of consequences besides constructive social action. The riots led a lot of congressmen and a lot of citizens to resist further federal programs for the cities. The riots led both police and citizens to arm themselves heavily, and led to a heavy vote for rightwing political candidates. The riots strengthened every rightwing extremist group in the country.

To cite only the favorable consequences of the riots and ignore the unfavorable is disastrously nearsighted. The provoking of fear is a dangerous form of brinksmanship. It may bring constructive results or it may unleash emotions that will lead to the suppression of all freedom.

I do not blame the ghetto residents

for being angry. I am with them. But they must not let their anger lead them into self-destructive moves. They must seek—as the college activists must seek, as we all must seek—a world in which man's destructive impulses are brought within a framework of law and rationality.

It is an old failing of the liberal that he has fantasies of a rather genteel revolution in which the revolutionaries stir up just enough turmoil to make comfortable people thoroughly uncomfortable. But you can't have revolution in carefully measured doses. Events will not be kind to those who unleash the furies of human emotion in the service of their own carefully calculated goals. Emotions get out of hand. No one knows what climax they will build toward, nor who will get hurt, nor what the end will be. Anyone who unleashes man's destructive impulses had better stand a long way back.

No society can give itself over to those whose purpose is civic tumult. The anarchist paves the way for the authoritarian. Either we will have a civil order in which discipline is internalized in the breast of each free and responsible citizen or we will see repressive measures designed to reestablish order. Everyone who cares about freedom will pray for the former and seek to avoid courses of action that lead to the latter.

For some years now the conscientious, generous-minded citizen has greeted each new outbreak of disorder with a determination to try even harder to correct the social injustices that seemed to lie behind such disorder. But correcting injustice is slow, and the disorders spread like summer grass fire. The serious citizen will have to learn a simple truth: one must act forcefully to combat injustice and *at the same time* one must oppose disorder and violence.

In conclusion, I would like to review very briefly our situation as I see it.

I have traveled to every corner of this nation studying our domestic problems; and I have had an exceptional opportunity to share in the varied attempts to solve those problems. In my judgment, the years immediately ahead will test this nation as seriously as any we have known in our history.

We must cope with social unrest that is greater in depth and intensity than any we have ever experienced. As part of the effort to cope with it, we must make progress in solving substantive problems of the utmost complexity and difficulty, particularly poverty and discrimination and the interlocking problems of the city.

We must repair the breakdown in the relationship between the individual and society.

And we must begin the exacting task of redesigning our society for continuous renewal.

I believe that we can do all these things. There are great constructive energies in the American people remaining to be tapped. We have strengths as a people that have not yet been tested. Out of this time of trouble can come a great new burst of vitality for this nation.

But not if we lose our heads and not if we delude ourselves. We shall accomplish none of the heroic tasks ahead without a tough-minded approach to the complexities of social change. Big talk won't get us there. Tantrums won't get us there. And we now know that we'll never make it on ideas without money, or money without ideas, or either without sound public management.

The substantive problems—housing, education, health, employment, discrimination, and so on—are numerous and exceedingly resistant to solution. And I have tried to suggest that they may in fact be insoluble until we make our society a better problem-solving mechanism. We must design new, more flexible, and far more effective federal-state-local relationships. We must design more fruitful relationships between the private and public sectors. We must devise new means of making government at every level more responsive. We must learn how to design large-scale organization that serves the individual. We must restore the sense of community.

We already have significant clues as to how we can accomplish these things. But there is heavy work ahead, work for able and courageous men and women who are willing to tackle the evils of the day in a problem-solving mood. We have plenty of debaters, plenty of blamers, plenty of provocateurs, plenty of people who treat public affairs as an opportunity for personal catharsis or glorification. We don't have plenty of problem solvers.

And the problem solvers need to be backed by a plentiful supply of Americans who are willing to acknowledge the grave difficulties facing this country. As a people we have a considerable gift for not being honest about our problems. We can look right at them and deny they exist, or deny that they're serious, or deny that any money need be spent to solve them. And those are forms of frivolity we can no longer afford.

We shall accomplish none of the significant tasks ahead if we count our short-term comfort as more important than our long-term future, if we are unwilling to tax ourselves, if we lack the courage to demand disciplined behavior of ourselves and others.

A relevant call to action would address itself first of all to that complacent lump of self-satisfied Americans who fatten on the yield of this society but never bestir themselves to solve its problems. It would address itself to the powerful men who rest complacently with outworn institutions when they have it in their power to redesign those institutions. It would address itself to those Americans who are still uncommitted to the values we profess to cherish as a people.

As a people, we still have a choice. If we want a society on the beehive model, all we need do is relax and we'll drift into it. If we want a society built around the creative possibilities of the self-directing individual, then we have tasks to perform.

Each of us has tasks to perform. Each of us is that self-directing individual. This free society begins with us. It mustn't end with us.

I am not proposing new duties; I am recalling old duties. Remember the Preamble to the Constitution? "We, the people of the United States, in order to form a more perfect union, establish justice, insure domestic tranquility, provide for the common defense, promote the general welfare, and secure the blessings of liberty to ourselves and our posterity. . . ." Great phrases, and the greatest of all is, "We, the people of the United States. . . ." Not, we, the public officials of the United States. Not we, the certified experts on public administration. Not we who happen to have time to think about these things when we're not busy running our businesses or practicing our profession. Just we, the people.

We have recently inaugurated a new president. No matter how gifted he may prove to be, he cannot save us from ourselves. He cannot function effectively unless we are actively and intelligently at work on our own problems.

No matter how accomplished our

public servants are, the inner mystery of democracy will always involve that old and good idea: "We, the people."

We, acting in our own communities across the nation, can pull this fragmented society together again. We can re-create an America in which men speak to one another in trust and mutual respect, sharing common objectives, working toward common goals. We can return this nation to a path of confidence and well-being. We can design a society capable of continuous renewal.

We can do these things. No one can do them for us.

27
President Johnson's Commencement Address at Howard University*

Dr. Nabrit, my fellow Americans: I am delighted at the chance to speak at this important and this historic institution. Howard has long been an outstanding center for the education of Negro Americans. Its students are of every race and color, and they come from many countries of the world. It is truly a working example of democratic excellence.

Our earth is the home of revolution. In every corner of every continent men charged with hope contend with ancient ways in the pursuit of justice. They reach for the newest of weapons to realize the oldest of dreams—that each may walk in freedom and pride, stretching his talents, enjoying the fruits of the earth.

Our enemies may occasionally seize the day of change. But it is the banner of our revolution they take and our

* [President Lyndon B. Johnson, "Commencement Address at Howard University," *The New York Times,* June 5, 1964.]

own future is linked to this process of swift and turbulent change in many lands in the world.

But nothing in any country touches us more profoundly and nothing is more freighted with meaning for our own destiny than the revolution of the Negro American.

In far too many ways American Negroes have been another nation, deprived of freedom, crippled by hatred, the doors of opportunity closed to hope.

In our time change has come to this nation, too. The American Negro, acting with impressive restraint, has peacefully protested and marched, entered the courtroom and the seats of government, demanding a justice that has long been denied.

THE CALL TO ACTION

The voice of the Negro was the call to action. But it is a tribute to America that, once aroused, the courts and the Congress, the president and most of the people, have been the allies of progress.

Thus we have seen the high court of the country declare that discrimination based on race was repugnant to the Constitution and therefore void.

We have seen in 1957, in 1960, and again in 1964 the first civil rights legislation in this nation in almost an entire century.

As majority leader of the United States Senate I helped to guide two of these bills through the Senate, and as your president I was proud to sign the third.

And now very soon we have the fourth—a new law guaranteeing to every American the right to vote.

No act of my entire administration will give me greater satisfaction than the day when my signature makes this bill too the law of this land.

The voting rights bill will be the latest and among the most important in a long series of victories. But this victory, as Winston Churchill said of another triumph for freedom, is not the end; it is not even the beginning of the end.

But it is, perhaps, the end of the beginning. That beginning is freedom and the barriers to that freedom are tumbling down.

THE RIGHT TO SHARE

Freedom is the right to share, share fully and equally in American society, to vote, to hold a job, to enter a public place, to go to school. It is the right to be treated in every part of our national life as a person equal in dignity and promise to all others.

But freedom is not enough. You do not wipe away the scars of centuries by saying now you're free to go where you want and do as you desire and choose the leaders you please. You do not take a person who for years has been hobbled by chains and liberate him, bring him up to the starting line of a race and then say, you're free to compete with all the others, and still justly believe that you have been completely fair.

Thus it is not enough just to open the gates of opportunity.

All our citizens must have the ability to walk through those gates and this is the next and the more profound stage of the battle for civil rights.

We seek not just freedom but opportunity. We seek not just legal equity but human ability. Not just equality as a right and a theory but equality as a fact and equality as a result.

For the task is to give twenty million Negroes the same chance as every other American to learn and grow, to work and share in society, to develop their abilities—physical, mental, and spiritual—and to pursue their individual happiness.

To this end equal opportunity is essential, but not enough, not enough. Men and women of all races are born with the same range of abilities. But ability is not just the product of birth; ability is stretched or stunted by the family that you live with and the neighborhood you live in, by the school you go to, and the poverty or the richness of your surroundings.

It is the product of one hundred unseen forces playing upon the little infant, the child, and finally the man. This graduating class at Howard University is witness to the indomitable determination of the Negro American to win his way in American life.

The number of Negroes in schools of higher learning has almost doubled in fifteen years. The number of non-white professional workers has more than doubled in ten years. The median income of Negro college women tonight exceeds that of white college women.

And there are also the enormous accomplishments of distinguished individual Negroes, many of them graduates of this institution, and one of them the first lady ambassador in the history of the United States.

NARROWING THE GAP

These are proud and impressive achievements. But they tell only the story of a growing middle class minority steadily narrowing the gap between them and their white counterparts.

But for the great majority of Negro Americans, the poor, the unemployed, the uprooted, and the dispossessed, there's a much grimmer story.

They still, as we meet here tonight, are another nation. Despite the court orders and the laws, despite the legislative victories and the speeches, for them the walls are rising and the gulf is widening and here are some of the facts of this American failure.

Thirty-five years ago, the rate of unemployment for Negroes and white was about the same. Tonight the Negro rate is twice as high.

In 1948, the 8 percent unemployment rate for Negro teen-age boys was actually less than that of whites. By last year, that rate had grown to 23 percent as against 13 percent for whites unemployed.

Between 1949 and 1959 the income of Negro men relative to white men declined in every section of the country. From 1952 to 1963 the median income of Negro families compared to whites actually dropped from 57 percent to 53 percent.

In the years 1955 through 1957, 22 percent of experienced Negro workers were out of work at some time during the year. In 1961 through 1963, that proportion had soared to 29 percent. Since 1947, the number of white families living in poverty has decreased 27 percent, while the number of poor non-white families decreased only 3 percent.

The infant mortality of nonwhites in 1940 was 70 percent greater than whites. Twenty-two years later, it was 90 percent greater. Moreover, the isolation of Negroes from white communities is increasing rather than decreasing, as Negroes crowd into the central cities and become a city within a city.

Of course, Negro Americans as well as white Americans have shared in our rising national abundance, but the harsh fact of the matter is that in the battle for true equality too many, far too many, are losing ground every day.

COMPLEX AND SUBTLE

We are not completely sure why this is. We know the causes are complex and subtle, but we do know the two broad basic reasons, and we do know that we have to act. First, Negroes are trapped, as many whites are trapped, in inherited gateless poverty. They lack training and skills. They are shut in slums without decent medical care. Private and public poverty combine to cripple their capacities.

We are trying to attack these evils through my poverty program, through our education program, through our medical care and our other health programs, and a dozen more of the Great Society programs that are aimed at the root causes of this poverty.

We will increase and we will accelerate and we will broaden this attack in years to come until this most enduring of foes finally yields to our unyielding will.

But there is a second cause much more difficult to explain, more deeply grounded, more desperate in its force. And it is the devastating heritage of long years of slavery and a century of oppression and hatred and injustice.

For Negro poverty is not white poverty. Many of its causes and many of its cures are the same but there are differences—deep, corrosive, obstinate differences—radiating painful roots into the community and into the family and the nature of the individual.

These differences are not racial differences. They are solely and simply the consequences of ancient brutality, past injustice, and present prejudice.

They are anguishing to observe. For the Negro, they are a constant reminder of oppression. For the white, they are the constant reminder of guilt.

But they must be faced and they must be dealt with and they must be overcome if we are ever to reach the time when the only difference between Negroes and whites is the color of their skins.

Nor can we find a complete answer in the experience of other American minorities. They made a valiant and a largely successful effort to emerge from poverty and prejudice. The Negro, like these others, will have to rely mostly on his own efforts, but he just cannot do it alone, for they did not have the heritage of centuries to overcome and they did not have a cultural tradition which had been twisted and battered by endless years of hatred and hopelessness.

DARK INTENSITY

Nor were they excluded, these others, because of race or color, a feeling whose dark intensity is matched by no other prejudice in our society. Nor can these differences be understood as isolated infirmities. They are a seamless web. They cause each other. They result from each other. They reinforce each other.

Much of the Negro community is buried under a blanket of history and circumstance. It is not a lasting solution to lift just one corner of that blanket. We must stand on all sides and we must raise the entire cover if we are to liberate our fellow citizens.

One of the differences is the increased concentration of Negroes in our cities. More than 73 percent of all Negroes live in urban areas compared with less than 70 percent for whites. Most of these Negroes live in slums. Most of these Negroes live together, a separated people, and men are shaped by their world.

When it is a world of decay ringed by an invisible wall, when escape is arduous and uncertain and the saving pressures of a more hopeful society are unknown, it can cripple the youth and it can desolate the men.

There is also the burden that a dark skin can add to the search for a productive place in our society.

Unemployment strikes most swiftly and broadly at the Negro. This burden erodes hope. Blighted hope breeds despair. Despair brings indifference to the learning which offers a way out, and despair coupled with indifference is often the source of destructive rebellion against the fabric of society.

There is also the lacerating hurt of early collision with white hatred or prejudice, distaste or condescension. Other groups have felt similar intolerance, but success and achievement could wipe it away. They do not change the color of a man's skin.

I have seen this uncomprehending pain in the eyes of the little young Mexican–American school children that I taught many years ago. But it can be overcome. But for many the wounds are always open.

Perhaps most important—its influence radiating to every part of life— is the breakdown of the Negro family structure. For this, most of all, white America must accept responsibility. It flows from centuries of oppression and persecution of the Negro man; it flows from the long years of degradation and discrimination which have attacked his dignity and assaulted his ability to produce for his family.

This, too, is not pleasant to look upon, but it must be faced by those whose serious intent is to improve the life of all Americans.

FAMILY IS CORNERSTONE

Only a minority—less than half of all Negro children—reach the age of eighteen having lived all their lives with both of their parents.

At this moment tonight, little less than two-thirds are at home with both of their parents.

Probably a majority of all Negro children received federally aided public assistance sometime during their childhood.

The family is the cornerstone of our society. More than any other force it shapes the attitude, the hopes, the ambitions, and the values of the child.

When the family collapses, it is the children that are usually damaged. When it happens on a massive scale, the entire community itself is crippled.

So, unless we work to strengthen the family, to create conditions under which most parents will stay together, all the rest—schools and playgrounds and public assistance and private concern—will never be enough to cut completely the circle of despair and deprivation.

There is no single easy answer to all these problems. Jobs are part of the answer. They bring the income which permits a man to provide for his family; decent home in decent surroundings and a chance to learn—an equal chance to learn—are part of the answer.

Welfare and social programs, better designed to hold families together are part of the answer. Care for the sick is part of the answer. An understanding heart by all Americans is another big part of the answer.

And to all of these fronts and a dozen more I will dedicate the expanding efforts of the Johnson administration.

But there are other answers that are still to be found, nor do we fully understand even all the problems. Therefore, I want to announce tonight that this fall I intend to call a White House conference of scholars and experts and outstanding Negro leaders of both races and officials of government at every level.

This White House conference theme and title will be to fulfill these rights. Its object will be to help the American Negro fulfill the rights which after the long time of injustice he is finally about to secure, to move beyond opportunity to achievement, to shatter forever not only the barriers of law and public practice but the walls which bound the condition of man by the color of his skin, to dissolve as best we can the antique enmities of the heart which diminish the holder, divide the great democracy, and do wrong—great wrong —to the children of God.

CHIEF GOAL OF PROGRAM

And this I pledge you tonight that this will be a chief goal of my administration and of my program next year and in the years to come. And I hope, and I pray, and I believe it will be a part of the program of all America.

For what is justice?

It is to fulfill the fair expectations of man.

Thus, American justice is a very special thing. For, from the first, this has been a land of towering expectations. It was to be a nation where each man could be ruled by the common consent of all—enshrined in law, given life by institutions, guided by men themselves subject to its rule. And all—all of every station and origin—would be touched equally in obligation and in liberty.

Beyond the law lay the land. It was a rich land, glowing with more abundant promise than man had ever seen. Here, unlike any place yet known, all were to share the harvest. And beyond this was the dignity of man.

Each could become whatever his qualities of mind and spirit would permit to strive, to seek, and if he could, to find his happiness.

This is American justice. We have pursued it faithfully to the edge of our imperfections and we have failed to find it for the American Negro.

So it is the glorious opportunity of this generation to end the one huge wrong of the American nation and in so doing to find America for ourselves with the same immense thrill of discovery which gripped those who first

began to realize that here at last was a home for freedom.

And all it will take is for all of us to understand what this country is and what this country must become.

The scripture promises "I shall light a candle of understanding in thine heart which shall not be put out." Together, and with millions more, we can light that candle of understanding in the heart of all America, and once lit it will never again go out.

28
*Strategies for Powerless Groups**
MORTON DEUTSCH

What can a less powerful group (Acme) do to reduce or overcome the defensiveness of a more powerful group (Bolt) and to increase the latter's readiness to share power? Suppose, in effect, that as social scientists we were consultants to the poor and weak rather than to the rich and strong, what would we suggest? . . . Given the resistance and defensiveness of those in high power, what can we recommend to those in low power as a strategy of persuasion? As Hovland, Janis, and Kelley[1] have pointed out, the process of persuasion involves obtaining the other's *attention, comprehension,* and *acceptance* of the message that one is communicating. The process of persuasion, however, starts with the communicator having a message that he wants to get across to the other. He must have an objective if he is to be able to articulate a clear and compelling message. Further, in formulating and communicating his message, it is important to *recognize*

*[Reprinted from *Journal of Social Issues,* Vol. XXV, No. 1, pp. 7–41 by permission of publisher and author.]
[1]Hovland, C. I., Janis, I. L. and Kelley, H. H., *Communication and Persuasion,* New Haven: Yale University Press, 1953.

that it will be heard not only by the other, but also by one's own group and by other interested audiences. The desirable effects of a message on its intended audience may be negated by its unanticipated effects on those for whom it was not intended. I suggest that the following generalized message contains the basic elements of what Acme must communicate to Bolt to change him and, in addition, it is a message which can be overheard by other audiences without harmful consequences. Admittedly, it must be communicated in a way which elicits Bolt's attention, comprehension, and acceptance of its credibility rather than in the abstract, intellectualized form in which it is presented below. And, of course, the generalized objective of equality must be detailed in terms of specific relations in specific contexts.

I am dissatisfied with our relationship and the effects it has. I think it can be improved in ways which will benefit you as well as me. I am sufficiently discontent that I can no longer continue in any relationship with you in which I do not participate as an equal in making the decisions which affect me as well as you, except as a temporary measure while we move toward equality. This may upset and discomfort you but I have no alternative other than to disengage myself from all forms of inauthentic cooperation: my dignity as well as pressure from my group will no longer allow me to engage in this self-deception and self-abasement. Neither coercion nor bribery will be effective; my self-respect and my group will force me to resist them. I remain prepared to cooperate with you as an equal in working on joint problems, including the problems involved in redefining our relationship to one another. I expect that changing our relationship will not be without its initial difficulties for both of us; we will be uncertain and perhaps suspicious, we will misunderstand and disagree and regress to old habits from time to time. I am willing to face these diffi-

culties. I invite you to join with me to work toward improving our relationship, to overcome your dissatisfactions as well as mine. I believe that we both will feel more self-fulfilled in a relationship that is not burdened by inauthenticity.

It would take too long to detail all the elements in this message and their rationales. But essentially the message commits Acme irreversibly to his objective; self-esteem and social esteem are at stake; he will be able to live neither with himself nor his group if he accepts an inferior status. This is done not only in words but also by the style of communicating which expresses a self-confident equality and competence. It provides Bolt with the prospect of positive incentives for changing and negative ones for not changing; Acme maintains a cooperative stance throughout and develops in action the possibility of a true mutual exchange by expressing the awareness that dissatisfactions are not one-sided. It also inoculates against some of the expected difficulties involved in change. It should be noted that Acme's statements of the threats faced by Bolt if change is not forthcoming (the instrumental threat of noncooperation, the moral threat that the status quo violates important social norms concerning human dignity and authenticity, the threat of resistance to coercion) are neither arbitrary, illegitimate, coercive, nor demanding to Bolt—i.e., they are not strongly alienating. . . .[2]

However as is often the case, the high power group may be unaffected by

---

[2] Editor's note: Elsewhere in his article Deutsch offers the following hypotheses about influence procedures likely to elicit resistance and alienation:

1   *Illegitimate techniques* which violate the values and norms governing interaction and influence that are held by the other are alienating (the greater the violation, the more important and the more numerous the values being violated, the greater will

the positive or negative incentives that the low power group control; it does not need their compliance. Universities can obtain new students; the affluent nations no longer are so dependent upon the raw materials produced in the underdeveloped nations; the white industrial society does not need many unskilled Negro workers.

WHAT CAN THE GROUP DO FOR ITSELF?

What can the low power group do in such situations? First of all, theoretically it may be possible to "opt out" more or less completely—to withdraw, to migrate, to separate so that one is no longer in the relationship. However, as the world and the societies composing it become more tightly knit, this option becomes less and less available in its

---

be the resistance). It is, of course, true that sometimes an adaptation level effect occurs so that frequently violated norms lose their illegitimacy (as in parking violations); at other times, the accumulation of violations tends to produce an increasingly negative reaction.

2 *Negative sanctions* such as punishments and threats tend to elicit more resistance than positive sanctions such as promises and rewards. What is considered to be rewarding or punishing may also be influenced by one's adaptation level; the reduction of the level of rewards which are customarily received will usually be viewed as negative.

3 Sanctions which are *inappropriate* in kind are also likely to elicit resistance. Thus, the reward of money rather than appreciation may decrease the willingness to cooperate with someone whose cooperation is engendered by affiliative rather than utilitarian motives. Similarly, a threat or punishment is more likely to be effective if it fits the crime than if its connection with the crime is artificial. A child who breaks another child's toy is punished more appropriately if he has to give the child a toy of his own as a substitute than if he is denied permission to watch TV.

4 Influence which is *excessive* in magnitude tends to be resisted; excessive promise or reward leads to the sense of being bribed, excessive threat or punishment leads to the feeling of being coerced.

---

extreme forms. Black communities can organize their own industries, schools, hospitals, shopping centers, consumer cooperatives and the like but only if they have resources, and these resources would be sharply curtailed if their relationship with the broader society were completely disrupted. Similarly, students can organize their own seminars, their own living communes, their own bookstores, but it would be difficult for them to become proficient in many of the sciences and professions without using the resources available in the broader academic community. . . .

Through building its own institutions and developing its own resources a low power group makes itself less vulnerable to exploitation and also augments its power by providing itself with alternatives to inauthentic cooperation. In so doing, it increases the likelihood that those in high power will be responsive to a change: the positive incentives for changing and the negative incentives for not changing take on greater value. Moreover, such self-constructive action may help to reduce the fears and stereotypes which underlie much of the defensiveness of high power groups.

In addition to the strategy of developing one's own resources and building one's own institutions, there are still other strategies that can be followed by a low power group in the attempt to influence a reluctant or disinterested high power group. The various strategies are not incompatible with one another. I list several of the major ones: (1) augment its power by collecting or activating subgroups within the high power group or third parties as allies; (2) search for other kinds of connections with the high power group which, if made more salient, could increase its affective or instrumental dependence upon the low power group and thus change the power balance; (3) attempt to change the attitudes of those in high power through education and moral persuasion; (4) use existing legal procedures to bring pressures for change; and (5) use harassment techniques to increase the other's costs of adhering to the status quo.

The effectiveness of any strategy of influence is undoubtedly much determined by the particular circumstances so that no strategy can be considered to be unconditionally effective or ineffective. Nevertheless, it is reasonable to assume that low power groups can rarely afford to be without allies. By definition, a low power group is unlikely to achieve many of its objectives unless it can find allies among significant elements within the high power group or unless it can obtain support from other ("third party") groups that can exert influence on the high power group. There is considerable reason to expect that allies are most likely to be obtained if: (1) they are sought out rather than ignored or rejected; (2) superordinate goals, common values, and common interests can be identified which could serve as a basis for the formation of cooperative bonds; (3) reasonably full communication is maintained with the potential allies; (4) one's objectives and methods are readily perceived as legitimate and feasible; (5) one's tactics dramatize one's objectives and require the potential allies to choose between acting "for" or "against" these objectives and, thus, to commit themselves to taking a position; and (6) those in high power employ tactics, as a counterresponse, which are widely viewed as "unfitting" and thus produce considerable sympathy for the low power group.

CIVIL DISOBEDIENCE

There is no time here to elaborate on procedures and tactics of building allies; this is what politics is all about. However, let me just comment about the nonviolent, civil disobedience, confrontation tactics which have been employed with considerable success by civil rights and student groups. These methods have tended, with continuing usage, to have less effect in arousing public response and sympathy for the low power groups involved. In part, this is because many of those in high power have learned that to employ coercion as a response to a nonviolent tactic of civil disobedience is self-defeating; it only serves to swing much of the hitherto uninvolved public behind the demonstrators. This is, of course, what happened in Selma and Birmingham as well as at Columbia University and Chicago when unfitting force was used. These techniques also have become less effective because repeated usage vulgarizes them; a measure which is acceptable as an unusual or emergency procedure becomes unacceptable as a routine breeder of social disruption. Let me note paranthetically that I have discussed "nonviolent, confrontation" tactics as a method for gaining allies and public support rather than as a procedure for directly changing the attitudes of those in high power who are strongly committed to their views. I have seen no evidence that would suggest it has any significant effects of the latter sort.

Finding allies and supporters is important not only because it directly augments the influence of a low power group but also because having allies enables the low power group to use each of the other change strategies more effectively. I shall not discuss the other strategies in detail but confine myself to a brief comment about each. A low power group can increase the dependence of a high power group on it by concentrating its power rather than by allowing it to be spread thinly. Thus, the political power of the Negro vote could be higher if it were able to decide the elections in a half-dozen states such as New York, California, Pennsylvania, Illinois, Ohio, and Michigan than if the Negro vote was less concentrated. Similarly, their economic power would be greater if they were able to obtain control over certain key industries and key unions rather than if they were randomly dispersed.

Education, moral persuasion, and the use of legal procedures to bring about social change have lately come into disrepute because these strategies do not bring "instant change" nor do they produce as much *esprit de corps* as strategies which give rise to direct action techniques. Nevertheless, it would be a mistake to underestimate the importance of beliefs, values, and the sense of legitimacy in determining individual and social action. Similarly, to engage in anti-intellectualism or to ignore the significance of intellectual work in establishing true knowledge is an error. Truth threatens arbitrary power by unmasking its unreasonableness and pretensions. Anti-intellectualism is a tool of the despot in his struggle to silence or discredit truth. Also, it would be a mistake to ignore the tremendous changes in beliefs and values concerning human relationships which have occurred during the recent past. Much of the evil which now occurs is not a reflection of deliberate choice to inflict such evil but rather the lack of a deliberate choice to overcome self-perpetuating vicious cycles. Obviously, a considerable educational effort is needed to help broaden the understanding of conflict and to accelerate growth in the ability to include others in the same moral community with oneself even though they be of rather different social, economic, and ethnic background.

HARASSMENT

Harassment may be the only effective strategy available to a low power group if it faces an indifferent or hostile high power group. Although sharp lines cannot be drawn, it is useful to distinguish "harassment," "obstruction," and "destruction" from one another. "Harassment" employs legal or semilegal techniques to inflict a loss, to interfer with, disrupt, or embarrass those with high power; "obstruction" employs illegal techniques to interrupt or disrupt the activities and purposes of those in high power; "destruction" employs illegal, violent techniques to destroy or to take control over people or property. Obstructive and destructive techniques invite massive retaliation and repression which, if directed against harassment techniques, would often seem inappropriate and arouse sympathy. However, a clearly visible potential for the employment of obstructive and destructive techniques may serve to make harassment procedures both more acceptable and more effective.

There are many forms of harassment which can be employed by low power groups: consumer boycotts; work slowdowns; rent strikes; demonstrations; sit-ins; tying up phones, mail, government offices, businesses, traffic, etc., by excessive and prolonged usage; ensnarling bureaucratic systems in their own red tape by requiring them to follow their own formally stated rules and procedures; being excessively friendly and cooperative; creating psychological nuisances by producing outlandish behavior, appearances and odors in stores, offices, and other public places; encouraging contagion of the ills of the slum (rats, uncollected garbage, etc.) to surrounding communities; etc. Harassment, as is true for most procedures, is undoubtedly most effective when it is employed to obtain well-defined, specific objectives and when it is selectively focused on key persons and key institutions rather than when it is merely a haphazard expression of individual discontent.

As I review what I have written, . . . where I have functioned as a self-appointed consultant to those in low power, I am struck by how little of what I have said is well-grounded in systematic research or theory. As social scientists we have rarely directed our attention to the defensiveness and resistance of the strong and powerful in the face of the need for social change. We have not considered what strategies and tactics are available to low power groups and which of these are likely to lead to a productive rather than destructive process of conflict resolution. We have focused too much on the turmoil and handicaps of those in low power and not enough on the defensiveness and resistance of the powerful; the former will be overcome as the latter is overcome.

29
The Strategy of Protest: Problems of Negro Civic Action*
JAMES Q. WILSON

The logical and empirical elements of bargaining are receiving increased attention as the effort proceeds to fashion an analytical tool useful for better understanding the nature of controversy. In many of these discussions, the focus has been on those who enter into the bargaining relationship out of either necessity or hope of gain (4, 9). The notion of bargaining is simplified if one assumes that the need for or desirability of bargaining is given. This is the case when two businessmen, for example, seek goals which are partially incompatible but individually attractive. Each stands to gain if his

*[Reprinted with permission from *Journal of Conflict Resolution,* Vol. 5, no. 3, September 1961, pp. 291–303.]

end can be realized, and to realize it he must deal with the other fellow. There is, in short, an inducement for each to bargain.

Equally interesting is the situation in which one party seeks a goal which it can realize without obtaining concessions from a second party. The second party opposes the realization of that goal, but has nothing which the first party needs or wants, and hence finds it difficult to place itself in a position in which the first party must bargain. This might be called the problem of the powerless. It arises, for example, when a disfranchised group seeks a law giving it the right to vote but, lacking the vote, has difficulty recruiting lawmakers who will support its cause. The most important group today which must act from a position of near powerlessness is the Negro. This article will (1) sketch some of the logical elements involved in attempts by the powerless to wield power, (2) relate these elements to certain empirical factors characteristic of the Negro in large northern cities. . . .

BARGAINING

By *bargaining,* I shall mean any situation in which two or more parties seek conflicting ends through the exchange of compensations. The ends must not be wholly incompatible (if they were, bargaining would be impossible) nor need the compensations be tangible. Intangible compensations are of importance as well. Bargaining will be distinguished from those cases in which one party seeks its ends by simply persuading the other party to accede by argument or rhetoric. It will also exclude cases of compulsion, in which one party endeavors to use physical force on a second party or so rearranges his situation that literally no alternative is open to him other than the one desired by the first party. The essential element in bargaining is that concessions are rewarded. The task is to find a mutually agreeable ratio for the exchange of those rewards.

These rewards may be either positive or negative. Banfield distinguishes between positive and negative inducements by noting that a *positive* inducement is given "if action in accordance with A's intention is made absolutely more attractive to B . . . and not because other possibilities have been made less desirable." In contrast, a *negative* inducement is given "if action in accordance with A's intention, although no more attractive absolutely than before the change was made, is nevertheless more attractive relative to the other possibilities that now exist" (1, 2). All other courses of action are made more disadvantageous than the desired course, which is also somewhat disadvantageous.

Certain individuals and groups may wish to bargain, but they may lack the resources to do so—i.e., they may lack any stock of inducements (positive or negative) which they can use to influence other parties to act in accordance with at least *some* of their intentions. Others feel no need to bargain with these people. The question then becomes, how such a group (which I shall call the "excluded" group) can acquire a supply of compensations such that others will want to bargain. In the typical case, the excluded group is separated from others by differences in status, class, caste, or authority, and thus neither persuasion nor compulsion is available as a tactic of influence. Bargaining is not available because the excluded group has nothing the others desire, either in relation to the issue in point or to any future issue which might arise.

It is, of course, not sufficient that the excluded group have some compen-

sations. The leaders of that group—the would-be bargainers—must show that they in fact control the resources and can "deliver" if they commit themselves. Negroes, for example, may represent customers or voters to businessmen and politicians, but if Negro leaders cannot alter the buying habits or switch the votes of their followers, the potential resources are useless. At this point, deception may become important. To the extent that Negro leaders are able to bargain at all, it is frequently a result of ignorance (or at least imperfect information) on the part of those with whom they are dealing. Since excluded groups (like Negroes) are often excluded precisely because of great status and class gaps, and because these gaps work to reduce information which each party has about the other, ignorance and deception can become very important factors in the strategy of Negro leadership.

Deception is of limited value, however, since it is easily exposed when the bargain is consummated. (It is nonetheless remarkable, the extent to which influence continues to be imputed to leaders of excluded groups even after their inability to deliver has been revealed. This may be a function of uncertainty as to their influence in future cases or a doubt as to whether the revealed failure was a valid test.)

PROTEST

The problem of many excluded groups is to create or assemble the resources for bargaining. Many often select a strategy of protest. *Protest* is distinguished from bargaining by the exclusive use of negative inducements (threats) that rely, for their effect, on sanctions which require *mass* action or response. Excluded groups often make up in number what they lack in resources, or their cause finds sympathizers among relatively large numbers of other groups. Bargaining might (as noted above) involve the use of negative inducements as compensation—i.e., a promise by one party *not* to act in a certain manner can be, relatively, a reward for the other party. This bargaining situation is based on protest only when these threats rely, for their effect, on the possibility of a mass response. The party against which the protest is directed values something which the excluded group can place in jeopardy. This could range from a certain reputation (which could be harmed by unfavorable publicity) to a business (which could be hurt by a boycott) and would include, in some cases, a desire to further some civic program without controversy.

There are various forms of protest action: verbal, physical, economic, and political. *Verbal* protest would include issuing denunciatory statements, mounting a campaign of adverse publicity, submitting petitions and memorials, holding mass meetings, and sending deputations to confront the other party. *Physical* protest would include picketing, sit-down strikes (as in places of business), "marches" (as the famous "March on Washington Movement" of 1940–1941 [5]), and (in the extreme case) violence (as in the Harlem race riots of the 1930's and later, which, in contrast with many riots in other places, were often initiated by Negroes). *Economic* protest characteristically involves a boycott or threat of a boycott (as in the "Buy Black" and "Don't Buy Where You Can't Work" campaigns in New York and Chicago in the 1930's) or a strike. *Political* protest requires voting reprisals, taken by either the excluded group or others who are sympathetic to its cause.

The strategy of protest requires more than the possibility of mass ac-

tion, however. First, there must be an agreed-upon goal on behalf of which mass action can be mobilized. Such goals may be either specific or general, defensive or assertive, welfare or status. The precise nature of the goal sought has important consequences for the kinds of incentives which can be distributed to generate and sustain mass action. A *specific* goal is more typical of successful protest (i.e., protest which in fact involved overt mass action and which thus created a situation with which other parties had to deal in some measure). The March on Washington Movement had the specific goal of securing the adoption of a fair employment practices law (or, failing that, an executive order to the same effect). The student sit-down strikes had the specific goal of inducing white proprietors to serve Negroes when seated at luncheon counters. Economic boycotts have the specific goal of inducing businessmen to hire Negroes or offer for sale products manufactured by companies which hire Negroes. At the same time, the specific goal is always related to a general, more vague principle. Each specific goal is the immediately sought application of some *general* notion concerning equality, opportunity, or status. This is essential, inasmuch as such principles are an essential incentive with which to mobilize large numbers of contributors to the protest action. Few will benefit personally from the attainment of the specific goal; therefore, general reasons of an ethical character must be offered to attract the support of the many.

The offering of general reasons for specific goals is an important constraint on the leaders of protest movements. It usually means that the specific goal is endowed with a moral or sacrosanct quality which renders it difficult to compromise. This suggests that the discretion of the protest leader to bargain after he has acquired the resources with *which* to bargain is severely limited by the means he was forced to employ in order to create those resources. Getting into a bargaining relationship for a leader of an excluded group often means, therefore, a reduction in his ultimate ability to bargain. This was revealed in the case of the Negro leader, A. Phillip Randolph, who organized the March on Washington Movement. He was heavily criticized by many Negro followers when the actual march was called off because President Roosevelt issued an executive order creating an FEPC. Some demands were made that the march be carried on for broader goals, demands which Randolph had to resist (5).

Goals may be either defensive or assertive. The excluded group may be seeking to defend itself against some maltreatment or injustice by seeking to block changes in the status quo (such as a land clearance project) or by demanding a redress of grievances (such as police brutality or racial violence). It may assert certain goals, such as a demand for certain jobs, public services, housing, an improvement in the quality of public facilities, or the passage of a law which will alter the status quo in favor of the excluded group.

Goals may involve either the welfare or the status of the group. Welfare goals refer to the direct, tangible improvement in the lot of the group or its members through providing some job, service, facility, or revenue. Status goals imply the elimination of barriers, the creation of opportunities which members of the group may or may not take advantage of. The choice between improving the quality of Negro schools and integrating all-white schools is an example.

A second requisite exists for protest action. There must be an identifiable group or agency or firm which is capable of granting the end sought. There must, in a sense, be not only a specific goal, but a specific *target*. An opportunity for bargaining cannot be created when the target of protest action does not have it in its power to respond to the demands made. A secondary relationship might, of course, be found. Demands might be made by A upon B through a protest strategy even though B cannot staisfy these demands. It may nonetheless be a valuable strategy if C can grant these demands and C is in a bargaining relationship with B. B, in effect, can be compelled to become an intermediary and extract concessions from C (on the basis of an exchange of rewards which B and C value) which are then made available to A.

The target of protest action must not only be capable of responding; there must be some likelihood that he can be induced to respond. Responses to protest can be conceived of as a weighing of the probable costs of enduring the protest against the probable costs of making the concessions. The cost of being the target of protest action depends on the situation. For government officials and politicians (at least in the North) it *may* mean the loss of votes from Negroes or from sympathetic whites, criticism by articulate elements in the community, adverse effects on the opinion of foreign allies, and so on. For private parties (businessmen, unions, etc.) the costs would involve a deterioration in public relations, a possible loss of business, a fear of government intervention, a loss of manpower, and the exposure to controversy and unpleasantness. (It should be counted as a gain for protest that it might enable some parties to implement goals they feel *ought* to be realized with the rationale that they were "compelled" to do it and hence should not be criticized by opponents of the protest group.)

LIMITS OF NEGRO PROTEST

It is clear to anyone who has investigated the matter even casually that there is today among Negroes, in both North and South, a quickened sense of mission and a rising level of expectations. More and more Negroes are expressing a deep discontent with their lot as individuals and as a group. The voices advocating "gradualism" and unhurried change have become fewer and fewer (even though the opinions behind these voices have not, in many cases, been altered). As the Negro has progressed, he has come to expect more and more in terms of equal treatment and improved conditions. . . .

[Organized protest has been more successful and until recently more prevalent in the South than the North.] This situation offers an opportunity to apply an analysis of protest strategy to an empirical situation to see if reasons can be found to account for the relatively low level of organized protest among northern Negroes. To begin, it is apparent that an improvement in the leadership skills and organizational resources of the Negro has occurred at a time when the goals of Negro public life have become less clear and the targets have become more uncertain. In northern cities in the past, and in the South today, most Negro community goals were specific, defensive, and of a welfare character. The Negro community responded to what were regarded as manifest injustices and public outrages. Anti-Negro violence, police oppression, the denial of ordinary public services, and other oppressions represented specific causes. They tended to unify the Negro community. Few could doubt that they were injustices. They touched, in a visible, direct, and personal manner the lives of identifiable individuals. Verbal forms of protest were often effective in branding the injustice and, given its character, the offense was usually condemned by the norms of the community. Newspapers and civic groups could not defend such offenses. Common decency seemed to demand a redress, and by simply calling attention to it in a forceful manner, some corrective action could be had—or at least (and this is what is important in this essay) responsible officials could be induced to deal in some manner with the situation. They could not easily avoid bargaining. They sought compensation—the prevention or cessation of criticism from the spokesmen for the community's mores. In an extreme case (such as a race riot), Negroes might organize (as they did on one occasion in Chicago) a picket line around the city hall in order to acquire bargaining resources in dealing with the police commissioner and the mayor.

Today, the ends which are receiving the greatest attention are those which are often general, assertive, and of a status character. Negroes seek changes in the status quo in their favor in the fields of housing and employment. The problems which are of most concern and which are frequently spoken of as appropriate issues for protest action involve an uncertainty as to specific goals. Nowhere is this more evident than in the field of housing. There is disagreement among influential Negroes as to the source of the problem, what ought to be done about it, and what can be done under the circumstances (12). There is considerable uncertainty as to what Negroes should protest *for*— liberalized mortgage requirements, more police protection in changing neighborhoods, the ending of restrictive real estate practices, legislation barring discrimination in sales and rentals, or some combination of all. Further, anti-Negro practices in real estate do not violate clear community norms as does violence or manifest oppression. In the great majority of cases, no moral stigma attaches to the man who refuses to sell his home to a Negro. The exposure of such acts, by public protest, rarely carries with it any effective sanction. Whites may grant that Negroes have a moral right to housing, but they usually insist with equal conviction that whites have a right to preserve the character of their neighborhoods.

Second, the targets of protest action have become unclear or ambiguous. In issues where the exercise of specific public powers or the making of definite private decisions were clearly adapted to the ends sought, the target was obvious. The police could be asked for protection, the hotel required to admit Negro guests, the bus line requested to hire Negro drivers, or the legislature asked to pass a law. As the goals of protest action become broader and more general, the targets of that action become similarly diffuse. What is the target for protests aimed at "equal opportunity in housing?" One cannot picket, or boycott, or send deputations to all the real estate brokers, all the mortgage bankers, all the neighborhood improvement associations, or all the community newspapers. If one selects a single target—one house or one block in a certain neighborhood—one *may* gain concessions, but these concessions will be limited to the specific case and will represent no change in policy. Discriminatory practices in housing, in brief, are not the product of public or private decisions by some identifiable decision maker. They are the result of an infinite number of social choices made by tens of thousands of home owners, landlords, realtors, bankers, loan officers, community groups, and individuals. Some practices undoubtedly can be curbed by legislation, but

since the housing market involves many forces beyond legislative control (or any centralized control), laws would be of limited value. This is particularly the case if the goal is *integrated* housing and not simply *more* housing for Negroes. Individuals can be compelled to show that a refusal to sell to a Negro is not based on racial grounds, but they cannot be compelled to remain in the neighborhood and live side by side with the Negro.

Third, some of the goals now being sought by Negroes are least applicable to those groups of Negroes most suited to protest action. Protest action involving such tactics as mass meetings, picketing, boycotts, and strikes rarely find enthusiastic participants among upper income and higher status individuals. Such strategies often require recruiting, through intangible appeals, lower income, lower status groups that do not consider mass action beneath their dignity. This was not crucially important when the Negro community could respond, with near-unanimity, to indisputable outrages—when, in short, they sought specific, defensive, welfare ends. Many of the goals being sought today, such as access to desirable housing in middle and upper income neighborhoods and employment in supervisory, skilled, or professional jobs, do not involve rewards for groups not equipped, by income, training, or disposition, to avail themselves of such opportunities. Even when the goal can be made specific, it becomes difficult to mobilize the masses when (1) the end sought clearly benefits, at least immediately, only middle and upper class Negroes and (2) no general, principled rationale can be developed which will relate the specific goal to the aspirations or needs of the rank and file. Indeed, as some recent cases suggest, there may be an actual conflict of ends between upper status and lower status Negroes (6, 8). . . .

Fourth, many specific goals toward which action can be directed occur in situations that place a negative value on protest. For example, when (as happened in Chicago recently) a builder proposes constructing a tract of homes in a white community which will be sold to whites and Negroes on a non-discriminatory basis, an intense controversy is immediately precipitated. Whites offer resistance. A specific issue is at stake—will or will not the houses be built. In this case, Negro protest organizations often feel, with some justification, that mounting a protest campaign against the whites would only aggravate the situation and reduce the likelihood of getting the homes built by giving credence to white fears that the integrated homes are part of a "conspiracy" created by the NAACP and other Negro organizations to "force" Negroes into white areas. Similar problems arise when a single Negro family attempts to buy and occupy a home in a white neighborhood. Often public officials come to the conclusion that the family's chances of establishing itself are reduced if Negro protest is organized in its behalf. Inducing whites to accept one Negro family is difficult; inducing them to accept a family which the whites believe was "planted" by the NAACP and is, thus, the vanguard of a host of Negro families is much more difficult. To be sure, there are some Negro leaders who seize upon such explanations as a rationale for not doing what they have no taste for doing anyway. But in many cases the problem is genuine. Protest appears to be dysfunctional in just those cases where a specific goal exists to make protest possible at all.

Fifth, Negroes are not organized on a continuing basis for protest activity. The on-going voluntary associations to be found in a northern Negro community are almost always led by middle class Negro business, professional, or church groups, with a sprinkling of labor leaders (10). These associations invariably lack a mass base. Even more important, those leaders who do command mass organizations are often under clear constraints to avoid protest tactics. At least two of the three principal Negro mass organizations (labor unions and political organizations) are part and parcel of citywide unions and political groups. They derive the incentives used to maintain their organizations (jobs, patronage, appointments to staff positions, money, slating for office, etc.) from sources controlled by whites. Negro labor leaders and politicians tend to reflect the character of labor and political movements in the city as a whole. It is only when the labor or political groups of the city are weak, divided, or faltering that Negro leaders in these organizations can act with some independence. (This is the case in New York, for example, in the relationships between Tammany Hall and Harlem.) It becomes very difficult to organize political or economic protest movements that require strikes or switching votes. To attempt this would involve challenging established leaders in these fields. Even assuming such leaders could either be induced to protest or somehow bypassed, it is not at all clear that traditional voting allegiances could be overcome in a manner that would permit protest leaders to threaten realistically election reprisals against public officials.

This means that Negro protest leaders, in dealing with white politicians, often must employ deception or rely on imperfect information when they suggest that they speak "for" Negro voters. Surprisingly, many politicians can be influenced, at least marginally, in this way. Doubts exist, if not as to which way Negroes will vote, then as to the size of that vote. Hopes exist of improving one's individual position with Negro voters. But these are minor bargaining resources. Usually both sides realize that no organization exists which can switch any significant number of Negro voters in a predetermined manner.

PROBLEMS OF COORDINATION

If these observations are correct, the prospects of vigorous, extensive, and organized Negro protest in large northern cities are poor. The danger confronting the Negro community in many places today is not extremism, but impotence. However, these conclusions regarding the logic and nature of protest do not cover all cases. Opportunities remain for this strategy, but these opportunities are of a limited character and present problems in themselves.

Protest action is best suited to situations in which the goal sought is defensive, specific, of a welfare character, relevant to the wants of the Negro rank and file, and has an explicit target. Such opportunities are found in greater number in the South than in the North today, but they are by no means absent in the North. Discriminatory practices are still to be found in many hotels, hospitals, restaurants, and places of employment. Existing voluntary associations in many, although not all, Negro communities are not absorbed in these tasks. For a variety of reasons— including the kind of people recruited to these agencies, the interests of the professional staffs, and budgetary needs — many of these associations are more concerned with broader problems involving goals which are assertive, general, of a status character, having multiple targets, and relevant more to the interests of the Negro middle and upper class. (This is not to dispute the pos-

sible validity of the argument that gains for middle class Negroes in the long run mean gains for Negroes as a whole, because of the precedent or symbolic value of such advances. But people are hard to mobilize for protest action aimed at goals which, for them, have only indirect or symbolic value.) This means that stimulating protest action may require, in many cases, focusing attention on goals of a lesser order than those now being discussed.

Further, it may well mean creating organizations specifically adapted to these protest ends. Neither the NAACP nor the Urban League,. in almost any city, is equiped to engage in such activity as it is now organized. Persons with the necessary leadership skills would, of course, be hard to find, as most are already either (1) committed to an existing Negro association, or (2) indifferent to civic action, or both. Further, the resources—in terms of time and money—for civic action are very scarce, and a new organization would only intensify the competition for these resources. At present, the NAACP is competent to issue verbal protests, provide legal assistance, and initiate court fights on behalf of Negroes, while the Urban League is sometimes able to negotiate (although usually with few, if any, bargaining resources). Other forms of protest are typically outside the province of most existing Negro associations as they are generally organized.

The task is to create the possibility of meaningful bargaining on a whole range of issues by being able to offer other parties the compensation of ending a protest campaign. This implies a division of labor between protest leaders and bargainers. In some cases, such a division in fact exists. In New York City, for example, the Urban League often finds itself presented with opportunities for negotiation because an extremist leader, such as Rep. Adam

Clayton Powell, Jr., has brought some city agency or private party under heavy fire. This is true even though many Urban League leaders often deplore Powell and his tactics; for them, Powell is a useful nuisance. An ideal strategy would include a protest organization campaigning against certain targets (a, b, and c) while another agency bargained for certain ends (A, D, and E). In one case, the target (a) and the goal (A) would be identical, and the strategy would be a *primary* one. If the goal (A) is conceded, the protest against the party which concedes the goal (the target, a) would be ended. In another case, the goal (D) differs from the target (b). Concessions from b would be extracted because b stands in some bargaining relationship with d, who can grant the goal (D). This would be a *secondary* strategy. For example, obtaining more middle income public housing units might be the goal, but the target would be an urban renewal program which would displace Negroes. The campaign against urban renewal would be reduced if the goal were granted. The bargaining linkage here might be between the Negro association which induces the backer of the urban renewal project to prevail upon the city housing authority to construct the housing project.

Some approximation of this does, in fact, occur on occasion. The difficulty is that it places a great premium on coordination among Negro leaders and organizations. This coordination is rarely easy to obtain. First, the various leaders may not agree on what goals should be sought. The would-be bargainers, in a typical case, might very well find more Negro public housing an objectionable goal since it might easily result in the placing of lower status Negroes in the neighborhoods of upper status Negroes. Second, the

protest association might well resist being "called off" for the price of a few housing units. This limited goal may not be sufficiently endowed with ideological significance to be the basis for mobilizing support for the campaign. The rank and file might feel that they were "sold out" by leaders who accepted such a concession rather than fighting the urban renewal project to the bitter end. The problem is to select a limited goal (so that there is some hope it can be obtained and so that it can plausibly be the subject of bargaining) and imbue it with enough significance so that it can provide incentives for action. Third, the protest and the bargaining groups would be radically different in character and thus find it difficult to work together comfortably. Each would be in competition with the other for scarce resources (personnel, contributions, publicity, etc.). Further, each would recruit members and leaders from different walks of life with differing temperaments and interests. There is no logical necessity that would prevent these two groups from coexisting peacefully and cooperating smoothly, but in fact cooperation (and sometimes even coexistence) seem impossible.

This raises a point about which Negro leaders themselves often speak. It is customary to assign to the NAACP and the Urban League, for example, distinctive roles and equal credit. Each has its function and each deserves support, one is told. One may prefer the league to the NAACP, but one recognizes the need for the other group. These amiable statements, however, often thinly conceal a great deal of tension between "league" types and "NAACP" types, particularly if (as is often the case) the leaders of the two organizations display strongly differing political styles (12). One group tends to be suspicious of the other. Normal organizational rivalries are intensified by tactical and temperamental differences. Suspicions are aroused about the motives and purposes of the other party. Cooperation becomes more difficult because one group has grave reservations about the ends and tactics of the other and thus finds a coordinated venture filled with uncertainties and possible risks.[1]

A strategy of secondary protest, with its attendant problem of coordination between two associations with differing end- and incentive-systems, points once again to the practical virtues of emphasizing narrow, specific goals with unambiguous targets. That such goals and such targets are to be found in abundance cannot be doubted. The immediate and tangible needs of Negroes, particularly for more and better jobs, are manifest. . . .

REFERENCES

1 BANFIELD, EDWARD C. "The Theory of Manipulation." (Mimeographed by Department of Government, Harvard University, 1956.)

2 ——. Political Influence. Glencoe, Ill.: Free Press. (Forthcoming.)

3 CLARK, PETER B. "Notes on Bargaining." (Mimeographed by Department of Political Science, Yale University, 1960.)

4 DAHL, ROBERT A., and LINDBLOM, CHARLES E. Politics, Economics, and Welfare. New York: Harper & Bros., 1953.

5 GARFINKEL, HERBERT. When Negroes March. Glencoe, Ill.: Free Press, 1959.

6 GLAZER, NATHAN. "Is 'Integration' Possible in New York Schools?" Commentary (September, 1960), 185–193.

7 LOMAX, LOUIS E. "The Negro Revolt Against the 'Negro Leadership,'" Harpers (June, 1960), 41–48.

8 MANNES, MARYA. "School Trouble in Harlem," Reporter (February 5, 1959), 13–19.

9 SCHELLING, THOMAS C. The Strategy of Conflict. Cambridge, Mass.: Harvard University Press, 1960.

10 SELZNICK, PHILIP. Leadership in Administration. Evanston, Ill.: Row, Peterson Co., 1957.

11 WILSON, JAMES Q. "Negro Civic Leaders." (A paper read before the annual meeting of the American Political Science Association, September 8–10, 1960, New York City.)

12 ——. Negro Politics: The Search for Leadership. Glencoe, Ill.: Free Press, 1960.

13 ——. "Two Negro Politicians: An Interpretation," Midwest Journal of Political Science (November, 1960).

[1] An apparent exception to the difficulty of coordinating protest action is the case of some southern sit-in demonstrations. In cities such as Nashville, Tenn., and Montgomery, Ala., the spontaneous student sit-in strategy caused deep concern among both white and "established" Negro leaders. The problem for the established Negro leaders (the lawyers, ministers, politicians, etc.) was to bargain with their white counterparts in order to gain some concessions in policies governing white lunch counters in return for ending the sit-in movement. Successful bargaining required that the Negro leaders be able to control the student demonstrators. In Nashville and other cities, when some agreement was reached, the sit-in strikes were in fact ended. This suggests a remarkable degree of coordination among Negro groups which, at the outset, were somewhat suspicious of one another and which had few common goals or common organizational memberships. I am told by certain southern Negro leaders that the device by which the "established" Negro leaders acquired control over the student strikers was the bail money which the arrested students could not furnish themselves. In Montgomery, for example, a large sum was apparently collected by Negro leaders to use on behalf of student strikers. It is reported that when some students showed a reluctance to agree to tactical moves suggested by adult leaders, a withdrawal of this financial support was threatened. The threat proved effective in most cases. Some student leaders attempted to assert their independence with the slogan, "Jail, Not Bail," but did not command a large following when it became apparent that a jail sentence could be for as long as thirty or sixty days.

30
*The Nonviolent Resistance Movement against Segregation**

JAMES W. VANDER ZANDEN

"Passive" or "nonviolent resistance" has become a major weapon in the arsenal of the Negro movement against segregation.[1] A dramatic and spectacular tactic, it found its first large-scale employment in a movement launched in late 1955 against segregation on city buses by Negroes in Montgomery, Alabama. The success of the Montgomery movement established passive resistance as a key weapon in desegregation efforts, and projected upon the national horizon a new group of militant Negro leaders represented by Rev. Martin Luther King, Jr. The movement places great stress upon nonviolent means such as boycotts and sit-ins, and nonviolent reactions in the face of attack.

Nonviolent resistance is a tactic well-suited to struggles in which a minority lacks access to major sources of power within a society and to the instruments of violent coercion. The stratification structure and the functional division of labor of a society are so constituted that a minority group undertaking "noncooperation," the withholding of its participation from certain essential areas of life, can exert considerable pressure upon the dominant group and extract concessions from them. By the same token, nonviolent resistance is less likely to bring direct retaliation from the dominant group than are tactics employing more directly aggressive forms of expression. Moreover, within the South, the mass character of the movement has posed particular difficulties to whites who would

*[Reprinted by permission from *American Journal of Sociology*, vol. 68, March 1963, pp. 544–549.]

undertake to punish the participants—for example, the relative infeasibility of mass imprisonments. During the past two decades vast social changes within the South have contributed to a redefinition of lynching as illegitimate. Simultaneously, within the larger American society, the Negroes' tactic of nonviolent resistance has gained a considerable degree of legitimacy. . . .

Although responses of overt, unaggressive accommodation to the racial structure generally prevailed among southern Negroes prior to 1954, various investigators noted that southern Negroes harbored considerable covert or latent aggressive impulses toward whites.[2] These feelings of latent hostility and aggression were not always manifest or conscious. From her psychiatric treatment of Negroes, McLean observed: "The intense fear of the white man with its consequent hostility and guilt may not be conscious in the Negro, but from my own psychoanalytic experience in treating Negro men and women, *I have yet to see a Negro who did not unconsciously have a deep fear of and hostility toward white people.*"[3] Karon, in a study of Negro personality characteristics in a northern and a southern city, concluded that Negroes in the South develop strong mechanisms of denial with respect to aggression, not only with respect to the race situation but to the whole of life. Compared with the Negroes in the northern city, the southern Negroes were characterized by a higher incidence in the number of people whose whole emotional life was colored by the struggle not to be angry.[4]

Within this setting, a program of nonviolent resistance to segregation offered a strong psychological appeal (in addition to its already-noted suitability as a tactic). On the one hand, there exist among Negroes considerable undercurrents of resentment toward whites and the southern racial structure. On the other hand, Negroes have been socialized generally in a tradition calling for the suppression of hostility and aggression toward whites, and also in a religious tradition stressing Christian love and tabooing hatred. Many Negroes have taken very literally the Christian doctrine that it is sinful to hate. Yet, they are placed in race situations in which hostility is an inevitable product; life confronts Negroes with circumstances that constantly stimulate aggressive thoughts and fantasies that are defined as sinful.[5]

The matter is compounded by widespread Negro feelings of self-hatred.[6] Within many minority groups there exist strong tendencies to accept the dominant group's evaluations and conceptions of the minority.[7] By virtue of his membership in the Negro group, the Negro suffers considerably in terms of self-esteem and has every incentive for self-hatred. In many respects, even good performance is irrelevant insofar as the Negro frequently gets a poor reflection of himself in the behavior of whites, regardless of what he does or what his merits are. Identified by society as a Negro, he, of necessity, so identifies himself. To compensate for this low self-esteem, the Negro identifies in part with whites and white values; for example, the success of the Negro cosmetic industry rests, in large measure, upon the considerable demand for skin bleaches and hair straighteners.[8] Hostility toward whites and simultaneous self-hatred and identification with whites are likely to intensify the internal turbulence which seeks for resolution.

Rev. Martin Luther King, Jr., has given articulate and forceful expression to these crosscurrents (the feelings of hostility toward whites on the one hand, and the dictates requiring suppression of these impulses on the other), and has posed a solution to the dilemma. He has told Negroes that they have long been abused, insulted, and mistreated, that they have been "kicked about by the brutal feet of oppression." In essence, he has repeatedly told his Negro audiences, using such veiled euphemisms as "protest," that it is permissible and legitimate for them to feel hostility and to engage in aggressive activities against the existing racial order.[9] In fact, an important theme in his speeches has been that Negroes have "a moral obligation" to fight segregation: "To accept passively an unjust system is to cooperate with that system; thereby the oppressed become as evil as the oppressor. Noncooperation with evil is as much a moral obligation as is cooperation with good."[10] He has thus defined the traditional pattern of acceptance and resignation as immoral.

Simultaneously, King and his followers have paid extensive homage to nonhatred, to Christian love: "Love must be our regulating ideal. Once again we must hear the words of Jesus echoing across the centuries: 'Love your enemies, bless them that curse you, and pray for them that despitefully use you.'"[11] In essence, King's message to Negroes has been that they can have their cake and eat it too; that they can "hate," but that really it is not animosity but "love." He has aided Negroes to redefine as moral and acceptable what otherwise would be defined as immoral and unacceptable. This is not to suggest hypocrisy; rather, it is an example of the facility with which humans can rationalize and legitimatize feelings, attitudes, and behavior that might otherwise be a source of emotional distress to them.

An incident at a Knoxville rally in support of the "Stay Away from Downtown" movement (part of the campaign to win the desegregation of that city's lunch counters) is illustrative. After a number of bitter, biting, and militant speeches, the chairman of the meeting came back to the microphone and reassuringly indicated, "We're making a lot of noise, but that doesn't mean we're angry at anybody. If you have no love in your heart, stay at home. Why, even Jack Leflore's got it now, a little bit!"[12] The assembled Negroes were permitted to vent their hostility but then, fittingly enough, were comforted, "We're really not angry." Further relief from the tension was provided by the good-natured ribbing of one of the community's Negroes.

The King appeal attempts to mediate between the conflicting traditions, of the accommodating Negro and the militant Negro. Ambiguously immersed within conflicting roles, the appeal looks in both directions, toward the suppression of hostility (the traditional approach), and toward its expression in a militantly aggressive social movement. Although such activities may be labeled "passive resistance," in reality they constitute what psychologists refer to as "passive aggression." Their net result is to challenge, to aggress against, existing patterns (and by implication the people who adhere to such patterns, e.g., the boycotted white merchants).

Yet as is so frequently the case rationalizations are not always completely successful in handling impulses defined as unacceptable. Bitterness, resentment, and hostility cannot be dispensed with so simply; protestations of love cannot totally veil aggressive impulses. The consequence is a wide prevalence of deep and disturbing guilt feelings. King has noted this in his own experience. Referring to his encounters with bus and city officials, he writes: "I was weighted down by a terrible sense of guilt, remembering that on two or three occasions I had allowed myself to become angry and indignant. I had spoken hastily and resentfully, yet I knew that this was no way to solve a problem.

'You must not harbor anger,' I admonished myself. 'You must be willing to suffer the anger of the opponent, and yet not return anger. You must not become bitter. . . .'"[13]

Prevailing guilt feelings caused by aggressive and hostile impulses seek satisfaction in the need for punishment. This probably accounts, in part, for the considerable premium assigned by the nonviolent resistance movement to suffering. In fact, the endurance of suffering and the "turn the other cheek" orientation have become exalted in their own right. King declares: "We will match your capacity [referring to whites] to inflict suffering with our capacity to endure suffering. We will meet your physical force with soul force. . . . Do to us what you will and we will still love you. . . . But we will soon wear you down by our capacity to suffer."[14] And "The nonviolent say that suffering becomes a powerful social force when you willingly accept that violence on yourself, so that *self-suffering stands at the center* of the nonviolent movement and the individuals involved are able to suffer in a creative manner, feeling that unearned suffering is redemptive, and that suffering may serve to transform the social situation."[15]

Similarly, it is not unusual to hear the movement's activists express their willingness to die for their cause, to suffer the severest form of punishment, a martyr's death. King, indicating his "personal sense of guilt for everything that was happening" as a result of the bus boycott (e.g., the violence that had ensued), explains that he "broke down" in a public meeting and then "in the grip of an emotion I could not control," exclaimed, "Lord, I hope no one will have to die as a result of our struggle for freedom in Montgomery. Certainly I don't want to die. But if anyone has to die, let it be me."[16] At times it appears that some members of the movement engage in subtle provocations, in a masochistic-like fashion, whereby they expect to bring about pain and degradation; they offer their "cheek" with the prospect of receiving a slap.

The emphasis upon suffering has still another source. Christianity teaches that voluntary submission to sacrifice, privation, and renunciation of gratification are preconditions for the attainment of the prospective goal, eternal happiness. Life is viewed as a brief period of affliction, to be replaced by eternal bliss for the righteous. The death of Christ upon the cross, the Savior's suffering, was the means by which the gates of paradise were opened.[17] Within this religious heritage, it is not difficult to make the attainment of an improved earthly future also contingent upon suffering. Suffering, and often merely its anticipation, clears the path to the fulfilment of otherwise forbidden values, the good life in which Negroes will enjoy a better future on earth. It is the Gandhian mandate that "Things of fundamental importance to people are not secured by reason alone, but have to be *purchased* with their *suffering*." The principle is seen in this illustration:

Once a pool driver [Montgomery Negroes established a car pool during the period of the bus boycott] stopped beside an elderly woman who was trudging along with obvious difficulty.

"Jump in, grandmother," he said. "You don't need to walk."

She waved him on. "I'm not walking for myself," she explained. "I'm walking for my children and my grandchildren." And she continued toward home on foot.[18]

Developments on the national and international scene have sharply posed the issue of the Negro's status within America. Within the context of these many crosscurrents, suffering provides a source by which Negroes may increase their self-esteem: First, one can appear uncommonly noble, gentle, and heroic through suffering and sacrificing one's own comfort and well-being for a cause. Second, suffering enables the Negro to feel that "we are after all the better men," "better" in the moral and spiritual sense. Christianity teaches that "He that humbleth himself shall be exalted" and "Blessed are the meek for they shall inherit the earth." Negroes can find a considerable sense of self-worth in these teachings, for "after all, we are the better Christians; in God's eyes we are honored." King indicates: "Since the white man's personality is greatly distorted by segregation, and his soul is greatly scarred, he needs the love of the Negro. The Negro must love the white man, because the white man needs his love to remove his tensions, insecurities, and fears."[19] Third, Negroes can enjoy the idea that they will finally triumph, that they will conquer their enemies. They can gain considerable satisfaction in the fantasy that the very society that neglects and rejects them now will see its sinful ways and repent. There is an inner expectancy and foreknowledge of coming victory.[20] Then "the last shall be first." Here again this sentiment finds frequent expression in King's speeches: "Before the victory is won some may have to get scarred up, but we shall overcome. Before the victory of brotherhood is achieved, some will maybe face physical death, but we shall overcome . . . behind the dim unknown standeth God within the shadows, keeping watch above His own. With this faith in the future, with this determined struggle, we will be able to emerge from the bleak and desolate midnight of man's inhumanity to man, into the bright and glittering daybreak of freedom and justice."[21]

A social movement as such offers certain rewards to a people weighed down by a sense of inferiority, powerlessness, and insignificance. In fusing oneself with a social movement external to the self, one can acquire the strength which the individual self lacks by becoming part of a bigger and more powerful whole. In so doing the individual may lose some of his personal integrity as well as some of his freedom, but he can also gain a new sense of strength and significance.[22] In this connection, one is struck by the intense exaltation and glorification of the leadership of the nonviolent movement by the rank and file, by its messianic character. Although mass meetings are frequently held during which the audience votes on various matters, their action is little more than a rubber stamp for the decisions made by the leadership and presented for perfunctory approval.[23] By the same token, a social movement helps to answer the question, "Who am I?" for a people whose social role is ambiguous and undergoing change. . . .

Whereas the South, until recently, rather formally and rigorously defined the position of the Negro within the region, the North did not do likewise. Within northern cities, Negroes, at least in theory, were the equals of whites, although in practice this was frequently not the case. Accordingly, it is understandable that many northern Negroes, especially among the lower socioeconomic groups, should become disillusioned and that they should turn their backs on integration for separatism. However, southern Negroes generally have not lost faith in the feasibility of the assimilationist approach; it has still to be tried. Furthermore, there is evidence that within the North the Negro church has lost its significance for many urban Negroes who seek to define their situation within religious terms.[24] This has not been the case within the South. A new group of Negro religious leaders, as represented by Rev. Martin Luther King, Jr., have undertaken to help the southern Negro define his situation within the terms of the church.

FOOTNOTES

[1] From 1954 to 1956 the author taught at an accredited Negro college with an interracial faculty in a Deep South state. By virtue of this position he was able to move rather freely within the Negro community. The interpretation advanced within this paper in large measure rests upon the observations made from this vantage point.

[2] John Dollard, *Caste and Class in a Southern Town* (3rd ed.; New York: Anchor Books, Doubleday & Co., 1957), p. 252; Abram Kardiner and Lionel Ovesey, *The Mark of Oppression* (New York: W. W. Norton & Co., 1951), p. 342; Guy B. Johnson, "Patterns of Race Conflict," in Edgar T. Thompson (ed.), *Race Relations and the Race Problem* (Durham, N.C.: Duke University Press, 1939), p. 126; Bertram P. Karon, *The Negro Personality* (New York: Springer Publishing Co., 1958), pp. 165–167; Helen V. McLean, "The Emotional Health of Negroes," *Journal of Negro Education,* XVIII (1949), 286; and Hortense Powdermaker, "The Channeling of Negro Aggression by the Cultural Process," in Clyde Kluckhohn and Henry A. Murray (eds.), *Personality* (2d ed.; New York: Alfred A. Knopf, Inc., 1956)', pp. 602–603.

[3] McLean, *op. cit.,* p. 286. My italics.

[4] Karon, *op. cit.,* pp. 165–167.

[5] Powdermaker, *op. cit.,* pp. 602–603.

[6] See Kardiner and Ovesey, *op. cit.,* p. 297; Kenneth B. Clark and Mamie P. Clark, "Racial Identification and Preference in Negro Children," in Theodore M. Newcomb and E. L. Hartley (eds.), *Readings in Social Psychology* (New York: Henry Holt & Co., 1947), pp. 169–178; Robert Johnson, "Negro Reactions to Minority Group Status," in Milton L. Barron (ed.), *American Minorities* (New York: Alfred A. Knopf, Inc., 1957), p. 205; Charles S. Johnson, *Growing Up in the Black Belt* (Washington, D.C.: American Council of Education, 1941), p. 259; and E. Franklin Frazier, *Negro Youth at the Crossways* (Washington, D.C.: American Council on Education, 1940), p. 180.

[7] Kurt Lewin, *Resolving Social Conflicts* (New York: Harper & Bros., 1948), pp. 186–200.

[8] For a discussion of Negro incorporation and distortion of white middle class values see E. Franklin Frazier, *Black Bourgeoisie* (Glencoe, Ill.: Free Press, 1957).

[9] There is reason to believe that Rev. Martin Luther King, Jr., himself, harbors considerable animosity toward whites; see Martin Luther King, Jr., *Stride toward Freedom* (New York: Balantine Books, 1958), pp. 71, 97, and 112.

[10] *Ibid.,* p. 173.

[11] *Ibid.*, p. 51.

[12] Merrill Proudfoot, *Diary of a Sit-in* (Chapel Hill: University of North Carolina Press, 1962), p. 118.

[13] King, *op. cit.*, p. 97.

[14] *Ibid.*, p. 177.

[15] King, "Love, Law and Civil Disobedience," *New South*, XVI (December, 1961), 6. My italics.

[16] King, *Stride toward Freedom, op. cit.*, p. 143.

[17] In this connection see Theodor Reik, *Masochism in Modern Man* (New York: Grove Press, Inc., 1941), pp. 319, 341–342, 428, 430–433.

[18] King, *Stride toward Freedom, op. cit.*, p. 61.

[19] *Ibid.*, p. 84.

[20] See Reik, *op. cit.*, pp. 319–322, 430–433.

[21] King, "Love, Law and Civil Disobedience," *op. cit.*, pp. 10–11.

[22] See Erich Fromm, *Escape from Freedom* (New York: Rinehart & Co., 1941), pp. 141, 151–156.

[23] See Jacquelyne Mary Johnson Clarke, "Goals and Techniques in Three Negro Civil-Rights Organizations in Alabama" (unpublished doctoral dissertation, Ohio State University, 1960).

[24] E. U. Essien Udom, *Black Nationalism: A Search for an Identity in America* (Chicago: University of Chicago Press, 1962), pp. 331–332.

PART FOUR
THE DYNAMICS OF CONFLICT

SECTION A

SOCIAL PROCESSES

ALTHOUGH conflicts may be very much affected by the ideology and kind of milieu and structure in which they occur, there is nevertheless often a sense of constant movement, change, and development over time as participants interact with each other. The organization of the conflict groups, the characteristics of activists, tactics, the conception a group has of itself and its opponents, and the intensity and extensiveness of the struggle may be in constant flux as the conflict develops over time.

In looking at ideology and the characteristics of activists or communities, we are usually cutting into social life at just one point in time and acting as if it were static. For some purposes this is adequate, yet it is also important to take a broad perspective and consider the developmental aspects of the conflict over time. When this is done, we are dealing with social process and our focus is on the often fluid, emergent, and shifting character of the conflict. It is with such dynamics that this section is concerned.

James Coleman's article on "The Dynamics of Controversy" is a superb example of this approach. The closer we look at conflict, or any social situation, the more complex and varied are the patterns we can uncover. Yet in abstractly considering a large number of cases, it is often possible to discover reoccurring themes and a limited number of typical patterns of development. One of the most interesting and important of these, because of its potential for extreme divisiveness, is considered by Coleman: community conflict which becomes polarized and relatively unrestrained. In such conflicts, where a disagreement between two groups eventually expands to include almost the entire community divided into warring camps, certain changes may regularly be observed. The basic issue in contention may shift from a specific grievance to a more generalized critique, new issues sometimes unrelated to the original one may emerge, and mere disagreements between people may give rise to intense feelings of antagonism. The very important point is made that "once set in motion, hostility can sustain conflict unaided by disagreement about particular issues." The conflict may continue after its initial cause is removed. Here unrealistic conflict becomes intertwined with realistic conflict.[1] It is this fusion which makes some conflicts so hard to resolve. As polarization develops, changes appear in social organization, there is increased reliance on informal communication, and the "vicious circles" and "runaway processes" characteristic of some conflicts may emerge. Coleman identifies a "Gresham's law of conflict" whereby moderate leaders are replaced by those less willing to negotiate and the emphasis shifts from winning to ruining the opponent.

Also taking a broad perspective that covers the entire course of the struggle, James H. Laue presents a model of civil rights change through conflict, abstracted from numerous southern communities during the early 1960's. He observes a pattern that moves from challenge by blacks, a period of overt community conflict leading to a crisis, the involvement of elements of the white power structure in negotiation to

---

[1] For discussion of these important concepts, see D. L. Coser, pp. 14–20 of this volume.

the emergence of some change. An important element in the changes that did emerge was a shift in the perceived self-interest of local whites with power; they may not like desegregation, but they like losing business, disruption, and bad publicity even less. More important was the fact that southern protests occurred within a national context essentially sympathetic to their ends. The richness and variability of any given instance of conflict is only partly described by such a model. A given conflict can stop at any stage, stages can be skipped, and such a model applies more clearly in the South than the North. Nevertheless it offers a framework for dealing with the developmental and social process aspects of a certain type of conflict.

The same thing is true of the article by John Spiegel, which deals with conflicts on college campuses. Spiegel identifies a pattern of development that characterizes many struggles and he gives a clear feeling of how a conflict evolves over time.

Tamotsu Shibutani and Kian M. Kwan consider a question which deals with cultural symbols and people's subjective perceptions: What kinds of conceptions of themselves and their opponents are people in conflict situations likely to construct and what are the implications of this? They observe that "contrast conceptions" may emerge in which one's own group is seen as noble and self-sacrificing, while the opponent becomes the personification of everything evil. This is made even easier when the difference between groups is seen as racial and genetic. Through selective perception, only those things consistent with their prior images may be perceived. A social process may be seen in the buildup of these conceptions as the conflict goes on. Such conceptions aid in drawing group boundaries and are one means by which solidarity

and cohesion within a conflict group are increased. They also are conducive to self-sacrifice and permit an ethical dualism, whereby any means can be used to subdue an opponent seen as beyond the pale of the human community. They are conducive to unrealistic conflict and an exaggeration of the actual extent of disagreement between groups. Though the rhetoric of contrast conceptions may sometimes substitute for actual conflict, it may also inhibit compromise and negotiation. Such conceptions are one aspect of the polarization process also considered by Coleman.

The last two articles in this section consider civil disorders that emerged in ghetto areas in 1964 and reached a high point during the summer of 1967. Louis G. Goldberg analyzes twenty-three civil disorders that occurred during 1967. This is a useful article because it attempts to deal with types of ghetto riot, rather than treating all riots as if they were the same.[2] Among types of riot noted are general social upheavals, political confrontations, expressive rampages, and those that seem to emerge in self-defense or are initiated by overly eager control forces anticipating a riot. Some ghetto uprisings may take on the character of a competitive game, in which youth attempt to humiliate the police.

Police are an important source of interracial conflict. Elements of unrealistic conflict, exaggeration, stereotyping, and scapegoating may be present on both sides. More clearly than is the case with many issues, struggles involving the police indicate how the authority relations stressed by Dahrendorf can be a major generator of conflict. The un-

[2] Variation in types of riot are also discussed in G. Marx, "Riots," *Encyclopaedia Britannica,* 1970, reprinted in P. Rose, *Study of Society* (New York: Random House, 1970); and G. Marx, "Issueless Riots," *Annals of the American Academy of Political and Social Science,* September 1970.

pleasant task given police of enforcing rules through coercion and force is bound to generate some opposition, particularly by those who are disadvantaged as a result of the social arrangements that police power maintains.

Conflicts with the police have involved disagreements over the enforcement of rules, particular instances of police brutality, a fight to gain or keep civilian review boards, efforts to change police employment and operating procedures, and demands for more and better policing. A large proportion of riots initially involved a police incident. In other racial conflict situations, even where police are not involved directly in the issue, they tend to become involved, and usually on a side against those protesting. This is a natural consequence of their being called out to keep the peace, regulate picket lines, or arrest those sitting-in or engaged in civil disorders.

In "Civil Disorder and the Agents of Social Control" I examine police behavior in ghetto riots. Here the dynamic and emergent quality of conflict can again be seen. The course and form of a riot involves elements that cannot very well be predicted by a consideration of static preriot variables such as the size of the economic gap between blacks and whites or the degree of pluralism in a community. Rather, attention must be directed to the interaction that occurs between controllers and rioters. The selection considers various ways in which police have been ineffective and even contributed to the disorders. Yet even when police behavior has been exemplary, this has not always stopped the disorders. For many blacks, police have become symbols of an oppressive white society. By the mere act of trying to maintain law and order, however fairly and impartially, they are also seen as maintaining the status quo.

31
*The Dynamics of Controversy**
JAMES COLEMAN

The most striking fact about the development and growth of community controversies is the similarity they exhibit despite diverse underlying sources and different kinds of precipitating incidents. Once the controversies have begun, they resemble each other remarkably. Were it not for these similarities, Machiavelli could never have written his guide to warfare, and none of the other numerous works on conflict, dispute, and controversy would have been possible.[1] It is the peculiarity of social controversy that it sets in motion its own dynamics; these tend to carry it forward in a path which bears little relation to its beginnings. An examination of these dynamics will occupy the attention of this chapter.

One caution is necessary: we do not mean to suggest that nothing can be done about community controversy once it begins. To the contrary, the dynamics of controversy *can* be interrupted and diverted—either by conscious action or by existing conditions in the community. As a result, although the same dynamic tendencies of controversy are found in every case, the actual development in particular cases may differ widely. In the discussion be-

*[Reprinted with permission of The Macmillan Company from *Community Conflict* by James Coleman. Copyright 1957 by The Free Press, a Corporation.]

[1] The one man who emphasized particularly the possibility of abstracting principles of conflict from particular situations of conflict is Georg Simmel, who wrote several essays on the subject. Unfortunately, Simmel never got around to writing a comprehensive theory of conflict, though he did set down a number of insights into particular aspects. See G. Simmel, *Conflict and the Web of Intergroup Affiliations*, Glencoe: The Free Press, 1955. Lewis Coser has brought together the best of Simmel's insights and elaborated on them. L. Coser, *The Functions of Social Conflict*, Glencoe: The Free Press, 1956.

low, the unrestrained dynamic tendencies will be discussed. . . .*

CHANGES IN ISSUES

The issues which provide the initial basis of response in a controversy undergo great transformations as the controversy develops. Three fundamental transformations appear to take place.

Specific to general

First, specific issues give way to *general* ones. In Scarsdale, the school's critics began by attacking books in the school library; soon they focused on the whole educational philosophy. In Mason City, Iowa, where a city-manager plan was abandoned, the campaign against the plan started with a letter to the newspaper from a local carpenter complaining that the creek overflowed into his home. This soon snowballed, gathering other specific complaints, and then gave way to the general charge that the council and manager were dominated by local business interests and had no concern for the workingman.

Most of the controversies examined show a similar pattern. (Even those that do not are helpful, for they suggest just why the pattern, *does* exist in so many cases. Political controversies, for example, exhibit the pattern much less than do disputes based primarily on differing values or economic interests. The Athens, Tennessee, political fight began with the same basic issue it ended with—political control of the community (Key, 1950). Other political struggles in which there is little popular involvement show a similar restriction to the initial issue.)

It seems that movement from specific to general issues occurs whenever there are deep cleavages of values or interests in the community which re-

quire a spark to set them off—usually a specific incident representing only a small part of the underlying difference. In contrast, those disputes which appear not to be generated by deep cleavages running through the community as a whole, but are rather power struggles within the community, do not show the shift from specific to general. To be sure, they may come to involve the entire community, but no profound fundamental difference comes out.

This first shift in the nature of the issues, then, uncovers the fundamental differences which set the stage for a precipitating incident in the first place.

New and different issues

Another frequent change in the issues of the dispute is the emergence of quite *new and different* issues, unrelated to the original ones. In the Pasadena school controversy, the initial issue was an increased school budget and a consequent increased tax rate. This soon became only one issue of many; ideological issues concerning "progressive education," and other issues, specific as well as general, arose. In another case, a controversy which began as a personal power struggle between a school superintendent and a principal shifted to a conflict involving general educational principles when the community as a whole entered in (Warner et al., 1949, p. 201–204). A study of the adoption of the city-manager plan in fifty cities (Stone, Price, and Stone, 1940, p. 34–38) shows that in one group of cities, designated by the authors "machine-ridden," the controversy grew to include ethnic, religious, political, and ideological differences. Political campaigns generally, in fact, show this tendency: issues multiply rapidly as the campaign increases in intensity.

There are two different sources for this diversification of issues. One is in a sense "involuntary"; issues which

* [Elsewhere in his book Coleman discusses situational restraints on controversy.]

could not have been raised before the controversy spring suddenly to the fore as relationships between groups and individuals change. We see how this operates in an argument between two people, e.g., in the common phrases used to introduce new issues: "I hesitated to mention this before but now . . ." or, "While I'm at it, I might as well say this too. . . ." As long as functioning relations exist between individuals or groups, there are strong inhibitions upon introducing any issue which might impair the functioning. In a sense the stable relation suppresses topics which might upset it. But once the stability of the relation *is* upset, the suppressed topics can come to the surface uninhibitedly. We suggest that exactly the same mechanisms are at work in the community as a whole; networks of relations, however complex, act in the same fashion.

But in many other cases, illustrated best by political disputes, the diversification of issues is more a purposive move on the part of the antagonists, and serves quite a different function: to solidify opinion and bring in new participants by providing new bases of response. Again, this is evident in the two-person argument: each antagonist brings to bear all the *different* arguments he can to rationalize his position to himself and to convince his opponent. Just the same thing occurs in community conflict: each side attempts to increase solidarity and win new adherents from the still uncommitted neutrals by introducing as many diverse issues as will benefit its cause. Both these functions —increasing solidarity among present members, and gaining new members— are vital; the first aids in the important task of "girding for action" by disposing of all doubts and hesitancies; the second gains allies, always an important aim in community conflict. . . .

Disagreement to antagonism

A third change in the nature of issues as a controversy develops is the shift from *disagreement* to *antagonism.* A dispute which began dispassionately, in a disagreement over issues, is characterized suddenly by personal slander, by rumor, by the focusing of direct hostility. This is one of the most important aspects in the self-generation of conflict: Once set in motion, hostility can sustain conflict unaided by disagreement about particular issues. The original issues may be settled, yet the controversy continues unabated. The antagonistic relationship has become direct: it no longer draws sustenance from an outside element—an issue. As in an argument between friends, a discussion which begins with *disagreement* on a point in question often ends with each *disliking* the other.[2] The dynamics which account for the shift from disagreement to antagonism are two: "involuntary" and deliberate. Simmel explains the involuntary process by saying that it is "expedient" and "appropriate" to hate one's opponent just as it is "appropriate" to like someone who agrees with you (1955, p. 34). But perhaps there is a stronger explanation: we associate with every person we know

[2] Conversely, a relationship which begins with two people *agreeing* in tastes and interests often ends with both *liking one another.* For a discussion of the process through which this occurs, see R. Merton and P. Lozarsfeld, "Friendship As a Social Process," in *Freedom and Control in Modern Society,* M. Berger, T. Abel, and C. Page (eds.), New York: Van Nostrand, 1954.

Georg Simmel notes the formal similarities between relations of positive and negative attachments, contrasting these with the *absence* of relationship. He suggests that the psychological processes generating antagonism are just as fundamental as those generating liking. Simmel also notes the difference between a negative relationship based on disagreement over an outside object, and one which needs no such object, but is directly antagonistic. See Simmel (1955, p. 34, 36, passim), and Coser (1956).

certain beliefs, interests, traits, attributes, etc. So long as we disagree with only one or a few of his beliefs, we are "divided" in our feelings toward him. He is not wholly black or white in our eyes. But when we quarrel, the process or argument itself generates new issues; we disagree with more and more of our opponent's beliefs. Since these beliefs constitute *him* in our eyes, rather than isolated aspects of him, his image grows blacker. Our hostility is directed toward him personally. Thus the two processes—the first leading from a single issue to new and different ones, and the second leading from disagreement to direct antagonism—fit together perfectly and help carry the controversy along its course.[3] Once direct antagonism is felt toward an opponent, one is led to make public attacks on him.

Perhaps it would be fruitful to set down a little more precisely the "involuntary" processes which we suggest operate to shift issues from one disagreement to a multitude, ultimately to antagonism. In a diagram it might look something like that shown below.

Men have a strong need (discussed in detail in the final chapter) for consistency. If I disagree violently with someone, then it becomes psychologically more comfortable to see him as totally black rather than gray.[4] This

drive for consistency may provide the fuel for the generalization processes in steps 3 and 4 below.

Apart from these "involuntary" or "natural" processes, the use of personal charges by the antagonists is a common device to bypass disagreement and go directly to antagonism. Sometimes consciously, often unconsciously, the opposing nuclei attempt to reach new people through this means, drawing more and more of the community to their side by creating personal hostility to the opponent.[5,6] In political disputes the degeneration to personal charges is particularly frequent. . . .

Changes in content and character of issues constitutes only one kind of change going on in the development of a controversy; at the same time, the

---

[3] It should be emphasized that these suggestions for processes are highly tentative; systematic research into the psychological dynamics involved in these changing relations would contribute greatly to our knowledge about the development of controversy.

[4] One might speculate that this tendency would be stronger among those who tend to personalize easily; they move more quickly perhaps from specific disagreement to hostility toward

the opponent as a whole. Feuds among hill people (who are highly "person-oriented"), for example, seem to bear this out. Thus the course of controversy may vary greatly in two communities, simply as a result of differences in "person-orientation."

[5] The general process by which new people respond to such appeals is discussed more fully later under the heading "Social relations as a basis of response."

[6] Whether or not persons previously neutral can be brought into the controversy seems to depend greatly upon the time at which they are confronted with the alternative. If the antagonists are too involved too early they are viewed with puzzlement and distaste and detachment by neutrals. The situation is much the same as confronts a man arriving sober in the middle of a drunken party; he cannot join in because these people are "too far gone" for him to experience the events of the party as they do. The similarity between an orgy of community controversy and a drunken orgy is more than superficial in this and other respects. People collectively "forget themselves" in ways they may be ashamed of later. One of the major questions of community conflict concerns the processes through which this "forgetting" occurs.

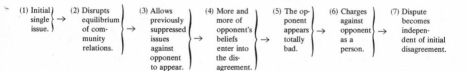

(1) Initial single issue. → (2) Disrupts equilibrium of community relations. → (3) Allows previously suppressed issues against opponent to appear. → (4) More and more of opponent's beliefs enter into the disagreement. → (5) The opponent appears totally bad. → (6) Charges against opponent as a person. → (7) Dispute becomes independent of initial disagreement.

whole structure of organizations and associations in the community is undergoing change as well. The nature of these changes is examined below.

CHANGES IN THE SOCIAL ORGANIZATION OF THE COMMUNITY

Polarization of social relations

As controversy develops associations flourish *within* each group, but wither *between* persons on opposing sides. People break off long-standing relationships, stop speaking to former friends who have been drawn to the opposition, but proliferate their associations with fellow-partisans. Again, this is part of the process of stripping for action: getting rid of all social encumbrances which impede the action necessary to win the conflict. Polarization is perhaps less pronounced in short-term conflicts, and in those in which the issues cut across existing organizational ties and informal relations. But in all conflicts, it tends to alter the social geography of the community to separate it into two clusters, breaking apart along the line of least attachment.

The formation of partisan organizations

In many types of community conflict, there are no existing organizations to form the nuclei of the two sides. But as the controversy develops, organizations form. In a recent controversy in Cincinnati over the leftwing political history of the city planning director, supporters of the director and of the councilman who hired him formed a "Committee of 150 for Political Morality."[7] This committee used considerable sophistication in the selection of a name and in their whole campaign. Rather than remain on the defensive, and let

[7] W. Hessler, "It Didn't Work in Cincinnati," *The Reporter,* IX, (Dec. 22, 1953), 13–17.

the opposition blanket the community with charges of subversion, this committee invoked an equally strong value —of morality in politics—and took the offensive against the use of personal attack by their opponents. This technique constitutes a way in which controversy can be held on a relatively high plane: by invoking community norms against smears, using these very norms as an issue of the controversy. If the norm is strong, it may keep the controversy "within bounds."

In general, as a dispute intensifies the partisans form *ad hoc* groups which have numerous functions while the controversy lasts: they serve as communication centers, as communication becomes more and more important within each side and attenuates between groups; they serve as centers for planning and organizing partisan meetings and other activities; and especially they can meet quickly—in a situation where speed is of utmost importance— any threat or challenge posed by the opposition.

The most common variation upon this theme is the union; in industrial disputes, the union is a defense organization *already* in existence; in a real controversy, it takes on all the aspects of the usual partisan organizations: secrecy, spirited meetings, pamphleteering, fundraising.[8]

The emergence of new leaders

As partisan organizations are formed and a real nucleus develops around each of the opposing centers, new leaders tend to take over the dispute; often they are men who have not been community leaders in the past, men who

[8] See Pope's graphic account of union operations in Gastonia, North Carolina, and Jones's discussion of union activity in Akron. L. Pope, *Millhands and Preachers,* New Haven: Yale University Press, 1942, A. Jones, *Life, Liberty and Property,* Philadelphia: Lippincott, 1941.

face none of the constraints of maintaining a previous community position, and feel none of the cross-pressures felt by members of community organizations. In addition, these leaders rarely have real identification with the community. In the literature they often emerge as marginal men who have never held a position of leadership before. A study of the fight against city-manager plans pictures the leaders of the opposition as men personally frustrated and maladjusted (Stene and Floro, 1953, p. 21–39). The current desegregation fights have produced numerous such leaders, often young, one a former convict, usually from the outside (*Life,* 1954; *Southern School News,* 1956).

The new leaders, at any rate, are seldom moderates; the situation itself calls for extremists. And such men have not been conditioned, through experience in handling past community problems, to the prevailing norms concerning tactics of dispute.

One countertendency appears in the development of these organizations and the emergence of their leaders. In certain conflicts, e.g., in Cincinnati, one side will be composed primarily of community leaders, men of prestige and responsibility in the community. Though such groups carry on the functions of a partisan organization, they act not to lower the level of controversy, but to *maintain* or raise it. As did the Committee of 150 (and the ADA in Norwalk, Connecticut, and other groups in other controversies), they attempt to invoke the community's norms against personal attacks and unrestrained conflict. Sometimes (as in Cincinnati) they are successful, sometimes not.

In the face of all the pressures toward increasing intensity and freedom from normal constraint this last development is puzzling. The source of the reversal

seems to be this: in certain controversies (particularly those having to do with the accusation of subversion), one side derives much of its strength from personal attacks and derogation, that is, from techniques which, were they not legitimated by patriotism or sex codes or similar strong values, would be outlawed by the community. Thus, to the degree that such methods are permitted, the attackers gain; and to the degree that community norms are upheld against these methods, the advantage is to the attacked. The more the attacked side can invoke the norms defining legitimate controversy, the more likely it is to win.

Invocation of community constraints is almost the sole force *generated by the conflict itself* which acts in a restraining direction. It is a very special force, and which appears to operate *only* under the conditions discussed above. Even so, it represents one means by which some controversies may be contained within bounds of normal community decision making.

Community organizations as the controversy develops

As conflict develops, the community's organizations tend to be drawn in, just as individual members are. It may be the American Legion, the PTA, the church, the local businessmen's association; if its members are drawn into the controversy, or if it can lend useful support, the organization will be under pressure from one or both sides to enter the controversy. This varies, of course, with the nature of the organization and the nature of the dispute.

At the same time there are often strong pressures, both within the organization and without, to remain neutral. From within: if its members hold opposing sentiments, then their disharmony forces the organization itself to remain neutral. And from without: the organization must maintain a public position in the community which might be endangered by taking sides in a partisan battle threatening to split the community. . . .

In sum, both community organizations and community leaders are faced with constraints when a dispute arises; the formation of a combat group to carry on the controversy and the emergence of a previous unknown as the combat leader are in part results of the immobility of responsible organizations and leaders. Both the new leader and the new organization are freed from some of the usual shackles of community norms and internal cross-pressures which make preexisting organizations and leaders tend to soften the dispute. . . .

The increasing use of word-of-mouth communication

As the controversy proceeds, the formal media of communication—radio, television, and newspapers—become less and less able to tell people *as much* as they want to know about the controversy, or the *kinds of things* they want to know. These media are simply not flexible enough to fill the insatiable need for news which develops as people become more and more involved. At the same time, the media are restricted by normative and legal constraints against carrying the kind of rumor which abounds as controversy proceeds. Word-of-mouth communication gradually fills the gaps, both in volume and in content, left by the mass media. Streetcorner discussion amplifies, elaborates, and usually distorts the news that it picks up from the papers or the radio. This interpersonal communication offers no restraints against slander and personal charges; rather, it helps make the rhetoric of controversy consistent with the intensity.

SUMMARY

Several characteristic events carry the controversy toward its climax. The most important changes in *issues* are: (1) from specific disagreements to more general ones, (2) elaboration into new and different disagreements, and (3) a final shift from disagreement to direct antagonism. The changes in the *social organization* of the community are as follows: the polarization of social relations as the controversy intensifies, as the participants cut off relations with those who are not on their side, and elaborate relations with those who are; the formation of partisan organizations and the emergence of new, often extremist partisan leaders to wage the war more efficiently; and the mobilization of existing community organizations on one side or the other. Finally, as the pace quickens and the issues become personal, word-of-mouth communication replaces the more formal media. It now remains to examine some of the reciprocal causations constituting the "vicious circles" or "run-away processes" so evident in conflict. These should give somewhat more insight into the mechanisms responsible for the growth of conflict.

RECIPROCAL CAUSATION AND THE DEVELOPING DISPUTE

The inner dynamics of controversy derive from a number of mutually reinforcing relations; one element is enhanced by another, and, in turn, enhances the first, creating an endless spiral.[9] Some of the most important

[9] The dynamics of controversy is a topic for the theoretician in sociology; it comes as close as any area of social life to constituting a closed system, in which all the effects are from variables within the system. When a theory of controversy does exist, the sets of mutually reinforcing relations like those examined in this section will constitute the heart of the theory.

relations depend heavily upon this reciprocal reinforcement; if one or more of these cycles can be *broken,* then a disagreement already on the way to real conflict can be diverted into normal channels.

Mutual reinforcement of response

Relations between people contain a built in reciprocity. I smile at you; if you smile back, I speak to you; you respond, and a relationship has begun. At each step, my reaction is contingent upon yours, and yours, in turn, contingent upon mine.[10] *If* you fail to smile, but scowl instead, I may say a harsh word; you respond in kind, and another chain of mutual reinforcement builds up—this time toward antagonism. It is such chains which constitute not only the fundamental character of interpersonal relations, but also the fundamental cycle of mutual effects in controversy. Breaking that cycle requires much effort. The admonition to "turn the other cheek" is not easily obeyed.

The direct reinforcement of response, however, is but one—the most obvious—of the mutually reinforcing relations which constitute the dynamics of controversy. Others, more tenuous, are more easily broken.

The mutual effects of social and psychological polarization

As participants in a dispute become psychologically "consistent," shedding doubts and hesitancies, they shun friends who are uncommitted, and elaborate their associations with those who feel the way they do. In effect, the psychological polarization leads

[10] Talcott Parsons who studies this characteristic of interpersonal relations in detail, speaks of it as the "double-contingency of interpersonal relations." Parsons has a full discussion of this aspect of relations between persons. T. Parsons, *The Social System,* Glencoe: The Free Press, 1951.

to social polarization. The latter, in turn, leads to mutual reinforcement of opinions, that is, to further psychological polarization. One agrees more and more with his associates (and disagrees more and more with those he *doesn't* talk to), and comes to associate more and more with those who agree with him. Increasingly, his opponents' position seems preposterous—and, in fact, it *is* preposterous, as in his own; neither position feeds on anything but reinforcing opinions.

The outcome, of course, is the division of the community into two socially and attitudinally separate camps, each convinced it is absolutely right. The lengths to which this continually reinforcing cycle will go in any particular case depends on the characteristics of the people and the community involved. . . . It is these characteristics which provide one "handle" for reducing the intensity of community conflict.

Polarization and intensity: within the individual and within each side

As the participants become psychologically polarized, all their attitudes mutually reinforcing, the *intensity* of their feeling increases. One of the consequences is that inconsistencies within the individual are driven out; thus he becomes even more psychologically polarized, in turn developing a greater intensity.

This chain of mutual enforcement lies completely *within* the individual. But there is an analogous chain of reinforcement on the social level. As social polarization occurs (that is, the proliferation of associations among those who feel one way, and the attenuation of association between those who feel differently), one's statements meet more and more with a positive response; one is more and more free to express the full intensity of his feeling. The "atmosphere" of the group is open for the kind of intensity of feeling that previously had to remain unexpressed. This atmosphere of intensity, in turn, further refines the group; it becomes intolerable that anyone who believes differently maintain association within the group.

These are examples of reciprocal causation in community conflict, as they appear in the literature of these controversies. They constitute the chains which carry controversy from beginning to end as long as they remain unbroken, but which also provide the means of softening the conflict if methods can be found to break them. It is important to note that these reciprocal relations, once set in motion by outside forces, become independent of them and continue on their own. The one continuing force at work is the drive of each side to win, which sets in motion the processes described above; it carries the conflict forward "under its own steam," so to speak. But reciprocal relations also affect the initial drive, amplifying it, changing it; no longer is it simply a drive to win, but an urge to ruin the opponents, strip them of their power, in effect, annihilate them. This shift in goals, itself a part of a final chain of reciprocal causation, drives these processes onward with ever more intensity.

Gresham's law of conflict

The processes may be said to create a "Gresham's law of conflict": the harmful and dangerous elements drive out those which would keep the conflict within bounds. Reckless, unrestrained leaders head the attack; combat organizations arise to replace the milder, more constrained preexisting organizations; derogatory and scurrilous charges replace dispassionate issues; antagonism replaces disagreement, and a drive to ruin the opponent takes the place of the initial will to win. In other words, all the forces put into effect by the initiation of conflict act to drive out the conciliatory elements, replace them with those better equiped for combat.

32
A Model for Civil Rights Change through Conflict*
JAMES H. LAUE

Viewing *power* as the *control over decisions,* and *social change* as the continuous process of *redistribution of power* within social systems, this essay examines the role of conflict in the extensive changes in American racial patterns in the last ten years. It develops a framework to help explain what has happened, and raises questions about the nature and directions of racial change today and in the next few years. The model[1] is intended to have general applicability to processes of change through conflict.[2]

I have seen communities go through a common sequence of stages in working out desegregation and elimination of certain discriminatory practices in response to challenges from minority groups. The phase-structure of social change presented here was developed in response to the data from my research on the direct action movement of the early 1960's in more than one hundred southern communities, with particular emphasis on the sit-ins and Freedom Rides.[3] In every community, the pattern seemed to be the same: challenge by the minority group, a period of overt community conflict cresting in a crisis, the drawing of hither-

*["Power, Conflict, and Social Change," by James H. Laue, is reprinted from *Riots and Rebellion: Civil Violence in the Urban Community,* edited by Louis H. Masotti and Don R. Bowen (1968) pp. 85–96, by permission of the publisher, Sage Publications, Inc.]

to uninvolved elements of white power into negotiation, and the working out of some change.

MINORITIES AND POWER

The model is called the 7 C's. It is an attempt to systematize the process which I saw occurring in city after city as desegregation was achieved. It starts with the assumption implied at the beginning of the essay, that significant social change takes place when new combinations of community power groups emerge to force an alteration in the perceived self-interest of the powerful and, therefore, a change in their priorities for actions. Direct action achieved success as a technique for forcing certain concessions because it developed a new source of power within groups which did not have sufficient amounts of the normal sources of power-for-change in a democratic system. Lacking sufficient political and economic power, Negroes used the only form remaining to them—their bodies. Through the testing and refining of direct action techniques (literally "putting your body on the line"), the movement developed negotiable forms of power. In turn, legislation and other action stimulated by the civil rights movement have begun to equip Negroes more adequately with the standard forms of political and economic power.

In explaining how redistribution of community power occurs through the 7 C's phase-structure, I begin with an eighth C: competition. Competition is a constant in all social interaction. All the stages of the model are varying forms of the competitive process. Competition is the process whereby persons quietly oppose one another in seeking the scarce rewards they have learned to want. It is, in this statement, close to what Sumner meant by "antagonistic cooperation."[4] It is a natural, ever-

present condition of all social interaction, and the starting point for any analysis of social change. The holders of power in all social systems try to suppress the notion that certain types of competition exist. The American race-related version, once restricted to the South but now heard increasingly in northern cities in only slightly altered language, is "our colored people are (or were) happy."

THE 7 C's

The 7 C's—the stages communities have transacted in working out change in racial patterns—are:

1 Challenge
2 Conflict
3 Crisis
4 Confrontation
5 Communication
6 Compromise
7 Change

1 *Challenge* is the open and dramatic presentation of demands and grievances by the minority, including the range from single specific grievances to an attack on the whole pattern of systematic discrimination in a community. The challenge is usually a last resort after less public approaches (educational and legal, for instance) have failed to bring significant communication or change. The classic example is the sit-in. Others are marches, picketing, or other well-publicized challenges to the status quo, such as lawsuits or boycotts.

2 *Conflict* is intensified competition of which a substantial proportion of the community is now aware. An accumulation of challenges brings ever-present competition to the surface, and it breaks through into overt conflict. Traditional mechanisms of social control are no longer able to manage the increasing frequency of challenges.

3 *Crisis* exists when elites with the power to change the discriminatory patterns challenged *define* the situation as severe enough to demand immediate action and rapid resolution. They have, that is, changed their perception of their own self-interest and what it will take to maintain and expand it. When the powerful decide to act, the crisis has been achieved.

Crisis thus is a subjective power-term, determined by the plans and actions of the powerful, rather than by the objective conditions of the situation. Some of the conditions which have persuaded the powerful to make the crisis-definition are demonstrations, boycotts, economic loss, damage to the city's image, a court decision on desegregation, violence—or the seriously anticipated threat of any of the above. Once the crisis-definition is made, for whatever reasons, the meeting of at least some of the demands presented in the challenge is inevitable, and the process usually hurries through the final stages to change.

4 *Confrontation* takes place when the decisionmakers being challenged recognize that the minority group has legitimate demands which can no longer be explained away, but which must be dealt with. If there is a stage in the process in which normative awareness develops on the part of the powerful, that is it. Awareness of the moral legitimacy of demands results from the harder realities of economic and political awareness learned in the previous stage. At least it may be said that the challenge-targets are more suggestible and more receptive to previously rejected change proposals and persons.

5 *Communication* is direct, face-to-face negotiation between the challengers and the dominant group(s), each now bargaining from a position of power. Postcrisis communication is always more frank and goal-directed than precrisis communication, for the powerful have been forced to drop defenses and take positive steps to remedy problems of which everyone is now consciously aware. The newfound power of the challengers consists of threats (to create further crises if certain demands are not met) and promises (*not* to create crisis if demands *are* met).

6 *Compromise* is a result of the bargaining which takes place in stage 5, and usually requires the enlistment (often covert) of community power resources beyond the parties in the communication process. There are victories and concessions for all communicating parties, with each faction usually asking for more than it expects to gain, in preparation for the anticipated giving in of the compromise stage.

7 *Change* is, by definition, the achievement by the protesters of at least some of the goals set forth in the challenge.

OTHER DIMENSIONS OF THE MODEL

There are several qualifications and subsidiary processes regarding the operation of this system. First, the model as outlined here recognizes that there are many centers and sources of power in communities and nations, and that the 7 C's process therefore operates simultaneously at many levels. Community power structure is not seen as monolithic, but rather as a series of interacting and interlocking systems—which means that the conflict process may operate within and between systems as well as in relation to the total community. It is macro as well as micro.

Second, the system *cycles*—that is, it runs its course on different issues over and over again in communities, with the stage 7 resolution of one conflict situation becoming the plateau upon which new challenges arise. A good example is Nashville, which in the years from 1960 through 1963 went through virtually the same process of appeal, Negro demonstration, white violence, boycott, arrests, community concern, and change on four different desegregation issues: lunch counters, theaters, retail employment, and the better restaurants. The emergence of the early stages does not always mean the cycle will run its course, however. It may get bogged down at any stage, then remain latent until sufficient challenges are taken up again. This was the case with Albany, Georgia, in 1961 and 1962, when the process never got past the conflict stage despite white retail losses of more than 60 percent. Local white influentials refused to make the crisis-definition, and eventually the movement lost momentum.

Lateral communication operates when nonconflict cities move to make change because of conflict and crisis in other communities. An avoidance model quickly develops. In Carolina and Virginia cities, significant changes which had been the object of protest for many months came about in a matter of days in mid-1963, because Birmingham was on. A typical northern example came from Philadelphia in August 1967 largely as a result of the message from Detroit. The city's business leaders discovered 1,200 jobs "for the idle poor" in response to the mayor's "call for help in easing ghetto tensions" and his statement that such hiring is "not now a matter of charity, but an investment in our community."[5]

Short circuiting is the process whereby communities move directly from stages 1 or 2 to stage 5 or even 6. They have recognized, based on previous local experience or contemporary lateral communication, that the change being demanded by the challengers is inevitable, and that it is in the self-interest of the powerful to move directly to communication (stage 5) or to the sixth stage of active reordering of priorities and enlistment of other community resources for change. A dramatic southern example is the immediate compliance of Albany, Georgia, officials, with the 1964 Civil Rights Act, telling newsmen, "Of course we're going to obey the law. We don't want Martin Luther King coming down here again."[6] Short circuiting of the change process also will be one result, I believe, of the current public and private sector activities responsive to the summer's urban racial violence.

The other side of the short-circuiting process, however, is the *neutralization of crisis*. Crisis tolerances change as communities learn to combat direct action and other forms of challenges. In most cities in the early 1960's, sit-ins were enough to stimulate a crisis-definition, but today they are dealt with as a matter of course and are generally not effective as a change technique. A surprising exception took place in early June 1967 in Boston, however, when policemen tried to disperse a group of welfare mothers sitting and lying-in overnight in a public building, and triggered two days of violent conflict between Negroes and the police.

From the viewpoint of systemic integration, it can be added that the operation of the 7 C's is, in the long run, a healthy process. Although conflict is disruptive in the short run, it serves to bring systemic stresses to the surface and forces communities to confront them and deal with them forthrightly, as Lewis Coser and others have pointed out.[7] Conflict is not the cause of social system stresses—rather it is a symptom, a process whereby the stresses may be transformed for remedial action. Andrew Young of the Southern Christian Leadership Conference has summed it up best in lay terms. "The movement did not 'cause' problems in Selma, as Sheriff Jim Clark and others claimed," Young says. "It just brought them to the surface where they could be dealt with. Sheriff Clark has been beating black heads in the back of the jail on Saturday night for years, and we're only saying to him that if he still wants to beat heads he'll have to do it on Main Street at noon in front of CBS, NBC, and ABC television cameras."

CASES IN POINT, SOUTH AND NORTH

There are other examples from hundreds of communities of how conflict-produced crises have forced white power to enable changes in racial patterns, a few of which may be mentioned here. Desegregation of lunch counters took place in more than two hundred southern cities within a year after the sit-in movement began in February 1960. The Freedom Rides took place in May of 1961, Alabama whites provided the violent counterpoint, the federal government intervened—and by November a Federal Communications Commissions order was issued (and enforced) banning discrimination in interstate transportation facilities.

Atlanta and Birmingham offer other instructive empirical cases. The different crisis-tolerances in these cities is directly reflected in the case with which change takes place, and the extent of the change. In Atlanta, a few sit-ins and arrests, SNCC picketing and Klan counterpicketing were enough to mobilize the necessary power centers for change. But in Birmingham it took Bull Connor, police dogs, fire hoses, 3,500 arrests, and pictures transmitted all over the nation and world before the "Committee of 100" got itself organized to make changes it had been capable of making all along.

It has worked in the North, too. In 1967 in Cleveland, Sealtest short-circuited the 7 C's by responding to the threat of a boycott with a $300,000 program for job training and community development in the Hough ghetto—a program it had been capable of delivering for some time. In Chicago, the Daley machine responded to SCLC's challenges in 1966 by giving minor concessions at the first push on housing inspection and enforcement and other targets. The Chicago Metropolitan Council for Open Cities, which is now working actively with the endorsement of corporate, labor, religious, and political elites, came into being after a summer of Negro open-housing demonstrations and violent white responses. The council was, in effect, a trade for King's agreeing not to lead a massive march into Cicero.

At a national level, the Civil Rights Act of 1964 and the Voting Rights Act of 1965 are direct results of the operation of the 7 C's process. After three years of direct action throughout the South, Birmingham produced a crisis-definition in the national administration in May of 1963. President Kennedy proposed the act within a month, communicated on nationwide television using ever-present but previously unused Biblical and constitutional value statements, and the administration

fought the bill through the compromise process of the Congress to enactment and the beginning of the change process within a year. The phase-structure of passage of the 1965 Voting Rights Act was much the same: the beating at the Selma bridge in March of 1965, a dramatic film clip on national television the next night, mobilization of national support by the movement, President Johnson going before the Congress and national prime-time television several weeks later to request legislation and say "We shall overcome," the passage of the act four months later in July, and the registration of more than 1.5 million new southern Negro voters within the next two years.

BUT DOES IT STILL WORK?

But a look at Congress, the urban violence, and the poll data on white attitudes today makes me seriously ask, "Do the 7 C's still work?" . . .

I question whether the model has long-range applicability as the racial focus moves urban and North because of two conditions which must be met if a social system is to achieve change through conflict:

1 The 7 C's can only operate in a social system in which the superordinate power *permits* conflict as a way of doing change. The 7 C's would not have worked in Nazi Germany; rather a kind of short circuiting from challenge (1) to repressive change (7) would have taken place.

2 It appears that the superordinate power must not only permit conflict, but must in fact, approve of the goals of the protesters.

What operated in the South, then, was a concessions model in which Negroes challenged politically expendable cities, counties, and states, while the federal government permitted the conflict process to run its course through to change, and tacitly (and often openly) supported the goals of the protesters as being consistent with basic American values. The permissive superordinate power was the federal government, supported by the mass media and the white liberal-labor coalition.

But now it is the superordinate power itself which is under attack. The targets now are the federal government, the large northern cities (with their nonexpendable Democratic machines), "white liberals," the mass media, judges who do not enforce housing codes, the real estate industry—in short, the whole middle class establishment, including people who write articles like this and people who read them. It was easy for the superordinate power in its various forms to support conflict in Alabama and Mississippi: the moral issues were seemingly clear, the devils were readily available in brutal sheriffs and unattractive politicians, and it was far away. But the same persons, newspapers, private organizations, and government officials who endorsed the movement's implicit use of the 7 C's process in the South, now confuse demonstrations with riots and label southern protest techniques turned northward as ill-considered and irresponsible.

An important theoretical question, then, is whether the American black movement needs and can find a higher superordinate power to legitimate and support its activities. Contacts of civil rights groups with revolutionaries and established governments in Africa and Latin America have been increasing in the last year. SCLC is beginning to convert its program to an international base, as presaged by the late Dr. Martin Luther King's antiwar activity and the continuing work of some SCLC staff members in Africa. And the movement has long considered soliciting United Nations support in the struggle against American racism.

In the light of these recent shifts in targets and allies—and of the urban racial violence of the past summers—an even more important question is "Under what conditions will the crisis-definition become repressive?" In the current statement of the 7 C's, the crisis-definition is essentially oriented to democratizing change. It assumes, within the context of a sympathetic superordinate power, that crisis always moves the targets of the challenge toward actions supporting desegregation and equal opportunity.

In addition to specifying the conditions under which the crisis-definition becomes repressive, we need to develop an alternate version of the stages following crisis.

Political and military reactions to the 1967 urban summer violence lead some to speculate that political leadership at both local and national levels is closer to a repressive crisis-definition in relation to an American minority group than at any time since the Japanese "relocation" in World War II.

"Don't reward the rioters" sentiment is high among whites, and black ghettos are full of rumors that the concentration camps are ready—and the wry comment that ghettos are too ecologically strategic for the Man to bomb the people.

The rise of black nationalism confirms the hostility of white leaders: "Look at all we have done for them in the last few years, and now they're saying maybe they don't even want integration!" To the consternation of whites, the slain Malcolm X is coming to be the same kind of hero for many black ghetto people that the slain John Kennedy is for many white liberals.

Despite the intensifying confrontation between white sentiment for law and order and black sentiment for change, there are some tentative signs that the 7 C's are operating for change on schedule, at least at the national level. . . .

But in the face of these positive change-oriented responses, we must raise the question of how long the essentially expressive violence of the summer outbursts will be tolerated by the national political system. We can predict with some degree of confidence that the system will soon develop repressive crisis-responses if the violence moves from the expressive level to the strategic or political. And with somewhat less certainty, I suggest that city and national administration leaders will not long permit the kind of massive applications of nonviolent direct action techniques to northern urban systems of government, transportation, and commerce that SCLS led in Washington, D.C., in the spring and summer of 1968.

THE THEORETICAL
TASKS AHEAD

I look forward to the unfolding of events in the next few years as they inform the unfolding of this particular change model. In summary, I believe that the next tasks in the theory's development are:

1 Develop a typology of the antecedent conditions which can predict whether the crisis-definition will be *democratic* or *repressive*, and develop an alternate version of the stages that follow a repressive crisis-definition.

2 Determine the social structural prerequisites for movement of the process from phase to phase.[9]

3 Develop a model to sort out the interaction patterns and interchanges within and between systems in conflict, with special attention to repressive and counterrevolutionary variables.

4 Develop a hierarchy of negotiable issues — and of meaningful concessions available to urban white power — as a guide to prediction of racial conflict and change patterns in the next few years.

If negotiable issues between urban blacks and whites can be found, then the 7 C's process will continue to oper-

ate in the urban North as satisfying concessions are elicited. If not — if the superordinate powers under attack move steadily toward repressive crisis-definitions — then the kind of conflict theory discussed here will seem pale in the face of the realities of violent change to come.

FOOTNOTES

[1] This paper's outline of the change-through-conflict process is consciously called a "model" rather than a "theory" because, at this level of its development, it provides only a set of sequential categories for understanding the process — not structural determinants for explanation and prediction.

[2] Other change processes involving lesser degrees of conflict include drift and rational means-ends chains (planned change through legislation or moderate private social reform measures).

[3] Data throughout this essay are drawn largely from my doctoral dissertation, "Direct Action and Desegregation: Toward a Theory of the Rationalization of Protest" (Harvard University, 1966) and from written and personal sources available to me in the course of my work in the Community Relations Service since 1965.

[4] William Graham Sumner, *Folkways* (New York: Dover, 1959; originally published in 1906), pp. 16–18.

[5] United Press International, August 10, 1967.

[6] Associated Press, July 3, 1964.

[7] Lewis Coser, *The Functions of Social Conflict* (New York: Free Press, 1965), and *Continuities in the Study of Social Conflict* (New York: Free Press, 1967); Kenneth F. Boulding, *Conflict and Defense* (New York: Harper and Row, 1962); and Thomas Schelling, *The Strategy of Conflict* (Cambridge: Harvard Univ. Press, 1960).

[8] This task, begun in my dissertation, is being expanded in *The Black Movement: A Social History of Protest in the 1960's* with Martin Oppenheimer, in preparation.

33
Stages in Campus Polarization*
JOHN P. SPIEGEL

In describing campus polarization, I shall treat it as a crisis occuring in four stages, each characterized by a sequence of actions and reactions. There is a risk of overgeneralization or unwarranted stereotyping in such an approach, but whether or not the four stages to be described really fit all situations is not so important as the advantage gained through imposing some clarity and order on the dynamics of the arousal, escalation, and decline of group hostilities.

THE COMING OF HOSTILITIES

The premonitory phase is characterized by slowly mounting resentment with a number of students whom I will call, for the sake of generalization, the "aggrieved" group. Their anger is aroused by the failure of the administration of the school to respond rapidly enough, or at all, to their expressed desire for change within the institution. The desired changes vary from school to school, but in general they revolve around administrative policy with respect to three substantive issues: (1) the quality of education for black and white students, including reforms of the curriculum; (2) policies related to the conduct of war in Vietnam and the involvement of the university with military research and training; and (3) the rights of students to have a part in the determination of institutional policy of all sorts.

In the minds of the aggrieved group there is no question of the legitimacy of the desired changes. Within the student body as a whole, however,

*[Reprinted with permission from *Trans-action*, October 1969. Copyright © October 1969 by Trans-action, Inc., New Brunswick, New Jersey.]

there is a spectrum of opinion ranging from active support through apathy to opposition. For this reason, the first administrative response to the proposals of the aggrieved group is likely to be perfunctory. Meetings between representatives of the aggrieved students and the administration, if they occur at all, are viewed by the administration mainly as opportunities for the students to express their feelings in hope that this will satisfy them. No real change is expected or envisioned by the authorities.

After a certain lapse of time without progress or change, the aggrieved students begin increasingly to see themselves in an adversary role vis-à-vis the administration. The current of the times asserts itself in the thinking of the aggrieved group, sometimes aided by visits from activist student groups at other institutions. Ideas originally defined as suggestions or proposals become talked about as "demands," and with this hardening and growing spirit of militancy within the aggrieved group come changes both within the general student body and within the administration. An increasing number of students identify themselves with the goals of the aggrieved students, though not necessarily with their activism, mainly because they share the others' resentment at the failure of the administration to consider requests for change with the proper seriousness. A large portion of the student body, in other words, feels vicariously slighted.

Representatives of the administration are usually aware of the changing attitudes of the students, but they tend to misinterpret them in the light of their own stake in avoiding rapid or abrupt change. Since the goals of change are still not taken seriously, administrators discount or dismiss the entire effort through a process of labeling designed to split the student body. Leaders of the aggrieved group are called "radicals," "anarchists," and a variety of other names. In private conversation they are often identified as spoiled, pampered products of well-to-do permissive parents or as disturbed youngsters in need of psychiatric attention. Their followers among the more moderate students are regarded as well-intentioned and essentially fair-minded romantic dupes. The labeling reflects the growth on both sides of the mistrust and disrespect whose unconscious origins I shall examine later in this essay.

Toward the end of the premonitory phase some subtle cleavages within the administration begin to appear, though they are still papered over with politeness. Some members of the administrative group, usually from the social science departments' faculty or from the counseling services, adopt a sympathetic, liberal attitude toward the changes requested by the students. They then urge, to the distress of others, that the college president, the deans, the school superintendent, or whoever stands for "officialdom," modify the rigid policy. These persons have usually been in face-to-face contact with some of the dissident students and perceive themselves as "honest brokers," presenting the students' case with intense sincerity and urgency. As a result of the advocate role of the "sympathizers," the spokesmen for the administration now shift their tactics to some degree. Representatives of the aggrieved group are seen and listened to more attentively. Some of their demands are accepted as potentially legitimate and the administrators promise to channel them through the bureaucratic machinery.

The crisis process is at this point in a paradoxical state. A temporary relaxation occurs because the aggrieved group of students believes it is finally making progress, while the administrators think they have finally defused a potential disruption. Actually, this is the calm before the storm. On both sides, the inevitable disappointment of unrealistically raised hopes is a guarantee of disaster. On the administrative side, the "channeling" procedure, at its best a clumsy matter, tends to get stalled because of uncertainties and disagreements about the best way of solving the problem or about whether it should be solved at all. In the students' view, the delays, mixed messages about what is taking place and the intimations of implacable rigidity behind a surface disguise of acceptance, all add up to a dead end: no possibility of progress.

INITIAL DISORDER

At this point, the crisis process moves toward the second phase: the initial disorder. Disillusioned, convinced that they have been deceived and that only the force of a dramatic act of protest can alter the situation in their favor, the aggrieved group begins to plan some form of disruption. At the same time, they elaborate and firm up previously (though tentatively) held hostile beliefs about the character and motives of the administration and of the social system it represents. The resulting ideological creed—for example, that the administration is authoritarian, bigoted, and hypocritical and that the social system is racist, oppressive, and resistant to change—thereupon is used to overcome moral scruples about the legal and ethical justification of the disruption being planned. (In saying this, I am not passing any judgment on the validity or lack of validity of the system of beliefs but merely describing a continuing process.)

So far all is prologue. The actual disorder that initiates the opening of the second phase may begin with a series of small demonstrations or with a major act such as seizing and holding a building. The students usually display contradictory moods that nevertheless fit together. They are excited and aggressive, even abusive, but fairly well-disciplined; exhibitionistic, but secretive; happy because they are finally taking action, but fearful of what it may lead to; defiant and uncommunicative, yet letting it be known that they would accept communication. An aura of unity and determination expressed in publicly stated "nonnegotiable demands" masks privately felt uncertainties and divisions of opinion. Despite these divisions, the aggrieved group is, at that moment, unified through the sharing of norm-violating behavior: they are all in the same boat.

The usual administrative response is shock. Under the impression that the new policy of bureaucratic openness to complaints has mollified the dissident students and reassured the moderates, the administration is unprepared for serious trouble. Still, some action must be taken, if only to relieve frustration and anger. Unfortunately, the administrators are faced simultaneously with two types of decisions, neither of which is easy to make: what to do about the "nonnegotiable demands" and how to deal with the disruption. Faced with this threat, the administrators have only a limited number of clear-cut options. They can:

Accept all the demands and ignore the norm-violating behavior. This capitulation by the administration promptly resolves the current situation. It is the least common solution.

Ignore the demands and throw out the offenders with the help of the police and other law enforcement agencies. Although this approach has been used, it brings about so many additional problems, particularly strong support for the militants by the moderates, that many administrators are reluctant to use it.

Ignore the norm-violating behavior while offering to negotiate the demands. Since this technique can easily be seen by the students as a "put-on" (with punishment to follow later) and since, from the side of the administration, it does not meet the challenge of illegal threat by the students, it is likely to result in a protracted stalemate. Nevertheless, it has been used.

Meet threat with threat by promising disciplinary procedures and punishments for the future while avoiding a confrontation and ignoring the demands, in the hope that the students will tire of their unproductive behavior and abandon it. Since they often do, this method can succeed.

Ignore both the norm-violating behavior and the demands by doing nothing and saying nothing. This produces an unsettling ambiguity and frustration for the students and gives the administration freedom to pursue any policy of punishment or nonpunishment or to sanction, negotiate, or deny any part of the demands, once the students abandon their norm-violating behavior. Any administration choosing this ambiguous policy must be certain of support from its various constituencies—faculty, trustees (or school committees), alumni, and the general public—who will probably not at all understand what the administration is doing. Because of the exacting conditions for its successful execution, this policy is seldom used.

Clear-cut as these policies may be, there is too much confusion and emotionalism and too little prior experience within the administration to permit the implementation of any one of them; also there are too many audiences to be taken into account. Instead, a seesaw struggle takes place around three, more intuitively developed positions: (1) a desire to support the goals of the aggrieved students while minimizing any loss of face to the institution for what may be interpreted as surrender. This position is usually termed "the soft line" advocated by the "doves." (2) A desire to defeat and punish the students while minimizing any loss of face to the institution for what may be interpreted as callousness or cruelty. This position is called "the hard line" advocated by the "hawks." (3) A middle ground, or temporizing position, which attempts to placate both the hawks and the doves in part and, again in part, to satisfy the demands of the students—a balancing process which requires the greatest diplomacy.

Since it takes some time for these positions to become crystallized, the administration is, for the time being, forced to delay action while contenting itself with ritualistic statements for public consumption, usually condemning the students' methods while expressing cautious sympathy for some of their goals.

MOUNTING POLARIZATION

The atmosphere now becomes increasingly acrimonious and conspiratorial; it is characterized by ad hoc committees, sudden summonses to meetings, secret emissaries mediating between rival factions, rumors and counter-rumors, student manifestos and the ever-present television crews and newspaper reporters on the lookout for interesting stories.

Polarizations grow by wild leaps into increasingly extreme positions: For the hawks any attempts to negotiate with the students *before* those "troublemakers" yield to punishment is anathema—a betrayal of everything the school as an intellectual establishment stands for. It is the end of reasoned inquiry, the death of scholarly detachment, the beginning of the politicalization of the school and thus the *finis* of academic freedom and dispassionate search for "the truth." For them, no decisions should be taken under threat of force. Nevertheless, they hold over the doves and the "temporizers" the threat of dire predictions. With thundering fervor, they foresee a general doom and schedule deadlines for specific catastrophes. Since, as they say, it is impossible to appease the students' hunger for violence and revolution, they guarantee that should their policy

lose out, another building will be seized, then another and another; next, the students will be running the institution, and in a year it will have collapsed altogether. To buttress the argument, analogies are summoned from all corners of history, with special emphasis on the Nazi and communist movements.

In addition to such fulminations, the hawks can scarcely conceal their contempt for the doves—those "bleeding hearts," those "masochists" who, perhaps unconsciously, are out to wreck the institution. On their side, the doves show a mild but persistent abhorrence of the wrath and, in their eyes, "sadism" of the hawks. Privately they tend to believe, for the moment at least, that most of the hawks are "paranoid personalities." In meetings and public discussions, however, they try to appeal to the hawk sense of reality by portraying in detail the way the aggrieved students have experienced the institution: its irrelevance, its arbitrary rules and regulations, and its unresponsiveness to student needs and especially to the need for shared communication. Such attempts at explanation are nevertheless perceived and dismissed by the hawks both as attacks upon the virtue of the academy and as apologies for deviant behavior.

Being men of the middle, the temporizers are not much persuaded by the logic of either the hawks or the doves. More realistic than the hawks about the actual extent of political influence present at the outset in the affairs of their institution, they are not so afraid of the loss of an already restricted academic freedom. Unlike the doves, they are worried by rapid social change of any sort, with its turbulence, its constant overhauling of administrative and appointment procedures, and its threat of loss of support from conservatives in the outside community. Moreover, they are drawn to the hawk position by a shared sense of indignation, though it is based on a different calculation. The temporizers have been impressed by the "liberalization" of American life in recent decades, the partial transformation of habitual "racist," "antistudent," or indifferent attitudes. Accordingly, they feel offended by the ingratitude of the aggrieved students, who in their view are "biting the hand that feeds them." This feeling is not shared by the hawks, who firmly believe that too much attention has been given the students to begin with; nor by the doves, who feel that the students have had too little attention. The function of this sense of betrayal, then, is to diminish the willingness of the temporizers to listen sympathetically to the students in the course of any negotiations—an effect in line anyway with their policy of delay. The sense of betrayal is shared by many persons in the general public who ask, with genuine annoyance and bewilderment, "What do those students want anyway?"

The polarization of the third phase is painful for most participants. Old friends find themselves unable to converse; people who have scarcely met fall into shouting matches; alliances hurriedly set up come crashing down, often undermined by gossipers. Meetings based on *Robert's Rules of Order* turn into travesties of rational discussion. Peacemakers by the dozen offer their own special formula for solving everything. No decision seems well-considered or objectively arrived at. The temptation to avoid or withdraw from the struggle is very strong.

RESOLUTION

Despite the appearance of chaos, the group process is actually moving toward resolution, the fourth phase of the crisis. The manner in which the crisis is re-

solved varies so much from institution to institution that no general description can be offered. The resolution can be either doveish, hawkish, or in line with the middle ground of the temporizers. But no matter which method resolves the crisis, there is likely to be some effort made to establish negotiations with the dissident students. The students, of course, do not acknowledge that such an event is occurring, since their demands are "nonnegotiable." Similarly, the administration must officially discount the process because they have usually stated publicly that no negotiation can take place under the condition of violence or threat. Accordingly, the contacts must be given another name, such as "explorations" or "clarification of demands."

There is no space to examine this process or to discuss the conflicts within the aggrieved group of students which it generates. Suffice it to say that if efforts actually are made to end the struggle, severe dissension occurs within the student group about how much or how little to settle for. Hardliners, often women adept at shaming the men, remind the group that *none* of the demands are negotiable. Moderates, arguing for a policy of realism, urge settling for what they regard as the administration's best possible offer. Extreme activists suggest escalating the disorder, while those with less taste for prolonged struggle indicate a reluctance to go on much longer. The hardening of attitudes within the student group about what policy to pursue is a process that Freud brilliantly described as "the narcissism of small differences."

An important aspect of the negotiations is the degree to which administration and student representatives at negotiating sessions miscommunicate. Identical words and expressions mean different things to the two parties. To the extent that this is the case, such sessions really *are* more for the sake of clarification than negotiation. In part, misunderstanding occurs because of the gap in values, beliefs, and experience separating the two groups. In part, the failure of communication is due to the novelty of such occasions and the absence of any traditional or agreed-upon style of conduct for the procedures, such as characterize labor bargaining sessions. But in large part, the communication failures are also the product of unconscious psychological processes. . . .

34
*The Formation of Contrast Conceptions**
TAMOTSU SHIBUTANI and
KIAN M. KWAN

From time immemorial men involved in conflict have committed the most vicious deeds against one another. They have fought with great courage and determination, only to wonder afterward whether victory was worth the sacrifice. This has happened over and over, and one wonders why men do things in the heat of conflict that subsequently fill them with amazement or remorse. Attempts have been made to explain atrocities in terms of sadistic instincts, but this is not sufficient. Such tendencies may very well exist in some individuals, but they are ordinarily suppressed. We must account for their being released under some circumstances and not under others. Since the things men do depend upon their definition of the situation, behavior in combat must be explained in terms of typical definitions formed in such contexts. Human beings interact in terms of the

conceptions they form of themselves and each other, and participants in conflict apparently construct typical personifications through selective perception. What is perceived often depends more upon the sensitivities of the perceiver than upon the attributes of the object. To what kinds of sensory cues are people in conflict situations sensitized? What kinds of conceptions are they likely to construct, even independent of the activities of their foe?

In conflict situations there tends to be a sharper definition of group boundaries and greater consciousness of kind. When the actual differences between opponents are slight, they tend to be exaggerated by accentuating status symbols. Ethnocentrism is intensified, and the disposition to evaluate the strange in terms of the known tends to convert the realization of differences into moral judgments.[1] Thus, in conflict situations there is a bipolarization of the participants into the good and the evil. A particularly fruitful concept is the *Gegenidee,* coined by Voegelin in an attempt to account for anti-Semitism in Germany. In building up the idea of the "Jew" attributes were selected that Germans unconsciously disliked in themselves. Only by attributing such qualities to someone else could a positive characterization of the ideal German be constructed. The Jew became the *Gegenidee,* the contrast conception, built up through the projection of all the traits rejected by Germans in forming their self-conceptions. Copeland subsequently used this concept to describe interethnic contacts in the American South. He believed that Negroes and white people were defined in moral

[1] G. P. Murdock, "Ethnocentrism," *Encyclopedia of the Social Sciences,* New York: Macmillan, 1931, vol. 5, pp. 613–614; and E. T. Thompson, "Race Relations in the Modern World," *Journal of Negro Education,* 1944, vol. XIII, pp. 270–279.

antithesis, white people attributing to Negroes all those traits that were the opposite of the qualities they valued in themselves.[2] But white people have not always conceived of Negroes in this manner—only when they were involved in conflict. When people are gripped with anxiety, they tend to see things in clearly delineated terms, and thinking generally becomes more stereotyped. The enemy is transformed into unrelieved evil, and one's own side is seen as possessing all the virtues.

People on both sides form similar conceptions of their opponents. In situations in which the color line is breaking down, those who are upwardly mobile insist that they are as worthy as members of the dominant group, although some of them may have inner doubts. Since they view themselves as equal, perhaps even as superior, they resent being relegated to inferior status. They are especially sensitive to slights. Some become so hypersensitive that they appear to be walking about with a "chip on their shoulder," looking for trouble. Any suggestion of inferiority, though unintended and without hostility, elicits sharp reactions. When a friendly white custodian refers to a Negro physician as a "boy" and to his colleague as a "gentleman," there is an angry explosion. Members of the dominant group, are defined as roadblocks, as barriers—in short, as frustrating objects. They are hated as tormentors —unfair, unjust, and indecent people who are deliberately attempting to hold down the deserving to perpetuate their own advantages. Even those who had not felt this way in the past develop such

views as the opposition between groups is intensified.

Members of the dominant group who accept the status quo are disturbed upon coming into contact with those of lower status who insist upon equal rights. Such individuals are viewed as a threat to their well-being. Much of what is commonly called "race prejudice" consists of the defensive hostility that might be expected of people who feel that their positions of privilege are in peril. They are convinced that minority groups are clearly inferior and that everyone could be happy if they would only be content to remain in their "place." The discontented few who threaten to upset the entire social order are viewed as dangerous objects—not only for what they might do for themselves but as agitators who might arouse others. Persons assuming a defensive stance become acutely sensitized to those qualities that make their opponents so formidable. They frequently charge that members of minority groups are clannish, that they work too hard, that they lie and cheat for each other, that they are unfair. Militant protest is condemned as "aggression," and insistence upon rights is dismissed as "insolence." In the American South a Negro with aspirations beyond his customary rank was accused of being "uppity," just as a Bantu in the Union of South Africa who was not subservient was called "cheeky." As long as American Negroes accepted their subordinate position, the prevailing attitude toward them was one of condescension and good will; when Negroes became upwardly mobile, however, this was transformed into hostility.

Participants in conflict situations characteristically impute vile motives to their opponents. Motive imputation is always inferential, and much depends upon the person who is making the inference. Since any overt act can be

[2] Lewis C. Copeland, "The Negro as a Contrast Conception," in E. T. Thompson, *Race Relations and the Race Problem, op. cit.,* pp. 152–179; and Eric Voegelin, "The Growth of the Race Idea," *Review of Politics,* II (1940), 283–317. Cf. Arthur Gladstone, "The Conception of the Enemy," *Journal of Conflict Resolution,* III (1959), 132–37.

interpreted in several ways, the identical deed may be seen as courageous or dastardly, depending upon the intention that is imputed. Each person is sensitized to those features in the behavior of others that will justify his feelings; of the hundreds of things an opponent does, one notices only those attributes that support his hatred, overlooking or explaining away everything else. Whatever the enemy does is interpreted in the least favorable light. If he fights courageously, he is called a fanatic; if he withdraws in the face of formidable opposition, he is called a coward. If he makes an honorable suggestion for a truce, it is viewed with suspicion and a search is made for ulterior motives. The result is that the other party is personified as the combination of the most horrible traits imaginable. Everything that is condemned within one's own group is imputed to the enemy. He is cruel, treacherous, sordid, perfidious, destructive; he is a fiend who commits atrocities against women and children, against the old and the blind.[3]

In contrast, one's own group and its allies are personified as noble and self-sacrificing people who fight only in self-defense. The contrast between friend and foe is enhanced as each combatant forms an idealized self-conception. Men rarely acknowledge fighting out of greed; they fight for lofty ideals—freedom, democracy, God. Divine justice is always on one's own side, the right side. That the opponent could make the same claim is inconceivable, for good is fighting against evil. Every form of common exertion has the blessing of all the holy sentiments, and steps sometimes have to be taken among Christians to calm the doubts of those who give the

Biblical injunctions against hatred and violence an inconvenient interpretation. As one Bantu in South Africa is quoted as saying, "You say the devil is black, but I picture a white man with blue eyes and yellow hair." According to one native preacher, "I know that the Lord Jesus Christ was a white man; yet I could not pray to Him and love Him as I do if I did not picture Him as black and with wool like myself."[4] In some parts of Asia and Africa, where hostility against white men has become intense, dark complexion has become a symbol of purity, a certificate of nobility, a passport to belonging. Some nationalist leaders have called for the unity of all men of color, as if they had something in common besides their grievances.

Once contrast conceptions are formed, they are continually reinforced through selective perception. Sensory cues inconsistent with expectations are overlooked. The manner in which convictions can be reaffirmed even in the absence of definite evidence is illustrated by Cameron's discussion of paranoid perspectives. A woman who has purchased a daringly new hat that may be too far ahead of the fashion trend is afraid that people will laugh at her. The first time she ventures into the street with it she encounters a strange man who is smiling. The man is smiling to himself about a practical joke that he had played on a friend the night before, but the woman concludes that he was amused at her hat and runs inside to change it. The difference between this woman and a person with paranoid delusions that FBI agents are following him is that she can communicate with her friends. When they reassure her that the hat is not comical, she can marshal her courage and venture forth again. But the person who is paranoid is iso-

[3] Cf. Harold D. Lasswell, *Propaganda Technique in the World War* (New York: Alfred A. Knopf, 1927), pp. 77–101; and Leo Lowenthal and Norbert Gutterman, *Prophets of Deceit* (New York: Harper, 1949), pp. 38–89.

[4] Olive Schreiner, *Thoughts on South Africa* (New York: Stokes, 1923), p. 127.

lated, and there is no one with whom he can check his impression. He suspects those who try to reassure him of being a part of the FBI conspiracy, and their testimony is discounted.[5] This is not to suggest that all people in conflict are paranoid, but they are cut off from their enemies in much the same manner. Those in minority groups who are convinced that members of the dominant group are out to "get" them frequently "test" the sincerity of others. If service in a restaurant happens to be slow—perhaps because it is a very busy day—this is interpreted as "discrimination." Attempts of the management to reassure them are rejected as "excuses." Rigidity of beliefs about others is often related to danger; the more frightened a person is, the more his ideas tend to become fixed.[6]

As conflict increases in intensity, the concept is further reinforced by sanctioned communication. What a person might say under ordinary circumstances is circumscribed only by considerations of good taste and tact, but in conflict situations there is additional pressure to say only good things about one's cause and bad things about the opposition. Thus, information that might correct contrast conceptions tends to be cut off. Since the enemy is diabolically clever and his propaganda is deadly, anyone who might say anything in his behalf is suspected of having been duped or even of complicity. Anyone who points out that his own side is not faultless is seen as a traitor and is sometimes ostracized. Not surprisingly, then, leadership on both sides tends to fall into the hands of extremists. Recognized leaders of minority groups find themselves under pressure to take a militant

stand. When the facts of the Nazi attempt to exterminate Jews became known after World War II, for example, American Jewish leaders found that they had to take a militant stand against anti-Semitism. Men who had changed their name and in private life put up with mildly anti-Semitic acquaintances found themselves making fiery demands in public. Had they not done this, they would have lost their following.[7] During the Mau Mau emergency in Kenya from 1952 to 1955, Jomo Kenyatta, the acknowledged leader of the Kikuyu, was reported no longer able to control the extremists. Had he arranged some kind of compromise with British authorities, he himself might have been slain by the Mau Mau.[8] As the desegregation issue became more intense in the American South, white people who took a moderate position were attacked as "nigger lovers." Similarly, a Negro who took a moderate view was attacked by other Negroes as an "Uncle Tom" or a "white man's nigger." Even the more conservative leaders of the NAACP were forced to take an outspoken stand.

Sumner long ago pointed to the utility of contrast conceptions. In conflict situations the differences between groups are so intensified that an ethical dualism becomes possible. The accentuation of differences is especially easy when people are already convinced that the opposition is genetically different. Since the enemy is viewed as something less than human—perhaps even as a threat to humanity—norms and obligations that hold in one's relationships with other human beings do not apply to him. A double standard of morality develops. Treachery, trickery,

[5] Norman Cameron, "The Development of Paranoic Thinking," *Psychological Review*, L (1943), 219–233.

[6] Cf. Forrest LaViolette and K. H. Silvert, "A Theory of Stereotypes," *Social Forces*, XXIX (1951), 257–262.

[7] David Riesman, "The Militant Fight Against Anti-Semitism," *Commentary*, XI (1951), 11–19.

[8] St. Clair Drake, "Some Observations on Inter-Ethnic Conflict as One Type of Inter-Group Conflict," *Journal of Conflict Resolution*, 1957, pp. 166–176.

bribery, anything to gain an unfair advantage—the very forms of conduct that would be severely condemned within the group—are highly praised when the victim is an opponent. In war men receive high decorations for doing the very things for which they would be incarcerated at home.[9] The most vicious carnage becomes possible because of the complete lack of identification. A machine gunner would have difficulty in strafing hundreds of women and children on the streets if he were able to identify with them. Thus, as conflict develops, contrast conceptions tend to make themselves come true. Each side is forced to act in ways that make the other angry, and hostility begets a hostile response. After a while, when the opponents attribute evil intent to each other, they are largely justified.

The construction of contrast conceptions also facilitates the mobilization of group solidarity. In large-scale conflicts sacrifices must be borne by a large number of people. Once contrast conceptions are widely held, men voluntarily join the struggle, and loyalty to one's ethnic group becomes an overriding consideration. They willingly do without items they need in order to enforce a boycott called against another ethnic group. Merchants whose livelihood depends in part upon trading with the enemy suffer heavy losses. Workers do not unite on a class basis. Where there is interethnic tension, the different groups maintain their distance, and employers have sometimes exploited such popular hatreds to maintain control. Labor unions in the South have faced special difficulties since the school desegregation issue attracted national attention. Since national officers of the AFL—CIO publicly supported desegregation, local leaders have had difficulty in recruiting and in

[9] W. G. Sumner *Folkways,* Boston, Ginn, 1906.

getting contributions for the union fund.

Contrast conceptions bolster determination to fight to the bitter end. There can be no thought of surrender to monsters; the fate of those who surrender would be worse than death. Hence, men prefer to die with honor than to give in to the forces of evil. There have been many wars in which hopelessly outmatched soldiers have fought on courageously to the last man. Even when there appears to be some possibility of compromise, combatants cannot be induced to consider it until they have been worn down to the point of exhaustion. Even then, negotiation is extremely difficult. When men distrust each other, anything that is suggested tends to be misinterpreted. Each party is so defensive that effective communication is almost impossible. When negotiations fail, this further reinforces the conviction that the enemy is vicious. In extremely bitter conflicts reconciliation is not possible until most of the active participants have died; then, members of a new generation who have only heard of the atrocities are able to reestablish communication.

A remarkable feature of conflict is that the conception of the enemy formed on one side is almost a mirror image of the conception formed on the other. Arabs and Jews have made somewhat different accusations against each other, but the presuppositions upon which each took action against the other are almost identical. The same can be said for the British and the Cypriots, the Indonesians and the Dutch, the Japanese and the Koreans. Similar personifications are also found in other kinds of conflict. Assumptions made about the opponent in strikes, in revolutions, in wars, and even in intense football rivalries are alike. In spite of the diversity of contexts the opposition is claimed to be immoral, unfair, vicious, and incapable of appreciating human sentiments. Many conservative Americans regard communists as devils. Communists have similar conceptions of their foes—"imperialists," "deviationists," and "counterrevolutionaries." Guerrilla fighters are often called "bandits" and are similarly characterized by the organized unit that hunts them down, whether it be the Japanese Army in Manchuria, the French Army in Indochina, or the U.S. Marines in Venezuela. One need only compare the assumptions made by many Jews about the "anti-Semitic Gentile" and the conception of the "Jew" held by Gentiles who are anti-Semitic; they frequently accuse one another of the same things! It is only natural that they dislike each other; no one could like human beings with the attributes that make up contrast conceptions.

But hatred is directed against an abstract object, and in many cases this does not interfere with actual contacts with friends and acquaintances on the other side of the color line. Except at the height of conflict, people in opposing ethnic groups continue to carry on their trade and other relationships as if nothing had happened. Contrast conceptions are artificial constructs; they are made up through selective perception, imagination, and the projection of rejected impulses to someone else. Concrete individuals who are well known are usually not associated with them; they are exceptions.

When peace is reestablished the combatants are invariably astonished to discover that their erstwhile foes are human beings after all. Upon meeting warriors from the other side, men discover that they are not fanatic cannibals. In prisoner-of-war camps guards and prisoners often discover that they have much in common—their dislike of military routine and longing for home, their dislike of petty and meaningless

tasks, the enlisted men's dislike of officers. The fact that they are so surprised is an indication of the inaccuracy of their working conceptions during combat.

Combatants often do have opposing interests, and much of their tenacity rests upon their correctly defining the enemy as an obstacle to their success. Nonetheless, much of the ferocity of conflict arises from the spontaneous reactions of men to images they construct in their minds. They invent frightful objects, become horrified, and then respond gallantly to the challenge to overcome them. They impute foul motives to people they do not even know and then react emotionally. Throughout history human beings have spent considerable time fighting against villains and ogres conjured in their imagination. . . .

35
Ghetto Riots and Others: The Faces of Civil Disorder in 1967*
LOUIS C. GOLDBERG

1. INTRODUCTION

Civil disorders in American cities in 1967 were not all of the same kind. The term "riot" has been too loosely applied to denote disturbances, often quite varied, which occurred last summer and in the previous three years.

*[This paper is based primarily on data published in *The Report of The National Advisory Commission on Civil Disorders* (New York: Bantam Books, 1968). The ideas for this particular analysis were formulated while I worked as a member of the social science research group of the commission. The group was directed by Dr. Robert Shellow and included David Boesel and myself as full-time analysts; Dr. Elliot Liebow, Dr. Gary Marx, and Dr. Derek Roemer as part-time analysts; and Drs. Neil Smelser, Nathan Kaplan, Ralph Turner, Kurt Lang, and David Sears as consultants. Nothing included here should be construed as the official

It has been used to refer to anything from a group of excited teenagers breaking windows after a dance, to a general social upheaval. All were civil disturbances; but only a few warranted the label "riot."

It is misleading also to think of the civil disturbances simply as "Negro riots." To do so suggests that the immediate responsibility for the course of the disturbances and the extent of damage lies solely with the Negro participants. It is necessary, of course, to underscore the reality of violent and aggressive mass actions involving looting, burning, and defiance of local authority within Negro areas; and the initiative of Negro rioters in events. But the threats to civil order and innocent life and property did not come only from the Negro side. In some cities, the behavior of various official control agents—police, national guardsmen, and the courts—in fact constituted official lawlessness: abuses of power in the name of law and order. ...

In other cities, "Negro riots" were more imagined than real. For such disorders, we must distinguish between *actual* collective violence by Negroes, and the *perception* of a riot by white authorities. There is much evidence that in several cities white anticipation

of Negro violence led to heavy-handed uses of official force that provoked violence which might not have otherwise occurred.

The news media, for their part, sometimes contributed to building expectations of community violence by overdramatizing disturbances and helping to create an emotional climate in which even minor incidents were seen as major riots.

2. PROMINENT FEATURES OF DISORDERS: CLASSIFYING THE "RIOTS"

A sample of twenty-three disturbances which occurred last summer shows clearly that the particular combination of circumstances in each city was to some extent unique.[1] But at the same time certain characteristics of different disturbances were so similar that we may *group the disorders, particularly the largest ones, on the basis of their most prominent features.*

2.1. General upheavals

Over a period of time a disturbance may develop into an upheaval which draws in thousands or tens of thousands of participants from a Negro ghetto, exhausts the resources of local police, severely taxes the capacities of city institutions, and involves an extraordinarily wide range of lawless activities on the part of both Negroes and control authorities. After the disorder has ended, an area often looks as if it has been through a state of civil warfare. Such was the case in Detroit and Newark, 1967, and in Los Angeles, 1965. These disorders were so massive, events so much beyond the control of either civil authorities or Negro community leadership, the points of street confrontation between police and Negroes so numerous and widespread, that it is difficult to characterize the whole complex of

view of either the social science group or the entire commission.

I should, however, like to express my debt to the entire staff of the commission, particularly the field teams who collected the data. Further, I should particularly like to thank my friend and partner David Boesel, who in certain respects must share equal responsibility for the ideas in this paper, for his encouragement and criticism. I also owe an idea to Professor Ralph Turner, and another to Betsy Jameson of Antioch College. Professor James S. Coleman of Johns Hopkins University was kind enough to express ambivalence toward an earlier version of this paper. While I would argue that objective evidence compels a harsher attitude toward civil and police authority stupidities in describing events than he would, I want to thank him for encouraging me to moderate the tone of the analysis.]

actions over the course of a disturbance in simple terms.

In all three cases, however, a similar pattern of development stands out: the violence in each went through two distinct phases. *In the first, widespread and aggressive action by ghetto Negroes overwhelmed local police forces, leaving them virtually powerless to enforce order in the streets. In the second, reinforced control authorities engaged in harsh retaliatory actions to reassert dominance.*

Phase 1: Negro rebellion In this phase *collective* violence was initiated by Negroes. In Detroit and Newark, as well as in Watts, aggressive action by Negroes escalated spontaneously from an initial confrontation with police into a highly generalized rebellion against white authority and white-owned property in the ghetto. In the face of an expanding rebellion, local police lacked the resources to act with the even-handed decisiveness necessary to bring the violence under control; their efforts inflamed rather than quieted Negro participants.

As the ability of police to enforce control of the streets diminished, more and more segments of the Negro community—older people, women, children—joined the young men who had been in the forefront. At the peak of this phase there was a euphoric realization among Negro rioters that they had nullified police control over their territory. Overwhelmed, the police floundered helpless and frustrated.

Phase 2: Control force retaliation Under the strain of widespread rioting, police order had begun to dissolve; many officers became subject to the same principles of crowd behavior that motivated Negro rioters. Deep-rooted racial prejudices surfaced. The desire to vent hostility, to reestablish domi-

nance, and to avenge police honor became compelling motives. Rumors and racist attitudes fed into each other as determinants of police behavior with the breakdown of routine arrest procedure, police communication systems, and police leadership control of their men on the street.

Once reinforcements arrived in the form of state police and National Guard units, the second phase of disorder was inaugurated. With police discipline severely weakened, many lawless acts initiated by lower-echelon police officers coincided with the reassertion of police dominance over Negro rioters. Many National Guardsmen, ill-disciplined and afraid, showed little restraint in using weapons in areas in which they were strangers. This period was characterized by a marked tendency among control authorities to treat all Negroes categorically as enemies. The presence of massive official force, or its withdrawal, or the exhaustion of Negro rioters and control authorities alike, would finally bring the violence to an end. . . .

2.2. Riots as political confrontations

Newark and Detroit are extreme examples of massive disorder in the summer of 1967. A few disturbances showed many of the characteristics of these general upheavals but developed over time in a distinctly political direction. As in the general upheaval, the level of disorder in the streets was quite large. *But in these disorders explicit political confrontation[2] between Negro leadership and civil authorities was at least as important a feature of the riot as violent street confrontation between Negro masses and the police.* This was true in such cities as Cincinnati and Plainfield.

On the first night of disorder in Plainfield, for example, a local Negro politician tried to steer the youth toward a meeting with the mayor to talk about their grievances. The meeting was held, but was unsatisfactory, the youth leadership representatives walking out twice, a minor riot occurring after the second walkout. On the next day, a meeting they were having in a park to formulate grievances and reduce them to writing was broken up by the police. Shortly thereafter violence rapidly escalated as a policeman was killed by a mob after he shot a youth, and the youths, fearing retaliation from the police, stole 46 carbines from a gun factory. Later, one of their representatives—a young man who has since become an important political figure in the community—attempted to use the possession of the guns as a bargaining tool, offering to exchange them in return for a sign of good faith from the authorities. An agreement was reached and Negro-initiated violence ceased, although the guns were not in fact returned. During a two-day period when police were kept out of the area of disturbance, the youths in effect took responsibility for keeping order. In the aftermath, the activities of the youth militants have involved the use of pressure group tactics in council meetings, their first victory being the defeat of an antiloitering amendment.

Unlike the general upheaval, events in Plainfield, although violent, were not entirely out of the control of community leaders. In Detroit, where there may have been tens or hundreds of bands of rioters at work, any kind of coherence or control over events was impossible. In Newark, the possibility for a political solution was quickly foreclosed by the severe political polarization between the mayor and the middle class Negro militants, and the lack of control of the latter over the young. But in Plainfield, the existence of a leadership group among the youth

who were rioting, and their willingness to negotiate, made possible a political compromise of sorts.

Indeed, a politicized focus and coherence to events occurred wherever rioters were sufficiently organized to "select" their own leadership for negotiation, or where there were leaders within the general community who would act and be accepted as "spokesmen." In such cases, militancy around the conference table would match, and often substitute for, militancy in the streets.

2.3. The riot as expressive rampage

While many of the larger disorders had pronounced instrumental and political components, there is also a type in which a quality of expressive rampaging on the part of the Negro participants was predominant. All of the ghetto riots involved the spontaneous gathering of an angry crowd in the first phase. But in this third type, the behavior of rioters gained little focus or direction over time. The clearest image is a wandering street mob, angry, drunken, milling about, lacking leadership or direction, engaged in breaking windows, or random acts of vandalism.

The riot in Dayton in 1966, which preceded two smaller disturbances during the summer of 1967, was of this type. From the start those engaged in the disturbance were a "bar crowd" of petty hustlers and drunks, marginal elements in the community. Efforts by the mayor to reach a "political solution" to the riot by negotiating with a militant civil rights leader on the scene was ineffective, because the rioting crowd was organized around drinking and chaotic emotional expression. Efforts to organize the crowd into a meeting to express grievance and negotiate failed totally. The disorder was finally suppressed by heavy arrests once local police were buttressed with National Guard forces.

2.4. The riot as fulfillment of anticipations

While the largest disorders generally began with an aggressive ghetto riot followed by a tough police response, there is another category of disturbance in which the flow of events proceeded in the opposite direction. *The first acts of collective aggression came not from Negroes but from control forces—subsequent Negro responses tending to be defensive, protective, or retaliatory.* In such cities as Cambridge, Maryland; Jersey City and Elizabeth, New Jersey, anticipations of Negro lawlessness, rather than actual lawlessness itself, led to periods of disturbance.

These were initiated by precipitous "riot control tactics" or "shows of force" by white authorities. Compared with cities that did have massive ghetto rioting, such disturbances remained fairly minor, although their actual proportions were often greatly exaggerated at the time they occurred.

In Cambridge, Maryland, the presence and speech of H. Rap Brown had a great effect in stimulating local authorities to acts of disorder against the Negro community. His mere presence evoked images in the minds of white leadership that there was an organized conspiracy afoot to lead Cambridge's Negroes in a rampaging pillage of the town's white business district. His inflammatory speech, although failing to galvanize Negro youth to start breaking things up, did produce a wave of hysteria in the Negro police officers who heard it. These reported that a riot was underway—thus confirming the worst fears of local white officials. At one point, after an injury to an officer, the local police chief wanted to go shooting into the area, and only restraints by state authorities prevented bloodshed. Later on, the white volunteer fire department refused to go into the Negro area to put out a small fire that finally spread into a blaze consuming a block of Negro businesses. This nonaction stemmed in part from a fear of a preplanned plot to "trap" fire department equipment in the Negro area, thus leaving the downtown area to be burned and plundered. . . .

In a few cities *joint expectations* held by *both* Negroes and whites that a riot was coming had something of a self-fulfilling character. However, in the absence of truly intense community polarization, the disturbances possessed a staged or simulated quality. The participants seemed to be going through the motions of a riot more than carrying out serious conflict. Lacking was the quality of vengeance and retribution which pervades so much of the behavior on all sides during a riot out of control.

Staged conflict in this sense occurred in New Brunswick, where youths put on a riot in the main street. An effective political response by the lady mayor brought a quick end to the disorder. The second night of rioting in Tucson was staged in another sense. Following queries by a newspaper reporter as to where and when they were going to riot that evening, youths put on a minor riot for the benefit of the press.

2.5. The riots that didn't happen: "mini-riots" and others

In most of the events in which anticipations of violence played an important role, the level of disorder on the Negro side was so minimal as to suggest calling these disturbances "Negro riots that didn't happen." There were also some low-level disturbances—"mini-riots" is an apt term—that reflected in germinal or aborted form dimensions more fully developed in the largest disorders.

The Atlanta and Tampa disturbances showed many characteristics in common with certain northern disorders. In Atlanta as in Newark and Detroit, a crowd formed in a community gathering place in a high density area. The scene in this instance was a neighborhood shopping center where police-related incidents had occurred the two previous nights. Stokely Carmichael, present to urge the crowd to take to the streets, found an audience willing to take matters into its own hands. But (1) the police immediately moved in with major force and were extremely effective; (2) the mayor quickly responded to the political aspect of the event by beginning visible construction the next day on long-delayed projects demanded by area residents; and (3) a newly formed Negro Youth Corps helped keep the rest of the summer cool.

In a northern city like Dayton, there was a significant potential in its two 1967 disturbances for a major Negro riot. The first disturbance followed a meeting protesting the cut of a grassroots poverty program. H. Rap Brown was the featured out-of-town visitor at the meeting. He excited youth who were already looking for an excuse to riot.

The second followed a bitter meeting protesting the release of a vice squad officer after a controversial killing of a middle class Negro professional. An initially decisive police response and the "cooling effect" of the Dayton White Hats in both cases rapidly attenuated the escalation potential in the disturbance.

Finally, in the category of "riots which did not occur" is the traditional race riot which has often marked American history. The potential nevertheless was there. In Cincinnati, New Haven, Newark, and Cambridge, whites were attracted to the scene, ready to take up the banner against Negroes and to defend white property. In such cities, effective police practice prevented

white outsiders from coming into Negro areas, thus aborting the race riot process. In Cambridge, where there has been a continuing danger of racial confrontation for several years, the state National Guard acted in its customary role as a buffer against violence.

3. PROCESSES IN DEVELOPING DISORDERS

3.1. Urban upheavals and satellite riots: the propagation of violence

As a nationwide phenomenon, the propagation of violence across the land follows the close link between major ghetto upheavals, or reports thereof, and "satellite" disorders in which authority overreaction occurs. The former has clearly acted as a trigger to the latter. In the wake of a disturbance the size of Newark or Detroit, rumors of small incidents in a local area become magnified as the beginning of a riot. On the white side, a climate of anxiety is produced by stories of planned violence, and fears of outside agitators and conspirators.

After the Detroit upheaval, eight other Michigan cities reported disorders. After the Newark riot, fourteen cities in the surrounding area had some sort of disturbance. *In at least two-thirds of fifteen cities studied in which disorders occurred shortly after major riots, the immediate precipitant of disorder seems to have been a police action prompted by ghetto violence elsewhere. . . .*

Another force in the proliferation of disturbances in the vicinity of the big city riots is the network of kinship and friendship relations between Negroes in major cities and outlying areas. For some it was literally true that "the brothers" in Newark or Detroit were "getting some of the action." Many people in Grand Rapids, for example, have relatives in Detroit. Reports that some of these relatives were killed in the Detroit riot increased tension and the potential for violence in that city.

The intensity of the flow of personal information from the Newark and Detroit ghettos to outlying areas at the peaks of the riots is indicated by the high number of out-of-town phone calls from the areas of greatest disturbance. These equaled top loads for a Mother's Day weekend, one of the periods in the year when telephone lines across the country become overloaded.

3.2. The media and the propagation of disorder

The majority of people in outlying areas and across the country do not, of course, learn about a riot through immediate personal information. TV can bring people hundreds or thousands of miles distant directly to the scene of a major disorder. *The effect can often be that of the crowd acting at long distance.* This was a typical feature of the nonviolent demonstrations of the civil rights movement at its peak. TV pictures of mob violence in the South would spark spontaneous sympathy demonstrations all across the North. And, in many instances, local civil rights movements would indigenously evolve from there.

In the case of the recent disorders, the "crowd at long distance" generated the impression that there was in fact a conspiracy some place for New Jersey to go up all at once. Actually, outbreaks of civil violence were quite spontaneous and unplanned—information from the media lowering the threshold for disorder all across an area.

One definite effect of the media seems to be the determination in time and place that latent tensions will surface into disorder. The potential for major riots in Plainfield and Detroit led by militant Negro youth had been there for some time. It was the Newark riot that dramatically changed "the

mood" in Detroit and helped galvanize Negro youths to aggressive action in Plainfield. They might have "blown" anyway, if not at that time, then perhaps at a later date. On the other hand, these cities went through crisis periods before in which a major disorder could have exploded, but did not. Perhaps if Newark had not occurred or if information about it had been totally suppressed, other cities might have weathered the storm—at least temporarily. Progress through institutional channels might have kept one step ahead of the chaos breathing on its heels.

3.3. "Outside agitators" and the spread of disorder

A discussion of the mass media effects in propagating disorder naturally leads into an examination of the actual influence over events of such nationally known, "headline-making" Negro radical leaders as Stokely Carmichael and H. Rap Brown. Their role in spreading disorder is by no means simple.

A cursory overview of the points where the distribution of disorder around the country crosses the distribution of appearances of Stokely Carmichael or H. Rap Brown would indicate that most disturbances occurred without their presence to help things along. Of twenty-three disturbances in our sample, in only six were either Carmichael or Brown around the scene at the time. And in only three of these were their appearance and rhetoric immediately linked with the immediate precipitants of disorder. In the other cities they arrived at the scene after action was already underway. In Cincinnati, for example, Brown's major role was presenting a list of some twenty demands from a nationalist group to a representative from the Human Relations Commission on the fourth day of the disturbance.

Thus the number of specific situations with which the presence of a national firebrand could be associated with disorder were very few. *And considering the large number of communities where Brown and Carmichael appeared which did not have riots, their "riot batting-average," if indeed their purpose was to provoke a disorder on the spot, was extremely low.* Nevertheless, Carmichael and Brown do have influence over some events, which stems from the particular way they lead people. Their leadership is symbolic rather than organizational. They cannot command others to riot—at least at this time—by coming in from out of town and passing down orders from the top. But as a symbolic focus for hopes and fears they can generate the emotional predisposition which might encourage disorder.

In this respect, a good deal depends on the mood of their audience when they arrive on the scene. In Atlanta, Carmichael's speech to a crowd suggesting that they force the police to work until they "drop in their tracks" brought a tumultuous response. In Dayton the youth were "looking for an excuse to riot" before Brown arrived. However, in Jersey City, Negro youth quickly fled a meeting at which Brown was speaking when a rumor spread that the police were coming. Brown reportedly left town muttering "the people here aren't ready."

White authorities, as the Cambridge and New Jersey cases illustrate, have often been emotional followers of the leadership of Brown and Carmichael, in the sense that fears of the influence or presence of the latter generated precipitous actions.

It should be stressed too that the influence process between audience and agitators is a two-way street. In Detroit it was an unknown local man who took upon himself the role of the agitator. But in so doing, he was responding as well to the mood of the crowd and a situation which commanded agitation. And while Brown and Carmichael have a utilitarian interest in seeing violence directed against white society's control of Negroes until equality is produced, most of the evidence indicates that crowds use them as much as they use crowds.

Like headliners and public men everywhere, they become tools of community groups in developing motivation and commitment in followers, creating resources, and getting actions going. Thus far, they have been the focal point for a great deal of emotional energies on the part of both Negroes and whites. It is easier, for example, for whites to see riots as caused by H. Rap Brown and Stokely Carmichael, with whom they are familiar, than by the conditions of local Negro communities, with which they are not. Negroes, for their part —especially the young—experience great jubilation in hearing a speaker "tell it like it is" and frighten whites in the process.

Whatever their role at a specific local disorder, however, the major source of influence of leaders like Brown and Carmichael over events is that the media provides them with a national audience. Brown and Carmichael have argued that violence is necessary—violence is occurring around the country—both are reported side by side on TV and in the press. Such a recurrent linking of spokesmen for disorder and actual violence produces cause and effect associations difficult to dispel. Brown and Carmichael become seen as having the extraordinary and dangerous power to spell-bind Negroes into rioting.

While such a conclusion greatly exaggerates their power, we must not underestimate the real importance of their posturing as revolutionaries in the creation of an emotional climate around the country which is conducive to violence. But here too they are not alone. The news media, the political authorities, the reports of the occurrence of actual riots are also central elements in creating a "riot climate."

It would, perhaps, be more appropriate to consider the development of a major ghetto riot, and the appearance of symbolic leaders arguing that violence is legitimate, as but different reflections of the processes of polarization going on throughout the society. It is the role of spokesmen for rebellion created by the fact that ghetto rebellions are occurring which is significant, and not Brown or Carmichael specifically. Previously that role was singularly filled by Malcolm X; now new men are moving to fill the gap, rushing to keep up with events more than they are guiding them.

The real source of Brown and Carmichael's influence thus far has been the failure of the white community to make their role irrelevant. Lacking recognition from the white community in other respects, without a place in society for themselves, young Negroes learn quickly that whites are afraid of Brown and Carmichael. *When whites fear your power to cause riots they take you seriously: that is the lesson of events. In this respect whites load the dice. The role of the militant demagogue and activist is rewarded again and again.*

3.4. Initial conditions in the spread of disorder

Loading the dice occurs within disturbances. At any phase, the events that have gone before shape the events that follow. This begins before actual violence erupts. If aspirations have been raised but community issues and conflicts continually find ghetto Negroes on the losing end, if a high degree of community polarization has developed, if racial solidarity and militancy within

the ghetto has been growing, if there is a large pool of aggressive and ambitious youth available for confrontation, it may be as difficult to contain a disturbance in its first phase as to contain an atomic chain reaction once the critical point has been reached.

This was the case in Detroit where events happened extremely fast, telescoping in a matter of hours community involvement processes that took three days to develop in Watts. In other cities where a truly explosive potential did not exist, it was very likely that a disorder would have died out of its own accord through normal processes of communal restraint without formal authority controls (e.g., mothers scold sons for rampaging, the youth not being serious about rioting, etc.).

Initial features of a disorder, where it was located, the time of day, who was involved, the weather, etc., also were important in determining the direction an incipient disturbance was to move. Rain stopped some incipient riots. Whether the people who initially became riotous were marginal elements of the Negro community or whether they were stable residents was an important consideration. Disorders that pulled in ambitious, achievement-oriented people were more violent.[3] Disorders that began near housing developments, shopping centers, or other places where ordinary people in the community gathered always had an extremely dangerous potential.

Grievances in the riot process Like the question concerning the role of Negro leadership in events, the question of the role of grievances, or the grievance process in disorders, is complicated. A popular model of riot causes sees a high level of unacted grievances, producing community tensions, which in turn produce riots. This theory is popularly held by people with programs or ideas they would like to sell that would ameliorate tensions by reducing grievances.

But there were cities in which the grievance level, in an absolute sense, was very high during the summer of 1967 which did not experience aggressive Negro riots. There were others in which the grievance level was much lower which did have aggressive ghetto rioting.

The importance of grievances in an event seems to be determined less by the *level of grievance* than the *kind* of grievance involved. People do not riot *for* better schools, but they will riot *against* the police and government as outside oppressors. Concerns for territory, domination, and hate of double standards (social injustice) run like a common thread through most of the largest disorders.

Item: In Plainfield, the double-standard issue of a policeman failing to make an arrest Negro youth thought he should have was the immediate precipitant.

Item: In Cincinnati, the issue of double-standards in the courts generated a sense of rage as a Negro was sentenced for murder and a white man for manslaughter within the same month. The first act of direct action was the stopping of delivery trucks by youths objecting to whites getting most of the jobs in Negro areas.

Item: In Detroit, the failure of a white newspaper to carry news of a Negro Vietnam veteran's murder at the hands of a white mob created bitterness as the local Negro newspaper reported the incident, including the miscarriage of the murdered man's pregnant wife, in full detail. A few weeks later and a short distance from where the murdered man lived a police raid in an afterhours club where a party for some Negro servicemen was in progress found an agitator haranguing an angry crowd that the police wouldn't do what they were doing in a white area.

Item: In Los Angeles in 1965, plaintive appeals of a Negro youth that he was not going to let the police take him to jail, aroused a tug-of-war between local community residents and white police which was the first incident in the Los Angeles riot.

Item: In Newark, a massive urban renewal project which would displace thousands of Negroes became the source of a bitter political struggle between the Italian political leadership and Negro militants, and was considered an important cause of the riot. Later, the belief of neighborhood residents that the police had not only beaten a taxicab driver but had beaten him before they got him to the police station catalyzed a mood of rebellion and community solidarity.

Grievances of one Negro group against another can also be considered as having a role in precipitating and shaping several disorders.

Item: Leadership competition between the Negro militants opposed to the mayor of Newark and the group of conservative Negro leaders who supported him in part prevented an effective counterriot response to the developing Newark crisis.

Item: In Cincinnati, the first outbreak of violence followed a speech by a Negro conservative at a protest rally which supported an antiloitering law and angered Negro youths.

Items: In Dayton's June 1967 disturbance, an intense controversy between militants and conservatives over the funding of an antipoverty program found a militant leader threatening a riot which shortly occurred.

Item: In Cambridge, white fear began to mount as two newly forming Negro groups, one conservative, one militant, began to compete for the leadership role left vacant since Gloria Richardson had left town.

Item: In Grand Rapids, entrenched vice elements in the Negro community, who were being threatened by the rising influence of poverty workers in the community, attempted to use the disorder to buttress their declining domination.

Item: In Detroit, a developing indigenous community organization leadership of a very militant character was threatening established middle class leaders who were well-incorporated into the Detroit political system. The latter were willing to go along with a policy of extreme repression the first day of the disturbance. Since the riot, they have been outraged at the willingness of city leadership to meet directly with lower class representatives, and have fought increases in power for the militant groups.

Finally, the *grievance process* — the effectiveness of the response of authorities to Negro grievances whatever these are — can be a crucial source of grievance itself. The substantive grievances (police practices, neighborhood services, schools, housing, etc) serve as indicators for measuring exactly how much and in what manner white authorities care about Negroes. They become tests of commitment.

In this respect, liberal or moderate cities are far more vulnerable to incidence of disorders than racially conservative ones. Examination of the twenty-three disorders in our sample indicates that those cities characterized by a general liberalizing, more humanitarian trend in elite attitudes — i.e., public recognition of the legitimacy of Negro complaints — are more likely to have the largest and most violent disorders. This is not surprising. Prolonged aggressive action by Negroes in racially conservative cities is less likely, because whites promise little, and what they do promise is immediate and extreme use of violent force to quell any disturbance at the outset, regardless of the merits of Negro complaints. In these cities, Negroes are continually reminded of "their place,"

and if some do not accept this definition they may be persuaded to refrain from violent protest anyhow.

The tokenistic pattern of race relations in more moderate or racially liberalizing cities encourages Negro demands for equalities, lifts the fear of extreme force (policemen increasingly attack the civil libertarian and community-relations emphasis of liberal government on the grounds that "law enforcement is being handcuffed"), yet generally fails to work great immediate changes in the conditions of ghetto life. Individual members of the group have greater mobility and opportunity than ever before, but many still lag behind, their increased desires for advancement unfulfilled. The dilemma of liberalizing governments is that lifting the more overt forms of repression and promises of equalities encourages a more rapid rate of change in the pyschology of Negroes than anything else. In such circumstances where old dominance relations are being undermined or are uncertain, grievances can be expected to escalate as Negroes test out white commitments in more and more areas. Growing black consciousness and sense of community increases the desire for action against obstacles that cramp ghetto Negroes in daily life, at the same time that white reaction to Negro "pushiness" invokes a sense of betrayal.

This seems extremely crucial for developing a mood of rebellion. Prior to the disorder there, Newark would have been considered a city undergoing racial liberalization. A Negro–Italian political coalition had put the mayor into office, and there had been many promises to the Negro community. Compared with other northern cities, the level of political access of Negroes in Newark might have been considered fairly high. But a split had developed in the coalition with the Italian political leadership, and Negro community elites engaged in bitter, emotionally charged disputes over police practices, a plan to tear down Negro-occupied areas to construct a medical complex, appointments to the board of education, and other issues. The Negroes saw broken promises, and an attempt by the Italians to establish their political hegemony at Negro expense. By the second evening of disorder in Newark, people were far beyond the stage where they would be willing to accept a token concession at the price of mitigating their righteous vengeance which had been so long in developing. Once that mood was there, a sudden concession itself triggered disorder as Negroes so to speak threw the concession of a Negro police captain back into the faces of the authorities with the attitude "keep it, you can't buy us that cheaply *now*."

3.5. The competitive process in developing disorders

Negotiations at such points fail because many people want combat more than peace. During a disorder itself, a competitive sense among Negro youths may become a powerful impetus to keeping the violence going. In Newark, some youths did not want to stop the riot because the score in deaths stood "25–2" with the police and guardsmen leading.

The game of riot: emasculating the police Within various groups on the street, people were quite conscious of the heroism and daring exhibited by young men. For Negro youth, challenging the police with taunts and dares involved a dangerous and dramatic competition. Their goal was to disrupt police order, to make the police "lose their cool," to produce situations in

which police worked until they "dropped in their tracks." Much of the behavior of the youth during a riot can be accounted for by this motivation: *they are interested not in killing policemen, but in humiliating them.* As Negroes have been rendered powerless for so long, as the police have continually disrupted the activities of the ghetto, the disorder becomes the grand opportunity to turn the tables.

In this respect, the riots also serve the functions of ritual ceremonies in which manhood is demonstrated. Many acts of confrontation (e,g., laying bare the chest and taunting police to shoot), which have a great intensity and seriousness about them are also dramatic posturing—open and public proof to both oneself and the police that things have changed. The test has dangers, but afterwards one can never go back to what he was before.

This form of street confrontation with the police, it should be noted, is not new. If we include the southern nonviolent movement, it has been going on for six years. In the South during 1962–1965 militant civil rights activists, many of whom were of northern background, became experts in the technique of disorganizing southern police through nonviolent demonstrations.

Negro youth in the North are now the aggressors. Instead of nonviolent demonstrations, breaking white property, setting fires, and racial taunting have become major aspects of the techniques of breaking up the police.

Much Negro youth crime has always had this quality of testing by street games with authorities. Confronting police and courts in efforts to construct a self-definition in which one does have some kind of place in society— if only a criminal one—does have a functional basis. Those who have served time return to their old associations with a new status as someone who is really tough and knows the ropes.

What is distinctive now is that this same process feeds into community confrontation. Traditional street-testing behavior by Negro youth is channeling into the disruption of city institutions. The massiveness of the disruption in a riot stems from the fact that a great number of youth are getting their badges of manhood all at once. Previously this occurred through the orderly and recurrent process of one-by-one confrontation which white institutions easily handled in the past.

Cross-city competition Evidence in our data indicate that cross-city competition among youth: "who holds the record, now?" becomes a salient force once control by police is lost. Cities that have already had major upheavals acquire symbolic value and become standards for comparison in other disturbances. For some participants there is a quite explicit desire to outdo New York, or Watts, etc. A Negro girl in Newark asked a reporter "Was the Harlem riot worse than this?" and assured that it was not, she cried, "that's good, that's great!"

Distinctive features of several major disturbances during the summer of 1967 can in part be attributed to the excitement generated among young Negroes that they were either doing something in a riot that had not been done before, or that they were doing it better than ever. Negro youths in Newark were quite proud that they were the first to ever lay siege to a police station. As the governor passed by in a National Guard tank, there were heated street side discussions on "How do you get into a tank with a Molotov cocktail?"

There is no reason to preclude the possibility of disruptive acts more consequential than any that have yet occurred. The first tank to be fire bombed, the first power station to be blown up, are but logical extension of the present pattern of disorder. "We're number one!" after all is an old American tradition.

FOOTNOTES

[1] This brief analytical summary is not meant to capture the richness and concrete details of the events. The reader is encouraged to refer to the excellent narrative of the Detroit, Newark, and other disorders provided in *The Report of the National Advisory Commission on Civil Disorders*, pp. 35–108.

[2] The use of the term "political" here is not meant to imply either (1) conspiracy, (2) prior organization to achieve specific political objectives through the use of violence (e.g., intimidating election opponents or forcing a city administration to grant a specific concession), or (3) a precipitant which was markedly "political." Nor is calling some disturbances "political riots" meant to imply that the general upheavals in Newark and Detroit lacked a powerful political component. A high level of political grievance on the part of Negroes, and the lack of significant responses by civil authorities contributed greatly to events in Newark and Detroit. But it would not do justice to the many nonpolitical aspects of generalized chaos in those cities to refer to their disorders as simply political riots. However, in cities like Plainfield and Cincinnati, the actions of Negro participants became directly focused at civil authorities. In turn, the responses of civil authorities to demands— particularly the demand for recognition— dramatically affected the level of aggressive action by Negro rioters.

[3] As in other areas of community life, the quality of a riot is affected by the level of energy and competency people bring with them. Those who participate in riots (see pp. 174–178 in *The Report of the National Advisory Commission on Civil Disorders*), as compared with those who do not, tend to be younger, better educated, more politically aware, more achievement oriented, more acculturated to the values of an industrialized urban society, and more dissatisfied with their place within it. Across cities, there is some evidence that the quality and character of Negro mass actions (political focus, degree of organization, volatility) is affected by differences in the level of unincorporated youthful talent.

36
Civil Disorder and the Agents of Social Control*,1
GARY T. MARX

Quis custodiet ipsos custodes? [*Juvenal (VI.347)*]

The mob quails before the simple baton of the police officer, and flies before it, well knowing the moral as well as physical force, of the Nation whose will, as embodied in law, it represents. [The Police and the Thieves, *1856*]

Most of our municipalities appear to be organized solely for social service. In the presence of a mob their police officers are as helpless as their school teachers or their hospital interns. [*Newspaper report on 1919 Riot*]

Now, I'm not saying that the community, the people in the community of Harlem, were blameless. There was bottle-throwing, but when people throw bottles, when they throw bricks, it's the responsibility of the police to arrest, or at least restrain the culprits, the guilty parties, not indiscriminately to shoot into hotel windows and tenement houses. Not to beat people who are merely walking down the street. [*James Farmer, 1964*]

Sure we make mistakes. You do in any war. [*Police Commissioner of New York City, 1964*]

I don't want to hear anything you [*Negro director of Human Relations Commission, counseling need to use black officers*] have got to say; you're part of the problem. We know how to run a riot and we are going to handle it our way. [*Deputy Chief of Police, Los Angeles, 1965*]

*[Reprinted by permission from the *Journal of Social Issues*, Vol. XXVI, no. 1.]
1 An earlier version of this paper was presented at the 1968 American Sociological Association meetings. I am grateful to the M.I.T.-Harvard Joint Center for Urban Studies for support and the National Advisory Commission on Civil Disorders.

[*The local police chief*] rushed into his office and, grabbing the rifle . . . and two boxes of ammunition, he shouted, "They've shot one of my officers. We're going to get every son-of-a-bitch down there. I'm getting god-damned tired of fooling around." [*State police report, 1967*]

If you have a gun, whether it is a shoulder weapon or whether it is a hand gun, use it. [*Director of Newark Police, over the police radio, 1967*]

To the [*riot*] commissioners and public alike we'd ask one question: When a law enforcement officer, faced with the extremely dangerous task of quelling what is in fact an armed rebellion, is the target of snipers' bullets, rocks, and bottles, just exactly what constitutes "undue force?" Were any of the commissioners who accuse police of using undue force on the firing line? Do they really know what they are talking about? Use of the term "undue force" is an exercise in tortured semantics that police refuse to accept. Not only is the charge without merit, it is an insult to brave men who risked their lives for the public and equally unacceptable to reasonable people. [*New Jersey State Patrolmen's Benevolent Association, 1968*]

In the final analysis [*in spite of poor judgment, excessive use of firearms, and a manifestation of vindictiveness on the part of police*] the responsibility for the loss of life and property that is the inevitable product of rioting and mass lawlessness cannot be placed upon those whose duty it is to enforce the law and protect the free of our society. [*Report of Essex County (N. J.) grand jury investigation of riot deaths, 1968*]

It seems . . . that it is not what you do, but how you do it and what you call it. [*John Steinbeck, 1961*]

The number of popular and scholarly perspectives that can be brought to bear on the interpretation of civil disorder seems limited only by the breadth of one's imagination and reading. Among some of the more prominent are those that stress the increased radicalism of social movements as they evolve, the relevance of a world revolutionary struggle, the importance of an external war, limited political access, various types of frustration, conspiracies, and agitation, the mass media, relative deprivation and heightened aspirations, frontier traditions and a history of racial and labor violence, lower class and criminal subcultures and youthful, Hobbesian, biological, or territorial man. Many of these factors can be fitted into Smelser's (1962) useful value-added model of the determinants of collective behavior.

Despite the undeniable relevance of some of these perspectives, they all focus on factors in the predisorder situation conducive to violence. They also tend to correspond to a particular left- or rightwing ideology. Thus conservatives tend to see disturbances as meaningless, irrational events caused by agitators activating the degenerate character of the lower classes, while liberals are more likely to see them as spontaneous patterned protests caused by deprivation. However, there is one perspective which finds support among both the extreme left and right, and which seeks the cause in the actual disturbance situation. This is the view which suggests that the police cause riots. (To be sure, these groups differ on the particular mechanism they emphasize—the right blaming the police for being too soft, the left blaming them for being too harsh.)

UNINTENDED CONSEQUENCES OF SOCIAL ACTION

One of the justifications for social research is that it goes beyond our common sense views of the world. Merton (1957) suggests that an important task of social research is to point out the latent or unintended consequences of human action. Thus, corrupt as early twentieth-century political machines were, they were important in the assimilation of Irish and other immigrants; and prostitution, whatever its moral implications, may make an important contribution to family stability. However, there are more interesting cases where unintended consequences are the direct opposite of intended ends. Thus we have learned that propaganda designed to reduce prejudice may actually reinforce it, that youth institutions may create juvenile delinquents who are later made into knowledgeable and embittered criminals by the prison system, that mental hospitals may encourage mental illness, that schools can impede learning, that welfare institutions may create dependency, and that doctors sometimes injure or even kill patients.

In the same fashion, a review of police behavior in civil disorders of a racial nature through the summer of 1967 suggests a number of instances where the behavior of some social control agents seemed as much to create disorder as to control it. . . .

This paper does not argue that police are the main *cause* of racial disorder. Indeed, police are one of the most scapegoated and stigmatized groups in American society and many parallels may be drawn between them and ethnic minorities. Yet, as Gertrude Stein noted, the answers one gives depends on the questions one asks. There are certain questions about civil disorders that can only be answered by considering the general nature of the police-black community relationship and the interaction that occurs between these groups during a disturbance. These questions have to do with the course, pattern, intensity, and duration of the disturbance.

As Park and Blumer and later students have noted, collective behavior has an emergent character to it. It involves elements that can't very well be predicted by a static consideration of the predisturbance variables mentioned in the beginning of the paper. Civil disorder involves a social process of action and counteraction. It is here that a consideration of police behavior is relevant.

As Allen Grimshaw (1963) has noted, police have been criticized for brutality and ineffectiveness in most twentieth-century racial disturbances. Any critical evaluation of recent control practices must first be put in historical perspective.

In reading about police behavior in earlier twentieth-century interracial violence, I found several reoccurring themes: (1) the police were sympathetic to (white) rioters and sometimes joined the riot themselves, (2) police often failed actively to enforce the law, and (3) when police did try to maintain law and order this often was not done in a neutral and impartial manner. . . .[2]

THE 1960s: SOME CHANGES IN POLICE BEHAVIOR

We have come a long way since the 1863 New York draft riot where when the president of the police board was asked about taking lawbreakers into custody he reportedly replied, "Prisoners? Don't take any. Kill! Kill! Kill! Put down the mob." Riots are now triggered when police kill or injure a Negro, rather than vice versa. Police have been much quicker to take action and this action has generally been more restrained than previously. The law has been enforced much more impartially. Particularly in the North, there are few reports of police failing to stop interracial assaults or of police firing

into unarmed noncombative crowds. Considering the absolute number, size, intensity, and duration of recent disorders, there has probably been much less police rioting, less brutality, and relatively less injury inflicted upon Negroes by the police; this is all the more salient since police have been provoked to a much greater extent than earlier and have many more opportunities to use force legally against blacks than they did in previous riots. . . .[3]

This is not to argue that police behavior has always been effective or humane. While the old adage told me by a veteran police official that in the past "the riot didn't start until the police arrived" may seem less true today, this is certainly not to say that the riot now always stops when the police do arrive. . . . It is ironic that although police are technically better prepared to control disorders and have a greater will to do so, they often have been unsuccessful. Control is more difficult now than in earlier race riots because of the greater use made of private weapons and the fact that merely separating whites from blacks and protecting black areas from white invasion is not sufficient for stopping the riot (Janowitz, 1968, p. 10). But in addition two important factors here are the general nature of police-black community relations and the actual behavior of police during the disturbance.

POLICE-COMMUNITY RELATIONS

In its riot analysis (inspired by what it felt were failings in the reports of the

---

[2] For a review of police behavior in earlier disturbances see pp. 22–31 of the original article, deleted here for reasons of space.

[3] Important factors in these changes, discussed at greater length in the original article are the state's increased monopoly over the means of violence, the extension of universal citizenship, greater police resources and professionalism, and the fact that maintaining law and order now means controlling blacks, rather than whites, as in earlier racial disorders.

New Jersey and National Riot Commissions) the New Jersey State Patrolmen's Benevolent Association (1968) finds a "growing disrespect for law and order" to be "one of the root causes" of recent civil disorders. While much in this document could be disputed by social scientists, there is an element of truth here, although the adjective "white" might have been added to "law and order." There may be less consensus among ghetto youth on the legitimacy of the police than in the past. Increasing technical proficiency and a more professional ethos are thus undercut by the decreasing respect potential rioters may hold for the police (Bouna and Schade, 1967).

Developments within the black community have meant that even the most "enlightened" police riot behavior has sometimes been ineffective. As blacks have gained in power and self-confidence through civil rights activity, and have become more politicized, the legitimacy granted police has declined. This is especially true for many of those most prone to participate in the disorders. For many of this group, police are seen as just a group of white men, meaner than most, who are furthermore responsible for the historical and current sins of their racial group. From the point of view of one youth in Watts, "The policeman used to be a man with a badge; now he's just a thug with a gun." This change in view is clearly in the eye of the beholder rather than in the behavior of the police. Though it may be true that relatively less capable people are being recruited for police work, by most criteria police are better than ever before. Ironically, indignation against the police has risen as police behavior has improved. During a five-year period in which the Chicago police department became increasingly professionalized, one study notes no change in police perception of how the public viewed them (Wilson, 1967).

To be sure, this negative view is held by only a minority of the black community, but it is held disproportionately by the most riot-prone group. For the general Negro community, complaints of police brutality are matched by the demand for greater police protection and indignation over the behavior of Negro lawbreakers.

The New Jersey Governor's Select Commission on Civil Disorder (1968) notes that "there was virtually a complete breakdown in the relations between police and the Negro community prior to the disorders. . . . Distrust, resentment, and bitterness were at a high level on both sides (p. 143)."

Indeed, for some blacks police come to be seen as an occupation army. Silver (1967) suggests the concomitant of this view when he notes that for many whites in the face of black unrest, "Police forces come to be seen as they were in the time of their creation—as a convenient form of garrison force against an internal enemy (p. 22)." As the various (largely unanalyzed) organizational ties between the police and the Department of Defense become stronger, the view of the police as a counterinsurgency force takes on added significance. In reviewing police preparations for future riots, a journalist notes, "One would think the police were readying for war. Or waging it (Wills, 1968)."

Useful parallels can be drawn to the way police were often seen in other ethnically mixed societies during tense periods (such as India and Pakistan in 1948, or Cyprus or Israel more recently). Police are viewed not as neutral representatives of the state upholding a legal system but as armed representatives of their ethnic communities. At this point, whatever obedience police can command emerges primarily out of gun barrels and not out of respect for them or the law and order they are enforcing. Even here the symbolic hatred that police may inspire can inhibit the effectiveness of threats of force. In such situations using ethnically alien police to stop an ethnically inspired riot may be equivalent to attempting to put out a fire with gasoline.

In such a context control agents may not be successful even when they "refrain from entering the issues and controversies that move the crowd, remain impartial, unyielding, and fixed on the principle of maintaining law and order"—one of "an effective set of principles for troops to control a rioting mob" suggested by Smelser (1962, p. 267). This is precisely because even in being neutral the police are in one sense not being neutral. By the mere act of maintaining white (or the status quo) law and order the police have in fact entered "the issues and controversies" and on a side likely to aggravate potential rioters. As Joseph Lohman, a former police scholar and official has noted, "The police function to support and enforce the interests of the dominant political, social, and economic interests of the town (Neiderhoffer, 1967, p. 13)."

POLICE BEHAVIOR IN RECENT DISTURBANCES

As noted, earlier police inaction in riots has generally given way recently to decisive police action. Yet many disorders have escalated, not as in the past because of what police failed to do, but precisely because of what they have done. Here racial liberals and conservatives have switched in their indictments of the police. Where liberals earlier complained that police were indecisive and not tough enough, complaints of excessive use of force are now common—while conservatives suggest the opposite. In another reversal the same U.S. marshals who were looked upon favorably by liberals when they protected civil rights activi-

ties in the South, became the enemy during the march on the Pentagon. Many conservatives who expressed pleasure over the presence of the marshals in Washington were indignant when they were in the South.

I have found it useful to organize police behavior that was ineffective or seemed to have the effect of creating rather than controlling the disorders into the following three categories: (1) inappropriate control strategies, (2) lack of coordination among and within various control units, (3) the breakdown of police organization. The remainder of the paper is concerned primarily with police behavior up to the end of the summer of 1967.

INAPPROPRIATE CONTROL STRATEGIES

Crowd dispersal[4]

Here I wish to consider ideas held by some control officials about disorderly crowds and the kind of police action that has flowed from such views. In the spirit of Gustav Le Bon it is sometimes assumed that crowds are uniformly like-minded, anarchic, irrational, and hell-bent on destruction. From this it may follow that all people on the street are seen as actual or potential rioters, that crowds must always be broken up, that a riot will not terminate unless it is put down, and that only a technical approach involving the use of massive force is adequate.

In all too many cases police have not

[4] Data on disorders in Plainfield, Jersey City, and Elizabeth, New Jersey; Cambridge, Maryland; Detroit, Newark, Cincinnati; Dayton, New Haven; Rockford, Illinois; and Milwaukee which are not referenced are from material in the files of the National Advisory Commission on Civil Disorders (Kerner, et al., 1968). Some of the ideas in this section have profited from discussions with and were jointly developed by Robert Shellow, Lou Goldberg, and Dave Boesel.

gone beyond a nineteenth-century riot manual (Molineux, 1884) which stated "crushing power, exercised relentlessly and without hesitation is really the merciful, as it is necessary, course to be pursued (cited in Garson, 1969)."

Police were often responsible for the formation of the initial crowd by responding to fairly routine incidents with a large number of squad cars with loud sirens and flashing lights. In some cities, applying the traditional strategy of dispersing the crowd had unanticipated consequences and served to escalate and spread the disorders. The control problem then shifted from a crowd to guerrilla-like hit-and-run activities more amenable (technically if not humanly, given innocent bystanders and the monor crimes) to city clearing tactics. In commenting on new riot training, a national guard officer stated, "We ran through all that crowd-control crap again. Hell, I was in Detroit two weeks and I never once saw a crowd (Wills, 1968, p. 55)."

While the formation of a crowd at the beginning seemed to be an important factor in most disturbances, it does not follow that crowds should always be dispersed, nor that when they are dispersed, force is the only means that should be used. While the crowd itself may be conducive to a lessening of inhibitions, the anger it feels may be heightened and released by precipitous police action. Here it may be useful to distinguish a series of precipitating or initiating events.

In New Haven in 1967, for example, after some initial minor violence the crowd's mood was still tentative. A small crowd walked down the street toward police lines. As the perimeter was reached, police fired three canisters of tear gas. The crowd then ran back breaking windows and began to riot seriously.

According to a report on the 1964 Harlem riot, following the efforts of New York City's tactical patrol force to clear an intersection by swinging their clubs and yelling "charge" as they plowed into the crowd and broke it into smaller segments, "Hell broke loose in Harlem (Shapiro and Sullivan, 1964)." The angry but otherwise peaceful crowd then began pulling fire alarms, starting fires, and beating whites.

In Englewood, New Jersey, police efforts to force Negro bystanders into houses, whether or not they were the right house, angered and sparked violence on the part of young men. In Rockford, Illinois, the first instances of rock and bottle throwing were inspired by police efforts to clear a late-night bar crowd off the streets.

A peaceful rally protesting school practices in Philadelphia was violently broken up by the civil disobedience squad using riot plan number three. This elicited a violent response from the Negro youth. The superintendent and the president of the school board subsequently blamed the police for starting a riot (*Philadelphia Inquirer,* Nov. 18, 1967).

Contrary to official riot control manuals and (usually) the wishes of higher authorities, as police encounter a crowd they may break ranks, raise their night sticks above their shoulders, and hit people on the head rather than the body.

Beyond the issue of police provoking a hostile but as yet nondestructive crowd to retaliatory violence or providing a symbolic act and serving as a catalyst for the expression of the crowd's anger, the members of the crowd, once dispersed, may do more damage than the crowd itself. This may be somewhat equivalent to jumping on a burning log in efforts to put out a fire, only to see sparks and embers scatter widely. In both Milwaukee and New Haven, disorders were spread in this fashion;

scattered bands of rioters presented police with a more difficult control situation than the original crowd.

An additional problem may emerge if police lack the power to clear the street or, as in Detroit, to control it once it has been cleared. In Newark after an angry crowd pelted the police station with rocks, bottles, and a few fire bombs, police made several sorties into the crowd using their clubs, and each time withdrew back to the station. Such a seesaw motion, in demonstrating police ineffectiveness and the crowd's parity with control officials, may have emboldened rioters.

Failure to negotiate

The treatment of disorders as strictly technical problems of law and order to be solved only by force has meant that negotiations and the use of counterrioters were often ruled out. Such iron-clad rules, popular in many police circles, completely obscure the variation in types of disorder. Where the disturbance seems apolitical, unfocused, and primarily expressive and is not related to current issues or demands, and where there is no minimal organization among rioters and no one willing to take counterriot roles, there would seem to be no alternative, from the perspective of the authorities, to the graduated use of force. However, where the disturbance develops out of a very focused context involving specific issues (the demand for finding promised jobs, a particular instance of police brutality, discrimination by a business firm, disagreement over school policies, etc.), where grievances are clearly articulated and demands are present, where there seems to be some organization among rioters, and where actual or would-be spokesmen and potential counterrioters come forth, the disturbance may be stopped or dampened by entering into a dialogue, considering grievances, and using counterrioters. To resort only

to force in such a situation is more likely to inflame the situation and increase the likelihood of future disorders.

The refusal to negotiate and use strategies other than a white show of force may have had disastrous consequences in Watts. The director of the Los Angeles Human Relations Commission had worked out a plan to send in 400 black plainclothes officers and several hundred antipoverty workers to make inconspicuous arrests and spread positive rumors ("the riot is over") and to withdraw white officers to the perimeter. Young gang leaders promised to use their influence to stop the riot and were led to believe that these conditions would be met.

The deputy chief of police rejected this proposal, stating among other things that he was not going to be told how to deploy his troops and that "Negro police officers are not as competent as Caucasian officers and the only reason for sending them in would be because they have black skins and are invisible at night." To the director of the Human Relations Commission he said, "I don't want to hear anything you have got to say, you're part of the problem. *We know how to run a riot* and we are going to handle it our way." In response to the promises of gang leaders to stop the riot, he stated, "We are not going to have hoodlums telling us how to run the police department." And, "We are in the business of trying to quell a riot and we haven't got time to engage in any sociological experiments (McCone, et al., 1965, pp. 59, 61, 63, 65)." Following this refusal a full-scale riot ensued.

All blacks as rioters

Just as it is sometimes erroneously assumed that all men at a gay bar are gay or all women standing on certain street corners at a particular time are prostitutes, so to the police any black person out on the street during a period of civil disorders may be suspect. In some cities, orders to clear an area and the panicky use of force (along with beliefs about the efficacy of getting tough) have resulted in the indiscriminate application of force to anyone with a black face, including innocent bystanders, government officials, policemen in civilian clothes, ministers and Negro youth trying to stop the disorders.

In noting police inability to differentiate rioters from spectators, an observer of the 1964 Harlem disturbance notes, "The result was injuries to spectators and, in many cases conversion of spectators into players (Shapiro and Sullivan, 1964, p. 57)." A factor related to failure to negotiate and the treatment of all black people on the streets as rioters involves official response to counterrioters. In many cases they were not used at all, or, once mobilized, their efforts were frustrated.

Previous role relationships have an important effect on behavior in disaster situations. While collective behavior is essentially defined by the emergence of new norms, it nevertheless occurs within a context of ongoing familial, religious, economic, political, and social relationships. In many cities the resources of the black community were effectively used in counterriot activities—quelling rumors, urging people to go home, and trying to channel indignation into less destructive protest. During the summer of 1967 in such cities as Tampa, Florida, and Elizabeth, New Brunswick, and Plainfield, New Jersey, police were even ordered out of the disturbance area and local residents successfully patroled the streets. The issue of whether or not police should be withdrawn is a complex one that far transcends the simplistic rhetoric of its opponents and supporters. While it was successful in the above cities, in several other cities it had the opposite effect. However, what is not

really at issue is the fact that there existed a sizable reservoir of counterriot sentiment that could have been activated in the place of, or along side of, other control activities. This counterriot sentiment was generally not counterprotest and in many cases represented considerations of strategy rather than principle. But motivation aside, failure to use counterrioters effectively may have prolonged a number of disturbances.

In Cincinnati, despite an agreement between the mayor and black leaders that the latter would be given badges and allowed to go into the riot area to help calm things, police refused to recognize the badges and arrested some of them on charges of loitering. A somewhat similar situation existed in Milwaukee. In Newark the mayor and governor gave permission to Negro volunteers to go among the people in efforts to calm the situation. Their activities were inhibited by enforcement personnel. According to the governor, they "were chased around so much by people who suspected them as participating in the riot that they had to abandon their efforts (Governor's Select Commission on Civil Disorders, 1968, p. 120)."

Beyond the general confusion in the disorders and a racially inspired (if not racist) inability to differentiate among types of Negroes, this police response was related to a view of the disorders as a technical problem to be met only by a show of force and a feeling that police competence and jurisdiction were being infringed upon. That counterrioters were often black activists, and in some cases gang youth, may have accentuated this feeling.

Official anticipation
Thus far, the disorders considered have involved the pattern of riotous or at least disorderly Negro behavior followed and sometimes encouraged by the

official response. However, there were other instances where the dynamics of the disturbance worked in the opposite direction. Here authorities (with poor intelligence reports) precipitated confrontation by anticipating violence where none was imminent and by overreacting to minor incidents that happened to occur during a major riot elsewhere.

While adequate planning and preparation are vital to effective control, they may help create a state-of-siege mentality, increase susceptibility to rumors, and exert a self-fulfilling pressure. This is particularly true when they are found with a get-tough, act-quickly philosophy. Following the Newark riot, fourteen cities in the surrounding area had some type of disorders; after Detroit, eight additional Michigan cities reported disorders. An important factor (rather than, or in addition to, psychological contagion) in the spread of violence from major urban centers to outlying communities was the expectation of a riot—and subsequent overreaction on the part of white authorities.

In New Jersey a month and a half before Newark erupted, there were reports of planned violence, and counterplans were designed. On June 5, 1967, the police chiefs of more than seventy-five New Jersey communitites met in Jersey City to discuss the supposed plans of militant blacks to foment violence. Jersey City, Newark, and Elizabeth were reportedly given "triple A" ratings for violence over the summer. Plans to coordinate control efforts were set up and procedures for calling in the National Guard and state police gone over. Riot control training was held in a number of communities.

When Newark finally erupted, prior rumors were confirmed in the minds of many local officials in other communities and fears of anticipated violence were acted upon. In one New Jersey city, officials reacted to the rumor that Stokely Carmichael was bringing carloads of black militants into the community, although Carmichael was in London at the time. In Jersey City, four hundred armed police occupied the black area several days before any disorders occurred. In Englewood, where police outnumbered participants three to one, black residents had earlier been angered by riot control exercises in which the wind had blown tear gas into surrounding Negro homes. In Elizabeth, police greatly increased patrols in the black area and residents expressed opinions such as, "The community felt it was in a concentration camp." The appearance of armed police patrols increased the likelihood of confrontation and greatly strained relations with local Negroes. Whatever an individual's feeling about civil rights, to have his neighborhood saturated with armed men in uniform in the face of minimal, sporadic, and even no disorders, often created indignation. A frequent demand was for police withdrawal or less visible show of arms. In six of seven New Jersey cities (that had disorders at the time of Newark) chosen for study by the riot commission, removal of police from the ghetto signaled an end to violence.

Sniping

While much sniping was attributed to control agents firing at each other, fire-crackers, and the snapping of broken power lines, response to the sniping that actually did exist was inadequate. Mass firing by men on the ground at buildings, often using their private weapons, without an adequate system of accounting for ammunition spent and not under the command of a superior officer, created much havoc, killed and wounded many innocent people, and helped escalate the violence. Such firing no doubt drew counterfire from angry Negroes bent on retaliation or who viewed their counterfire as self-defense, in some cases creating the very sniper fire it was supposedly trying to stop. The fact that changes in policy from not shooting to shooting looters during the Detroit riot were not announced may have increased the death toll. In a related context, if people don't hear an order to disperse because they are too noisy, that doesn't affect the legality of their arrest—according to guidelines put out by the San Francisco police department (1963, p. 4).

The use of force

In the use of force in quelling a disturbance, the police have traditionally faced a dilemma. To underreact out of concern with heightening tensions, because of technical incapacity, or because the seriousness of the situation is not appreciated may permit disorders to spread rapidly as new norms conducive to disorderly behavior emerge and as people see that they can break rules without fear of being sanctioned. On the other hand, to use too much force too soon may create incidents and escalate the disorders as bystanders become involved and the already involved become ever more indignant. In cities such as Watts, Newark, and Detroit, police departments moved from a pattern of underreaction to overreaction, in each case inadvertently contributing to the disorders.

In Detroit a factor that came to be known as the "blue flu" may have been relevant. Prior to the riot, in an abortive unofficial strike many officers had called in sick. It has been suggested that some policemen in their anger and in order to demonstrate their importance to the city went beyond the policy of departmental restraint in underreacting during the initial disorders, in some cases even encouraging people to loot. This police strike did not have the tragic consequences of the 1919 Boston police strike. In fact, according to several

preriot sources, reports of crime actually went down when the police were out on strike.

There are two independent issues in the much-debated role of force in quelling civil disorders. One has to do with the effect of threats of force on the outbreak of disorders and the other with its effect on the course of a disturbance once it has started.

The tensions which generate riots are not likely to be reduced by a tough-talking mayor or police chief. Such rhetoric would seem to have little deterrent value and may help further to polarize the atmosphere and create fear in blacks of genocide and plans for self-defense (which are then likely to be taken by police as proof of the need to be even tougher). However, once disorders have begun, a get-tough policy may be more "effective." (Although the criteria of effectiveness are by no means clear; and effectiveness, if defined simply as the cessation of the disorders, may conflict radically with other cherished values of the society.)

The example of Milwaukee shows that an early display of overwhelming force can stop the disorders—though the closing of airports and highways, the presence of 4,800 national guardsmen, 800 policemen, and 200 state police after about 150 youths broke windows and looted after a dance seems rather out of proportion. Similarly, indiscriminate lethal force will temporarily scatter a crowd. A group of angry blacks protesting a segregated bowling alley in Orangeburg was broken up (in the largest single bloodletting thus far) when state police fired without warning into the unarmed group, killing three and wounding twenty-seven others (many of whom were shot in the back).

While such force may temporarily break up the crowd (ethical considerations aside), it may create martyrs and symbolic incidents which galvanize social-movement support. Witness the cases of Lafayette and the Parisian National Guard firing on unarmed demonstrators in 1791, the Boston Massacre in 1770, the calvary's riding down peaceful demonstrators at Peterloo in 1819, the firing on unarmed petitioners at the Winter Palace in 1905, and General Dyer's massacre of Indians at Amritsar. A fruitful area of study is the sociology of martyrdom and the conditions under which repression will arouse sympathy on the part of larger audiences. Important issues here would seem to be whether the repression is directed against nonviolent or violent demonstrators and whether the protest involves a moral issue easily seen to be consistent with the basic values of the larger society.

Unfortunately, it can't very well be said scientifically that those control practices most offensive to humane sensibilities are also those least likely to be effective, although neither can the opposite be said. Strong moral grounds clearly exist for opposing such policies, but very little is known about the likely short- and long-run consequences of different control strategies.

We can hypothetically differentiate between control practices that may have no effect on the disorders, those that cause them to escalate, and those that reduce or stop them. Empirically trying to sort these out is, however, very hard. Given the lack of sophisticated analysis with a reasonable sample, examples can be selectively chosen to show the effectiveness or ineffectiveness of almost any given strategy. In the case of the "get-tough perspective" these often are embarrassingly time-bound. Thus two cities often cited, Miami (whose police chief stated, "When the looting starts, the shooting starts") and Philadelphia ("They take your attempts to meet their demands

as a sign of weakness; you have to meet them with absolute force") subsequently have experienced disorders.

There is a curious confusion in the image of man held by proponents of a get-tough policy. On the one hand, they assume that the potentially riotous individual is cold and calculating, carefully weighs the consequences of his actions, and hence will be frightened by the potentially strong sanctions. On the other hand, rioters are simultaneously thought of as completely wild and irrational people caught up in an "insensate rage."

In a related context students of criminal behavior in American society have consistently noted that harsh sanctions and capital punishment are not effective deterrents for many offenses. Some research in other countries has reported curvilinear relationships between hostile outbursts and repression (LeVine, 1959; Bwy, 1968). Student and antiwar protests are beyond the scope of this paper, yet much of what has been said about police behavior during city racial disorders applies here as well. As a brief aside we can particularly note their role in aiding the success of student protests.

The state of our social engineering knowledge is admittedly limited; however, if one wanted to structure the world to be sure that university disturbances would occur, one could learn a lot by watching the unintended consequences of the behavior of university administrators. One pattern that applied to a great many disorders up to 1968 is as follows. A small number of students, often with a cause or issue that doesn't actively interest the mass of their fellows, plan or actually carry out limited peaceful protest action. The university administration tries to restrict the protest; it prevents freedom of speech and action, or it arbitrarily and without due process singles out certain activists for punishment, or it calls the police to break up a demonstration. With these administrative actions the nature of the unrest changes quantitatively and qualitatively. A basic issue now becomes free speech or police brutality or rights of due process. Latent tensions may result in additional issues such as the quality of education coming to the surface, issues which had nothing to do with the original problem or the university response. Greater unity among the protestors develops; the mass of uncommitted moderate students are drawn to their side (often in spite of initially opposing them or being indifferent to the original issue); liberal faculty and organizations in the outside community respond in like fashion. The dynamics of the situation thus involve the move from a small peaceful protest to a large disorderly and disobedient protest. (In student demonstrations abroad, use of police has often had similar consequences; in the case of France and Germany, see Crozier, 1968, and Mayntz, 1968.)

In this move from limited to general protest, aged if sometimes crew-cut university administrators, confronted with a novel situation, are pulled between conservative boards of regents, trustees, and public, and the liberal academic community. They vacillate, act inconsistently and unpredictably, and may fail to grasp the essence of the situation they are confronted with; they may make undocumented (and certainly unwise) statements about the role of communists, off-campus agitators, and troublemakers; they may be unable to differentiate kinds of student demonstrators. Various deans and university officials make statements and offer interpretations that may contradict each other; agreements reached between student and authorities may be overruled or distorted by other authorities. As at Berkeley and Columbia, admin-

istrators may fail to accept the recommendations even of their own faculty or faculty-student committees set up to deal with the crisis. Students perceive university administrators as being confused, bungling, arrogant, hypocritical, and acting in bad faith; this strengthens student feelings about the legitimacy of their cause.

Finally, when authorities do act by calling in the police, police often conform to the strategy of the demonstrators, seemingly unaware that such a strategy, if not completely self-defeating, at best has no win consequences for the authority structure. There are two important issues in using police in campus disorders: first, the fact that the conflict is stopped by the naked power of the state, contrary to hallowed ideals of a liberal university; and second, the fact that insulted and provoked police sometimes lose control and use undue and indiscriminate force, thus greatly increasing the disorders. Some private schools such as Chicago, Brandeis, Roosevelt, and Reed where the police have not been called in to "solve" conflicts (partly because such schools are not under as stong external pressure from the public and government to do so) have avoided the degree of disruption and disorder, the residue of bitterness, and the concessions to students that have been present at schools such as Berkeley, Wisconsin, San Francisco State, Columbia, and Harvard where the police were called in.

LACK OF COORDINATION AMONG CONTROL UNITS

The historical fact that the United States did not develop a specialized national riot police as in France and Italy has probably meant prolonged disorders and greater injury and death. The constitutional delegation of the police function to states and our forty thousand separate police units means that initially each city must rely on its own inadequate resources.

In the face of major, unanticipated disorders involving a wide area and large numbers of people engaged in hit-and-run guerrilla-like tactics, local decentralized autonomous American police, organized primarily to fight crime, control traffic, and keep the peace were usually ineffective. The control of such disturbances requires training and activity that are almost opposite in nature to those needed for normal police operations (Turner, 1968), and necessitates calling in other control units differing in training, organizational structure, ethos, and familiarity with the local area. Not surprisingly difficulties often emerged as a result.

Whereas the inability to admit failure, bureaucratic entanglements, petty rivalries, and political considerations all delayed the calling out of higher levels of force, the lack of prior planning and an unclear chain of command meant further delays once other control agents finally did arrive on the scene. Local, state, and national guard units did not merge easily. Guard units, accustomed to acting in patrols, were fragmented and guardsmen were isolated from commanding officers; police, who were usually organized as one- or two-man autonomous patrol units, were to become disciplined members of military units, relying on commands from superiors and not on their own discretion. While officers from different units were together, they were often responding to separate orders. In Newark the three enforcement agencies were issued separate orders on weapons use. In commenting on the use of his men, a National Guard commander in Detroit noted, "They sliced us up like baloney. The police wanted bodies. They grabbed guardsmen as soon as they reached armories, before their units were made up, and sent them out—two on a firetruck, this one in a police car, that one to guard some installation." This meant that "a young man without a car or radio, without any knowledge of the city, could get stranded far away from any officer, without food or cigarettes, convinced (often rightly) that no one remembered where he was. . . . The guard simply became lost boys in the big town carrying guns (Wills, 1968)."

Technical as well as social communications problems contributed to ineffective coordination of control activities and clearly furthered the disorders. Regular radio frequencies were heavily overtaxed, and local police, state police, and the National Guard operated on different frequencies. Though this had been a problem two years earlier in Watts, little had changed by the time of Detroit and Newark. In the beginning stages of the latter, state police were unable to get a clear definition of riot perimeters or where activity was heaviest. They could not obtain information about the movement of local police patrols or citizens' calls and were obliged to follow local police and fire trucks responding to calls (Governor's Select Commission, 1968). Inability to communicate was a factor in police and guardsmen firing at each other and in the belief in widespread sniping.

Poor communication within departments also had serious consequences (Cohen and Murphy, 1967; Conot, 1967). One reason the Los Angeles police department failed to employ sufficient manpower when needed was the reluctance of subordinate commanders to expose themselves to ridicule and downgrading by possible overreaction. While the Los Angeles police possessed some of the most skilled investigators in the world, trained to deal with master criminals, they could not get a true picture of what was happening in the early stages of Watts. Early on the third day of the riot, field forces knew the situation was out of control but the downtown command post was still optimistic. This is the classic problem of information flow in a bureaucracy. This highly professional department was unable to admit that a handful of what it considered hoodlums could create a major disturbance that it couldn't control.

In Plainfield, contrary actions by county and city police greatly inflamed the disorders. Plainfield had a relatively political disturbance with meetings and negotiations between blacks and city authorities alternating with violence. At one such meeting, under the auspices of community relations personnel and with city police understanding, several hundred men gathered in a county park to discuss their grievances and to choose leaders to represent them. During the meeting the violence had greatly subsided. However, this was shortlived, as the meeting was abruptly terminated by county police who said they could not meet in the park without a permit. This incensed the young men. Within an hour violence flared—that night a patrolman was killed and the destruction reached its highest point.

Further conflict among different levels of authority emerged in Plainfield between the police and local and state officials. Police felt "left out," "tired," and "poorly treated," and threatened to resign en masse (and to some observers almost mutinied) following their exclusion from negotiations which led to the release of arrested rioters, a policy of containment following the killing of a fellow officer, and the stopping by a state official of a house-to-house search for stolen carbines. The New Jersey riot inquiry felt that the circumscription of local police activities was such "as virtually to destroy the department's morale . . . [and]

to limit seriously the effectiveness of the force (Governor's Select Commission, 1968, pp. 150, 153)."

In still other cases, as in Los Angeles, Boston, and New York, agreements reached by mayor's special representatives, human relations officials, and police-community relations officers who had rapport with rioters were not honored by other policemen, creating great indignation and a sense of betrayal. In Los Angeles, the police-community relations inspector was reportedly not called into the inner circle of police advisors. The chief of police was unaware that his department had been represented at an important community meeting held during the riot. A potentially ugly incident might have emerged in Detroit (May 21, 1968) when mounted police outside a building tried to drive supporters of the Poor People's March back into a building, while police on the inside were trying to drive them out. In Rockford, Illinois, in 1967, as people poured out of bars that were closing, police tried to drive them off the street that other police had already barricaded. In Birmingham in 1963, police circled several thousand blacks, on one side swinging their clubs and from the other side turning water hoses on them, catching bystanders as well as protesters—though this was no doubt all too well-coordinated.

BREAKDOWN OF POLICE ORGANIZATION: ONE RIOT OR TWO?

An additional source of police ineffectiveness and abuse stems from the breakdown of organization within enforcement agencies. In most discussions of recent riots, undue emphasis has been given to the behavior of rioters. The normal concepts used to analyze collective behavior have been applied to them—emotional contagion, the spread of rumors, panic and the expression of frustration, the lessening of inhibitions, and innovative efforts to handle certain kinds of strain. Yet in several major disturbances, this perspective might equally be applied to the police. Police, lacking training and experience and often uncertain of what they were to do, sometimes became fatigued (frequently working 12-hour or more shifts with insufficient rest periods and nourishment); they were thrown off balance by the size of the disturbance and by being drawn frantically from' one area to another, in some cases for false alarms seemingly coordinated with attacks and looting. As large numbers of people taunted, defied, insulted, and attacked them and they saw their fellows injured and in some cases killed, patience thinned and anger rose. Rumors about atrocities committed against them then spread.

Police may come to take violent black rhetoric and threats (which are partly related to expressive oral traditions, ritual posturing, and political in-fighting) too literally—as the lack of police killed by snipers and even reports that some snipers may have misfired on purpose, and the lack of attacks on known racists might imply. The belief may spread that they are in a war and all black people are their enemy. Traditional misconceptions about riotous crowds may contribute to an exaggeration of the dangers confronting them. As police control of the "turf" is effectively challenged and rioters gain control of the streets by default, the word may spread (as in Watts, Newark, and Detroit) that rioters have "beat the police." Losing face, humiliated by their temporary defeat and with their professional pride undermined, police may have a strong desire for revenge and to show their efficacy.

In a context such as the above, superior officers may lose the power to control their men. The chain of command and communication between and within enforcement agencies, often unclear to begin with, may completely break down. The most dangerous part of the disturbance is now at hand as the environment changes from a riot to a war. Some police behavior seems as much, or more, inspired by the desire for vengeance, retaliation, and "to teach the bastards a lesson" as by the desire to restore law and order.

The words of Lee and Humphrey, written shortly after the 1943 Detroit riot, are clearly relevant twenty-six years later: "War is to the army much what civilian outbreaks are to the police. Both offer socially acceptable outlets for the residuum of aggressiveness characteristic of each (Lee and Humphrey, 1943, p. 114)."

On the third day of the Detroit riot, an officer was overheard telling a young black on a newly stolen bicycle, "The worm is turning." And turn it did as the police took off their badges, taped over squad car numbers (this, of course, greatly reduced the number of complaints filed), and began indiscriminantly and excessively using force against rioters, bystanders, and in some cases each other. The death and injury toll climbed rapidly. Some of the firing stopped only when control officials ran out of ammunition. At this time the Algier's Motel killings and "game" occurred. One of the police officers involved in this incident stated, "there was a lot of rough-housing, you know, everything just went loose [following the killing of a police officer on the third day of the riot]. The police officers weren't taking anything from anyone (Hersey, 1968, p. 134)." This would seem to be something of an understatement.

According to one high police official

in secret testimony, by the fourth day of the riot "the police were out of control." There are some reports of police keeping looted goods taken from prisoners, robbing them, and of doing damage to "soul brother" stores spared by the rioters (Governor's Select Commission, 1968). Claims of brutality filed included charges of the mistreatment of women and the carving of initials on prisoners. It should be noted that such behavior occurs in spite of official riot control manuals stressing restrained use of force, and (usually) in spite of the wishes of higher authorities. Recent control manuals, while leaving something to be desired in their conceptual approach to collective behavior, stress the controlled and graduated use of force (Federal Bureau of Investigation, 1967; Mombiosse, 1967; also see Westley, 1956).

The attacking of fellow officers took two forms. It was either accidental or willful—as in the case of the beating of Negro police officers thought to be civilians because they were in plainclothes. For an example of the beating of an off-duty officer in Newark (*New York Times,* July 14, 1967) and the case of two black plainclothes officers beaten when the New York tactical patrol force "stampeded a crowd, . . . flailing vigorously with clubs," see Shapiro and Sullivan (1964, p. 93). A related incident not involving force occurred in Watts where a Negro plainslothesman (sent incognito to scout the Watts riot) hailed a radio car to make his report. The officer inside leaned out and asked him, "What you want, shitass jigaboo? (Wills, 1968)."

The chairman of the Newark Human Rights Commission reported that ". . . men were being brought in, many of them handcuffed behind their backs, being carried like a sack of meal, and the fifth policeman would be hammering their face and body with a billy

stick. This went on time after time. Many times you would see a man being brought into the police station without a mark on his face and when he was taken out he was brutally beaten (Governor's Select Commission, 1968, p. 118)." It has been said in jest, although there is an element of truth in it, that Newark was a classical race riot except the Italians wore blue uniforms.

Police may come to see rioters and suspected rioters, like those convicted of crimes, as having forfeited their civil rights. In Watts an officer responded to a black pedestrian who complained about being stopped on his way home from work: "Don't yell at me; you lost your rights a couple of days ago (Cohen and Murphy, 1967, p. 195)."

There often seemed to be a tendency for police behavior to become progressively worse as the disorders wore on. In Watts, Newark, and Detroit this was partly related to the entrance of higher level control units into the disturbance. The assignment of guardsmen to accompany policemen may be seen by the latter as offering a chance to reverse earlier humiliation and gain revenge for injury and death suffered by the police. At the same time, inexperienced guardsmen, isolated from the authority of their commanding officers, may become subject to the same collective behavior phenomena as police and blacks, further adding to disorder-creating activities.

The head of the Detroit police, a former reporter, was hesitant to call out the guard, noting, "I've been on too many stories where the guard was called up. They're always shooting their own people"; and "Those poor kids were scared pissless, and they scared me (Wills, 1968, pp. 43, 44)." Calling them out was, however, a necessity to gain federal troops.

What is especially tragic is that the

symbols of police legitimacy become the cloak under which much indiscriminate force is exercised upon the Negro community. It is a mistake to attribute such behavior only to the desire for revenge or to a hatred of Negroes, because part of it would seem to be equivalent to the behavior of front line soldiers who in their first combat experience kill many of their own men. That the breakdown of police organization transcends racism may also be seen in police response to student protests (such as at Columbia University) and various antiwar demonstrations.

It is important to recognize that not only was police behavior in the latter stages of several major riots brutal and probably ineffective, but that such acts were not idiosyncratic or random. They were woven into a social fabric of rumor, panic, frustration, fatigue, fear, racism, lack of training, inexperience, and the breakdown of police organization. While such a situation creates widespread fear in the Negro community and may inhibit some rioters, it can lead to (and partly results from) escalation in the level of black violence. There is an interaction process with gradual reciprocal increases in the severity of action taken on both sides. The fact that police abuses were most pronounced in Newark and Detroit, where disturbances were the most serious, does not imply a one-sided causal interpretation. Here we see the emergent character of the disorders.

Just as the belief that blacks want to kill police spreads among police so the opposite view may spread among black people. According to one account, Negro spectators in Harlem were "convinced that the policemen were the aggressors, in spite of the bricks, bottles, rubbish cans, and Molotov cocktails which flew around the intersection." According to an elderly woman, "They want to kill all of us; they want

to shoot all the black people." A man agreed: "They wouldn't do all this gunslinging and clubbing on 42nd Street (Shapiro and Sullivan, 1964)."

An additional element in the misuse of official force is the view held by some policemen that they can (and indeed must) "hold court in the street," given the presumed leniency and complexity of the legal system (Reiss and Bordua, 1967). Gathering evidence that will hold in court during mass disorders and demonstrations is difficult; those arrested can often be charged with nothing more than a misdemeanor; sentencing for riot offenses tends to be lighter than for similar offenses committed in nonriot situations. The use of violence in such situations may also be related to the policemen's effort to save face and their belief that respect for their authority must be reestablished (Westley, 1953).

The breakdown of police organization and misuse of force did not happen to anywhere near the same extent in all cities that had disturbances. An important question for analysis is why in Watts, Newark, and Detroit—but not in Cincinnati or Boston? The conditions under which such police behavior appears are not well-understood. There would seem to be a relationship to things such as training, the extent to which the police share social characteristics with and disagree with or are threatened and offended by the issues raised by protestors, the extent of injuries and provocation faced by police, the size and stage of the riot, the clarity of orders stressing restraint, the tightness of the command structure and whether civilian monitors and high level government and police officials are on the scene, whether or not it is made clear to police that they will be punished for misbehavior, and whether or not police expect disturbance participants to be sufficiently punished by the legal system. That there was a breakdown of police organization in two of the most "professional" (according to the standards of the International Association of Chiefs of Police) departments in the United States, Los Angeles and Chicago, suggests that this issue goes beyond what is usually understood as police professionalism. In fact it may even be that less "professional" police departments such as Boston's have greater flexibility and a less zealous approach to potential threats to "law and order," permitting them to show greater restraint and making them more effective during a tense period.

QUIS CUSTODIET IPSOS CUSTODES?

One of the central intellectual problems for social analysis is the basis of social order. If one resolves the question of social order by relying on shared values and the internalization of standards, then this is not seen as an issue. Yet even those who answer the question of social order by stressing the importance of external force usually ignore it. In several of the major disturbances, after a period of time the tragic answer to the question of "who guards the guards" almost seemed to be "no one."

In at least one case, however, the answer to this question was higher level authorities. In a border city whose chief of police wanted ". . . to get every son-of-a-bitch down there; I'm getting goddamned tired of fooling around," the highly professional restraint of state police and National Guard commanders seemed to prevent a police-initiated slaughter in the aftermath of minor disorders following a speech by H. Rap Brown. In the judgment of these higher level commanders, the best control of the disorders was seen to lie in controlling the local police. The original disorders to an important extent grew out of exaggerated fears that Negroes were planning an attack on the downtown area and a state-of-siege worldview among white authorities. The police chief was enraged by the wounding of a police officer which had followed instances of "white nightriding" and several shots fired by a deputy sheriff at H. Rap Brown as he walked toward the dividing line between the white and black areas. The white local volunteer fire department refused to put out a fire of unknown origin at a Negro school that had been the center of controversy, resulting in several square blocks being burned down. The National Guard then effectively neutralized the local police force and protected the Negro community, action which clearly contradicts the view of a monolithic, oppressive white control force. In another instance—the 1964 Harlem disturbance—James Farmer felt "the police were hysterical" and reportedly appealed to Governor Rockefeller to send the National Guard to "protect the citizens of Harlem (Shapiro and Sullivan, 1964, pp. 71, 83)."

One of the manifestly unfair aspects of social organization is that those with official power are usually also those (or are intimately tied to those) who possess the power to sanction the misuse of this power. One means by which the police traditionally have been controlled is through the courts by the *exclusionary rule,* whereby illegal means used in gaining evidence or making arrests are grounds for the dismissal of a case. However, this rule only applies when convictions are sought (a factor often beyond the control of the police). In addition many police abuses do not involve the gathering of evidence. The closeness of the police to the courts and their interdependence may inhibit the regulatory role of the former, particularly at lower levels.

Individuals can also bring costly and time-consuming civil damage suits against the police, although those most likely to need redress may be least likely to have the resources necessary for a long court struggle—and establishing proof is difficult. The anonymity and confusion of a crowd situation and the tendency to remove badges make identification of offending officials unlikely. In the rare cases where police are criminally prosecuted for riot offenses, juries tend to find in their favor.

Police have also been controlled through direct political means. The rise of "good government"-inspired civil service reforms and the decline of the urban political machine makes this less likely today. Most of the now defunct Civilian Review Boards met with great police resistance, had no formal enforcement power, and could not initiate inquiries.

The means of control favored by the police is self-regulation, in a fashion analogous to specialized professions such as medicine or law. It is argued that police work is highly technical and only those who practice it are competent to judge it. Internal review mechanisms have been inadequate to say the least; there is evidence to suggest that, like the rest of us, the police can resist anything but temptation. Knowledge that they are unlikely to be subjected to postriot sanctioning may have lessened restraints on their use of violence. In many departments there is a strong norm of secrecy surrounding police misbehavior; even when known, infractions often go unpunished.

The consequences, costs, and benefits of various means of regulating the police have not been carefully studied. It is clear from some of the data considered in this paper and from more recent events such as the Chicago Democratic Convention, the People's Park episode in Berkeley, and attacks on groups such as the Black Panthers that the control of the police is sometimes not much affected by the courts, various other checks and balances, internalized norms of fair play, nor internal police organization. The question of control and responsiveness of the police is certainly among the most pressing of domestic issues.

It has been often suggested that the most hideous crimes have been committed in the name of obedience rather than rebellion. In the Gordon Riots of 1780, demonstrators destroyed property and freed prisoners but evidently did not kill anyone, while authorities killed several hundred rioters and hanged an additional twenty-five. In the Réveillon Riots of the French Revolution, several hundred rioters were killed, but they killed no one (Couch, 1968). Up to the end of the summer of 1967, this pattern was being repeated; police, not rioters, are responsible for most of the more than one hundred riot deaths that have occurred. To an important extent this pattern stems not from differences in will, but from the greater destructive resources of those in power, associated with their holding power to begin with, and from their ability to sanction. In a related context, the more than one hundred civil rights murders of recent years have been matched by almost no murders of racist whites. (Since 1968, this pattern may be changing.)

As long as racism and poverty exist American society needs relentless protest. It also needs police. It is increasingly clear that police are unduly scapegoated, stereotyped, and maligned; they are, as well, underpaid, undertrained, given contradictory tasks, and made to face directly the ugly consequences of the larger society's failure to change. It is equally clear that solutions to America's racial problems lie much more in the direction of redistributing power and income, eliminating discrimination and exploitation, than in changing the police. Nevertheless, one important factor in heeding the Kerner Commission's plea (1968) to "end the destruction and the violence, not only in the streets of the ghetto but in the lives of the people" is surely more enlightened police behavior.

REFERENCES

BLUMER H. "Race Prejudice As a Sense of Group Position." *Pacific Sociological Review,* 1958, **1,** 3–7.

BOUNA, D., and SCHADE, T. "Police Riots and the Inner City and Police and Urban Unrest." Unpublished manuscript, Western Michigan University, 1967.

BWY, D. "Dimensions of Conflict in Latin America." *American Behavioral Scientist,* 1968, **2,** 39–50.

CHICAGO COMMISSION ON RACE RELATIONS. *The Negro in Chicago.* Chicago: University of Chicago Press, 1923.

COHEN, J., and MURPHY, W. *Burn, Baby, Burn.* New York: Avon, 1967.

CONOT, R. *Rivers of Blood, Years of Darkness.* New York: Bantam, 1967.

COUCH, C. "Collective Behavior: An Examination of Stereotypes." *Social Problems,* 1968, **15,** 310–321.

CROZIER, M. "French Students: A Letter from Nanterre Ca Folie." *Public Interest,* 1968, No. **13,** 151–159.

DAHLKE, A. "Race and Minority Riots— A Study in the Typology of Violence." *Social Forces,* 1952, **30,** 419–425.

FEDERAL BUREAU OF INVESTIGATION. *Prevention and Control of Mobs.* Washington, D.C., 1967.

FOGELSON, R. "Violence As Protest: An Interpretation of the 1960's Riots." *Proceedings of the Academy of Political Science,* 1968, **29,** 25–42.

FRANKLIN, J. H. *From Slavery to Freedom.* New York: Knopf, 1965.

GARSON, D. "The Politics of Collective Violence." Unpublished doctoral dissertation, Harvard University, 1969.

GOVERNOR'S SELECT COMMISSION ON CIVIL DISORDERS (New Jersey). *Report for Action,* 1968.

GRENLEY, W. "Social Control in Cicero." *British Journal of Sociology,* 1952, **3,** 322–388.

GRIMSHAW, A. "Actions of Police and the Military in American Race Riots." *Phylon,* 1963, **24,** 271–289.

HERSEY, J. *The Algiers Motel Incident.* New York: Bantam, 1968.

JANOWITZ, M. *Social Control of Escalated Riots.* Chicago: Univ. Chicago Center for Policy Study, 1968.

KERNER, O., et al. *Report of the National Advisory Commission on Civil Disorders.* New York: Bantam, 1968.

LEE, A. M., and HUMPHREY, N. O. *Race Riot.* New York: Dryden, 1943.

LEVINE, R. "Anti-European Violence in Africa: A Comparative Analysis." *Journal of Conflict Resolution,* 1959, **3,** 420–429.

MARSHALL, T. "The Gestapo in Detroit." *Crisis,* 1943, **50,** 232–234.

MAYNTZ, R. "Germany: Radicals and Reformers." *Public Interest,* 1968, **No. 13,** 160–172.

MCCONE, J. A., et al. "Governor's Commission on the Los Angeles Riots." *Volume II: Chronology.* Los Angeles, 1965.

MERTON, R. *Social Theory and Social Structure.* Glencoe, Ill.: Free Press, 1957.

MOLINEUX, E. L. "Riots in Cities and Their Suppression." Boston: Headquarters, First Brigade, 1884.

MOMBOISSE, R. *Riots, Revolts, and Insurrections.* Springfield, Ill.: Thomas, 1967.

NEIDERHOFFER, A. *Behind the Shield.* New York: Doubleday, 1967.

NEW JERSEY STATE PATROLMEN'S BENEVOLENT ASSOCIATION. *A Challenge to Conscience.* Maplewood, N.Y., 1968.

OSOFSKY, G. "Race Riot, 1900, a Study of Ethnic Violence." *Journal of Negro Education,* 1963, **32,** 16–24.

REISS, A., and BORDUA, D. "Environment and Organization: A Perspective on the Police." In D. Bordau (Ed.), *The Police.* New York: Wiley, 1967.

RUDWICK, E. *Race Riot at East St. Louis, July 2, 1919.* Cleveland: World, 1966.

SAN FRANCISCO POLICE DEPARTMENT. "Police Control of Riots and Demonstrations." San Francisco, 1963.

SELIGMANN, H. J. "Race war." *New Republic,* 1919, **20,** 48–50.

SHAPIRO, F. C. and SULLIVAN, J. W. *Race Riots.* New York: Crowell, 1964.

SHELLOW, R., and ROEMER, D. V. "The Riot That Didn't Happen." *Social Problems,* 1966, **14,** 221–233.

SHIBUTANI, T., and KWAN, K. H. *Ethnic Stratification.* New York: Macmillan, 1965.

SHOGAN, R., and CRAIG, T. *The Detroit Race Riot.* Philadelphia: Chilton, 1964.

SILVER, A. "The Demand for Order in Civil Society: A Review of Some Themes in the History of Urban Crime, Police, and Riots." In D. J. Bordua (Ed.), *The Police.* New York: Wiley, 1967.

SMELSER, N. *Theory of Collective Behavior.* New York: Free Press, 1962.

TURNER, C. C. "Planning and Training for Civil Disorder." *The Police Chief,* 1968, **35,** 22–28.

WASKOW, A. I. *From Race Riot to Sit-in: 1919 and the 1960's.* Garden City, N.Y.: Doubleday, 1966.

WENKERT, R., MAGNEY, J., and NEEL, A. *Two Weeks of Racial Crisis in Richmond, California.* Survey Research Center, Univ. of California, Berkeley, 1967.

WESTLEY, W. A. "Violence and the Police." *American Journal of Sociology,* 1953, **59,** 34–41.

WESTLEY, W. A. *The Formation, Nature, and Control of Crowds.* Defense Research Board, Canada, 1956.

WHITE, W. F. "Chicago and Its Eight Reasons." *Crisis,* Oct., 1919, **18,** No. 6.

WILLS, G. *The Second Civil War.* New York: New American Library, 1968.

WILSON, J. O. "Police Morale, Reform and Citizen Respect: The Chicago Case." In D. J. Bordua (Ed.), *The Police.* New York: Wiley, 1967.

SECTION B
CASE STUDIES: THE ANALYSIS CONFLICT

CAREFUL attention to the material presented thus far will have suggested a number of the factors that are important to consider in analyzing the emergence, form, course, and consequences of racial conflict. Among important ways in which conflict situations differ from each other are their context, the characteristics of involved groups and individuals, the nature of the issue, and the means used. In approaching any given conflict certain questions should be asked, though answers may often be limited or difficult to come by. Among a large number of questions that might be asked and which may help sensitize us to factors most relevant for sociological understanding are the following:

Group Structure

What sources of cleavage beyond racial group serve to divide the involved groups, such as social class position, age, region, sex, religion, or ideology? Or, conversely, what characteristics do combatants have in common?

Is the dispute generated by deep cleavages in the community or relatively superficial ones?

Are the parties to the conflict tightly or loosely integrated into the dominant institutions and organizations of the society? What is the class base of the involved leaders and followers?

Are the involved groups internally homogeneous and subject to the control of a strong leader, or is each group internally fragmented?

Does the conflict occur within a close-knit communal group or between formally organized voluntary associations?

Is the conflict between a dominant and subordinate group, two more or less equally subordinate groups, or within one of these?

Is the conflict between two private groups or a private group and the government?

Are there strong disinterested third parties present who wish to see the conflict resolved?

Are there other third-party groups with needed resources that can be drawn to the side of the less powerful group?

Is a central power structure with the capability of decisive action present?

Are there mechanisms present such as courts or boards of appeal which can channel and limit the conflict?

Is the conflict of a face-to-face nature or mediated through third parties?

What lines of communication exist between involved groups?

How many clearly distinct groups are a party to the controversy?

How many other minority groups are there in the community in question?

What proportion of the population belongs to the minority community?

What proportion of the minority and dominant group becomes involved in the conflict?

The Issue

How great is the felt gain to the dominant group and cost to the minority? What proportion of each group feels strongly affected by the issue?

How clearly defined are the goals of the involved groups? How clearly can responsibility be fixed for the situation that a group finds intolerable? Does the goal sought have a specific or diffuse character?

What is the relative mix of realistic and nonrealistic conflict elements? Is the degree of emotional involvement around the conflict high or low?

How consistent are the goals of the minority group with the dominant values of the society?

Does the conflict occur within a broad framework of consensus, or is it over the very basis of consensus?

Do the involved groups disagree about one issue or a large number of issues?

Is the issue one of a "zero sum nature" whereby if one group gets its way the other group must lose totally, or does the issue involve the possibility of negotiation and partial gains for each group?

Is the group initiating the conflict seeking to veto a decision, or does it seek some new direction for policy?

Is the issue one which can be shown to directly benefit more people than just the minority—such as all the poor, all people with children, everyone in a given region, etc.?

Within the minority group, is it an issue that affects all members more or less equally (denial of right to vote or sit anywhere on the bus), primarily the poor (inferior schools, union discrimination), or primarily the rich (discrimination by country clubs and expensive hotels)?

Is the conflict initiated because the minority group is questioning the racial status quo, or because the dominant group through attacks and exploitation seeks new gains, to maintain the status quo, or even to restore a declining color line?

Within that institutional setting does the conflict occur—schools, universities, factories, retail merchants, unions, police, churches, welfare and housing bureaucracies, legislative or judicial bodies?

What is the substantive nature of the issue? Are issues of class, status, or power most clearly involved? How close does the issue come to involving social interaction between blacks and whites at an equal status level?

Does the conflict primarily involve a struggle after scarce resources, the clash of divergent beliefs, or an effort to directly injure one's opponent?

Tactics

What kind of resources does the less powerful group have access to beyond its ability to disrupt? How easily can it organize itself for conflict action and how great are the risks it faces in so doing?

What are a group's traditions regarding the use of violence and working outside the system?

To what extent is the conflict bound in by rules, and are the means used seen as legitimate by members of the dominant society?

What conflict means are used: elections, the courts, lobbying, strikes, demonstrations, sit-ins, boycotts, riots, guerrilla warfare?

Is there a division of labor among the leadership, with charismatic- and bureaucratic-task-oriented roles performed by different people?

Are followers motivated to carry on the struggle primarily by ideology or by concrete material rewards?

Have dramatic and symbolic events occurred which groups can capitalize on to inspire followers and gain needed support through the mass media?

What images does a group hold of itself and its opponents at various stages of the conflict?

How are conflict actions labeled by various interested parties (e.g., as justified protest, crime)?

To what extent is a life cycle model of breakdown, chaotic disruption and mass unrest, organized protest, social change and the disappearance of protest present, as against continued conflict and intermittent disruption?

If the conflict terminates, what form does it take and what is responsible: complete victory for one side, compromise resulting in partial gains for each side, stalemate and truce, fatigue when one or both sides give up or withdraw, arbitration, the shifting of attention to other issues, repression of the weaker group, attack by some third party which binds previous antagonists together?

Does the conflict stop with the immediate issue at hand, or does it also result in setting up new mechanisms for resolving future disputes?

The above questions were not chosen at random. Rather they deal with many of the elements of conflict emphasized in the theoretical literature. Given answers to some of the above questions, the empirical case of interest can be considered in light of various propositions about conflict.

Through considering a number of such empirical cases, it is possible to offer support or cast doubt on a given hypothesis. Listed below are some theoretical propositions about how conflict elements affect each other. They make predictions about conflict's form, intensity, patterns of development, and consequences. By offering a limited but still systematic framework, they help explain conflict and give unity at a more general level to a number of discrete phenomena. They may also help structure our observations of conflict situations.

The following are among a large number of available propositions which receive some support from impressionistic observations and occasionally the systematic collection of data. It should be stressed that these are by no means iron laws, but merely hypotheses that seem reasonable and may help in understanding conflict.[1] Implicit in them is the condition "all other things being equal." These propositions focus primarily on factors affecting conflict once it emerges, rather than on those affecting the likelihood of its occurrence as in Part IIB. In most cases hypotheses already offered in the text such as in the articles by Coleman, Laue, Breed, or Coser are not repeated. In observing particular current examples of racial, or other kinds of conflict, an effort should be made to apply these propositions as well as to ask the questions just mentioned.

PROPOSITIONS

Forms and Patterns of Development

To the extent that major sources of social differentiation (such as class, race, religion, territory) overlap rather than criss-cross each other, conflict is likely to be more intense. A society faces maximum likelihood of massive conflict (or of political disruption) when the various lines of differentiation of values, interests, and collectivity memberships coincide among the same population aggregates (R. Williams, 1969).

Group conflicts are at their strongest, are most likely to develop and least likely to be dissipated, when no internal conflict is felt within the person (J. Coleman).

Periods of intense conflict are more likely when prolonged periods of rising expectations and gratifications are followed by short periods of sharp reversal (Davies).[2]

The intensity of conflict accompanying social change is likely to be greatest when the change is extensive, occurs suddenly, and when those implementing the change circumvent public opinion and work outside existing institutions (Suchman et al.).[3]

The greater the conflict between dominant and minority group, the lesser the conflict within these groups.

The greater the conflicts between racial and ethnic groups, the lesser the class and religious conflicts, and vise versa.

Among the members of any dominant group the greatest incidence of conflict behavior toward a given minority will be found among those classes which are most vulnerable to competition from the minority (R. Williams, 1947).

The larger the number of parties, the more difficult it will be to discover a common solution in which all parties can achieve at least some gain over previous power positions (Mack and Snyder).

[1] For more comprehensive inventories see R. Williams, *The Reduction of Inter-group Tensions* (New York: Social Science Research Council, 1947); R. Mack and R. Snyder, "The Analysis of Social Conflict—Toward an Overview and Synthesis," *Journal of Conflict Resolution* (June 1957); B. Berelson and G. Steiner, *Human Behavior: An Inventory of Scientific Findings,* (New York: Harcourt, Brace, & World, 1964); M. Sherif, *In Common Predicament,* (Boston: Houghton Mifflin, 1966); H. Blalock, Jr., *Toward a Theory of Minority Group Relations* (New York: Wiley, 1967); L. Coser, *The Functions of Social Conflict* (New York: Free Press 1954), and *Continuities in the Study of Social Conflict,* (New York: Free Press, 1967); W. Gamson, *Power and Discontent,* (Homewood, Ill.: Dorsey Press, 1969); C. Fink, "Some Conceptual Difficulties in the Theory of Social Conflict," *Journal of Conflict Resolution* 12, no. 4; M. Deutsch, "Conflicts: Productive and Destructive," *Journal of Social Issues* 25, no. 1; R. Williams, "Conflict and Social Order: Some Complex Propositions for Sociologists Who Live in Interesting Times," unpublished paper, 1969; R. Dahrendorf, *Class and Class Conflict in Industrial Society* (Palo Alto: Stanford Univ. Press, 1959); and the additional articles in footnote 2 of the Introduction.

[2] J. Davis, "Toward a Theory of Revolution," *American Sociological Review* (February 1962).

[3] E. Suchman *et al., Desegregation: Some Propositions and Research Suggestions* (New York, Anti-Defamation League, 1958).

There is a persistent tendency to reduce multiple-party conflict to two-party conflict via coalitions and blocs (Mack and Snyder).

The larger the number of issues on which a group is divided, the more prolonged and intense the conflict (Deutsch).

The more loosely connected and separable the issues, the easier the conflict will be to resolve, particularly if opponents value issues differentially (Deutsch).

Small conflicts are easier to resolve than large ones. Conflict is enlarged by dealing with it as a conflict between big rather than small units (as a conflict between two individuals of different races or as a racial conflict), as a conflict over a large substantive issue rather than a small one (over "being treated fairly or being treated unfairly at a particular occasion"), as a conflict over a principle rather than the application of a principle, as a conflict whose solution establishes large rather than small substantive or procedural precedents (Deutsch).

Escalation of conflict will be more likely and more rapid when one or more of the contending groups lacks a hierarchy of power and authority or a clear structure of representation. Escalation in demands and in resort to obstruction and force is favored by:

1 multiple contenders for leadership
2 rapid turnover of both leaders and followers
3 lack of definiteness in powers, rights duties, and privileges of spokesmen, organizers, representatives

(R. Williams, 1969)

Collectivities whose members lack multiple responsible involvements and commitments in the major activities of the community or society are likely to be extreme in their demands and tactics in disputes (R. Williams, 1969).

In the absence of a superordinate source of constraint, conflicts often are subject to escalation in severity or ferocity . . . a tendency for increasingly drastic means to drive out the less drastic, resulting in the sovereignty of the least moral participant (R. Williams, 1969).

Violent conflict is more likely when the government, or another third party, is unable or unwilling to intervene.

The greater the resources a group has to use in its struggle, the less likely that it will publicly use means seen as questionable by the dominant segments of the society.

Conflict is likely to be more intense in close-knit groups and in those organized in a rigid way (Coser, 1956).

Conflicts are likely to be more intense and more violent to the degree that the struggle is waged for the sake of superindividual rather than personal ends (Coser, 1956).

The greater the absence of conditions which allow groups to develop organizations to struggle for goals through established channels, the greater the likelihood of violent conflict (Dahrendorf).

Conflict is likely to be bound in by rules when the following are present: institutional forms such as collective bargaining and adjudicative systems; roles such as mediators, conciliators, referees, judges, and policemen; norms stressing "fairness" and "nonviolence"; and specific rules for conducting negotiations (Deutsch).

Adherence to rules limiting conflict is more likely when (1) rules are known, unambiguous, consistent, and unbiased; (2) the other side adheres to the rules; (3) violations are quickly known by significant others; (4) there is significant social approval for adherence and significant social disapproval for violation; (5) adherence to the rules has been rewarding while uncontrolled conflict has been costly in the past; and (6) one would like to be able to employ the rules in future conflicts (Deutsch).

Outcome

In a society such as the contemporary United States, the challenges of relatively powerless groups are likely to meet with the greatest degree of success to the extent that:

1 Their demands can be seen as consistent with the broader values of the society.

2 They can gain the support of more powerful third parties and/or show how their demands will benefit other groups as well.

3 Their demands are concrete and focused.

4 The more clearly they can fix responsibility for the situation they are protesting (e.g., protest against an urban renewal project as compared to protest over inadequate housing).

5 Pressure is brought to bear on the responsible party, and there is minimum discomfort to those not responsible.

6 They adopt new techniques which authorities have not had experience dealing with.

7 Neutral third parties are present who have an interest in restoring harmony.

8 The powerless group is willing to negotiate, and its demands do not have a zero-sum quality.

9 Their demands involve a request for acceptance of social diversity, equal treatment, or inclusion, rather than domination over, or change in the practices of, the dominant group towards itself, or fundamental redistributions of income and power.

10 The powerless group seeks to veto a proposed policy rather than to see a new policy implemented.

11 The further a demand is from involving equal social status contact with whites (e.g., greater resistance to residential and school integration than a demand for improving black schools and building new low income housing in a black area).

12 The less the perceived cost to white society.

13 The lower the status of the white group most likely to be hurt by the challenge.

14 The minority population is large enough to organize itself for conflict but not large enough to be perceived as a serious threat to the dominant group.

The following case studies report a small number of racial conflict situations. The case studies presented here vary considerably from each other with respect to region (North, South, rural, urban), institutional area where the struggle occurs (the legislature, the schools, the police, the economy, the streets), the means (voting, lobbying, boycotts, sit-ins, persuasion, threats, violence), and the groups involved (minority versus majority or within these groups), and outcome. However in each instance many of the same analytic areas can be identified: some scarcity of resources or the clash of beliefs, varying mixtures of realistic and nonrealistic conflict, ideas which justify struggle, social conditions which operate to encourage or inhibit it and push the struggle in one direction or another, and interaction among participants and the development of the conflict over time.

In the 1950's and middle 1960's, schools were almost always a locus for conflict as they were one of the most visible of segregated American institutions. The 1954 Supreme Court decision and the actions of the federal government in the South legitimated the struggle for integrated schools. However as appreciable resistance was met and schools in the North became more, rather than less, segregated, the black community increasingly turned inward, and school controversies began to emerge over the issue of community control of schools and demands for a black curriculum.

Given the presence of large numbers of young people who can rather easily be mobilized for action on one side or the other, and the school's crucial role of socializing the young and transmitting basic values and worldviews, it is not surprising that school controversies have often been intense and prolonged.

R. Crain, in his discussion of a San Francisco school controversy, cites many of the basic elements—such as school officials who see themselves alone as possessing the technical expertise needed to make complex school decisions; splits within the minority community and the large number (nine) of civil rights groups that school officials had to deal with at one time or another; the use of a law suit, threats, and disruption to force negotiations; the importance of the role of misunderstanding; the reflexive emergence of an anti-integration citizens group; the appointment of a study committee; the emergence of newer issues; and the role of third parties. As the conflict escalated it became very confusing and more difficult to understand. The NAACP appears to have switched its position from goals of a status nature involving symbolic affirmation of the principle of nondiscrimination to goals of a welfare nature such as the building of new essentially segregated schools in ghetto areas. There is some tension between full integration and the development of a strong ethnic power base.

Michael Lipsky considers the 1963 and 1964 Harlem rent strikes led by Jesse Gray by examining some of the constraints faced by low income protestors.[4] Although the rent strike resulted in some marginal changes, it failed to obtain its fundamental goal. Protest by low income groups is seen as an unreliable political tactic, particularly in the long run, although it may be useful in raising issues. Such protest groups are at a competitive disadvantage in terms of skill and resources relative to the powerful groups they challenge. A protest leader also must try and appeal to diverse groups

[4] The issue of substandard housing or exorbitant rents involved in a rent strike or exploitation by merchants and employers are, in a strict sense, class rather than racial issues. The white poor and other low status minorities face many of the same problems as blacks. However, because the landlords, merchants, and employers are usually white and blacks are more likely to be renters, customers, and employees, such issues in fact come to be defined as racial issues. Racial factors are, of course, also relevant in accounting for the development of this consistent pattern of racial subordination.

such as his own grassroots supporters, the mass media, interested third parties, and those who have the power to give him what he wants. For example, to hold his followers he must often be militant, particularly if he can offer them few tangible rewards, yet this may alienate third parties whose support is vital. On the other hand, if his need for militant rhetoric and the demands of the press for newsworthy material do not prevent him from communicating his willingness to negotiate, the subsequent need to bargain and compromise may alienate many of his followers.

The article by Howard Hubbard contrasts the success of civil rights protest in Birmingham with its failure in Albany, Georgia. Though Martin Luther King was prominently involved in both struggles, they had very different consequences. A crucial factor is seen to be the different tactics adopted by police. In Birmingham, unlike Albany, the conflict occurred in a context where violence was perpetrated by authorities. Here dramatic incidents and the creation of martyrs and symbols are seen to be important to the mobilization of mass support. This also indicates the emergent character of the conflict and how the results, depending on the nature of the interaction between opponents, can often not be predicted.

Rita James Simon and James W. Carey consider the controversy that developed around an incident of alleged discrimination against black athletes at the University of Illinois. They indicate some of the confusion that is often present in conflict situations, which even subsequent investigation by the researchers could not untangle. They show the important role the mass media has in turning a minor charge into a dramatic conflict and how some men come to play stylized roles. In noting intragroup conflict between the NAACP and the black athletes they suggest the importance of a personal vendetta between two leaders, feelings of superiority on the part of the NAACP, the interest of the latter in finding an issue that would call attention to the general situation of blacks on the campus, and the dependence of black athletes on white coaches and the athletic association. The specific incident that triggered the dispute was the vehicle for a consideration of more general issues involving blacks on the campus. From the perspective of the blacks the ending of the conflict seems rather unsuccessful; it simply dropped out of sight. Perhaps because blacks took no coercive action, little change emerged.

Most of the articles in this book take a rather tough-minded perspective to human society. In Dahrendorf's term, they emphasize the coercive side of society, focusing on power, pressure, force, and division. However, as Dahrendorf also notes, there is a consensus or integration side of society as well. Leon Mayhew emphasizes this side by showing how shared values of an abstract nature can be used by a group to obtain social change. He examines the history of the passage of a full employment practices bill in Massachusetts and considers the interplay between formal laws, unwritten values, and organized interest groups. He makes the important point that "the civil rights lobby did not prevail simply because it was organized; it prevailed because it was organized to express and enhance community values." He shows the importance of creating the appearance of a broad base of public support and the crucial importance of support from powerful third parties who offer needed resources and help legitimate the claims of the minority. In the interest of self-determination and community building, the importance of coalitions is now

underplayed by some segments of the black movement. This article stresses the role of law in bringing about change. Though its impact may not be felt immediately and uniformly and its effect is easily exaggerated, it has a symbolic meaning, helps legitimate demands for change in policy, and if strong enforcement agencies are set up, can have an important effect on behavior.

The case study by Harold A. Nelson deals not so much with a single direct clash involving particular demands but with the emergence and consequences of an informal black police organization. There are some interesting parallels here to the Black Panthers, who emerged in a similar fashion, and to the white organization started by Tony Imperiale in Newark. The emergence of such groups in the face of a situation defined as unsatisfying is wholly consistent with an American frontier, self-help ethos. If schools and police in low income areas are seen as unsatisfactory and impossible to change, then do not change them but create your own. There are of course great problems with obtaining the resources needed to do this, and there may be much resistance from the traditional institutions.

The emergence of the Defenders, the group described by Nelson, led to important changes on the part of police and the cessation of white harassment of blacks. The mere threat of their presence was sufficient for change without physical conflict actually occurring. This illustrates a subtle point about conflict: the winner does not necessarily win because he physically or financially destroys his opponent; rather he gains his desired end through threatening to do so and making it clear that he means business. To a weaker or outflanked opponent this may be sufficient for change. The role of threats, assessment of the opponent's strengths, how serious he is, and how far he will go to gain his ends are important parts of the conflict process.[5]

Yet the emergence of such parapolice groups does not always have the positive ending described by Nelson. Struggles over police issues may be particularly intense because they involve coercion and direct physical controls over people. For one thing such groups may help to sharpen conflict by organizing a previously unorganized group. The chance of violent clashes with the police or organized ideological opponents may be greatly increased. Even if this isn't the case, applying the perspective of Dahrendorf, many of the problems facing police stem from the mere exercise of authority. A conflict potential is inherent in this kind of relationship no matter who exercises authority.[6] There are also interesting questions about who controls this new group of controllers who have emerged to control the excesses of the old controllers.

In the evolution of the black struggle from working primarily in the courts in the 1950's to the nonviolent direct action of the early 1960's to spontaneous ghetto violence in the last half of the 1960's, a progression toward ever increasing militancy may be seen. If one were to apply a rigid evolutionary model, the next step would clearly seem to be from mass violent unrest to planned uprisings and guerrilla warfare. Many observers of all political persuasions see this coming. Already there are isolated guerrilla-like attacks on police, firemen, and other officials servicing ghetto communities, as well as attacks on courts, schools, and downtown business areas.

Martin Oppenheimer asks a hard question: What are the real prospects for organized mass violence and guerrilla warfare in the urban black ghetto? In a useful historical review, he notes a number of problems that urban insurgency movements face, including the lack of a logistical base and territorial isolation. More difficult for the government to deal with is a revolutionary underground that includes terrorism, sabotage, and perhaps small mobile guerrilla bands. The threat of violence and an occasional attack initially may be relevant to some change. However as attacks escalate and fear spreads, the ultimate consequence, according to Oppenheimer, is likely to be the suspension of the Constitution, an American police state, and the turning of ghettos into concentration camps, though such repression for some might have the consequence of furthering the will to insurrection.

Racially linked conflict is currently too often conceived of in terms of a homogeneous black group challenging the traditional forms of social stratification in a monolithic, white-dominated society. To be sure this is currently the most newsworthy form of race conflict. But such challenges meet with response and generate resistance. The white counterprotest is a crucial and all too neglected phenomenon, as is variation and conflict within the white community between different regional, religious, ethnic, class, ideological, and age groups. Equally of interest is conflict within the minority community. Many of the articles in this section touch on these types of conflict as well, particularly the articles by Walker and Rogers on blacks and by Skolnick and Goldberger on whites.

That American blacks, coming from different parts of Africa with different

---

[5] T. Schelling, *The Strategy of Conflict* (Cambridge: Harvard University Press, 1960).

[6] A consideration of the issues raised by such groups may be found in G. Marx and D. Archer, "Citizen Involvement in the Law Enforcement Process: The Case of Community Police Patrols" (Paper presented at 1970 meetings of American Political Science Association, Los Angeles, Calif.).

cultures, languages, and tribal attachments, were forged into an ethnic group by their American experience, has, according to many observers, led to a lesser degree of solidarity and unity than among ethnic groups such as the Italians, Irish, or Greeks who have a very different American experience. The encouragement by powerful whites of division within the black group, going back to the distinction between house and field slaves, and the few meager resources available to blacks have been a source of much intragroup competition and rivalry. One theme of the black movement is, of course, black unity.

Contrary to the assumption often made that a powerless minority must maintain unity and solidarity if it is to be effective, Jack L. Walker, in analyzing a controversy over discriminatory hiring in Atlanta, observes certain benefits in disunity. He argues that it may help, rather than hinder, social change by inspiring the competing groups to greater efforts and by making moderate leaders more acceptable (by contrast to radicals) to those with power. In this instance student protest leaders forced a crisis through direct action techniques. However, conservative black leaders, accepting the student goals but not their means, were crucial to the emergence of negotiations. The protest of the students is seen to occur in a "righteous vacuum," necessitating the help of conservative black leaders who are seen as reliable and responsible by whites. Some of the conflict dynamics noted by Coleman may be observed in this article.

However in another example, Ray Rogers examines a conflict between the Black Panthers and a black group known as "US," which has anything but the positive consequences observed in Atlanta. He describes the conflict between the groups that resulted in two killings on the UCLA campus. These groups are somewhat similar in terms of the social basis of their support and overall ideology, though one identifies with cultural nationalism and the other with political nationalism. The conflict involved a power struggle over who would control resources on the UCLA campus and in the Los Angeles black community. The Panthers have accused US of being a police-front organization. Here we see that one of the consequences of the slight loosening up of white-controlled purse strings for Office of Economic Opportunity projects, increased foundation grants, black studies programs, and the like has been an increase in conflict within the minority community (and between them as well as the struggles among blacks, Puerto Ricans, Mexicans, and Indians in various parts of the country indicate). Apparently benign ameliorative efforts may have the consequence of a divide and rule strategy, particularly when funding is still relatively low.

The remaining four articles in this section focus more on actual conflict groups than particular instances of conflict. In a historical sense appreciably more violent conflict has come from those who felt threatened by a challenged status quo than by those who challenge it. Here we again see interaction whereby a move by one group leads to counter moves by another.

Skolnick examines the counterprotest activities of southern groups such as the Klan and the National States Rights Party. He considers the history of the Klan, its social base, its relationship to those with power, and its changing nature. He suggests that the hostility of the marginal and economically insecure Klansmen partly stems from a sense of impotence and competition with blacks. The Klan has been encouraged by the fact that local authorities were often ambivalent about them, if not highly cooperative. As the article by Nelson suggests, to many blacks there seemed slight difference between the Klan and law enforcement officials. According to one of Skolnick's informants, "the establishment fears war between the races less than an alliance between them." Here intergroup conflict between those with many of the same problems of poverty and powerlessness may help perpetuate the very system that disadvantages both.

Contemporary violent white counterprotest is certainly not limited to the South. As blacks have made some gains, used what a majority of the population sees as questionable means, and received much publicity, and as politicians have begun to make use of the law and order theme, the deep resentment toward blacks on the part of many urban, working class, white ethnic groups from Southern and Eastern Europe has become apparent. Ironically these groups, who as immigrants were themselves earlier victims of prejudice and nativism on the part of the predominantly Anglo-Saxon Protestant Klan, American Protective Association, and Know-Nothings have come to show some of the same attitudes and behavior. In dealing with their racism and counterprotest, it is important to understand the strains, tensions, and fears that affect their behavior. An important generator of conflict on the part of lower status whites is competition, or the fear of it, from blacks. Robert Wood, a former secretary of HUD, writes:

Let us consider the working American— the average white ethnic male:

He is the ordinary employee in factory and in office. Twenty million strong, he forms the bulk of the nation's working force. He makes five to ten thousand dollars a year; has a wife and two children; owns a house in town—between the ghetto and the suburbs, or perhaps in a low-cost subdivision

on the urban fringe; and he owes plenty in installment debts on his car and appliances.

The average white working man has no capital, no stocks, no real estate holdings except for his home to leave his children. Despite the gains hammered out by his union, his job security is far from complete. Layoffs, reductions, automation, and plant relocation remain the invisible witches at every christening. He finds his tax burden is heavy; his neighborhood services, poor; his national image, tarnished; and his political clout, diminishing . . . one comes to understand his tension in the face of the aspiring black minority. He notes his place on the lower rungs of the economic ladder. He sees the movement of black families as a threat to his home values. He reads about rising crime rates in city streets and feels this is a direct challenge to his family. He thinks the busing of his children to unfamiliar and perhaps inferior schools will blight their chance for a sound education. He sees only one destination for the minority movement—his job.

Paul Goldberger in his discussion of Newark's North Ward Citizens' Committee founded by Tony Imperiale observes many of these themes. There are interesting parallels between this group and the "Defenders" studied by Nelson. Of particular interest is the "hot line" between Imperiale's office and LeRoi Jones's Spirit House in the black central ward.

Inga Powell Bell offers a sociological analysis of a southern CORE chapter in the early 1960's. She considers the organizational structure of CORE, the social characteristics of activists, the relationship of the group to whites, to various other Negro groups, and to the Negro community in general. A small number of individuals united by strong primary group ties were often sufficient for successful direct action. She contrasts these CORE members with older, more conservative leaders who work through institutionalized political channels.

Harry Edwards specifically deals with variation in the black community by seeking to delineate major types of activism among black college students, a group in many ways in the vanguard of the black and more general student movements. Based on his participation in, and research on, the black student movement, he discusses the philosophies held by different types of students, their background characteristics, and the roles they may play at different stages in a given struggle.

Many of the articles included here stress the importance of coalitions, allies, and interested third parties to the success of a minority group struggle. One of the ironies of efforts to abolish a color line is that success is rarely obtained without considerable cooperation from some members of the dominant group and in spite of the efforts of some members of the minority group, though to be sure the former situation may involve considerable tension, as the withdrawal of whites from SNCC and CORE in 1966 indicated.

In "Majority Involvement in Minority Movements," Michael Useem and I examine the relationship between dominant and subordinate group activists in the civil rights, abolitionist, and untouchable movements. Here we focus on common sources of conflict internal to these movements. Three sources of conflict are identified. The first two involve elements of realistic conflict: ideological differences and the struggle over power within the organization. The third tends to involve "unrealistic" conflict elements of a subjective nature such as displaced aggression, suspicion, and stereotyping. Some of the dissension may be seen as an example of Coser's observation that conflict, when it emerges, is likely to be particularly intense in close-knit groups. Out of the

observation that similar conflict themes appear in these diverse movements, scientific generalizations and propositions about such movements may emerge.

37
Conflict and School
Desegregation in
San Francisco*
R. CRAIN

In the other cities we have seen how concern over a particular school can escalate into a full-scale assault on de facto segregation (Baltimore and Newark are examples). In both these cases, the rejection of the specific demands led to increased pressure for more general solutions. In San Francisco we see an unusual reversal of this pattern; a specific demand was made and it was more or less met by the school board without reducing any of the pressure for a more general solution. San Francisco is in some ways our most important case, for it points out better than any other city that there is no necessary relation between the actual number of students in integrated schools, or the school's willingness to take concrete steps to integrate schools, and the ability of the school system to avoid conflict.

From the beginning, the San Francisco schools and the civil rights leaders were poles apart in ideology. Like the Bay City movement, San Francisco's civil rights leaders wanted to talk about de facto segregation in the abstract; the school administration would have no part of such a discussion.

At the January 1962 school board meeting, two white liberals, Mrs. Beverly Axelrod, representing CORE, and

*[Reprinted from Robert L. Crain, *The Politics of School Desegregation* (New York: Doubleday Anchor Books, 1969). Copyright © 1968 by National Opinion Research Center. Reprinted by permission of the author and Aldine-Atherton Publishing Company.]

Frank Quinn of the Council of Civic Unity, an interracial human relations organization, presented statements. CORE asked for a racial census; the council added a request that a board-appointed citizens' committee and the superintendent each prepare a report on de facto segregation.

The board asked Superintendent Harold Spears to reply, and his report, presented on June 19, was a complete disappointment to the civil rights groups. Spears began by saying. "Although the question of racial interaction in any area of civic affairs has its emotional overtones, the subject can lend itself to rational and deliberate treatment. The point of departure in this investigation has been the educational implications, since the function of the American public school is the effective instruction of the pupils therein. . . ." He then went on to discuss in detail the changing racial composition of the city and the way in which attendance boundaries are set, and reviewed the census data (for nonwhites including Orientals, rather than Negroes) for different parts of the city. Although the superintendent noted that busing to relieve overcrowding sometimes resulted in integration, he added that he did not (and by implication, should not) consider racial integration as even a secondary goal of the transportation of pupils to relieve overcrowding. He also stressed that busing weakened the home-school tie, and noted that busing was inconvenient to Chinese children who were in a hurry to reach after-school classes in Chinese culture.

He then stated the school system's philosophy on the issue of the racial census of pupils:

We are now faced with the movement to emphasize differences in the color and race of pupils, with teacher, parent, and child. In some eastern school systems, such records are now prepared annually. One asks for what purposes do we so label a child, and in turn, post a sign on his school, indicating the racial makeup of the student body at the moment?

If we were preparing to ship these children to various schools, in predetermined racial allotments, then such brands would serve the purpose they have been put to in handling livestock. But until somebody comes up with an educationally sound plan for such integration, then this racial accounting serves nothing but the dangers of putting it to ill use. . . .

It is quite apparent that as more courts face the technicalities of the issue, we should expect the injection of the question of the purpose of the American public school, a matter that has been somewhat ignored up to this point.

Without a doubt, state school codes do not speak of social adjustment as a purpose in the establishment of public schools. Instead, they speak specifically of subjects to be taught. . . .

It is true that any school or any classroom provides a social situation, for when two pupils or more are grouped for instruction the element of human relationships enters the picture. But this social situation has never been stated in law as a purpose of a school. Rather it is a condition that arises because efficiency of school operation demands that children be grouped for instructional purpose, rather than to be tutored individually. The teacher naturally takes advantage of the group situation to teach beyond the subjects which constitute the curriculum, but nobody has ever justified through public expenditure the organization of schools primarily for the social purpose.

The school is an instrument through which society both preserves the culture and brings out social change. The school is actually an instrument of social change, but as such an instrument, the children are not to be used as the tools. . . .

The Brown case in 1954 and the Taylor

case in 1961 were both concerned with the civil rights of individuals. As there is an attempt to push broader interpretations in the court cases ahead, then the child's educational rights must be brought out in relationship to his civil rights, lest there be possible conflict. Certainly such refinement of issue will demand the opinion of the educational profession as well as that of the legal profession. . . .

Returning to the specific case at hand, I have no educationally sound program to suggest to the board to eliminate the schools in which the children are predominantly of one race, as has been suggested to the board by the Congress of Racial Equality. If such schools are educationally unsound, as has been charged by the Bay Area Human Relations Council, then certainly any program to improve the situation would need to be educationally sound if established by official board action.

CENTRAL JUNIOR HIGH SCHOOL

At the same time, the Central Junior High School issue came to life. Central Junior High was a new name for the old building originally used by the elite Lowell High School. The area around the proposed Central Junior High School had experienced a steady increase in Negro population from approximately 8 percent in 1950 to 35 percent in 1960, resulting in overcrowding in Franklin Junior High School, an overwhelmingly Negro school. With the opening of the new school, several predominantly Negro elementary schools could be redistricted to relieve this overcrowding. Although we have no racial data on the schools for that time, it appears that Central Junior High School would have been approximately 60 percent Negro when it opened. The new boundaries also included two predominantly white schools which would be transferred from a white middle income junior high school. One was

Gratten, serving a predominantly white area adjacent to the University of California Medical School. The community included moderate and high income whites and Negroes and a number of local civil rights leaders. By May, the Gratten Parents and Friends Committee has been organized to protest that their children were being transferred into a racially imbalanced school and that panic-peddlers were already ringing doorbells through the Gratten area. Spears had incurred the wrath of one of San Francisco's most articulate and outspoken neighborhoods. Since Mrs. Axelrod was one of the Gratten group, CORE was quick to back them. The Gratten group was not, however, completely trusted by the NAACP. Gratten, after all, had a choice: they could simply try to get out of the predominantly Negro school themselves or they could choose to stay in Central but press for a redrawing of boundaries to increase the number of whites in the school. They chose the latter tack and thus established themselves as integrationist, rather than merely anti-Negro.

The Gratten group asked for and received a hearing at the June board meeting. More than three hundred persons were in the audience. The board listened with some sympathy to the Gratten parents. Hcwever, they also noted that this was their last meeting before adjourning for their July vacation. At first they proposed to postpone the matter until they had developed a general policy in September. This would, of course, be after school opened. Then the board decided to hand the responsibility for a decision over to Spears and instructed him to meet with the Gratten parents within ten days; they further instructed Spears that he should feel free to take any action he wished on the matter. The board themselves had not gone on record whether they favored or disapproved of taking race into consideration in setting school boundaries. Granted, the school board did have a policy of general support for neighborhood schools, but within these rather vague bounds, they were in effect empowering Spears to make policy on this matter while the board was on vacation. Spears was reluctant to accept this carte blanche position.

At this meeting with them, Spears apparently managed to conciliate some of the parents by promising to keep the school under review during the first semester it was open. But there was also a good deal of misunderstanding. Apparently an agreement was reached with the Gratten parents which collapsed the next day. In any case, by the end of July, an impressive array of statements and threats had been made. *The San Francisco Chronicle* called for elimination of every predominantly Negro school and strongly backed the Gratten parents. Terry Francois of the NAACP spoke to the Gratten parents and urged them to consider filing suit, picketing, and boycotting the school. CORE began a sit-in. The Gratten parents won the support of Mayor Christopher, the San Francisco Labor Council, and the Teachers' Union. In August, the *Examiner* joined the *Chronicle* in urging that the racial imbalance of Central be improved.[1] That same day the NAACP announced that it would boycott the school and would arrange for volunteer teachers to maintain a private school for the Central students. On August 14, Spears announced that Central Junior High School was a temporary expedient. This is the first public hint that the school system was considering not opening the school at all. But as Spears was making this statement,

the Gratten parents announced that they would participate in the NAACP boycott. The next day they filed suit against the schools. The suit was hurriedly drafted and was not taken very seriously by any of the participants; however, it did provide the mechanism for negotiations. When the Gratten attorneys appeared before Judge Alfonso D. Zirpoli, Zirpoli refused to set a date for the hearing, but instead urged the board to meet with the plaintiffs. The parties agreed to try to settle out of court. School board attorney Breyer had originally asked that hearings be put off until after the special September 18 meeting of the board, but Judge Zirpoli merely postponed the hearing until after the regular August 21 board meeting. Although no agreement was made at this meeting with Judge Zirpoli, the Gratten representatives did mention that they would be satisfied if the Central plan was scrapped completely.[2] Board president Ladar stated he was willing to meet with the Gratten group, and a meeting was set for three days later. Meanwhile, the noise level increased steadily. An anti-integrationist group, the Citizens Committee for Neighborhood Schools, was organized and released a series of statements. This group, which drew much of its strength from the all-white areas just beyond Gratten, was arguing that any move to redistrict Central to improve racial balance would be illegal discrimination against whites. If Central were to be balanced, their children would be likely candidates for transfer into it.[3]

---

[1] *The Examiner* called for the addition of three all-white schools to the Central district. The result was to add impetus to the organization of a segregationist group in that area.

[2] Judge Zirpoli was in a strong position to chair the negotiating session. As a liberal Democrat on the Board of Supervisors, he had had previous experience dealing with the school board and the civil rights leaders.

[3] It should be noted that the congruence of neighborhood of residence and civil rights ideology was by no means perfect. As seems to be the usual case, those persons who were faced with problems of retaining whites in an integrated neighborhood were supporting integration,

In the midst of this, Ladar met with the Gratten group's attorney (who had a few days earlier been quoted as advocating a campaign of harassing board members with phone calls at home). He later said that the meeting had been friendly and helpful.

The August 21 board meeting, like the preceding two, was held in the school system's auditorium. This time there were 1,200 persons in the audience. At the meeting, Spears informed the board that community pressures had made it impossible to maintain an educationally sound program at Central, and he recommended that plans for opening the school be dropped. Ladar stated that this represented no victory for anyone but would settle the issue, and the board voted unanimously to leave Central vacant.

Everyone expressed a little bit of dissatisfaction with the situation. Spears had stuck to his position that the schools were only concerned with education by giving an "educational" reason for changing policy on the school. The NAACP expressed concern that many of the Negro pupils would be in a less-balanced school than Central if they were returned to Franklin. And the Citizens for Neighborhood Schools accused the board of giving in to anarchy. The board, and particularly Ladar, had continued to maintain a good image with the civil rights groups, but Spears remained very much a target now. In any other city the solution of the Central School issue would have been viewed as a radical integrationist act, for many of the students were reas-

signed into white junior high schools, including one in the heartland of the Citizens for Neighborhood Schools. However, the civil rights groups were still on record as opposing busing.

THE "DE FACTO" SEGREGATION ISSUE CONTINUES

The school segregation issue was still very much alive. Spears told a teachers group that they could expect the civil rights movement to pick out more schools for attack. At the September 18 meeting, demands were made that the board call for a racial census, adopt a statement endorsing "maximum" integration as a goal, and appoint a citizens' committee. The board took no action on the first two demands, but appointed a board committee composed of Mrs. Claire Matzger, James E. Stratton (the board's Negro member), and Joseph Moore to make a report. The following month the NAACP filed suit, asking the court to order the school system to present a plan to eliminate de facto segregation.

The board's committee reported six months later in April 1963. The committee endorsed the idea that race be considered when new school sites were selected, and advocated redrawing of school boundaries to reduce segregation. It also advocated the open enrollment of all high schools and the appointment of an assistant superintendent for racial problems. The report went on to reject the possibility of busing as a solution to racial imbalance. (At that time the schools were still transporting to relieve overcrowding, moving three thousand students, many of whom were Negroes attending white schools.) The NAACP endorsed the report as a "delightful surprise." The board discussed the recommendations, and only one board member, Adolfo De Urioste, was critical of it. He joined

---

and those groups who had not yet had Negroes move in were segregationists. But this does not mean that every member of the Gratten group was a loyal civil rights activist: the chairman of the Citizens Committee for Neighborhood Schools—Leon Markel—was the extreasurer of the integrationist Council for Civic Unity and a well-known supporter of a state FEPC law.

the rest of the board in an unanimous vote adopting it.

During the next two years, the school desegregation issue moved along in a slow-paced fashion. The NAACP suit was pursued unenthusiastically, since its legal position was ambiguous. Meanwhile, the civil rights movement was busy demonstrating on the employment front. The school system implemented its high school open enrollment plan in the fall of 1963. A minor explosion occurred in 1964 when the board voted four to three to take no position on the referendum to repeal the state fair housing ordinance, and a board meeting was picketed shortly thereafter.

In the spring of 1964, only a few days before the deadline for submitting propositions for the November election, Spears presented the board with plans for a bond issue for new school construction. The board and the community reacted with surprise and some confusion. Since the plan called for a high school in a location which would result in it "being properly integrated," Spears commented that he expected the civil rights groups to "go along with it." In fact, the movement at this point was in no mood to go along with anything. The NAACP finally decided to oppose the bond issue. Bond issues require a two-thirds vote, so the NAACP opposition would be a serious threat to passage. In addition, the Central Labor Council announced that it would oppose the bonds unless the NAACP agreed to support them. Spears met in a pair of meetings with the NAACP. The agreement reached was a strange one, for the meeting found Spears opposed to building permanent schools in the ghetto and the NAACP in favor. The result was that Spears modified the plan to include construction of schools that Spears said he "would have never dreamed of asking for."

In the summer of 1965, after another round of picketing, Spears agreed to meet one of the demands presented in January 1962 and took a racial census of the schools. The census found that the eight high schools ranged in their Negro populations from 4 to 34 percent. The fifteen junior high schools ranged from 2 to 90 percent, but only two were more than 50 percent Negro. Of the ninety-five elementary schools, all had some white students. Using the 10 percent point as a threshold, nine of the elementary schools would be classified as segregated Negro, compared with eighty-five where Negroes attended school with whites. One school of the ninety-five had no Negro students at all. Seventy-six percent of all San Francisco Negro pupils were in integrated elementary schools. (For St. Louis and Baltimore, the figures are 14 percent and 20 percent.)

INTERPRETATION

The civil rights movement's unfriendly critics sometimes accuse it of provoking conflict for no apparent reason. The San Francisco story helps us to understand why school integration conflicts sometimes appear this way. As the conflict escalated, it became easier and easier for new demonstrations to break out. It also became harder and harder to understand what the fights were about. On two occasions Spears told his board that they could expect the civil rights movement to support a particular proposal. In the first case he was planning to reduce overcrowding in a school by transferring students into a new, integrated school nearby. That was Central Junior High School. In the second case, he was planning the construction of a new, integrated high school. That was the 1964 bond issue. Spears can be forgiven for not understanding the civil rights movement. On the other hand, there is a steady underlying theme of the conflict that does make sense. It would be difficult for any civil rights movement to be at peace with the San Francisco schools.

At the most concrete level, Central Junior High School and the 1964 bond issue were not primarily civil rights issues. The Gratten neighborhood saw the threat of engulfment by the ghetto and asked for, and received, relief. As in Baltimore and Newark, it was easy for a liberal and militant integrated neighborhood to incorporate its demands into the policy of the civil rights movement, and thus it was easy for the movement to support them in turn. As we have now seen in four cities, the people who feel they have the most to lose from segregation are whites who are forced into predominantly Negro schools. But the Gratten demands were met. In the bond issue, the NAACP took a stance apparently in rejection of integration, and demanded ghetto schools.

But in the abstract, the demands of civil rights movement were fairly consistent, and these demands were never agreed to. It is important to recognize that the civil rights leadership is not, and does not attempt to be, the general leadership of the Negro community. Whereas the general leader must work toward a variety of goals to meet the many needs of a neighborhood or a community, the civil rights movement has a much more restricted task. To oversimplify considerably, their aim is to eliminate racial discrimination and to create the symbols of racial nondiscrimination—in other words, to establish racial equality in both the concrete and the abstract. The San Francisco movement recognized from the beginning that there would be little if any actual discrimination against Negro pupils in school districting. They therefore focused on asking the school board to recognize that racial integration was a positive value, by drawing up a plan to intentionally integrate schools. Like the other northern movements, they did not feel it necessary to actually achieve anything resembling total integration. At the minimum, they wanted a statement of policy endorsing integration as a positive value, and some evidence that this statement was being implemented in good faith. In fact, the movement waited from January 1962 until April 1963 when the board subcommittee reported for the policy statement that merely committed the board to consider integration as a goal in new school construction and redistricting. Even after that, they complained that Superintendent Spears was not enforcing the new policy. At this level, it is understandable why the issue exploded as it did.

If this interpretation is correct, then we see why in San Francisco, as in other cities, compensatory education cannot be considered a substitute for integration. Compensatory education may be good for Negroes, but it does not help to meet the specific goals of the civil rights movement. Thus compensatory education is more or less irrelevant. But this line of reasoning leads us to another question. Why did the civil rights movement oppose the bond issue and demand ghetto schools? One tentative explanation is that the NAACP, like the Urban League, is not single-mindedly concerned with civil rights. The Urban League was originally developed as a social welfare agency and has only recently become an accepted member of the civil rights community. The NAACP is in many cities a well-established organization with a large membership which is the spokesman for the Negro community on many issues.[4] Thus it tends to supply general leader-

[4] Lewis M. Killian (1965) has said that it is ". . . a peculiar product of the minority community. If it must be compared to any institution of the white community, it has corresponded most closely to government."

ship rather than civil rights leadership. In addition, the NAACP concentrates on legal action, and thus becomes the natural home of Negro lawyers—some of whom expect to become holders of political office. But political leaders are by definition general leaders. Throughout our story, the San Francisco NAACP was badly split between the militants and moderates. The militants may have been reluctant to support anything the school board did, but after having taken the leap into opposing the bond issue, needed to think of some compromise which would enable them to support it. A campaign against the bonds would have been a serious drain on organization resources. With the NAACP board evenly divided between militants and moderates, some compromise device was in order—the construction of new schools was an obvious candidate, and it was attainable. Of course, schools must sometimes be built in racial ghettos; if François, as supervisor, had asked for this, no one would have been surprised; what is surprising is that the NAACP elected to play François' role.

This switch from "status" to "welfare" goals is only one of the ways in which the San Francisco civil rights movement was unstable. It was also in a state of organizational flux: Spears was forced to deal with at least nine different civil rights groups.[5]

From this viewpoint, Spears' 1962 report, from which we quoted, is very important. In the report, he refused to

set racial integration as a goal of the schools and dismissed it as irrelevant. In addition, he accused the civil rights leadership of having illegitimate values —of wanting to stigmatize children by conducting a racial census.[6] Thus in this speech he managed to reject entirely the basic goal of the movement —to establish the symbols of racial equality. Despite this, we have no reason to think that he was in any way anti-Negro. Spears had apparently no hesitation at all about sending Negro children into all-white schools, including schools in recognizably anti-Negro areas. But he insisted that this was by accident; he simply did not believe that he, as an educator, should do anything to increase integration. Spears has articulately presented a point of view which seems to be shared by many school administrators—that the details of school operation are matters which laymen are ill equipped to consider. The civil rights leadership was simply not qualified to make sound decisions on questions of school organization. Or as Spears told a teachers group, "We are the ones who know about teaching and about the best way to group children for learning."

Spears' aggressive response is reflected in two public comments that the school system could expect more difficulty with the civil rights movement. In the speech just referred to, given during the moratorium on direct action which was in force during the Johnson-Goldwater campaign, he told the teachers to expect a boycott. Earlier, at the end of the Central Junior High School issue, he had predicted that the movement would not be content, but would go looking for another school to make into an issue.

---

[5] In addition, *The San Francisco Chronicle* was responsible for much of the confusion about busing. Its editorial, during the Central Junior High School controversy, called for total integration—meaning the same white-Negro ratio in every school. In its way, the *Chronicle* is as flamboyant as any blood-and-gore tabloid, except that the *Chronicle* gets its headlines from (sometimes ridiculous) civic crusades. It may be that the *Chronicle* is a prototype of the future American newspaper, in which civic affairs, rather than sex, becomes amusement for the masses.

[6] More practically, Spears was also concerned that white parents might start running from schools where the head count showed a high Negro enrollment.

If Spears was a political martyr, he was martyred as much by his school board as by the movement, for the school board was surprisingly conservative for cosmopolitan San Francisco, and, more important, it seemed to be consistently reluctant to take action. It was Spears who conducted the actual negotiations over the bond issue. The board instructed Spears to take whatever action he wished in the Central issue and then dawdled through the summer until the issue nearly exploded. Spears was not insulated by his board from the civil rights issue; he made many of the major decisions. It is fashionable now for critics of the schools to accuse professional schoolmen of arrogance. But as Joseph Pois suggests in his intelligent study of Chicago (1964), the superintendent-dominated system is often the result, not of an arrogant superintendent, but of a weak board.

The reason for the relative impotence of the board lies in its complex, semipolitical recruitment structure. Between 1962 and 1965, the board included four Republicans and three Democrats; three Protestants, two Catholics, and two Jews; two women and five men; one Negro, one labor leader, and at least two members who were active in Republican party politics. With a seven-member board, it is not easy to construct such an arrangement and still guarantee the presence of enough skilled and energetic persons to make up a leadership core. Since we did not trace the history of the board, we do not know how rigid this appointment formula was. It may have been partly a consequence of the fact that Mayor George Christopher, who appointed this board, was planning to run in the Republican primary for governor. But it is traditional in San Francisco to appoint a religiously balanced board that contains some civic leaders but that is, politically, as much bipartisan

as it is nonpartisan. Before the appointment of the board's first Negro, Stratton, there were three white Protestant Republicans. In order to maintain the same religious and political composition, the Negro would have to replace one of these.[7] In addition, Christopher needed Negro support in his forthcoming attempt at the governorship, and Stratton was going to campaign for him. It is easy to find a Negro Protestant, but harder to find one who is active in Republican politics.

Assuming that we are correct in describing the rules for balancing the board, such an appointment formula would be tight enough to make it difficult for the mayor to select a board with a strong core or leadership. The appointment formula would also naturally result in a very heterogeneous board. Four members (the two white Protestants and the two Jews) are unusually wealthy—probably wealthier than any of the board members in the preceding six cities. The other three members are a social worker, a small businessman, and a union official.

Bipartisanship also results in a board that is heterogeneous on ideological lines. The result is that the board has at times had difficulty agreeing on policy. The racial issue has tended to divide the board on ethnic lines; for example, the board voted against opposing the constitutional amendment prohibiting fair-housing legislation by a four-to-three vote, with the two white Protestants and the two Catholics outvoting the two Jews and the Negro.[8]

[7] We are told that Negro leaders were invited to ask the Jewish leadership to surrender a seat. This may have been a facetious statement.

[8] The San Francisco school board was strongly criticized for taking this position. In California, governmental agencies take positions on referenda frequently. In addition, the civil rights movement argued that since the board had blamed de facto segregation on housing patterns, it was incumbent upon it to lend its support to any movement to break down housing discrimination.

Finally, several of the board members are politically active, although none of them can be considered to be purely political appointees. One of the board members is a member of the Republican National Committee; others apparently have participated in political club or fund-raising activities. Although four board members are wealthy, only two can be considered active members of the "civic elite" who are involved in community "projects." In neither of the two western cities studied is there a clear line separating the political activists from the civic elite. Thus, although this is not the usual "political" board, it cannot be considered "nonpolitical," either.

Again we see that a principal factor in deciding the course of the school integration issue is the composition of the board. In San Francisco, an inarticulate board passed a good deal of responsibility on to the superintendent. He took an extremely "professional" stance, which in turn resulted in his being accused of arrogance. However, his ideological position is really not much different from that of other superintendents who are protected by their boards.

The San Francisco board is above average in its degree of acquiescence to civil rights demands. If we look only at action, not words, the San Francisco board and Superintendent Spears have probably gone as far as any of our cities in integrating their school system. Had they not been confronted by a very militant civil rights movement, they would have had less difficulty. But San Francisco did make a serious mistake in not realizing that while action may speak louder than words, words speak also.

38
Case Study of a Harlem Rent Strike*
MICHAEL LIPSKY

The poor lack not only money, but power. Low income political groups may be thought of as politically impoverished. In the bargaining arena of city politics the poor have little to trade.

Protest has come to be an important part of the politics of low income minorities. By attempting to enlarge the conflict, and bring outside pressures to bear on their concerns, protest has developed as one tactic the poor can use to exert power and gain greater control over their lives. Since the sit-in movement of 1960, Negro civil rights strategists have used protest to bring about political change, and so have groups associated with the war on poverty. Saul Alinsky's Industrial Areas Foundation continues to receive invitations to help organize low income communities because it has demonstrated that it can mobilize poor people around the tactics of protest.

The Harlem rent strikes of 1963 and 1964, organized by Jesse Gray, a dynamic black leader who has been agitating about slum housing for more than fifteen years, affected some tenants in approximately 150 Harlem tenements. Following the March on Washington in August 1963, the rent strikes played on the liberal sympathies of New Yorkers who were just beginning to reexamine the conditions of New York City slums. Through a combination of appeal and threat, Jesse Gray mounted a movement that succeeded in changing the orientation for some city services, obtained greater *legal* rights for organized tenants, and resulted in obtaining repairs in

---

*["Rent Strikes: Poor Man's Weapon." Reprinted with permission from *Trans-action,* February 1969. Copyright © February 1969 by Trans-action, Inc., New Brunswick, New Jersey.]

a minority of the buildings in which tenants struck. Along with rent strikes conducted by Mobilization for Youth, a prewar poverty program, the rent strikes managed to project images of thousands of aroused tenants to a concerned public, and to somewhat anxious reform-oriented city officials.

The rent strikes did not succeed in obtaining fundamental goals. Most buildings in which tenants struck remained in disrepair, or deteriorated even further. City housing officials became more responsive to housing problems, but general programs to repair slum housing remained as remote as ever. Perhaps most significant, the rent strike movement, after a hectic initial winter, quickly petered out when cold weather again swept the Harlem streets. Focusing upon the rent strikes may help explain why this protest failed, and why protest in general is not a reliable political weapon.

PROTEST HAS LONG-RANGE LIMITS

Protest as a political tactic is limited because protest leaders must appeal to four constituencies at the same time. A protest leader must:

1 *nurture and sustain an organization composed of people who may not always agree with his program or style*

2 *adapt to the mass media—choose strategies and voice goals that will give him as much favorable exposure as possible*

3 *try to develop and sustain the protest's impact on third parties—the general public, sympathetic liberals, or anyone who can put pressure on those with power*

4 *try to influence directly the targets of the protest—those who have the power to give him what he wants*

The tensions that result from the leader's need to manipulate four constituencies at once are the basic reason why protest is an unreliable political tactic, unlikely to prove successful in the long run.

Protest activity may be defined as a political activity designed to dramatize an objection to some policies or conditions, using unconventional showmanship or display and aimed at obtaining rewards from the political system while working within that system. The problem of the powerless is that they have little to bargain with, and must acquire resources. Fifteen people sitting in the mayor's office cannot, of themselves, hope to move city hall. But through the publicity they get, or the reaction they evoke, they may politically activate a wider public to which the city administration is sensitive.

The tactic of activating third parties to enter the political process is most important to relatively powerless groups, although it is available to all. Obviously any organization which can call upon a large membership to engage in political activity—a trade union on strike, for example—has some degree of power. But the poor in individual neighborhoods frequently cannot exert such power. Neighborhood political groups may not have mass followings, or may not be able to rely on membership participation in political struggles. In such cases they may be able to activate other political forces in the city to enter the conflict on their behalf. However, the contradictions of the protest process suggest that even this tactic—now widely employed by various low income groups—cannot be relied upon.

Take, for example, the problem of protest leaders and their constituents. If poor people are to be organized for protest activities, their involvement must be sustained by the symbolic and intangible rewards of participation in protest action, and by the promises of material rewards that protest leaders extend. Yet a leadership style suited to providing protesters with the intangible rewards of participating in rebellious political movements is sometimes incompatible with a style designed to secure tangible benefits for protest group members.

Furthermore, the need of protest leaders to develop a distinctive style in order to overcome the lack of involvement of potential group members diffuses as well as consolidates support. People who want psychological gratification (such as revenge or public notice and acknowledgment), but have little hope of material rewards, will be attracted to a militant leader. They want angry rhetoric and denunciation. On the other hand, those people who depend on the political system for tangible benefits, and therefore believe in it and cooperate with it to some extent, are likely to want moderate leadership. Groups that materially profit from participation in the system will not accept men who question the whole system. Yet the cohesion of relatively powerless groups may be strengthened by militant, ideological leadership that questions the rules of the game, that challenges their morality and legitimacy.

On the other hand, the fact that the sympathies and support of third parties are essential to the success of protesters may make the protesters' fear of retribution, where justified, an asset. For when people put themselves in danger by complaining, they are more likely to gain widespread sympathy. The cattle-prod and police-dog tactics of Alabama police in breaking up demonstrations a few years ago brought immediate response and support from around the country.

In short, the nature of protesters curtails the flexibility of protest leadership. Leaders must limit their public actions to preserve their basis of support. They must also limit protest in line with what they can reasonably expect of their followers. The poor cannot be expected to engage in activities that require much money. The anxieties developed throughout their lives—such as loss of job, fear of police, or danger of eviction—also limit the scope of protest. Negro protest in the South was limited by such retributions or anxieties about facing reprisals.

Jesse Gray was able to gain sympathy for the rent strikers because he was able to project an image of people willing to risk eviction in order to protest against the (rarely identified) slumlords, who exploited them, or the city, whose iceberg pace aided landlords rather than forced them to make repairs. In fact, Gray used an underutilized provision of the law which protected tenants against eviction if they paid their rent to court. It was one of the great strengths of the rent strikes that the image of danger to tenants was projected, while the tenants remained somewhat secure and within the legal process. This fortunate combination is not readily transferable to other cases in which protest activity is contemplated.

Apart from problems relating to manipulation of protest group members, protest leaders must command at least some resources. For instance, skilled professionals must be made available to protest organizations. Lawyers are needed to help protesters use the judicial process, and to handle court cases. The effectiveness of a protest organization may depend upon a combination of an ability to threaten the political system and an ability to exercise legal rights. The organization may either pay lawyers or depend on volunteers. In the case of the rent strikes, dependence on volunteer lawyers was finally abandoned—there were not enough available, and those who were willing could not survive long without payment.

Other professionals may be needed in other protest circumstances. A group trying to protest against an urban renewal project, for example, will need architects and city planners to present a viable alternative to the city's plan.

Financial resources not only pay lawyers, but allow a minimum program of political activity. In the Harlem rent strikes, dues assessed against the protesters were low and were not collected systematically. Lawyers often complained that tenants were unwilling to pay incidental and minor fees, such as the $2 charge to subpoena departmental records. Obtaining money for mimeo flyers, supplies, rent, telephones, and a small payroll became major problems. The fact that Jesse Gray spent a great deal of time trying to organize new groups, and speaking all over the city, prevented him from paying attention to organizational details. Furthermore, he did not or could not develop assistants who could assume the organizational burden.

Lack of money can sometimes be made up for by passionate support. Lawyers, office help, and block organizers did come forth to work voluntarily for the rent strike. But such help is unreliable and usually transient. When spring came, volunteers vanished rapidly and did not return the following winter. Volunteer assistance usually comes from the more educated and skilled who can get other jobs, at good salaries. The diehards of ad hoc political groups are usually those who have no place else to go, nothing else to do.

Lack of money also can be overcome with skilled nonprofessionals; but usually they are scarce. The college students, Negro and white, who staffed the rent strike offices, handled paper work and press releases, and served as neighborhood organizers, were vital to the strike's success. Not only could they communicate with tenants, but they were relatively sophisticated about the operations of the city government and the communications media. They could help tenants with city agencies, and tell reporters what they wanted to hear. They also maintained contacts with other civil rights and liberal organizations. Other workers might have eventually acquired these skills and contacts, but these student organizers allowed the movement to go into action quickly, on a citywide scale and with a large volume of cases. One of the casualties of black power has been the exclusion of skilled white college students from potentially useful roles of this kind.

Like the proverbial tree that falls unheard in the forest, protest, politically speaking, does not exist unless it is projected and perceived. To the extent that a successful protest depends on appealing to, or perhaps also threatening, other groups in the community, publicity through the public media will set the limits of how far that protest activity will go toward success. (A number of writers, in fact, have noticed that the success of a protest seems directly related to publicity outside the immediate protest area.) If the communications media either ignore the protest or play it down, it will not succeed.

When the protest *is* covered, the way it is given publicity will influence all participants including the protesters themselves. Therefore, it is vital that a leader know what the media consider newsworthy, and be familiar with the prejudices and desires of those who determine what is to be covered and how much.

MEDIA'S DEMANDS MAY BE DESTRUCTIVE

But media requirements are often contradictory and hard to meet. TV wants spot news, perhaps thirty seconds' worth; newspapers want somewhat more than that, and long stories may appear only in weekly neighborhood or ethnic papers. Reporters want topical newsworthiness in the short run—the more exciting the better. They will even stretch to get it. But after that they want evidence, accuracy, and reliability. The leader who was too accommodating in the beginning may come to be portrayed as an irresponsible liar.

This conflict was well-illustrated in the rent strike. Jesse Gray and the reporters developed an almost symbiotic relationship. They wanted fresh, dramatic news on the growth of the strike—and Gray was happy to give them progress reports he did not, and could not, substantiate.

Actually, just keeping the strikes going in a limited number of buildings would have been a considerable feat. Yet reporters wanted more than that—they wanted growth. Gray, of course, had other reasons for reporting that the strike was spreading—he knew that such reports, if believed, would help pressure city officials. In misrepresenting the facts, Gray was encouraged by sympathetic reporters—in the long run actually undermining his case. As a *New York Times* reporter explained, "We had an interest in keeping it going."

Having encouraged Gray to go out on a limb and overstate the support he had, the reporters later were just as eager for documentation. It was not forthcoming. Gray consistently failed to produce a reliable list of rent strike buildings that could withstand independent verification. He took the reporters only to those buildings he considered "safe." And the newspapers that had themselves strongly contributed to the inflation of Gray's claims then helped deflate them and denied him press coverage.

The clash between the needs of these two constituencies—the media and the protesters—often puts great strain on leaders. The old-line leader who appeals to his followers because of his apparent responsibility, integrity, and restraint will not capture the necessary headlines. On the other hand, the leader who finds militant rhetoric a useful weapon for organizing some people will find the media only too eager to carry his more inflammatory statements. But this protrayal of him as an uncompromising firebrand (often meant for a limited audience and as a limited tactic) will alienate him from people he may need for broad support, and may work toward excluding him from bargaining with city officials.

If a leader takes strong or extreme positions, he may win followers and newspaper space, but alienate the protest's target. Exclusion from the councils of bargaining or decision making can have serious consequences for protest leaders, since the targets can then concentrate on satisfying the aroused public and civic groups, while ignoring the demands of the protesters.

What a protest leader must do to get support from third parties will also often conflict with what he must do to retain the interest and support of his followers. For instance, when Negro leaders actually engage in direct bargaining with politicians, they may find their supporters outraged or discouraged, and slipping away. They need militancy to arouse support; they need support to bargain; but if they bargain, they may seem to betray that militancy, and lose support. Yet bargaining at some point may be necessary to obtain objectives from city politicians. These tensions can be minimized to some extent by a protest organization's having divided leadership. One leader may bargain with city officials, while another continues rhetorical guerrilla warfare.

Divided leadership may also prove useful in solving the problem that James Q. Wilson has noted: "The militant displays an unwillingness to perform those administrative tasks which are necessary to operate an organization." The nuts and bolts of administrative detail are vital. If protest depends primarily on a leader's charisma, as the rent strikes did to some extent, allocating responsibility (already difficult because of lack of skilled personnel) can become a major problem. In the rent strike, somebody had to coordinate court appearances for tenants and lawyers; somebody had to subpoena Building and Health Department records and collect money to pay for them; and somebody had to be alert to the fact that, through landlord duplicity or tenant neglect, tenants might face immediate eviction and require emergency legal assistance. Jesse Gray was often unable, or unwilling, to concentrate on these details. In part failures of these kinds are forced on the protest leader, who must give higher priority to publicity and arousing support than to administrative detail. However, divided leadership can help separate responsibility for administration from responsibility for mobilization.

Strain between militancy to gain and maintain support and reasonableness to obtain concessions can also be diminished by successful "public relations." Protest groups may understand the same words differently than city officials. Imperatives to march or burn are usually not the commands frightened whites sometimes think they are.

BARGAINING IS FOR INSIDERS

Protest success depends partly upon enlarging the number of groups and individuals who are concerned about the issues. It also depends upon ability to influence the shape of the decision, not merely whether or not there will be a decision. This is one reason why protest is more likely to succeed when groups are trying to veto a decision (say, to stop construction of an expressway), than when they try to initiate projects (say, to establish low cost transportation systems for a neighborhood).

Protest groups are often excluded from the bargaining arena because the civic groups and city officials who make decisions in various policy areas have developed relationships over long periods of time, for mutual benefit. Interlopers are not admitted to these councils easily. Men in power do not like to sit down with people they consider rogues. They do not seek the dubious pleasure of being denounced, and are uneasy in the presence of people whose class, race, or manners are unfamiliar. They may make opportunities available for "consultation," or even "confrontation," but decisions will be made behind closed doors where the nature of the decision is not open to discussion by "outsiders."

As noted before, relatively powerless protest groups seldom have enough people of high status to work for their proposals. Good causes sometimes attract such people, but seldom for long. Therefore protest groups hardly ever have the expertise and experience they need, including professionals in such fields as law, architecture, accounting, education, and how to get government money. This is one area in which the "political impoverishment" of low-income groups is most clearly observed. Protest groups may learn how to dramatize issues, but they cannot present data or proposals that public officials consider "objective" or "reasonable." Few men can be both passionate advocate and persuasive arbiter at the same time.

Ultimately the success of a protest depends on the targets.

Many of the forces that inhibit protest leaders from influencing target groups have already been mentioned: the protesters' lack of status, experience, and resources in bargaining; the conflict between the rhetoric that will inspire and hold supporters, and what will open the door to meaningful bargaining; conflicting press demands, and so on.

But there is an additional factor that constrains protest organizations that deal with public agencies. As many students of organizations have pointed out, public agencies and the men who run them are concerned with maintaining and enhancing the agency's position. This means protecting the agency from criticism and budget cuts, and attempting to increase the agency's status and scope. This piece of conventional wisdom has great importance for a protest group which can only succeed by getting others to apply pressure on public policy. Public agencies are most responsive to their regular critics and immediate organizational allies. Thus if they can deflect pressure from these, their reference groups, they can ease the pressure brought by protest *without meeting any of the protest demands.*

At least six tactics are available to targets that are inclined to respond in some way to protests. They may respond with symbolic satisfactions. Typical, in city politics, is the ribbon-cutting, streetcorner ceremony, or the mayor's walking press conference. When tension builds up in Harlem, Mayor Lindsay walks the streets and talks to the people. Such occasions are not only used to build support, but to per-

suade the residents that attention is being directed to their problems.

City agencies establish special machinery and procedures to prepare symbolic means for handling protest crises. For instance, in those New York departments having to do with housing, top officials, a press secretary, and one or two others will devote whatever time is necessary to collecting information and responding quickly to reporters' inquiries about a developing crisis. This is useful for tenants: It means that if they can create enough concern, they can cut through red tape. It is also useful for officials who want to appear ready to take action.

During the New York rent strikes, city officials responded by: initiating an antirat campaign; proposing ways to "legalize" rent strikes (already legal under certain conditions); starting a program to permit the city to make repairs; and contracting for a costly university study to review housing code enforcement procedures. Some of these steps were of distinct advantage to tenants, although none was directed at the overall slum problem. It is important to note, however, that the announcement of these programs served to deflect pressure by reassuring civic groups and a liberal public that something was being done. Regardless of how well-meaning public officials are, real changes in conditions are secondary to the general agency need to develop a response to protest that will "take the heat off."

Another tactic available to public officials is to give token satisfactions. When city officials respond, with much publicity, to a few cases brought to them, they can appear to be meeting protest demands, while actually meeting only those few cases. If a child is bitten by a rat, and enough hue and cry is raised, the rats in that apartment or building may be exterminated, with much fanfare. The building next door remains infested.

Such tokenism may give the appearance of great improvement, while actually impeding real overall progress by alleviating public concern. Tokenism is particularly attractive to reporters and television news directors, who are able to dramatize individual cases convincingly. General situations are notoriously hard to dramatize.

To blunt protest drives, protest targets may also work to change their internal procedures and organization. This tactic is similar to the preceding one. By developing means to concentrate on those cases that are most dramatic, or seem to pose the greatest threats, city officials can effectively wear down the cutting-edges of protest.

As noted, all New York City agencies have informal arrangements to deal with such crisis cases. During the rent strikes two new programs were developed by the city whereby officials could enter buildings to make repairs and exterminate rats on an emergency basis. Previously, officials had been confined to trying to find the landlords and to taking them to court (a time-consuming, ineffective process that has been almost universally criticized by knowledgeable observers). These new programs were highly significant developments because they expanded the scope of governmental responsibility. They acknowledged, in a sense, that slum conditions are a social disease requiring public intervention.

At the same time, these innovations served the purposes of administrators who needed the power to make repairs in the worst housing cases. If public officials can act quickly in the most desperate situations that come to their attention, pressure for more general attacks on housing problems can be deflected.

The new programs could never significantly affect the 800,000 deteriorating apartments in New York City. The new programs can operate only so long as the number of crises are relatively limited. Crisis treatment for everyone would mean shifting resources from routine services. If all cases receive priority, then none can.

The new programs, however welcomed by some individual tenants, help agencies to "cool off" crises quicker. This also may be the function of police review boards and internal complaint bureaus. Problems can be handled more expeditiously with such mechanisms while agency personnel behavior remains unaffected.

Target groups may plead that their hands are tied—because of laws or stubborn superiors, or lack of resources or authority. They may be sympathetic, but what can they do? Besides, "If-I-give-it-to-you-I-have-to-give-it-to-everyone."

Illustratively, at various times during the rent strike, city officials claimed they did not have funds for emergency repairs (although they found funds later), and lacked authority to enter buildings to make emergency repairs (although the city later acted to make emergency repairs under provisions of a law available for over sixty years). This tactic is persuasive; everyone knows that cities are broke, and limited by state law. But if pressure rises, funds for specific, relatively inexpensive programs, or expansion of existing programs, can often be found.

Targets may use their extensive resources and contacts to discredit protest leaders and organizations: "They don't really have the people behind them"; they are acting "criminally"; they are "leftwing." These allegations can cool the sympathies of the vital third parties, whether or not there is any truth behind them. City officials, especially, can use this device in their contacts with civic groups and communication media, with which they are mutually dependent for support and assistance. Some city officials can downgrade protesters while others appear sympathetic to the protesters' demands.

Finally, target groups may postpone action— time is on their side. Public sympathy cools quickly, and issues are soon forgotten. Moreover, because low income protest groups have difficulty sustaining organization (for reasons suggested above), they are particularly affected by delays. The threat represented by protest dissipates with time, the difficulty of managing for constituencies increases as more and more information circulates, and the inherent instability of protest groups makes it unlikely that they will be able to take effective action when decisions are finally announced.

SURVEY RESEARCH AS PROCRASTINATION

The best way to procrastinate is to commit the subject to "study." By the time the study is ready, if ever, the protest group will probably not be around to criticize or press for implementation of proposals. The higher the status of the study group, the less capable low-status protest groups will be able to effectively challenge the final product. Furthermore, officials retain the option of rejecting or failing to accept the reports of study groups, a practice developed to an art by the Johnson administration.

This is not to say that surveys, research, and study groups are to be identified solely as delaying tactics. They are often desirable, even necessary, to document need and mobilize public and pressure group support. But postponement, for whatever reason, will always change the pressures on policymakers, usually in directions unfavorable to protest results.

Groups without power can attempt to gain influence through protest. I have argued that protest will be successful to the extent that the protesters can get third parties to put pressure on the targets. But protest leaders have severe problems in trying to meet the needs and desires of four separate and often conflicting constituencies—their supporters, the mass media, the interested and vital third parties, and the targets of the protest.

By definition, relatively powerless groups have few resources, and therefore little probability of success. But to survive at all and to arouse the third parties, they need at least some resources. Even to get these minimal resources, conflicting demands limit the leader's effectiveness. And when, finally, public officials are forced to recognize protest activity, it is not to meet the demands, but to satisfy other groups that have influence.

Edelman has written that, in practice, regulatory policy consists of reassuring mass publics symbolically while at the same time dispensing tangible concessions only to narrow interest groups. Complementing Edelman, I have suggested that public officials give symbolic reassurances to protest groups, rather than real concessions, because those on whom they most depend will be satisfied with appearances of action. Rent strikers wanted to see repairs in their apartments and dramatic improvements in slum housing; but the wider publics that most influence city officials could be satisfied simply by the appearance of reform. And when city officials had satisfied the publics this

way, they could then resist or ignore the protesters' demands for other or more profound changes.

Kenneth Clark, in *Dark Ghetto,* has observed that the illusion of having power, when unaccompanied by material rewards, leads to feelings of helplessness and reinforces political apathy in the ghetto. If the poor and politically weak protest to acquire influence that will help change their lives and conditions, only to find that little comes from all that risk and trouble, then apathy or hostility toward conventional political methods may result.

If the arguments presented in this article are convincing, then those militant civil rights leaders who insist that protest is a shallow foundation on which to build longterm, concrete gains are essentially correct. But their accompanying arguments—the fickleness of the white liberal, the difficulty of changing discriminatory institutions as opposed to discriminatory laws—are only part of the explanation for the essential failure of protest. An analysis of the politics involved strongly suggests that protest is best understood by concentrating on problems of managing diverse protest constituencies.

It may be, therefore, that Saul Alinsky is on soundest ground when he recommends protest as a tactic to build an organization, which can then command its own power. Protest also may be recommended to increase or change the political consciousness of people, or to gain short run goals in a potentially sympathetic political environment. This may be the most significant contribution of the black power movement— the development of group consciousness which provides a more cohesive political base. But ultimately relatively powerless groups cannot rely on the protest process alone to help them obtain long-run goals, or general improvements in conditions. What they need for long-run success are stable political resources—in a word, power. The American political system is theoretically open; but it is closed, for many reasons suggested here, to politically impoverished groups. While politicians continue to affirm the right to dissent or protest within reason, the political process in which protest takes place remains highly restricted.

39
From Failure to Success— Albany to Birmingham*
HOWARD HUBBARD

The organized militant phase of the civil rights struggle coincides in most persons' minds with the series of long hot summers which began in Birmingham in the spring of 1963. In fact, however, Martin Luther King's Birmingham campaign was preceded by a less well-known effort in Albany, Georgia, in the summer and fall of 1962. Significantly, by Dr. King's own admission the Albany operation was a failure.

When, in Albany, Georgia, in 1962, months of demonstrations and jailings failed to accomplish the goals of the movement, reports in the press and elsewhere pronounced non-violent resistance a dead issue.

There were weaknesses in Albany, and a share of the responsibility belongs to each of us who participated. However, none of us was so immodest as to feel himself master of the new theory. Each of us expected that setbacks would be a part of the ongoing effort. There is no tactical theory so neat that a revolutionary struggle for a share of power can be won merely by pressing a row of buttons. Human beings with all their faults and strengths constitute the mechanism of a social movement. They must make mistakes and learn from them, make more

*[Reprinted from Public Interest, No. 12, Summer 1968, pp. 4–8. Copyright National Affairs, Inc. 1968.]

mistakes and learn anew. They must taste defeat as well as success, and discover how to live with each. Time and action are the teachers.

When we planned our strategy for Birmingham months later, we spent hours assessing Albany and trying to learn from its errors.[1]

The implication of the passage quoted is that Albany really was a failure, but that "weaknesses" and "errors" uncovered there helped perfect the theory that was applied successfully in Birmingham. King nowhere gives explicit details of how his Birmingham strategy benefited from the Albany experience, but the lesson learned from Albany can be inferred from the following passage, in which "Bull" Connor's initial tactics are compared with those of Pritchett.

Birmingham residents of both races were surprised at the restraint of Connor's men at the beginning of the campaign. True, police dogs and clubs made their debut on Palm Sunday, but their appearance that day was brief and they quickly disappeared. What observers probably did not realize was that the commissioner was trying to take a leaf from the book of Police Chief Laurie Pritchett of Albany. Chief Pritchett felt that by directing his police to be non-violent, he had discovered a new way to defeat the demonstrations. *Mr. Connor, as it developed, was not to adhere to nonviolence long; the dogs were baying in kennels not far way; the hoses were primed. But that is another part of the story.*[2]

Evidently the reason King failed in Albany was that Chief Pritchett used force rather than violence in controlling the situation,[3] that is, *he effectively*

[1] Martin Luther King, Jr., *Why We Can't Wait* (New York: Signet Books, 1969), p. 43.
[2] *Ibid.*, p. 69. Emphasis mine.
[3] The riot control strategy that emerged during the riots which occurred in the wake of Dr. King's assassination essentially duplicates this technique. Troops in sufficient numbers dominate

reciprocated the demonstrator's tactics. King's Birmingham innovation was preeminently strategic. Its essence was not merely more refined tactics, but the selection of a target city which had as its Commissioner of Public Safety "Bull" Connor, a notorious racist and hothead who could be depended on *not* to respond nonviolently.

When the demonstrations began, Connor was a lame duck, having been defeated by Albert Boutwell, a "moderate," in a runoff election April 2, 1963. Knowing that Connor's term would soon expire, eight Birmingham clergymen took newspaper space to ask, not unreasonably, that Dr. King desist until Boutwell had been given an opportunity. King's answer was his celebrated "Letter from a Birmingham Jail,"[4] which, though admirable as rhetoric, comprised a somewhat hawkish response to the ministers' proposals. King declined their suggestion that he negotiate forthwith, saying that nonviolent direct action must first "create such a crisis and foster such a tension" that meaningful negotiation would be assured. He also stated that "one has a moral responsibility to disobey unjust laws," citing as an example the local parade ordinance, a deliberate breach of which had resulted in his incarceration.[5]

After eight days, Dr. King emerged from jail to initiate on April 20, a new operational phase which enlisted school-age children in large numbers and sought to "fill the jails." This tactic was gradually intensified until, on May

2, more than a thousand young demonstrators were jailed.

Finally, on Friday, May 3, "Bull" Connor "abandoned his posture of nonviolence." King's account is unfortunately not clear as to whether "some few spectators" who "reacted to the brutality of the policemen by throwing rocks and bottles" precipitated the employment of dogs and hoses or vice versa. In any event, pictures of the resulting violent confrontation, which culminated in the brutal use of high pressure hoses on the demonstrators, shocked and outraged the United States and the rest of the world on Saturday morning. This episode is at least superficially familiar to anyone who took an interest in the matter at the time, and most persons' curiosity concerning it has long since ceased.

However, the events of the next three days, Sunday, Monday, and Tuesday (May 5, 6, and 7) impart a curious off again/on again quality to the proceedings and, though quite significant, have seemingly gone unnoticed.

Dr. King tells in his book how, on Sunday afternoon, the Reverend Charles Billups led another massive march, proceeding down a Birmingham street across which Connor and his men had taken up positions, deployed their hoses, etc. When the marchers drew near, Reverend Billups "politely refused" Connors' order to turn back, whereupon "Bull Connor whirled on his men and shouted: Dammit. Turn on the hoses."

Then, according to King, occurred "one of the most fantastic events of the Birmingham story." The marchers, many of whom had been on their knees, stood up and advanced. Connor's men fell back, "their hoses sagging uselessly in their hands," while several hundred Negroes marched past them without interference to hold a prayer meeting "as planned."

---

the situation without resort to firearms. Firearms are the equivalent in a riot environment of dogs, fire hoses, and cattle prods in the context of a nonviolent demonstration.

[4] *Ibid.*, Chap. 5.

[5] His conviction was appealed to and ultimately upheld by the Supreme Court, and Dr. King served a well-publicized five-day sentence in August 1967—reading William Styron's *Confessions of Nat Turner.*

Now King's account differs in several important respects from *The New York Times* version. According to *The Times,* the demonstrators knelt to pray directly in front of Connor's "barricade," whereupon Reverend Phillips *(sic)* declaimed "Turn on your water, turn loose your dogs, we will stand here till we die." No such orders were forthcoming, however, and after an interval during which police made no attempt to disperse them, the demonstrators proceeded not toward the jail, their supposed goal, but to a nearby park where they held their prayer meeting.

Whichever version one accepts, the point is that Connor evidently apprehended the unwisdom of bowling over nonviolent demonstrators with high pressure hoses for a third straight day. The next day, Monday, one thousand more Negroes were jailed, 40 percent of them juveniles. A Negro woman was photographed being held down by five white policemen. Dick Gregory was arrested. However, authorities announced their intention to use "no more force than necessary," and, as on Sunday, hoses were not employed. On Tuesday, "police and firemen drove hundreds of rioting Negroes off the streets with high pressure hoses . . . after 2,500 to 3,500 persons rampaged through the business district in two demonstrations." Thus provoked, Connor reverted to his original conspicuously oppressive and brutal fire-hose tactic, although a measure of restraint prevailed inasmuch as cattle prods and police dogs were not reintroduced. On Wednesday, a moratorium was declared on demonstrations, and negotiations began on Thursday.

Now there are several illuminating perspectives one can open up and many issues to examine in the light of the preceding accounts.

A moral and intellectual paradox is that the Albany campaign—where nonviolence was reciprocated—failed, whereas Birmingham—where violence was nonviolently provoked—was interpreted as a great success. The demonstrations had to provoke a violent response in order to succeed. According to Arthur Schlesinger, Jr., "the Attorney General three times counseled the Birmingham leaders not to force issues while Bull Connor was still in charge."[6] But after the conspicuous brutality of dogs, fire hoses, and cattle prods, no one cared to examine the fine structure of the gamelike tactics and strategy that brought it about.

An advocate of nonviolent techniques might simply regard Birmingham as a more skillful and therefore successful application of "moral jujitsu," secure in the knowledge that the cause was ultimately just so that the rest was merely "tactics." But for an objective observer, the interesting questions are: Why didn't Connor inquire of Albany's Chief Pritchett concerning his methods? Why didn't Pritchett volunteer them? On the other hand, maybe he did and the answer is: "Bull" Connor didn't get his nickname for nothing. How, after the example of Albany, could sheriffs consistently fail to cope with King's tactic as most of them did?

The following three propositions are advanced as working hypotheses:

1 King's skill consisted mainly in his ability to *contrive*—in the best Machiavellian tradition—a situation in which he was the injured party (an interpretation quite inconsistent with the popular verdict at the time). He did not anticipate beforehand everything that this would entail. His tactics emerged in a series of existential command decisions.

2 Such a strategy depends for its success on certain gaps and discontinuities in communication. (If Connor had understood King's method earlier, he would have behaved differently—albeit hypocritically.)

3 Where public opinion arbitrates, sentiment rallies to the victim—which idea

[6] *A Thousand Days* (New York: Houghton, 1965), p. 988.

the victim may exploit, *as long as he does so discreetly.* To appreciate the last qualification is to appreciate some of the costs incurred by the movement, now that riots sometimes appear instrumental and deliberate. To arrange to have violence visited upon oneself reflexively for the benefit of an influential audience is an exercise in public relations—but, to be effective, must not appear as such.

Birmingham left such a vivid sense of outrage hovering over the country that Negro leaders organized the March on Washington, which provided an outlet for the powerful resentment that was engendered during the latter part of the summer of 1963. The following spring witnessed the passage of the Civil Rights Bill of 1964. In the interval after Birmingham, President Kennedy remarked to Dr. King: "Our judgment of Bull Connor should not be too harsh. After all, in his way, he has done a good deal for civil rights legislation this year."[7]

40
*The Phantom Racist**
RITA JAMES SIMON and JAMES W. CAREY

In 1963 three freshmen Negro athletes at the University of Illinois at Urbana sought out a Negro graduate student and complained to him about racial discrimination against them. Specifically, they said, a member of the football staff had urged them to stop dating or being seen with white girls. The Negro graduate student arranged for the athletes to sign affidavits charging the Athletic Association, which administers intercollegiate athletics at Illinois, with discrimination.

This was the precipitating incident in the search for what we call the "phan-

[7] King, *op. cit.,* p. 132.
*[Reprinted with permission from *Trans-action,* November 1966. Copyright © November 1966 by Trans-action, Inc., New Brunswick, New Jersey.]

tom racist." He is a phantom because the specific charges of discrimination were never proven, but neither were the issues he raised ever resolved. They underscore the continuing problems of Negro students at the university.

First, some background about the University of Illinois must be considered:

There are approximately 350 Negro students at the University of Illinois. The estimated number is surprisingly small considering that nearby Chicago has the second largest Negro population in the United States. Negroes are approximately 1 percent of the university enrollment.

Among the 350, about thirty-five have athletic scholarships. Though athletes must meet minimum standards of academic achievement, they are chosen principally for athletic ability.

Few Negro students at the University of Illinois are active in civil rights organizations or have participated in civil rights demonstrations. Some went South to serve in the Mississippi summer projects and voter registration drives, but few have taken action directly focused on campus and community conditions. Civil rights groups made attempts to end "white only" membership in fraternities and sororities and to end discrimination in privately owned rooming houses. (These demands were met when the university set a date for the removal of discriminatory clauses and required nondiscrimination from any landlord renting to university students after January 1, 1966.)

Independent studies have indicated that Negroes, in general, do not consider the university or its environs as a congenial place for them.

After the complaint of discrimination was made in 1963, the following sequence of events occurred.

FUMBLE ON FIRST DOWN

Armed with the affidavits from the three freshmen athletes, a group of graduate students, most of them Negro and members of the campus chapter of the NAACP, formed an ad hoc committee of Students for Human Dignity and Social Peace. The committee approached the *Daily Illini,* the student undergraduate paper, and asked to have the charges of discrimination publicized. The editor of the *Daily Illini* doubted the charges and delayed printing them. Word of the committee's attempts leaked to the Athletic Association and to other Negro athletes, who had not been informed.

One football player, a self-appointed spokesman for the other Negro athletes, contacted the *Daily Illini* editor and certain members of the ad hoc committee. The athlete disputed the charges and threatened to discredit them and the ad hoc committee if the Athletic Association and the coaching staff were harmed. He contended that if the athletes were warned about dating it was because their classwork was suffering and the coach was merely trying to help them. He pointed out that a large number of Negro athletes dated white girls and received no warning from the coaches.

Members of the ad hoc committee, in a subsequent interview, said that the coach was responding to pressure from the town, which found the sight of Negro boys and white girls together repugnant and that talking to the athletes about their social life was *prima facie* evidence of discrimination.

After some deliberation, the *Daily Illini* refused to run the story. Lacking support from the Negro athletes and the student daily, the ad hoc committee changed its strategy.

The ad hoc committee decided to gather additional evidence of the mistreatment of Negro athletes in particular and of Negro students in general. To that end the committee took testimony from Negro athletes for presentation to the university administration. The football player who had threatened to discredit the ad hoc committee was one of those who testified. This athlete later said his testimony was directed solely against the Department of Physical Education on the campus. The athletes

did contend, however, that the University of Illinois was not a good school for Negroes; they said that the atmosphere was hostile and they had been humiliated by teachers, coaches, other athletes, and white students. They said that when they were used by the Athletic Association to recruit other Negro atheletes, they had a difficult time, in good conscience, urging them to come. Much of their testimony was about the bad climate for Negro students in general — not just Negro athletes.

The evidence was presented to the university administration and to the all-university Committee on Race Relations in December of 1963. A subcommittee of the race relations committee investigated the Department of Physical Education and the Athletic Association. As a result, the provost issued a statement in September 1964 that did not specifically confirm the ad hoc committee charges, but did warn against discrimination against Negro athletes. It directed staff members to refrain from using racially demeaning expressions, to cease interference in the social activities of athletes, and to discourage white athletes from intruding into the private affairs of Negro athletes.

Members of the university administration later commented that they felt that the investigation had substantially improved the racial climate on the campus, that particularly objectionable practices had been stopped, and that the Negro students themselves were satisfied.

INTERFERENCE CALLED

But following the close of the football season in 1964, members of the ad hoc committee received evidence that the provost's directive was being ignored. A Negro athlete confided to a Negro graduate student that he had been warned against interracial dating, and that his choice of courses was interfered with. At this time, the campus chapter of the NAACP entered the conflict in defense of the Negro athletes. Many members of the ad hoc committee had left the university and those who remained decided to turn over all the committee's materials to the NAACP and have them continue where the committee left off. Distrustful of the administration and its motives, the NAACP took its case directly to the public.

Until January 1965, the conflict between Negro students and the university had been a private matter. Persistent rumors had circulated but most of the faculty, students, and community were unaware of the conflict. The NAACP made the conflict a public matter by releasing to the press a resolution which charged:

For the last several years complaints have been lodged with this office alleging that the University Athletic Association and members of the Physical Education Department including some coaches, have been guilty of racially discriminatory policies. . . .

A special committee, appointed by the president's office, found that many of the allegations were true. . . . But the NAACP has learned that Negro athletes are still being subjected to such discriminatory practices.

The NAACP also sent approximately forty letters to high schools throughout the nation urging Negro athletes not to come to the university.

Three days later a statement, claiming to represent the opinions of all Negro athletes on campus, was released to the news media. It denounced the NAACP and defended the coaches and the Athletic Association.

We, the Negro athletes of the University of Illinois, do, without qualification, fully denounce recent allegations made by the Uni-

versity of Illinois chapter of the NAACP concerning alleged discrimination against university athletes.

First, the Negro athlete on the University of Illinois campus is articulate, he is well aware of his position as an individual and as a member of the Negro race, he is, further, aware of his position as a member of a team which represents the U. of I. He does not need an organized spokesman, whether it be the NAACP or some other organization.

Negro athletes at the University of Illinois feel their civil rights have been violated by the NAACP in their failure to seek our counsel, both as a group and as individual citizens before taking the irresponsible action of attacking the U. of I. Athletic Association.

The day has long since passed when the philosophy of "protecting our little brown brother" is needed. The Negro athlete at the U. of I. is a student first. He is to receive an education at one of the nation's finest universities. He is not a shuffling, grinning "Uncle Tom" as the NAACP's action would indicate. . . .

We feel, moreover, that the national organization of the NAACP should publicly censure the U. of I. chapter for their action.

We categorically deny the existence of any segregationalist measures on the part of any member of the U. of I. coaching staff.

In making this statement Negro athletes wish to make very clear that their remarks represent the opinions of every Negro athlete without exception.

Following the exchange of charges, other organizations and groups entered the conflict: the local chapter of the American Association of University Professors, the public relations office of the university, the provost's office, and many members of the faculty, fraternities, sororities, and student groups. Press and television coverage continued for almost three weeks.

The day after release of the resolution reportedly representing all Negro athletes the NAACP stated:

We, the University of Illinois chapter of the NAACP, are disheartened, but not surprised, by the repudiation of our recently passed resoltion purporting to speak for all of the Negro athletes, past and present. We do not choose to engage in any internecine debate with this group. However, we stand on our resolution.

CHARGES OF UNNECESSARY ROUGHNESS

Later the NAACP claimed to have affidavits describing specific discriminatory practices by certain coaches and professors. (None of these affidavits were ever made public.) Other campus organizations joined in support of the NAACP—the executive council of the Friends of SNCC, and two Negro sororities and fraternities.

A few days later the NAACP spokesmen charged that the athletes' statement denouncing them was a fraud. They claimed that the athletes never saw it before it appeared in print, and that it was the work and opinion of only one man—the athlete spokesman who in the past had both supported and denounced the university's policies. No one they said—not even the athletes themselves —had ever seen a copy of the statement with the signature of all the Negro athletes on it. Even the director of public information at the university, who announced that twenty-five of the twenty-seven Negro athletes on campus had attended a meeting and signed the statement, was unable to produce a signed copy for more than a month after it was released. When the statement was finally produced the NAACP charged that the signatures were obtained under duress, that it had taken the Athletic

Association a month to get the athletes to sign.

The story was picked up by the national news services and publicized across the country. Sports columnists on both coasts commented on potential loss of athletes; national civil rights leaders deplored continuance of discrimination at the Illinois campus. Locally, the *Daily Illini* editorially bewailed the absence of information and continued suspicion and distrust.

And then, without formal charges ever being made, without identification of either the racist or the athletes, without resolution of the issues, without adjudication of the charges, the case dropped from public view. It left behind suspicion, consternation, and damaged reputations.

ANALYZING THE PLAYS

Acting independently, we attempted as researchers to determine what the facts were, to understand how the situation had become as confused as it was, and to unravel the snarled communications. We interviewed members of the NAACP, Negro athletes, and concerned members of the faculty, hoping to disentangle fact from fiction. Although partly successful in gathering facts, we could not resolve basic issues; and here lies much of the significance.

Our procedure was straightforward. We interviewed two officers of the NAACP (both Negro graduate students), and the author of the statement from the Negro athletes, a graduating senior on the football team. We read all published accounts and interpretations, talked with past and current faculty members close to the students involved. Most important of all, we interviewed, by anonymous questionnaire, fifteen of the twenty-seven Negro athletes at the university (nine of them had attended the meeting during which plans to publish a denunciation of the NAACP were supposedly formulated).

When the NAACP took the issue to the media, the case became part of the great public drama of civil rights. That is, the case became subject to the laws of drama rather than the laws of reason. Men had to cast themselves in roles appropriate to the drama—as gods and devils, racists, integrationists, or liberal fools. Because mass exposure makes celebrities overnight, vanity and ego got locked into the discussion. For example, as the charges and counter-charges were hurled we became increasingly suspicious, on the basis of our interviews, that part of the trouble was caused by a personal vendetta between two Negroes—the leader of the athletes and one of the leaders of the NAACP.

Because the case of discrimination expressed much more than concern for a few athletes and because the media turned the case into a dramatic conflict, it became virtually impossible to resolve the issue, to interpret the events, or even to get a consistent rendering of the facts.

Some things did emerge clearly, however. The whole episode was precipitated by the complaint of a single Negro athlete. One of the NAACP officers revealed to us his name and the nature of his complaint.

But the NAACP refused to make any of this information public—because the athlete did not want it made public. He was *not* graduating and fearful of retaliation. According to the NAACP, he had been told to stop dating white girls and had been pressured to major in physical education although he preferred to study something else and had already been accepted by the other school.

According to the NAACP, this complaint fit a pattern. The complaints

investigated by the provost's office a year and a half earlier, also involved interference by the staff in the social activities of Negro athletes. The provost's directive of September 1964 had not been heeded.

Two questions still remained:

Why hadn't the NAACP reported the complaint to the university before it contacted the high school athletes and the press?

Why didn't the NAACP try to get endorsement from at least some of the Negro athletes—or at the very least inform them—before publicizing their resolution?

Our informants claimed that one member had talked to someone on the president's staff and was told that the NAACP should document the incident. Two other representatives of the NAACP then offered to bring the complaining student to testify directly if the administration would guarantee his immunity.

But, our informants said, the university refused to "promise anything"; also the university spokesmen played down the seriousness of the charge. The NAACP therefore felt that even if they did produce the student, the university would not take a serious view of the matter, and he might lose his athletic scholarship or be otherwise penalized. They believed that the university had not enforced its 1964 directive and could not be trusted now. (The university claims that such an encounter never took place; that casual mention had been made of a developing incident, but that none was ever specifically outlined, no charges ever made, and that the university at all times offered complete protection to any Negro wishing to protest.

As to the second question, in a sense the NAACP was acting as an unauthorized spokesman for the athletes. (A charge later leveled at the NAACP was that they ignored the athletes, because, to put it mildly, they looked down on them, considered them dull, unable to understand the issues, in need of defense by more intelligent and articulate Negroes.)

But the NAACP did not feel they needed endorsement—one case of discrimination, when discrimination clearly violates rules and official policy, is sufficient cause for complaint. They also believed that by leaving the athletes out, they were actually protecting their best interests. One put it this way:

They really would rather not get involved and this is quite understandable. If you are on a team no one wants to be caught in a controversy involving that particular party and his immediate superiors—his boss, in other words. That is what the relationship really amounts to.

The NAACP thus felt they were being sensitive to the conflicting demands on the Negro athletes and did not want to hinder their careers. But they also believed that they had the implicit support of the Negro athletes, that privately the athletes would applaud them. They had listened to the athletes complain many times about unfair and discriminatory practices, and of their helplessness to do anything about it as long as they wanted to play.

Our informants thought, therefore, that the athletes wanted and needed their help—even though, as one acknowledged, none of the Negro athletes were members of the NAACP.

THE DEFENSE DIGS IN

The NAACP was surprised and angered when the statement reportedly signed by the Negro athletes was published. One said:

At first, after this thing broke and the resolution was released, I was very angry with all of them. I had heard these groups com-plain many times ever since last spring. Then they turn around and take a position like this. I was pretty angry and I decided that I would help the people that . . . wanted to be helped, and as for the other people, it's just too bad. If they want to be kicked around, they have that right. I just don't want them coming to me anymore saying what "the man" is doing to them.

But, he said he later found that the statement was "in fact the opinion of only one man." Two of the athletes who attended the meeting came to see him afterward and told him that the group had agreed upon a short statement which exonerated a few coaches and stated that as individuals they had not experienced discrimination by the Athletic Association. But that at no time did the athletes attack the NAACP nor deny the existence of discrimination by coaches.

So much for the NAACP's position. What of the other side? Did the athletes agree with the counterresolution? Did they condemn the NAACP's action? We have two sources of information— our interview with the organizer and author of the statement and the responses of fifteen other Negro athletes to an anonymous questionnaire.

The author said he believed that "the coach (Pete Elliot) and his staff did not use discriminatory practices and that the NAACP's attack on the staff as a whole was unjustified and untrue." As soon as he read the NAACP's resolution in the newspaper on Friday (the first he knew of it), he phoned Elliot to apologize and to express his loyalty to him. During the conversation he told Elliot that he was pretty sure the other Negro athletes agreed, and he would find out by calling a meeting. On Sunday evening, the local radio and television stations announced and read in full the resolution expressing the sentiment of the Negro athletes against the NAACP. The author claims that it reflected accurately the opinions expressed during the meeting, and that most (although not all) athletes read and signed it before release. The only reason all did not sign was simply because he could not locate them in time; all had agreed that the resolution should be written and publicized.

At this point, the NAACP used this athlete's earlier words against him. A few months before he had taken part in a student discussion on the "impressions, attitudes, and feelings of the Negro athlete," and the tape recording of this discussion had been presented to the administration as evidence of discrimination. Now his remarks were publicized by the NAACP. He had complained that at the Rose Bowl game the previous winter, a white all-American had called him a "black nigger." He said:

The thing that hurt me most was . . . the position the coaches took. The actual blame was placed on me. The coaches made an attempt to persuade the rest of the Negroes on the team that it was my fault and due to my nature; I was told that I should make a statement to try to soothe the feelings of the team. I didn't see what I could say to the team other than I was sorry he called me a black nigger. The issue was never really covered over. I think this is an example of the type of situation on our team. I think this is true in the administration. I think this is true in the various schools on campus, especially the school of Physical Education and I think that something has to be done. . . .

Now you ask me why I wouldn't recommend this type of school to another Negro student. . . .

I think the most disgraceful lack of administration here at the University of Illinois is that it is not geared at all for the Negro student. This is not just the athlete. . . . The Negro athlete and the Negro student is com-

pletely without facilities; completely without anything to do unless we go to town or unless we go to some activities that are off-campus.
. . .

The tape proved, as it was intended to, that the author was inconsistent. But that still does not answer the basic question: did the resolution published in the name of all the Negro athletes actually represent their views?

We decided to contact the athletes directly. It turned out that this was the most difficult and complicated task in the entire fact-finding operation. They were extremely loath to talk even when assured that no one would be quoted, and that we did not represent the university in this matter. We finally had to get the NAACP and the leading Negro athlete to act as intermediaries.

Of the fifteen respondents (not including the author of the resolution, but including the original complainant to the NAACP) fourteen answered that they disagreed with the NAACP statement. All fifteen said they thought the NAACP should have talked with the Negro athletes before releasing the story—and thirteen said the fact that they did not was important: "Everyone should have a chance to voice his own opinion"; "Athletes, Negro or white, aren't dumb. We can speak for ourselves"; "The statement isn't true." Some said "the NAACP challenged the maturity and intelligence of every Negro athlete on campus." All stated that they disapproved of the NAACP writing letters to Negro high school athletes.

On the other hand, only ten of the fifteen athletes who filled out the questionnaire had actually attended the Sunday meeting. About half of the total respondents said they had seen the NAACP resolution and talked about it beforehand. When asked to describe what they understood the group had decided to do, nine of the ten who attended said "write a letter of rebuttal," or "go on record in defense of the Athletic Association," or "make up a statement in which each sport where there are Negro players individually clear that sport." One said "talk the situation over with the NAACP."

All but one claimed that everyone in the group went along with the decision to censure the NAACP publicly. Of the ten, seven said they saw and signed the statement later that evening. Two said they signed it several weeks later after they had seen it in print. One said he never signed it because he did not have the chance to. Three of the five who did not attend the meeting saw and signed the statement at a later time.

Only one of the respondents who attended the Sunday meeting believed that the statement did not reflect the group decision and he did not sign. He felt that the author's attack on the NAACP did not reflect either the group's or his own feeling. He wrote:

The NAACP is the strongest organization for Negroes. Why should I hurt them? I am not trying to help the Athletic Association by hurting the NAACP.

When asked if they had spoken to members of the NAACP since the two statements appeared, five said yes. But only one—the one quoted above—said that he felt apologetic toward the NAACP.

PENALTIES FOR NEGRO PLAYERS

Had they *personally* experienced any discrimination at the university? Seven answered "yes," seven "no," and one said "it is difficult to answer." Those who answered "yes" said "from other students," and also said "from other athletes and the physical education faculty." Specifically they endured: name calling, warnings by coaches not to become "involved" with white girls,

receiving lower grades in physical education classes than they felt they deserved, and hearing teachers tell "Uncle Tom" jokes.

When asked: "If you had the chance to do it over, which university would you most like to attend?" eight chose the University of Illinois. Of those choosing other schools, five gave as reasons: "a more liberal racial climate," or "you can go places with a white girl without being disliked or looked at too hard."

In summary: The NAACP attacked the Athletic Association because they felt they had evidence of a continuing pattern of racial discrimination within the coaching staff, and that they could convince the university administration of it only if they galvanized public sentiment. A strong majority of the Negro athletes, organized and led by one of their colleagues, resented the NAACP's intrusion into their affairs, particularly without consultation, advice, or consent.

But a number of vexing and significant questions still remain: Was the case against the university and the Athletic Association strong enough to stand up in a formal public hearing? Why did the Negro athletes seem, relatively, to be so cool to civil rights issues? Why *didn't* the NAACP discuss the matter with some of the Negro athletes before acting?

To take the case to the public without securing the support of the athletes was politically foolish—in Lenin's terms, it was "political adventurism"—leading a revolution with no following. But this action did not cause the rupture between the NAACP and the athletes—rather it was a manifestation of other disorders, and a symptom of the social distance that separates Negroes from their leadership. We believe that this gulf is, most regrettably, grounded in the stigma of intellectual inferiority.

The cliche that beefy athletes recruited to play in highly commercialized college sports, especially football, whether Negro Americans from the slums or white Americans from the mines and fields, are stupid, lower class, and uncouth is certainly not new and not based on race. Athletes, white and black, are frequently referred to by other students as "animals." But the white student does not feel that the behavior of white athletes reflects on him; while the tenuous intellectual identity of Negroes makes them fear being classified with Negro athletes, and resaddled with this stigma.

But the stigma of inferiority also infected the Negro athletes, whether it seemed to come from the whites or their own people, and whether it was addressed to them as Negroes or as athletes.

But while this resentment may explain the rupture between the two groups, we are still left with the fundamental indifference of the Negro athletes here (and perhaps in general) to civil rights. Most athletes agree, it seems to us, that they had suffered discrimination from coaches and fellow students. Most believe that the Athletic Association and the Department of Physical Education give them lower grades than they deserve, prevent them from gaining recognition in certain sports, and police their social activities.

But in spite of these facts, Negro athletes, if they had not been organized, would have stayed out of the conflict. Why—especially if, in fact, many of the athletes believe in the truth of the NAACP charges? We do not accept the argument that they were coerced by threats from the university that they would lose their athletic scholarships (many of them were graduating seniors) or in other ways suffer if they did not announce their disapproval.

DIFFERENT GOALS FOR ATHLETES

We think that the most reasonable explanation lies in the image that the athletes have of themselves, and in their goals. Unlike many of the other Negro students on the campus they do not come from middle class families; almost all of them are from lower class families, from southern rural areas or big city northern slums. They are college students and not common laborers or high school dropouts because they are athletes. Their hopes for the future are tied to success in collegiate and professional sports—an industry dominated by whites. As individuals, many may resent strongly the discrimination they perceive all too clearly, but they see little to be gained by joining an organization which might protect them from verbal barbs, but hurt their chances of success in the one area in which they are skilled.

Success in athletics depends on individual achievement and recognition by the coaches and managers of the sport. The crucial figures in the lives of the athletes are the coaches and trainers who work with them. If they are to permanently escape from their backgrounds, they must have support. The NAACP and other civil rights organizations cannot write their ticket for social and financial success. So they identify with, they spend their time with, and they attach their hopes to the world of sports and to people who can train and grant them recognition in that world.

Further, we received the continuous impression—though it was only an impression—that an athlete senses discrimination to the degree he is unsuccessful in athletics. If he is doing well he is not likely to feel any discrimination. Moreover, he is likely to be happy with the university. But if he is doing badly in athletics, feelings of antagonism and insecurity are likely to be expressed as feelings that he is being discriminated against both by the coaching staff and by teachers and students. (In a separate study, a student in one of the author's classes interviewed some of the white athletes. He reported that many of them believe that the Negro players receive preferential consideration from the coaches and teaching staff, and "get all the breaks.")

Finally, the alleged discrimination within the Athletic Association was an issue seized upon to express symbolically an ineffable and inchoate feeling of mistreatment. There was much more than a case of discrimination at issue here. The attack on the Athletic Association expressed a real grievance, albeit not the grievance specifically charged. The Athletic Association served as a symbol which coalesced and expressed the Negroes' general alienation from, and unhappiness with, the university. The NAACP was not out in this case to save the athletes from themselves or the Athletic Association, but to galvanize public sentiment behind the general plight of the Negro at the University of Illinois and not the specific plight of an athlete warned about dating white girls.

The move backfired. First, because the Negro athletes did not share the same sense of alienation—they were better integrated into the structure of the university because of their involvement in athletics, and especially because they knew that success in sports, and not other Negroes, would determine their futures. Second, because the administration was too near-sighted to be able to distinguish between a demand for sympathy and understanding for the Negro student with a demand for the resolution of a particular case.

The NAACP never asked for a judi-cial hearing in which to present charges. In all probability, they could not have presented a clear case. But even more than that, perhaps, they did not want a judicial victory. What they wanted was proof that the university understood the problems of Negro students, and was on their side—but they did not get it.

41
The Role of Moral Values in the Passage of Equal Opportunity Laws*
LEON MAYHEW

It works because we are asking for what everyone pays lip service to. The legislature isn't actually convinced about the bills. [A civil rights lobbyist]

PASSAGE OF THE EMPLOYMENT LAW

The passage of a law proscribing discrimination is the end product of one phase in the institutionalization of equal opportunity. This section outlines the history of the original passage of the Massachusetts Fair Employment Practices Bill in 1946. . . . From this outline will emerge a picture of the role of established and emergent interests in permitting or stimulating the legal institutionalization of an ideal. The account will also show the crucial importance of the existence of the ideal itself. . . .

Massachusetts did not escape the malaise and discontent that gripped the American Negro at the outset of the defense boom of the early forties. There, as elsewhere, the Negro did

*[Reprinted by permission of the publishers from pp. 75-90, 98–101 of Leon H. Mayhew, *Law and Equal Opportunity*, Cambridge, Mass.: Harvard University Press, Copyright 1968, by the President and Fellows of Harvard College.]

not feel that he was sharing in the general recovery. Depression conditions lingered in the Negro community and Negro leaders sought relief from the racial barriers that seemed to be responsible.

Governor Saltonstall responded by establishing a Commission on the Employment Problems of Negroes. The commission studied the distribution of the Negro population, the occupational and industrial distribution of Negro workers, the extent of Negro employment and unemployment, employer attitudes, the Negroes' relations with organized labor, and the role of the United States Employment Service. The commission concluded that the Negro was economically disadvantaged and faced racial barriers in employment. In 1942 its members passed on to the governor a set of recommendations for strengthening existing legislation against discrimination in state employment, public works, public utilities, and licensed employment agencies, and for bringing to the governor's office and other state offices a greater recognition of problems of equal opportunity.[1]

These recommendations fell short of calling for the legal prohibition of discrimination in private employment. However, the report constituted official recognition of the problem, and some of the recommendations recognized the need for some sort of efficient *enforcement procedure* if civil rights laws were to make a significant contribution to solving problems of Negro employment. The labors of the commission did not produce any immediate results.

In 1943 a nationwide outburst of riots and violence gripped the country, producing in their wake numerous committees designed to investigate the causes of racial tension and to mediate racial conflict. Boston's most dramatic outburst of intergroup tension was a disturbing wave of anti-Semitic vandalism. As in the case of a number of sister communities, the response was the establishment of a special committee, the Massachusetts Committee on Racial and Religious Understanding, created by Governor Saltonstall in 1943.[2]

The function of this committee was to carry out investigations of discriminatory situations and to sponsor and assist educational programs designed to combat discrimination. Once formed, the committee supported passage of a Fair Employment Practice Act.[3]

The legislature, prodded by the FEPC movement which had turned its attention to the states, gave full consideration to a permanent FEPC law in 1945. The New England Division of the American Jewish Congress introduced a bill similar to the Ives-Quinn Bill which was being considered in New York. The AJC was able to secure support from a variety of sources. Indeed, the suporters of the legislation succeeded in shaping such a powerful image of the moral sense of the community that some political analysts thought the bill was sure of passage.[4]

The legislature's Committee on State Administration sent the bill to the House Ways and Means Committee where it suffered a blow from which it never recovered. On June 9 the committee recommended rejection and substituted a measure calling for a special legislative commission to study antidiscrimination legislation.[5]

The matter was considered on the floor of the House on June 20. In a session described as the "wildest of the current session" the House approved the idea of a special commission of inquiry by a roll call vote of 117 to 103. The Ways and Means Committee of the Senate swept aside the House recommendation and recommended consideration of the original legislation, but the motion was killed on the Senate floor by a 17-to-17 tie vote, with Senate President Arthur Coolidge casting the ' decisive vote.[6]

Political techniques

The story of the successful effort of the following year deserves presentation in some detail. The techniques used in securing passage of antidiscrimination legislation reveal the interplay between written statutes, unwritten values, and organized interests.

The political methods of the unsuccessful 1945 campaign were not ill-conceived. The winning effort in 1946 was based on the same principles.

A veteran civil rights lobbyist outlined the principle to the author in succinct and frank terms:

It [our method] works because we are asking for what everyone pays lip service to. The legislature isn't actually convinced about the bills.

The technique involves a paradoxical principle: the value system can be used as a tool to secure legislation designed to create compliance with values, even though the attitudes or the behavior of the community deviate from value ideals. The activities of the civil rights lobbyists are designed to make maximum use of the compulsive power of abstract values.

These activities can be divided into two categories:

1 Programs designed to reinforce and interpret the values. Such programs must create an image of value consensus and community support for the lobbyist's interpretation of the values. This is the technique used at public hearings. One musters support from as many sections of the community as possible and sends witness after witness to the stand to testify as to the moral necessity of immediate action. Preferably, the witnesses have a structural position that permits them to speak for a large segment of the community or for an important organization that has the function of a moral caretaker.

2 Programs designed to put decisionmakers into a position where they must either act on behalf of the legislation or create an appearance of public disavowal of the values that have been established by the programs described above. For example, a legislator may be confronted by a delegation purporting to represent the moral sense of the community, and told that he must take a stand. Such a technique is not irresistible, but it puts the decisionmaker on the moral defensive and prevents him from handling the matter behind the scenes where pressures from powerful interests can win the day.

Let us turn to an account of the 1946 campaign and see these techniques at work.

In the fall of 1945, Governor Tobin, with the support (in fact the prodding) of Republican Lt. Governor Bradford, created a Committee to Study and Recommend Fair Employment Practice Legislation. Former Mayor Frederick W. Mansfield was appointed chairman. The group was to study existing legislation and other proposals and work out a satisfactory statute for Massachusetts. . . .

The study committee unanimously backed a proposed statute and Governor Tobin introduced it in the legislature.

The fight for passage was engineered by Henry Silverman, executive director of the New England Division of the American Jewish Congress, in an ad hoc role as chairman of the steering committee of the Committee for a Massachusetts FEPC.[7]

The proponents of the bill adopted a strategy involving what they termed a "people's lobby." Developing a people's lobby involves enlisting the support of a wide variety of groups and organizing local committees for support of particular pieces of legislation. The year before, the push had come from Boston alone. This time, committees were formed in thirty other communities. Religious groups, labor, veterans, minority groups, civic, business, and political organizations were involved in the campaign. A complete list of all the groups would be quite long. . . .

Throughout the campaign legislators were invited to meet with the FEPC committee and explain their views. If they opposed passage, attempts were made to persuade them to change. In each case the committee demanded public commitment.

The first task was to obtain a favorable report from the Committee on State Administration. This committee held a public hearing on February 6, 1946, in Gardner Auditorium at the State House. Supporters of the bill packed the galleries with seven hundred spectators, who watched fifty persons testify in favor of the bill. Senator Saltonstall, busy fighting for federal FEPC in Washington, sent a telegram of support. Mayor Mansfield of the drafting committee reported that he had held eight public hearings on the subject and had heard over two hundred witnesses testify in favor of the legislation as against only one witness who had been opposed.

Henry Turner, chairman of the New York Commission, commented on his experiences, pointing to the success of conciliatory efforts and the infrequent use of the law's compulsive powers. High Boston officials of the Episcopal, Methodist, Unitarian, Congregational, Baptist, and Presbyterian churches spoke in favor of the ordinance as did representatives of the Massachusetts Council of Churches and the Greater Boston Ministerial Alliance.

Labor was represented by the Massachusetts Federation of Labor, the state CIO, and several locals. Of course, minority group representatives also spoke in favor of the bill.[8]

February 18 was set aside for the testimony of opponents. Only one witness made an appearance. Jarvis Hunt, former president of the Massachusetts Senate, spoke as legislative agent of the Associated Industries of Massachusetts.[9] Mr. Hunt thought that the law would be a burden on business. He claimed that the employers of New York and New Jersey had found it intolerable and had had to stoop to under-the-counter dealing in jobs. Newspaper advertising had to be given up in favor of private reference systems. According to Mr. Hunt, the best legal minds in the commonwealth had challenged the constitutionality of the proposed law.

The witness felt that Massachusetts was free of bias; he knew of no cases of discrimination. He complained that the governor had stacked the cards against the opposition by appointing a committee to decide what kind of legislation to pass rather than to determine whether legislation was needed. This had made the opponents feel that opposition was useless, and that, he alleged, was the reason why more of the many opponents of the bill had not come to speak against it.

Mr. Hunt was not correct in this judgment. More people did not come to speak against the bill because the proponents had taken the moral offensive. To speak against the bill was to take on the combined religious and civic organization of the community. The position of the Associated Industries seemed hopeless, not because of the type of committee the governor had appointed, but because the committee for a Massachusetts FEPC had created the appearance of an inexorable tide of organized public opinion. They had created the organizational symbols of the moral support of the community. Passage of some sort of act seemed inevitable to most observers,[10] but that did not mean the opponents had given up, as Mr. Hunt suggested. It merely seemed safer to work behind the scenes to force obstructive legislative maneuvers or eviscerating amendments, than to publicly oppose a bill of impeccable moral intentions.

The upshot of the public hearing was a unanimously favorable committee report. Even the two members of the Committee on State Administration who had opposed the 1945 bill went along this time. Support seemed to be mushrooming. The avowed support of leaders of both political parties and the unanimous committee recommendation heartened the pro-civil rights faction and analysts began to regard passage as a certainty.

Business became concerned. The Boston Chamber of Commerce conducted a poll of their membership and found that passage of the bill was opposed by a nine-to-one margin. Having discovered the degree of business opposition, they decided to work against passage. Warnings concerning the effects of the proposed laws on business practices were widely circulated. For example, the rules promulgated by the New York Commission were used as a weapon. The success of the New York law had been used as a debating point in Massachusetts. When the chamber looked into the New York situation, they discovered that the commission had been very strict in enforcing a ban on any kind of preemployment inquiry that might betray the race, religion, or national ancestry of the applicant. Even the question, "where were you between 1914 and 1918," was officially forbidden. The chamber circulated New York's published rules as an example of how far a commission would go in interfering with everyday business practices.

Despite their efforts and the efforts of the Associated Massachusetts Industries, a vocal and organized opposition, comparable in breadth and energy to the Committee for a Massachusetts FEPC, did not develop. Businessmen confined themselves to behind-the-scenes maneuvers. They did not try to organize a massive grassroots effort.

The public temper regarding open expressions of antiminority-group feeling had been made quite clear by an event in March. In the course of debate on a proposal to teach racial tolerance in the public schools, Representative Charles H. Taylor is reported to have remarked, "This is just an attempt to whitewash the nigger." "What?" demanded a colleague. "I said 'whitewash the nigger,' with two G's."[11] Minority groups set up a public clamor demanding Representative Taylor's immediate impeachment; his home was picketed and in less than a week he had been forced to an abject apology. "No offense was intended," he claimed. According to Taylor, in the district of Pennsylvania where he was raised, Negroes call each other "nigger" without rancor. He announced that he had "nothing but good will toward my Negro brother."

The lesson seemed plain. It would not be safe to oppose the forthcoming legislation by direct appeals to prejudice.

The next problem for the Committee for a Massachusetts FEPC was to move the bill out of the House Ways and Means Committee. On May 6, Ways and Means sat down to discuss the bill. In the words of one reporter:

What started out to be a leisurely discussion of the merits of the bill rapidly transformed into a one-hour bedlam on the fourth floor of the State House yesterday with three hundred white, yellow, and Negro citizens confronting legislative chiefs with a demand that the measure be brought out from the committee at once.[12]

The shouting crowd demanded that Senate President Coolidge, Representative Roy Smith, Chairman of the Ways and Means Committee, and House Speaker Frederick B. Willis state their views. Then the group demanded that all members of the Ways and Means Committee come in and state their views. President Coolidge thought this a highly irregular procedure. He alleged that the legislative leaders thought that they were only being asked to come into the room to hear the views of several distinguished citizens who had helped to draft the bill. It was, said President Coolidge, as improper to ask a presiding officer his views as to ask a judge how he felt about a case under consideration.

The Boston Herald reported that *all* legislators agreed that the demonstration had done no service to the cause. It was thought that the measure might pass eight-to-seven and a supposed lineup was reported. In reading the newspaper analysis of the day, we get the impression of a very close fight, suddenly jeopardized, perhaps fatally, by the massive attempt to influence the legislators.

Despite all the legislators' agreement that the supporters' tactics had not aided their cause, the Ways and Means Committee passed the measure to the floor with a favorable report, not by a vote of eight to seven, but *without dissent.* In fact, the vote in executive session *had* been eight to seven, but none of the seven opposers were willing to have their dissent recorded.

The floor battle began in the House on May 8. In a 4½-hour debate before packed galleries, Representative Robert Connolly led the opposition with dogged determination. Several members registered their opposition to the extensive lobbying efforts of the supporters of the bill.

Agitation from the outside is trying to drive us to do something we don't want to do. [13]

We saw an expression of mob rule led by a man who wants to get on the public payroll, wants to get his nose in the trough, wants one of these three jobs on the proposed commission which would administer this law. [14]

The comments of one representative who had voted against the bill the previous year indicates both a clear understanding of the tactics of the Committee for a Massachusetts FEPC, and a felt inability to escape them:

This legislature is on the spot, and rather than putting us in the position of saying that we are in favor of discrimination, we ought to pass some sort of bill here today. [15]

Representative Connolly was well aware of his opponents' tactics and attempted to counter them with an unprecedented motion that the house rules be suspended to permit Australian ballot on the issue rather than the usual roll call:

I have so moved because I believe that the secret ballot would give a true expression of the sentiment of this house and an accurate expression of public opinion. . . . We have been subjected to pressure groups and I think that by voting secretly we will vote as we think. [16]

In other words, the only way to escape the pressure of mobilized public morality is to escape public visibility so that the forces of the established structure can operate in their usual fashion.

The motion was declared in order but was defeated after the floor leaders of both parties had argued against it.

A second strategy of the opponents involved bringing other value traditions to play on the issue. Massachusetts had never before established a quasi-judicial administrative agency, and administrative procedure eliminates some traditional rules of evidence, some traditional legal rights such as trial by jury, and the rigid structural separation of prosecution and judgment. In fact, the legality of the measure under the state constitution could be attacked. Questions of private property were also raised. The opponents could thus muster reasonable arguments to the effect that although discrimination is reprehensible, it should not be battled at the expense of traditional legal protections. The satisfactory experience of federal administrative agencies, operating under similar provisions and subject to similar judicial controls, helped to counter this argument. A substitute measure to simply declare discrimination a crime punishable according to ordinary procedures, thus defeating the easy administrative remedy that lay at the heart of the legislation, was defeated.

One tactic for demonstrating adherence to the principle of nondiscrimination and at the same time attempting to defeat an effective statute is to propose a substitute measure with weaker provisions, but the Committee for a Massachusetts FEPC had made it clear that only a vote for the measure *as written* was a vote against discrimination. Various weaker substitutes were defeated in early tests of strength.

Debate continued on May 14. The legislature spent nearly the whole day attacking and defending the techniques of the minority group leaders who were pressing passage of the bill. A full gallery kept the pressure up. One representative attacked the gallery in these words:

It is discriminating for you to expect the Massachusetts legislature to pass an unjust, unworkable, discriminating act just as you have written it. [17]

Another legislator complained,

. . . unless you vote for House bill 1704, the CIO will get you.

Representative Connolly called attention to the ethnic origins of the bill.

I'm interested in who filed this bill. . . . Last week the galleries were filled with Negroes but was this bill originated by Negroes? No, it was filed by Jewish people because the Negroes wouldn't have the ten cents carfare to come up here and file the bill. Somebody put up the money. [18]

Connolly received a gubernatorial rebuke for his intemperate language. His attempt to turn the pressure tactics against the backers of the bill by pointing to the extent of Jewish support was unsuccessful. After beating down half a dozen amendments and substitute bills, the act passed the final test in the House. By a vote of 164 to 59 the House voted not to refer the bill to the next session, whereupon the bill was engrossed by voice vote. . . .

With the exception of Mr. Connolly's vituperative outbursts, the opposition's tactics, their motions, and their amendments were designed to escape the dilemma created by the Committee for a Massachusetts FEPC. Their actions professed great sympathy for the *goals* of the act but argued that the *means* were not appropriate. As one legislator expressed it:

I will vote against this bill because it will retard the cause of racial tolerance just as prohibition retarded the cause of temperance. [19]

Passage in the House set the stage for a repeat performance in the Senate. On May 15, even before the bill came to a first reading, the senators of both parties had caucused outside the Senate chamber. The decision of the caucus was to send the bill to the state Supreme Court for an opinion on its constitutionality. The idea of requesting an advisory opinion from the Supreme Court had been suggested to the senators by the Massachusetts Associated Industries.

When Silverman's forces got wind of this development, they swung into action. Any delay was to be avoided and consideration by the Supreme Court would be risky. A telegram campaign was begun and an ad hoc group began a twenty-four-hour State House vigil. On May 17, the Senate galleries were packed for the beginning of consideration of the bill. The Senate, *in open session,* could not carry out its caucus decision. After two hours of debate a motion to send the bill to the Supreme Court for answer to sixteen questions of constitutionality failed in a very close vote, seventeen to fifteen. Fourteen of nineteen Republicans supported the motion and twelve of thirteen Democrats opposed it. This was the closest to a party-line vote that had yet occurred and the supporters prevailed only because they were able to hold on to five Republican senators.

On May 20 the Senate, to gallery applause, again refused to send the bill to the Supreme Court by the same seventeen-to-fifteen vote. The bill was then sent to the Senate Ways and Means Committee where it appeared that the chairman would delay the bill by not allowing it out of committee. The chairman was immediately asked to pay another visit to the people's lobby and the bill was reported out of committee less than fifteen minutes after it had been referred to them. The report was favorable and there was only one dissenting vote. The bill came out of committee so unexpectedly that it went through three readings on the Senate floor and was engrossed by voice vote before anyone remembered to ask for a roll call. A roll call was duly requested and the measure was passed twenty-two to eleven, twelve of twelve Democrats and ten of twenty-one Republicans favoring passage. . . .

Thus, despite numerous defensive and dilatory strategies, an unwilling legislature passed the Fair Employment Practices Bill. It passed because the people's lobby mobilized the symbols of public consensus at every strategic juncture. Every hearing, every motion to table, every motion to substitute, every referral to committee, and every other parliamentary device encountered the public scrutiny of the people's lobby. Every morally feasible objection to the

law was successfully defined as tantamount to rejection of the expressed ideals of the community. . . .

The passage of antidiscrimination statutes is one element in the institutionalization of equal opportunity. Through legislation, one interpretation of the value tradition is given official normative expression and specified kinds of deviance become subject to official sanctions. Legislation may not immediately remake the society but it can provide both an enforceable interpretation of the value tradition and administrative machinery for the enforcement process. Legislation puts the organized power of the community at the service of those elements in the community with an interest in implementing equal opportunity.

It was the groups who received access to legal power that brought about passage of the law. Legislation is not a simple emanation from the value system. It is a product of an organized effort by groups with ideal and material interests in the equalization of opportunity. The success of the movement had a number of structural sources. The "liberal" groups were able to prevail because the opposition was not able to organize effectively. Lack of organization, in turn, was not a mere consequence of carelessness or sloth; it had a structural basis. The natural organizational sources of opposition are the groups whose activities will be regulated. These groups were not united in intense opposition. Many members either gave the issue a low priority or supported passage.

In short, the ideal had already achieved some measure of institutionalization. Some of the targets of the law already had psychological commitments to, or interests in, equal opportunity.

To say that legal institutionalization depends on an appropriate organization of interests in the community is not to say that the value tradition was not involved. The movement was not a mere power struggle. Much of the latent power of the opposition was enclosed in a moral muzzle. The civil rights lobby did not prevail simply because it was organized; it prevailed because it was organized to express and enhance community values. The value tradition gave the movement justification and a leverage on the status quo. The movement used the value tradition to prevent the forces of the status quo from achieving political expression.

It is important to recognize that packed galleries do not, by themselves, produce desired legislation. Just two months before FEPC carried, an unruly crowd of five hundred veterans jammed into a hearing to demand passage of a bill to provide a $900 bonus to all veterans, to be financed by a state lottery. Their efforts were unsuccessful, but the full galleries at FEPC hearings and debates did not represent mere political pressure; they symbolized the voice of moral obligation. The legislator might have his own opinions on the moral dimensions of the issue, but the FEPC lobby forced him to compare his views with those of the community's specialists on religious and civic morality.

The same principle used in attracting support within the legislature also operates in building pressure outside the legislature. The individual minister, civic leader, or official may be uncertain or lukewarm on the legislation, but unable to find a satisfactory way of refusing to participate in the movement. In fact, it was alleged on the floor of the legislature that the governor and the lieutenant governor did not really want to see the bill passed.

The movement mushrooms on the same principle that supports southern segregation. Only certain sentiments are expressible. The southern moderate and the northern racist are prevented from introducing their views into discussion. As a result they come, for lack of social support, to underestimate the degree of public support for their position. . . .

It would not be accurate to state that the supporters of the bill won because they discovered an effective rhetoric. The roots of their success lay deeper than mere rhetoric. Almost any cause, including bonuses for veterans, can be provided superficial garb from the value tradition at a merely rhetorical level, but the organizational devices of the civil rights movement effectively symbolized a deeply rooted and compelling strain on the American ethic. . . .

FOOTNOTES

[1] John Duffy, *State Organization for Fair Employment Practices* (Berkeley, 1942), pp. 26–27.

[2] Interview with Chairman Mahoney.

[3] *Boston Globe,* February 6, 1946, p. 1.

[4] *Boston Herald,* June 20, 1945, p. 1.

[5] *Ibid.*

[6] *Boston Herald,* June 21, 27, 28, 1945, p. 1.

[7] Henry Silverman, "How We Won in Massachusetts," *New Republic,* July 8, 1946, pp. 10–11.

[8] *Boston Herald,* February 7, 1946, p. 1.

[9] This is the Massachusetts counterpar of the National Association of Manufacturers.

[10] The passage of the bill was throughly reported in the Boston daily papers in February, March, April, and May 1946.

[11] *Boston Herald,* March 8, 1946, p. 22.

[12] *Boston Herald,* May 7, 1946, p. 1.

[13] *Boston Herald,* May 9, 1946, p. 1.

[14] *Ibid.*

[15] *Ibid.*

[16] *Ibid.*

[17] *Boston Herald,* May 15, 1946, p. 1.

[18] *Boston Herald,* May 15, 1946, p. 1; June 21, 1945, p. 1.

[19] For example: "Let these minority groups wait another hundred years."

42
The Defenders: A Case Study of an Informal Police Organization*

HAROLD A. NELSON

I. INTRODUCTION

In many southern communities, the concept of "law and order" has one meaning for whites and another for Negroes. In oversimplified terms, whites tend to equate it with adherence to traditional southern mores. These mores *are* the law regardless of what judges, federal officials, or Congress may have said to the contrary. Order exists when community behavior patterns are in strict compliance with the dictates of the mores. Primary responsibility for maintaining this order rests with local law enforcement agencies. It is their responsibility to protect the "southern way of life" by crushing any challenge to it which may arise in the community.

Negroes equate this definition of law and order with the determination of whites to maintain a system which operates solely for their own benefit and which is rooted in illegality and brute force. They see themselves confined to a world governed not by law and order but by a vicious white populace which maintains its dominant position because it holds a monopoly of power. Law enforcement agencies are nothing more than the "white man's army" committed to protecting the "white man's society"

by any means they choose to employ. These agencies function not for the protection and welfare of all citizens but for that of whites alone. No agency exists for the protection of Negroes from the dominant group and no mechanism is provided within the mores whereby they may challenge the monopoly of power held by whites.[1]

At issue is whether a group which perceives itself thus victimized can alter this situation. If it is denied services normally provided by law enforcement agencies, can it provide at least some of them for itself? More generally, can such a group develop a mechanism by which it can successfully confront the monopoly of power arrayed against it and effectively challenge the mores which govern the community?

This paper is concerned with the efforts of Negroes in a southern community to accomplish these goals. It describes the development of an informal police organization which not only provided certain services to Negroes, but also acted as the vehicle whereby traditional mores were challenged and a redistribution of power in the community was effected.[2]

*[Reprinted from Harold A. Nelson, "The Defenders: A Case Study of an Informal Police Organization," *Social Problems* 15, no. 2, (Fall 1967) pp. 127–147. I wish to acknowledge the many contributions of "William Smith" to my understanding of the Defenders. Not only did he spend long hours educating me in the general area of racial problems in the South, but he gave extended assistance in the preparation of this paper. I am deeply indebted to him, for without his aid, this paper could not have been written.]

[1] There is considerable evidence to justify this belief, evidence with which white Americans in general have only recently become acquainted. . . .

[2] Data for this paper were gathered over a four-year period. Included is material obtained both prior to the inception of the Southville Action Organization and the Defenders and following their creation. . . . The data were gathered in several ways. Material collected on various facets of the Southville Action Organization were gained as a result of my participation in that organization from its inception. Additional data were accumulated through many long conversations held with both SAO leaders and members. . . . Additional information on the perspectives of movement and nonmovement Negroes resulted from my participation in meetings held in Southville and throughout the state. . . .

Material on the Defenders was obtained in several ways. Participation in SAO resulted in my friendship with William Smith before he assumed leadership of the Defenders. When he

II. ORIGIN OF THE DEFENDERS

Southville is located in a deep southern state. Its population of 50,000 persons includes 18,000 Negroes. It is the largest city in a county of 100,000 persons, approximately one-third of whom are Negroes. While the county is heavily agricultural, Southville is sufficiently industrialized to rank as one of the important industrial areas of the state. Prior to 1964, the city maintained the traditional patterns of segregation characteristic of most southern communities. Local law enforcement agencies employed only white persons and were disliked and distrusted by the city's Negro population. A long-time and widespread dissatisfaction with racial conditions was shared by the community's Negroes, but prior to 1964 no organized attempt was made to change this situation. In that year, a Negro minister was installed in one of the largest Negro churches in Southville with the understanding that he would also act as a civil rights leader. With the aid of several ministers and laymen, he organized the Southville Action Organization, which initiated a series of mass meetings and freedom

schools. After several months, SAO drew up a list of demands for changes in the city's segregation practices and presented them to the city commission. The commission rejected the demands, and SAO countered by holding Southville's first protest march. Law officers and SAO leaders agreed in advance on procedures to be followed during the demonstration. Although the marchers adhered to these procedures, police used electric cattle prods and night sticks to harass the protesters.

Response to SAO and the demonstrations by white public officials was predictable. Communist influence was suspected and "outside agitators" were seen as stirring up "a few dissidents" who in no way reflected the dominant mood in the Negro community. Calls were issued for the restoration of "harmony between the races." This could best be accomplished, it was held, by disbanding SAO and removing its minister-leader from his pulpit and from the city. These expressions faithfully reflected the mood of most of Southville's white citizens. While the great majority was passive in its response, the Ku Klux Klan applauded the public pronouncements and publicly dedicated itself to firm opposition to the activities and demands of SAO. Civil rights activists interpreted this as confirmation of their belief that there was no important difference between the belief-systems and objectives of public officials and those of the Klan. Law officers were especially distrusted. Many were believed to be Klansmen and the rest were seen as Klan sympathizers.[3] Almost all were believed to be prepared

---

founded that organization, this relationship allowed me access to it which might have been impossible otherwise. This included not only contact with Smith but with other members of the organization as well. Smith was willing to discuss the Defenders in detail with me and to permit the presentation of this material in written form. He did so because he believed it important that others understand the necessity of organizations such as the Defenders, given the racial conditions of the South. He also felt that there was a widespread misunderstanding of the purposes of such organizations, and he hoped to see this corrected. Because of this, not only did I have the opportunity to observe the Defenders in the performance of their more obvious duties, but was permitted to be present during some of their less public activities as well.

Various persons who provided information for this paper did so with the understanding that, insofar as possible, anonymity would be preserved. Therefore, the names of persons and places appearing herein are fictitious.

[3] This was hardly an unfounded belief. The police chief had told his officers that he wanted no Klansman on his force, but he possessed neither complete knowledge of Klan membership nor sufficient power to compel resignation. Many Negroes believed that he also lacked the desire and that his statement was merely a subterfuge to "cool them out."

to carry out any orders issued by the Klan. Negro activists were certain that the officers were eagerly awaiting an opportunity to conduct Klan inspired violence against them.

During the next three months, SAO activity increased. New and stronger demands were made, stores were boycotted, marches were held with increasing frequency, violence against the activists accelerated and tensions in the community increased. Finally, city officials announced a ban on further demonstrations and charged the police with enforcing it. To SAO leaders, this was the same as announcing a ban on change in favor of tradition and charging the Ku Klux Klan with enforcing it. They announced that they would defy the ban, and a date was set for the proposed march.

More than a thousand persons appeared for the demonstration. As the leaders led the marchers out of the church they were confronted by police, sheriff's deputies, firemen, and "special deputies," some of whom were suspected of being Klansmen. The leaders were promply arrested. Immediately thereafter, law officers charged the demonstrators, forcing them back into the church with nightsticks, cattle prods, fists, and water hoses. Tear gas was shot into the building, and the officers continued their attack as the demonstrators fled from the gas-filled church. As the protesters dispersed, they were chased into neighboring areas. Homes of those living nearby were invaded, and persons not involved in the demonstration came under indiscriminate attack. Numerous arrests were made, and several of the demonstrators were hospitalized as a result of beatings and gasing. Word of the incident spread rapidly. Stories of police brutality against men, women, and children circulated throughout the Negro sections of the city. The police had,

in the eyes of the Negroes, confirmed that if they were not Klansmen, they might as well be, and that they would use any measures of force and violence they wished against those who dared defy white southern racial mores.

When Southville's evening newspaper carried a distorted account of the events together with a justification of the actions of the law officers, Negroes interpreted this as proof that the officers had been carrying out the orders of the "white power structure." This seemed to be the opening shot in an all-out war to kill the civil rights movement in the city. Faith in the effectiveness of the nonviolent posture of SAO was seriously undermined, and most of its leading spokesmen were in jail. That evening, Negroes armed themselves, some waiting for an expected nightride of Klansmen through their neighborhoods, others hoping to ambush police cars, and still others planning to go to the business district of the city and burn it to the ground. In the early evening hours, an unstructured, unorganized violent retaliation seemed certain. While the total number of Negroes planning to take part in offensive violence was not large, it would have been sufficient to destroy much of the downtown area of Southville and to cause widespread injury and death to whites.

At this same time, one of the SAO members began taking steps to thwart the impending riot. He did this not because he feared violence or was opposed to it in principle, nor because he believed massive retaliation was not merited, but because he felt it was futile. He opposed it because it was unstructured, disorganized, lacking in plan or lasting value and because it would result in death and injury to a great many innocent persons. It was his desire to translate the prevailing mood into something which could permanently restrict the activities of police and Klan, and which would provide a forceful mechanism for changing the community's power distribution. He called together several close friends, convinced them that a disorganized riot would serve no useful purpose, and together, they set out to find the rioters-in-waiting to convince them also. One by one they were found and the case was argued. The message was simple: "If we're going to do this thing, let's do it right"; and "right" meant organization and planning. One by one, the potential rioters were persuaded to surrender their arms on the promise that the weapons would be returned at a meeting which would be held that night. So great was the respect commanded by this small group, and especially by its leader, that the riot was averted.

The meeting held that night centered on proposed retaliation for the day's events. A major source of bitterness was the abject failure of law officers to perform their duties in even a minimally acceptable manner. Under prodding by the meeting's chairman, immediate retaliation became less important in the minds of those in attendance than a basic alteration in the power distribution in Southville. The chairman argued that if the police failed to perform their duties, either they would have to be forced to do so, or someone else would have to perform them. If the Klan was determined to run rampant, someone would have to control it. If men, women, and children were to be beaten, someone would have to prevent it. The meeting ended with the agreement that that "someone" would have to be a new organization dedicated to bringing about a basic redistribution of power in the city. A meeting was called for the following night to establish such an organization.

The second meeting was attended by some three hundred persons. They included gang leaders and members, white collar and blue collar workers, the highly educated and the uneducated. Chairing this meeting, as he had the first, was William Smith, who had led the effort to thwart the riot. Almost immediately, the question arose as to who should be the leader of the new organization. Smith's name was suggested and there was no dissent. At this point, Smith advised the meeting that he would accept only on condition that he be allowed to choose a small executive board which would devise a series of qualifications for membership and evaluate the candidacy of each applicant. His and the board's decisions would be final. Further, he stated that all decisions regarding policy would be set by the board and would be binding on all members. Finally, he said that all members would be required to pledge their lives to him and the organization. He asked for a formal vote on whether those in attendance still wished him to head the organization. He was unanimously elected. He then announced that the organization would be called the Defenders.

III. ORGANIZATIONAL STRUCTURE

Smith patterned the organization along the lines of a military combat unit. Four levels were established: the leader, his executive board, a cadre of lieutenants, and the rank-and-file membership. The leader and his executive board were designated as policymakers, strategists, and final authority for tasks to be undertaken by the organization. The lieutenants were assigned some limited authority, primarily in conducting investigations, and the rank and file were to carry out assignments handed down from the executive board.

From the three hundred persons attending the organizational meeting, one hundred were selected for membership, and the organization has remained approximately at that number since then. Roughly one-half the membership may be described as "hard-core" and is distributed throughout all four levels. The remaining fifty members are utilized for special assignments, usually when large numbers of persons are needed for some task. At any time, the leader can mobilize fifty members and have them prepared for a task in less than two hours.

Membership in the Defenders is conferred only after a thorough investigation. . . . No one is admitted to candidacy unless he has served at least six weeks under active war combat conditions. . . . A second requirement is that the potential candidate be married and, preferably, have a family. Meeting this requirement indicates to the organization a willingness to assume responsibility. . . .

The candidate's personal conduct must be above reproach. A rigid code of personal morality is applied as a standard, and any deviation from it effectively eliminates him from consideration. . . .

Membership in the organization is drawn from a wide range of occupations, educational backgrounds, ages, and areas of residence. By maintaining a heterogeneous membership, as representative as possible of the Negro population, the information network nurtured and maintained by the organization is made as inclusive as possible. . . .

The organization functions in a semisecret manner. It operates on the principle that those who need to know of its existence do know or will be informed of it. . . . One reason for this is because of the kinds of investigations it conducts and data which it gathers. Another reason is the belief that the whites will be more amenable to pressure and compromise if they are assured

that the general public is not aware they are yielding to such pressure.

IV. ORGANIZATIONAL ACTIVITIES

The tasks which the organization has undertaken include protection, investigation, intelligence, and a form of "crime" prevention.

The immediate impetus for the creation of the Defenders was provided by the perceived failure of law officers to perform their role adequately for Negro citizens. While this failure was most obvious in conjunction with civil rights activities, it was not limited to them. A long-standing complaint against the police was that *no* Negro could be certain he would receive the same treatment, concern or respect as would a white person. The organization conceives of its duty, therefore, as more encompassing than concern with massive civil rights demonstrations alone. Rather, it holds the prerogative to choose to assume responsibility in any situation in which a person has suffered some injustice for which law officers would normally be expected to take some action but where it is not expected that they will perform their role adequately. The organization may become involved either at the request of an individual or without such request if the situation seems to have important implications for other persons in the community. (In one instance, dynamite was set off near a group of homes. Without waiting for a specific request for aid, the organization concerned itself with the situation.) Should an individual request the aid of the Defenders, it may or may not be given. Representatives of the organization must be satisfied that the party requesting aid has suffered some injustice and that he was not the instigator. It must also be satisfied that the complainant is willing to give his full cooperation to the organization, including providing all information which he possesses. Should the organization conclude that the complainant is withholding information, it may refuse to enter the case. Should it enter and then conclude that he is the offending party, it may withdraw. At this point, the Defenders must act in a suprapolice function. Differing from the police, the organization has no court system to determine ultimate guilt or innocence, hence it must accept some responsibility in this area. Since it must do so, it is important that the Defenders obtain all available information. If it is convinced that some of this information is being withheld by the complainant, the most "responsible" decision it can make is that some presumption of guilt thereby exists and on this basis it withdraws. Since most of its activities center about allegation of Negroes against whites, it seeks to be absolutely certain of its "legal" (i.e., moral) position before it moves against offending whites.

At the organization's inception, it was faced with two immediate problems. To that time, segregation and its attendant patterns of white supremacy had been enforced formally by law enforcement agencies and informally by the Ku Klux Klan. When law was not sufficient to do so, extralegal methods were employed to establish and maintain an atmosphere of fear and intimidation. No effective counterforce or neutralizing agent existed; the test of the Defenders' viability was whether it could establish itself as such a force. Smith saw the organization's first task as eliminating the Klan as a force in Negro life and the second as restricting the police to their normal duties. If the police could not be forced to fulfill their legal role, they *could* be blocked from performing an extralegal one. Klan and police, then, had to be

confronted with sufficient power to limit effectively their sphere of influence. The mere announcement to these agencies of the formation of a "protective organization" was not sufficient, nor was it expected to be. The dominant stereotype of Negroes held by these groups as docile, fearful, cowardly, and deathly afraid of police and Klan necessitated direct confrontation to disprove the stereotype.

Two incidents were of major importance in limiting Klan activities. From the inception of SAO, it had been the practice of the Klan leader to be near the scene of any movement activity. At any time a meeting was held he would "patrol" the area in his car. This gesture expressed his contempt for SAO and his stated conviction that the Klan, not SAO, would be the dominant force in Negro life. One evening as he began his vigil, armed Defenders appeared in front of the meeting place. As the Klansman began to drive by, he saw that they were prepared to fire at him and he quickly maneuvered his car so that a truck was between him and the church and immediately left the area. Not only did he "run," but he never again appeared at the site of SAO activity.

By this single act, the organization had demonstrated publicly to its own members, civil rights activists, Negro townspeople, and the Klan leader and fellow Klansmen that the old order had changed, at least partially. If the organization was prepared to confront the Klan leader, it was obvious that it was equally prepared to confront lesser Klansmen. From the date of this incident, the number of Klan cars seen in Negro neighborhoods decreased considerably, and those which did appear passed through quickly. The Klan relinquished its control over these areas, but sought to limit the Defenders to these same neighborhoods. On another evening, in a peripheral area of the city, a car loaded with Klansmen opened fire on a car holding Defenders. One of the members noted later that "they shot too soon," and when the Defenders' car pulled closer, its passengers returned the fire and the Klansmen fled. These two incidents demonstrated to the Klan the determination of the Defenders to eliminate Klan influence among Negroes and to insert itself into the power structure of the community. Although other incidents did occur, for all intents and purposes, large scale organized semipublic Klan activity against Negroes ended with these incidents. Negro neighborhoods were now effectively closed to Klansmen. Neither did they attempt to intimidate the Defenders again.

While the police officially recognized the organization's formation, they opposed its existence and sought to discredit and destroy it. Official recognition came in the form of a meeting between Smith and a high-ranking police officer. The official told him the organization could gain no power, would accomplish nothing, and would not be tolerated by the police. His statements, on the surface, constituted a dismissal of the organization as inconsequential, but carried the deeper message that the police would not permit their own power to be challenged or restricted. The police set out to do what the Klan had failed to do—to frighten the Defenders into submission. Individual members were subjected to various forms of harassment. When this failed, the police increased their pressure. A critical point was reached early one morning when a number of police cars appeared at Smith's home. Crouched behind their cars with weapons drawn and spotlights directed at the front door, the police ordered "the occupant" of the house to come out.

When he did, they demanded his name and he pointed to a sign on the lawn which carried his name and house number. Again they demanded his name and he told them to look at the sign. The question was repeated several times, always with the same answer. The incident ended with the police finally asking him if he were a "John Greene" for whom they were allegedly looking. He replied that his name was on the sign and that, further, they knew full well who he was. At this, the police claimed a case of mistaken identity and left. Smith is convinced that the police had so acted in the hope of frightening him into running or making some other move which would have given them a "justification" for killing him. When he did not, they lost their nerve and, in some confusion, withdrew. Failing to frighten and thereby to discredit the leader, they arrested a number of his members. Smith countered by informing the chief that unless his men were released, he would "turn loose" the remaining members of the organization. The arrested men were immediately released. Smith then met with the chief and told him that the organization would remain in existence, that its members could not be frightened, and that if any harm came to them or their families, "blood would flow." He stated his intention to see that extralegal activities carried out by police against Negroes were stopped by any means necessary. Subsequent to this meeting, not only did harassment of the Defenders cease, but reports of police brutality against Negroes in general declined rapidly.

The first task of the organization had been accomplished. The Klan had been defeated and its effectiveness as a social control mechanism among Negroes severely diminished. No longer could it operate openly as a public, unofficial arm of the police. Secondly, the police had been confronted and their extralegal power to a great extent stripped from them. The organization had inserted itself into the power structure of the city and had to be considered by any group planning activity against Negroes. In effect, a "war of fear" had been waged to determine the order of power not only in the Negro sections of the city but over the lives of Negroes in general. The Defenders had clearly won.[4]

With their failure to destroy the Defenders, the police resorted to a different strategy. Rather than actively opposing those connected with civil rights activities, they passively refused to perform any meaningful functions whatsoever regarding them. Apparently, it was assumed that by so doing, mobs of whites would control the activities of the activists. This was a miscalculation which inserted the Defenders directly into the role of policemen and thereby increased the organization's role and broadened its sphere of influence and power. Adoption of this passive role coincided with the "testing" of a restaurant to determine if it would comply with the newly passed Civil Rights Act of 1964. The owner did comply by serving the testers. However, in the process, a group of whites began to gather in front of the business. Although some police were present, they made no attempt to dis-

perse those gathering. In a short period of time, approximately six hundred whites appeared, and the crowd began defacing the business. Still the police took no action, nor did they threaten any arrests. As the crowd developed into a mob challenging the testers to come out, the police informed the testers that they could not control the mob nor guarantee the safety of those inside the building, thus washing their hands of the whole affair. Smith was notified of the situation and immediately dispatched several cars to the scene. Defenders spirited the testers to the cars and they drove off. The cars went immediately to a prearranged location which had been "staked out" by other members of the organization. Had the mob followed, which it did not, it would have been caught in a trap. The Defenders had not only provided the police function of protection but had also constructed its own form of "crowd control."

Protection quickly became a major function of the organization. A great many civil rights activists had received anonymous threats of violence and death. Law enforcement agencies were unwilling to provide protection for the persons involved, their families or their homes, therefore the Defenders assumed this responsibility.[5]

The organization's protective role extends to whites as well as Negroes. A few white persons had acted in concert with SAO and hence were no more

[4] The vast majority of the white population was not aware of the Defenders' existence. The news media published no stories and no public officials made mention of it during the conflict. After the Defenders' victories over Klan and police, it is doubtful that those whites who knew of the battles wished to publicize their results. One candidate for public office did try to make the organization an issue. The reaction of the white community in general was disbelief that such an organization existed. One might hypothesize that the thought of such a militant organization of indigenous Negroes was so at variance with their stereotype of Negroes as docile, fearful, and "content with their lot" as to prohibit its acceptance even as a possibility.

[5] Had the police assumed this role, it is still likely that the organization would have provided protection, since one of the agency's activists believed that what they needed protection *from* was the police. Teams of guards were assigned to homes under the threat of violence, and a number of "squad cars" toured Negro sections of the city each night watching for suspicious persons. Any who were found were ordered out of the area. The presence of this force acted as a deterrent to violence although on one occasion it became necessary to use force to stop a group intent upon assassinating the leader of SAO.

assured of police protection than were Negro activists. Streets on which they lived were patroled by car, they were guarded when they were in places of potential danger, and, in general, were given the same services provided Negro activists. Smith pointed out on several occasions that when a member swore to "be his brother's keeper" this meant "his brother regardless of race."[6]

Organizational protection also extends to visitors to the city who might be in danger because of their support of the civil rights movement. On these occasions, the Defenders have supplanted the police in providing escort and protective services. On one such occasion, aides to the white person involved were put in contact with the leader. Smith shared their doubts as to the probable dedication of the police to protecting the person in question. When asked whether he would provide the protection he agreed, but only under certain conditions. Smith and the aides were to agree upon a detailed timetable of the activities of the visitor while he was in Southville. Once he arrived, he and his associates were to be subject to any orders Smith gave them. When this was agreed to, Smith took the schedule of events to an organizational staff meeting. There decisions were made as to the number of Defenders needed, which members would be used, and what the specific duties of each would be. Late one evening, a "dry run" was held to determine the adequacy of the plan. Alternate plans were worked out in the event of a crisis, and plans were made for the disposition of any persons attempting to disrupt the activities. Some three

hours before the visitor arrived in the city, each member was in his assigned position and various buildings had been inspected to assure that they were secure. Occasionally, police appeared near scenes of the activities, but at no time did they attempt to assert a special prerogative to be present. The members, in turn, regarded them with the same degree of watchfulness they reserved for any suspicious white persons. At no time were weapons displayed, but in the words of one member, "A man *might* get one shot at . . . but he'd never get the second one off." Only when the visitor had been escorted out of Southville did the organization cease its alert.

At times, the organization goes beyond normal protective duties. In one case, a family in a community some twenty miles from Southville was being subjected to a serious form of harassment. Both husband and wife had been physically assaulted by whites, and the husband had been hospitalized as a result of the attack. His wife contacted members of SAO who in turn contacted Smith. He met with her and it was agreed that neither she nor her children were safe in the community, therefore it was decided to bring them to Southville. The Defenders assumed responsibility for moving her and her family to the city, securing a house and assuring financial support of the family until a job was found for her eldest son. When doubts arose as to whether her husband was receiving proper medical treatment, a Southville doctor was contacted who agreed to treat the man if he were transferred to the city's hospital. Smith then contacted a local ambulance service and received assurance that it would transfer the man at any time it was deemed necessary.[7]

---

[6] In order to carry out this protective function efficiently, the organization utilizes not only weapons of various kinds but walkie-talkies, two-way radio-equipped cars, and a number of other devices. It is safe to say that most equipment which is employed by the standard police department is also present in the Defenders' arsenal.

[7] This illustrates a major canon of the organization: "Once we agree to take something on, we go all the way with it." Members of the organization scorn no one so much as the person who

A second broad task of the organization, closely related to protection, is that of investigation. The purpose is to insure as complete knowledge as possible of plans and activities of anyone or any group having any relation to Negroes, civil rights advocates, or their opponents. This includes any information which could conceivably relate to potential organizational duties and tasks. The insistence of the leader that the organization have as complete and accurate data as possible regarding any incident *before* the Defenders enter a case makes investigation of great importance and places great responsibility upon the men selected to do the investigating. The men charged with this task constitute the organization's intelligence unit.

As soon as Smith is informed of an incident with which the Defenders might become involved, he dispatches investigators to interview witnesses and to gather any other pertinent information. Seldom do investigators make public their duties. Rather, interviewing and data gathering are carried on without revealing that an investigation is under way or that the organization is in any way involved in the situation. Not infrequently, Defenders are present with the police and both agencies collect information at the same time.[8]

In addition to the mechanism for specific investigations, the organization maintains a highly efficient and effective permanent data-gathering system. This system has provided sufficient

information to permit quick identification of automobile ownership from license numbers and, in many cases, from description of the car when the license is not available. Dossiers are maintained on all persons with whom the organization has had dealings or with whom it is felt it might come in contact at some later date. These dossiers include not only addresses, descriptions, and information on current activities, but also rather extensive background data including past behavior and activities. The organization has demonstrated the ability to obtain data which is kept in locked files in public and private offices and which is, supposedly, unavailable to the public.

Historical records are also maintained and investigations of incidents which occurred long before the organization's creation have been carried out. In one case, a record has been compiled of a lynching which occurred in Southville thirty years ago. Included in the record are the names of persons, including many still alive, who took part in the planning and actual lynching of the victims and who went unpunished at the time. Included is information on the present whereabouts of several key figures who left Southville shortly after the murders. Only when the last of the major figures in the case has died will it be marked "closed." Records are also maintained on important public figures who have had some connection with Southville. These include information not only on current activities but on activities in which they participated as much as thirty and forty years ago. These current and historical records are maintained because of the possibility that they may, at some time, be of value in providing information regarding some incident or event of interest to the Defenders. Hence, they might provide important data regarding the decision to enter a case and the type of action to be taken.

accepts responsibility and then fails to carry it through to completion. Smith is firm in his insistence that the Defenders not commit itself to any project unless it is prepared to do anything and everything to bring it to successful conclusion. Once committed, the organization is completely committed up to and including the lives of its members.

[8] This is possible since the police know only part of the Defenders' membership list and are generally not aware of the investigators who may be present in such guises as "curious neighbors" or "helpful friends."

The "crime prevention" phase of the Defenders' duties also illustrates the high degree of organization of the group. Smith was aware from the outset that at times the organization would have "no choice" but to act, to commit its resources and the lives of its members to some task. However, he wanted to insure that this would occur only when absolutely necessary and when he could be satisfied that no other method for handling the situation was available. Investigation makes it possible for him to determine if there is just cause for action. Intelligence makes it possible for him to become aware of developing, potentially dangerous situations. With this knowledge, he may act to prevent an incident from occurring, rather than being limited to acting only after some incident has occurred which demands a form of retribution. A critical component of this prevention function is the Defenders' surveillance team which is maintained in all Negro sections of the city. This team is comprised of members, each of whom has been assigned responsibility for a particular Negro neighborhood. These persons are to keep fully informed about the activities of residents of the neighborhoods, especially those activities which might result in some kind of racial incident. Primarily, members of the team are to identify potential "troublemakers" and observe their activities. Should these persons become a "threat to the peace," a report is made to Smith, and representatives of the organization talk to the person involved, explaining to him that his activities may cause a serious situation if continued. So great is the respect for the Defenders that this action has been sufficient to control such persons. This form of prevention seeks to assure, insofar as possible, that Negroes will not be the cause of racial incidents and that the organization will not have to become involved in situations which could have been avoided or handled in a peaceful way.[9]

To a major extent, the organization is the creation of William Smith and reflects both his personality and his belief system. Others in positions of authority in the organization closely mirror many of his own characteristics. Prominent among these are a dislike of emotional displays, a strong emphasis on rationality, decisiveness of action, and a controlled anger at the racial situation in the state and nation. Smith and most of the members give the impression of being introspective, intelligent, articulate, highly rational, and decisive. Not only do individual members reflect his own personality system, but the organization itself reflects his beliefs and goals to the extent that a knowledge of the man contributes to a clearer picture of the organization, its self-conceived duties, and its goals. . . .

VI. CONCLUSION

Although the Defenders does not seek publicity, it is well known among Negroes in Southville. It enjoys great respect and is a source of considerable pride, primarily because it is proof that white southern mores can be successfully challenged and that a change in the distribution of power can be effected. Violence, so often employed by whites, is revealed as a two-edged sword. With considerable pleasure, Negroes note that "white men are not as tough as they thought they were," and that Negroes, in the person of the Defenders, have proved themselves

---

[9] It is true that the Defenders could refuse to enter a situation which had been provoked by a Negro. However, if the situation had resulted in an overly severe response by the police, for example, their serious mistreatment of the offender, the organization might be forced to act to remind the police that their extralegal activity was restricted.

more than a match for violent white power. They are aware that it is now much less likely that they will be the victims of arbitrarily administered white violence. They know also that they have a champion which will extract a heavy price from the perpetrators of any such violence. For Negroes in Southville, this represents a most important and valued kind of social change.

The nonviolent SAO also welcomes the Defenders, whose existence has strengthened their bargaining position. Prior to the creation of the Defenders, white officials were confronted solely by the alternatives of accepting or rejecting SAO demands. Subsequent to its creation, additional variables had to be considered. The alternative to SAO demands no longer is the maintenance of the status quo but the possibility that the city may be transformed into a battlefield which will destroy Southville. Formerly, acquiescence to SAO demands had been the less attractive alternative. The Defenders has served to make the nonviolent SAO considerably more attractive to white officials than it once was.

Ridicule has replaced fear as the dominant reaction of Negroes to the Ku Klux Klan. While the Klan continues to issue pronouncements reaffirming its dedication to southern white mores and predicting victory in the struggle to maintain them, Negroes view these statements with contempt. Occasional pronouncements by the Klan leader that the Klan is nonviolent are viewed with amusement. Considering the Defenders' existence and the Klan's unwillingness to confront that organization, there is no other choice. While the Klan still inspires hatred, its power to control the action of Negroes is rapidly vanishing. In Southville, the Klan has become little more than a social club, without the power

to enforce its desires. It is now much more concerned with national politics than with local racial conditions. Its failure to control these conditions has forced it to look elsewhere if it is to *seem* an active organization.

The role played by law enforcement agencies has undergone considerable change. These agencies are much less a "white man's army" and much more in conformity with the normal police role. While individual officers may continue as Klansmen, the quasipublic relationship between the Klan and law agencies has ceased. On occasion, officers do overstep the boundaries of their role, but when this occurs, they are much more likely to be censured by their superiors. In one instance, an officer made a racial slur against Smith. Immediately, Smith registered a complaint with the officer's superiors. The issue was resolved when both the officer and the police chief apologized for the remark. In the main, white officers maintain a distant and "correct" attitude toward the Defenders. However, two newly employed Negro officers have reacted somewhat differently. They have talked with Smith and have asked for any assistance the Defenders would be willing to give in maintaining peace and order in Negro sections of the city.

The vast majority of white persons remain unaware of the Defenders' existence. They speak of the recent past as a time of "racial unrest" and are pleased that this is no longer the case. They tend to attribute this change to the "inherent good will between the races" which exists in the city. They accept the desegregation which has occurred as proof of the good will of whites, and attribute the impetus for this change to the basic decency of white persons rather than to efforts by Negroes. SAO is viewed not only as unnecessary but as having introduced conflict where none should have been. Change has been accomplished more despite that organization than because of it. Whites are proud of their law enforcement agencies, reject any allegations of brutality against Negroes, and credit much of the return of peace to the "professionalism" of law enforcement agencies. These agencies are praised for their impartiality, good sense, and good will toward all citizens. Neither the newspaper nor white officials have sought to advance any other explanation for the changes which have occurred in Southville.

The Defenders was organized to alter the distribution of certain types of power in the community. It removed the threat of fear, intimidation, and violence from the lives of Negroes. As a result, it became a kind of referee enforcing a set of rules by which SAO and white officialdom would confront each other on the subject of social change. So long as organized violence was the sole prerogative of the white population, SAO was overmatched in the struggle. The presence of the Defenders removed the threat of violence and permitted SAO's nonviolent methodology to confront a Defenders-insured nonviolent white opposition. This permitted the issues of racial change to be debated and settled within the framework of peaceful coexistence. The Defenders' continued existence acts to insure that violence will remain neutralized in the struggle.

Members of the Defenders believe that Southville is a microcosm of the total society. Throughout the nation, they see the commitment to nonviolence among Negroes diminishing rapidly. No longer is it possible to rely upon a nonviolent response to white violence and police brutality. They see the issue not as whether there will be violence but the form that violence will take. Unless organizations such as their own which lend support to the more broadly based nonviolent movement become the rule, there will be an ever increasing random violence. This random, goalless, and widespread violence will be the result of the abandoning of hope that a redistribution of power is possible in the American society.

It is the Defenders' belief that their organization has prevented this kind of desperate violence because it has proved to Negroes in Southville that it is possible to challenge successfully the monopoly of power held by whites. The organization is firm in its belief that it has accomplished this because it speaks the only kind of language many persons in power understand.

43
*The Black Guerrilla**
MARTIN OPPENHEIMER

What are the real prospects for guerrilla warfare in the urban black ghetto? A 1967 Harlem handbill states, "There is but one way to end this suffering and that is by black revolution. Our revolution is a unity of the black man wherever he may be. . . . When we unite we can end our suffering. Don't riot, join the revolution!" I. F. Stone, on August 19, 1968, commented: "We must be prepared to see first of all that we face a black revolt; secondly, that the black ghettos regard the white police as an occupying army; thirdly, that guerrilla war against this army has begun. . . . The effect of the ambushes which have begun to occur in various cities is to deepen police hatred . . . and therefore to stimulate those very excesses and brutalities which have made the police a hated enemy."[1]

On the other extreme, as it were,

*[Reprinted by permission of Quadrangle Books from *The Urban Guerrilla* by Martin Oppenheimer, Copyright © 1969 by Martin Oppenheimer.]

are warnings emanating from police and army circles. *The New Republic* (January 27, 1968) quotes a Colonel Robert B. Rigg, writing in the January 1968 *Army* magazine, as predicting "scenes of destruction approaching those of Stalingrad in World War II." Colonel Rigg's viewpoint seems to be that ". . . in the next decade at least one major metropolitan area could be faced with guerrilla warfare requiring sizable United States army elements. . . ."

If we assume there will in fact be further disorders in our urban ghettos in the years to come, given the general failure of society to solve the problems of the poor and of the black community, and that some of these disorders may well take the form of paramilitary outbursts, what is the prognosis for such insurrectionary attempts?

I assume first of all that a black rebellion would be a genuinely popular uprising and might be able to take over militarily the black ghetto areas of some cities. But if this were to take place, it would be without any logistical base in the countryside or abroad, and the urban uprisings would be territorially and logistically isolated. A further assumption is that of the black power advocates themselves, namely, that we live in a basically racist society which would not hesitate to counter with a reactionary, completely military solution to black paramilitary activity. There is ample evidence to support the idea that even racially and culturally similar groups do not balk at such measures. If a serious insurrection were to take place, there is little doubt (at least in my mind) that this would unleash the barely latent hostilities of a large sector of white society, which would support repressive measures. In addition to being isolated in the cities, the black guerrilla would confront a government more or less in a

position to move in a unified fashion against him. In brief, the black guerrilla is in as bad a position as some of the worst examples of revolt in history (for example, the Warsaw Ghetto) and is certainly in no way analogous to the more optimal situations (Caracas in 1958, or Petrograd in 1917).

The latter were offensive (revolutionary) in the sense that the existing government was to be replaced; a black rebellion would in all likelihood be, like the Warsaw Ghetto uprising, *defensive,* meaning that it would be a reaction to further encroachments on the ghetto population by the status quo—hence an insurrection of desperation. (An alternative strategy, that of the "interurban guerrilla," will be explored later.)

A brief examination of some cases that roughly approximate the situation of the defensive black guerrilla in the United States will show, I think, that unless the social structure becomes far weaker than we have reason to believe it will in the near future, a defensive black insurrection is doomed from a military point of view.

Some information was gathered covering six cases of urban uprisings, all but one in this century. Excluded from these cases were such short-lived risings as those in Berlin and Poznan in June 1953 and June 1956, respectively; also excluded were general rebellions of which the urban uprising was only one part—for example, the Hungarian rebellion of 1956 or the Irish Revolution of 1919—and urban uprisings such as Petrograd and Caracas, where the rebels were neither isolated nor confronted with a unified power structure.

The following criteria were used in this selection, which, it should be emphasized, is illustrative rather than a sampling. First, each uprising was at minimum a guerrilla outbreak, backed

TABLE 1

Case	Dates	Casualties
The Paris Commune	March 28–May 28, 1871	20,000 to 30,000 dead versus 83 officers and 794 men of the Versaillese government
The Easter Rising (Dublin)	April 24–29, 1916	No figures available
Shanghai, China	February 21–April 13, 1927	About 5,000 dead
Vienna, Austria	February 12–17, 1934	1,500 to 2,000 dead versus 102 Heimwehr
Warsaw Ghetto	April 19–May 15, 1943	Several thousand allied, 56,000 deported, versus about twenty Germans
Warsaw Uprising	July 31–October 2, 1944	100,000 to 250,000 dead

by a significant sector of the local urban population—that is, each was a genuinely popular "rising." Second, in each case the rising developed into a rebellion which successfully took over an entire city or a large sector thereof. Third, the rebels in each case were isolated, either acting totally alone, or effectively separated from outside support. Fourth, in these illustrations the government continued to function effectively at least outside the city, and managed to move in a unified fashion against the rebels within a short time. These are, in fact, the conditions confronting black power strategists when they talk about paramilitary activity of an insurrectionary kind.

1. THE PARIS COMMUNE, MARCH 28–MAY 28, 1871

After the capitulation of Paris to the Prussians on January 8, 1871, the Prussian troops remained on the outskirts of the city, preferring to let the conservative Thiers government disarm the more popularly based National Guard which was mainly working class in composition. When the government attempted to do so on March 18, the National Guard resisted, and on the 28 the commune was proclaimed. The official government withdrew to Versailles, and together with the Prussians

beseiged the city. The commune held fast for two months but was finally overwhelmed by the troops of Versailles, with the Prussians playing a relatively passive role. A brutal massacre followed; Frank Jellinek has pointed out that the whole Jacobin "terror" during the French Revolution executed 2,596 people in Paris; in the commune between 20,000 and 30,000 men, women, and children fell. How many of these were victims of the massacre is unknown. Over 30,000 people were subsequently imprisoned. The Versaillese forces lost 83 officers and 794 men killed.[2]

2. THE EASTER RISING, DUBLIN, APRIL 21–29, 1916

Intense repression of Irish Nationalism from 1914 to 1916 had built up considerable resentment in the population, and by the fall of 1915 the Irish Volunteers, military arm of the Irish Republican Brotherhood, were drilling and marching openly in many parts of the country, including Dublin. An uprising was fixed for Easter Sunday 1916, but was countermanded at the last minute by the national organization, led by moderates. The Dublin organization, James Connolly's working class-oriented Citizens' Army, determined to go ahead anyway, and the rebellion broke out on

Monday, April 24, with the swift seizure of the Post Office and other key points, and the proclamation of the republic. Some one thousand to fifteen hundred armed men and women participated. British troops were rushed to the city from thoughout the country, and they gradually forced their way into insurgent areas, backed by artillery fire and raiding parties which took heavy casualties among civilian noncombatants. On Saturday, April 29, the surviving Citizens' Army soldiers surrendered. Connolly himself was severely wounded. Courts-martial quickly followed, and from May 3 to 12, fifteen of the ringleaders, including Connolly, were executed. In 1919 the armed struggle was renewed on a nationwide basis, resulting two years later in an ambiguous treaty with the British. This was followed by a civil war which lasted two more years. Precise casualty figures on the Easter rising are not available.

3. SHANGHAI, FEBRUARY 21– APRIL 13, 1927

In response to Chiang Kai-shek's military advance from the north with a revolutionary army, the workers of Shanghai staged a general strike on February 19, 1927, to undermine the local warlord and aid Chiang. In response, execution squads were set up on the streets, and after this terror an insurrection began on February 21. Chiang, who was basically hostile to the working class forces, waited on the outskirts of the city, and the insurrection was suppressed two days later. While Chiang continued to engage himself in moppingup operations outside the city, the workers again struck on March 21. Again Chiang did not move. This strike also led to an insurrection which succeeded in taking over the city, and Chiang was welcomed as a liberator. But on April 12 Chiang, aided

by foreign troops and gangsters, began a reign of terror against working class, trade union, and communist organizations. After sporadic resistance, the revolutionists were wiped out by Chiang's forces within twenty-four hours. O. Edmund Clubb estimates that about five thousand radicals, unionists, and the like were massacred.[3]

4. VIENNA, FEBRUARY 12–17, 1934

The Austrian Socialist party had been desperately trying to work out a common front against the Nazis with the Dollfuss regime, despite the latter's physical attacks on the socialists in various parts of the country. The Viennese socialists, representing the city's working class in the main, finally agreed to rise in arms if the Dollfuss government attempted further suppression of workers' organizations in the city. On February 12 the Heimwehr, Dollfuss' military arm, raided Viennese workers' clubs and arrested many leading socialist figures. Armed resistance began when Dollfuss invaded, interestingly, the worker-controlled public housing projects and fired on the project with howitzers and mortars. After three days of heavy fighting the survivors were forced to surrender or were overpowered, with some leaders fleeing the country. Nine leaders of the defensive "insurrection" were immediately hanged and thousands were imprisoned in concentration camps. Some fifteen hundred to two thousand people had been killed, as against 102 soldiers of the Heimwehr.

5. THE WARSAW GHETTO, APRIL 19–MAY 15, 1943

In the fall of 1942, after only 70,000 of an original population of 400,000 remained in the Jewish ghetto of Warsaw, the Jewish organizations decided to resist further deportations militarily. The ghetto was more or less in Jewish hands to begin with, and when Weapons-SS raiding parties entered to liquidate the population on the 19, they were met with gunfire. Only some fifteen hundred Jews were organized into military units, with less equipment among them than in a company of infantry (about a hundred rifles, a few machine guns, a few hundred revolvers). SS and police units numbered two to three thousand. Several thousand Jews were killed in the fighting, some five to six thousand escaped into the surrounding countryside (many to be captured and killed later), and 56,000 were deported to extermination camps. When the Russians arrived in January 1945, only two hundred Jews remained alive in the city.

An interesting historical note for those who believe that in some sense ghetto home rule (including self-policing) is desirable, is that the Warsaw Ghetto was, from 1940 to 1943, virtually a Jewish state. "Yiddish-speaking policemen were a direct consequence of the German decision to establish a ghetto, and in that respect they became as necessary as any other group. . . ."[4] This self-rule, wherever it existed among Jews, actually contributed to their destruction by creating a mechanism which the Nazis could and did use to do their work. A similar example occurs in the story of *The Bridge on the River Kwai*, when the discipline and morale infused by a British officer are used by the Japanese to help their military efforts in destroying other British units.

A ghetto is particularly vulnerable to hunger and disease, especially when enforced by a besieging army (as in Warsaw or the Paris Commune). In Paris the people ate rats and shoelaces; in Warsaw hunger and typhus resulted in five thousand deaths each month in the year prior to the ghetto uprising.

"By decreasing and choking off the food supply, the Germans were able to turn the ghettos into death traps. And that is what they did."[5] Raul Hilberg reports that in the winter of 1941–1942 the sewage pipes froze, toilets became useless, and human excrement was dumped into the streets with the garbage. Cases of cannibalism were reported. Between 500,000 and 600,000 Jews died in Polish ghettos and labor camps *before* the extermination camps went into operation.

6. THE WARSAW UPRISING, JULY 31–OCTOBER 2, 1944

As Russian troops approached Warsaw, an underground army, with agreement of the Soviets, rose up to throw out the Germans and divert German troops from the Russian flanks. Preparations were relatively open, as the Germans ignored violations of many regulations. There was a virtual vacuum of power in the city, and the underground was able to take over large sectors of it very quickly. The Russians, however, did not come to the aid of the uprising for political reasons, and the German occupying troops were soon able to make serious inroads into the city. Despite several extremely risky British and American air drops of supplies (and ultimately even Russian ones, though they neglected parachutes so that all supplies were destroyed as they hit the ground), the underground was forced to surrender. The Germans had deported some 200,000 hostages to nearby concentration camps by this time; estimates of total Warsaw casualties for the two-month battle range from 100,000 to 250,000 killed.

Note that in most of these cases the rebels had no illusions about winning without outside aid. In three of the cases (the Easter Rising, Shanghai, and the Warsaw Uprising) the rebels moved on the false assumption that aid would be forthcoming, and in two others they moved only in desperation, with no real hope of success. Even the Paris Commune hoped that the remainder of the country would organize communes to come to its aid. Furthermore, in five of the six cases, the actual outbreak of the rebellion took place only as a defensive measure against severe encroachments by the dominant power, and would probably not have occurred at all without this repression. The Warsaw Uprising is the only exception to this. And, in three of the cases, the rebellion was against foreigners. Perhaps it can be argued that the American white power structure is basically foreign to the black population, but having a clearly foreign oppressor does seem to make it easier to unite the population for rebellion.

Given this sort of dismal evidence, why has so much attention been given by the white press, and by some spokesmen in black power circles, to paramilitary potentials? There are three possible interpretations for this fascination (apart from the view that the police and the military display alarm in order to justify their existence and their appropriations). First, paramilitary affairs in the black ghetto may be largely a creation of the press which has resulted in a self-fulfilling prophecy. For the white community, which seems to require a rationale for abandoning the civil rights movement and refusing significant aid to urban areas, the urban riot has become highly functional. The attention given by the white press to what has been until recently the peripheral phenomenon of paramilitary black power is equally if not more functional. For lower middle class people in the suburbs who have long-repressed itchy trigger fingers, talk of urban risings by the black population affords an outlet for repressed hostilities which can

only be exceeded by an actual outbreak of warfare. For the black community, the large-scale attention focused upon a small minority of paramilitary types seems evidence that such activity may in fact be dangerous, hence effective as a threat with which to coerce white power structures. Such a view is useful for paramilitary recruiters.

A second, related interpretation deals with the psychological drawing power of all violent, action-oriented movements. It has to do with the "machismo" so important to downtrodden males in any oppressed culture.

A third interpretation, which is by now a cliche in social science as well as informed lay circles, has to do with the desperation born of the apparent failure of both conventional politics and nonviolent direct action to secure significant changes in the condition of the American Negro. As a result, many black leaders have been forced to the conclusion that, for the time being at least, the civil rights movement is dead and that black power—the cultural, social and economic autonomy (and, given the ghettoized character of the black population, territorial autonomy) of blacks—is the only viable strategy. Black power is a vague concept because it is a new movement. It should not be surprising that some of its advocates demand violent or military tactics. We must remember that it took from about 1825 to the publication, in 1896, of Herzl's *The Jewish State* for Jews even to begin to clarify the issue of "Jewish power," and that almost from the beginnings of Zionism, many Zionist as well as non-Zionist ghetto groups had paramilitary auxiliaries.

A SCENARIO

Despite the pessimistic military prognosis for a black revolution, it "might be attempted in the face of overwhelming odds and without regard to the terrible consequences."[6] Let us see, by the use of a crude scenario, how a defensive black insurrection, born of desperation, might develop. Obviously, any knowledgeable person could add all sorts of complications and refinements to such a scenario by including various technological considerations. Nevertheless, I believe the basic issues can be clearly made to appear in such a semifictional presentation.

It was a hot Friday evening in August 1969, in the north Philadelphia ghetto. In the third incident in as many weeks, police halted a car belonging to members of the "Black Liberation Front," and, when one of the blacks was slow to get out of the car, police opened fire. Two of the car's occupants were hit; a third returned the fire with an automatic carbine, and an officer was hit. An "assist officer" call went out and soon a several-block area was surrounded by "red cars." Meanwhile, the surviving BLF fighter disappeared. The appearance of the police cars drew catcalls from the young people of the area, and when police attempted to place two youngsters under arrest, a minor riot broke out. Other BLF members had by then been alerted, and within a half-hour a small mob was moving onto the precinct station.

Meanwhile, a half-dozen "triads" of BLF irregulars opened fire on traffic patrolmen and police cars at as many locations in north and west Philadelphia, and other units of less than a dozen men each began to smash store windows along Columbia and Ridge Avenues, the principal ghetto merchant centers. An outraged mob of blacks, at a BLF street-corner rally at 52nd and Market Streets, occupied the train station there and took over the control point of the suburban trains. A trained BLF technician halted the Paoli (suburban) Local.

Almost simultaneously, "Radio Black Liberation" went on the air to declare martial law in north and west Philadelphia, and to announce the formation of a revolutionary government for the defense of the area against further atrocities by the white police "pigs." Control points were established, and whites attempting to enter the area by car or bus were fired on and turned back. Radio Black Liberation announced the capture of over one thousand white businessmen and professionals from the Paoli Local. The North Philadelphia Station of the Pennsylvania Railroad was captured after an exchange of gunfire with railway police, and train service to New York City was cut. Irregular BLF units intercepted underground telephone and electricity conduits, and all electricity in Philadelphia, plus a ten-county area in southeastern Pennsylvania and southern New Jersey, was cut off. City hall, some fifteen blocks from the rebel-held area, was attacked by terrorist groups, and an explosion rocked the police station at 8th and Race, a similar distance from the north Philadelphia ghetto. The police communications system was knocked out, and there were heavy police casualties. North and west Philadelphia, with a total black population of about 400,000 (and less than 100,000 whites), was effectively under rebel control.

BLF activities had been under surveillance for some time. Months before, the Philadelphia police commissioner had developed contingency plans in case of a serious uprising, in careful collaboration with state and federal officials. Hints of black unrest had appeared in the local press, and the usual electronic devices, though unconstitutional, kept interested parties informed of most BLF activities. Gun sales in the suburbs and white areas adjacent to the ghetto rocketed; when the Paoli Local was stopped, a few white businessmen even took revolvers and carbines from their attache cases and managed to scare the rebels off the train station platforms. Thus, while the train remained an isolated hostage in a hostile ghetto, it remained "free." The passengers went hungry that night and the succeeding day; a handful of black passengers was executed.

National Guard units "trained up" to urban guerrilla warfare duty, and virtually all white, were moved in quickly to confront the rebel control points all along the borders between north and west Philadelphia and the rest of the city. Police cut off the city water supply to the ghetto area, and auxiliary electricity and telephone systems restored service to the remainder of the city and outlying counties. Special Forces units moved by boat to the bridges of the Schuylkill River and cut off communications between north and west Philadelphia. Helicopters began twenty-four-hour surveillance of the rebel areas—the rebels managed to shoot down several of them. By 4 A.M. Saturday morning the rebel area, cut in half, lay in total darkness, surrounded by a division of the Pennsylvania National Guard. Radio Black Liberation was effectively forced off the air as its generators carried it only to a fifty-block area. No food supplies of any kind were delivered to the ghetto area Saturday. The Paoli Local, isolated but free, was soon reinforced by pinpoint parachutists of the 110th Airborne, who shot their way out of the station to "liberate" a block area on each side. Helicopters using flamethrowers prepared the way; extensive fires soon raged in west Philadelphia— there was of course no fire service, and no water.

By noon Saturday, dissension in rebel ranks began to build as deputations of neighbors pleaded for surrender. There was no milk, no bread, no water; the sewage system was hopelessly backed up, and the almost negligible medical personnel left in the area warned of imminent epidemics. Looting of stores was complete, but the food supplies could not last long. Outbreaks in other northern cities, which the BLF had hoped for, either failed to materialize or were similarly isolated. In any case, the rebels received no accurate information from the outside, and they could not even know of the protests entered on their behalf by several African nations. (The Soviet Union remained silent, having just suffered a reprimand from the United Nations General Assembly for its intervention in the internal affairs of Rumania.)

At 2 P.M. on Saturday, deputations of National Guard officers, including Negro officers, made appearances in both west and north Philadelphia. Upon being taken to rebel headquarters, they stated that unless the rebels surrendered unconditionally by 5 P.M., artillery units would proceed to demolish north Philadelphia block by block. The rebel command repeated the famous utterance made by the United States commander at Bastogne, in World War II, adding, "What the hell, it's cheaper than urban renewal."

Meanwhile, however, two other events in the city came to light in the press (which appeared that day as usual, with appeals for law and order which were dropped into the ghetto area). First, south Philadelphia, the location of Philadelphia's third black community, was placed under martial law—a pass system was instituted, and several hundred potential "troublemakers" were quickly arrested and shipped to a neighboring county jail, which had been taken over by a National Guard battalion. Second, at the border of north Philadelphia and neighboring

Kensington, National Guard units were alternated with units of the Kensington Citizens' Militia, which, unlike the National Guard, began a tactic of quick hit-and-run invasions of the rebel-controlled area. Several dozen blacks were killed in these raids, which demolished, by explosive, several tenements. Eleven militiamen fell casualty to the rebels. By 3 P.M. Saturday, eight blocks were evacuated and left in the hands of the Kensington Militia, while no blocks were gained anywhere against the National Guard and the Airborne troops.

Promptly at 5 P.M. a field artillery battalion of the 1st Army, headquartered at Fort Dix, entrenched itself in a schoolyard ten blocks below the ghetto area and proceeded to level the area bordered by Broad, Columbia, 15th and Jefferson Streets, in the heart of north Philadelphia. A half-hour later an Air Force jet dropped napalm on the Muslim Mosque on Lancaster Avenue in west Philadelphia, starting an uncontrollable fire.

Events after that time were indistinct. It would seem that a crowd of black women, some armed, overran the rebel post at Presbyterian Hospital in west Philadelphia and surrendered to the National Guard. Except for one public housing project, in which snipers continued activity until Sunday morning, west Philadelphia was occupied by midnight. North Philadelphia held out longer because of fear of the Kensington Militia, but word of this finally leaked out through the city's Human Relations Commission, and the militia was withdrawn: a committee of Negro ministers surrendered the area to the guard in a brief, prayerful ceremony at noon Sunday. The "Philadelphia Commune" was over, less than forty-eight hours after it began.

More than two thousand "rebels," most of them women and children, perished, as against some one hundred guardsmen (mostly victims of sniper fire), some dozen airborne and two dozen civilians (in the battle of the Paoli Local), eleven Kensington Militiamen, and twenty police officers.

This sort of outcome has been the common fate of isolated urban uprisings. Coordinated uprisings in many cities would complicate matters, of course; so would supporting paramilitary actions (including, perhaps, seizures of public buildings and even police stations) by leftwing students. But so long as the general public (including about 800,000 members of the National Rifle Association) is prepared to support the government, even a larger-scale uprising can have hardly any other result.

There is a possible exception; if, in a preconsensus "liberal" stage the government acts inconclusively, the rebellion might last longer. But, again given the prognosis of general public hostility to the aims of the rebels, pressure on the government from the right would probably be so extreme that a military solution might be forced. If the government continued to vacillate, a threatened rightwing coup (or, at minimum, rightwing vigilante action) would force the government to "clean up the mess" rather than be forced from office.

Let us suppose, however, that the Philadelphia Commune had been able to hold out for a few more days, and that the government had proposed a negotiated settlement. What might the rebels have demanded? It is difficult to say, particularly since the black community is itself divided on broad strategy. But one might suppose the following kinds of demands: (1) Self-government with the election of a black mayor and council in the black-held area. (2) Expropriation of all white-owned businesses with ownership passing to the community (socialization). (3) Black autonomy over all institutions in the rebel area, including public schools, welfare institutions, and housing. (4) Political recognition as a separate city-state, or perhaps in cooperation with other such communes, as a nation, with diplomatic representation. (5) Free passage to and from work in white areas, with economic relationships roughly approximating those of the "common market," i.e., a common monetary standard, trade agreements, no tariffs, and so on.

Such an arrangement is not dangerous to white society in any fundamental way, and in fact is one of the establishment strategies. . . . Demographically black government is in the cards for many American cities anyway, so long as city-county consolidation (the abolition of artificial city boundaries) is resisted by the suburbs. With the exception of the landlord and small-merchant class (and a few larger distributors like those of dairy products, who would have to give way to black cooperatives), the advantages to the economy would probably outweigh the disadvantages. White society might still be able to hire black mercenaries to fight its colonial wars. And a wasteful welfare establishment could be dismantled in much the same way as with a guaranteed minimum income, except that the black community alone would have to generate that income rather than the whole nation.

In the short run, most of the economic disadvantages of the plan would be to the black community. Many more would be unemployed before whites caught on to the advantages (and basically harmless nature) of the balck-controlled internal neocolony. It would take some years before enough capital could be generated inside the black community to reach the "takeoff" point of economic development, and black businesses (whether privately controlled or socially owned and controlled) would

then have to confront the problem of competition with white businesses which would probably be discriminatory. This new discrimination could only be overcome by competing economically, which would in all probability mean cutting labor costs and installing labor-saving machinery. The black community would then have an unemployment rate roughly similar to its rate at present, but at a higher level of expectation. In terms of *general* economic conditions it would continue to be dependent on the white economy because of its need to trade with the outside world.

Trotsky once said you cannot have socialism in one country. Nor can you have it, isolated, in one ghetto or even in a set of ghettos. The economic future of the black American is, for better or worse, tied to a national and, in fact, an international economy. Separate economies are no longer viable even if they were not prevented by the dominant social order for racist reasons. (One can imagine how racists would use the fact that blacks were economically and politically no longer a part of the United States.)

Black power circles have mentioned an alternative form of paramilitary activity in the urban context—the longer-range revolutionary underground, possibly including terrorism, sabotage, and even small, mobile guerrilla bands, all of this being carried on over a longer period of years. The objective of such a strategy would be similar to that of Debray in Latin America: to create such social havoc that the structure of society would be subverted. With such subversion, and the inability of the regime to cope with the problems created by it, other elements of society would also become disaffected, and the guerrilla movement would in this way gradually grow to a point where an attempt to overthrow the entire government might be made. The strategy would assume some allies among whites.

Such a prognosis makes more sense. "The new concept is lightning campaigns conducted in highly sensitive urban communities with the paralysis reaching the small communities and spreading to the farm areas. . . . It dislocates the organs of harmony and order and reduces central power to the level of a helpless, sprawling octopus. . . . The factory workers will be afraid to venture out on the streets to report to their jobs. . . . Violence and terror will spread like a firestorm. A clash will occur inside the armed forces. . . . U.S. forces will be spread too thin for effective action. . . . The economy will fall into a state of chaos."[7] The obstacles to this strategy, unlike that of the insurrectionary outbreak as such, are not as serious as the House Committee on Un-American Activities might think—it is questionable that "there is little doubt that such an uprising could be effectively and quickly controlled." It is not true, either, that "the ghetto could be isolated and the guerrillas effectively bottled up," unless all ghettos were turned into concentration camps—which would create precisely the conditions for immediate, widespread insurrection that some militants might like. Nor is it true that "a guerrilla war based on racial lines would never be supported by any sizable number of Negroes . . . ," especially if the committee's suggestion that the ghetto should be isolated and "search and seizure operations . . . instituted" is followed.[8]

What HCUA has done is to support the idea that an actual outbreak of insurrection at present would be suicidal. But it has not effectively demolished the arguments for a gradual build-up, beginning with terrorism and sabotage on a small scale. Indeed, it supports such a strategy by pointing

(accurately, I think) to the way our government would react once such a campaign were begun: "most civil liberties would have to be suspended . . . the population of the ghetto would be classified through an office for the 'control and organization of the inhabitants. . . .'" We might even see the institution of puppet governments, and puppet police, and, of course, "The McCarran Act provides for various detention centers. . . ." This, then, is the sure road to the subversion of the country and to a revolution—or a counterrevolution. Who will have been chiefly responsible, the rebels or the police state created to control them?

FOOTNOTES

[1] *I. F. Stone's Weekly,* August 19, 1968.

[2] Frank Jelhnek, *The Paris Commune of 1871,* London, Gollancz, 1937.

[3] O. Edmund Clubb, *Twentieth-Century China,* New York, Columbia University Press, 1964.

[4] Gerd Korman, "The Setting," *New University Thought,* vol. 6 (March-April 1968), Special Commemoration Issue for the Twenty-fifth Anniversary of the Warsaw Ghetto Uprising, 7.

[5] Raul Hilberg, *The Destruction of the European Jews,* Chicago, Quadrangle Books, 1961, pp. 168–174.

[6] Lewis M. Killian, *The Impossible Revolution: Black Power and the American Dream,* New York, Random House, 1968.

[7] Robert F. Williams, quoted in Committee on Un-American Activities, U.S. House of Representatives, *Guerrilla Warfare Advocates in the U.S.,* Washington, U.S. Government Printing Office, 1968, p. 19.

[8] Committee on Un-American Activities, pp. 57–58.

44
The Functions of Disunity: Negro Leadership in a Southern City*

JACK L. WALKER

INTRODUCTION[1]

During the last five years waves of Negro protest demonstrations have swept across the southern states. Incidents like the Montgomery bus boycott, the freedom rides, and the sit-ins have spread with amazing speed, provoking racial crises in numerous towns and cities, even in the Deep South, and often taking the white leaders by surprise. From these crises a new type of Negro leadership seems to be arising: one dedicated to protest rather than accommodation and determined to press its demands for equality with a wide range of weapons including economic boycotts, civil disobedience, and political reprisals, tactics that southern Negroes have never used in the past.

As the new, more militant leaders have arisen in Negro communities, the established leadership has usually offered resistance, and as a result many southern Negro communities have been torn by disunity and internal conflict. Lewis M. Killian and Charles U. Smith in investigating Tallahassee, Florida, following a sharp dispute over bus segregation in the city found that the more militant, "protest" leaders had completely displaced the established Negro leadership. They found that after the crisis had passed, not one of the six persons named by a panel of both whites and Negroes as the top Negro leaders before the dispute were included as top leaders after the dispute. Also not one of the five persons that the panel named as top Negro leaders after the dispute had been ranked among the first ten before the dispute took place. Even the old, established leaders seemed to be aware that they had been displaced, and the study also indicated that a majority of the Negro community had shifted their allegiances to the protest leaders. Killian and Smith argue that:

. . . the new leaders are becoming permanent leaders not because of the attractiveness of their personalities or their skill at organizing, but rather because they adhere rigorously to the form of militant leadership which is becoming the trend for Negroes throughout the United States.[2]

The situation in Tallahassee, however, does not seem to have been duplicated in all other southern cities, or even in all those that have experienced a racial crisis within the last five years. Leslie Dunbar in commenting on the findings of Killian and Smith has argued that:

There is some evidence in the stories of how a number of southern cities have desegregated lunch counters to suggest that the older Negro leadership and the protest leaders can and do fruitfully complement each other, though coordination and mutual trust have sometimes been hard come by. My guess would be that this is the true interpretation. Negro leadership in the South is being broadened by an infusion of new elites.[3]

The subject of this essay is the relations between the established Negro

*[Reprinted with permission from the *Journal of Negro Education*, XXXII (Summer 1963), pp. 227–236.]

[1] The research on which this essay is based was financed by a grant from the Iowa Citizenship Clearing House and the National Center for Education in Politics. Neither of them, of course, is responsible for any errors of fact or interpretation in this study.

[2] Lewis M. Killian and Charles U. Smith, "Negro Protest Leaders in a Southern City," *Social Forces* (March, 1960), p. 257.

[3] Leslie Dunbar, "Reflections on the Latest Reform of the South," *Phylon,* 22:253, Fall, 1961.

leadership and the new protest leaders in a southern city, the issue raised by Dunbar, Killian, and Smith. The analysis is based on a case study of the sit-in controversy in Atlanta, Georgia, and is concerned particularly with the social and economic factors associated with the leaders' differing attitudes towards goals and techniques of social action. It will be argued that both the conservative and the protest leaders can play an important part in such racial disputes, and unless the conservatives are completely displaced by the protest leaders, disputes among the leadership tend to increase, not decrease, the effectiveness of the Negro community's battle against the institutions of segregation.

SIT-INS IN ATLANTA: A CASE STUDY[4]

On February 1, 1960, several Negro students sat down at a lunch counter in Greensboro, North Carolina, and refused to leave when told that the store did not serve Negroes. The manager is reported to have said: "They can just sit there. It's nothing to me." But within a week similar groups were sitting down in protest all over the South, and a major social movement was underway. The sit-ins spread even into the Deep South, and in response to fears and rumors that sit-ins were being planned the Georgia legislature passed a special trespass law on February 17, 1960.

Their fears were well-founded, for as early as February 4 students at Atlanta University were planning demonstrations, but they were persuaded by faculty members and an apprehensive administration to postpone their action

[4] This case study is based on the record of the controversy found in the files of *The Atlanta Constitution, The Atlanta Journal, The Atlanta Daily World,* and *The Atlanta Inquirer,* and on a series of interviews with the principal actors conducted during April and May of 1962.

until they had drawn up a statement of their grievances. This statement was quickly completed and printed in the form of a full-page advertisement in all local newspapers on March 9, 1960, under the title: "An Appeal for Human Rights." The advertisement caused a sensation in the state and it was commented on by politicians and public figures all over the country. This was followed on March 15 by the first widespread sit-in demonstrations in Atlanta in which seventy-seven students were arrested under the new Georgia trespass law.

While their cases were pending in court the students began to work on several other projects. They mounted picket lines against food stores which had large Negro clienteles yet did not hire Negroes above the menial level, they held a series of meetings in Negro churches explaining the student movement and asking for support, they began publishing a weekly news sheet that eventually became a full-fledged weekly newspaper, and on May 17, 1960, they gathered 1,400 students together to march on the State Capitol in downtown Atlanta to celebrate the Supreme Court's 1954 antisegregation decision. This march was diverted by Atlanta's Chief of Police to prevent the students from meeting a large, ugly crowd that had gathered at the capitol. When the students left for summer vacation tension was running high in the city.

During the spring of 1960 there was considerable dispute among adult Negroes about the student movement. Although there were few who spoke out directly against the students, there were those who expressed their disapproval by keeping silent or withholding praise. The conservative adults, many of whom were businessmen, were opposed on principle to the students' use of picket lines and boycotts against businesses which practiced discrimination in hiring. They were also apprehensive when they understood that the students were not satisfied with their first sit-ins and their march on the State Capitol, but were planning repeated demonstrations in an effort to force the issue. The adult community began to divide on their support for the students and rumors that all the Negro adults did not approve of the students' efforts passed through the white community.

Regardless of the criticism, the leaders of the student movement continued organizational and propaganda work during the summer. On June 27 they met privately with the president of the city's leading department store who tried to convince them to give up their demonstrations promising that he would consider their grievances later on after the schools had been safely desegregated. This meeting broke down into a heated argument in which the student leaders are reported to have threatened the merchant with a boycott and the merchant shouted: "I don't need Negro trade!"

Following this incident conservative Negroes came into the open with criticisms of the students, and a few even made public speeches attacking their methods. But even so, after the students had returned for the fall term, on October 19, 1960, widespread sit-ins were mounted once again, and once again large numbers of demonstrators were arrested.[5] The students refused to leave the jail on bail at this time. Once again tension built up in the city. At this point the mayor asked for, and was granted, a thirty-day truce period in which he promised to try to reach a settlement of the dispute.

[5] These demonstrations received nationwide attention, especially because of the arrest of Martin Luther King, Jr., and the series of events that led to the famous phone call to the King family from John F. Kennedy.

The mayor's efforts were completely unsuccessful. The leading merchants were in no mood to compromise with the demonstrators and were suspicious of the mayor who was quite anxious to get a settlement and whose political power rested firmly on Negro support. When the mayor called a meeting of the downtown merchants in his office, only the small ones attended who depended heavily on Negro trade and feared a boycott.

On their own the leading merchants decided to try informal methods to bring an end to the disturbances. The conservative leaders of the Negro community, those who had criticized the students during the summer and who had been considered the "spokesmen" of the Negro community in the past, were asked to attend a private meeting with the merchants. The meeting was secret but it seems that the Negroes were being asked to use their influence to persuade the demonstrators to cease their efforts and to wait until after the schools were desegregated to discuss the issue of lunch counter desegregation. After meeting twice they decided to invite one adult Negro leader who had been a close advisor of the students, and the most influential student leader to a secret meeting in the Negro section of town so that the white merchants could offer their proposals. When these two men were contacted, however, they immediately became suspicious of the proceedings and decided to expose them. They made a public announcement that they were not a party to these secret negotiations, and when the conservative Negroes and the whites arrived at the meeting place television cameras were already set up and reporters were everywhere clamoring for statements.

After this incident, on November 25, 1960, the students resumed their sit-ins and also organized a full-scale boycott of the downtown shopping area. A stalemate continued through the months of December and January, during which most of the lunch counters remained closed and the boycott of the downtown stores remained in effect.

Throughout this three-month period of stalemate the students, equiped with shortwave radios, had been sitting-in at lunch counters all over the city without incident. Either they had been ignored, or the counters had been closed, but on February 7, 1961, one restaurant manager in a federal office building invoked the trespass law and had the demonstrators arrested. During the next three days arrests continued daily with the students refusing once again to come out on bail. A protest march and rally was planned to take place in front of the jail on February 19, and it was feared that such a demonstration might result in a riot.

At this tense moment the student leaders themselves turned to one of the oldest, most respected Negro leaders and asked him to try to get negotiations started again. This man had made public statements backing the students at the beginning of the movement, but he was also widely considered to be a conservative and had attended the secret meetings with the white merchants in November 1960. At this juncture, however, by utilizing friendships he had with influential white leaders, he was able to get negotiations started which eventually led to a settlement of the controversy. The agreement was announced on March 7, 1961. It called for desegregation of the lunch counters after the school desegregation had been completed during the fall of 1961, and, except for the firm agreement that the counters would be desegregated, it was essentially what the merchants had pressed for from the beginning. The actual desegregation took place on September 27, 1961.

THE FUNCTIONS OF DISUNITY

The sit-in controversy in Atlanta took place in a community which is still basically segregated. Although a few of the barriers have been broken down during the past five years there are still almost no social contacts between the leadership of the two racial groups and residential segregation places their homes far apart. This isolation of the leadership of the two communities from each other is a potentially disruptive element in the social structure of the city. If a crisis arises involving the crucial issue of race, communication between the leaders of the two racial groups, which is normally tenuous and rather formal, becomes very hard to maintain, and it is even more difficult to establish the circumstances in which negotiation of the difficulties that caused the crisis can take place.

During the controversy over the sit-in demonstrations in Atlanta such a breakdown in communications between whites and Negroes occurred, and at the same time relations among the Negro leaders were strained because of their disagreements over tactics. The conservative Negro leaders are primarily older businessmen, although there are also social workers, college administrators, and ministers in this group. The more liberal group is made up of students, members of the staffs of various Negro improvement groups, college teachers, younger businessmen, and ministers.[6]

The dispute within the Negro community revolves around the use of protest demonstrations and economic

[6] The principal actors in the sit-in controversy were interviewed at length, and frequently they voluntarily described themselves with such terms as "conservative" or "liberal." These self-identifications were used, along with an analysis of each participant's actions and statements during the dispute to decide which were conservatives and which were protest leaders.

boycotts to press the attack on segregation. The conservatives never questioned, throughout the sit-in controversy in Atlanta, the goals of the students, and even when they agreed to attend secret meetings with the merchants they never failed to inform the whites that they thought the students' demands were justified, even if they did not approve of their methods.[7] The conservatives oppose boycotts and protest demonstrations primarily because they feel these public displays of discontent cause bitterness and rancor and tend to destroy the cordial, settled atmosphere which they feel is a necessary precondition to effective negotiations. They also fear economic retaliation more than the protest leaders, not only because of their own business, but also because they have worked hard to build institutions such as the YMCA, the Urban League, and many churches which depend heavily on contributions from influential whites. During the boycott that accompanied the sit-in affair in Atlanta some of these organizations began to lose white contributors as tension mounted. To some extent the conservative leaders have each made adjustments to the traditional position of the Negro in southern society. Although none seem completely satisfied, in varying measures they have given up efforts to penetrate the dominant white society and consequently they have a

greater commitment to the institutions within the Negro community.

The businessmen among the conservatives have frequent dealings with influential whites in the city; both the bank and savings and loan association operated by Negroes in Atlanta have very sizable deposits from white customers. In fact, to a large extent, the power of the conservatives depends on their influence with the white community. They are spokesmen for the Negro community primarily because they have gained white recognition and favor, although their own achievements placed them in a position to be chosen for this role. Because of this process of selection, the protest leaders regard the conservatives with almost the same hostility they have for the whites, if not more so. They complain that the conservatives' power is based essentially on the Negro's fear of the power of the white man. They think that the established leaders have profited from the injustices of segregation by trading their human dignity for the opportunity to represent the whites within the Negro community.

The protest leaders are not so directly engaged in activities and institutions that serve the whole community as are the conservatives, and they deal more exclusively with the Negro community than the conservatives. Yet even so they do not feel as much committed to its maintenance; in fact they hate all that it stands for. Their work brings them into closer contact with the social, economic, and political deprivations suffered by the Negro, and they tend to concentrate on these injustices and have fewer reasons to try to protect institutions, both charitable and commercial, that presently exist in the Negro community. They are under less compulsion than the conservatives to act with restraint or to compromise their demands in order

---

[7] It should not be surprising that the older leaders would be in sympathy with the goals of the students because the students' protests did not grow out of alienation from any of the society's basic orienting values except those, such as white supremacy, that underpin segregation. Searles and Williams found that the student protests "were precipitated by Negro students' reference to the white middle class as a standard of comparison. . . ." They also discovered that: "Far from being alienated, the students appear to be committed to the society and its middle class leaders." Ruth Searles and J. Allen Williams, "Negro College Students' Participation in Sit-ins," *Social Forces,* 40:219, March, 1962.

to make limited material gains or to promote the fortunes of Negro businessmen. In this sense they stand outside the economic and social life of the established community and they try to keep the dominant leaders, both white and colored, at arm's length, guarding against being too friendly with politicians and certainly never asking them for favors or help of any kind. They try to conduct their affairs strictly on the basis of their moral principles, and for these reasons conservatives frequently regard them as "irresponsible" and find their attitudes toward politics and community leaders "unrealistic" or "hateful." One conservative leader in Atlanta, who has a reputation as a good tactician and organizer, acknowledged the importance of the student protests in bringing "more integration is less than two years than we gained in ten," but he also argued that "they will never get anything done on their own because they are cut off; they work in a righteous vacuum over there."

The protest leaders and the conservatives manifest considerable suspicion for each other, and in Atlanta a complete breakdown in relations between them is prevented primarily by the existence of several influential men who stand between these two groups and are not so deeply committed to either political style, or who are caught in ambiguous circumstances that prompt them to maintain contact with both protest and conservative leaders. These men tend to bind the Negro community together by providing lines of communication between leaders of all persuasions.

Even though the conservative and protest leaders distrust each other, during the Atlanta sit-in controversy at least, their efforts were complementary. In fact, if the Negro community

is conceived of as a system designed to fight the institutions of segregation each of these groups performed a function in this situation. The students and the adult protest leaders, by organizing demonstrations and economic boycotts, created a crisis which had to be resolved, even if in doing so they raised the level of tension between the two racial groups in the city and caused a rather dangerous breakdown of communications. But the leaders of the protests did not have the power to resolve the crisis they had created because they had no basis for contact with the dominant white leaders. As James Q. Wilson suggests, one of the inherent difficulties of protest action is "that the discretion of the protest leader to bargain after he has acquired the resources with which to bargain is severely limited by the means he was forced to employ in order to create those resources."[8] From the beginning of the dispute the leading merchants refused to negotiate directly with the demonstrators whom they considered to be irresponsible troublemakers. In fact, the tactics pursued by the protest leaders were almost certain to antagonize the dominant whites. As Killian and Smith point out in describing the political style of the protest leaders:

This new leadership is not of the accommodating type. It seeks gains for the Negro community through formal demands and requests, boycotts, lawsuits, and voting. The protest leaders are not concerned with whether or not the whites high in the power structure know, like, or want to deal with them.[9]

The more conservatively inclined leaders, utilizing their reputations and the connections they had built up with

[8] James Q. Wilson, "The Strategy of Protest," *Journal of Conflict Resolution* (September, 1961), p. 293.
[9] Killian and Smith, *op. cit.,* p. 257.

the community through the years, had the function of resolving the crisis situation created by the protest leaders. In this case even the antagonism between the two groups was functional because it made the conservatives seem more reliable and responsible in the eyes of the whites, and so they were still able to act as negotiators when both sides were ready to compromise.

Those leaders in the middle, who did not identify completely with either the conservative or the protest leaders, had the function of moderating this conflict over tactics. Some individuals find themselves in this situation because they are subject to cross-pressures which restrain them from becoming attached to either side in the controversy. Others are not committed because they have a flexible attitude toward social action which prompts them to regard all tactical weapons as potentially useful. Regardless of the influences that put them in this position, however, these leaders in the middle provide both formal and informal links between the conservative and protest leaders.

The situation in Atlanta does not seem to have been unique. Something of this same kind of unanticipated cooperation and sharing of functions between protest and conservative Negro leaders seems to have taken place during the sit-in controversy in Knoxville, Tennessee. Negotiation began initially there without any demonstrations, but broke down after four tedious months of talks. Sit-ins began on June 9, 1960, and a boycott was started five days later on June 14. Merrill Proudfoot describes a meeting of the executive committee of the protest movement which took place on July 2, 1960, after about three weeks of demonstrations. The meeting was attended by the president of Knoxville College, who had not been involved in planning or staging the

demonstrations, and he revealed that he had been contacted by an official of the Knoxville Chamber of Commerce who informed him that there was a movement underway to reopen negotiations. Proudfoot rather indignantly comments:

The circuitous means of communicating with one another has lent a comic-opera aspect to the way this major community problem has been handled. It would seem sensible for one of the merchants to have called Crutcher or James [the leaders of the demonstrations] and said, "Come on down and let's talk!" Instead the merchants hint to the Chamber of Commerce official that they might be willing; he contacts not Crutcher or James, but Colston—the one person in the Negro community who has the greatest status . . . and he in turn makes the contact within the Negro community.[10]

Also when a negotiating team was formed to formulate the final agreement to desegregrate, Colston was included once again, but this time he was accompanied by Crutcher. Although the description is not so complete it seems that a similar process operated at Winston-Salem, North Carolina, where the agreement to desegregate the lunch counters was not formulated by the protest leaders. Clarence H. Patrick reports that:

The demonstrators several times sought unsuccessfully for someone to organize and mediate a meeting between them and the store managers in an attempt to resolve the antisegregation movement on the basis of some mutual agreement. The leaders of the protest never met, as a group, with the managers of the stores where the protests occurred.[11]

[10] Merrill Proudfoot, *Diary of a Sit-in,* Chapel Hill: University of North Carolina Press, 1962, pp. 111–112.

[11] Clarence H. Patrick, *Lunch Counter Desegregation in Winston-Salem, North Carolina* (Pamphlet Distributed by the Southern Regional Council, 1960), p. 7.

CONCLUSION

The evidence presented here suggests that not all southern Negro communities have experienced the same changes in leadership that Killian and Smith detected in Tallahassee. In some cases it seems that a kind of tactical balance exists with both conservative and protest leaders playing a part in the fight for equality. However, there is no evidence that the period of change and transition in Negro leadership in Atlanta has ended. In fact, a major unsettling force seems to be developing beneath the level of leadership. Almost all the leaders interviewed, including the conservatives, felt that expectations are rising perceptibly throughout the Negro community as a result of recent successful attacks on the institutions of segregation. The Negro masses, who have traditionally been apathetic toward politics and efforts to fight segregation, seem to be gaining hope that change is possible and are shaking off the mood of cynical resignation that has paralyzed them in the past.

Looking forward, these circumstances suggest a prediction that the drive to break down racial barriers will not stall once a few victories are won, but will continue and intensify in the foreseeable future. However, there are some uncertain features of this development. First of all, it is unclear whether the conservatives, who were once the dominant leaders within the Negro community, are being completely supplanted by the protest leaders, or whether in the future there will continue to be a mixture of conservative and protest elements in Atlanta's Negro leadership. It is uncertain, because of increasing demands for equality from the masses, whether the aging conservative group will be replaced with leaders of similar stature and influence within the Negro community. If this does not occur, the present tactical balance within the Negro community will be altered in favor of the militants.

The full impact of such a change in Negro leadership on race relations in the city would depend in large measure on the reactions of the whites. Several local observers, when asked to comment on this prospect, emphasized that a new, younger, and more liberal group of white leaders is emerging in the city to replace the older, more conservative whites. There is also a widely held impression in Atlanta that the majority of the white population has accepted, or at least is resigned to, the end of segregation. These observers saw a prospect of diminishing resistance from the whites, faster integration, and improving race relations as the younger leaders of both races take control.

The accuracy of this prediction depends, to a large extent, upon the nature of the issues that face the community in the future, and upon the pliability of the whites as the Negroes begin agressively attacking segregation in such potentially explosive areas as housing and employment. It also seems likely that in the future the Negro community may become more united behind the protest leaders, but this may not automatically result in an increased effectiveness in gaining their ends. This study brings into question the assumption commonly made that a weak minority within the society must maintain unity and solidarity if it is to be effective in gaining its objectives.

It seems clear that the Atlanta Negro community became more effective in breaking down the barriers of segregation after the militant, protest leaders came on the scene, even though their arrival caused considerable bickering and disunity among Negro leaders in the city. However, the protest leaders' outspoken desire to destroy the institutions of segregation, their habit of treating all issues in moral terms, and their willingness to employ force in the form of economic boycotts to gain their objectives alienated them from the dominant white leadership. The conservative leaders were much more acceptable to the whites because they tended to concentrate primarily on improving the economic welfare of the Negro without demanding an immediate end to segregation. The conservative Negro leaders' primary interest in maintaining the institutions within the Negro community along with their antipathy for the protest leaders and their obvious disapproval of boycotts and demonstrations made them seem "responsible" in the eyes of the whites, and thus acceptable as bargaining agents. Therefore, it would seem that a Negro community in a southern city is likely to be more effective in eliminating the institutions of segregation if it has both conservative and protest elements within its leadership. Without the protest leaders it will lack the capacity to precipitate tension through the use of boycotts, demonstrations, and other direct action techniques. And without the conservative leaders it is in danger of losing contact with the dominant white leaders and being unable to negotiate a peaceful, compromise solution to a racial crisis. Seen in this light, there seems to be a part to play in the Negro's fight for equality for both the more accommodating, conservative leaders and the liberal, protest leaders. As long as a broad agreement exists on the ultimate goals of equality and an end to racial discrimination, some disunity over the proper methods of social action may be positively desirable.

45
Intraminority Violence: US and the Panthers at UCLA*
R. ROGERS

In the black liberation movement, where relationships and alliances change from issue to issue, militant advocates of the seizure of power have literally fought and killed one another for control. Ideological imperatives may be claimed, but behind these is the fact that whoever controls this movement will participate in the direction of millions of dollars worth of black programs that are now being situated on college campuses everywhere in the country. And anyone, or any black nationalist organization for that matter, threatening to expose or interfere with this power move may expect to suffer dire consequences.

At UCLA, two of California's most militant factions—the Black Panther Party and Maulana Ron Karenga's US organization—were brought together in the choosing of a director for the school's newly founded Afro-American Studies Center. The leaders of the Black Students Union (BSU) had hoped that their presence would help "keep the school's administration honest." However, everyone overlooked one potential source of trouble: the Panthers and US have been archenemies for a long time. While the Panthers [stress their role as] black revolutionaries, US, a tightly knit cultural nationalist organization, has demonstrated an ability to overwhelm if not usurp other black nationalist organizations. And as a result, Panthers John Jerome Huggins and Alprentice (Bunchy) Carter were shot to death by members of US.

During the weeks before the shooting, a good deal of anxiety had built up

*[Reprinted with permission from *The Nation*, May 5, 1969, Vol. 208, no. 18, pp. 558-560.]

because a number of other "students" were toting guns around campus. Consequently, some leaders in the BSU thought it would be wise to invite a black "coalition" on campus to tranquilize the situation. This coalition consisted of local community leaders, in addition to a member of the UCLA faculty and Karenga himself. Some of the members were not completely awake to the urgent need for this coalition, and participated lethargically.

Consequently, Karenga and the coalition's organizers more and more controlled the direction of the group. It was supposed to be acting in an advisory capacity, but when it stepped into the situation, the coalition brought its own candidate for the job of director, and insisted that he was so highly qualified that he must be paid $23,000, the salary of a full ᴬrofessor, and several thousand dollars moᴸ than the school had expected to pay. The administration was disposed to hire the coalition's nominee, but negotiations hung fire on the matter of salary, Chancellor Charles Young feeling that the man did not have the academic credentials to warrant the sum asked.

While these talks were going on, some factions became highly suspicious of the coalition's motives for insisting that their candidate should get the job. It was suggested that through him the coalition expected to control the millions of dollars that would be directed into the program.

Huggins and Carter were UCLA students, as well as Panthers, and immensely popular on campus. They were loud in their opposition to the coalition nominee, and many black students sided with them. They were opposed by a minority who were adamant supporters of US. At a meeting off-campus, Karenga is purported to have told the students that if the administration did not accept the coalition's candidate, they should "investigate" the possibilities of "disrupting the school."

Meek in the face of this hostility, the students maintained that they should have more time to study other candidates. On top of their other suspicions, they doubted that the man being pushed was sufficiently "community conscious" for the job. As late as the day of the shooting, January 17, the students were still hassling over the qualifications they expected the director to possess. On a Campbell Hall bulletin board they had outlined these qualifications: "Academic: political science; Ph.D. Emotional (soul): student interest, community commitment."

Later in the day, a meeting agreed on these qualifications, and after it the students were filing out, laughing and talking. Then without warning the gunfire broke out and Huggins and Carter fell dead. After secret, two-day Los Angeles County grand jury hearings, tightly guarded and designed to eliminate any possibility of retaliation against witnesses, five high-ranking members of US were indicted on charges of conspiracy and murder of the two Panthers. The conspiracy charge stems from testimony that the assassinations were planned well in advance. Of the five men named in the grand jury indictment, the police so far have been successful in arresting only two. George (Ali Sultani) Stiner, and his brother, Larry (Sakia) Stiner. Larry, according to the police, had a bullet wound in his right shoulder when he surrendered to the police three days after the shooting, and it is believed that Carter pulled a gun and fired just before he was hit.

The fear that swept the campus after the shooting still hangs in the air. One young woman who was outspoken against the intrusion of Karenga and the coalition has had to change her address. At first the shooting stalled efforts to establish the Afro-American Studies Center, at a time when similar programs for other minorities were well on their way to becoming part of the university's American Cultures Institute for Research and Community Action.

Since the UCLA assassinations there have been several more shootings, one of which was almost fatal to another Panther. It has been established that US was also behind these attacks. Police say that they are hindered in their attempts to stop the assaults by interference from Mayor Yorty's staff. On several occasions this interference has come on the heels of a "good arrest," the US member being out of jail shortly after he was booked. The Stiner brothers were booked late last year for a $4,000 Santa Ana armed robbery, felonious assault, and kidnap, but when the UCLA shooting occurred they were loose on $31,250 bail provided by a left-wing organization. On March 21, they were convicted of the Santa Ana charges and sentenced to from fifteen years to life.

If it is true that Yorty's office is solicitous of the welfare of US members, there are probably two reasons. Karenga is adamantly anticommunist, as is the mayor, and his organization, though not large (perhaps two hundred members), is tightly disciplined and capable of providing Yorty with a political wedge into the black community. Karenga was known as Ron Everett when he graduated cum laude from UCLA a few years ago. He flirted for a time with the Muslims while employed by the county as a welfare case worker (there are Muslim overtones to his demands upon his followers for self-sacrificing and unquestioning loyalty, and in some of the cultural aspirations of his creed). Shortly after the 1965 Watts riots, US and Karenga won national attention with a *Life* cover story.

Although the Panthers have achieved much notoriety as perhaps the best armed black nationalist organization in America, police say that US is as formidable. Karenga, however, claims to deplore violence.

Sometimes brothers get so hung up in the myth of revolution that they talk about bringing America to her knees, and they can't even wipe out one police station.

A lot of brothers play revolutionary: they read a little Fanon, a little Mao, and some Marx. Although this information is necessary, it is not sufficient, for we must develop a new play of revolution for black people here in America.

US members are divided into "tribes" and given Swahili names. They are instructed to live by the tenets of *The Quotable Karenga* (their leader has also read a little Mao) which directs them along a "Path of Blackness," an alternative to the standards of the white society. "The sevenfold path of blackness is think black, talk black, act black, create black, buy black, vote black, and live black."

(As for voting black, it was reported that during the weeks before the Los Angeles mayoral primary, Karenga was approached by a Yorty staff member and asked to support the mayor over Thomas Bradley, a black candidate. Karenga turned him down.)

The first serious clash with the Panthers occurred in 1967 on a Los Angeles street. Guns were drawn but the somewhat mysterious confrontation ended without a major incident. The second clash was no mystery; it came about over a difference of strategy. During the planning of a fund-raising rally for Huey P. Newton at the Los Angeles Sports Arena, the Panthers insisted that the police should not be allowed in the building, since this would be an affront to the major figures in the black liberation movement who would be present—

Stokely Carmichael, James Forman, and Rap Brown, as well as Reies Tijerina of the Federal Alliance of Land Grants movement. Eldridge Cleaver, minister of Panther information, asked Karenga to intercede with the police on behalf of the Panthers, but Karenga refused. This made Cleaver and the Panthers angry. Apparently, they had been under the impression that they could get anything they wanted from any organization in the movement.

The next evening some two hundred black people gathered in the basement of a Baptist church to hear Carmichael and Tijerina recite the plight of the black and brown peoples. While Carmichael, honorary prime minister of the Panthers, was speaking, Karenga and some of his followers entered the auditorium. The Panthers bristled. A Panther official approached the stage and whispered something in Carmichael's ear. The speaker tried to brush aside the interference, but the man persisted. He took Carmichael by the arm and gently pulled him off the stage. Later, it was learned that the Panthers had refused to allow the meeting to proceed while Karenga and his lieutenants were in the auditorium.

There is no discernible difference of ideology or goals between these two organizations; the "sevenfold path of blackness" can be walked as readily by a Panther as by one of Karenga's tribesmen. . . . They are testing each other to see which shall seize the power, and they have the guns with which to make the tests terribly rigorous. As of now, neither the Panthers nor US (nor for that matter any other organization) has come up with satisfactory answers to all the existing problems. And until they settle the pecking order among themselves, they are not apt to provide them. Karenga, an articulate and eloquent man, says that black people must banish the white frame of reference from their minds because it excludes the concept of blackness. But that, clearly, is too simple a prescription for the social and political complexities of black liberation.

46
White Militancy*
JEROME SKOLNICK

The idea of "militancy" suggests the activities of blacks, students, antiwar demonstrators, and others who feel themselves aggrieved by the perpetuation of old, outworn, or milignant social institutions. The historical record, however, indicates that considerably more disorder and violence have come from groups whose aim has been the preservation of an existing or remembered order of social arrangements, and in whose ideology the concept of "law and order" has played a primary role. There is no adequate term to cover all of the diverse groups who have fought to preserve their neighborhoods, communities, or their country from forces considered alien or threatening. The lack of a common term for Ku Klux Klansmen, Vigilantes, Minutemen, Know-Nothing activists, and anti-Negro or anti-Catholic mobs reflects the fact that these and other similar groups have different origins, different goals, and different compositions, and arise in response to specific historical situations which repeat themselves, if at all, only in gross outline.

Still, certain patterns stand out in the history of white militancy. In the past, the white militant was usually—though not always—an Anglo-Saxon Protestant, and the targets of his protest included other white ethnic groups. Today, while the WASP remains a

*[Reprinted from *Politics of Protest*, pp. 210–211, 214–224 by permission of Simon and Schuster. This paper is informed by the work of David Chalmers.]

major figure in the overall picture of white militancy, much of the white protest, especially in the urban North, comes from ethnic groups—especially Southern and Eastern European—which were themselves former targets of nativist agitation. Another change is more subtle. Until recently, the violent white militant acted, very frequently, with the assistance, encouragement, or at least acquiescence of more "stable" elements of the population, and quite often in concert with the militant and nativist aims of the American political and legal order. Today this is considerably less true. With the exception of some areas of the country—notably parts of the South—the violent white militant has become a minority, and operates beyond the pale of the law and the polity, both of which he tends to distrust in proportion to his lack of political efficacy or influence. . . .

A combination of public and private action has characterized the expression of white militancy in the South, where the Ku Klux Klan has intermittently arisen in the context of a social order which has given official and widespread approval to the exploitation and subordination of the black population. The Klan arose in the aftermath of the Civil War, when emancipation, the fourteenth amendment, and the ravages of the war itself had disrupted the traditional caste order and weakened, to some extent, the effectiveness of the black subordination. To many white southerners, the limited gains of the southern blacks represented a state of fearful disorder. Woodward has described this atmosphere and the early legislation aimed at reestablishing social control along caste lines:

The temporary anarchy that followed the collapse of the old discipline produced a state of mind bordering on hysteria among southern white people. The first year a great

fear of black insurrection and revenge seized many minds, and for a longer time the conviction prevailed that Negroes could not be induced to work without compulsion. Large numbers of temporarily uprooted freedmen roamed the highways, congested in towns and cities, or joined the federal militia. In the presence of these conditions the provisional legislature established by President Johnson in 1865 adopted the notorious Black Codes. Some of them were intended to establish systems of peonage or apprenticeship resembling slavery.[1]

After the Black Codes were struck down, the Klan emerged to drive the freedmen out of politics and restore power and control to the dominant white leadership. The nightriding assaults on blacks, northerners, and their southern sympathizers were justified as "the necessary effort to prevent crime and uphold law and order."[2] The first Imperial Wizard of the Klan, General Nathan B. Forrest, explained the need for the Klan in these terms:

Many northern men were coming down there, forming leagues all over the country. The Negroes were holding night meetings; were going about; were becoming very insolent; and the Southern people . . . were very much alarmed . . . parties organized themselves so as to be ready in case they were attacked. Ladies were ravished by some of these Negroes. . . . There was a great deal of insecurity.[3]

While Klan leadership was often held by men of substance, the rank-and-file Klansman was most often a poor white fearful of black economic competition. Klan violence, like western vigilantism, more often than not received support from significant segments of the dominant population.

Acts of violence were usually applauded by the conservative press and justified then, and afterwards, by the always allegedly bad reputation of the victims.[4]

The typical weapon of the Reconstruction Klan and subsequent white terrorists was lynching. The Tuskegee Institute has kept a record of lynchings in the United States since 1882 which gives an indication of the extent of white violence and serves as a reminder that the white militant has been the single most violent force—outside of war—in American history. For the period 1882–1959, Tuskegee has recorded a total of 4,735 lynchings, of which 73 percent were of Negroes and 85 percent of which took place in the southern and border states.[5]

Again, it should be stressed that terrorist violence was only the leading edge of southern anti-Negro militancy, which, in an important sense, was itself only the most blatant element of an endemic national racism and nativism. The revived Ku Klux Klan of the 1920's, which mixed anti-Negro, anti-Semitic, and anti-Catholic agitation, spread throughout the country and rose to a membership of several million. It was deeply entwined with several local and state governments.

Klan violence in California was as brutal as anywhere in the South, and in the town of Taft, in Kern County, the police and best citizens turned out to watch an evening of torture in the local ball park. When an anti-Klan candidate won the Republican primary in Oregon, the Klan jumped to the Democratic party and helped capture the governorship and enough of the legislature to outlaw all parochial schools. In Colorado, the Klan, with business support, elected two U.S. Senators and swept the state. When the Grand Dragon, a Denver doctor, was accused of having forced a high-school boy into marriage by threatening him with castration, the governor appointed the Klan leader aide-de-camp, as a show of confidence.[6]

In part, the rise of the later Klan was influenced by D. W. Griffith's racist epic, *Birth of a Nation,* which portrayed the early Klan as a romantic defender of southern white womanhood against the ravages of the freed blacks. Such nostalgia was not confined to the poor, the uneducated, and the parochial. Woodrow Wilson, on seeing the picture, was reported to have been much impressed: "'It is like writing history with lightning,' he said, 'and my only regret is that it is all so terribly true.'"[7]

In addition to the resurgence of the Ku Klux Klan, the era during and after World War I saw an eruption of vigilante activity against numerous groups, often backed by constituted authority or the highly placed. During a wave of agitation against German–Americans during the war, Theodore Roosevelt advocated shooting or hanging any German–American who proved to be disloyal.[8] A private organization called the American Protective League, operating as a kind of quasi-official adjunct to the Department of Justice, engaged in various acts of physical force against German–Americans, unionists, and draft evaders.[9] Vigilante violence against IWW organizers in the Pacific Northwest took place in the context of a judicial system explicitly hostile to unions and largely controlled by business interests.[10] In some of the postwar race riots, like that in Washington in 1919, police and the military joined with other militant whites in assaults on the Negro community.[11] Where nativist violence was not officially sanctioned, whole communities sometimes rose up against "alien" elements:

During the night of August 5, 1920, and all through the following day hundreds of people laden with clothing and household goods filled the roads leading out of West Frankfort, a mining town in southern Illinois. Back in town their homes were burning. Mobs bent on driving every foreigner from the area surged through the streets. For-

eigners of all descriptions were beaten on sight, although the Italian population was the chief objective. Time and again the crowds burst into the Italian district, dragged cowering residents from their homes, clubbed and stoned them, and set fire to their dwellings. The havoc went on for three days, although five hundred state troops were rushed to the scene.[12]

The militant violence of white vigilantes, then, has not operated as a peripheral phenomenon in isolation from the major currents of American history. Rather, vigilantism represented the armed and violent wing of national tendencies toward racism, nativism, and strident Americanism which have been present since the nation's beginnings. With sporadic acceptance by dominant, largely Anglo-Saxon and Protestant population in substantial control of much of the American political, military, and legal apparatus, private violence was a significant factor in thwarting the democratic aspirations of minorities. Today, the violent or potentially violent white militant tends to speak from a position of relative political impotence, and his militancy must be seen as in large part a protest against that impotence and the insecurity which accompanies it. Nevertheless, in some instances, the militant white receives at least qualified support from—and sometimes achieves influence in—local or regional political structures. In other instances, white militants have adopted American political rhetoric and used it to structure the expression of their own discontents. On the other hand, national politics has seemingly adopted some of the rhetoric of white militancy. In all instances, the fabric of American social and political institutions has created the context in which contemporary white militancy flourishes. All of these phenomena are evident in the contemporary South.

THE SOUTH

The advancement of the nigra can be solely attributed to the sincerity of the southerner. [Robert Shelton]

In 1928, a leading historian characterized the South as "a people with a common resolve indomitably maintained—that it shall be and remain a white man's country."[13] Despite a number of social and economic changes, on balance the South remains distinct in the degree to which it remains commited to the preservation of the "white man's country," and in many areas of the South official politics and private violence interact to make the South the great regional fortress of white racism.

The flourishing white violence in the South must be seen against the background of major social and economic changes which have produced in many areas of the region a dispossessed and insecure class of marginal whites. Increasing industrialization has shifted the center of influence to a rising middle class, frequently Republican and increasingly affluent. At the same time, industrialization has effectively begun to undermine the caste order in the economic realm, a process noted by students of the South some years ago.[14] Jobs formerly "white" have been entered by Negroes, especially in the burgeoning area of the southern economy composed of industries working in part on government contracts.[15] At the same time that caste controls over black economic competition are crumbling under the impact of economic rationalization, a pervasive economic insecurity exists throughout much of the still essentially underdeveloped region. Coupled with a decreasing effectiveness of white sanctions over black social and political behavior—resulting partly from urbanization and industrialization and partly from civil rights activity—these events have accentuated a traditional sense of power-lessness and insecurity on the part of those marginal whites who historically have owned little else than their white skin and controlled little more than the local behavior of blacks.

The plight of the marginal white reflects a more general marginality and primitivism characteristic of large areas of the entire region. Culturally, parts of the South remain shot through with a strident fundamentalism and distrust of everything foreign; politically, parts of it remain dominated by self-serving cliques whose power rests primarily on the traditional political exclusion of blacks; its economic stagnation in many areas combines with its politics to pro-duce in several places a depressingly high rate of malnutrition, infant mor-tality, and disease. These conditions affect both poor black and poor white. It is in this context that white terrorists, abetted in some areas by an affluently racist middle class and a political and legal order committed to the mainte-nance of caste domination, have per-petrated repeated violence against blacks, civil rights workers, and others.

It should be stressed that in the South it is particularly difficult to sepa-rate the phenomena of official and pri-vate violence. Southern police have traditionally condoned private violence in many areas. In other areas, white vigilante groups have drawn consider-able membership from police forces.

Much of the militant white violence in the South has come from organiza-tions such as the several Ku Klux Klans and the National States Rights Party, although considerable violence has been done by apparently unaffiliated whites, such as the Florida group who recently kidnapped a young black who was "beaten to an unrecognizable pulp" with a machete on the mistaken belief that he had had sexual relations with a white girl.[16] There is some evidence that the various militant white organiza-tions differ in the degree to which they have espoused or participated in violent action.

The National States Rights Party, with headquarters in Birmingham and a membership in several nonsouthern states, is like the Klan, anti-Semitic as well as anti-Negro. It is an outgrowth of an earlier guerrilla group in Georgia called the Columbians, which in the late 1940's organized an armed plot to over-throw the Georgia state government. Though small, the NSRP has been ex-tremely active in southern racial vio-lence.[17]

The largest of the Klan organiza-tions, the United Klans of America, headed by Robert Shelton of Tusca-loosa, Alabama, has striven for a re-spectable image, and Shelton has re-portedly discouraged the use of violence by members. Nevertheless, Klan ideol-ogy and organizational structure are neither oriented toward nor capable of control over the activities of local groups and individuals. The murders of Lemuel Penn in Georgia and of Mrs. Vi-ola Liuzzo in Alabama were the by-product of relatively disorganized patroling efforts by such local units. Further, even the "official" advocacy of nonviolence is qualified in view of the Klan's conception of the imminent danger which black gains pose to south-ern order. "We don't want no violence," Shelton has said, "but we ain't gonna let the niggers spit in our face, either."[18]

The unaffiliated Mississippi White Knights of the Ku Klux Klan has been the source of much of the violence against civil rights workers in the state. The group arose during, and in response to, the intensive civil rights activity in Mississippi, after a long period in which Klan activity in the state had been dor-mant. Thirty-six White Knights have recently been arrested on charges of terrorism, including suspicion of at least seven murders. Much of this terrorist activity took place during the "long hot summer" of 1964. The group has been held responsible for the killing of three civil rights workers in Neshoba County, Mississippi, during that summer; and its leader, Sam Bowers, along with Neshoba Deputy Sheriff Cecil Price, is now appealing federal conviction. The involvement of the Neshoba Sheriff's Department in the murders indicates the degree to which the Mississippi Klan has drawn membership and support from law enforcement. No state charges were ever brought against the Neshoba group.

The Mississippi White Knights have remained in the forefront of white violence. In 1966, the head of the Hattiesburg chapter of the NAACP was killed in a shooting and firebombing attack on his home by carloads of White Knights. In 1967, the head of the NAACP's Natchez chapter was blown to bits when a bomb was planted in his car. The White Knights are suspected of burning some seventy-five churches, a fact which contrasts peculiarly with the group's justification of violence in terms of Christian duty:

As Christians we are disposed to kindness, generosity, affection, and humility in our dealings with others. As militants, we are disposed to the use of physical force against our enemies. How can we reconcile these two apparently contradictory philosophies, and at the same time, make sure that we do not violate the divine law by our actions, which may be held against us when we face that last court on the Day of Judgement? The answer, of course, is to purge malice, bitterness, and vengeance from our hearts. To pray each day for Divine Guidance, that our feet shall remain on the Correct Path, and that all of our acts be God's will working through our humble selves here on earth.[19]

The White Knights have stressed that the major source of their effectiveness is favorable public opinion. "As long as they are on our side," Bowers has written, "we can just about do anything to our enemies with impunity."[20] As a general rule, Klan success throughout the South has come primarily in those areas where state and local leaders and police have been most militant in resisting civil rights activity. In the Klan's center of strength in Alabama, a square in the center of the state including Tuscaloosa, Birmingham, Anniston, and Montgomery, the tacit encouragement of police and political leaders has significantly abetted Klan violence.

When it came down to bombings and beatings, the Negroes of Birmingham claimed, it was sometimes difficult to distinguish between the Klansmen and the deputies. Also within the Klan's charmed geographical quadrilateral was the governor's mansion in Montgomery where Alabama governors John Patterson and George Wallace refrained from giving the impression that prosegregation violence was completely distasteful.[21]

Local and state juries and courts have acquired an impressive record of failing to indict or convict in crimes against civil rights workers. For that matter, the federal government was not overly quick to step in against white violence until the summer of 1964.[22] There are signs, however, that the attitude of many elements of the South is in transition. New civil rights laws, Supreme Court decisions, and increased FBI surveillance have combined with local resistance to Klan violence. The convictions brought by an all-white federal jury in the Neshoba case are one such indication; another is the increasing pressure by Mississippi police against the terrorist activity of the White Knights of the Ku Klux Klan.[23]

The Klan and other militant white groups, both organized and ad hoc, have operated as the "dirty workers" of a system of caste domination. In an important sense, southern racism has successfully channeled the political protest of the marginal white into expressions which support the existing political and social arrangements of the South. In the process, the actual sources of the grievances of the marginal white have gone uncorrected. Klan violence represents the thwarted and displaced political protest of whites acting from a context of economic insecurity, threatened manhood, and inability to influence local and national political structures.

A study of Klan membership in the late 1950's described it as largely composed of marginal white collar, small business, and skilled workers occupying an intermediate position between clear-cut blue collar and clear-cut white collar positions.[24] An assessment of present Klan membership would not show much change. Among the recent leadership of various state and national Klan organizations are numbered a truck driver, a crane operator, a barber, a former rubber plant worker and later salesman, a former bricklayer and lightning-rod salesman, a machinist, a paint sprayer, and several evangelical ministers, among others. The seven Klansmen convicted in the Neshoba County slayings included three truck drivers, one trailer salesman, a chemical plant worker, a deputy sheriff, and a vending-machine distributor. In contrast to the middle and upper middle class membership of the vigorously racist Citizens' Councils of the Black Belt South,[25] the typical rank-and-file Klansman is subject to the vicissitudes of southern economic insecurity and to a large degree excluded from the benefits of industrialization accruing to the new middle class.

In addition to economic insecurity and marginality, the grievances of the rank-and-file Klansman include a strong sense of diminished manhood. The rhetoric of southern white militancy, like that of black militants, is suffused with a sense of the decline of male effectiveness and the restorative functions of militant action: "Step out from behind the petticoat and be a man."[26]

Klan rhetoric reflects the strong sense of distributive injustice common to the marginal southern white. Klansmen have criticized the extent of federal antipoverty funds given to blacks in the face of white poverty, and complain that riots have brought blacks federal largesse while the law-abiding poor white must work and receives no federal attention. "Health, education, and welfare is nigger health, nigger education, and nigger welfare; they have done nothing about yours."[27] The Grand Dragon of the North Carolina Klan has complained that "the only contact with the federal government is the FBI bug" and that the government has never approached him to discuss constructive measures for poor whites.[28] Another Klan complaint has been that those whites who advocate integration are those who are able to afford to send their children to private schools, thus shifting the burden of accommodation to the poor white.[29]

The racist thrust of southern white protest has largely obscured the syndrome of genuine grievances which have indeed been largely ignored, on both local and federal levels. For some areas of the South, it may be the case that, as one critic has suggested, "The establishment fears war between the races less than an alliance between them."[30] In any case, under present political conditions in many areas, the channeling of the marginal white protest into anti-Negro directions serves to buttress a system of political and economic stagnation in which the poor of both races lose. Whether this condition can be altered is largely dependent on the sensitivity of efforts to deal with the grievances of the poor white. For the moment, the white protest remains at the level of a crude racism, well-expressed in one of the Klan's recordings:

You have to be black to get a welfare check
and I'm broke
No joke
I ain't got a nickel for a coke
I ain't black you see
so Uncle Sam won't help poor nigger-hating
me.[31]

FOOTNOTES

[1] C. Vann Woodward, *The Strange Career of Jim Crow* (New York: Galaxy Oxford University Press, 1966), p. 23.

[2] David M. Chalmers, *Hooded Americanism* (Chicago: Quadrangle Paperbacks, 1968), p. 20.

[3] Quoted in Chalmers, pp. 20–21.

[4] Chalmers, *op. cit.,* p. 18.

[5] United States Civil Rights Commission Report, *Justice* (Washington, D.C.: U.S. Government Printing Office, 1961), pp. 266–268.

[6] Chalmers, *op. cit.,* p. 3.

[7] Quoted in Chalmers, *op. cit.,* p. 27.

[8] John Higham, *Strangers in the Land* (New York: Atheneum, 1963), p. 104.

[9] Higham, *op. cit.,* p. 212.

[10] Patrick Renshaw, *The Wobblies* (Garden City, N.Y.: Doubleday, Anchor, 1967), pp. 163–167.

[11] Arthur I. Waskow, *From Race Riot to Sit-in* (Garden City, N.Y.: Doubleday, 1966), chap. 3.

[12] Higham, *op. cit.,* p. 264.

[13] U. B. Phillips, quoted in Woodward, *op. cit.,* p. 8.

[14] Allison Davis, "Caste, Economy, and Violence," *American Journal of Sociology,* II, No. 1 (1945), pp. 7–15.

[15] James W. Vander Zanden, *Race Relations in Transition* (New York: Random House, 1965), pp. 6–7.

[16] *Baltimore Sun,* September 18, 1968.

[17] California Department of Justice, *Paramilitary Organizations in California* (California: Report to the State Legislature, 1965).

[18] Quoted in Chalmers, *op. cit.,* p. 372.

[19] *Los Angeles Times,* quoting Bowers, July 29, 1968.

[20] *Los Angeles Times,* quoting Bowers, July 29, 1968.

[21] Chalmers, *op. cit.,* p. 373.

[22] See Chalmers, *op. cit.,* chap. 4.

[23] *Los Angeles Times,* July 29, 1968.

[24] Vander Zanden, *op. cit.,* p. 43.

[25] Vander Zanden, *op. cit.,* p. 26.

[26] Quoted in Peter Young, "Appendix to Consultant's Report," Task Force I, this commission, p. 6.

[27] Quoted in Young, *op. cit.,* p. 14.

[28] Quoted in Young, *op. cit.,* p. 20.

[29] Quoted in Young, *op. cit.,* p. 21.

[30] Quoted in Young, *op. cit.,* p. 32.

[31] Quoted in Young, *op. cit.,* p. 26.

47
Tony Imperiale Stands Vigilant for Lawandorder*
PAUL GOLDBERGER

It was a warm Sunday evening in May, and the crowd, jammed elbow-to-elbow in the tavern parking lot, was wildly enthusiastic. "Give 'em hell, Tony," an old man shouted. "Tell 'em where to go."

Tony began quietly. "I didn't see any flags in the city of Newark lowered to half mast when Governor Lurleen Wallace died," he said. "Why not, when they could do it for that Martin Luther Coon?" The audience cheered, and Tony gained momentum. "When is it gonna stop?" he cried. "Everybody says, 'Don't bother 'em now. Leave 'em alone, and they'll calm down.' Well, it took riots that burned down half of a town before we learned."

Tony is Anthony Imperiale—5 feet 6¾ inches, a tough-muscled 230 pounds, 39 years old. That evening in Nutley, N.J., five miles north of Newark, he was hailed as a savior by hundreds of white residents who are convinced that the Negro is taking away everything the white man has earned. Tony isn't going to give it up without a fight—and Tony is their man.

Imperiale is the organizer of Newark's North Ward Citizens' Committee, which claims a dues-paying membership of two hundred and thousands of enthusiastic followers. In their leader's view, they are "defenders of law and order," banded together in the wake of last summer's Newark riots to stand up to communist-inspired racial pressures. In the view of Governor Richard J. Hughes, they are "vigilantes."

They own guns and take karate training from Imperiale, a Black Belt in the art. Ten of their radio-equipped cars patrol the North Ward each weekday night (17 on weekends) to ward off criminals and/or invaders from the adjacent Central Ward, the black ghetto. Chapters in five suburban towns, including Nutley, mount their own patrols. Imperiale used to boast loudly that the committee owned a helicopter and an armored car, and he insisted that members on patrol wear fatigues—but he has of late soft-pedaled these matters.

Last month the windows fronting the committee's cinder-block headquarters on North Seventh Street were shattered by three explosions. No one was injured in the 1:20 A.M. bombing, but it was a close call. "If a guy hadn't talked me into taking another drink at a bar I was in," Imperiale says, "me and my wife Louise would have been sitting right where that plate-glass window was torn out." He has few doubts about who placed the dynamite, and he has doubled the night patrols. He has also expressed uncertainty about his ability to control committee members: "If this kind of thing happens again, I won't be responsible for what these people here will do."

Tony Imperiale is not alone in America 1968. In Detroit there is Donald Lobsinger, chairman of a six-year-old organization called Break-

through. His formula for security "Study, arm, store provisions, and organize." In Warren, Michigan, druggist Ronald Portnoy leads a group known as Fight Back. Its literature proclaims: "The only way to stop them is at the city limits." In Oakland, California, the leader of the Home Defense Association is Herbert Clark. It has published a manual recommending firearms and ammunition and containing chapters on "Defense of an Individual House" and "Neighborhood Perimeter Defense."

Not many of these men, however, have built up the support or strength of Newark's Imperiale; in fact, there is often an element of bosh about the private vigilance business. Ernest Bradow, for example, a 26-year-old member of the John Birch Society who lives in North Bergen, N.J., created something of a stir in July when he claimed that his group, People's Rights Enforced Against Riots and Murder, had 319 members patroling eleven towns. Bergen County Prosecutor Guy W. Calissi ordered an investigation that turned up only one member of PRE-ARM. His name was Ernest Bradow.

Imperiale is of another stripe. Last month he sought election to a council that will oversee administration of the federal model cities program in Newark. There were four posts open in each of thirteen districts—248 candidates for 52 seats. Imperiale not only won in his district but polled more votes than any other candidate in the city. He called his victory "an affirmation of the people's desire for law and order." Now he is running for the city council, and his eye is on the office now occupied by Mayor Hugh J. Addonizio.

The Imperiale platform is basically the same cry for law and order that sets crowds cheering wherever he speaks. Some of the planks:

"The American people are very gullible. They let the politicians yield to the racial. And the Communists take the radical and exploit him. . . . In the riots, billions of dollars of property was destroyed, and the Constitution of the United States was thrown into the gutter. When is Washington gonna put down their foot and say, 'Look, law and order must prevail'?"

"We look at the policemen—they've been abused, they've been harassed, they've been rubbed under the nose with anything that these radicals wanted to do, and they got away with it. Because the quislings, the politicians with no guts, were selling the decent people out. . . . The first thing I'm gonna do is take politics out of the Police Department. . . . And I intend to fight any group who tries to tie the hands of the police by shouting 'police brutality' or this or that. I'm gonna fight you, tooth and nail."

"They oughta register Communists, not guns."

"Are there no poor whites? But the Negroes get all the antipoverty money. When pools are being built in the Central Ward, don't they think the white kids have got frustration? The whites are the majority. You know how many of them come to me, night after night, because they can't get a job? They've been told, 'We have to hire Negroes first.'"

"The church has no right getting into this (ghetto educational and recreational programs sponsored by Catholic parishes). They just take an interest because they think there's a threat of whites no longer coming to church. . . . Churches shouldn't get tax exemptions. When they begin to get involved in private enterprise, they should be taxed, and taxed to hell."

In the view of Imperiale's constituency, he tells it like it is. The large majority of the ward's 43,000 residents are Italian–American, though there has been something of an influx of Negroes since the 1960 census, when the proportion of Negroes was 17.6 percent.

White Protestants have been leaving the area, the Roman Catholic population has increased and some Negro congregations have taken over property formerly owned by white Protestant churches.

It is a shabby neighborhood, once firmly middle class, now in the grip of a slow but insistent deterioration. The percentage of owner-occupied homes has dipped. Many single-family homes have been converted to multiple-occupancy dwellings. There is a crowded, ticky-tacky feeling about it all.

Perhaps the most unhappy facet of the North Ward, however, is a pervasive —and in many ways valid—mental set. The people sense that their backs are to the wall, that conditions are worsening, and no help is on the way. There are state and federal funds being poured into Newark, but they are being spent elsewhere; for bad as the ward's problems may be, they don't compare to the problems of the city's black ghettos.

More than half of Newark's 400,000 residents are Negroes. A third of the city's housing is substandard; unemployment in black areas such as the Central Ward is officially set at 12 percent, unofficially as high as 20 percent; there are 17,000 households "living" on incomes of less than $3,000 a year. Newark leads all cities of the nation of its size in crime and venereal disease and maternal mortality rates.

When the city celebrated its tricentennial in 1966, it adopted the slogan, "Pride in Newark." But the statistics above don't lend themselves to being pointed to with pride; Tony Imperiale and his followers point to them with fear and anger, and the presence of black faces in their North Ward is a constant reminder that "it could happen here."

It is not, Imperiale insists, that he and the members of the committee are racists. He tells of inviting a Negro neighbor and his family over for a meal.

When a Negro woman died in his neighborhood this summer, he took in her 7-year-old boy for several days; the boy still spends as much time with the Imperiales as with his own family, Imperiale says.

But Imperiale is quick to defend whites who attack Negroes entering the ward ("The colored just come looking for trouble"), and he is convinced that the Negro is incapable of dignified living ("Look at this," he says, pointing to a 15-year-old photograph of a North Ward neighborhood. "And look at it now, with garbage on the streets." A committee member adds, "They don't know how to live here; they have no pride." Later, a tour of the neighborhood turns up only a few signs of deterioration. "The garbage man must have just been here," the committee member quickly explains.)

Imperiale and his wife, Louise, live in a small, two-story house on an integrated block not far from committee headquarters. They have four sons, ranging in age from eleven to three, and another child is on the way. The neighborhood, like the house, is short of space, and Imperiale's radio-equipped 1959 Cadillac is often double-parked. He shows visitors through the house with pride, pointing out the prefabricated wood paneling he installed himself. He is proud of his gun collection, too, which fills most of the dining room. Some of the more up-to-date models are kept loaded. He is likely to speak with visitors at the dining room table, fiddling with a toy machine gun as he talks.

The son of Italian immigrant parents, he has lived virtually all his life in the North Ward. He joined the National Guard at the age of sixteen, two years later entered the Marines, where he had two tattoos stitched in his arms. One is made up of a pair of lovebirds with an inscription that reads "Louise

and Tony"; the other, labeled "Death Before Dishonor," is a dagger piercing a heart. (His taste for personal adornment has continued—he uses Man-Tan and wears a toupee.)

Imperiale served four years with the Marines, has since done private detective work as well as operating the Imperiale Association of Judo and Karate and the Tomar Construction Corporation, a patio-building firm (both situated in the committee headquarters). He wanted to become a policeman, but he claims that he was rejected because of his height. (He is too short by a quarter of an inch.)

There are charges that Imperiale has been or is a member of the New Jersey Ku Klux Klan. John Behringer, the state's Grand Dragon and a former police officer, claims he inducted Imperiale at a ceremony in West Caldwell in April 1967. Behringer elaborates: "I had my red robe and my mask on." Robert Kohler, director of the Newark office of the Anti-Defamation League, is inclined to believe the charge on the basis of his investigations: "On the face of the evidence, either Mr. Imperiale or Mr. Behringer is lying. I see no reason why Mr. Behringer should lie in this case."

Imperiale hotly denies any Klan connection; that, it would seem, is going too far. But, though he says he is not a member of the John Birch Society, he "wouldn't be ashamed to be one." There are many Birchers in his committee. Imperiale voted for Barry Goldwater in 1964, but now considers the Arizona Republican "too wishy-washy." His choice for 1968 is George Wallace. "I think he's the answer to a lot of problems," Imperiale says, problems he feels might also be solved by "about forty more Joe McCarthys."

In his determination to stand in for Joe in Newark, Imperiale has made a conscious effort to improve his vocabulary and life style—so that he can better deal with the world outside the North Ward. Thus, when an aide automatically sought to prevent a *New York Times* reporter from seeing Imperiale because the paper is "a little too far left for us," Imperiale intervened and arranged the interview. His new political career is part of a program to prove that he is a responsible person, that he wishes to operate within the establishment. ("A Negro lady came to see me just the other day and told me I'm going to get Negro votes. You see, there are conservative and moderate Negroes who want law and order just like us.") The image change is slow in coming, though, and the Imperiale language and syntax still have a way to go.

Any uneasiness Imperiale may reveal in his forays into the outer world vanishes when he makes the rounds of his own small world of the North Ward. His natural life style blossoms, as it did one warm, humid evening recently during a committee patrol.

Patrols start at headquarters, a one-story building that contains a small office with radio equipment and several telephones. Behind the office is a multipurpose room, once the karate school gymnasium, the walls of which are painted bright orange. A bulletin board is posted with clippings—pro and con—about the organization. Judo posters line one wall, and literature published by black militants is displayed on another. Street maps abound. A sign beside the door reads: "No profanity. Fine 25 cents."

The office is usually staffed by neighborhood housewives while their husbands patrol the streets and their young children play hide-and-go-seek around the building. They are, respectively, members of the North Ward Women's Auxiliary and the North Ward Junior Auxiliary. The most singular artifact in the office is a telephone directly connected to LeRoi Jones's Spirit House in the Central Ward.

This is Newark's famous "hot line," suggested by Police Director Dominick A. Spina, that is used in the event of threatening racial violence to link Imperiale and Jones—the Black Belt and the black nationalist leader and poet. The two men are on first-name terms. "I don't say I love LeRoi," says Imperiale, "but I respect him. I would meet with the devil himself to hear what he had to say." Jones says, "At least Tony Imperiale is an authentic spokesman for his people."

The hot line has been used several times to head off trouble when rumors of impending race war have filled the North and Central Wards. "There was an incident one night," Imperiale recalls, "when we were supposed to have done something. The hot line rings. It's Kamil Wadu [Jones's Chief of Security]. Immediately through our radios we dispatch one of our cars, check it out, and find it's a fallacy. In the meantime Kamil's people are in the area, checking out the same thing. We dispel the rumor together, before all our people take to the street and start something."

Most of the members of the patrol are young, and the cars they drive tend to be old. As dusk falls, the street in front of headquarters comes alive with the roar of faulty mufflers and the impatient engine revving of youth craving excitement. They wear black construction hats decorated with the committee's initials, NWCC, embossed in white. They talk together with a kind of false bravado.

Imperiale gives the word, and the four-man patrols move out. They follow carefully planned routes, studying the scene, looking for signs of trouble. At first, the police used to stop the cars to search them for weapons, and some such searches still occur. "They never find any guns," says Imperiale, "because we never carry any. It would be stupid." The patrol is intended to prevent conflict, he says, not start it.

For Imperiale, a patrol consists of driving from one corner gathering of white youths to another. Invariably he is recognized, and he knows most of the boys by their first names. "Hi ya, Angelo." "Waddaya doin', Stevie?" He urges them to stay cool, stay out of trouble. Older residents often spot his elderly black Cadillac. "Go get 'em, Tony," they shout. "They're out to get you." The bombing of committee headquarters is fresh in their minds.

Police calls, monitored at headquarters, are relayed to Imperiale over his car radio. If the call is for a location on his patrol route, he drives over; otherwise, he instructs the headquarters operator to dispatch a nearer car (the patrol assignments are charted on a large map of the city at headquarters).

The crackling of the radio provides a steady punctuation for conversation in the Imperiale Cadillac. He and his followers have absorbed the jargon of radio communications; it pervades their speech. And thus far everything has been 10-4 (OK) for the organization— since the patrols began, they have never been involved in a blameworthy incident. Actually, though the potential for excitement is most obviously there, the patrols tend to be boring.

Imperiale has time to relax and talk. He notes an unfamiliar Negro face in his ward: "See that guy over there? We don't know who he is, so we keep an eye on him for a while. We'll drive back here later and see if he's still around." (He wasn't.)

The car draws up to the rear of a pizza palace on Bloomfield Avenue; this is where the white youths of the ward hang out, a good spot to keep track of the action. Everybody knows Imperiale (they call him "Big T"),

and he seems to know everybody. He favors one boy with a characteristic playful cuff on the cheek (sometimes the cuffs are pretty hard, but no one seems to mind). "Are you OK? Did you keep the job I told you about?" To another he says, "Jerk, I saw you and those other bums hot-rodding. What did I tell you about that?" They crowd around him in obvious awe and affection, and when Imperiale singles out a boy for attention, the youth revels in the sensation.

At 11 P.M., back on patrol, a police report is relayed about a prowler at a nearby address. The car moves off to the site, within the speed limit. A look around—nothing—the patrol resumes.

Toward midnight, the tour of duty ends. Most of the patrol members drift back home, but a handful return to headquarters. There they sit around with Imperiale, talking things over, working out small improvements in their strategy and logistics. In an emergency, he says, the committee could have fifty patrols on the streets.

Because of such patrols and the other activities of the committee, Imperiale believes, an all-out race war in the city and suburbs can be avoided. "It doesn't necessarily have to come to that," he says. "We're showing the radical blacks that there's whites that will stand up. We're proving that it can be prevented."

This optimistic outlook is not shared, however, by all of Imperiale's followers. Tom Benecchi, the former coordinator of the committee's Nutley chapter who has withdrawn to form his own group and do his own thing, views his role mainly as that of delaying race war, not preventing it. "It's bound to come," he says. "Some crazy colored bastard, a Negro militant, will start shooting at whites, and then some crazy white bastard will start shooting back. But maybe when they see five hundred of us with guns, maybe then they'll think twice about coming into our town."

Imperiale's May speaking engagement in Nutley illustrated his empathy with the up-tight suburban minority. It is a town of 30,000 with a goodly number of WASP commuters, though the largest ethnic grouping is Italian. The meeting was publicized by means of handbills distributed on Nutley's streets by children; the handbills urged citizens to "Support Law and Order" by going to the Riviera Tavern, an unprepossessing bar in a poor section of town.

By 8 P.M., the scheduled starting time, a crowd of three hundred (police estimate) or seven hundred (Benecchi estimate) had gathered. Whatever the numbers, they were sufficient to cause the meeting to be switched to the tavern parking lot.

Imperiale arrived at 8:30. Attired in an iridescent brown suit and black turtleneck, he climbed atop an old wooden table, a microphone in his hand. Benecchi and an aide stood guard. Imperiale introduced himself, apologized for not having an American flag on display and launched upon his standard speech. A few excerpts:

"You've been fortunate not to have been hit by a riot yet, because you know that the enforcement of law is what the taxpayer depends upon. This is how we feel safe. This is that one thin line between us—law and order, the boys in blue. . . . If Chief Justice Earl Warren, if the Supreme Court is gonna continue to pass laws to benefit the commies, to benefit the radicals who are bent on the destruction of the United States, then it is up to you, the decent citizens, to stand up and be counted. Because when you're not watching, they're sneaking the commies and the radicals right in under you. And it's happening in your town as well as mine."

The crowd thoroughly enjoyed

Imperiale's talk; it was not so friendly, though, to some of those present. Two bearded college students, quietly watching, were roughed up as Imperiale spoke, but he urged the crowd to desist. "It's the oldest commie trick in the world," he said, "to try and break up the meeting. But there's too many decent people here." He advised the students "to hold your tongue or you're liable to get yourself busted up."

A reporter for *The Nutley Sun*, the local weekly, was questioned about his use of a portable tape machine to record the meeting. When Imperiale's talk came to an end, the reporter was asked to leave before he had a chance to talk to any of the group's organizers or to listen to the many citizens who stayed to offer support, congratulations, and advice.

Mayor Harry W. Chenoweth, visibly upset at the sudden rise of militancy in tranquil Nutley, later threatened the Riviera with loss of its liquor license if another such meeting were held.

"I was deeply concerned to think that this organization had moved out into the suburbs where there was no need for it," Chenoweth said. "The law enforcement agencies of Nutley, with the cooperation of neighboring towns and the backup of county and state police, are adequate to handle any sort of problem. These groups are trying to take over enforcement of the law." Last April, the Nutley Town Commission appropriated $40,000 for the purchase of riot-control equipment.

Tom Benecchi dismissed the mayor's charge. "We're not trying to take over the police work," he says. "We just want to help them. Nutley doesn't have enough police protection, and sometimes we see things before the police do. But when we do, we give them credit."

Late in June, Imperiale was the guest of honor of the Nutley–Belleville Citizens' Committee, Benecchi's splinter group, at a rally at the Elks Lodge in Belleville, a town which lies between Nutley and Newark. The Imperiale performance followed the usual pattern, with this added touch of audience participation:

Imperiale: "I'm against the radical, black or white. I've never made a racist statement, I've never told anyone to kill a nigger, like I've been accused of."

A Member of the Audience: "You should!" (Loud laughter and applause.)

Imperiale: "But if a radical comes to your house, defend your property and shoot him dead." (Prolonged cheers.)

There are, however, various groups of citizens with whom Imperiale is not so popular. Clergymen, for example, and not simply because of his tax-exemption position. His followers have been accused of throwing rocks at priests attending a rally, and Imperiale has minced no words in his condemnation of the clergymen who protested a North Ward committee proposal for a police canine corps: "Don't think that because a man wears the cloth of God, he hasn't his hates and prejudices. We knew there was a shortage of policemen and that dogs had proved in other places to be an asset. We didn't make an issue out of it; the clergy did. They came to the city council and said: 'These dogs will be used against the Negro.' That's a controversy they had no business getting involved in."

City and state officials are not among Imperiale's strongest supporters. Governor Hughes, who sees the committee as analogous to burgeoning Nazi groups in Germany in the 1930's, has submitted a bill to the New Jersey legislature making it illegal to belong to any organization "with two or more persons who assemble as a paramilitary or parapolice organization." The bill was passed by the Senate but has been locked up since July in committee in the Assembly.

The governor has also requested Imperiale to disband voluntarily; Imperiale has refused.

Mayor Addonizio, a former congressman, says Imperiale's group is a "problem." He adds: "Any group that walks around in paramilitary uniforms is undesirable." And he believes that Newark has had a quiet summer this year "in spite of" the North Ward committee which has "acted to further separate the black and white communities."

Addonizio is in the unenviable position of being attacked by the black community as a rightist and the militant white community as a leftist. "When we elected a man who fourteen years served in Congress with an honorable record," Imperiale says, "how were we to know he would turn quisling. Who bothered to check to see if he was lefty?"

Addonizio and Imperiale do have in common, though, their belief that Police Director Spina has been wrongly indicted by a grand jury for "willfully" refusing to enforce the state's gambling laws in Newark. This in spite of the fact that Imperiale was not pleased by police response following the bombing of committee headquarters. When police were unable to turn up much evidence in the hours after the blast, Imperiale commented, "If this happened in the Central Ward, they'd a had one hundred cops and one hundred leads by now."

The mayor has to date taken no specific action against the committee. Indeed, Donald A. Malafronte, administrative assistant to Addonizio and administrator of the model cities program, feels that Imperiale has not had an entirely bad effect on the city. "In some ways he relieves tension among his own people because he tells whites what they want to hear," Malafronte says. "We don't believe Imperiale ever laid a hand on anybody. Like LeRoi Jones, he belongs in Newark, but on the fringes. We want to forge them both together, with Imperiale on one wing and Jones on the other, but none in center stage, because Newark isn't *all* Anthony Imperiale or LeRoi Jones."

Malafronte added, however, that the city is "concerned" about white militancy, and that the North Ward Citizens' Committee is under constant surveillance by the Newark police department: "We have the organization so completely penetrated with police that Imperiale can't sit down without our knowing about it."

Perhaps the most dedicated Imperiale opponents are the members of the state's American Civil Liberties Union (which Imperiale calls "nothing but a communist front—they took prayer out of the schools and all that"). The ACLU has filed suit in federal court charging, among other things, that Imperiale is in collusion with the Newark police department to prevent Negroes from achieving equality.

The suit grew out of an incident preceding the New Jersey ACLU's annual meeting last April at the Military Park Hotel, Newark. As Mrs. Rita D'Joseph, the group's education director, entered the hotel to make last-minute preparations for the meeting, she was greeted by pickets at the entrance.

"There were men in fatigues, and some women," she recalls. "It was a boisterous scene. The pickets' signs read, 'ACLU Are Pinks' and 'Untie Policemen's Hands.' As I left my car, I heard shouts of: 'There she is! Get her! Kill her!' I was surrounded. A man tried to grab the signs I was carrying, and pushed me back and forth. People shouted: 'Commie bastard!' It was Anthony Imperiale who was leading the picket line."

When Mrs. D'Joseph got inside, she telephoned Henry di Suvero, then the group's executive director and now head of the Emergency Civil Liberties Committee in New York City. Di Suvero arrived shortly thereafter, and he and Mrs. D'Joseph asked a uniformed police officer to arrest the picketer who had abused her. The officer refused. Immediately afterward, according to Di Suvero's testimony in court, Donald Mangione, an offduty Newark policeman, stepped from the picket line and arrested Di Suvero. Di Suvero states that he was then struck by Imperiale, and taken to the Third Precinct in a paddy wagon.

In late July, United States District Court Judge James A. Coolahan denied the ACLU's bid for a preliminary injunction against Imperiale. The full trial of the case, as well as of Di Suvero's criminal indictment (on the charge of threatening the life of a policeman), has yet to take place.

Despite the setback, Di Suvero feels that the court proceedings have served to temper the militant group. "In a sense it was a battle for shaping the consciousness of the community to what was happening," he said. As a result of the suit, Attorney General Arthur Sills instigated a full-scale investigation of the North Ward committee. The United States Attorney's office in Newark has also begun an investigation.

Meanwhile, with court cases pending and proposed legislation hanging fire and investigations proceeding, all directed against him, Imperiale continues to organize his patrols and recruit new members for his organization. And he has begun his campaign for city council. Most political observers expect him to win.

"Maybe I can't do much in the council," Tony Imperiale says, "but you're gonna hear my voice." Of that, there can be little doubt.

48
Case Study of a Southern
CORE Group*
INGA POWELL BELL

"I've been waiting two years for this. We've been working for it for two years, and I want to stay here until we find out what happened tonight." This was the thought shared by the nineteen members of the CORE chapter of "Southern City," gathered in a Negro Baptist church for their weekly meeting on a humid July evening in 1962; victory in their lunch counter desegregation campaign seemed, incredibly, only hours away.

Everyone was acutely conscious that a Negro negotiating team was sitting across town with representatives of the white business community to set the date for simultaneous desegregation of all lunch counters in the city. CORE's two representatives were to report back to the CORE meeting as soon as the negotiations were completed. Then the chapter, restless under a suspension of direct action during the negotiating period, could begin organizing testing teams to ensure compliance.

For the past two years, Southern City CORE had weathered police harassment, arrest, violence, ridicule, and hostility as they picketed and sat-in at lunch counters in the downtown area. Even the established Negro leadership had frequently discouraged their effort and shown hostility to it. But the campaign had succeeded. There was no doubt about CORE's accomplishment. This small determined band had brought the white business community to the negotiating table and had made it willing to talk to "anybody who can stop these demonstrations."

But more was at stake than the lunch

*[From *CORE and the Strategy of Non-Violence* by Inge Powell Bell. Copyright © 1968 by Random House, Inc. Reprinted by permission of the publisher.]

counter victory. The unity of the Negro community was also on trial. For CORE, despite its often rancorous disagreements with older leaders of the Negro community, had voluntarily invited the Negro "establishment" into the negotiating committee. They felt that this was necessary to Negro unity although they continued to regard their Negro allies with suspicion. . . .

DIRECT ACTION TACTICS

In order to appreciate the barriers to unity in the Negro community, it is necessary to grasp the great sociological and philosophical differences that separate those individuals who work in a direct action group like CORE from those who participate in the more traditional groups that work through established, "institutionalized" political channels. The central difference between institutional and direct action lies in the mechanism through which decisions are influenced. "Mechanism" means the power that is mobilized and brought to bear on decisionmakers. Institutional political action revolves around the struggle for control over governmental bodies and public policy. Its pivotal instrument is the vote. In order to influence elections, groups that use institutional means must develop some type of broad consensus sufficient to give them numerical strength at the polls. In the case of direct action, power lies in having an organization capable of inflicting financial loss on businessmen or creating disturbances and embarrassment for public officials. This may be accomplished by boycott, which requires a disciplined activist group plus fairly broad support in the Negro community, or by sit-ins that disrupt business or harm a firm's reputation; this tactic requires only small numbers of highly dedicated persons. This is essentially a process of coercion, although a certain amount of legitimation is necessary in order to persuade the majority and its political representatives to tolerate it. Such toleration may be achieved, however, far short of majority consensus on the changes brought about by the direct action. . . .

BACKGROUND OF CORE MEMBERS

In the case of groups following an institutional political strategy, leaders are typically persons of prestige and power within the segment of the community they represent. They are also moderates in the sense that they are not drawn from the most extreme or militant portion of their constituency, but are close to the political position of the middle-roaders and the moderate wing of the opposing camp.

In the case of direct action, on the other hand, the activists are typically persons who are isolated from prestige and power within their own constituency and who represent the most radical and militant wing of their camp. This difference follows naturally from the fact that institutional leaders must win over to their camp the middle-roaders and moderates in the opposing camp, whereas activists must be persons who are sufficiently alienated from the prevailing consensus to risk condemnation and more serious sanctions resulting from a frontal, coercive attack on the opposition.

The membership of Southern City CORE fit the picture of a typical direct action group. There were about thirty members, fifteen of whom were part of the group's active nucleus. Of this nucleus, ten were college students, two were not working and were living at home during an interim in their studies, and three worked in semiskilled and service occupations. Most of the members' families had lived in Southern City for one or two generations. Except

for two in white collar jobs, the fathers of all the nucleus members were unskilled laborers. Most of the members, even two couples who were married and had children, lived with their parents. Typically, their home was a railroad flat composed of four or five rooms arranged in bead-string fashion without hallways. Furnishings were usually old and sparse. There were few rugs. The number of persons in a household ranged from six to ten or twelve. There were usually other grown siblings, who either attended college or worked, generally in white collar jobs. Most of the mothers worked as domestic servants, waitresses, and the like. All the households that I visited gave the impression of having high morale and strong family organization. All were extremely neat and clean despite the poor quality of housing and furniture. In all these households the children, though frequently numerous, were making plans to move into white collar and professional occupations.

Clearly then, these CORE members stemmed from the "upper lower" class within the Negro community's system of social stratification. Their parents were members of the unskilled but steady and respectable working class. The CORE members themselves were upwardly mobile, but still in an interim position where their future prospects did not yet accord them any real status of their own other than the nebulous one of being students.

Another characteristic that defined CORE members as persons removed from positions of power and prestige was the age composition; all the members of the active nucleus were under twenty-five. The chairman was twenty-three and the two past chairmen were even younger, whereas almost all the "established" Negro leaders were middle-age.

During these two years of operation,

the CORE chapter had only a handful of white members. There were four whites in the original group and about the same number in subsequent groups, but their turnover was very great. Of five former active white members on whom it was possible to gather information, two were undergraduate students at a "liberal-to-moderate" white college of high academic standing, two others were graduate students at the same college, and one was a professor at the state university. Three of the five were northerners; the other two came from border states. Parents' occupations ranged from skilled laborer to wealthy contractor.

Thus, although the Negro members of CORE were, by virtue of their background and age, truly outside of, and isolated from, the conservative influences of the elements of prestige and power in the Negro establishment, they did have roots within what may be termed the Negro masses: the great bulk of the city's Negro population. The white CORE members, on the other hand, were complete outsiders in the white community because they were all from outside the city and region and were unconnected with any segment of the white community except the academic subculture from which all of them were recruited.

STRUCTURE OF CORE

Organizations geared to institutional political strategy typically emphasize a large membership with minimal participation by most members. The group is usually a typical secondary organization with loose, formally structured ties. In contrast, the ideal direct action group has a small, highly dedicated and involved membership united by strong primary-group ties. The reasons for this difference again follow from the central difference in the two strategies. A large,

minimally involved membership is the best way to build up the widespread but relatively shallow commitment needed for numerical strength at the polls. Direct action, on the other hand, requires only small numbers of persons, but these must be so highly motivated and involved that they are willing to risk the great hardships involved in direct action.

Southern City CORE typified this generalization. In its internal structure, it was a cross between a political organization and a college friendship clique or neighborhood gang. On the formal side, there were five elected officers, an executive committee, and several operating committees. There were also regular weekly membership meetings, where all the members were entitled to discuss and vote on the group's business. The attendance at these meetings usually numbered around twenty people. However, the real work and day-to-day decision making was carried on by the active nucleus of officers plus a few other active members, all close personal friends who saw each other almost daily. Most active members reported that all their closest friends were in CORE, and although personal friendship was an important factor in binding the group together, it was the CORE bond, rather than any other common interest, that undergirded the relationships and loyalties of the group.

When CORE members got together, CORE business—past, present, and future—was virtually the only topic of conversation. CORE activities were so time consuming that most of the purely social activities occurred as by-products of CORE business: coffee after meetings, supper to discuss the newsletter, a party after a direct action project, or dropping over to discuss an impending action.

The active nucleus was a true primary group. Most members were emotionally "available" for such close ties because they were becoming independent of their parental households but had not yet established families of their own. More important, perhaps, the nature of direct action invariably bound the participants in close emotional ties. In the words of one CORE member: "We feel we are one family. We have the closeness of a family. We ran from the same things together. We've been implicated in the same things—we're constantly in touch with each other."

In terms of time spent in the group, then, to its active members CORE was truly a total-involvement organization. All those I queried said that they spent at least ten or fifteen hours a week on CORE activities. Some said that they spent almost every hour of their non-working or nonstudying time in CORE. This is probably no exaggeration if we include the sociability interwoven with CORE activities. Only one member reported considerable involvement in another organization, and no member was more or even equally involved in any other activity. Beyond mere time commitment, it appeared that under the pressure of Southern conditions CORE usually became an overriding obsession with its members. One student who quit CORE to catch up on his graduate work reported:

It wasn't so much the time it took as the emotional involvement. I just couldn't stop thinking about it and start thinking about something else. We were having so much trouble organizing the community effectively that I would find myself always thinking of evolving strategy.

And another student said:

Since the arrest for handing out leaflets my whole life was covered with CORE. I suppose I spent almost every minute of my

time involved in it. If I wasn't going to meetings I was talking to people here on campus. People would come up to me all the time if they wanted to know anything about what was going on. Everybody knew I was in it. My schoolwork went way down. I was continually on the spot. That's why I'm reluctant to go down there now and get into it again—because I know I'll get involved in it like this, totally.

In its isolation from other organizations, in the strong radicalism of its convictions, and in the semi-illegal nature of many of its activities, the group was bound by all of the forces that unite members of a political sect on the one hand and a juvenile gang on the other. But the negative features that become divisive in these other groups were counteracted by the peculiar combination of features in CORE. The powerlessness of the political sect, which results in a turning inward of hostilities in the form of philosophical disputes and heresies, was counteracted in CORE by the constant outlet for activity offered by direct action. The complete illegitimacy of a gang in the eyes of the outside world—and to a large extent in the eyes of its own members—results in the members fearing and resenting gang involvement at the same time that the condemnation of the outside world forces them further into the gang.[1] In CORE, on the other hand, the condemnation of the outside world could not be turned into resentment of the group because of the group's strong sense of moral legitimacy, a sense that was reinforced by the group's contacts with national CORE.

RELATIONSHIP TO WHITE COMMUNITY

Established Negro leaders whose organizations combine some forms of direct pressure with attempts to influence the white community and thus gain advantages for the Negro through institutional political action typically depend upon alliances with white liberal groups. They come into minimal contact with conservatives and archsegregationists. This pattern of persuasive contact underlies the weakness of such organizations because white liberals are few in number and lack real political and economic power. By contrast, the direct action group in the South engages in direct confrontations with conservative and segregationist power figures in both the political and the economic hierarchies of the city. The nature of this direct action contact is purely coercive and often violent. Contrary to the idealized version of direct action strategy as enunciated in the philosophy of nonviolence, there is no genuine attempt at communication, persuasion, or consensus building between these two conflicting groups. There is pushing and shoving and, eventually, bargaining, but there is no dialogue. Because the direct action strategy depends on coercion for its results, CORE groups have little tactical use for coalitions with white liberals, who may, at times, help to persuade the white community to initiate or accept reforms but who have little direct influence on the process of decision making. . . .

CORE's contact with white liberals and moderates in Southern City was ex-. tremely minimal because Negro leaders were isolated from these people. Most of the white liberal groups were oriented toward influencing white opinion and putting pressure on political leaders. In this enterprise, support from Negro leaders could only weaken their position, and interracial memberships were considered politically impossible. One must add that, given the atmosphere in the city, social contact between Negroes and "respectable" whites

was so difficult as to be almost non-existent. . . .

CORE, on the other hand, did not need such groups to carry out its strategy. Its direct action tactics automatically excluded it from gaining their support. But, more important, CORE was not basically concerned with influencing white public opinion through persuasion, education, or propaganda. It aimed directly at certain "power targets," such as businesses. The fact that the direct action campaign had some educational impact upon the white public was an inevitable by-product of the group's activities, and what was gained here did not require alliance with white liberal and moderate groups. In the context of this strategy the liberals were "counted out."

RELATIONSHIP TO NEGRO COMMUNITY

Throughout its brief history in Southern City, the CORE chapter's contacts with established groups and leaders in the Negro community were almost entirely negative, reflecting both a conflict of organizational interests and a clash of viewpoints.

In the late summer of 1960, when CORE was planning its first sit-in, the NAACP approached the group in the role of mediator between CORE, the mayor's office, and the dime store managers. The NAACP was motivated by its interest in peaceful school desegregation, which its legal actions had brought to a head and which was scheduled to begin in September. NAACP leaders promised to set up a negotiating session between CORE and the business leaders under the auspices of the mayor's office. At the negotiating session CORE representatives found that only the political authorities were present. The store managers had already been "talked to," and CORE was asked to hold off its picketing for a year in the interests of ensuring peaceful school integration. The group refused this proposition and voted to proceed with sit-ins immediately.

The next important contact with established Negro groups was in a newly formed organization set up in December 1960. The organization was composed of about one hundred Negro leaders representing various groups in the Negro community, including CORE. During December 1961, CORE had succeeded in getting the backing of some Negro churches, and a few ministers had actually joined the CORE picket lines to protest lunch counter segregation. The leaders of the CORE chapter were trying, with some hope of success, to get the backing of this organization and of more Negro ministers.

But in January an event occurred that destroyed these small efforts at cooperation with a broader spectrum of Negro groups. The local Negro newspaper printed a bitterly worded letter in which CORE was accused of promoting interracial romances of the white male-Negro female variety, which have extremely unsavory overtones of concubinage in the Negro community. As a result of this letter, the ministers withdrew their support, and the newly formed organization decided to withhold its endorsement of the picketing.

The only interracial civil rights group in the city besides CORE was a human relations council. At the time of this study, the council had held only a few meetings. It was composed of the welfare-minded, rather impotent white liberals and a small group of "establishment" Negroes—all very light-skinned and obviously recruited from the highest echelons of the Negro community. The group was considering working on improving vocational and technical training in Negro high schools.

CORE was invited to join it, but they sent only an occasional representative.

The CORE chairman's judgment on this council reveals the extent to which social class tensions affect the relations between CORE and established Negro leaders. Significantly, the negative reaction to the council was based solely on the character of the Negro members; the white members were completely ignored.

At the human relations council—we've been asked to come to this kind of thing now, but we're out of place—we're strictly low-brow. Most of us don't know how to act there, and, you know, we think different. M [the CORE group's lawyer] of course is an exception. His parents weren't middle class, but he's moved up, being a lawyer—although he doesn't belong to any of their social clubs because he thinks they're a bunch of phonies. Anyway, I don't think you can hope for much to come out of a group like that.

The various other Negro groups, the established Negro ministers, the so-called Negro leaders, the "black bourgeoisie," and the "old family group" all merged into a single category referred to by CORE members as the Negro establishment. This was the group against which CORE members expressed the most frequent, and by far the most vehement, hostility. These were CORE's real adversaries in the ideological struggle. For it was here, within the Negro community, that CORE engaged in its significant dialogues. Here, in battle against the relatively conservative and established groups, they attempted to create a new and more militant consensus of Negro opinion.

A fairly large proportion of CORE members had been recruited out of the NAACP Youth Council. Their defection to CORE resulted from their own belief in greater militancy, and they continued to resent the council as a roadblock to the growth of the direct action movement. One such member said of the council:

They were always discussing their next party —or they are raising money to send delegates to the national convention. They are just social. They can't do anything that isn't approved by the adults. We used to always go asking them to help us picket. Once they came out—a couple of them. But they were never here when we needed them.

Another CORE member said of the established Negro leaders:

Look, I'll give you an example of the way our so-called Negro leaders act. We asked them to picket the stores with us, so this thing would have more prestige. They refused— never a one came out. But when the city refused to let one of the nationally known integration leaders speak in the city auditorium they were all out there picketing— because they thought this was a big national thing and would be in all the newspapers.

The response of the established Negro leadership to CORE was equally vehement. One NAACP leader said:

CORE groups have blackmailed Negro leaders all over the country. The attack which CORE has made has been equally vicious against segregation and the white leadership and the established Negro leadership. The NAACP has been pushed into the position of having to prove that it's liberal. We've lost membership in many places because of the way CORE has blackmailed us and pushed us. After all we can't come out in opposition to CORE—we're afraid to come out in opposition to them. . . .

While the Negro establishment represented a competitor for the leadership of the Negro community, CORE had to draw for its members and supporters on the average Negro, whose thinking it hoped to reshape. CORE's disappointment with its constituency was reflected by a fairly high incidence of unfavorable comment. The criticisms were mainly that the average Negro was too cowardly to stand firm, too brainwashed by the white culture, and too apathetic to support the militant movement. Although these comments were occasionally very bitter, as when members recalled how Negroes crossed their picket lines or slammed doors in their faces during voter registration drives, they were often tinged with understanding and humor. There was a sense that "this is the sad condition from which we have just emerged ourselves." This story, told at a CORE gathering, illustrates this attitude:

We were going through some small town on the bus and we saw this Negro lady walking along the street—and there were nothing but whites around her—and Alice yells out the window, "Hey, lady, are you a New Negro or an Old Negro?" and the lady scrunches herself all up and says, "I'm an ooooold Negro!"

Attitudes toward Black Muslims were almost equally divided between favorable and unfavorable. Muslims had one temple in the city but were not very strong. However, CORE members had considerable contact with them because they moved in the two strata where Muslims make their greatest impact: lower class groups and student groups. CORE members reported frequent conversations with Muslim members and sympathizers and had invited a Muslim speaker to one of their meetings. In the struggle to radicalize the Negro community, Muslims were seen more as allies than as competitors. Like CORE, they were trying to undo white brainwashing and to undermine the prestige of the middle class Negro leadership. They were admired for their dramatic exposure of racist myths and for their ability to appeal to lower class Negroes. Although Muslims were criticized for their "inverse racism" and their goal of a segregated society, these criticisms were not usually very vehement.

The commitment to interracial groups was the one radical value of national CORE that conflicted directly with the inclination of the lower class Negro community and the black nationalists. This was also the one radical value that was most expendable to Negro leaders of Southern City's CORE, as was indicated by the reaction of Negro members to the letter in which the local Negro paper criticized CORE members for interracial dating. The article, as will be recalled, injured CORE's position in negotiations for support of picketing with other Negro groups. These events precipitated a crisis within the group: white members insisted that interracial socializing was central to CORE's goals, while most Negro members felt that this was peripheral and expendable if it hurt the group's standing in the Negro community. As a result of this dispute most white members left the group.

CORE's cooperative or relatively sympathetic contacts in the Negro community suggest that the direct action movement, although largely a generational phenomenon, is also very closely tied to social class. Within the student generation, it was, as we have seen, the students from working class homes who most frequently participated. On the other hand, cooperation and understanding between CORE and the consumer's group was great despite the age difference, largely because the consumers were a working class group. Membership in the Muslims is young and predominantly lower class, and both of these characteristics—youth and lower class status—tend to isolate the individual from contact with, and sympathy for, the prestige and power structure of the Negro and white communities.

STRUGGLES FOR CONSENSUS WITHIN THE NEGRO COMMUNITY

Throughout CORE's campaign to desegregate lunch counters, members of white churches and moderate organizations summarily condemned the direct action, and reaction among Negro leaders was mixed. The leading white daily newspaper at first refused to cover the arrests and later covered them too thoroughly, giving names and addresses of those arrested. All the editorial comment was negative.

The decision to negotiate desegregation of the lunch counters did not stem from any liberalization of local white public opinion or from any change of policy on the part of white political leaders. The initiative for bringing about the negotiations between storeowners and Negro leaders stemmed, rather, from the nationwide chain stores, which feared the economic losses and adverse publicity of the demonstrations on a national level.* Thus, a small nucleus of fifteen to thirty persons plus a temporary following of perhaps forty more —all lacking prestige or influence in the existing leadership structure of the city, but all armed with the willingness to expose themselves to arrest, violence, and condemnation—had, over the course of two years, created a completely new bargaining position. This bargaining position was so strong that conservatives in the white business community were willing to deal with them and insisted on dealing first and foremost not with "influential Negroes" but with "whoever can stop these demonstrations."

To this point, CORE consistently appeared as a direct action group organizing coercive strength against the

*During the southern sit-in movement of the previous summer, these chains had suffered financially from disruption in their southern stores and from sympathy boycotts of their northern outlets.

white community while engaging in little communication with them. Within its own racial community, CORE allied itself with other youthful and lower class groups while carrying on its ideological struggle against the established, older, middle class Negro leadership. Yet at the point where CORE was asked to enter into negotiations with white merchants, it suddenly began to play a new role that appeared to contradict the picture developed earlier. Although the merchants had made it clear that they only wanted to talk with the groups responsible for the direct action, CORE invited the established Negro leaders to join the Negro negotiating team.

Thus, they brought in the very establishment that they so greatly opposed ideologically: leaders of moderate Negro groups, leaders of Negro churches, and the publisher of the Negro paper. CORE had only two persons on the seventeen-member team: the chairman of the chapter and one of lawyers connected with CORE, who served as chairman of the entire Negro negotiating team. Why, just when it had created an independent bargaining position, did CORE bring in these other elements?

A partial reason lies in the fact that the cooperation of these persons was needed. The editor of the Negro newspaper was brought in to prevent publicity leaks. Both Negro and white members were afraid that news of the negotiations might encourage the White Citizens Council to organize countermoves. The consumers' group, which had been picketing intermittently for jobs, had to be brought into the agreement in order to put an effective moratorium on all demonstrations during the course of the negotiations. To bring in their representatives was not enough; CORE leaders felt that they should also bring in two established Negro leaders who controlled the consumers' group's funds and could better influence its conduct. However, these reasons do not seem

sufficient to account for the large amount of power that was literally given away by the group. They were presented as explanations for a decision that the CORE leaders did not themselves fully understand. During the course of the six-month negotiations, CORE negotiators were frequently infuriated because they felt that they were being held up and sabotaged more by their fellow Negroes than by the whites sitting across the table. Yet they continued to defend the necessity of having included "the Negro power structure" in the negotiations.

Actually the decision seemed to stem largely from an unwillingness to take power because of the low status of the CORE members within the Negro community. A revealing quotation from one CORE leader reflects this lack of confidence:

The merchants never said who should be on the Negro negotiating team. We could have had seventeen CORE members on it if we had wanted to, but we had to get broad representation. The only thing the merchants were interested in was that they were talking to the right people—that is, the people who could stop the demonstrations. We had to get the other because we were vis-a-vis the power structure of the whole community, not just dealing with the merchants on the main street. The Chamber of Commerce was involved, and many prominent persons like bank presidents. So we had to have the power people in the Negro community.

In CORE's invitation to the established Negro leaders we see the organization in an unfamiliar role: as compromiser and consensus builder. The established Negro leaders lived in a defined situation that included white prestige figures (and indeed the white community) among their reference groups. Just as this relationship inclined these leaders to trade away part of their power position for the good opinion of the white leadership, so the CORE leaders—cut off from the white leadership by a great gulf of class, age, and ideology, and hence quite unwilling to give way to them—inevitably had to include within their defined situation the established Negro leadership simply as a reference group. They, too, had to trade away part of their power position in return for the prestige and sense of security they borrowed from the endorsement of established leaders.

Within the Negro community, then, CORE's role, despite the harsh aspect of its ideological attacks on the established Negro leadership, was, at times, a consensus-building one in its attempts to organizationally and ideologically mobilize its own "side" for attack on the white community. Vis-a-vis the white community, it played a wholly radical role in that it used power against white targets without real attempt at legitimation. Through the coercive power generated by direct action, the burden of adjustment to an unwanted situation was shifted from the Negro community to the white community.

Were CORE the only element at work in such a situation, the result would be a rapid breakdown of consensus and order in the entire community. However, it has generally been noted that direct action sets off new processes within the white community that prevent the complete breakdown of consensus. Liberal and moderate groups suddenly emerge and try to readjust the white community to the changing circumstances. At the same time, established Negro leaders, pushed from behind by the young radicals and encouraged by the emergence of the white liberals, take a stronger tone in their attempt to reeducate the white community. Both elements are able to emerge under the "cover" provided by the extreme radicalism of direct action, in other words, as a lesser evil. Within this process, the breakdown of the consensus-building mechanisms and the

development of an acute Negro-white polarization remains a constant and threatening possibility.

FOOTNOTE

1 For a discussion of the group's legitimacy as it applies to the delinquent subculture, see Albert K. Cohen, *Delinquent Boys: The Culture of the Gang* (New York: Free Press, 1955), pp. 67–69.

49
The Reluctant Revolutionaries: Types of Black Student Activists*
HARRY EDWARDS

Since the fall of 1967, many whites and Negroes in America have accepted the image of the politically active black student as he has been portrayed in the mass media—a bearded, doped-up, wooly-headed, bead-wearing savage with a gun in one hand and a molotov cocktail in the other who is dead set on burning the colleges and universities of America to the ground to secure relatively insignificant gains or simply to see them burn. The picture had changed since the late 1950's and early 1960's when many people, whites in particular, regarded blacks as innately nonviolent, Bible-quoting, childlike figures, striving to be recognized as full-fledged human beings. Needless to say, the latter image is just as distorted as the former. In the black student movement today, there exist several distinct and sometimes conflicting political perspectives among the active participants in the student revolt. . . .

The following categories of student types participating in the Black student revolt are developed from qualitative and ethnographic data gathered by the author while lecturing to and organizing

* [Reprinted with permission of the Macmillan Company from *Black Students* by Harry Edwards. Copyright © 1970 by The Free Press, a Division of the Macmillan Company.]

black student groups on over sixty pre-dominantly white college (two-year and four-year schools) and university campuses across America during the three-year period from summer, 1966 to summer, 1969. . . . Although the following typologies are certainly ideal and relatively general, the component characteristics of each are sufficiently specific to render each type identifiable in any black student population.

The participants in the black student revolt comprise five types: the radical activist, the militant, the revolutionary, the anomic activist, and the conforming Negro.

THE RADICAL ACTIVIST

The radical activist is the third smallest group of black students active in the revolt. Of the 378 students upon whom attention was focused fifty-six fit this category. These people typically have relatively long histories of activism in the liberation struggle, usually dating back to participation in SNCC activi-ties during that organization's pre-black power days. Thus they usually are so-phisticated in organizing and mobilizing people and have a substantial amount of firsthand experience in confronting en-trenched, legally established institutions and authorities.

The radical activist is usually older— both academically and chronologically —than his black student peers. He may be a senior or graduate student in his middle or late twenties. He usually comes from a middle class Negro family and first entered college by qualifying under traditional or "normal" standards for entry. Sometime early in the course of his undergraduate career, however, his primary goal of getting a college de-gree became secondary to a growing in-terest and participation in political activities revolving around the struggle of black people for freedom and justice.

In other words, somewhere along the line, he discovered that he, too, was black. As he became more and more involved in political activities, his pre-occupation with academic goals became tenuous, as did his ties with his middle class Negro parents, who often neither understood nor favored his involvement. Consequently, his academic career, undergraduate and sometimes graduate, was prolonged.

In 1966 and 1967, heeding the call for black power, the radical activist black student returned to the college campus. It was he who spearheaded the shift in areas of confrontation from segregated public facilities to the col-lege campus. It was the radical activist —the former staunchly nonviolent activist turned radical by his experiences during the integration-oriented phase of the movement—who brought the messages of Malcolm X, Stokely Car-michael, and others back to the college campuses of America. And, it was he, too, who first began to agitate for and to organize what have come to be known generally as black student unions.

In the black student movement, the radical activist is more politically sophis-ticated at the domestic level, more experienced, and has more organiza-tional ability than any of the other types. For these reasons, during the early or-ganizational lives of black student or-ganizations, it is usually the radical activists who politicize the members, organize and run most meetings, define political issues, and either occupy them-selves or delegate to others positions of authority and power in the organiza-tional hierarchy.

In the truest sense of the word, the radical activist is a politician. He is willing to create and compromise on relatively insignificant issues in order to achieve more significant goals. Looming as somewhat of a vestige of his involvement in the "nonviolent" phase of the student movement is his uneasiness about using premeditated violence or destruction as means to be employed in the struggle. He will, however, use such means if he perceives himself as having been pushed to it by authorities in the course of a confrontation. For the radical activist is, basically, a reformer. And except for the fact that he realized the necessity of black separatism during the current phase of the struggle and is willing to employ means more radical than nonviolent direct action, his orientation differs little from the reformist orientation exhibited by him earlier in political activities. He still believes that America, despite her severe afflictions and institutionalized ills, is worth saving. And what is more, he believes that it can be done without resort to wholesale violence and destruction. But for the radical activist, the ultimate determiner of what means will be employed in the black student movement rests with the authorities who preside over the nation's campuses. If they do not resort to violence and brutality in their dealings with black people, then he will not respond violently in his dealings with them. . . .

THE MILITANT

Once the demand for more liberal college entrance standards had increased the number of young black students on the nation's college campuses, the leadership days of the radical activist were numbered. And under the circumstances, this result was predictable. For these new students emerged mostly as militants. The militant type is by far the most numerous in the black student movement. Of the student population studied here 154 of 378 emerged as militants. He, too, is a reformer. But he differs from the radical activist in several significant respects. For the

militant is the "nouveau noir" of the black student movement.

First of all, he tends to be younger, both academically and chronologically, than the radical activist, usually an undergraduate in his late teens or early twenties. He typically possesses neither practical experience in dealing with political issues nor any cohesive philosophy that might guide him in moving politically in a manner relevant to the problems of Black people. For he has, in many instances, just recently begun to discover that he himself is black and not a Negro. This being the case, the campus militant at first does no organizing. Rather, militants are organized and politicized by the radical activists and others. Primarily because he has been "turned on to blackness" by radical activists and others active in the black student revolt, the militant picks up and freely uses all the current rhetoric of the movement. He also is the type most likely to wear the latest in "African" styles, which afford him a means of exhibiting his militancy both for the sake of his own ego and to intimidate whites. But the militant's first priority remains a college education. Participation in political activities aimed at bringing about relevant changes in the educational process that will facilitate the solving of problems faced by black people is secondary. Hence, despite his threatening rhetoric and appearance, the militant is not disposed to get involved in any type of action which will jeopardize his educational future, although he may give lip service to such action. He attempts to rationalize this disposition with the claim that he is "going to return to the black community" to put to work the skills that he masters during his college career. But the fact of the matter is that the militant has not yet completely accepted the philosophy of black power. His goal is to force the white racist establishment in America to allow greater mobility for blacks in the existing social order. His immediate aspirations are for a high-paying job and the best house that he can afford. And while he may certainly choose a job where blacks are the primary recipients of his services, the militant is by no means enthusiastic about the idea of actually living in a hard-core black community. In fact, unlike the radical activist and other types who either have had a great deal of experience in working and organizing in the black communities of America or who are products of those communities, the militant cannot technically "return" to the black community, because typically he has never lived or worked there. He has typically been "protected" from such experiences by his Negro parents, who have maintained very tight control over him. His close ties with his middle class Negro family are continued throughout the militant stage of his political development.

Initially, the militant seldom attends black student union meetings. And although he may endorse the programs of the organization, he leaves most of their implementation to the radical activist. He almost never volunteers for committees or other positions vital to the functioning of the union. At some point, however, the militant does become more actively involved, usually as a result of some particular issue which catches his fancy or because something develops that threatens his own personal goals. It is at this point that the militant snatches the reins of power from the radical activists.

The militants typically wrestle power from radical activists by means of a crude type of plebiscite. The radical activist gains control of black student organizations through his proven ability to mobilize and move people toward defined goals. His success in these efforts makes the exercise of this power legitimate. Under the radical activist, a black student union functions as sort of a benevolent dictatorship. When the militants take power, however, democratic rule, with all its necessary, but monotonously slow, rules of order and regulations, replaces the efficiency and speed of the radical activist's one-man decision-making authority.

With the militant at the helm, means become less radical, the immediate issues around which he organizes programs of action become less relevant to the black community, and a premium is placed upon threatening rhetoric and cultural exhibitionism while meaningful political action of significance in achieving the long-range goals of freedom and justice for the black masses is minimized. In adopting such tactics, militants seek both to participate in the black student movement and simultaneously to protect their own personal educational goals. . . .

THE REVOLUTIONARY

There are few revolutionaries in the black student revolt and in the broader black liberation struggle. But the significance of the revolutionary political perspective is not determined by the relative numerical strength of its adherents. For what the revolutionaries lack in numbers, they make up in zeal.

The revolutionaries are the second smallest group active in the black student revolt, only forty-seven of the 378 black students studied here. Like the radical activists and the militants they place a high value on black pride, on Afro-America's cultural and historical ties with Africa, and on reaffirming the contributions that black people have made to the growth of America. But, unlike the radical activists and militants, the revolutionaries repudiate almost all means except premeditated and calculated violence as legitimate tactics in the black liberation struggle. In fact, the black revolutionary is as far to the political left of the radical activist and the militant regarding tactics as the latter two groups are to the left of traditional Negro leaders on the issue of black separatism and nonviolence. It is the revolutionary who has both popularized and who staunchly believes in the implications of the statement that "more political solutions have come from the barrels of guns than from the halls of the United States Congress." But, the revolutionary Black student is also unique on other respects.

The socioeconomic class origins of the revolutionary seem not to conform to any distinguishable pattern. He may come from either the lower classes of black society or from the Negro middle class. Of all the types discussed here, he is the most well-read and also the most dogmatically ideological. Although he not infrequently has had some firsthand experience in the integration-oriented phase of the black liberation struggle, he usually has become alienated from the more traditional directions and slow pace of the movement.

The academic and chronological variables of age also tend to defy easy categorization as far as the revolutionary is concerned. He may be among the youngest black students active in the revolt or he may be among the oldest. But, usually, the older he is, academically and/or chronologically, the more adamant, the more ideologically dogmatic, and the more dedicated he is to the notion that only violent revolutionary upheaval can achieve true liberation for black people in America. For the revolutionary, unlike the militant and the radical activist, is not a reformer. He holds that blacks cannot liberate black society either through nonviolent, direct action or through shrewd, po-

litical maneuvers calculated to reform. In his way of thinking, the entire institutional structure of America must be totally and irreversibly destroyed, so great is the depth of the nation's corruption, oppressive tendencies, and racist orientation. Unlike the radical activist and the militant, who pursue traditional academic goals while simultaneously trying to bring about changes from within the educational institution, the revolutionary relies chiefly upon self-education as his main avenue of intellectual development. He distrusts much more than the radical activist and militant both the motives for and the content of more established educational curricula. Graduation from college, for him, means little. For of what value is a college degree from a school which has functioned as a major component of a racist and oppressive society when that society is inevitably going to be destroyed? The chief justification for the revolutionary being in college is that the educational institutions of America provide him with a forum and a stage from which to politicize other young black people. Because he is typically well-read, articulate, and usually enrolls only in those courses which interest him politically, he does well in school. However he makes little progress toward fulfilling the course requirements for graduation and thus he tends to become a "professional student." He feels that it is essentially from the ranks of black students that the intellectual and analytical skills will come which are so necessary to mounting a successful revolution. In short, the revolutionary sees it as no coincidence that the world's most successful modern revolutionaries —Che Guevara, Mao Tse-tung, and Fidel Castro, among others—were all students at the time that they began to formulate their revolutionary ideologies.

Like the radical activist, the revolutionary may enter college under more traditional entrance standards. For he is often adept at both reading and writing, the two basic guides to assessing the potential of prospective college students. But he may also enter college under more liberalized minority group entrance standards.

The revolutionary tends to break off all ties with his family if he is from the Negro middle class, for the political and social perspectives of his Negro parents relative to the masses of black people are repugnant to him. If he is from the lower classes of black society, his family ties tend to be lax anyway, because his family, and his parents in particular, can neither discuss with him nor understand the political, intellectual, and analytical foundations of his revolutionary attitudes and actions. In both cases, however, he soon loses almost all contact with his family, and for extended periods of time his parents may know neither of his whereabouts nor of his activities.

Because of his devotion to revolutionary ideologies and dogmatic dedication to the ideas of men such as Malcolm X, Huey Newton, and Stokely Carmichael, the revolutionary student tends to be somewhat of an internationalist. Unlike the militant and the radical activist, who see a possibility for reforming America's institutional structure in order to save the black masses, the revolutionary believes it necessary to destroy America in order to make the world safe—not only for Afro-Americans, but for all nonwhite peoples. The revolutionary sees America not only as domestically oppressive, but as the major power oppressing and thwarting the efforts of peoples around the earth to escape from colonialism, exploitation, and racist white domination. Because of his internationalist perspective, the revolutionary often makes the mistake of dogmatically accepting revolutionary philosophies and tactics which have been successful in developing

agrarian societies as applicable to the highly urbanized and industrialized societal conditions under which black people live in America. And from the perspective of many blacks who listen to his hymn of violent revolution, herein lies the Achilles heel of the revolutionary's entire argument. As one young militant stated, "Russia and China combined would form the most powerful military force in the world and even they are not attacking the USA. I'd be a fool to get out there with *a* pistol or *a* rifle and try to overthrow this country violently."

In the black student organization, the revolutionary seldom becomes active until a crisis arises. For the deliberately slow pace and politically dubious orientation of organizational activities and programs are often intolerable for him. He agitates among and prods black student union members and elected militant leaders to become more radical. The revolutionary is seldom elected to positions of authority in the black student organization, and when he is his tenure in office is usually short-lived. For he tends to push the militant membership at too fast a pace and in too radical a direction to suit the political fancies of the militants. But once a crisis arises, particularly under circumstances where campus authorities have threatened to call in police, and violence against black student union members seems imminent, the militants often turn to the revolutionary for advice on tactics and strategies for self-defense. If such tactics of self-defense are deemed by the militant majority as insufficient in the face of mounting police power and brutality, they may turn over all decision-making authority to the revolutionary and leave it to him to decide the best strategy for dealing with the police. In such cases, the end product of revolutionary leadership is usually revolutionary action—the burning and bombing of college buildings and offices and armed confrontations between police and black students. Usually, the most powerful force that impels militants either to overtly or covertly relinquish control of black student organizations to the black revolutionary is the fact that college administrators and civil authorities usually resort to overkill tactics in the face of relatively insignificant militant threats.

The revolutionary, regardless of whether he originates from the lower classes of black society or from the Negro middle class, knows black people and the black community. Although it is from among the black students of the nation that he hopes to draw the necessary intellectual inspiration to mount a revolution, it is from among the ranks of the oppressed and angry lower classes of blacks that he hopes to draw the soldiers who will destroy America through the use of violent force. Typical of the prospects for this revolutionary army is the black anomic activist.

THE ANOMIC ACTIVIST

The black anomic activist is the epitome of the "rebel without a cause." At least he is not conscious of the exact dimensions of his cause. He is simply in a state of rebellion against America and his position in the nation. But nevertheless, he has a role—and a very vital role—to play in the black student revolt. Numerically, the anomic activist type of black student is the least represented type in the black student revolt (only twenty-two of the 378 students studied here.) However, like the revolutionary, what the anomic activist lacks in numerical strength he more than makes up for by his zeal for radical action. He, like the revolutionary, has been made the stereotype for the black student by sensation-seeking, white journalists.

The anomic activist, more so than any of the other types we have mentioned, is a product of the naked and unadulterated black experience in America. Before arriving on the college campus, he may have belonged to one of the thousands of juvenile gangs which proliferate in the black communities of America. He may also have been charged with several juvenile crimes by the police in his home town. For him, his secondary education was irrelevant both to his future and his then current activities. He usually managed to win a high school diploma because of compulsory attendance regulations, the fact that he did passable work in school, parental pressure to remain in school or leave home, and the fact that his teachers were usually only too happy to see him "graduate" just to get rid of him. . . .

The anomic activist is typically among the youngest participants in the black student movement, both academically and chronologically. His academic immaturity tends to be perpetuated by the fact that he typically makes little progress up the academic ladder from freshman to senior or graduate status, partly because he does poorly scholastically but also because he is not hesitant about leaving one school and enrolling in another. When he does so, he usually finds that many of his poor grades are not transferable. Or, he may apply to a school and simply not admit that he had been enrolled previously at another four-year institution. Whether he loses or retains his hard-earned academic credits is of little concern to him, because he feels that he has little stake in either the educational process or in the functioning of any particular college. And his tendency to leave one college and enroll in another is made easy by liberal admissions policies for prospective black students and financial aid programs. . . .

Within black student organizations, the anomic activist's almost compulsive orientation toward action and rebellion is the determining factor in his activities.

He seldom attends organizational meetings and almost never holds any position of authority. He is usually apathetic about the activities and functions of such groups until a crisis arises. He is seldom concerned about the relative importance of issues. Rarely does he take the time to analyze them. Means-ends relationships or goal-directed action are irrelevant. He is always prepared to take the "whole trip" regardless of the issues involved or the consequences of his actions. He would as soon burn down a college as not. In short, his behavior within the context of the black student revolt is systematically functional but individually aberrant. Usually, the militant majority active in black student organizations can effectively suppress and may even denounce the anomic activist. But he becomes an extremely valuable "brother" in crisis situations when police power is brought brutally and forcefully to bear upon black students.

As we mentioned earlier, the militants may turn to the revolutionaries for advice or leadership in crisis situations. If self-defense tactics clearly are inadequate, the revolutionaries assume complete authority and decision-making power in the group and offensive action becomes the prime means of retaliating against the police. The individuals who carry out the most radical measures are the anomic activists.

Unlike the revolutionary, the anomic activist adheres to no coherent, philosophical ideology. Virtually his entire existence has been marked by diffuse anger and rage. So when campus and civil authorities react to more restrained black student activities with overkill responses born of ignorance, racist attitudes, and conservative or reactionary traditionalism, they inadvertently fan to life the anomic activist's smouldering hate and fury. Violence follows, against college communities and facilities. There is literally no limit to the means which the anomic activist is willing to employ, given access to an appropriate arsenal and knowledge of how to utilize it. He can sit-in, disrupt gatherings, commit arson, or bomb as he feels the occasion may demand. But usually the more radical and direct the means employed, the more likely he is to become involved in their implementation.

The anomic activist usually has virtually no ties with his family. Coming from hard-core black society and often from a single-parent, multiple-sibling family, the tight-knit, traditional, nuclear family style of life has never been a reality for him. In a very real sense, his "family" has always been his peer group on the "block"—that frustrated, angry, and disinherited group in black society from whose ranks come the thousands who yearly fill the nation's alcoholic and narcotics hospital wards and local, state, and federal prisons.

So the anomic activists have finally achieved the relevance and purpose which they have so often sought in the greater society—as the shock troopers of the present phase of the black student revolt. Drawing guidance from the black student revolutionary and legitimacy from the exaggerated responses of college and civil authorities, he has at long last found a relevant role in life.

THE CONFORMING NEGRO

The type of student termed here the conforming Negro constitutes the second largest group of participants in the black student revolt, ninety-eight out of the 378 students studied. . . .

The conforming Negro student most closely epitomizes the philosophies, values, and attitudes of the traditional middle class Negroes, . . . although this type of student does not usually come from a middle class background. His family most likely has existed on the fringes of the socioeconomic boundaries that separate the lower middle class from the lower classes in black society. He usually comes from a "respectable," hard-working, church-affiliated family, which has managed to survive just above the poverty level. He generally has completed high school with decent grades and may have spent the first few years immediately following high school graduation working at some unskilled job or fulfilling his military "obligations." But with the liberalization of college admittance standards and readily available financial aid, an opportunity for him to obtain a college education has opened up, and he has taken it.

If two words can capture the essence of the conforming Negro's life style on the college campus, those words are "individual achiever." His sole purposes for being in college are to obtain a college degree and, hopefully, at least the rudiments of the educational expertise which that degree supposedly symbolizes. He may be the only person in the history of his family ever to finish high school, and the first person in his community ever to attend college. As a result of these distinctions, he is usually a source of pride to his parents and a special person in his neighborhood. He thus feels an obligation to his parents, to his community, and to himself to complete college. Hence, he perceives himself as having a stake in the maintenance of the established educational institution in America as it now functions. His long-term goals center upon getting a high-paying job and buying a big house, preferably outside of the black community. He makes no pretensions about returning to the black community from which he came. For unlike the militant, the conforming Negro is blatantly honest about his intentions and goals.

Thus, for the reasons we have just listed, the conforming Negro is highly critical of the activities of the other black students on campus. For they could and often do disrupt class schedules and sometimes close the college completely. In either case, the conforming Negro recognizes that such activities could extend his college career beyond the timetable which he has outlined for himself. And then, too, as one such student stated recently at Cornell University, the activities of militant black students "make all Negroes look bad." He failed to complete his statement, which would have revealed what he really meant—that black students make all Negroes look bad in the eyes of white people. And this omission perhaps says more about the conforming Negro than does his conformity to the traditional Negro role and orientation and lack of concern about the plight of the masses of Afro-Americans. He never criticizes white or Negro college administrators or civil authorities for their intransigence on issues which clearly must be changed if black people are to receive a relevant education. He is usually too busy being appreciative toward whites for being permitted to attend "their" college. . . .

The conforming Negro attends no black student organization meetings on his campus and is usually ostracized by blacks who do—as are all proven and discernible Negroes. As a result, the conforming Negro student typically associates only with whites or with other Negroes. Today, more than at any other time in history, young whites, in particular, are only too happy to dine, date, and otherwise fraternize with Negroes, given the fact that black people are advocating black separatism. . . .

Despite the fact that he is typically lumped together with black college students by whites, the conforming Negro, upon occasion, serves a useful purpose for the white establishment. Sometimes he publicly denounces the activities of black students in the mass media, particularly on television, and this helps to create the fallacy that such activities are the work of a few radical malcontents and that the majority of black students are appalled by such acts and repudiate them. . . .

These, then, are the five major types of students participating, passively or actively, in the current phase of the black student revolt.

50
Majority Involvement in Minority Movements: Civil Rights, Abolition, Untouchability*

GARY T. MARX and MICHAEL USEEM

An issue that leftist movements in America have continually confronted concerns the disadvantaged position of various racial and ethnic groups. Awareness of the discrimination, exploitation, and indifference long faced by black Americans was a primary catalyst in the creation of the new left in the past decade. However, as the history of the civil rights movement of the sixties has shown, this concentration of energy on the situation of an oppressed minority was not without severe problems. In particular, sharp conflict developed over the participation of whites in organizations whose resources were primarily devoted to working for and within the black community. As the civil rights effort evolved the position of

whites in the movement took on an increasingly ambiguous nature, eventually culminating in the exclusion or voluntary withdrawal of whites from central roles in the struggle and the emergence of the ideology of black power. Was this development entirely unique to the civil rights movement? Perhaps there are structural elements in this type of political movement which would inevitably lead to acute tension between dominant and subordinate group activists.

One manner in which to deal with this question is through the comparative analysis of similar movements. Our interest is in the role played by outsiders in other people's struggles, individuals who don't share the stigma or socially debilitating attribute and who don't stand to gain in the same direct way from the desired social change. There are of course an immense variety of political movements in which both insiders and outsiders played important roles. However for direct contrast with the civil rights effort we sought movements whose primary concern was altering the depressed condition of a minority group defined along racial or ethnic lines. Two efforts seemed particularly well-suited for a comparative analysis: the movement to end untouchability in India, and the abolitionist movement in this country. In a cursory examination of these movements and the civil rights effort we were struck by the poignant and ironic parallels in the conflict that often developed between blacks and whites or untouchables and caste Hindus working together in a common movement to bring about change. All three movements were intensely committed to ending the oppression of a relatively small ethnic or racial minority (whose condition was also of significant societal wide concern), all were predominantly left-

*[Reprinted with permission from the *Journal of Social Issues*, Vol. XXVII, No. 1. A number of colleagues graciously offered useful comments on this paper but we are particularly indebted to August Meier, Elliot Rudwick, and David Riesman for their extensive critiques. We are grateful to the Joint Center for Urban Studies and the Clark Fund for support. An earlier version was read at the American Sociological Association annual meeting, Washington, D.C., 1970.]

liberal in ideology and strategy but included strong radical currents, all had histories stretching over at least several decades, all took on a variety of organizational forms involving large numbers of people, all had both minority and dominant group members active in the struggle. . . . In this essay we attempt to draw out several sociological themes which appear to be typically associated with outsider involvement in minority movements.

Before examining these movements, some possible problems of method and evidence should be noted. The empirical foundation on which our argument rests could be appreciably stronger. Historical material on the untouchable movement is sketchy, and sociological analysis of all three developments is limited. This has necessitated reliance on observations and personal accounts of movement participants, especially activists from the minority group. Using such subjective assessments presents certain problems, although such evaluations reflect an important social reality. The degree of accuracy in personal accounts may vary considerably between observers, and more systematic data are needed to transform the suggestive findings of this paper into firm conclusions. For example, assertions about ideological differences between insiders and outsiders require verification through standard survey methods (a possibility in the cases of untouchability and civil rights). It should also be noted that we will be discussing modal tendencies and do not mean to imply that all white involvement in black movements or caste Hindus in untouchable movements has met with conflict, nor that differences characterizing the insider and outsider groups apply to all members taken individually, nor that other sources of conflict unrelated to race were not often present (e.g., class-based tensions have often been

attendant). In addition we are dealing with relations among activists and not uninvolved minority or majority group members, and not the way in which the movements relate to the broader society. We have tried not to magnify the degree of internal tension in these movements by only considering extreme examples, but in emphasizing some of the themes we have at times been somewhat selective in the presentation. A paper focusing on intergroup cooperation in these movements would no doubt deal with a number of issues and data we neglect.

FOUR CONFLICT THEMES

A comparative assessment of these three movements—abolition, civil rights, untouchable—will be undertaken along four themes. The first considers lines of ideological disagreement which have often distinguished insiders from outsiders. Frequently (though certainly not always) minority group activists have held somewhat more radical and militant attitudes than their majority group colleagues, at least with respect to the struggle around the oppression of that particular racial or caste group. Outsiders, on the other hand, have often affiliated with a broader set of political causes and movements. Even if there is a consensus on questions of ideology and strategy a second and third source of conflict stems from the fact that social movements are in many ways microcosms of the larger society. The divergent background and experiences of activists from the two groups may have important effects on the internal structure and culture of the movements. Structural conflict at times has arisen because dominant group activists, usually from more privileged backgrounds, have tended to come to the movement with more of the skills and experience which are important for the success of the movement such as writing, internal organizing, planning strategy, and fund raising, but perhaps a lesser commitment to the goals of that particular struggle (though not necessarily a lesser commitment to changing the system). These initial differences may result in disproportionate numbers of outsiders being in decision-making positions and may inhibit the development of similar skills among insiders. A third source of tension, cultural conflict, may arise because movement members have often been the carriers (if in a somewhat diluted form) of the prejudices and hostilities of the larger social milieu from which they came. Suspicion, distrust, and scapegoating on the part of the minority group, and stereotyping, patronization, and paternalism on the part of the dominant group have resulted in some cases. These two general types of conflict roughly correspond to Simmel's distinction between realistic and nonrealistic conflict (see Coser, 1956). The final theme to be considered concerns the development of these conflicts over time. Outsiders frequently have played critical roles in the early phases of these movements, but as the struggle has gained strength (and/or failed to bring about meaningful change) the latent conflicts between the two groups have tended to become more visible. Pressures develop on outsiders to reduce their level of involvement or to withdraw altogether.

IDEOLOGICAL CONFLICT BETWEEN MINORITY AND OUTSIDERS

In the civil rights, abolition, and untouchable movements, political divisions have been pervasive, perhaps a characteristic of most intense political movements. Some differences were benign and readily resolved, but others remained sharp and created consider-able internal conflict, and at times these ideological divisions paralleled the internal social cleavage between activists from the dominant and subordinate groups. A theme running through all three movements has been the occasional tendency for minority group activists to adopt a somewhat less reformist and more revolutionary perspective on the liberation of their own group, or at least to develop critiques of dominant group activists in these terms. Many instances of conflict between the two groups of activists could be traced to disagreements over the timetable for change, how far one should go in compromises and the extent to which noninstitutionalized protest means were acceptable. There has also been a tendency for outsiders to maintain interest in a wider variety of causes, which have often included the situation of women, the working classes, the poor, depressed castes and other ethnic minorities; they have lacked strong personal identification with any single issue.

Within the civil rights movement, for instance, this pattern was evident in CORE from its original inception until the middle 1960's. Rudwick and Meier (1969) observe that at the time of CORE's founding in 1942 the whites had interests ranging from nonviolence to racial equality, whereas involved blacks were primarily concerned with fighting racism. Two decades later this ideological divergence was still evident in CORE, as a study in the sixties reports: "Whites generally came to the movement with fairly stable, well-defined liberal views. . . . Their participation in the movement, which usually overshadowed other commitments, was one of a range of liberal political activities. . . . Negroes, however, required no elaborate liberal conditioning to bring them into the movement. The movement was their cause. . . . Negroes were always under direct emotional pressure resulting from segregation and discrimination. Therefore, the potential for great radicalism was present in their personal relationship to the issue (Bell, 1968, pp. 126–27)."

The untouchable movement, which has been influential in India since at least the turn of the century, evidences a parallel source of tension. B. R. Ambedkar, the foremost leader in the untouchable movement until his recent death and himself an untouchable, and Mahatma Gandhi, a caste Hindu, were frequently at odds over the proper solution of untouchability. Gandhi was associated with a wide variety of causes including ending British colonialism, encouragement of village industry, and uplifting the untouchables and women, while Ambedkar was concerned almost entirely with the condition of the untouchables and related depressed classes in India. The two leaders also differed on the amount of change needed to improve the situation of the untouchables. Gandhi felt that caste Hindus could be persuaded to accept the depressed classes as part of the Hindu fold, but Ambedkar maintained that the prospects for this were dim and that only through the application of political pressure could the rights of the untouchables be secured (Zelliot, 1966). Disagreements also occurred over the effectiveness and acceptability of various protest means. In the 1920's and 1930's direct action campaigns were often conducted against various restrictions faced by untouchables. Typical action included the collective drinking from community wells normally off-limits to untouchables and the entry of temples reserved for use by caste Hindus. These tactics were less acceptable to caste Hindus engaged in the movement than their untouchable allies. The series of events surrounding these steps of direct ac-

tion are remarkably similar in form to the events and aftermath of the freedom rides of CORE and sit-ins of SNCC in the early part of the sixties in this country.

Within the abolitionist movement white militancy was not lacking, as evidenced by the actions such as those of John Brown, but many black abolitionists at times urged more radical strategies on the overall movement and expressed a greater sense of urgency over the termination of slavery. In 1829 an early call to arms was issued by the black abolitionist, David Walker, which was frank in its encouragement of violent forms of action if circumstances were appropriate. Walker's "Appeal" was widely circulated and caused much consternation in the white antislavery camp. "A more bold, daring, inflammatory publication, perhaps never issued from the press of any country," asserted the white abolitionist publisher Benjamin Lundy. "I can do no less than set the broadest seal of condemnation on it (quoted in Litwack, 1961, p. 234)." Though the position was denounced by many whites in the antislavery cause, a little over a decade later another black abolitionist, Henry Highland Garnet, delivered an address before a national black antislavery convention which strongly echoed Walker's tone and included the exhortation, "It is your solemn and imperative duty to use every means, both moral, intellectual, and physical that promises success (1843)."

Black abolitionists tended to have a shorter timetable for change than their white coworkers. This difference became sharper as the antislavery movement increasingly sensed that its decades of effort had made little headway, particularly with the Dred Scott decision (1857) and the Fugitive Slave Act of 1850. Militancy increased among blacks as they wearied of "exhortations to be patient and await that 'impartial and just God' who would inevitably rid the nation of slavery (Litwack, 1965, p. 151)." By the critical decade of the 1850's black circles were openly discussing the encouragement of slave insurrections and forceful opposition to such legislation as the Fugitive Slave Law, and some even advanced the view that the entire political structure of the country should be overturned if necessary for the abolition of slavery. The more radical orientation of blacks in the movement extended beyond the issue of formal bondage to the situation of the free black in America. Many blacks in the antislavery crusade felt that the reformist instincts (in some cases encompassing a variety of issues) of their white colleagues prevented them from confronting subtler but nonetheless pervasive forms of racial oppression faced by those not in formal bondage. White abolitionists were quite sensitive about publicly advocating or evidencing a belief in full social equality and interracial mixing, and even black membership in some abolitionist societies was at times a hotly debated issue (Meier and Rudwick, 1966; Litwach, 1965).

A major strategic fracture at times overlapping the division between insiders and outsiders concerns attitudes toward self-help. Minority group activists have often argued that the process of struggling for one's freedom is a necessary prerequisite for fully ending oppression. Conversely, outsiders have tended to stress the strategic advantages of involving majority group activists. This is seen to increase the legitimacy of the movement as well as offering essential resources, such as financial backing.

Frederick Douglass expressed a view shared by many black abolitionists that "the man who has *suffered the wrong* is the man to *demand redress*—

that the man *struck* is the man to *cry out*—and that he who has *endured the cruel pangs of slavery* is the man to *advocate liberty* (1847)." At times white support was viewed more favorably since white activists were essential for gaining further white converts to the antislavery cause. However, as momentum gathered in the decades just prior to the Civil War black activists increasingly asserted their special standing within the movement. A black abolitionist conference announced in 1854 that "the time is come when our people must assume the rank of a first-rate power in the battle against caste and slavery; it is emphatically our battle; no one else can fight it for us, and with God's help we must fight it ourselves (quoted in Litwack, 1965, p. 155)." White abolitionists, on the other hand, often conceived of the black role as essentially symbolic and useful at ceremonial occasions but secondary to the real political effort.

Similar themes are present in the Indian movement. Many untouchable leaders felt that the efforts of high status Hindus inherently crippled the cause because their presence meant the untouchables would be denied control over even their own movement (Rudolph and Rudolph, 1967, p. 141). Ambedkar adamantly opposed top-down reform and was strongly committed to the central involvement of untouchables in the struggle. In his own acrid assessment: "The work of the Harijan Sevak Sangh [a prominent caste Hindu dominated organization working to alleviate the depressed position of the untouchables] is not to raise the untouchables. Gandhi's main object, as every self-respecting untouchable knows, is to make India safe for Hindus and Hinduism. He is certainly not fighting the battle of the untouchables. On the contrary by distributing through the Harijan Sevak Sangh petty gifts to petty untouchables he is buying, benumbing, and drawing the claws of the opposition of the untouchables which he knows is the only force which will disrupt the caste system and will establish real democracy in India (1943, p. 69)."

Similar tensions have been present throughout the recent history of the civil rights movement, culminating in the ascendance of the idea of black power and the partial withdrawal of white activists. A variety of arguments have been advanced against having outsiders engaged in a movement working primarily in black communities (though combating racism in white contexts may be appropriate). As in the case of the untouchable leaders, black activists were fearful that reform from above would ultimately leave black communities in a state of dependency.

It was argued that the society's dominant white institutions had yielded only limited reform in the past and there was little reason to expect them to be a major impetus in the future behind the more massive changes critically needed. Furthermore, whatever improvement in the condition of black people these institutions already could be credited with was viewed as little more than a response to pressures from below. The mobilization of the black community was therefore viewed as essential at minimum for prodding those with power to create reformist changes. But if the mustering was effectively accomplished there were additional benefits which were unachievable under top-down reform. It may help produce a sense of pride, self-reliance, and confidence within the black community which is a desirable end in itself. In addition, the new political awareness may eventuate in more intense and lasting pressure for radical change. White activists of course did not formally represent the

dominant white power structure, but symbolically they did to many and their presence in the movement impeded the creation of the desired self-confidence and political consciousness. The civil rights movement was attempting to relate to black people, but blacks had difficulty shaking loose of deferential tendencies around whites, no matter how well-intentioned the whites were. White workers, for instance, were at times able to get rural blacks to register to vote after black workers had failed. As the movement evolved many minority group activists came to feel that the early benefits of outsider involvement were outweighed by detrimental effects of this sort. Many of the negative aspects are summarized in a position paper of a SNCC-affiliated group (written just prior to the emergence of the black power ethos), which argues strongly for a black-led, black-staffed, and black-financed movement for organizing within their own communities. The rationale includes: "The inability of whites to relate to the cultural aspects of black society; attitudes that whites, consciously or unconsciously, bring to black communities about themselves (Western superiority) and about black people (paternalism); inability to shatter white-sponsored community myths of black inferiority and self-negation; inability to combat the views of the black community that white organizers, being 'white,' control black organizers as puppets; . . . whites, though individual 'liberals,' are symbols of oppression to the black community—due to the *collective* power that whites have over black lives (Vine City Project, 1967, p. 97)."

THE PRIVILEGED POSITION OF THE OUTSIDERS

Almost by definition outsiders in these movements tended to have privileges and opportunities that were systematically denied most members of the subordinate group. Consequently outsiders were often more skilled in a variety of ways relevant to the needs of the movement, and this initial difference often created a situation in which outsiders occupied a disproportionate share of high status positions and exerted what was seen as an excessive influence on decision making. In this respect the internal structure of the movements reflected in microcosm many of the intergroup patterns typical of the broader society. This was tolerated and even accepted as necessary for a limited period, but many minority group activists came to conclude that such an arrangement inhibited the growth of the movement, was incongruent with its basic aims, dampened militancy, and reduced the opportunity for developing political competence among minority group activists.

This pattern is most apparent in the antislavery cause. In the signing of the constitution establishing the New England Anti-Slavery Society only a quarter of the signers were black, and only three blacks were officially present at the 1833 conference which formed the American Anti-Slavery Society. In the early phases of the abolitionist effort those organizations that were integrated were prone to relegate blacks to peripheral roles requiring little more than a black skin or a personal history of former bondage. As people truly representative of those in bondage they performed useful symbolic functions on ceremonial occasions, but most other roles, such as propagandizing, organizing forums and conventions, and raising financial support, were assumed by whites. With the exception of the underground railway (which involved comparatively few whites) this marginal role for blacks persisted throughout the antislavery movement.

Black abolitionists painfully sensed their exclusion; Martin Robinson Delany (1852) critically observed that white "abolitionists have each and all, at different times presumed to *think* for and *dictate* to, and know better what suited colored people than they knew for themselves. . . ." Frederick Douglass corroborates this view as late as 1855: "Our oppressed people are wholly ignored . . . in the generalship of the movement to effect our redemption (quoted in Meier and Rudwick, 1966, p. 105)."

There are similarities, if less extreme and more benign, in the civil rights efforts of the 1960's. Writing of his own experience in the South, Staughton Lynd notes that "many of us had drifted into administrative roles . . . not because we wanted to be leaders, but because we were obviously better able to write press releases and answer the telephone than to approach frightened black people in remote rural communities. The objective result, however, was that we made more decisions than we should have made (Lynd, 1969, p. 14)." Several participant observers noting the same pattern suggest that an additional factor may lie in differences in cultural style revolving around the supposed greater emphasis whites placed on punctuality, structure, and organization (Keller, Mabutt, and Ruhe, 1965). The influx of skilled whites into the movement and their assumption of authority roles created considerable resentment. In some cases local activists withdrew from the movement and many blacks came to feel that as always whites were trying to take things over to serve their own ends. An important role in decision making by whites dates far back in the civil rights movement; for instance, Ralph Bunche in the early 1940's saw white involvement to have a powerful indirect effect on keeping interracial organizations moderate, since blacks in the organizations often felt compelled to defer to white opinion (Myrdal, 1942).

A second structural source of tension in such movements may lie in what is perceived as the differential levels of commitment of the two types of activist. Regardless of background, people enter social movements for a variety of reasons and these may change over time. Yet the minority group activist is working for the liberation of himself and the community with which he is politically, culturally, and personally identified. In most cases he can never leave his ascriptive minority group status and should he wish to give up full-time involvement he may have fewer opportunities in the larger society. He thus may be seen as more reliable and accountable for his actions than an outsider who can leave the struggle more easily. For dominant group activists abstract moral principles may be more important as a guiding motive since neither they, nor their community of origin, stand to gain in the same direct way from involvement. Furthermore the very political principles that brought the outsider to the ethnic movement in question may at a later date direct their energies into other causes. The overall commitment of outsiders to the creation of social change may be equivalent to that of the minority group activists, but it may be less identified with any single movement.

Adequate empirical evidence on differential commitment is lacking, yet common to all three movements is a questioning of the motives and degree of commitment of activists from the dominant group. In the case of the southern civil rights movement there are data indicating that many whites had a short period of activism. According to one study, only 7 percent of whites who went South during the summer of 1965 remained there during the fall. Only one out of four white volunteers definitely planned to return to the South to work with the movement, and only a tenth of those in the study reported considerable guilt about leaving the struggle (Demerath, Marwell, and Aiken, 1968). Unfortunately comparable turnover rates for blacks are not available. Even when whites remained in the South there was resentment over the perception that they could more readily play two roles. Julius Lester comments: "Sure whites came South. They got a little taste of jail, got beaten, but they were white. That meant they could go back home and not have to worry as they walked down the street. . . .[N]o matter where they were in the South, they could sneak off and go to a nice white restaurant or the movie theatre. . . . They could drive down the highway and if they were not known as civil rights workers, their minds could be easy (1968, p. 103)." Furthermore, some whites became engaged in civil rights for reasons only indirectly relevant to the concrete struggle of blacks. In one study, among reasons given by whites for their involvement were: "the opportunity for active rebellion against everything from the oppression of capitalism . . . to my parents," "I like Negroes . . . relationships with them are not neurotic and are free of deception," and "to make a witness to what I believe (Pinkney, 1968, pp. 97–100, 180)." Though similar motives might characterize some blacks they were not as apparent or suspect because of the minority group members' direct personal stake in the struggle. Some blacks felt they were being used as therapy by conscience-stricken white activists.

The abolitionist movement also saw some whites involved for diverse reasons and short periods of time. An historian reports the presence of those for whom the movement represented "a release for private devils," and the cause was not without its "summer soldiers who after a season disappeared in the shadows (Quarles, 1969, p. 53)." There was a tendency for the commitments of some whites to be dictated more by a general social conscience than a deep radical determination to overthrow slavery, and at times this led to a greater concern with assuming a proper moral posture than in obtaining the movement's goals; a prominent white abolitionist observed, "My friends, if we never free a slave, we have at least freed ourselves, in the effort to emancipate our brother man (quoted in Quarles, 1969, p. 53)." Such sentiments were a factor in the widespread dismay blacks felt with their white allies in the later decades of the movement. Speaking in 1837 a black minister declared that in the early days there were few white antislavery advocates and their commitments were clear and deep, but "now a man may call himself an abolitionist and we know not where to find him (Wright, 1837)."

Many untouchable leaders were also suspicious of caste Hindus concerned with the condition of the untouchables. They felt their commitment was never transformed into anything but promises after Gandhi assumed leadership in the 1920's. This led to considerable disillusionment among untouchable activists (Heimsath, 1964, p. 252). Suspicion of outsiders' motives was manifest in debates on whether the untouchables in India ought to elect solely their own representatives (separate electorate) or if both caste and noncaste voters should collectively help to select the person to serve as representative of the untouchables (joint electorate). Ambedkar was vehemently opposed to the joint scheme since he felt that untouchable background was essential for a person to represent authentically the interests of his class (Ambedkar, 1943, pp. 26ff.). This deep distrust of outsiders is shared by the politically conscious sector of a large untouchable community recently studied. Lynch notes a widespread feeling that only untouchable leaders could "really understand and achieve empathy" with the community, a sentiment reflected in the strong identification with Ambedkar's movement at the national level (1969, pp. 137ff.).

BRINGING IN CULTURAL PREJUDICES

Independent of the structural conflicts in the movement, interpersonal relations within the movement may inadvertently manifest many of the social patterns of the greater society. Though the most virulent and blatant forms of group prejudice were not in evidence among the three movements, mild negative group attitudes and a sense of inferior or superior group status was manifest, and condescension, patronization, paternalism, and stereotyping on the part of the outsiders were frequently noted. Like Captain Lingard in Joseph Conrad's The Rescue, the dominant group activist too often "prided himself upon having no color prejudice and no racial antipathies . . . only he knew what was good for them." At times this was reciprocated by passive acceptance of an inferior social position on the part of activists from the subordinate group, although enmity toward the dominant group coworkers has often been a simultaneous development. This was further exacerbated by a feeling among insiders that many dominant group activists behaved hypocritically; they espoused a creed of egalitarianism within the movement yet often denied it in practice. Many of these deeply felt tensions between the two types of activists were sharpened by a tendency noted by Coser (1956) for conflict to be particularly pronounced in close-knit groups.

There is much evidence that the internal culture of the abolitionist movement was pervaded by both racial and class prejudice to a much greater extent than in the civil rights movement. The sense of racial superiority was retained by many of even the most ardent white abolitionists, and the "patronizing air of the uplifter" toward the "downtrodden and unwashed" frequently characterized the manner in which whites in the movement related to free blacks (Pease and Pease, 1965, pp. 685ff.). Whites often offered advice and observations on a variety of matters in a fatherly and demeaning style to their black colleagues. An exceptional black received more than exceptional praise from some white abolitionists, perhaps reflecting their mild astonishment in encountering a black person with ability. The effects were not lost on the black abolitionist who often complained that the antislavery cause itself was psychologically oppressive; racial prejudice pervaded much of the atmosphere. A black minister warned an antislavery convention that "abolitionists must annihilate in their own bosoms the cord of caste. We must be consistent—recognize the colored man in every respect as a man and brother (Wright, 1837)." Another source of tension was the feeling that white abolitionists oftentimes were guilty of discrimination outside of the movement. Many abolitionists bitterly denounced the system of slavery and devoted much energy to its eradication but drew back from behavior that suggested social acceptance of the free black. In some public places, the home, and other private settings white abolitionists often were sensitive to charges of racial mixing, and their social associations were something less than fully

integrated. Furthermore, free blacks in the North faced serious economic discrimination. Many whites active in the antislavery struggle were successful businessmen and yet they frequently failed to make efforts to hire blacks or did so only for the most menial positions (Litwack, 1965, pp. 141–143).

A caste Hindu activist frankly assessed the lingering prejudices many brought to the untouchable movement. "It will take some time before *even the best amongst us* begin to look upon Harijans as an important and integral part of the great Hindu community. *Even the most enlightened amongst us* perfectly unconsciously recognize inwardly the distinction between Harijans and non-Harijans (quoted in Sanjana, 1946)." Accusations of hypocrisy and inconsistency were also directed at caste Hindus.

Like some of the white abolitionists, various Congress spokesmen were quick to denounce the sins of untouchability but were hesitant to transgress traditional taboos against socially mingling with untouchables. Some simply refused to share dinners with members of the depressed classes when invited or, if unavoidable, shunned too close a seating arrangement (Natarajan, 1959, pp. 148–152). When they did join in such dinners they often later underwent symbolic acts of disavowal. Gandhi insisted that orthodox Hindu communities should not be distressed by the process of reform and when he made the removal of untouchability a part of the Congress program he explicitly excluded interdining.

Similar sources of friction along racial lines have also been evident in the civil rights movement. On a number of projects whites felt themselves to be more skilled than their black leaders and refused or were reluctant to follow orders they perceived as unnecessary or wrong. As one activist indicated,

"I felt like the master's child coming to free the slaves," a feeling sometimes revealed in behavior. Levy reports the case of a civil rights office that was managed by a black activist but which included some white workers. When several whites unfamiliar with the office entered they directed their initial queries for information to the white person rather than the black in charge (1968, p. 78). Even with the best of intentions race has a persistent relevance that is hard to overcome. Traditional social forms and etiquette, as well as stereotypes, facilitate (or at least do not directly counter) usual patterns of dominant-subordinate relations, even among those committed to a more equalitarian society. One volunteer recalls: "A white man never turns black in Mississippi. . . . [Y]our secret belief [does not disappear] . . . that you are, after all, superior . . . you're still college-educated, still play acting, and still white (Sutherland, 1965, p. 58)." Everyday language in an interracial setting often came to have unintended implications. "Following a marvelous dinner at the house of your local landlord, you hear yourself say, 'Boy, was that a great dinner' and you choke involuntarily on the expletive. You can't forget that you're still white . . . (Sutherland, 1965, p. 59)."

However, social expectations may also ensnarl even the most tolerant, if in a reverse fashion, in the process Goffman has called "deminstrelization" (Goffman, 1963, p. 110). Some whites overcompensated in trying to deny their outsider and middle class backgrounds. Whites in overreacting to the racism of the larger society occasionally adopted a subordinate position and hid skills that would be inconsistent with this, or refused to argue with blacks, even if strongly provoked. Some gave away personal possessions and were unable to deny any black request. A

white volunteer in the South recalls "we've sort of laid down and let them run over us." In another case a white took over the job of toilet cleaning in a civil rights office to prevent blacks from assuming a stereotyped role (Levy, 1968, pp. 110–111). The effort to appear as nonwhite as possible may also be seen in the adoption of aspects of black and working class culture (Marx, 1967a; Warren, 1965). Hard work by whites for the movement, partly inspired by a desire to prove their commitment, was sometimes seen instead as proof that they were trying to take things over. Interracial sexual affairs were seen by some as a way of transcending race and, for whites, demonstrating their lack of prejudice, but often they were felt to be strategically unwise, were a source of anxiety and jealousy, and were seen to be detrimental to the development of black pride. Activists were also affected by some of the sexual mythology and fears of the larger society. Thus a white staff member of an organization dedicated to "accomplishment of a completely integrated society" on hearing the screams of a girl at an evening conference, reports that his "immediate reaction was that one of the Negroes was raping the shit out of her (Levy, 1968, p. 81)."

In addition to being suspicious of outsiders, some minority group activists displaced their general antiwhite feelings onto the white workers. Robert Moses notes that "it's very hard for some of the students who have been brought up in Mississippi and are the victims of this kind of race hatred not to begin to let all of that out on the white staff (quoted in Warren, 1965, p. 96)." In the face of numerous frustrations, whites were accessible and provided a relatively safe target, unlike most members of the dominant group. The sense of collective guilt which initially brought many outsiders into the movement in some cases predisposed them to passively accept or even seek this scapegoating.

Even if in their face-to-face interaction whites and blacks can relate authentically and avoid the kinds of conflict mentioned here, the culture of the outside world, as it impinges on the movement may create internal conflicts. For instance, in the South white activists arrested often faced more tolerable jail conditions, and national indignation over the few whites martyred in the civil rights struggle has been far greater than over the much larger number of blacks. Though one reason for involving whites in the summers of 1964 and 1965 was the desire to draw national attention, when this attention came many blacks were resentful and took it as one more manifestation of American racism. Survey data reveals that many white activists sensed distrust and hostility from black activists (Demerath, Marwell, and Aiken, 1968; Pinkney, 1968, pp. 114ff.). However, the attitudes of black activists on these issues may be very different from those of the masses of uninvolved blacks. Thus, surveys frequently find the overwhelming majority of the black population look favorably on white participation in civil rights activity (Marx, 1967b; Campbell & Schuman, 1968).

THE CHANGING ROLE OF OUTSIDERS—INDEPENDENCE NEEDS OF OPPRESSED MINORITY

Thus far we have focused primarily on the static question of insider-outsider discord. Certain structural features of the movement have been seen to have various consequences. We now turn briefly to the more dynamic social process question of the evolution of conflict over time.

Rarely have oppressed minorities been *entirely* responsible for their own liberation. Privileged groups played prominent roles in the ending of slavery in Greece and Rome, were conspicuous in the French and Russian revolutions, and at least since the time of Karl Marx observers have noted a tendency for some members of the privileged to defect and take up the cause of the oppressed. In the movements examined here and in others of a similar type it appears that the role of outsiders may be critical in the early phases of the struggle. The more oppressed the minority group, the more essential may be aid from members of the dominant group in initiating the liberation movement. However, as the movement gathers strength the importance of outsiders is often greatly reduced, at times leading to their complete withdrawal. Caste Hindus initiated many of the early efforts aimed at ameliorating the condition of the untouchables, and white abolitionists were primarily responsible for the formation of many of the early antislavery societies and for hooking these into a national system. In the case of civil rights, whites played a crucial active role in the founding of the NAACP, the Urban League, and CORE, although not in organizations emerging later such as SNCC and the Black Panthers (Kellogg, 1967; Meier and Rudwick, 1969; Farmer, 1965).

Outsiders generally have had greater command over resources, have been freer to act, were likely to be close to centers of power, and have often had essential organizing experience. Their presence in the struggle may add an aura of legitimacy to the protest movement's goals, and when they are harassed or killed in the cause the situation is dramatized far beyond what happens when minority group members face similar brutalization. In addition, in the germinal phase many members of the oppressed group may be isolated from alternative definitions of the situa-

tion and in the absence of a strong protest tradition may not actively question the legitimacy of the system, and
of course some may have a vested interest in maintaining the status quo.
Thus the important, often even predominant, role of outsiders in the beginning stages of these movements is
not surprising. However, an additional
factor in the early involvement of outsiders in some organizations such as
CORE and the British Committee
Against Racial Discrimination is an ideology that defined interracial cooperation as an end in itself.

Once outsiders are into this type of
effort, however, their presence is potentially problematic for reasons discussed above. Some of the advantages
of having outsiders involved in the
beginning stages may come to be seen as
liabilities as the movement evolves.
Several developments facilitate the separation of minority and majority group
activists. First of all, with engagement
in the movement insiders acquire necessary skills and confidence, and become
less dependent on outsiders. Second, the
latent structural conflicts become more
manifest with continued interaction
of the two groups. Third, as the objectives are not reached or even approached despite intense activity and
sacrifice, militancy and susceptibility
to new strategies may increase, as well
as internal scapegoating. Finally, as
the movement recruits new members
from the oppressed group and the character of its membership shifts, it may
become increasingly less dependent on
manpower from outsiders. Thus, structural aspects of such movements are
likely to give rise to severe conflict
and this in turn helps generate beliefs
justifying the separation of minority
and dominant group activists. On the
other hand the adoption of such beliefs
may in some cases precede internal conflict and hasten the division of the move-

ment. Ideology may diffuse between
movements, as seems to have occurred
in Britain where a black power perspective and symbols have been adopted by
some blacks in an effort to oust whites
from CARD, the major civil rights organization.

The processes noted here are not
irreversible. The American left has
vacillated between emphasizing the
uniquely racial as against the shared
economic class aspects of the situation
of blacks in America. In parts of the
1930's and the past two decades the
class component has been ascendent,
but at other times the racial line has
been considered prime. Concomitantly
tactics have shifted between a racially
separate movement and a common integrated struggle. In the 1960's, particularly with the rise of the black power
movement, the unique ethnic aspects
of black subordination were stressed.
Associated with this trend has been the
tendency among whites who left the
black movement to become engaged
in social movements in which they no
longer were defined as outsiders (e.g.,
campus issues, the antiwar movement,
draft resistance, women's liberation,
ethnic associations). More recently
much leftist thought has argued that
the problems of blacks and other ethnic
groups, the white working class, females, and to some degree even those
of students, stem from shared economic
and political oppression. With this
perspective goes an emphasis on cooperation in a common struggle. Similarly various periods in American history show blacks moving toward and
then away from inclusion depending on
the receptiveness of the dominant
group. Beyond the internal sources of
tension noted here, when the dominant
group's supposed receptiveness proves
illusory, blacks have increasingly turned
inward and in a separatist direction.
For instance, the hopes raised by the

Civil War and World War I led to an initial emphasis on inclusion; the shattering of those hopes facilitated the ascendance of separatist leaders such as Booker T. Washington and Marcus Garvey.

The future of the relationship between the white left and the black movement in America is hardly clear at the present. Tensions and impediments to interracial cooperation remain present. Yet movements do not exist in a vacuum. While both the white left and the black movement are made up of highly diverse groups, important segments of each are coming to reflect a growing ideological similarity which stresses the presence of a common enemy and the need for cooperation to build an interracial society free of exploitation and racism. This is apparent in the coalitional ties which have been developing over the past few years between the Black Panthers and various white radical groups, though the relationship yet remains an ambivalent one. Thus the tendency for interracial movements to splinter along racial lines may be followed by a tendency to regroup as the limits of independent action and separatism are realized and because of solidarity created by shared repression at the hands of the government and other powerful institutions in the society.

IN CONCLUSION

A comparative look at these three movements reveals several recurrent themes of intergroup tension. There is much variation depending on the time period and the segment of the movement involved, yet ideological cleavage frequently exists between dominant and minority group activists. When conflict of an ideological nature along this line emerged there was a tendency for insiders to see themselves as more radical and committed than outsiders; more eager to create changes immediately than gradually, less willing to compromise their program for the sake of expediency, less hesitant to use non-institutionalized protest means, less concerned with a variety of political movements, and more likely to espouse a creed of self-help. As microcosms of society these movements often developed internal authority and skill structures resembling in diluted form the subordinate-dominant relations characteristic of the broader societal context, as well as atmospheres containing many of society's intergroup hostilities and prejudices. Over time many of these latent conflicts became manifest, and dominant group activists who played an important role in the formative phases of the movement were excluded or forced to assume greatly reduced roles.

In making inferences concerning these patterns to other social movements generalizations must be undertaken with caution since the civil rights, untouchable, and abolitionist causes represent responses to somewhat similar forms of oppression with both insiders and outsiders actively engaged. However, a very impressionistic look at related movements such as those of Mexican–Americans in this country, the Burakumin in Japan, blacks in South Africa and the Caribbean, and Asians and Africans in England suggest many of the same themes. The interaction between insiders and outsiders in a variety of other movements not involving race or ethnicity, such as nonworking class activists in the labor movement, men in the feminist movement, and colonials in nationalist movements may also show similarities. It would be interesting to examine movements where the source of outsiderness stems not from race and ethnicity but from characteristics such as sex, class, age, religion, or past experience (e.g., those without a record of confinement active in the prison or mental hospital reform movement). A variety of other issues might also be pursued. We have focused mainly on factors conducive to conflict and separation of insiders and outsiders. An important question for further analysis would be the factors facilitating cooperation among such activists, and the stages in a movement's life history when such conditions occur. For instance, strong external pressures from an unsympathetic and occasionally repressive dominant society have often been conducive to intergroup solidarity. Numerous examples of interracial cooperation are described in the growing literature on the civil rights movement (Zinn, 1964; Pinkney, 1968; Sutherland, 1965; Sugarman, 1966; Belfrage, 1966). Another important question has to do with differences in the extensiveness of conflict and separation of activists in diverse organizations such as NAACP, CORE, and SNCC which are part of the same general social movement. Rudwick and Meier note that beyond difference in constituency and top leadership, the strong bureaucratic structure of the NAACP may have made it more stable and resistant to the separatist thrust that completely changed CORE (Rudwick and Meier, 1969). Finally, it would be interesting to explore whether the internal tensions of a movement preview broader societal changes. The activists' awareness of ideological and interpersonal strains in their movement may encourage many people outside of the cause to become conscious of similar factors in their own lives.

In contrast to the untouchable and abolitionist movements, the civil rights struggles of this decade are still very much with us, and perhaps one indirect benefit of comparing these three movements is to make our own period of history a little more intelligible, though this is a comment on neither the morality nor strategic value of these developments. Many whites who had contributed much to the civil rights movement were initially shocked, angered, and bewildered at the development of the black power movement. Some sought explanations in terms of the presumed unstable personalities of radical blacks rather than in terms of the social structure of the movement. However, similar processes in the three movements examined here suggest that tension among activists and the rise of the black power movement were in part a response to political differences and interpersonal conflicts common to this type of social movement. An identification of historically recurring conflict themes generated by the structure of such movements might also help future movements avoid or minimize the conflict that ironically may develop among those of different backgrounds committed to common goals of social change.

REFERENCES

AMBEDKAR, B. R. *Mr. Gandhi and the Emancipation of the Untouchables.* Bombay: Thacker, 1943.

BELL, I. P. *CORE and the Strategy of Nonviolence.* New York: Random House, 1968.

BELFRAGE, S. *Freedom Summer.* Greenwich, Conn.: Fawcett Publications, 1966.

CAMPBELL, A., and SCHUMAN, H. *Racial Attitudes in Fifteen American Cities.* Ann Arbor: Survey Research Center, 1968.

COLES, R. "The Search for Community," *The New Republic.* February 26, 1966, 154, 12–14.

COSER, L. *The Functions of Social Conflict.* New York: Free Press, 1956.

DELANY, M. R. *The Condition, Elevation, Emigration and Destiny of the Colored People of the United States, Politically Considered,* (Philadelphia: Author, 1852). Preface reprinted in H. Aptheker (ed.), *A Documentary History of the Ne-*

gro People in the United States: From Colonial Times through the Civil War. New York: The Citadel Press, 1968, 326–327.

DEMERATH, N. J., III, MARWELL, G., and AIKEN, M. "Tactics and Tensions in a Summer of Yesteryear: Results of a Panel Analysis of 1965 Southern Civil Rights Workers." Paper presented at the annual meeting of American Sociological Association, Boston, Massachusetts, 1968.

DOUGLASS, F. The North Star (editorial), December 3, 1847. In H. Aptheker (ed.), op. cit., 266.

FARMER, J. Freedom When? New York: Random House, 1966.

GARA, L. "Who Was an Abolitionist?" In M. Duberman (ed.), The Antislavery Vanguard: New Essays on the Abolitionists. Princeton: Princeton University Press, 1965, 32–51.

GARNET, H. H. "An Address to the Slaves of the United States (1843)." In H. Aptheker (ed.), op. cit., 226–233.

GOFFMAN, I. Stigma: Notes on the Management of Spoiled Identities. Englewood Cliffs, N.J.: Prentice-Hall, 1963.

HEIMSATH, C. Indian Nationalism and Hindu Social Reform. Princeton: Princeton University Press, 1964.

KERR, D. Dr. Ambedkar: Life and Mission (2d ed.). Bombay: Popular Prakashan, 1962.

KELLER, A., MABUTT, F., and RUHE, D. "Summer 1965: The White 'Freedom Fighters' in the South." Kansas Journal of Sociology, 1965, 1, 119–122.

KELLOGG, C. NAACP: A History of the National Association for the Advancement of Colored People. Baltimore: Johns Hopkins, 1967.

LESTER, J. Look out Whitey! Black Power's Gon' Get Your Mama! New York: Grove Press, 1968.

LEVY, C. Voluntary Servitude: Whites in the Negro Movement. New York: Appleton-Century-Crofts, 1968.

LITWACK, L. "The Emancipation of the Negro Abolitionist." In M. Duberman (ed.), op. cit., 137–155.

——North of Slavery: The Negro in the Free States, 1790–1860. Chicago: University of Chicago Press, 1961.

LYNCH, O. M. The Politics of Untouchability: Social Mobility and Social Change in a City of India. New York: Columbia University Press, 1969.

LYND, S. "The Movement: A New Beginning." Liberation, May 14, 1969, 7–20.

MARX, G. "The White Negro and the Negro White." Phylon, 1967a, 28, 168–177.

——Protest and Prejudice: A Study of Belief in the Black Community. New York: Harper and Row, 1967b.

MEIER, A., and Rudwick, E. M. "How CORE Began." Social Science Quarterly, March, 1969, 49, 789–799.

MYRDAL, G. An American Dilemma. New York: Harper and Row, 1944, 2 vols.

NATARAJAN, S. A Century of Social Reform in India. Bombay: Asia Publishing House, 1959.

PEASE, W., and PEASE, J. H. "Antislavery Ambivalence: Immediatism, Expediency, Race." American Quarterly, 1965, 17, 682–695.

PINKNEY, A. The Committed: White Activists in the Civil Rights Movement. New Haven: College and University Press, 1968.

POUSSAINT, A. "Problems of White Civil Rights Workers in the South." Psychiatric Opinion, 1966, 3 (6), 18–24.

QUARLES, B. Black Abolitionists. New York: Oxford University Press, 1969.

RUDOLPH, L. I., and RUDOLPH, S. H. The Modernity of Tradition: Political Development in India. Chicago: University of Chicago Press, 1967.

RUDWICK, E. M., and MEIER, A. "Organizational Structure and Goal Succession: A Comparative Study of the NAACP and CORE, 1964–1968." Social Science Quarterly, June, 1970.

SANJANA, J. E. Caste and Outcaste. Bombay: Thacker, 1946.

SUGARMAN, T. Stranger at the Gates. New York: Hill and Wang, 1966.

SUTHERLAND, E. (ed.). Letters from Mississippi. New York: McGraw Hill, 1965.

VINE CITY PROJECT. "Whites in the Movement." In M. Cohen and D. Hale (eds.), The New Student Left. Boston: Beacon Press, 1967.

WARREN, R. P. "Two for SNCC." Commentary, 1965, 39, 38–48.

WRIGHT, T. S. "Address to the New York State Anti-Slavery Society Convention, Utica, New York, September, 1837." In H. Aptheker (ed.), op. cit., 169–173.

ZELLIOT, E. "Buddhism and Politics in Maharashtra." In D. E. Smith (ed.), South Asian Politics and Religion. Princeton: Princeton University Press, 1966.

ZINN, H. SNCC: The New Abolitionists. Boston: Beacon Press, 1965.

PART FIVE
CONSEQUENCES OF
CONFLICT

ONE of the important ideas developed by Karl Marx and held by many social analysts and activists (not necessarily always dissimilar groups) is the role of conflict in generating change. Implicit in many of the articles read thus far is the notion that parts of society are in a tension with each other and out of their clash emerges a new order, although perhaps one containing different contradictions. The case studies suggest that change often does follow a challenge.

One of the main themes in the current sociology of conflict is an emphasis on its unrecognized positive functions. In the face of the preponderant view that conflict is uniformly a bad thing, such an emphasis is a helpful corrective. Yet if applied too dogmatically, it can inhibit understanding and lead to unrealistic assessments. Although Frederick Douglass' stirring words, "power concedes nothing without a demand, it never did and it never will . . . men may not get all they pay for in this world, but they must certainly pay for all they get," cannot help but stir strong feelings in those aware of American society's many failings, the link between protest and change is by no means always perfect.

A particularly important question for those concerned with racial injustice in American society has to do with the consequences of current racial conflict. What is the link between conflict and change? How much can it accomplish? What are its limits? How much has conflict accomplished? What changes have there been in the distribution of scarce resources and the means by which these are distributed? Beyond the issue of change, what other functions or consequences of conflict may we observe?

To talk about the consequences of conflict we must first specify the level at which we wish to look: the society as a whole, the dominant group, the minority group, the world community, various institutions, the values of the society, or the individual personality. Consequences will not necessarily be uniform either within or between these units.

What are the consequences for the entire society? Does the conflict bind the antagonists together and serve to activate shared moral values of equality and brotherhood, or does it lead to polarization? Does it lead to redistribution of desired resources and new ways of allocating scarce goods? As role models, what effect has the black questioning of traditional social forms, the demand for dignity and participation, and direct action tactics had on other groups in American society, or indeed the world? One need only look here at the liberation movements of other ethnic minority groups, students, women, homosexuals, and the antiwar movement to get some sense of this.

As the social order is questioned by blacks, does the dominant group experience an increased sense of cohesion? Are white groups which were previously somewhat beyond the pale, such as Italians and Jews, suddenly more acceptable? Or does the dominant group become internally fragmented as its various parts take different sides in the racial struggle?

Among the most interesting of consequences are those for the minority group. Whatever its effect in redistributing resources or on legislative programs, recent racial conflict has had an important effect on the personality and on the internal organization of various black communities. That black demands for change have often fallen far short of their goals does not mean that conflict has been insignificant. The very fact of struggle may change the way a group thinks of itself and the nature of its interaction with others. At the personality level, the struggle for equal rights has had an important effect on black self-image and feelings of pride. The civil rights struggle and the more recent black power movement seem to have greatly increased feelings of unity and solidarity among blacks and have given rise to numerous black advancement organizations. Here we see how external conflict and what may be perceived as a common enemy may bind a group together. On the other hand, as several of the case studies suggested,

as the group meets with some success, internal conflict and competition may greatly increase as new resources become available. An increase in frustration over failure to obtain its goals may have similar consequences. It is also possible that to protest and not be successful may reinforce feelings of powerlessness, apathy, and despair.

Within which institutional areas does conflict first lead to change? Does resistance to change increase as the psychological closeness of whites to blacks increases, as Gunnar Myrdal suggested? Do conflict-created changes in one institutional area such as the law or the economy reverberate throughout the system and lead to changes in other areas, without conflict necessarily occurring there? For example, a successful fair housing campaign may mean not only better housing but an increase in black economic position, as individuals move closer to jobs not available in the inner city. Or better jobs for blacks gained through a boycott may also mean an increase in status.

Even within the same institutional area a demonstration or a riot that produced change in one community, through a spinoff effect, was sometimes able to produce like changes in other communities, without any overt conflict having occurred. By the mere fact of raising issues and making well-publicized demands, awareness of the problem may be increased and the behavior of others not directly involved in the controversy affected. The 1960's and 1970's are clearly periods of heightened consciousness regarding racial inequality. Much change, often unnoticed, has emerged from this awareness triggered by conflicts and specific demands elsewhere. Here the threat of conflict, whether real or imagined, and sometimes a resurgence of conscience have brought about change. A reverse effect may also be noted—increased efforts at repression in response to fear of expected conflict.

We lack satisfactory answers to most of the above questions. Recent social analysts have tended to stay away from them—perhaps because change may be looked at on so many levels, and there appears to be much variation between place and time with respect to the conflict-change link. It is often difficult to sort out correlation from causality. As will be suggested, even where conflict and change are found together they may both be produced by some third factor. There may also be a time lag. Thus a given demonstration may set changes in motion which don't surface for several years.

There can be little doubt that some major changes have occurred, particularly in our legal and political structures, and in the South. The nation has in principle, through its legal system, Congress, and the executive, committed itself to equal treatment of all its citizens. The Supreme Court in the school desegregation case of 1954 and other decisions since then, the Civil Rights Acts of 1964 and 1965, various state and local laws, numerous executive orders, and even an occasional show of force have declared de jure segregation and discrimination to be illegal.

Formal, legally sanctioned segregation and the elaborate system of etiquette that supported the caste system are clearly on the retreat. In the South transportation facilities, lunch counters, libraries, playgrounds, hotels, restaurants, universities, and some schools have been desegregated. There has also been noticeable desegregation in some small and moderately sized northern communities. Many changes at a symbolic level have occurred such as spelling "Negro" with a capital "N" and addressing blacks as "Mr." or "Miss."

There has also been a pronounced redistribution of power in many parts of the country. The national political parties at least now endorse the idea of equal rights. The power of the national government relative to the states has increased. Change is quite visible in the area of political participation, particularly in the South. In 1964 about two million southern blacks were registered to vote. Only four years later, with population size remaining constant, this figure increased to three million. In 1969 the number of blacks holding elected office in the South was almost four hundred, an increase of more than one-half over the number just a year before. The number of blacks elected mayors, city councilmen, school board members, and the like is increasing steadily, if not necessarily dramatically, as is the number of blacks in appointive positions.

The educational and economic position of blacks has improved greatly, particularly in an absolute sense.[1] Though quantity is not equivalent to quality of education, the gap in median years of education completed between young blacks and whites is one-half a year. Between 1960 and 1966, the percent of nonwhite males completing high school increased from 36 to 53, and the proportion of black youth completing college almost doubled. Between 1940 and 1968, black income increased from $3.5 billion a year to $32 billion. In 1959, 55 percent of nonwhite families were below the poverty level as defined by the government; in 1967, the number was approximately 35 percent. In 1966, 23 percent of nonwhite families had incomes over $7,000 (in the North this

[1] For example, see Urban America, Inc. and the Urban Coalition, One Year Later (New York: Praeger, 1969); Social and Economic Conditions of Negroes in the United States, U.S. Dept. of Labor (October 1967); N. Glazer, "America's Race Paradox," Encounter (October 1968); and Gary Marx, "Perspectives on Racism" in M. Wertheimer et al., Confrontation: Psychology and the Problems of Today (Chicago: Scott, Foresman, 1970).

figure was 38 percent), as compared with only 9 percent in 1956, using dollars of the same value. Though relative to the even greater improvements in the position of whites these changes are much less impressive. The most important measure for conflict and felt deprivation is the position of blacks relative to whites.[2]

One area where the decline of racism is perhaps most clearly documented is at the attitudinal level. In interview situations, the proportion of whites accepting crude stereotypes, believing in innate racial differences, and supporting segregation has consistently declined.[3]

If the nation has not yet seen a shift in its priorities from the arms race and the space race to the human race or mobilized its resources to attack poverty and racism the way it potentially could, there have nevertheless been sizable increases in expenditures for manpower programs, education, health, and welfare. For example, according to the Kerner Commission,

Federal expenditures for manpower development and training have increased from less than $60 million in 1963 to $1.6 billion in 1968. The president has proposed a further increase to $2.1 billion in 1969.

Federal expenditures for education, training, and related services have increased from $4.7 billion in fiscal 1964 to $12.3 billion in fiscal 1969.

Direct federal expenditures for housing and community development have increased from $600 million in fiscal 1964 to nearly $3 billion in fiscal 1969.

Public institutions including the schools, police, and welfare organizations have undertaken agonizing reappraisals of their agency's effectiveness, with some changes of policy. Efforts have been undertaken to recruit new minority group employees and upgrade old ones, as well as to sensitize the agency to the problems faced by blacks.

In the private sector as well, there are countless new and often unheralded (and unfortunately all too often unsuccessful) programs—for example, efforts by business to provide new training and jobs. Blacks are no longer so invisible in the mass media and are shown in a fuller range of roles, from judges in soap operas, to the beer drinkers, cigarette smokers, denture and girdle wearers, and body-odor-stomach-ache-headache

---

[2] Comparisons between blacks and whites tell a very different story. Approximately 35 percent of blacks, against 10 percent of whites, have income below the poverty level. Although nonwhite unemployment rates are half of what they previously were, they still are consistently two to four times as high as those of whites. In some urban areas the rate for young nonwhite males is 40 percent, with many more underemployed or working full time for below-subsistence pay. About one in three experienced black workers was out of work some time in 1968. A black has one-third as much chance of completing college, and if he does, he can expect to earn less than a white with only a high school diploma. A black baby has a three times greater chance of dying in infancy than a white baby: if he survives, he can expect to live seven years less than his white counterpart. In 1967, blacks were 11 percent of the population, yet had only 1 percent of the seats in Congress and 1.5 percent of all elected offices. In some ways the gap between whites and blacks is increasing. The gap between the death rates for white and nonwhite infants increased from 66 percent in 1950 to 90 percent in 1964. In 1967 black median income, though higher than ever before, had decreased from a previous high of 57 percent of white median income to 53 percent.

[3] In 1942 more than half the whites questioned in a national poll expressed a belief in innate racial learning differences. By 1968, a national CBS poll found only 14 percent of whites agreeing that "white babies usually have more natural intelligence than black babies," though twice as many had no opinion. In 1942 only 30 percent of a national sample felt that whites and blacks should go to the same schools; in 1956 it was 61 percent, and in 1965, 67 percent; in the same period those who said that they would not object to a black neighbor of their social class rose from 35 percent to 64 percent and those who favored integrated seating on buses rose from 44 percent to 78 percent. See P. Sheatsley, "White Attitudes toward the Negro," *Daedalus* (Winter 1966), pp. 217–238.

sufferers who populate the plastic world of American advertising. More subtle changes such as the way minorities are treated in school textbooks may also be noted.

It is of course probably impossible to sort out precisely what role conflict, or the threat of it, has played in facilitating these changes. There is no single reason for the various advances that have occurred. Increases in the gross national product and migration out of the South and to cities (as industrialization spread and agriculture declined) until recently were important factors in the improved educational, economic, and political situation of blacks.[4]

The increased power of the federal government relative to that of the states and the greater integration of the South into the national life are also relevant to the changes that have occurred. One factor encouraging change from the top has been the new significance American color problems gained as nations of Asia and Africa emerged from colonial rule. It became difficult to expouse American ideals in the cold war, while denying them so thoroughly in practices at home. Moral appeals to conscience and shared values stressing equality and brotherhood have also played some role,[5] though for political reasons the goodwill of a benevolent elite is often overstressed. However, as blacks took to the streets and engaged in

nonviolent direct action (in the early 1960's), the momentum of change increased noticeably, though as this gave way to violent outbursts the tempo of change has slowed noticeably and many losses have occurred.

In a very general sense both racial conflict and changes in race relations may stem from the same broader phenomena such as changes in technology, urbanization, or the spread of new ideas. Some of the changes in the position of blacks are consistent with broader trends that have been occurring in the last several centuries in industrialized countries, as certain value themes such as universal rather than particular standards of judgment come into greater prominence and ascriptive bases of solidarity such as race, religion, and ethnicity decline,[6] with a concomitant emphasis on a more rational use of human resources.

The impersonality, anonymity, and mobility of large urban areas that tend to go along with industrialization make it difficult to maintain an elaborate caste system. The rise of the idea of citizenship and the extension of political, economic, and welfare rights had led to the partial inclusion of many previously excluded lower status groups. As new resources of lower status groups mix with their new aspirations and a sense of relative deprivation, protest emerges which in turn generates further change. Although conflict may speed up a given change, certain changes may have a dynamic of their own that transcend (and make easier) the actions of conflict groups demanding inclusion.

If change may come from sources other than conflict, it is not true that conflict always leads to change.[7] In an

[4] Ironically an important impetus to this migration was the greater demand for black labor during World Wars I and II and the Korean War. Blacks have made their greatest economic gains relative to whites during periods of war. This is certainly not an argument for continuing wars, but indicates what full mobilization of national resources and their more rational use can accomplish. If the same concerted efforts that characterized the society in wartime were directed at the equally insidious enemies of racism, poverty, and indifference, significant progress could be made.

[5] Cf. G. Myrdal's stress on the contradiction in the American value system, G. Myrdal, *An American Dilemma* (New York: Harpers).

[6] T. Parsons, "Full Citizenship for the Negro American? A Sociological Problem," *Daedalus* (Fall 1965).

[7] The importance one gives to conflict in bringing about change also depends on the causal model adopted to explain the current position of

age where the gap between our ideals and our practices is so apparent, it is painful to acknowledge that human institutions may change rather slowly. One can decry it or welcome it, depending on his or her political perspective and interests, yet, as Robert Nisbet has observed, "persistence and fixity are very powerful realities. . . . Habit, custom, adaptation even to the absurd and potentially lethal use and wont, and sheer inertia are . . . strongly built into the socialization process."[8] There are as well powerful vested interests which often oppose change. Yet social change does occur. An awareness of its complexities and sources of resistance is certainly no justification for not seeking it. However, realistic expectations are likely to lead to more effective strategies and less likely to lead to frustration, with its potential for apathy and withdrawal from the struggle or wanton violence.

It is easy to overemphasize the benefits from recent violent confrontations. There may be a diminishing returns effect. An initial disruption may have a communications function, and in the chaos concessions may be granted. Then, as authorities learn to cope with such actions, they may stop listening. Even though riots have visibly and forcefully brought the problem of unequal opportunities to national atten-

tion, they have not resulted in appreciable change.

Perhaps nothing can do so in a fundamentally conservative country where almost 90 percent of the inhabitants are white and there are certain gains for them in having a large black underclass. One of the tragedies of American race relations is that when blacks work within the system and play the game according to the traditional rules, they may get rather little. Yet when blacks operate outside the system and disrupt it, they do not necessarily have any better results. At the national level, following the riots of 1967, Congress did not significantly increase expenditures for domestic programs; some appropriations were even reduced. It did, however, pass an antiriot bill. Partly in response to black and student demonstrations, the late 1960's saw a shift to the right politically in numerous state and local elections. That 20 percent of the American population seriously considered voting for George Wallace in the 1968 election is not insignificant.

Under some conditions, conflict initiated by the minority group may lead to a hardening of attitudes, retrenchment, and repression or may have no effect. Among some factors crucial to the outcome of protest action seem to be (1) the type of demand and goals, (2) the means adopted, (3) the context of the protest including the extent of mass mobilization, and (4) response of authorities to the actual protest.

The protest actions that have met with the most success have been nonviolent southern demonstrations against segregation. The seemingly greater effectiveness of southern than northern black protest appears to be related to the fact that the goals sought by southern blacks were consistent with the broader moral values of the society. Southern protestors were demonstrat-

---

blacks in America. If problems are seen to stem largely from the self-conscious actions of a racist elite, then struggle will be seen as essential. If however emphasis is placed on what are seen as internal weaknesses of the black community—its family structure, lack of education, training and competitive work habits (factors generally acknowledged to have come about as a result of *past* oppression)—then the main task will be seen as building up the black community rather than struggling with white opponents, though even here conflict may be involved in the struggle over the resources needed to do this.

[8] R. Nisbet, *The Social Bond* (New York: Random House, 1970), p. 307.

ing on behalf of rights seen as legitimate by the nation at large. Demands for the legally and morally well-established right to vote or attend a public university are very different from the demands for community control, preferential treatment, reparations, or abstract dignity that often characterize recent northern racial conflict. Also relevant is the concrete, less costly, and more easily granted nature of many southern demands.

With the help of the national media and using nonviolent means, southern demonstrators turned police into the aggressors, and martyrs were created. Confrontations involving aggressive violence by demonstrators are likely to arouse very different sentiments in the community at large. Beyond these factors the greater complexity of northern industrial centers and the more diffuse and insulated nature of their power structures may make them less vulnerable to direct protest action.

The articles in this last section touch on some of the themes considered above. Joseph S. Himes, writing about the early 1960's before ghetto violence appeared, asks whether organized conflict initiated by blacks makes any contribution to, or has any positive consequences for, the functioning of the larger American society. He observes that such conflict may alter the social structure, increase interracial communication, increase solidarity and affirm ultimate values of American society, and have an important identity function for blacks. His article is a useful summary of many of the positive aspects of conflict.

One of the functions of conflict is its potential for binding a group together. The article by Fredric Solomon et al. observes an unintended or latent consequence of conflict—that during periods of organized nonviolent protest

there may be a decline in crimes of violence by blacks. There are some parallels here to the argument of black psychiatrist Franz Fanon writing about the colonial struggle in Algeria against the French.[9] He stated that through struggle the native gains a sense of manhood and channels his energy in the direction of attacking oppression rather than in the direction of crime or intragroup attacks.

Irving Howe takes a more questioning approach to the positive functions of conflict if it is carried out through confrontation tactics likely to alienate a majority of the population. Although such tactics may bring about change, they may also lead to backlash and repression unless certain conditions are present.

One official response to crisis and conflict is to study it. This may give the impression that something is being done while costing relatively little. Michael Lipsky and David Olson analyze some of the constraints under which a commission such as the National Advisory Commission on Civil Disorders operates. In so doing they indicate why commissions often disappoint their critics.

INTERRACIAL COOPERATION AND THE LIMITING OF VIOLENT CONFLICT

Between a mass media that is all too often sensation-seeking and the distortions of white and black nationalist ideologies, it is easy to forget or even deny the unheralded and undramatic, but quantitatively much more prevalent, examples of interracial cooperation, or at least nonantagonism, as well as the variation that exists within racial groups. That race, at least in the United States, is an important factor in identity

[9] F. Fanon, *The Wretched of the Earth* (New York: Dial Press, 1967).

does not mean it is the only factor. Human beings are also united and divided by many factors which far transcend race, such as their generational, social class, regional, national, religious, and sexual identities, as well as their identification with various ideologies and special interest groups. As suggested in the last section, to the extent that these potential sources of cleavage (e.g., between the young and the old or between those who live in urban and rural areas) cross cut rather than overlap with racial grouping, conflict is less likely. Men of different racial and ethnic groups but of the same social class, age, and region are likely to find they have more in common in terms of life style and political interests than those with whom they merely share racial identity but differ markedly from with respect to the above characteristics. Those who fantasize about a final American racial armaggedon where lines of struggle are determined only by color deny the deep divisions and heterogeneity within racial groups.

Beyond this, even where race is a salient factor in a person's identity or in a social situation, this does not therefore preclude harmonious relations with outsiders. The mere existence of difference need not imply conflict. Under various conditions similarly marked birds may indeed flock together, though opposites as well may be attracted to each other or differences may be seen as irrelevant.

Given the pressure of recent current events, most research and public attention have focused on racial conflict and discord. Yet countless thousands of harmonious interracial contacts in schools, factories, supermarkets, playing fields, and the like daily go unnoticed. There is a considerable body of literature on the psychology and sociology of racial cooperation. Studies have been done on the relatively suc-

cessful integration of the armed services and some neighborhoods and schools.[10] Many studies, such as those discussed by Rabb and Lipset in Part I, have shown that positive racial feelings often result from interracial contact which occurs in an equal status setting, in a context where norms of tolerance are stressed. Attitude research reveals sizable reservoirs of good will on the part of a large majority of the black population and a goodly proportion of the white population as well.

This is by no means to suggest that American society is one big, happy, tolerant, racially mixed family where things are uniformly getting better all the time. The depth of racism and resistance to change among certain segments of the white population and the quickening pace of the bitterness felt among certain segments of the black can hardly be denied. Yet little is gained and much may be lost in the form of self-fulfilling effects by overemphasizing the extensiveness of, and potential for, racial conflict and the impossibility of any reconciliation between blacks and whites.[11]

As the articles in this book of readings suggest there are clearly many grounds for racial conflict. A more

[10] For example, C. Moskos, Jr., "Racial Integration in the Armed Forces," *American Journal of Sociology* (September 1966); and B. Hesslink, *Black Neighbors: Negroes in a Northern Rural Community* (Indianapolis: Bobbs-Merrill, 1968). On the effects of interracial contact, see G. Simpson and M. Yinger, *Racial and Cultural Minorities* (New York: Harper and Row, 1965), pp. 503–511.

[11] For a discussion of the self-fulfilling prophecy, see R. Merton, *Social Theory and Social Structure* (New York: Free Press, 1957), pp. 421–436. Self-fulfilling effects refer to situations where men's actions on a given erroneous belief result in the belief being made true. For example, the widespread belief that narcotics addicts steal often results in their being denied jobs, which then may lead many to steal. Or the erroneous belief that most blacks favor racial separation, are militantly antiwhite and pro-violence may lead to racial policies which in fact bring these about.

racially just American society will not be achieved without struggle, though struggle alone is not sufficient.[12] Yet in applying a conflict perspective to society what exists of consensus and cooperation should not be ignored. Careful understanding certainly requires appreciation of the necessity of conflict. Yet there is more, actually and potentially to American race relations than this, even if it often remains obscured.

These facts aside, violent conflict might be greatly reduced were scare resources more equitably distributed and national priorities shifted more from defence and space to social needs. It is not clear at what point the granting of concessions may cease to raise aspirations and cause demands to escalate. The most important argument for bringing about racial change should not be that it will necessarily stop conflict and disorder, but that it is just and moral and consistent with the unique values upon which this country was founded. However it is clear that greater inclusion of lower status groups, their more cohesive and forceful organization into interest groups, effective mechanisms for the expression of grievances, the strong legitimation of the need for change rather than its exploitation by calls only for law and order on the part of government officials, impartial law enforcement, the development of nonviolent alternatives for coping with crisis situations, greater restraints on the use of official violence, and greater controls over the availability of weapons would reduce the probabilities of conflicts which result in violence.

51
The Functions of Racial Conflict*
JOSEPH S. HIMES

When one contemplates the contemporary American scene, he may be appalled by the picture of internal conflict portrayed in the daily news. The nation is pictured as torn by dissension over Vietnam policy. The people are reported being split by racial strife that periodically erupts into open violence. Organized labor and management are locked in a perennial struggle that occasionally threatens the well-being of the society. The reapportionment issue has forced the ancient rural-urban conflict into public view. Religious denominations and faiths strive against ancient conflicts of theology and doctrine toward unification and ecumenism. Big government is joined in a continuing struggle against big industry, big business, big finance, and big labor on behalf of the "public interest."

The image created by such reports is that of a society "rocked," "split," or "torn" by its internal conflicts. The repetition of such phrases and the spotlighting of conflict suggest that the integration, if not the very existence of the society is threatened. It is thus implied, and indeed often stated, that the elimination of internal conflict is the central problem for policy and action in the society.

These preliminary remarks tend to indicate that there is widespread popular disapproval of social conflict. In some quarters the absence of conflict is thought to signify the existence of

*[Reprinted from *Social Forces*, Vol. 41, no. 1, pp. 1–10 by permission of the publisher, University of North Carolina Press. Presidential address delivered at the annual meeting of the Southern Sociological Society, New Orleans, April 8, 1966. I am indebted to Professors Ernst Borinski, Lewis A. Coser, Hylan G. Lewis, and Robin M. Williams, Jr., for their critical reading of this manuscript.]

[12] See K. Clark, *Dark Ghetto* (New York: Harper and Row, 1965), chap. 8.

social harmony and stability. According to the human relations theme, conflict, aggression, hostility, antagonism, and such devisive motives and behaviors are regarded as social heresies and therefore to be avoided. Often the word conflict is associated with images of violence and destruction.

At the same time, in contemporary sociology the problem of social conflict has been largely neglected. As Coser, Dahrendorf, and others have pointed out, this tendency issues from preoccupation with models of social structure and theories of equilibrium.[1] Conflicts are treated as strains, tensions, or stresses of social structures and regarded as pathological. Little attention is devoted to the investigation of conflict as a functional social process.

However, some of the earlier sociologists employed social conflict as one central element of their conceptual systems. Theory and analysis were cast in terms of a process model. Conflict was viewed as natural and as functioning as an integrative force in society.

To Ludwig Gumplowicz and Gustav Ratzenhofer conflict was the basic social process, while for Lester F. Ward and Albion W. Small it was one of the basic processes. Sumner, Ross, and Cooley envisaged conflict as one of the major forces operating to lace human society together.[2] Park and Burgess employed social conflict as one of the

processual pillars of their sociological system.[3]

At bottom, however, the two analytic models of social organization are really not inconsistent. Dahrendorf argues that consensus-structure and conflict-process are "the two faces of society."[4] That is, social integration results simultaneously from both consensus of values and coercion to compliance. Indeed, in the present study it is observed that the two sources of social integration are complementary and mutually supporting.

Coser has led the revival of sociological attention to the study of social conflict. In this task he has injected the very considerable contributions of the German sociologist Georg Simmel into the stream of American sociological thought. Ralf Dahrendorf, among others, has made further substantial contributions to the sociology of social conflict. One latent consequence of this development has been to sensitize some sociologists to conflict as a perspective from which to investigate race relations. Thus race relations have been called "power relations" and it has been proposed that research should be cast in terms of a "conflict model."[5] This approach is consistent with Blumer's thesis that race prejudice is "a sense of group position" and that empirical study

---

[1] Lewis A. Coser, *The Functions of Social Conflict* (Glencoe, Illinois: The Free Press, 1956), p. 20; Ralf Dahrendorf, *Class and Class Conflict in Industrial Society* (Stanford: Stanford University Press, 1959), chap. 5.

[2] William Graham Sumner, *Folkways* (Boston: Ginn, 1906); Edward Alsworth Ross, *The Principles of Sociology* (New York: Century, 1920); Charles Horton Cooley, *Social Process* (New York: Charles Scribner's Sons, 1918), and *Social Organization* (New York: Charles Scribner's Sons, 1909).

[3] Robert E. Park and Ernest W. Burgess, *Introduction to the Science of Sociology* (Chicago: University of Chicago Press, 1924).

[4] Dahrendorf, *op. cit.,* pp. 157–165. Arthur I. Wastow makes the same point in his concepts of "church," "state," and "government" as models of social integration. See *From Race Riot to Sit-In. 1919 and the 1960s: A Study in the Connections Between Conflict and Violence* (New York: Doubleday & Co., 1966).

[5] Lewis M. Killian and Charles M. Grigg, *Racial Crisis in America* (Englewood Cliffs, N.J.: Prentice-Hall, 1964), p. 18 ff.; H. M. Blalock, Jr., "A Power Analysis of Racial Discrimination," *Social Forces*, 39 (October 1960), pp. 53–59; Ernst Borinski, "The Sociology of Coexistence—Conflict in Social and Political Power Systems," unpublished, pp. 6–7; Wilson

involves "a concern with the relationship of racial groups."[6]

In the present discussion the term "racial conflict" is used in a restricted and specific sense.[7] By racial conflict is meant rational, organized, overt action by Negroes, initiating demands for specific social goals, and utilizing collective sanctions to enforce these demands. By definition, the following alternative forms of conflict behavior are excluded from the field of analysis.

1 The aggressive or exploitative actions of dominant groups and individuals toward minority groups or individuals.

2 Covert individual antagonisms or affective compensatory or reflexive aggressions.

3 Spontaneous outbursts or nonrationalized violent behavior.

As here treated, racial conflict involves some rational assessment of both means and ends, and therefore is an instance of what Lewis Coser has called "realistic conflict."[8] Because of the calculating of means and ends, racial conflict is initiating action. It is a deliberate collective enterprise to achieve predetermined social goals. Of necessity, conflict includes a conscious attack upon an overtly defined social abuse.

Merton has pointed out that groups sometimes resort to culturally tabooed means to achieve culturally prescribed ends.[9] Under such circumstances one might assume that if legitimate means were available, they would be employed. But, Vander Zanden has observed, "Nonviolent resistance is a tactic well suited to struggles in which a minority lacks access to major sources of power within a society and to the instruments of violent coercion."[10] He goes on to add that, "within the larger American society the Negro's tactic of nonviolent resistance has gained a considerable degree of legitimacy."[11] Three principal manifestations of Negro behavior fit this definition of racial conflict.

1 Legal redress, or the calculated use of court action to achieve and sanction specific group goals. Legal redress has been used most often and successfully in the achievement of voting rights, educational opportunities, and public accommodations.

2 Political action, or the use of voting, bloc voting, and lobby techniques to achieve legislative and administrative changes and law enforcement.

3 Nonviolent mass action, or organized collective participation in overt activity involving pressure and public relations techniques to enforce specific demands.

This essay examines some of the social functions of conflict as here defined. It is asked: Does realistic conflict by Negroes have any system-maintaining and system-enhancing consequences for the larger American society? To this question at least four affirmative answers can be given. Realistic racial conflict (1) alters the social structure,

---

Record, *Race and Radicalism* (Ithaca: Cornell University Press, 1964); Ernst Borinski, "The Litigation Curve and the Litigation Filibuster in Civil Rights Cases," *Social Forces,* 37 (December 1958), pp. 142–147.

[6] Herbert Blumer, "Race Prejudice as a Sense of Group Position," in J. Masuoka and Preston Valien (eds.), *Race Relations* (Chapel Hill: The University of North Carolina Press, 1961), p. 217.

[7] In much authoritative literature the concept conflict in racial relations is used in various other ways. See for example, George Simpson and J. Milton Yinger, *Racial and Cultural Minorities* (New York; Harper & Row, 1965), chap. 4; Killian and Grigg, *op. cit.;* Leonard Broom and Norval D. Glenn, *Transformation of the Negro American* (New York: Harper & Row, 1965), esp. chaps. 3 and 4.

[8] Coser, *op. cit.,* pp. 48–55.

[9] Robert K. Merton, *Social Theory and Social Structure* (Glencoe, Illinois: The Free Press, 1957), pp. 123–149.

[10] James W. Vander Zanden, "The Non-Violent Resistance Movement Against Segregation," *American Journal of Sociology,* 68 (March 1963), p. 544.

[11] *Ibid.,* p. 544.

(2) enhances social communication, (3) extends social solidarity, and (4) facilitates personal identity. Because of space and time limitations, considerations of societal dysfunctions and goal achievements are omitted.

STRUCTURAL FUNCTIONS

H. M. Blalock has noted that within the American social structure race relations are power relations.[12] Thus, realistic social conflict is an enterprise in the calculated mobilization and application of social power to sanction collective demands for specific structural changes. Yet, because of minority status, Negroes have only limited access to the sources of social power. Robert Bierstedt has identified numbers, resources, and organization as leading sources of power.[13] Of these categories, resources which Bierstedt specifies as including money, prestige, property, and natural and supernatural phenomena, are least accessible to Negroes.

Perforce then, realistic racial conflict specializes in the mobilization of numbers and organization as accessible sources of power. Thus a boycott mobilizes and organizes numbers of individuals to withhold purchasing power. A demonstration organizes and mobilizes numbers of individuals to tap residual moral sentiments and to generate public opinion. Voter registration and bloc voting mobilize and organize numbers of citizens to influence legislative and administrative processes. Legal redress and lobby techniques mobilize organization to activate legal sanctions or the legislative process.

The application of mobilized social

power in realistic racial conflict tends to reduce the power differential between actors, to restrict existing status differences, and to alter the directionality of social interaction. First, in conflict situations, race relations are defined unequivocally in power terms. Sentimentality and circumlocution are brushed aside. The power dimension is brought into central position in the structure of interaction. The differential between conflict partners along this dimension is thus reduced. The power advantage of the dominant group is significantly limited. In this connection and perhaps only in this connection, it may be correct to liken embattled Negroes and resisting whites to "armed camps."

Second, alteration of the power dimension of interracial structure tends to modify status arrangements. In the traditional racial structure, discrimination and segregation cast whites and Negroes in rigid and separate orders of superiority and inferiority. The limited and stylized intergroup contacts are confined to a rigid and sterile etiquette. However, in realistic conflict initiating actors assume, for they must, a status coordinate with that of the opposition.[14]

Status coordination is one evident consequence of power equalization. Moreover, it is patently impossible to make demands and to sanction them while acting from the position of a suppliant. That is, the very process of realistic conflict functions to define adversaries in terms of self-conception as status equals. Martin Luther King perceives this function of realistic conflict in the following comment on the use of nonviolent action and deliberately induced tension.[15]

---

[12] Blalock, *op. cit.*, pp. 53–59.

[13] Robert Bierstedt, "An Analysis of Social Power," *American Sociological Review*, 15 (December 1950), pp. 730–738. Bierstedt argues that numbers and organization as sources of social power are ineffectual without access to resources.

[14] Thomas F. Pettigrew, *A Profile of the Negro American* (Princeton: D. Van Nostrand Co., 1964), p. 167.

[15] Martin Luther King, *Why We Can't Wait* (New York: Harper & Row, 1963), p. 81.

Nonviolent direct action seeks to create such a crisis and foster such a tension that a community which has constantly refused to negotiate is forced to confront the issue. It seeks so to dramatize the issue that it can no longer be ignored.

That is, social power is used to bring interactors into status relations where issues can be discussed, examined, and compromised. There are no suppliants or petitioners and no condescending controllers in a negotiation relationship. By the very nature of the case, interactors occupy equal or approximately equal positions of both status and strength.

Third, power equalization and status coordination affect the interactional dimension of social structure. The up and down flow of interaction between super- and subordinates tends to level out in relations between positional equals. That is, rational demands enforced by calculated sanctions cannot be forced into the molds of supplication and condescension.

The leveling out of social interaction is inherent in such realistic conflict mechanisms as sit-ins, freedom rides, bloc voting, voter registration campaigns, and boycotts. Thus, for example, the interruption of social interaction in a boycott implies an assumption of status equality and the leveling of interaction. The relationship that is interrupted is the up and down pattern inherent in the status structure of inequality. No relationship is revealed as preferable to the pattern of supplication and condescension. Whether such structural functions of realistic conflict become institutionalized in the larger social system will depend on the extent of goal achievement of the total Negro revolution. That is, structural consequences of conflict may be institutionalized through the desegregation and nondiscrimination of education,

employment, housing, recreation, and the like. Changes in these directions will provide system-relevant roles under terms of relatively coordinate status and power not only for the conflict participants, but also for many other individuals. Developments in these directions will also be influenced by many factors and trends apart from the process of realistic racial conflict.

We may now summarize the argument regarding the structural functions of realistic racial conflict in a series of propositions. Realistic conflict postulates race relations as power relations and undertakes to mobilize and apply the social power that is accessible to Negroes as a minority group.

In conflict, the traditional interracial structure is modified along three dimensions. The power differential between interactors is reduced; status differentials are restricted; and social interaction tends to level out in directionality. Whether these structural consequences of realistic conflict become institutionalized in the general social system will depend on the extent and duration of goal achievement in the larger social structure.

COMMUNICATIONAL FUNCTIONS

It is widely claimed that Negro aggression interrupts or reduces interracial communication. Whites and Negroes are thought to withdraw in suspicion and hostility from established practices of communication. The so-called normal agencies and bridges of intergroup contact and communication are believed to become inoperative. Such a view of conflict envisages Negroes and whites as hostile camps eyeing each other across a "no man's land" of antagonism and separation.

It is true that racial conflict tends to interrupt and reduce traditional communication between whites and

Negroes. But traditional interracial communication assumes that communicators occupy fixed positions of superiority and inferiority, precludes the consideration of certain significant issues, and confines permitted interchanges to a rigid and sterile etiquette. "The Negro," write Killian and Grigg, "has always been able to stay in communication with the white man and gain many favors from him, so long as he approached him as a suppliant and as an inferior, and not as a conflict partner."[16]

It will be evident that intergroup communication under such structural conditions is both restricted in content and asymmetrical in form. However, our analysis indicates that realistic conflict functions to correct these distortions of content and form and to extend the communication process at the secondary mass media level.

First, realistic racial conflict heightens the individual level and extends the social range of attention to racial matters. Individuals who have by long custom learned to see Negroes only incidentally as part of the standard social landscape, are brought up sharply and forced to look at them in a new light. Persons who have been oblivious to Negroes are abruptly and insistently confronted by people and issues which they can neither avoid nor brush aside. Many individuals for the first time perceive Negroes as having problems, characteristics, and aspirations that were never before recognized, nor at least so clearly recognized. Racial conflict thus rudely destroys what Gunnar Myrdal aptly called the "convenience of ignorance."[17]

In *Freedom Summer,* Sally Belfrage gives a graphic personal illustration of the attention-arresting function of realis-

tic racial conflict.[18] In the most crowded and hottest part of an afternoon the daughter of one of Greenwood's (Mississippi) leading families walked into the civil rights headquarters. In a lilting southern voice she asked to everybody in general: "I jus' wanted to know what y'all are up to over here."

At the same time the "race problem" is brought into the focus of collective attention by realistic conflict. Negroes as well as their problems and claims insist upon having both intensive and extensive consideration. To support this contention one has only to consider the volume of scientific, quasi-scientific, and popular literature, the heavy racial loading of the mass media, and the vast number of organizations and meetings that are devoted to the racial issue.

Further, realistic racial conflict tends to modify both the cognitive and affective content of interracial communication. Under terms of conflict whites and Negroes can no longer engage in the exchange of standardized social amenities regarding safe topics within the protection of the status structure and the social etiquette. Communication is made to flow around substantive issues and the calculated demands of Negroes. Communication is about something that has real meaning for the communicators. It makes a difference that they communicate. In fact, under terms of realistic conflict it is no longer possible to avoid communicating. Thus Martin Luther King argued that nonviolent mass action is employed to create such crisis and tension that a community which has refused to negotiate is forced to confront the issue.[19]

In conflict the affective character of communication becomes realistic. The communicators infuse their exchanges of cognitive meanings with the feelings

---

[16] Killian and Grigg, *op. cit.,* p. 7.
[17] Gunnar Myrdal, *An American Dilemma* (New York: Harper & Bros., 1944), pp. 40–42.

[18] Sally Belfrage, *Freedom Summer* (New York: The Viking Press, 1965), p. 48.
[19] King, *op. cit.,* p. 81.

that, within the traditional structure, were required to be suppressed and avoided. The Negroes are permitted, indeed often expected to reveal the hurt and humilitation and anger that they formerly were required to bottle up inside. Many white people thus were shocked to discover that the "happy" Negroes whom they "knew" so well were in fact discontented and angry people.

Thus the cognitive-affective distortion of traditional interracial communication is in some measure at least corrected. The flow of understanding and affection that was permitted and encouraged is balanced by normal loading of dissension and hostility. The relationship thus reveals a more symmetrical character of content and form.

Finally, attrition of primary contacts between unequals within the traditional structure and etiquette is succeeded, in part at least, by an inclusive dialogue at the secondary communication level. The drama of conflict and the challenges of leaders tend to elevate the racial issue in the public opinion arena. The mass media respond by reporting and commenting on racial events in great detail. Thus millions of otherwise uninformed or indifferent individuals are drawn into the public opinion process which Ralph H. Turner and Lewis M. Killian have analyzed as defining and redefining the issue and specifying and solving the problem.[20]

Much obvious evidence reveals the secondary communication dialogue. Since 1954 a voluminous scientific, quasi-scientific, and popular literature on the race issue has appeared. Further evidence is found in the heavy racial loading of newspapers, magazines, television and radio broadcasting, and the motion pictures. The race problem has been the theme of numerous organizations and meetings at all levels of power and status. From such evidence it would seem reasonable to conclude that few if any Americans have escaped some degree of involvement in the dialogue over the race issue.

We may now summarize the argument briefly. Realistic racial conflict tends to reduce customary interracial communication between status unequals regarding trivial matters within the established communication etiquette. On the other hand, conflict tends to extend communication regarding significant issues with genuine feelings and within noncustomary structures and situations. At the secondary level both the volume of communication and the number of communicators are greatly increased by realistic conflict. These observations would seem to warrant the conclusion that communication within the general social system is extended by realistic racial conflict.

SOLIDARITY FUNCTIONS

A corollary of the claim that racial conflict interrupts communication is the assertion that conflict also is seriously, perhaps even radically, disunifying. Struggles between Negroes and whites are thought to split the society and destroy social solidarity. It is at once evident that such a claim implies the prior existence of a unified or relatively unified biracial system. Notwithstanding difference of status and condition, the racial sectors are envisaged as joined in the consensus and structure of the society.

A judicious examination of the facts suggests that the claim that racial conflict is seriously, perhaps even radically, disunifying is not altogether correct. On the one hand, the image of biracial solidarity tends to be exaggerated. On the other, realistic racial conflict serves

[20] Ralph H. Turner and Lewis M. Killian, *Collective Behavior* (Englewood Cliffs, N.J.: Prentice-Hall, 1957), chaps. 11 and 12.

some important unifying functions within the social system.

As Logan Wilson and William Kolb have observed, the consensus of the society is organized around a core of "ultimate values."[21] "In our own society," they assert, "we have developed such ultimate values as the dignity of the individual, equality of opportunity, the right to life, liberty, and the pursuit of happiness, and the growth of the free personality."

Far from rejecting or challenging these ultimate values, the ideological thrust of realistic racial conflict affirms them.[22] That is, the ultimate values of the society constitute starting points of ideology and action in racial conflict. As Wilson Record and other have observed, Negro protest and improvement movements are thoroughly American in assumption and objectives.[23]

This fact creates an interesting strategic dilemma for the White Citizens Councils, the resurgent Ku Klux Klan, and similar manifestations of the so-called white backlash. The ideology of racial conflict has preempted the traditional high ground of the core values and ultimate morality. The reactionary groups are thus left no defensible position within the national ethos from which to mount their attacks.

One consequence of realistic racial conflict, then, is to bring the core values of the society into sharp focus and national attention. People are exhorted, even forced to think about the basic societal tenets and to consider their meaning and applications. A dynamic force is thus joined to latent dedication in support of the unifying values of the society. Thus, as Coser has observed, far from being altogether disunifying,

realistic conflict functions to reaffirm the core and unifying values of the society.[24] In other words the "two faces of society" are seen to be complementary and mutually supporting.

The primacy of core values in realistic racial conflict is revealed in many ways. Martin Luther King places the ultimate values of the society at the center of his theoretic system of nonviolent mass action.[25] In his "Letter from Birmingham Jail" he refers to "justice," "freedom," "understanding," "brotherhood," "constitutional rights," "promise of democracy," and "truth." See how he identifies the goal of racial freedom with the basic societal value of freedom. "We will reach the goal of freedom in Birmingham and all over the nation, because the goal of America is freedom."[26]

One impact of realistic racial conflict is upon interpretation of core values and the means of their achievement. Thus, the issue is not whether or not men shall be free and equal, but whether these values are reserved to white men or are applicable to Negroes as well. Or again, the phrases "gradualism" and "direct action" depict an important point of disagreement over means to universally affirmed ends. But, it may be observed that when men agree on the ends of life, their quarrels are not in themselves disunifying.

Further, the very process of realistic racial conflict is intrinsically functional. Participants in the conflict are united by the process of struggle itself. The controversy is a unique and shared social possession. It fills an interactional vacuum maintained in the traditional structure by limited social contacts and alienation.

At the same time, as Coser has argued, a relationship established by

---

[21] Logan Wilson and William L. Kolb, *Sociological Analysis* (New York: Harcourt, Brace & Co., 1949), p. 513.

[22] Pettigrew, *op. cit.*, p. 193.

[23] Record, *op. cit.*; Pettigrew, *op. cit.*; Broom and Glenn, *op. cit.*

[24] Coser, *op. cit.*, pp. 127–128.

[25] King, *op. cit.*, pp. 77–100.

[26] *Ibid.*, p. 97.

conflict may lead in time to other forms of interaction.[27] It is conceivable that Negroes and whites who today struggle over freedom and justice and equality may tomorrow be joined in cooperation in the quest of these values.

Conflict is also unifying because the object of struggle is some social value that both parties to the conflict wish to possess or enjoy. The struggle tends to enhance the value and to reveal its importance to both actors. A new area of consensus is thus defined or a prior area of agreement is enlarged. For example, that Negroes and whites struggle through realistic conflict for justice or freedom or equality tends to clarify these values for both and join them in the consensus regarding their importance.

"Simultaneously," as Vander Zanden observes, "within the larger American society the Negro's tactic of nonviolent resistance has gained a considerable degree of legitimacy."[28] That is, conflict itself has been defined as coming within the arena of morally justifiable social action. The means as well as the ends, then, are enveloped within the national ethos and serve to enhance societal solidarity. In this respect realistic racial conflict, like labor-management conflict, tends to enter the "American way of life" and constitutes another point of social integration.

Many years ago Edward Alsworth Ross pointed out that nonradical conflicts may function to "sew" the society together.[29]

Every species of conflicts interferes with every other species in society . . . save only when lines of cleavage coincide; in which case they reinforce one another. . . . A society, therefore, which is ridden by a dozen oppositions along lines running in every direction may actually be in less danger of being torn with violence or falling to pieces than one split just along one line. For each new cleavage contributes to narrow the cross-clefts, so that one might say that society is sewn together by its inner conflicts.

In this sewing function, realistic racial conflict is interwoven with political, religious, regional, rural-urban, labor-management, class, and the other persistent threads of struggle that characterize the American social fabric. What is decisive is the fact that variously struggling factions are united in the consensus of the ultimate societal values. The conflicts are therefore nonradical, crisscrossing, and tend to mitigate each other.

The proposition on the solidarity function of realistic racial conflict can now be formulated briefly. The claims that racial conflict is disruptive of social solidarity, though partially true, tends to obscure other important consequences. Conflict not only projects the combatants into the social consensus; it also acts to reaffirm the ultimate values around which the consensus is organized. Moreover, conflict joins opposing actors in meaningful interaction for ends, whose importance is a matter of further agreement. From this perspective and within a context of multifarious crisscrossing threads of opposition, realistic racial conflict is revealed

---

[27] Coser, op. cit., pp. 121–122.
[28] Vander Zanden, op. cit., p. 544.
[29] Ross, op. cit., pp. 164–165. Dahrendorf, op. cit., pp. 213–215, argues that conflicts tend to become "superimposed," thus threatening intensification. "Empirical evidence shows," he writes, "that different conflicts may be, and often are, superimposed in given historical societies, so that the multitude of possible conflict fronts is reduced to a few dominant conflicts. . . . If this is the case, (class) conflicts of different associations appear superimposed;

i.e., the opponents of one association meet again—with different titles, perhaps, but in identical relations—in another association." (Pp. 213–214.) Such an argument, however, fails to recognize that conflicts may superimpose along religious, regional, ethnic, or other fronts and thus mitigate the strength of the class superimposition.

as helping to "sew" the society together around its underlying societal consensus. We now turn to a consideration of certain social-psychological consequences of realistic racial conflict.

IDENTITY FUNCTIONS

The fact is often overlooked that realistic racial conflict permits many Negroes to achieve a substantial measure of identity within the American social system. This function of racial conflict is implied in the foregoing analyses of communication and solidarity. However, the analysis of the identity function of racial conflict begins with a consideration of the alienation of the American Negro people. Huddled into urban and rural slums and concentrated in menial and marginal positions in the work force, Negroes are relegated to inferior and collateral statuses in the social structure. Within this structural situation discrimination prevents their sharing in the valued possessions of the society. Legal and customary norms of segregation exclude them from many meaningful contacts and interactions with members of the dominant group.

Isolated and inferior, Negro people searched for the keys to identity and belonging. The social forces that exclude them from significant participation in the general society also keep them disorganized. Thus identity, the feeling of belonging and the sense of social purpose, could be found neither in membership in the larger society nor in participation in a cohesive racial group. Generation after generation of Negroes live out their lives in fruitless detachment and personal emptiness. In another place the alienation of Negro teenagers has been described as follows.[30]

The quality of Negro teenage culture is conditioned by four decisive factors: race, in-feriority, deprivation, and youthfulness. Virtually every experience of the Negro teenager is filtered through this complex qualifying medium; every act is a response to a distorted perception of the world. His world is a kind of nightmare, the creation of a carnival reflection chamber. The Negro teenager's culture, his customary modes of behavior, constitute his response to the distorted, frightening, and cruel world that he perceives with the guileless realism of youth.

Yet the search for identity goes on. It takes many forms. In the Negro press and voluntary organizations it is reflected in campaigns for race pride and race loyalty. One sector of the Negro intelligentsia invented the "Negro history movement" as a device to create a significant past for a "historyless" people. For the unlettered and unwashed masses the church is the prime agent of group cohesion and identity. The National Association for the Advancement of Colored People and other militant organizations provide an ego-enhancing rallying point for the emancipated and the aggressive. The cult of Negro business, escapist movements like Father Divine's Heaven, and nationalist movements like Marcus Garvey's Universal Negro Improvement Association, and the Black Muslims provide still other arenas for the Negro's search for identity.

Despite this variegated panorama of effort and search, the overriding experience of Negroes remains isolation, inferiority, and the ineluctable sense of alienation. Whether involved in the search or not, or perhaps just because of such involvement, individuals see themselves as existing outside the basic American social system. Vander Zanden puts it this way: "By virtue of his membership in the Negro group, the Negro suffers considerably in terms of self-esteem and has every incentive for self-hatred."[31]   Thus self-conception

---

[30] Joseph S. Himes, "Negro Teen Age Culture," *Annals*, 338 (November 1961), pp. 92–93.

[31] Vander Zanden, *op. cit.*, p. 546.

reflects and in turn supports social experience in a repetition of the familiar self-fulfilling prophecy.

In this situation, collective conflict had an almost magical although unanticipated effect upon group cohesion and sense of identity among Negroes. Group struggle, as Coser and others have pointed out, functions to enhance group solidarity and to clarify group boundaries.[32] The separations among collective units are sharpened and the identity of groups within a social system is established. In the course of conflict collective aims are specified, defined, and communicated. Cadres of leaders emerge in a division of labor that grows clearer and more definite. Individuals tend to find niches and become polarized around the collective enterprise. All participants are drawn closer together, both for prosecution of the struggle and for common defense.

As the racial conflict groups become more cohesive and organized, the boundaries with other groups within the American social system become clearer. The distinction between member and nonmember is sharpened. Individuals who stood indecisively between groups or outside the fray are induced or forced to take sides. The zones of intergroup ambiguity diminish. Internally, the conflict groups become more tightly unified and the positions of members are clarified and defined more precisely.

Further, conflict facilitates linkage between the individual and his local reference group as the agent of conflict. The individual thus achieves both a "commitment"[33] and a "role" as a quasi-official group representative in the collective struggle. Pettigrew writes:[34]

Consider the Student Nonviolent Coordinating Committee (SNICK). . . . The group is cohesive, highly regarded by Negro youth, and dedicated entirely to achieving both personal and societal racial change. Recruits willingly and eagerly devote themselves to the group's goals. And they find themselves systematically rewarded by SNICK for violating the "Negro" role in every particular. They are expected to evince strong racial pride, to assert their full rights as citizens, to face jail and police brutality unhesitatingly for the cause. . . . Note . . . that these expected and rewarded actions all publicly commit the member to the group and its aims.

In the general racial conflict system individuals may act as leaders, organizers, and specialists. Some others function as sit-inners, picketers, boycotters, demonstrators, voter registration solicitors, etc. Many others, removed from the areas of overt conflict, participate secondarily or vicariously as financial contributors, audience members, mass media respondents, verbal applauders, etc.

In the interactive process of organized group conflict self-involvement is the opposite side of the coin of overt action. Actors become absorbed by ego and emotion into the group and the group is projected through their actions. This linkage of individual and group in ego and action is the substance of identity.

Paradoxically, the personal rewards of participation in conflict groups tend to support and facilitate the larger conflict organization and process. Edward Shils and Morris Janowitz have noted this fact in the functions of primary groups in the German Army in World War II.[35] That is, for the individual

---

[32] Coser, *op. cit.,* p. 34.

[33] Amitai Etzioni employs the concept "commitment" to designate one dimension of cohesiveness and operational effectiveness in complex organization. See his *Complex Organizations: A Sociological Reader* (New York: Henry Holt Co., 1961), p. 187; and *A Comparative Study of Complex Organization* (Glencoe, Ill.: The Free Press, 1961), pp. 8–22.

[34] Pettigrew, *op. cit.,* pp. 165–166.

[35] Edward A. Shils and Morris Janowitz, "Cohesion and Disintegration in the Wehrmacht in World War II," *Public Opinion Quarterly,* 12 (Summer 1948), p. 281.

actor the sense of identity is grounded and sustained by gratification of important personal needs.

In the case of realistic racial conflict, group-based identity functions to facilitate sociopsychic linkage between the individual and the inclusive social system. It was shown above that racial conflict is socially unifying in at least two ways. First, the conflict ideology identifies parties to the conflict with the core values of the social heritage. Thus sit-inners, and demonstrators and boycotters and all the others in the drama of racial conflict conceive themselves as the latter-day warriors for the freedom, justice, and equality, and the other moral values that are historically and essentially American. For many Negroes the sense of alienation is dispelled by a new sense of significance and purpose. The self-image of these embattled Negroes is consequently significantly enhanced.

Second, the conflict process draws organized Negroes into significant social interaction within the inclusive social system. Some of the crucial issues and part of the principal business of the society engage Negroes of all localities and stations in life. Though often only vicariously and by projection, life acquires a new meaning and quality for even the poorest ghetto dweller and meanest sharecropper. The sense of alienation is diminished and the feeling of membership in the inclusive society is enhanced.

We may now formulate the argument as follows. Intense alienation kept alive the Negro's quest for identity and meaning. Miraculously almost, realistic racial conflict with its ideological apparatus and action system functions to alleviate alienation and to facilitate identity. Conflict enhances group solidarity, clarifies group boundaries, and strenthens the individual-group linkage through ego-emotion commitment and overt action. In-group identity is extended to the larger social system through the extension of communication, the enlargement of the network of social interactions, and ideological devotion to national core values. It may be said, then, that through realistic racial conflict America gains some new Americans.

52
Civil Rights Activity and Reduction in Crime among Negroes*

FREDRIC SOLOMON, WALTER L. WALKER, GARRETT J. O'CONNOR, and JACOB R. FISHMAN

INTRODUCTION

In this preliminary report, data are presented on a possible reduction in crime among Negroes in certain cities during periods of organized community action for civil rights in those cities. The existence of such a phenomenon has been remarked upon by leaders of "direct action" civil rights groups in several communities. Yet, to date there has been no documentation of this phenomenon except for newspaper accounts of the one-day "March on Washington for Jobs and Freedom" of August 28, 1963.

According to *The Washington Evening Star,* there were only seven "major crimes" recorded by the District of Columbia police in the 24-hour period ending at 8:00 A.M. on August 29, 1963.[1] The *Star* noted that during the same time period in the previous week, there had been nineteen such crimes. Thus, reported major crime in Washington apparently dropped 63 percent

*[Reprinted by permission of the American Medical Association from *Archives of General Psychology,* Vol. 12, March 1965, pp. 227–236.]

for the day of and the night after the march.

Somewhat more surprising is an article which appeared in *The New York Times*. A reporter spent most of August 28 in Harlem and then wrote a story about the serious but happy mood that seemed to pervade Harlem on that day.[2] The story in the *Times* concluded with the following:

Police cars patrolled Harlem's streets all day, thinking it would be a big day for robberies, with so many Negro residents away from home, for the trip to Washington.

But in the evening, the desk sergeant of the 26th Precinct reported no robberies or other crime.

It has been our opinion that in the long run, the effects of the civil rights movement on the self-image and social behavior of the American Negro will be as important as the movement's direct effect on segregation patterns. Two of us have already written extensively about the student civil rights demonstrators themselves—their attitudes, behavior and motivations, and the psychological significance of anti-segregation activities in their life histories to date.[3–5] The present paper represents the initial phase of an inquiry into possible communitywide "side effects" of the civil rights movement.

Data will be presented which, in a preliminary way, tend to document the existence of an association between well-organized direct action for civil rights and a substantial reduction in crimes of violence committed by Negroes. We shall discuss the findings, their limitations, and their implications and shall offer some thoughts about further research. . . .

METHODOLOGY

For three cities (two in the Deep South and one in a border state) data were collected from various sources, including official crime reports, medical records, newspaper accounts, and individual interviews with residents. . . . A general problem in the crime statistics which we *were* able to obtain was the absence of racial breakdown in most of the data.

Two central crime information agencies were contacted for their help —the Uniform Crime Reporting Section of the Federal Bureau of Investigation and the Crime Information Center of the National Council on Crime and Delinquency. They were of limited assistance; and we have drawn some inferences from data from several cities; but we have found only one southern city with the kind of published crime reports that would be maximally useful to us in this research, and that is "city Z." Using an alternate approach, we have obtained hospital emergency room statistics and other relevant data from a small town which we shall call "town X," and we have a fairly reliable picture of developments there. Finally, via interviews, we collected some important anecdotal material which describes direct interaction between delinquent gangs and a young civil rights leader in "city A."

In evaluating crime data our focus has been upon major crimes committed by Negroes, with special emphasis upon aggravated assaults. There are several reasons for this focus. Local police departments report major crimes to the FBI under the heading of "Part I Offenses. . . ." Of major crimes against persons, aggravated assault is by far the most frequent, so that variations in the number of assaults from year to year (or month to month) are likely to be statistically more meaningful than would be variations in homicide or rape, for example. Furthermore, aggravated assaults frequently result in some kind of medical attention to the victims; so medical personnel in hospital emergency rooms may keep records that may usefully supplement what appears (or does not appear) in police reports. Finally, as the FBI *Manual on Uniform Crime Reporting* states, assaults are a fairly sensitive "index of social disorder in a community."[6] One must always keep in mind that, except for homicide and armed robbery, *all* crime statistics are reflecting merely the top of an iceberg of unreported crime. It has been suggested that most criminal acts never come to the attention of the police. . . .[7]

CITY Z

City Z is a large industrial and educational center located in the Deep South. The city has had a reputation for being "progressive," within the confines of segregation. Many of the city's Negro college students come from the North. The city has a well-established Negro middle class. Although the police force is interracial, the Negro officers customarily restrict their arrest power to Negro suspects.

The civil rights movement in city Z, according to local citizens, began in 1960 primarily as a student movement in response to the initial sit-ins in Greensboro, N.C. However, the white community's reaction to the students' increased pressure for equality soon welded the whole Negro community (and its established leaders) into a unified force in support of direct action.

Two economic boycotts of downtown stores with segregated facilities and employment practices were nearly 100 percent effective in terms of participation. In the Christmas season of 1960 and again at Easter of 1961, reportedly no more than a handful of Negroes could be seen shopping downtown on any given day. In response to this boycott by the whole Negro community, as well as in response to numerous public demonstrations by stu-

dents, the major downtown stores finally did upgrade employment opportunities for Negroes, and all their lunch counters were desegregated by the end of 1961. There was virtually no organized civil rights protest activity in 1962, in sharp contrast to the extremely active years of 1960 and 1961. (Late in 1963, public protests resumed, focusing upon segregated eating places.) . . .

Various direct action protests were common occurrences in city Z in 1960 and 1961; there were no such activities in 1959 and very few in 1962. Table 1 shows that in 1960 the number of Negro versus Negro assaults coming to the attention of the police decreased 31 percent from the 1959 figure. During 1961, the Negro versus Negro assaults remained at this low 1960 figure. However, in 1962—a year which saw civil rights activity in only one month—the annual rate for Negro versus Negro assaults returned to the 1959 figure.

Aggravated assaults within the white community did *not* vary in the same manner as did the Negro versus Negro assaults. On an annual basis, the figures for cross-race assaults are too small to be particularly noteworthy.

The known offense data concerning aggravated assault cases are reported not only annually but also on a month-by-month basis. Such figures would appear useful in making a closer inspection of the possible relationship between variations in civil rights activity and changes in Negro crime rates. These *monthly* data, however, are not broken down by race, as were the *annual* data reported in Table 1. Therefore, any inferences from these data of an association between civil rights activity and assaults by Negroes must be based on the knowledge that whites account for only a small proportion of the total reports of aggravated assault. For the period 1959–1962, only 16.5 percent

TABLE 1   Aggravated Assaults (Known Offenses, by Race)

	1959	1960[a]	1961[a]	1962
Negro attacks Negro	531	371	373	536
White attacks white	85	79	100	101
Negro attacks white	8	9	13	19
White attacks Negro	5	5	5	9

[a] Years of sustained civil rights activity.

of the reported and recorded assaults were attributed to whites; thus, in any given month, one might assume that Negroes account for about four out of five of the "known offenses" in the aggravated assault category.

It is of some interest to note, as in the top line of Table 2, monthly averages for assaults in city Z. In the period 1959 through 1962 there were sixteen months in which newsworthy civil rights protest activity occurred (fifteen months in 1960 and 1961, one month in 1962). The average number of assaults in these "civil rights months" was thirty-nine; the average number of assaults in "non-civil rights months" was fifty-two, one-third higher than in the "civil rights months."

Of all the forty-eight months from 1959 through 1962, only three had less than thirty reported assaults. These were the months of October 1960 (twenty-seven), November 1960 (twenty-three), and January 1961 (twenty-five). It turns out that this period (October 1960–January 1961) was an especially significant one in terms of the history of city Z's civil rights movement. We have already noted the successful boycott of downtown stores which occurred

from about December 15, 1960 to January 15, 1961. But this was preceded by a peak of mass activity in October and November 1960. Mass arrests of demonstrators and the confinement of the city's civil rights leaders both took place during these two months of unusually low rates of assault.

It is also interesting to note that except for the period just mentioned it was largely in the warmer months of 1960 and 1961 that most of the civil rights activity took place. Crime, especially assault, is at its greatest during the warmer months. The months of May, June, and July in both 1960 and 1961 were all months of civil rights activity, whereas these same months in 1959 and 1962 were inactive, as far as direct action for civil rights is concerned. The average number of assaults in these civil rights months, compared with these non-civil rights months was forty-six versus fifty-six. . . .

CITY A

Our second, designated city A, is in the Deep South not far from city Z. It has a population of 60,000, virtually no Negro middle class, and a reputation

TABLE 2   Aggravated Assaults (Known Offenses)

	1959	1960[a]	1961[a]	1962
Monthly average (all races)	52	38	41	59
Annual assaults by Negroes	539	380	386	575
Annual assaults by whites	90	81	105	110
Annual grand total	629	464	491	711

[a] Years of sustained civil rights activity.

for police brutality and unequal administration of justice. Details of the crime picture are not available from its police department. City A is brought up here only because the young leader of the civil rights movement there has been quite successful in converting members of delinquent juvenile gangs into nonviolent workers for civil rights. The leader was interviewed several times, and his reports were corroborated by others familiar with his work.

The leader's work with the gangs grew out of necessity, not design. Soon after he had begun organizing meetings and protest marches and had come into conflict with the police, he discovered that his group's activities were receiving unasked for "protection" of a violent sort. For example, young people from delinquent gangs would "protect" a civil rights meeting in a church by standing outside throwing bricks at white policemen. Soon the civil rights leader—a former seminary student—was able to persuade the delinquents that they were needed instead as guards *against* violence, assigning them the job of "policing the area to make sure no violence occurred and to make sure nobody was waiting outside who should be inside at the meeting."

Over the next two years, about two hundred members of four different gangs of out-of-school, out-of-work Negro teenagers received some training in nonviolent techniques and have become rather effective workers for voter registration, thus aiding the regular members of the local civil rights group, most of whom are in school or have jobs. Reportedly, delinquency among the gang members has diminished markedly, although sometimes the civil rights leader has had to personally "cool off" gang wars and personal rivalries to avert the bloodshed that used to be the order of the day.

TOWN X

Town X, which has a population of less than twenty thousand, is situated in a rural part of a border state. The Negro population is about one third of the total. The town is controlled by a small number of wealthy whites who are adamant segregationists. . . .

The spring of 1963 heralded the arrival of Congress of Racial Equality (CORE) officials and members of student organizations. The local nonviolent action group was under new leadership, and demonstrations were in active progress by May. A mass arrest took place, which highlighted the movement in the national press. In June, the Negro community had an explosive reaction when two teenagers were sent to reform school for illegal demonstrating. Prior to this incident, some local leaders had experienced difficulty in raising crowds to demonstrate; but now, they had to beseech them to remain in their homes, lest violence should ensue from inadequately planned demonstrations. An army of police reinforcements occupied the town and the situation resembled one of martial law for much of the summer. Gradually, the mutual fear of violence eased, and negotiations were resumed. Demonstrations were suspended in August and September while a temporary compromise was being worked out. . . .

Because of the longitudinal nature of the civil rights action outlined above (five months of maximal organization in 1963, some activity in 1962, none in 1961), town X was thought to be a propitious place to investigate the incidence of crime among Negroes in temporal relation to the movement. For the purpose of the study it was decided to investigate the period of May through September for the years 1961,

1962, and 1963. It is felt that this period reflects the situation in terms of a progression from virtual inactivity to explosive action. This progression seems to be reflected in data on major crime in the town. The police reports of town X for the months of May through September show that the number of Part I Offenses recorded during this five-month period in 1963 was thirty-one, a very low figure. During this period in previous years, records show forty-nine reported offenses in 1962 and seventy-three in 1961. By way of contrast, the number of reported offenses in the four months *before* direct action began in 1963 and in the three months after it had subsided, showed approximately the same crime rate as the previous two years (see Table 3). Unfortunately, these figures do not include reports of assaults, and there is no racial breakdown, although it is known that Negroes *normally account for about* 50 percent of the arrests for "major crime" in town X.*

Because the relevant police records with racial breakdowns are unavailable, we thought of studying the emergency case records of the General Hos-

pital in an effort to estimate the number of injuries resulting from assaults by Negroes during the time periods in question. Table 4 shows the incidences including those arising from racial rioting and police violence. The last line in Table 4 is corrected to exclude these cases, and represents the "routine" number of cases treated. Both tables exclude assaults perpetrated in the local labor camps, as it is felt that those were essentially nonconnected with the movement. We were told that the Negro migrant workers, who come to the area during the summer months to harvest the crops, would not associate themselves in any way with the movement, and, in fact, stayed away from the town because they were "scared." (Parenthetically, it *is* interesting to note that the incidence of assault among the migrant workers showed no appreciable change. Indeed a slight increase was apparent, whereas the "routine" cases from local Negroes diminished sharply.)

While it is felt that these figures do not represent the total number of assaults, they would seem to reflect a fairly constant proportion of the incidences and thus be suitable for our purposes. The one Negro physician in the community quite independently

---

* An examination of Magistrate's Court's gross records of people arraigned on a variety of crimes indicates a similar trend. In the summer of 1962, 53 percent fewer *local Negroes* were arraigned on the various charges than were arraigned in the summer of 1961. The summer of 1963 saw a slight rise in the total, in that a reduction of only 25 percent below the 1961 figure was apparent. It is fair to assume, though, that the reason 1963 showed more cases than 1962 is that a substantial num-

ber of disorderly conduct and trespass arrests took place as part of 1963's civil rights effort by local Negroes. (The 1962 civil rights arrests, it will be recalled, were largely of people from out of town, though that year's efforts were obviously watched by the local populace with avid interest.)

TABLE 3   Town X Part I Offenses (Murder, Robbery, Burglary, Larceny)

	1961	1962	1963
May–September	73	49	31
January–April	38	49	35
October–September	21	31	30
Total (annual)	132	129	96
Total adult arrests by the police force—all offenses	(Data missing)	386	429

TABLE 4   Town X Emergency Room Cases—Assaults by Negroes[a]

	May	June	July	August	September	Total
1961	1	7	7	2	4	21
1962	1	4	0	7	1	13
1963 All cases	0	1	4	4	1	10
1963 "Ordinary" cases	(0)	(0)	(0)	(4)	(1)	5

[a] This table represents the number of injury cases arising from assaults by Negroes in town X, which were treated in the emergency room of the local public general hospital. The figures include only assaults which occurred within the city limits and do not take into consideration the assaults perpetrated by members of the migrant labor force (see text). The bracketed figures in the last row are corrected to *exclude* assaults directly connected with civil rights action—e.g., injuries incurred during clashes with the police. The period represented is May through September of 1961, 1962, and 1963.

supported the accuracy of the trend shown in these hospital records in stating that "during the summer of 1963 I stitched only three or four cases, when in others years I would have seen a dozen in the same period of time."

Many local leaders were interviewed in conjunction with the study, and their anecdotal impressions are of some interest. For example, the Public Health Inspector, whose duty it is to control the spread of venereal disease, particularly among crime-prone lower class Negroes well known to him, observed: "Many of the contacts I sought, who would normally have been in jail, were living at home or could be found with their friends."

One of the principal Negro leaders estimates that there was much less crime in general: "People became interested in the movement, and were reluctant to do anything to jeopardize its progress. Most of the 1962 arrests were Freedom Riders—not locals. By 1963 there was a unification of common interest, and people who before were indigent and depressed, suddenly found that they had something to live and fight for."

Another local movement leader had anticipated trouble from the "winos" (alcoholics) and for this reason she felt that they should not be included in the protest marches. However, she was surprised to find that with special attention from the sober and more responsible members, they behaved themselves admirably and turned out to be exemplary, if somewhat passive, demonstrators. A student leader attests to this and quotes the case of a young alcoholic who had a long history of arrests. "He apparently was accustomed to being in the county jail, but while the movement was strong and active he never was in trouble, although he continued to drink." When the student returned to the town later in the year, months after all activity had ceased, he met the man leaving the jail; he had just been released and was heading for a bar.

Many factors may influence this apparent decrease in the incidence of crimes involving personal violence. Most of the local people quoted above mentioned that a temporary ban on retail sales of alcohol and the imposition of a curfew were important inhibitors. One reliable report, however, indicates that "bootlegged" alcohol was readily available for anyone who wanted it. Group identification and interest in the cause, strengthened by the persuasion of the leaders, were the factors most commonly selected for mention. One leader said that during the marches, "We found ourselves breaking ranks to intervene in sidewalk scuffles and family squabbles, so that there may well have been more than an indirect influence. . . ."

COMMENT

The material we have presented raises many questions, certainly more questions than it has answered. We hasten to state categorically that the findings are suggestive, but by no means conclusive.

There seem to us to be four areas that warrant discussion and exploration:

1 To what extent are the data reliable?
2 Assuming the data *are* reliable and suggest a diminished incidence of crime committed by Negroes during periods of direct action for civil rights, what are the possible explanations for this relationship?
3 What implications might all this have for an understanding of violence in populations of the poverty-stricken and socially disadvantaged?
4 What further research is indicated to shed light on the effect of organized social movements on the behavior of lower class populations?

We have already remarked that probably the majority of criminal acts go unreported and that collection of crime data by police departments is often quite unreliable. One can never be sure what factors, including chance, may be operating to influence the crime reporting process. Even when one finds a police department (such as the one in city Z) that prides itself on its crime reporting, there is still much to be desired in the uniformity of crime reporting from city to city.

Nonetheless, even taking these limitations into account, it is interesting that the statistics we have collected show the definite trend that they do, and that supplementing the police statistics with hospital Emergency Room records (as we have done in town X) reveals the same trend. It is possible to argue that this apparent trend is based on a change in contact between the police and the Negro community. Perhaps the police were so busy with civil rights demonstrators that their contact with or recording of crimes of violence within the Negro community was altered; i.e., their attention and concentration of forces were elsewhere. Or, perhaps, during economic boycotts Negroes are more careful to shield crime from the eyes of the police and white authorities. If these be so, any drop in crime rate is more illusory than real.

While these are real possibilities, there is at least anecdotal evidence to the contrary. During periods of "racial tension" in the South, the police force generally pays particularly close attention to the Negro sections of town and keeps a close vigil for potential violence of all kinds. Furthermore, where we have been able to supplement police data with medical information, as in town X, the incidence of medically recorded injuries resulting from personal violence has shown a decrease during civil rights activity.

Obviously, it would further strengthen the case for our hypothesis if we could present parallel data from comparable communities which have had no direct action civil rights programs. Unfortunately, we have not yet been able to obtain appropriately comparative data.

Assuming for the time being, then, that the reduction in the incidence of crime was *real,* not merely apparent, how might this be explained?

Perhaps when there are important events upon which the attention of any community is focused there is distraction from the forms of behavior which might otherwise lead to crime. Is the reduction of crime in these instances an epiphenomenon of the focusing of group attention on unusual public events? (There are some reports, for example, that crime in Washington, D.C., was reduced somewhat during the period following President Kennedy's assassination. Would the same have been true of the 1962 Cuban crisis or of a World Series?)

Or, perhaps the explanation lies in a deterrent effect of the increased number of policemen on patrol during periods of protest, or the potentiality of such an increase. In city Z, at least, this "deterrence" could not have been a large factor in the sustained diminution of assaults during 1960 and 1961. The major form of protest during that time was an economic boycott which did not involve the local police very extensively.

There is some sociological and psychological data that might suggest a basis for the possible existence of a causal relationship between organized direct action for civil rights and reduced crime among Negroes. A long-term effect of segregation upon lower-class Negroes has been a blocking off of their social and self-assertion—economically, socially, and psychologically.[8,3,5] Open expression of their resentment against second-class status has been blocked off in both South and North. We would agree with other authors that this damming-up of resentment is one reason for the high incidence of crime among lower class Negroes;[8,9] this is further supported by the fact that the vast majority of violent acts by Negroes are directed toward other Negroes. To put it another way, one might say that for the lower class Negro, avenues have been closed off by the social structure, so that violent crime against members of his own race is one of the channels of least resistance open to him for the expression of aggression. When he becomes aggressive *against segregation,* the Negro's sense of personal and group identity is altered; race pride partially replaces self-hatred, and aggression need not be directed so destructively at the self or the community. The concept of "prosocial acting out" has been set forth elsewhere[3,4] to describe risky, aggressive, somewhat impulsive actions which the actor sees himself taking "for the good of society." These actions are thus distinguished from the diffuse lashing out against social institutions that characterizes "antisocial acting out"—

although in some cases, the psychodynamic roots of the two types of behavior may be quite similar.

When large-scale direct action civil rights activities are launched in a community, the leaders face a herculean task of community organization. The members of the community must be recruited, trained, and organized into a disciplined, nonviolent army. Networks of communication and transportation must be arranged, for large numbers of people must be united behind a single effort. It is the pooling of resources, the setting up and certifying of goals, priorities, and methods in a community effort to produce social change that draws neighbors together in an organization whose very existence would tend to discourage crime (particularly crimes of violence against each other). If the community organization process is successful, each man, through the combined strength of his and his neighbors' efforts, can have that seat at the "community bargaining table" that has traditionally been denied him. Each man learns that possibly his personal welfare and certainly the welfare of the movement requires unity in the Negro community. As a result of the need for unity, people begin to know their neighbors and their neighbors' problems. A spirit of common concern pervades the community and serves to discourage crimes of violence. . . .

The data we have presented do not indicate any long-lasting effect of organized civil rights activity upon the crime pictures of city Z and town X—although seemingly permanent gains have been made with the juvenile gangs of city A. In looking at the crime data from city Z and town X, it is clear that after the major civil rights action had ceased, the number of reported crimes by Negroes returned fairly promptly to the frequency that was customary before the "movement" began. It is impressive, though, that a reduced crime rate for Negroes was sustained in city Z for two full years before going back up to former levels. Furthermore, when crime rates returned to frequencies comparable to earlier years, there was no "re-bound phenomenon" of a net *increase* in violence which (had it occurred) might have been attributed to frustration of hopes which had been "stirred up" by the civil rights movement. Indeed, in city Z the 1962 frequency of assaults by Negroes is somewhat *below* what one would expect in view of the increase in population over 1959.

This brings us to our concluding remarks. We feel it should be emphasized that if our findings are verified, there is then a very strong argument that the kind of community organization and psychological mobilization inherent in the civil rights struggle may be of prime importance in the development and implementation of various crime prevention programs and antipoverty programs. It would appear that such programs—which, after all, are often aimed at lower class Negroes—could learn a great deal from the interactional and motivational processes involved in the direct action civil rights movement.

REFERENCES

1 "Crime Drops Overnight, March Plans Credited," *Washington Evening Star,* Aug. 29, 1963, p. B-1.

2 TALESE, G.: "A Happy Day in Harlem," *New York Times,* Aug. 29, 1963, p. 19.

3 FISHMAN, J. R., and SOLOMON, F.: "Youth and Social Action: I. Perspectives on Student Sit-In Movement," *Amer. J. Orthopsychiat.,* 33:872–882, (Oct.) 1963.

4 SOLOMON, F., and FISHMAN, J. R.: "Youth and Social Action: II. Action and Identity Formation in First Student Sit-In Demonstration," *J. Soc. Issues,* 20: 36–45, (April) 1964.

5 SOLOMON, F., and FISHMAN, J. R.: "Psychosocial Meaning of Nonviolence in Student Civil Rights Activities," *Psychiatry,* 27:91–99. (May) 1964.

6 FEDERAL BUREAU OF INVESTIGATION: "1964 Manual for Uniform Crime Reporting," Department of Justice.

7 PEARL, A.: personal communication to the authors.

8 KARDINER, A., and OVESEY, L.: *Mark of Oppression: Psychosocial Study of American Negro,* New York: W. W. Norton & Company, Inc., 1951.

9 MYRDAL, G.: *American Dilemma,* New York: Harper & Brothers, 1944.

53
The New "Confrontation Politics" Is a Dangerous Game*
IRVING HOWE

A new term has entered the American language—"confrontation politics," the equivalent in public life of Russian roulette in private life. Some who play this new political game are authentic desperadoes, mostly young Negro militants; others are white middle class students acting—or acting-out—a fantasy-wish of revolution.

For the black desperadoes, "confrontation politics" can bring large risks: prison, violence, death. For the white students, the risks until recently were small; but now, after the ghastliness of Chicago and the growing popular obsession with "law and order," they will surely increase. For the country as a whole, the problem is perplexing. At a time of social disorder, when gross injustices continue to plague us, there arise combative minorities charged with moral idealism and apocalyptic emotion, which have developed tactics of protest going beyond the usual democratic methods yet short of the usual insurrectionary ones.

Like many other new left notions, "confrontation politics" has not been well-articulated as a theory. It is a kind of politics that grows up through improvisation, and it has been improvised as a way of getting around the sense of futility which has usually beset American radicalism. It has been choreographed as an out-of-doors explosion, a sort of real-life theater.

The purpose is to prod and incite a dormant, insensitive society into recognizing its moral failures. No longer committed, as were the Marxists, to the idea that the proletariat would be the crucial lever for the transformation of history, the young semi-anarchists who practice "confrontation" see themselves as a minority probably doomed to remain one for a long time. They have no expectation of creating new electoral majorities and small expectation of persuading large numbers of people; for they see the mass of Americans as brainwashed by "the media" (the very media which give them vast amounts of publicity). Their politics is a politics of desperation, at best moral shock and at worst nihilist irritation. They assign to themselves the task of sacrifice and assault, as a self-chosen vanguard which must destroy the complacence of "corporate liberalism."

What makes this task seem especially urgent is the feeling that in Vietnam the United States is conducting an immoral war which the ordinary democratic process is too slow and cumbersome to cope with.

One source of confrontation politics, seldom acknowledged, is the strategy worked out by the civil rights movement in the South during the fifties. Under strong pacifist guidance at that point, the civil rights movement "confronted" southern institutions through direct action—that is, through demonstrations, parades, lunch counter sit-ins. Conceived as a way to force the South into recognizing that Negroes would no longer be dormant, these actions involved a degree of "obstruction" (Jim Crow arrangements in stores were upset) and a kind of "confrontation" (nonviolent minorities exposed themselves to beatings by police and mobs).

The success of such actions depended on the following conditions:

The demonstrators were demanding rights which had already been recognized, both in law and moral consensus, by the nation as a whole. Despite failures by the federal government to enforce antidiscrimination laws, the demonstrators could count on at least some practical help from the Kennedy and Johnson administrations, as well as large amounts of support from many northerners. And while the southern police often remained brutal, it was no longer possible for municipal state governments in the South to destroy Negro protest through sheer terror.

The demonstrations came at a time when there were growing differences of response among southern whites. A majority may still have remained convinced that Jim Crow was a practical convenience, but a growing minority seems to have felt it was morally indefensible. Even if that minority did not always act with courage, it did begin to break the monolithic front which the white South had put up for decades. Doubt and guilt pierced the hard shell of white superiority.

The unconditional nonviolence practiced by Dr. King and his friends was a principle that sections of the middle class South had to respect—indeed, to respect almost as much as white northerners came to admire. The sight of men willing to turn the other cheek is one that must move, or at least disturb, people who retain even the flimsiest connections with Christianity. Tactically, it bewildered the southern police who would have been delighted to trade one hundred blows for one, but didn't know how to cope with men going limp under beatings.

While the southern demonstrators sometimes broke local ordinances, their actions were justifiable by democratic standards. For they had long been deprived of the right to vote and thereby participate in changing policies through peaceful means—which meant they now had a certain sanction for resorting to partly coercive but completely nonviolent forms of direct action. Furthermore, they were struggling for the enforcement of national laws superceding local ordinances, many of which were deliberately contrived to circumvent federal legislation and were commonly felt to be of dubious constitutionality. Indeed, one reason for breaking local ordinances was to challenge their constitutionality.

The power of southern protest derived partly from its alliance with major forces in the North: liberals, unionists, churches, and academicians, all pressing for civil rights legislation. One reason the Selma march proved to be so valuable was that it came just at the moment when it could most dramatically induce popular support for the Voting Rights Act. By contrast, demonstrations leading only to other demonstrations, or demonstrations lacking clearly defined goals (e.g., "justice"), or demonstrations with hopelessly unrealizable goals (e.g., a "black republic" in the South) will result in a dissipation of energies. The civil rights marches during the fifties and early sixties, however, were directed toward concrete local aims and in support of proposed national legislation.

Now all these favorable circumstances were special to the South, and it would be naive to suppose they can now be duplicated on a national scale. When certain kinds of demonstrations are held by Vietnam protestors—especially if they are feckless enough to include Vietcong banners—it can hardly be said that they act in behalf of moral-political opinions shared by a large majority of the people but thwarted by a sectional minority; or that they have been significantly deprived of their right to organize and protest; or that they act out of a principled devotion to nonviolence.

These are not new problems, either in the development of radical movements or the history of democratic states. There are historical precedents, and something can be learned from glancing at them.

Shortly after the Russian Revolution there appeared tendencies within the communist movement, opposed by Lenin and Trotsky, which led to a strategy of constant assault: endless demonstrations, unremitting "offensives," indeed a precursor of confrontation politics. Some ultra-left German communists even gave this strategy a name, the "theory of electrification." Through reckless self-sacrifice, the party would "electrify" the masses into revolution. Predictably, this led to disasters in Germany and elsewhere during the early twenties—brave but suicidal coups by communist combat groups which failed to gain the support of the workers. About the "theory of electrification" Trotsky remarked with asperity that the probable consequence was that the electrifiers would burn themselves.

In the immediate pre-Hitler period, there was an even more senseless turn toward a kind of confrontation politics. The communists came up with the insane notion of "social fascism," according to which the Social Democrats, and not the Nazis, were the main danger in Germany. (Today, it is "the liberals" who are the main danger. . . .) The communists kept staging endless demonstrations which, in Trotsky's phrase, "succeeded only in irritating all classes without winning over any." They antagonized the middle classes; they wore out the patience of the workers; they exhausted their own cadres. They made loud noises about "taking power" but never came within reach of power. Inevitably there appeared a force calling for the restoration of "law and order," behind which a large segment of the population united, actively or passively. It would be an exaggeration to say that the communist tactics caused the rise of Hitlerism, but no exaggeration at all to say that they helped the Nazis come to power.

Taken simply as a syndrome of going into the streets (what has been called the "theory of permanent demonstrations"), the politics of confrontation would not be a very serious matter. Demonstrations can be useful; demonstrations can be self-defeating. Opposition to the Vietnam war was surely rallied and increased through demonstrations; but some of them, by allowing themselves to be linked with the Vietcong and overtaken by anti-American hatreds not at all essential to the cause of peace, had a counterproductive effect, stiffening the hostility felt by millions of Americans toward dissent. About such matters we can only make estimates based partly on our sense of what the country is like. There is, finally, no science for measuring the consequences of going into the streets.

Far more serious is the political outlook which inspires confrontationist acts. As developed by Herbert Marcuse, the current new left guru, this political outlook advances the following propositions: We live in an advanced stage of capitalism, a mass society providing bread, circuses, and technology, which has tamed the forces of opposition and thereby undercut hopes for "transcendence." There is no great likelihood, in Marcuse's view, that we will soon witness an end to a social oppression sustained by material plenty but yielding no spiritual gratification. Efforts at reform tend to be superficial, and many of the values of liberalism—tolerance, free speech, electoral activity—are depreciated as devices for adjusting people to the status quo.

Revolution thus being declared all but impossible and reform all but ineffectual, Marcuse's doctrines justify those radicals who turn away from both traditional Leninism and social democracy, in order to launch a series of adventures or "raids," perhaps to usurp, perhaps to unsettle established power, but clearly without much concern for democratic processes. The claim here is that the society can be shaken into change, if shaken at all, only through attacks by marginal groups: the outraged poor, alienated hippies, rebellious students.

Whatever one may think about the analytical portions of Marcuse's thought, his political conclusions offer a simultaneous rationalization for withdrawal and wildness, copping-out, and turning-on. Precisely insofar as numbers of students have come under Marcuse's influence, the picture of society he draws seems less and less valid. Men are not slipping into apathy and somnolence, at least not yet; they are disturbed, restless, worried. In the last decade the United States has not become stultified, immobile, and indifferent. The *cul-de-sac* of historical stagnation posited by Marcuse is indeed

a nightmare haunting every sensitive man, but one must be able to distinguish between the fears of the dark and the facts of day.

Still, if you hold a version of Marcuse's ideas and believe liberalism is exhausted or corrupt or inseparable from "racist imperialism," if you further conclude that no major social classes within society can be expected significantly to transform it; you then have no serious alternative to either a Salinger-like withdrawal or the political equivalent of guerrilla raids. By this last phrase I don't mean literally shooting it out—though there are a few freelance lunatics advocating as much—but rather a series of actions, dramatic, desperate, and provocative, which keep the society in a state of constant turmoil and the university in a state of constant chaos.

This strategy, in my view, can lead only to disaster and a backlash of terrifying proportions. The signs of it are everywhere about us.

A tacit premise behind "confrontation politics" is that the university largely resembles the surrounding society or is even identical in nature with it. The result is to damage academic life and distort political action.

Within the university the new left students engage with more or less liberal faculties, and behind these engagements there is often the assumption that, finally, the university will behave like a middle class parent. When sometimes it does not, there follow among students considerable shock and rage. At Columbia the students who seized buildings and declared "communes," were engaged in a quasi-revolutionary action—or so some of them said. But when the Columbia administration (quite stupidly, I think) retaliated with the police force which new left theory says is inevitable but which new left feelings are often not really prepared for, the students cried foul. They invoked the traditional view of the university as a cloister of intellect from which police should be barred.

At this point they were caught in a dilemma. If they believed it proper to transform the campus into a training ground for revolutionary action, they could hardly complain when the powers-that-be retaliated with force. If they genuinely believed (as I, for one, believe) that the campus should be a center of learning from which the police are barred, then they could hardly treat the university as if it were *no more than* a microcosm of capitalist society. True, they might argue with much cogency that many universities have been contaminated and should be returned to their true purposes of scholarship and teaching; but to say that would be to accept—O, dreadful prospect—a view of the university close to that of liberalism.

The analogy between university and society breaks down in a still more serious way. One reason the tactics of the Students for a Democratic Society have worked on certain campuses is that implicitly they count on that mixture of affection and irritation many faculty people feel toward "the students." In good measure the politics of confrontation as practiced on the campus depends on a benevolent or indecisive response from the liberal professors whom the new left treats with such contempt. But once such tactics are transferred to the society at large, the result is going to be very different. The professors, who count for a good deal on the campus, count for fairly little in the society; and the society itself is not nearly so pacific or indulgent as are most professors. One needs a talent for self-delusion to say that in the United States liberalism—for all its many faults and failures—represents the main danger to humane aspirations.

No; this society retains large poten-

tials of hatred and violence, its capacities for tolerating what it regards as disruption have a visible limit, and its response to confrontation tactics could well be a crushing display of force which would harm many people who have nothing to do with the new left. I say none of this by way of approval, only by way of describing hard facts which those of us who believe in radical politics must take into account.

If anything should give the new left pause, it is the fact that according to the polls, a clear majority of the American people approved of Mayor Daley's treatment of the Chicago demonstrators. I don't mean it should give them pause on their opposition to the Vietnam war, an opposition I share; but that it should stir them into rethinking the value of confrontation methods.

Now, when arguments of this kind are put forward in debates with the new left, one of the usual replies goes like this: "You liberals, you Social Democrats are always trying to hamstring protest by raising the specter of backlash. But where is the backlash? Is it perhaps just a bogy with which you're trying to frighten us? And if we pay attention to it, how can we ever mount an effective protest?"

The backlash is everywhere. Some of us, raised on memories of earlier decades, carry a mental picture of reactionary mobs and American Legionnaires assaulting radicals in the street: that was true in the twenties and thirties; it may yet prove true in the next few years. But just as everything else in modern society becomes bureaucratized, so has backlash. Instead of the swarming mobs, there are now trained police. The white workers of Italian or Polish or Slavic origin who have managed to save up enough money to buy themselves little homes in the suburbs aren't likely to organize mobs to invade the black ghettos—at least not yet; but they are inclined, many of them, to vote for George Wallace in the name of "law and order." That some 20 percent of the American electorate could even consider voting for Wallace —surely that's a sufficient sign of backlash.

Is the answer, then, for dissidents to crawl into holes and keep silent? Of course not. But in order to protest the Vietnam war it isn't necessary to rouse all the prejudices millions of Americans hold, and it isn't even necessary to outrage their sincere patriotic sentiments. In order to fight for Negro rights, it isn't necessary to talk blood or to call white men "honkies" and policemen "pigs." That's a way of blowing off steam, and the resulting profit goes to George Wallace.

One aim of confrontation politics is the "polarization" of society. In plain English, this means that by constant assault the activists hope to drive a segment of the liberals into radicalism; thereupon the "mushy middle" of the country will be broken up; and we can then look forward to an apocalypse, with two extremes hardened and ready for a final conflict.

When they invoke this vision the confrontationists are drawing upon political emotions that have been very powerful in the twentieth century— emotions concerning "the seizure of power," a political second coming. Having shared these emotions and still being susceptible to them, I can appreciate their force. But I must nevertheless ask: what, in the present circumstances, would be the likely outcome of such a "polarization" in the United States?

Were anything of the sort to happen, millions of ordinary Americans—for whom student protest-drugs-hippiedom-Negro rioting forms a stream of detested association—would also be activated. Lower class white ethnic groups would

be stirred up. *Lumpen* elements would be emboldened. Both respectable and marginal classes would turn to demagogues promising order in the streets.

Despite its talk about "the power elite" and the idiotic notion it sometimes proposes that we live under "liberal fascism," the new left clings to an excessively optimistic view of American society. Its spokesmen have neither memory nor awareness of what fascism—the real thing, *fascist* fascism— would be like. They fail to recognize that there are sleeping dogs it would be just as well to let lie. And they are shockingly indifferent to the likelihood that the first victim of a new reaction in America would be the universities in which they now find shelter.

Only in terms of a theory of "polarization" can one explain the peculiar intensity with which new left students kept trying to break up the meetings of Hubert Humphrey, while virtually ignoring those of Richard Nixon. (I am against breaking up anyone's meetings.) They were acting on the premise that liberalism is their main enemy, and some of them have even said that they would find attractive an alliance between far left and far right.

Such notions tacitly continue the old Stalinist tradition of "the worse, the better" and the *"Nach Hitler, uns."* Yet all of recent history enforces the lesson that misery cannot be the seedbed of progress or chaos of freedom. Polarization helps, not the left, but the right; not those with grievances, but those with guns. In any case, is the prospect of polarization an attractive one? How many of us would like to face a choice between an America symbolized by George Wallace and an America symbolized by Tom Hayden? Morally, because he is against racism, Hayden is superior, but politically, neither has much respect for democracy. I for one would fear for my safety almost as much with one as with the other. Wallace might have me pistol-whipped as a communist, and Hayden have me sent to a labor camp as a Social Democrat. Hayden would be more accurate politically, but what sort of consolation would that be?

For a while confrontation politics seems to work. Caught off balance, the enemy panics. College administrators aren't sure how to cope with students who seize buildings. But in time, for better or worse, they are going to figure out a way of dealing with this problem.

There is some truth in the claim— it constitutes a damning criticism of our society—that provocative demonstrations spilling over into violence have a way of gaining attention, certainly from TV, which programmatic and disciplined protest does not. But it is a truth easily overstated. The ghetto riots in Detroit and Watts have not brought notable improvements to their communities; they have not led to those increased federal appropriations which are the only serious way of starting to clear the slums. At best they have enabled those communities, at enormous cost to themselves, to gain a slightly larger share of the funds already available. And as the California election of Ronald Reagan showed, the violence helped set off an electoral trend which can only signify a tight-fisted and mean-spirited policy toward the blacks.

Concerning this, let me quote from a discussion between Bayard Rustin, the Negro leader, and myself in the November *Dissent:*

Howe: I keep encountering the argument in regard to riots: "We know in principle it's not a good thing. But when you have a society that is not susceptible to pressure or moral appeals, the only way you can get them to pay attention is through raising hell."

Rustin: There are two tragedies here. One is that to some extent they're right. You don't get concessions until there's been trouble. . . . The second tragedy is that

although we receive minor concessions from the establishment, once the rioting reaches a certain point there will be repression against the entire Negro community.

Howe: Raising the ante indefinitely isn't going to work. . . .

Rustin: Right. To repress one-tenth of the population will require an assault on the civil liberties of everyone. And in such an atmosphere, no genuine progress in redistribution of wealth can take place. . . . There's another factor. Sooner or later the unity of the Negroes, small as it is, in making demands on the whole society will be splintered, because the Negro community gets into a debate— are you or are you not for violence?— instead of uniting around a fight for political and economic objectives.

The advocates of "confrontation" seem undisturbed by the fact that they are setting precedents which could lead to a major crisis for democracy. If it is permissible for opponents of the war to burn government records, why may not neo-Fascists do the same thing a few years later? If it is permissible for leftwing students to seize buildings in behalf of virtuous ends, why may not their action become a precedent for doing the same thing in behalf of detestable ends? At the very least, such problems must be discussed.

Some will say that violence and illegality are already rampant in the society, and that they are merely responding to its official use. This has a measure of truth. But I would reply that democratic procedures, incomplete as they may still be, have been established only after decades of struggle, and that it would be feckless to dismiss them as mere sham. Those of us who see the need for radical change have the most interest in preserving democracy.

A few years ago Staughton Lynd wrote about an antiwar demonstration in Washington: "It was unbearably moving to watch the sea of banners move out . . . toward the Capitol. . . . Still more poignant was the perception that as the crowd moved toward the seat of government . . . our forward movement was irresistibly strong . . . nothing could have stopped that crowd from taking possession of its government. Perhaps next time we should keep going, occupying for a time the rooms from which orders issue."

One must ask Staughton Lynd: under whose mandate were the marchers to occupy the government? And if they did "perhaps next time" arrogate to themselves the privilege of a *coup d'état*, even a symbolic one lasting five minutes, how will they keep other crowds, other causes—equally sincere, equally "moving"—from doing the same "perhaps the time after next?"

The politics of confrontation bears an inherent drift toward antidemocratic elitism. Electoral processes are declared irrelevant, majorities mere formalities. Once such notions are indulged, the choice is either to sink back into apathy with pot or to plunge into a desperate elitism which dismisses the people as boobs and assigns the "tasks of history" to a self-appointed vanguard. And in the current atmosphere, it isn't hard to drift from elitism to talk of violence. Mostly, so far, it is talk.

But there are troubling signs. This past summer, the office of Stanford University's president was set afire, an event that followed in time a season of student sit-ins. I see no reason to connect these two, and would never have dreamed of doing so had I not read the following in a new left paper, *The Mid-peninsula Observer:*

Most leftists in this area seem to feel that the fire was politically motivated, and a split of opinion has developed with regard to the tactical efficacy of the act. Some believe that the fire was an effective attack on state power and that it was a logical extension of the leftist activity that has been going on at and around Stanford. Others think that the fire itself was a mistake . . . since it is not clearly connected with a political movement and since most of the people who might be educated by such an act are gone for the summer.

Significant here is not the speculation that the fire was politically motivated—a speculation I refuse to accept —but the argument offered by those leftists opposed to setting fires. They seem to have a seasonal theory of the revolutionary uses of arson. In the winter, apparently, when more people can be "educated" by such an act, these critics would find arson more acceptable. The whole thing, I must say, reminds one of Dostoyevsky's "The Posessed"—as also of George Orwell's caustic remark that a certain kind of infantile leftism is "playing with fire on the part of people who don't even know that fire is hot."

Or here, to cite another instance, is an August 25 report by Robert Maynard in *The Washington Post* about a feud between SNCC and the Black Panthers. At a meeting between leaders of the two groups, writes Maynard, there was a sharp dispute which "resulted in Panthers drawing guns on James Forman," the SNCC leader. Another SNCC leader, Julius Lester, is quoted by Maynard as having written: "The shoot-out was averted, fortunately, but there was no doubt . . . that whatever merger or alliance may have existed was finished."

As a sign of the fraternal spirit induced by black power, this isn't much more convincing than the civil war in Nigeria. No doubt, much of this gun drawing is a kind of play acting; but play acting can lead to acting.

Nor is the rhetoric of violence likely to diminish soon. The new left will continue to talk blithely about revolution, but the police will do most of the shooting. Might it not, therefore, be in order to plead with the young confrontationists that if the ethic of democracy seems to them hollow or irrelevant, they at least think in terms of common prudence? And perhaps that they take off an hour to read Lenin's "Left-Wing Communism: An Infantile Disorder" in which the great revolutionist explains why compromise and even retreat is sometimes necessary?

One defense sometimes offered for confrontation politics is that, effective or not, it provides a dramatic way of releasing emotions. Of all the arguments, this seems to me the least tolerable. It means that in behalf of self-indulgence one is ready to bring down on oneself and others the forces of repression, of which the first victims would surely be the Negroes about whom the new left declares itself so deeply concerned. This is a form of middle class frivolity: a politics of the kindergarten. About such carryings-on (Yippies' trippies) I would cite a remarkable statement recently made by the English writer, David Caute, himself a new left sympathizer, after his return from Czechoslovakia:

These observations reveal to me a certain perversity in my own attitude. Nostalgia for student riots, clashes with the police, and totally exposed thighs suggests a false romanticism, irritable desire to inflict on an ostensibly sane society a form of chaos which, as a way of life, is superficial and nihilistic. The manner in which young Czechs are conducting themselves is really a model of civic control and enlightenment, whereas we have become alcoholic on sensation and violence.

Far more serious are those who advance the view that as a matter of conscience and regardless of consequences, they must break a given law. If a man finds the Vietnam war a moral crime and says he cannot serve in the Army even though the result be his impris-

onment, then I think he merits respect and, often, admiration. He is ready to accept punishment for his behavior, ready to pay the price of his convictions. His violation of the law is undertaken in behalf of a higher principle and out of respect for law in general; he hopes to stir the conscience of society or, failing that, to live according to his own. Such a version of civil disobedience, Spiro Agnew notwithstanding, is a legitimate act when seriously undertaken in a democratic society.

What is not legitimate is to use tactics that look like civil disobedience but are meant to further "revolutionary" ends (e.g., blocking draft boards), since these can only lead to displays of impotence and are likely to harm those who genuinely care about civil disobedience. Nor is it legitimate to resort to civil disobedience, or a tactic easily confused with it, every Monday and Thursday morning. Acts of conscience violating the law can be taken seriously only if they are concerned with the most fundamental moral issues. And there is also, I think, an obligation to obey many laws one dislikes, in order to preserve the possibility of peacefully changing them.

This is a bad moment in American politics. The Vietnam war is a scandal and a disaster; social obligations pile up shamefully in the cities; radical measures are called for; the exploited cannot remain silent. Militant protest is therefore needed. Yet we must try to make certain that the methods we use to fight against injustice do not give the opponents of liberty an occasion for destroying both the struggle for justice and the procedures of liberty. That would be to invite disaster through a celebration of mindlessness.

54
*Riot Commission Politics**
MICHAEL LIPSKY and DAVID J. OLSEN

Speaking before the National Commission on Civil Disorders, better known as the Kerner commission, Kenneth Clark wondered aloud about the usefulness of what the commissioners and their staff were doing. There had been previous riot commissions Clark reminded his audience, and they too had issued reports. But the whole undertaking had, for him, an Alice-in-Wonderland quality about it, "with the same moving picture reshown over and over again, the same analysis, the same recommendations, and the same inaction."

Kenneth Clark's skepticism is widely shared. But should we despair with him that riot commission reports are irrelevant? Or should we agree with public officials that riot commissions provide an invaluable service for helping society understand complex events? Or should we think cynically that riot commissions are no more than the tools by which chief executives placate and arouse people? These questions may only be answered by examining the place and function of riot commissions in the political life of the country. What do they really do? And how do they do it? How does one account for the great differences between expectations and results in the lives of recent riot commissions?

These questions open wide areas of disagreement, of course. But generally speaking, riot commissions are usually described in one or more of the following terms:

1 Government officials, it is sometimes thought, create riot commissions to provide authoritative answers to social and economic questions posed by riots, and to provide authoritative recommendations for preventing them in the future. This is certainly what commissions are *supposed* to do, as can be gleaned from reading the formal "charge" to any recent riot commission.

2 Others feel that riot commissions are simply a convenient way for public officials to buy time in which to formulate public policy. A harsher variant of this viewpoint has public officials creating commissions in a deliberate effort to evade political pressures and avoid coming to grips with the problem. A more sophisticated variant has the officials buying time so as not to have to deal with the passions *of the moment*. In the immediate aftermath of a riot, political executives have to conclude that neither the intense anger of blacks nor the intense fear and anger of whites are appropriate pressures or reliable indicators of what they should do.

3 It is said, also, that riot commissions are simply created to exonerate public officials from responsibility for the situation leading to the riot or for their behavior during it. In the recent past a number of commentators have inferred that riot commissions have "whitewashed" public officials.

4 Independent of the validity of the above three positions, it is said that riot commissions are irrelevant to the political process. Essentially this seems to have been the position of Kenneth Clark in his influential commission testimony.

5 Regardless of the reasons for initiating riot commission activity in the first place, it may be said that riot commissions essentially function as interest groups, competing with other interest groups in attempting to influence the political environment in ways favorable to their general orientations.

In recent research on the National Commission on Civil Disorders (Kerner commission), the Governor's Select Commission on Civil Disorder of the State of New Jersey (New Jersey commission), and postriot politics in Newark, Detroit, and Milwaukee, we have tried to develop a framework for analyzing some of the above considerations.

*[Reprinted with permission from *Trans-action*, July/August 1969. Copyright © July/August 1969 by Trans-action, Inc., New Brunswick, New Jersey. This article is part of a larger study of the political impact of riots on American cities. The study has been supported by the Harvard-M.I.T. Joint Center of Urban Studies, by *Trans*-Action, and by the Institute for Research on Poverty, University of Wisconsin.]

We conclude that formation of riot commissions gives rise to public expectations which cannot be fulfilled and that riot commissions are charged with incompatible goals which cannot meaningfully be reconciled.

Insofar as this is the case, riot commissions are most profitably viewed as participants in the ongoing political struggle of American race relations. They may make marginal contributions to that struggle by providing status and support for interpretation of riots which may affect the decisions of other political actors. They may also provide information about riots that will influence others, and may lend legitimacy to information which is already available. Riot commissions further may help structure the terms in which debate over issues relating to riots will be pursued. They are initiated by public officials as part of the executive function, but they are transformed by their constituents and, by virtue of the involvement of commissioners in commission business, they transform themselves into pressure group competitors in the political process. . . .

The research strategy of the Kerner commission was highly complex and difficult to implement. The president charged it with a number of independent and delicate tasks. The first was to describe accurately what happened in each riot city, and to do it despite an extraordinary diversity of testimony. Adequate handling of this task alone would have had severe political implications. The finding of a conspiracy, for example, would support those skeptics of recent black political developments who would like to discount reports of widespread discontent among black people in American cities. A finding that no conspiracy existed, on the other hand, would lead analysis into the tangled network of social causation in racial matters about which there

is great controversy. The president also asked the commission to explain why riots took place in some cities but not in others, even though previous studies on this question had proved to be singularly unsuccessful. Finally the president requested proposals on how to prevent future riots. This may have been the most politically perilous charge of all. It demanded a review and evaluation of reform planning that would have to be convincing to (first) the commissioners and (then) the public. The peril lies in the fact that such a task raises questions of the capacity of this system to respond to social needs and the adequacy of previous programs. This diffuse research agenda had to be accomplished *in less than a year.*

RIOT COMMISSIONS AS ORGANIZATIONS

1. The scarcity of time and resources

Such tight schedules are not peculiar to riot commissions, but the Kerner commission and other recent riot commissions seem particularly hampered by these constraints. It is uncertain whether any riot commission could adequately fulfill the research goals with which they are charged. Almost as soon as commissions are convened, their directors find themselves confronted by critical deadlines. They must hire staff quickly without the luxury of fully assessing their qualifications and before the research agenda has even been completed. One consequence is that generalists, such as lawyers, may be hired over specialists, since staff directors may not know precisely what they want to do. The Kerner commission was especially hampered because in late August talented people in the academic world were already committed, and because hiring had to proceed in the face of widespread skepticism such as that expressed by Kenneth Clark.

As soon as staff is hired, the pressure is on to collect the data. Investigation must follow quickly upon the occurence of riots because of the need to interview witnesses while memories are still fresh and because proposed solutions presumably depend upon a research effort. The Kerner commission decided to obtain information on riots in twenty cities, including environmental background features and interviews with key people, from city officials to militant civil rights activists. The data-gathering teams went into the field at a time when December 15 was considered the target date for an "interim" report. This meant they had about two months in which to uncover the facts about the riots, the cities in which they occurred, and possible explanations for their occurrence. Obviously, this was too short a time period to obtain sufficient data to develop well-rounded studies, a fact confirmed by the Kerner commission's decision not to develop all these profiles for publication. The New Jersey commission, given less than three months to hire staff and conduct and assemble research, was similarly constrained by time.

Another consequence of having to produce reports under this kind of pressure is that the staff is almost obliged to develop (or simply accept) a general working theory of riot causation to guide the research. The outlines of the theory are familiar to anyone who has looked into almost any recent commission report. It holds that systematic deprivation and discrimination in the past, when added to reasonable expectations of positive change and when accompanied by continued indignities and community resentments, become focused by a single incident or series of incidents into behavior that takes the form of looting and other hostile activities. As a general theory this is perfectly serviceable, but it hardly accounts

for the varieties of civil disorders, which presidents, governors, and others are concerned about. Social scientists, especially, must find this unsatisfactory, since they are interested in explaining variation, rather than explaining why something does or does not exist. The questions of why riots occurred in some cities and not in others, or why riots varied in form and intensity, can be sensibly addressed only through a more rigorous comparative analysis than there was time to undertake in the work of recent riot commissions. Farming out research to social scientists was one way the Kerner commission attempted to deal with research difficulties, but this was not entirely satisfactory.

As individuals with public constituencies, commissioners have to be assured that their decisions rest upon irrefutable and unambiguous evidence. The time problem intrudes when commission staffs anticipate these needs and try to "build a case," an effort that detracts in some ways from an open research strategy and diverts staff members from other duties. Staffers on the Kerner commission, for example, had to return to the field to obtain affidavits from witnesses on whose testimony the narrative summaries of disorders rested. Staff investigators of the New Jersey commission were required to file individual memoranda on every person with whom they talked on commission business. "Building a case" and good research procedures are not necessarily incompatible. But a strain is placed upon mutual satisfaction of both these goals when time is short. Statistics without relevance are collected; time-consuming procedures are honored to make an impression of thoroughness; theories with potential validity are rejected since they cannot be adequately tested, and so on.

Related to the demands for building a case is what happens when commissions begin to focus attention on the single task of producing the final document. At this point, other talents, perhaps antithetical to those of the researcher, are demanded of the staff. These are the ability to work all day and night, the capacity to absorb endless criticism without taking personal affront, and the ability to synthesize the sentiments of the commissioners, or to anticipate their sentiments regarding various issues. These qualities are those of lawyers, of advocates who work under pressure for clients regardless of personal interests or allegiance to material. In this respect commission staff-domination by lawyers may be a necessary rather than an accidentally perverse quality of commissions. But the point remains that those best able to gather and interpret socially relevant data may not perform well in accommodating to the pressures that are brought to bear in writing the final report.

The pressures of time are also incompatible with a rational search for answers. Under rational procedures, study should be followed by conclusion, followed by program suggestions relating to those conclusions. But lack of time required recent riot commissions to formulate their programs at the same time as they were analyzing causes. This is not to say that their conclusions do not follow from the analysis. But this dynamic helps explain why there need not be a relationship between the factual analysis of events and commissions' proposals for change.

Scarcity of resources also contributes to the typical shakiness of the organization of riot commissions. Commissions enjoy no regular budgetary status, nor do they continue to enjoy top executive priority after their creation has served to reassure the executive's constituency that he has acted on the problem. The Kerner commission, for example, was originally promised sufficient funds to accomplish their task, but it was later discouraged from seeking more money because in late 1967 it had become presidential policy to seek no supplementary appropriations from Congress, and because federal agencies were reluctant to contribute to the commission from their diminished budgets.

2. Developing commission integration
It is the peculiar dilemma of riot commissions that commissioners are apparently chosen for the diversity of interests they represent, while at the same time they are expected to agree on, and support, a meaningful report about a complex problem with clear ideological overtones. This circumstance sometimes leads the public to assume, quite understandably, that the final report of any given commission will be little more than a collection of bland generalities, or an out-and-out whitewash. If it is the first, it will be because the commissioners were in fact representative of diverse and conflicting interests and were unable to agree on anything controversial. And if it is the second, it will be because they were really chosen by the political leadership for the basic congruence of their views. Either way, the appointment of riot commissions has led to rather unflattering expectations of their work, and often justifiably so, given the extent to which recent commissions have been made up of incumbent or former public officials and bona fide members of high status organizations such as trade unions, financial conglomerates, or the press.

Riot commissions are made up of men chosen for diversity of interests, and they are inherently temporary. Thus riot commissions are confronted in extraordinary fashion with the problems inherent in all complex organizations—the development of mechanisms of socialization and the development of group norms and values which may overcome tendencies toward fragmentation and disintegration. In practical terms, tendencies toward fragmentation and disintegration in riot commissions may take the forms of developing minority reports and developing destructive tensions between commissioners and staff. . . .

But, in a sense, a minority report is an ultimate weapon. One must still account for how commissioners with diverse interests and viewpoints come to identify themselves with the final product of a commission. Under what circumstances do such men permit themselves the luxury of political compromise in endorsing views to which they may not totally subscribe?

One way to explain the surprisingly provocative quality of both the Kerner commission and the New Jersey commission reports, given the essentially conservative cast of their members, is that their staff directors explicitly encourage and engineered the development of *a sense of urgency* within these commissions. Direct exposure to ghetto conditions was perhaps the most successful technique to this end. Members of the Kerner commission conducted two-day tours of riot areas, sometimes even without the company of the press corps or the guiding hands of city officials. One of the most successful of these took place in Cincinnati on August 30 when Mayor Lindsay and Senator Fred Harris, two of the most liberal members of the commission, met alone with a group of black nationalists. They were frankly informed of the group's dedication to the destruction of American society as now constituted. The confrontation apparently was particularly meaningful for Lindsay and Harris because the nationalists were highly educated men, and so could not be dismissed as being merely frustrated because of restricted mobility.

By the same token, the New Jersey commission staff arranged for their commissioners to divide into teams of two and accompany antipoverty workers into Newark ghetto homes, bars, and barber shops. Most participants, including chairman Robert Lilley, credited these tours with creating the sense of awareness and alarm about ghetto conditions that was ultimately reflected in the final report.

This facet of commission procedure in part was born of political necessity. Staff research was not immediately available to the commissioners, yet they had to demonstrate to the public that they were doing *something*. One way to do this was to study conditions firsthand. Happily, this also permitted commissioners to learn about ghetto conditions and agree on the nature of ghetto existence before policy papers were prepared and before it became necessary to "take sides."

Exposure to formal witnesses with dramatic testimony was also useful in creating a sence of urgency. Kenneth Clark's appearance before the Kerner commission was considered influential in offering perspective to the commissioners on their activity. The same effect was produced when the staffs of both the Kerner commission and the New Jersey commission circulated articles by Robert Blauner and by Robert Fogelson that were highly critical of the McCone commission. These articles alerted everyone to the potential public criticism of "wishy-washy" riot reports. Many New Jersey commissioners reported being heavily influenced by the testimony of black shopkeepers whose stores were shot up by New Jersey policemen; shopkeepers, after all, were not likely to be malcontents.

Problems of potential fragmentation threaten commission unity at all stages. Initially, the problem is one of getting commissioners to think of themselves as *commissioners,* not as individual politicians. This is helped, as we saw, by creating a sense of urgency among commission members. In later stages, the problem becomes one of conflicts arising from the fact that commissioners must begin to take stands on matters of public policy.

Considerable conflict did develop in the work of recent commissions at the writing stages, but these conflicts did not erupt to the extent that minority reports were filed or that serious public displays of conflict emerged in the press. The Kerner commission did not break up over the appropriateness of criticizing major social institutions or over the ultimate tone and emphasis of the report summary, although these were issues of considerable conflict within the commission. Neither did the New Jersey commission break up over the issue of recommending governmental consolidation for Essex County, although the commission was significantly divided over this issue. Commissioners clearly preferred to accept compromise rather than diminish the total impact of the report because of open conflict or sniping at the document. Members of both commissions have refrained from dissociating themselves from aspects of the reports, and many have actively defended them, despite the controversies they have set off.

Although there were considerable disagreements on the various commissions, what is significant were the areas of agreement. So far as we can discover there was little dispute over the causes of riots. The commissioners agreed that the riots were not results of conspiracies nor mass behavior dominated by criminal or quasi-criminal elements. Rather, these men (and one woman) chosen for their community standing and their connection with established institutions—people, in other words, who were rela-

tively conservative in the literal sense—attributed the riots to long-standing factors of discrimination, deprivation, and neglect. They condemned violence and criminal behavior, but they recognized that riots could be understood as products of central tendencies in American life.

There was also no question that extraordinary measures would have to be taken if the country wanted to deal seriously with the social bases of urban unrest. What debate there was concerned the kinds of measures that would have to be undertaken, and the kinds of criticism of American institutions appropriate for public discussion. But on the whole, these disagreements over the nature of the recommendations are less significant than the commissioners' agreement on the necessity for radical departures from existing public policy. When viewed in the light of the political and social legitimacy commanded by recent riot commissions, this is the significance of recent commission reports.

Apart from the danger of conflict among the commissioners, there is also the possibility of conflict between them and their staffs. In this regard, an important point of tension is the commissioners' need to feel reassured that staff members are free from bias and are presenting their work free from ideological distortion. Commissioners' suspicions apparently focus upon two possibilities. On the one hand, some staff members are feared to be overzealous for social reform, with a corresponding bias emerging in their work. This possibility is somewhat reinforced by the nature of lower-level staff recruitment, where an interest in social reform may be significant in the type of person willing to work for commissions on short notice. The field staff of the Kerner commission, for example, was made up to a significant degree of young lawyers and returned Peace Corps volunteers. On the other hand, formally bipartisan commissions encounter suspicion that top staff members are really very partisan and have been selected to whitewash elected officials.

The dangers of failure to allay commission suspicions that the staff is over-zealous or partisan are two: The commissioners may reject staff work and in the end develop conclusions independent of staff analysis; or, in anticipation of commission antagonism, staff work may be screened to provide commissioners with only "acceptable" material. In either case, the commission runs the risk of staff revolt, the erosion of organizational loyalty among the staff, and divisive public debate inspired by discontented staff. . . .

Ideological splits between commissioners and staff are more difficult to control and can be quite damaging to ultimate commission influence. The prestige of the McCone commission, for example, was severely undermined by critics who argued that the conservative cast of the commission substantially ignored the findings of its social science staff and consultants. The writings of Robert Blauner, Robert Fogelson, Paul Jacobs, and Harry Scoble reflect this. During the life of the Kerner commission, as well, major difficulties emerged over staff suspicions that their analyses were being rejected on conservative grounds.

The most obvious and best publicized example of this commissioner-staff tension revolved around the rejection of a document entitled, "The Harvest of American Racism" drafted by social scientists employed by the Kerner commission. From all indications, it appears that this draft was rejected for inclusion in the final report not only because its conclusions were radical, but also because documentation for its underlying theory of riot causation was lacking. There was also a problem of communication within the commission. The social scientists were shocked to find the document that they considered only a draft treated as a final product. This was devastating because the social scientists assumed it was clear that adequate documentation had not yet been appended to the theoretical analysis. On the other hand, the chief staff directors of the commission were no less dismayed to received what they considered an unsubstantiated theoretical piece. The staff directors argued that for commissioners to accept a provocative analysis required, at the very least, that it be grounded in a solid evidential base.

Very shortly after the "Harvest" draft was rejected, the commission changed its timetable to eliminate the interim report and released most of the staff, about one-hundred people. For some staff members, these three events confirmed their suspicions that the commission was exploiting them without respect for their skills and was leaning toward development of a conservative report that was at odds with the staff members' analysis. Leaks to the press followed, and at least one commission consultant held a press conference to discuss these matters publicly. Thus, for a period in the latter half of December the Kerner commission was under considerable pressure in the press to deny charges that it was heading in a conservative direction.

Release of the final report allayed these fears. Previously critical staff members now acknowledge this and, indeed, that much of their analysis was woven into the final document. By taking their fears to the press, these staff members may have contributed to the outcome by putting pressure on the commission at a critical time.

3. The development of political legitimacy

Initially, riot commissions are charged with generating objective analysis and impartial recommendations based upon this analysis. Initially, commissioners are recruited because of their status, their imputed objectivity and responsibility, and the extent to which they appear to be representative of a spectrum of diverse interests. We have suggested, however, that if commission efforts are to be successful, commissioners must give up some of their self- and occupational role interests and develop orientations toward the commission as an organization with a life of its own. As this happens riot commissions adopt strategies to maximize the impact of the final report. We have already mentioned the example of staff directors formulating procedures to discourage minority reports. They recognize that a commission that appears to be substantially divided merely testifies to the complexity of the issue and is supportive of many viewpoints.

An insight into the efforts of riot commissions to develop legitimacy can be found in the tension between pursuit of a "scientific" research strategy (or "scientific" legitimacy) and the political needs of commission work (or "political" legitimacy). Staffs must conduct inquiries so that the commission appears comprehensive in searching for explanations and program proposals, reliable in presentation of evidence, and cognizant of advanced work in various research and program areas. This image must be secured by the staff for the commission whether or not information so obtained is related to questions or answers of commission interest. . . .

Besides establishing their "scientific" legitimacy, commissions must give the impression that all political groups are given their day in court. Sometimes the motives for hearing certain witnesses are transparently political rather than educational or evidential. The Kerner commission, for example, took the testimony of many of the black militants whose names appear on the witness list at a period when many chapters in the report already had been approved in relatively final form.

So far, we have been building an argument that the internal political dynamics of riot commissions can be characterized as the gradual development of *a pressure group*. This is particularly curious because, in the first place, riot commissions are established by public officials as objective instrumentalities to provide authoritative answers to questions of concern (thus, they are *government* organizations); and, in the second place, because riot commissions are specifically designed for the representation of *diverse* interests when originally formed.

Nevertheless, this view of riot commissions as developing into pressure groups may help explain both their strengths and weaknesses. Insofar as a diverse group of implicitly responsible, high status individuals subscribe to one interpretation of civil disorders and subscribe to a single set of recommendations, riot commissions may claim a high degree of political legitimacy. This is their strength. But insofar as a riot commission must compete in the political arena without being able to rely upon the organizational status of individual commission members, riot commissions enter an ideological arena where they must compete with other groups in the political process. In that competition, the impact of commissions is predictably marginal. The executive who creates a riot commission assigns to it the function of authoritatively articulating goals for the alleviation of problems of civil disorders. But the goals become authoritative for the larger political system only insofar as they are accepted by other groups for conversion into public policy. In the absence of such acceptance, the recommendations remain only as political demands. They are purely recommendatory or advisory unless supportive relations can be established with interest groups and other key actors.

RIOT COMMISSION STRATEGY

In attempting to develop political coalitions and influence the political process, riot commissions adopt a variety of strategies to overcome their relatively powerless status. These strategies include: (1) maximizing the visibility and controlling the exposure of the reports; (2) competing for legitimacy; (3) affecting the political environment; and (4) assisting the implementation process.

1. Maximizing visibility

Riot commissions are concerned with creating favorable images of their activities, and attempt to do so by giving maximum visibility to their reports. The tone adopted in the reports reflects this concern. Both the Kerner commission and the New Jersey commission elected to develop what appear to be hard-hitting documents. In the Kerner commission report, as everyone recalls, "white racism" was identified as the overriding primal cause of conditions leading to riots. This was sensational, assuring a maximum impact for the commission's labors. At the same time, however, the commission report contained almost no criticism of established institutions or programs. Criticism of national-level programs is largely lacking—despite the fact that the federal government is the only locus for the kind of effort that is called

for in the report—and criticism is minimized of trade unions, big-city mayors, and other groups who might be expected to do something about the alleged "racism. . . ."

2. Competing for legitimacy

In attempting to influence other political actors on behalf of their report, riot commissions, as we have seen, try to establish firmly their claims as the authoritative interpreters of civil disorders and as authoritative planners for preventing future civil disorder. These claims do not go uncontested. Other groups have access to the same symbols and similar grounds of legitimacy.

Simply stated, one riot commission often begets another, or two, or three. The competing riot commissions have less claim to objectivity or being "official," but they have greater claims to reliable constituencies and the group status that results. These constituencies are, for one reason or another, determined to undermine the monopoly of legitimacy asserted by the riot commissions and attempt to establish legitimacy of their own. They adopt the commission inquiry form in order to capitalize on the acceptability of this political instrument.

The political logic appears to be as follows: if it can be shown that opposite conclusions can emerge from the same kind of investigation of civil disorders, then it can be argued that the conclusion of the authoritative commission was the product of the biases of commissioners. This is all quite explicit, and antagonistic interest groups don't hesitate to use the tactic even when it is patently clear that the "competing commission" is undertaking a biased investigation. Take, for example, the remarks of John J. Heffernan, President of the New Jersey State Patrolmen's Benevolent Association, when he "predicted" the findings of his association's investigation: "We are appalled at the findings of the [New Jersey] riot commission, especially in the interests of law and order. The PBA riot study and investigation committee is certainly going to come up with different findings."

After President Johnson issued an executive order creating the Kerner commission, the United States Senate authorized the Permanent Subcommittee on Investigations of the Committee on Government Operations (McClellan committee) "to make a full and complete study and investigation of riots . . . and measures necessary for their immediate and long-range prevention." The McClellan committee's investigations have attempted to undermine the findings of the Kerner commission by centering on Office of Economic Opportunity personnel involved in riots, hearing witnesses who allege that there is a conspiracy behind the riots, and generally giving a hostile reception to other witnesses not sympathetic with the committee's more conservative views. That President Johnson himself tried to undermine his own Kerner commission is perhaps not surprising. The fact that he included in his charge to the (Milton) Eisenhower commission on the Causes and Prevention of Violence the duty to investigate civil disorders is consistent with his other acts of unsympathetic reception of the Kerner report. The New Jersey commission's "Report for Action," released in February of 1968, shortly thereafter triggered the New Jersey State Patrolmen's Benevolent Association's Riot Study Commission report entitled "A Challenge to Conscience." In Detroit, Jerome P. Cavanagh's Mayor's Development Team represented a public response

to local civil disorders with most commission members drawn from city agencies and the mayor's office. But the Development Team was soon challenged by the New Detroit Committee, a private counterthrust to the public commission. In California, the conservative McCone commission was countered, both as to its findings and its recommendations, by the California Advisory Committee to the United States Commission on Civil Rights.

These competing commissions employ many of the same strategies and tactics as official riot commissions in manipulating the symbols of legitimacy. They follow closely the procedures of the initial commissions, including assembling a staff, holding formal hearings, conducting investigations, hearing witnesses, collecting documents, and offering recommendations. In fact, they are often the same witnesses, the same documents, and similar investigations. But their findings and recommendations vary considerably from the conclusions of initial commissions. Riot commissions, whether initial or competing, thus represent ad hoc devices by which on-going antagonistic interests compete for political legitimacy.

3. Affecting the political environment
In content, commission reports can be analyzed as attempts to reassure various publics in an otherwise unsettled environment. These reassurances may take the form of dispeling popular rumors and myths, or they may take the form of interpreting disturbing events in ways that can be absorbed within traditional American beliefs.

Efforts to reassure various publics begin as soon as commissions are formed. Early testimony plays an important part in giving the appearance that significant interests are being represented. J. Edgar Hoover's statement that he had no evidence of a conspiracy was the only testimony released officially during the first set of Kerner commission hearings. . . .

Beyond dispeling myths such as those of conspiracy, riot commissions also reaffirm traditionally accepted views of society. They uniformly condemn violence and reaffirm the principles of law and order. They also commonly invoke that series of beliefs in the American creed pertaining to "equality" and "integration." Note the concluding sentence to the Kerner commission's chapter on the history of Negro protest: "Negro protest for the most part, has been firmly rooted in the basic values of American society, seeking not their destruction, but their fulfillment." Which values? Which America? The statement may have empirical validity when interpreted, but here it has primarily inspirational value. . . .

4. Strategies for implementation
It is appropriate to conclude by mentioning a number of explicit strategies that riot commissions adopt to affect the reception of their product in the political arena. Riot commissions have recently advocated extending commission life in one form or another. The McCone commission, for example, chose this means for advancing its recommendations. Near the end of the New Jersey commission's deliberations, a request was made to Governor Richard Hughes to establish an ongoing review body including some members of the commission. A commissioner on Mayor Cavanagh's Development Team indicated that after the MDT issued its report, it was decided that an executive committee composed of the mayor and five of the mayor's top assistants should meet periodically to review what was happening to the MDT report.

The major drawback to this approach has been the lack of power of the commissions once reports are issued. If riot commissions themselves have relatively little power, then a few of the commission members meeting periodically have even less power in the implementation process. . . .

Commissioners as individuals have attempted to exert pressure on public officials for implementation. In New Jersey, for example, Governor Hughes was threatened by individual members of the commission with public criticism if he continued his failure to respond. Shortly thereafter, the governor and his staff received members of the commission and in an all-day session virtually wrote the governor's special message to the legislature. This message, which called for expenditures of $126.1 million on welfare housing education law enforcement, and urban problems, incorporated most of the commission's recommendations pertaining to New Jersey state government.

FUNCTIONS OF COMMISSIONS

Let us now try to evaluate the assumptions about riot commissions that were identified at the beginning of this essay.

1 Riot commissions are inherently incapable of providing sophisticated answers to the most important questions relating to riots. As government agencies limited in time, resources, and staff, riot commissions can contract for a limited number of empirical studies, investigate the validity of some rumors and myths surrounding civil disorders, and make relatively intelligent judgments in describing riot occurrences. They can also make sound program proposals, though they must do so before critical research has been completed. Recommendations of riot commissions may be said to be authoritative in the sense that they are comprised of high-status individuals and are accorded high status by the fact that they were created by the chief executive. But their recommendations are authoritative only insofar as the chief executive moves to implement them.

To the extent that the chief executive fails to move toward implementation

—as in the case of President Johnson— or to the extent that recommendations go beyond the scope of executive powers —as in the case of the New Jersey recommendations regarding Newark corruption—riot commissions must be seen not as authoritative but as competitive pressure groups in the political process. As such their influence is restricted to the legitimacy that they can capture and the political skills of individual commissioners who attempt to affect implementation.

2 It is rather fruitless to enter the murky area of the motivation of executives who create riot commissions. But our analysis does permit us to say a few things. Whether or not riot commissions are created in order to buy time, it is unquestionable that they do permit public officials to avoid immediate pressures for action and to postpone decisions for many months. Not only does the creation of a commission deflect pressures from the chief executive, but it also improves his bargaining position in a conservative direction by permitting him to claim that he is constrained by other political pressures over which he has little control. In the intense crisis following the riot, people seem to appeal instinctively to the chief executive for leadership. But the opportunity for decisive leadership, for making qualitatively different decisions about national priorities, based on opportunities available only in crisis situations, may not be what the politician desires. Postponement permits the chief executive to wrap himself in the usual constraints of office where politics as usual will continue to obtain. Riot commissions also contribute to cooling of tensions by reassuring various publics in a symbolic way that their needs are being met. This may take the form of calling witnesses representative of various positions, making hortatorical appeals for justice and nonviolence, and so forth.

3 Is there something inherent in riot commissions that supports allegations that they are established to whitewash public officials? We may ask this apart from the question of whether some commissions are made up of members picked primarily for their unquestionable support of a chief executive. We think there is a builtin tendency toward the whitewash, to the extent that riot commissions minimize criticism of the public official to whom they must look for primary implementation of the report. Further, for the sake of commission solidarity and to avoid diminishing the report's impact by the airing of dissension, riot commissions minimize criticisms of institutions with which individual commissioners are intimately associated. To some extent, public officials attempt to influence commissions in favorable ways through appointments of political allies and "reliable" individuals to the commission. As we have suggested, however, this strategy will have limited returns because of the fears of partisan bias and the need to make the commission appear "representative."

4 and 5 Kenneth Clark's skepticism over the relevance of riot commissions is essentially justified. Riot commissions are not the authoritative program planners for a community torn by crisis and harvesting the fruits of past social injustice. Neither are they accorded the status that might accrue to them by virtue of the prestige of individual commissioners or the expertise that they command. Rather, starting from the myth that riot commissions will provide authoritative answers to questions of social concern, and that these answers will be widely accepted by politicians who will move to implement them, riot commissions move through a process in which they become just another pressure group among many in the political process. And in influencing that process, their resources are insufficient to prevail in the competition.

The allegation that commissions have repeatedly come to the same analysis, recommended similar programs, and failed to produce action is true, but as criticism it is misdirected. It is not the commissions themselves to which one must look to understand the "Alice-in-Wonderland" atmosphere that Kenneth Clark perceived. One must look to the political process itself—that greater wonderland in which riot commissions play only a marginal role.